D1713336

The Working Class in European History

Syndicalist Legacy

Syndicalist Legacy

Trade Unions and Politics in Two French
Cities in the Era of World War I

Kathryn E. Amdur

University of Illinois Press
Urbana and Chicago

Publication of this work was supported in part by a grant
from the Andrew W. Mellon Foundation.

©1986 by the Board of Trustees of the University of Illinois
Manufactured in the United States of America
C 5 4 3 2 1

This book is printed on acid-free paper.

LIBRARY OF CONGRESS CATALOGING-IN-PUBLICATION DATA

Amdur, Kathryn E., 1947–
    Syndicalist legacy.

    (Working class in European history)
    Bibliography: p.
    Includes index.
    1. Syndicalism—France—History—20th century.
2. Confédération générale du travail—History—20th
century. I. Title. II. Series.
HD6684.A52 1986   335'.82'0944   86-1633
ISBN 0-252-01238-0

For My Parents

Contents

List of Tables and Graphs

Abbreviations Used in the Text

AIT   Association Internationale du Travail. Anarchist International at Berlin, formed in 1922.

CDS   Comité de Défense Syndicaliste. Left-wing syndicalist group formed in 1917 and led by Raymond Péricat; same name used for the anti-Communist group formed within the CGTU in 1922 and led by Pierre Besnard.

CFDT   Confédération Française Démocratique du Travail. New secularized name of the CFTC as of 1964.

CFTC   Confédération Française des Travailleurs Chrétiens. Organization of Catholic trade unions founded in 1919.

CGT   Confédération Générale du Travail. Central confederation of French trade unions, founded in 1895 and merged with the Fédération des Bourses du Travail in 1902.

CGTSR   Confédération Générale du Travail Syndicaliste Révolutionnaire. Third trade-union confederation, founded in 1926 by anarcho-syndicalists who opposed the "Bolshevization" of the CGTU.

CGTU   Confédération Générale du Travail Unitaire. Dissident trade-union confederation composed of Communists and anarcho-syndicalists who quit the CGT in 1921–22.

CI   Comité Intercorporatif. Group formed in 1917 in the Loire (and dissolved in December 1919) to link the unions in the "war industries" of metals and construction and to take the lead in organizing protests against the war.

CRRI   Comité pour la Reprise des Relations Internationales. First antiwar group of French Socialists and syndicalists, formed in 1916 and led by the Parisian metalworker Alphonse Merrheim.

CSR   Comité Syndicaliste Révolutionnaire. Group of dissident (minoritarian) syndicalists within the CGT, formed in October 1920 and forerunner of the CGTU.

GSR   Groupe Syndicaliste Révolutionnaire. Group of dissident syndicalists within the CGTU, formed in 1923 to oppose the unions' "Bolshevization."

ISR   Internationale Syndicale Rouge. Also called the Profintern, the trade-union wing of the Communist International.

PCF   Parti Communiste Français. French Communist Party, created by the schism in the Socialist Party in December 1920.

PLM   Paris-Lyon-Méditerrannée. Railway line; the Union PLM was the group linking the unions of employees on this line in the railway federation of the CGT. Saint-Etienne railroad workers were part of this group.

PO   Paris-Orléans. Railway line; the Union PO was the group linking the unions of employees on this line in the railway federation of the CGT. Limoges railroad workers were part of this group.

PUP   Parti d'Unité Prolétarienne. Dissident party formed of former Communists in 1930.

SFIC   Section Française de l'Internationale Communiste. French section of the Communist International; alternate name for the PCF.

SFIO   Section Française de l'Internationale Ouvrière. French section of the Socialist International; official name of the Socialist Party in France (during the life of the Socialist International), formed by the unification of diverse socialist groups in 1905.

UD   Union Départementale. Departmental grouping of unions in the CGT (or CGTU), representing the regional dimension of trade-union organization, in contrast to the industrial dimension, which was represented in national federations for each industry or trade.

UR   Union Régionale. Regional grouping of unions in the CGTU, which replaced the UDs after 1925.

USC   Union Socialiste-Communiste. Dissident party formed by the schism in the PCF in 1923.

For abbreviations used in the notes, see the separate list immediately preceding the notes.

Acknowledgments

It is a most pleasant duty for me to thank those whose generous gifts of time and energy have helped to bring this project to completion. I wish to express special gratitude to Professor (Emeritus) Gordon Wright for sparking my interest in French history, for leading me to this topic, and for helping to see the project through to the end. I would also like to thank other teachers and colleagues for their helpful comments and suggestions at various stages of this project: Carolyn Lougee, Albert Camarillo, Rondo Cameron, Joan Wallach Scott, Michael Hanagan, John Merriman, Christopher Johnson, Irwin Wall, Jolyon Howorth, Andrew Pitt, Daniel Colson, Yves Lequin, Annie Kriegel, and the late Jean Maitron. In addition, I wish to acknowledge my debt to those institutions that helped to fund the research for this project: the Council for European Studies; the Georges Lurcy Memorial Foundation; the French government; the Mrs. Giles Whiting Foundation; the Emory University Research Committee; and the National Endowment for the Humanities.

While in France I had the privilege of meeting many people whose knowledge of French labor politics helped me to bridge the gap that faces Americans who try to study a foreign culture. In addition to those French scholars noted above, I wish to thank Antoine Perrier, Francine Bourdelle, Andrée Dujacques, Janet Jacobs, Michelle Zancarini, and Monique Luirard for sharing the product of their own researches; Michel Laguionie and Antoine Laval for lending their personal papers and for putting me in contact with local trade unionists; and Roger Penot, Jean Pralong, and Jean Seigne for agreeing to discuss their personal experiences in the labor movements in Limoges and Saint-Etienne. I am also grateful to the public archivists in both cities and in Paris for facilitating my use of their resources; to the librarians at the Chamber of Commerce at Saint-Etienne for permitting me to consult their private collections; and to the administrators of the Syndicat CGT de la Chaussure and the Syndicat CGT du Livre at Limoges, as well as those of the Bourse du Travail at Saint-Etienne, for granting me access to their archives of union minutes and other reports. The managements of the Haviland porcelain company and the Heyraud and Vincent shoe companies at Limoges must also be thanked for opening their personnel files and for helping me to look for other materials to use in this study. These personal contacts supplemented the insights to be gleaned from the public record and vastly enriched my sojourns in France.

I wish lastly to thank those whose moral support and practical assistance were indispensable in the final stages of this project. Patricia Stockbridge valiantly typed the manuscript and patiently endured its several revisions. My close friends outside the historical profession prodded me to express my ideas in less specialized terms and joined me in celebrating the partial victories as the goal came within sight. Perhaps above all, my parents cheered me on and showed the pride (and the patience) that saw me through the project's long gestation and birth pangs. It is to them I dedicate this volume—in the hope that it may merit their "grandparental" love.

Syndicalist Legacy

Introduction

In 1914 the French labor movement seemed on the verge of full conversion to reformism. The influence of revolutionary syndicalist ideology, of uncertain extent even in its peak years, was by then unmistakably on the decline. Labor's decision, with the Socialists, to support the government's wartime appeal for "Sacred Union" should have come as no real surprise to anyone.

The experience of protracted war, however, was devastating at every level of European society and was especially critical for working-class politics. French workers, convinced that they bore the major burden of their country's war effort, reacted to acute economic and psychological tension by launching massive waves of strikes. Many workers urgently began to question the politics of Sacred Union. The Russian Revolution also highlighted the possibility of revolution by a self-conscious and war-wearied proletariat. While the military victory of 1918 temporarily distracted the labor movement from more revolutionary concerns, its failure to bring the anticipated release from economic hardship stirred new waves of protest in 1919 and 1920. The resurgence of left-wing extremism was institutionalized in the split within the Socialist Party (SFIO) and the creation of a Communist Party (PCF) in December 1920.

In many ways parallel to this political schism was the split in the General Confederation of Labor (CGT) in the winter of 1921–22. The left wings of both the SFIO and the CGT used similar reasoning to reject the class collaboration of the war years. Many left-wing unionists rallied to the new Communist Party and demanded adhesion to the Profintern, the new trade-union international formed by the Bolsheviks. The most obvious difference between the two left wings was one of strength: while the schismatic forces grew to be a majority in the old Socialist Party, they remained a minority in the CGT.

The labor schism was further complicated, however, by the revival of a dormant anarcho-syndicalist current, which demanded labor's independence not only from Socialist reformism but from any form of political tutelage. The militant minority that broke off to form the CGTU ("Unitaire") was, despite the body's new name, divided internally between Communist and syndicalist factions. These groups competed for leadership of the new organization until the Communists consolidated their control, both nationally and locally, in 1923–24. In response, many syndicalists quit the CGTU to form autonomous unions, some of which grouped in a third confederation, founded in 1926, the CGTSR ("Syndicaliste Révolutionnaire"). The second schism showed how problems of doctrine and strategy had been only partially resolved by the first.

These events—the war, the labor schism, and the troubled history of the CGTU—form the outline of the present study. Some of the story has already been told elsewhere, although more from the perspective of party politics than from that of labor unionism and the working-class experience.[1] The change in perspective raises new questions that other studies have not satisfactorily answered: How parallel were in fact the trade-union and the party schisms? How did unionists, in comparison to party activists, feel the effects of the Russian Revolution and World War I? Beyond political issues, how was the labor movement shaped by changing industrial conditions and demographic factors in the wartime and immediate postwar period? Above all, which groups of workers—in which industries and localities—supported the various labor factions? These questions seek to transcend the record of decisions by labor organizers in Paris—or in Moscow—to explore the behavior of local workers, both on the job and in local politics. The local emphasis permits a close look at the labor movement in action: the unions' membership and recruitment, their strike behavior, and their relations with leftist parties before and after the birth of the Communist Party in France.

The focus on trade unionism shows first of all that the CGT schism was more than a mere echo of the earlier political rupture. Left-wing unionists shared some of the same concerns of left-wing party leaders, who looked to communism to resolve the dilemmas of revolutionary strategy that had been posed by the experience of war.[2] Most unionists, however, found it difficult to accept permanent collaboration with any leftist party, whether Socialist or Communist. The idea of independent unionism, enshrined in the CGT's Amiens Charter (1906), remained very much alive after 1918. It survived despite the growth of prewar reformism and wartime party-union collaboration, and despite the pleas of those party leaders who viewed trade-union autonomy as a useless anachronism characteristic of a "Latin" personality or a backward economy.[3] As a result, postwar syndicalists faced more than a simple choice between socialism and communism, or between reformism and revolution. They had also to decide what kind of revolutionary strategy to adopt: with or without party collaboration; by mass organization or by small-scale active minorities; and with centralized decision making or with federalist structures and local autonomy. These issues, not altogether new but posed with increased urgency, forced unionists to decide what kind of labor movement best suited postwar circumstances. The questions, and the syndicalists' answers, showed that prewar doctrines still seemed relevant to postwar conditions, at least in certain industrial and geographic sectors of France.

These issues, and their continued importance, prompt a further consideration of the syndicalist phenomenon. Although sometimes dismissed as "a cause without rebels," even in the prewar era,[4] syndicalism was rooted in specific features of the French economic and political environment, many of which continued to prevail after the war. These roots can best be explored by examining both the strategies or doctrines of French syndicalism and their actual impact on union activities in specific local and industrial contexts. Such an examination can also help to determine in what way any labor ideology—syndicalist, Socialist, or Communist— becomes meaningful in practical terms.

As a political doctrine, revolutionary syndicalism stressed above all the value of union independence from party politics. Rather than depend on party leadership or parliamentary negotiation to gain benefits, syndicalists proposed a strategy of "direct action," including sabotage and the general strike.[5] Syndicalists rejected parliamentary politics for two main reasons: the parties' electoral preoccupations seemed to make them irrevocably reformist, and the attempts by competing socialist factions to dominate the unions risked imposing harmful divisions on the working class. But what if there were a truly revolutionary party, one that could overcome simple electoralism and also unite the laboring masses behind it? When such a prospect was offered by the newly formed Communist Party, most syndicalists were temporarily enthusiastic but ultimately found it at best a partial answer. Even those who welcomed the idea of a truly revolutionary party could not accept Lenin's reversal of syndicalist theory, when he claimed that the party must lead since the unions were too reformist to make the revolution on their own. In fact, syndicalists came to stress union autonomy above revolutionary commitment, when they chose collaboration with postwar reformists in place of continued subordination to the Communist Party. Still, these syndicalists believed that a middle ground might exist between the comparable evils of the CGTU and the CGT.

As seen from the unionists' perspective, the Communist Party was less a revolutionary alternative to Socialist politics than an extreme version of the Socialists' stress on organization and political leadership. Like prewar Guesdists, the Communists wished to subordinate the unions to the direction of a revolutionary avant-garde. Party leaders also espoused a doctrine of centralization, in which tactics would be designed by the central leadership and only carried out by the local branches. Local spontaneity, or sensitivity to unique local conditions, would thus be subordinated to the perceived needs of the revolution on a national—or international—scale.

This pattern of centralization conflicted with the syndicalist traditions of local autonomy, which had shaped the federalist structure of the prewar CGT. Local associations of unions (Bourses du Travail), federated loosely on the national level, at first made most of the important decisions, as in the timing or execution of strikes. Then parallel to this system of Bourses grew a network of national federations that grouped unions of the same trade or industry. These federations gained increasing authority as unionists—and party supporters—came to recognize the importance of Paris as the seat of government action in the national economy.[6] Still, syndicalists who disputed such parliamentary activity also questioned the need for centralized institutions, which were of limited value in direct dealings with industrial employers—except those similarly organized on a national basis, such as the steel industry with its Comité des Forges.

Many syndicalists also questioned the party's attempt to speak for the mass of French workers. Indeed, they had often admired the Communists' disdain for compromise for the sake of building a mass organization, and they shared Lenin's apparent faith in a small-scale movement that would retain its revolutionary purity by excluding all but the most dedicated activists from its ranks. Some carried this faith to its logical extreme by willingly breaking with all rivals—even those in the Communist Party—to form their own groups, however tiny. The idea of schism may in fact be seen as a syndicalist concept, while the Communists—after completing the rupture of the party organizations—instead urged trade-union unity, if only to let themselves eventually win control of the union movement as a whole.

The idea of schism and minority unionism might seem to contradict the principle of proletarian unity, which for revolutionary syndicalists had been the main argument for preserving union autonomy from the divisive effects of party politics. Few syndicalists actually preferred schism to unity, although their extremism helped to provoke the schism, while their militant methods became all the more necessary to compensate for the unions' small size. Most syndicalists accepted the principle of mass unionization, but only if their ideals could remain uncompromised. Whatever the theories, in practice the syndicalists spoke only for a small group of workers, although even the early Communists likewise won little mass support.

Beyond its political dimensions, syndicalism must thus be examined as an economic program that represented specific groups of workers. Despite their frequent sectarianism, most syndicalists did defend the workers' practical interests, which they thought were ignored by partisan politicians and by national leaders unfamiliar with specific local needs. Even workers who were more immediately concerned with practical issues of wages or working conditions than with abstract party ideologies could respond to the syndicalists' strategic decisions on when or how to strike. By looking at these strategic issues, as argued by different groups of workers, it is possible to discover how far their choices of strategy or program were determined by their economic position, and how far political divisions within the labor movement corresponded to social and economic divisions within the working class.[7]

The fact of social or economic divisions among workers conflicted, of course, with the ideal of working-class unity. These divisions could follow skill or wage levels, sex or geographic origins, or "corporate" distinctions among workers in different trades. The term "corporatism," as applied to the labor movement, commonly implies a certain reformism because it suggests the possibility of social harmony between workers and their employers in a given industry, plus the existence of craft divisions among workers that would impede class solidarity.[8] Even "revolutionary" unionists could be highly corporative, however, if they stressed their own interests as skilled craftsmen rather than the needs of the unskilled masses. Despite the idea of industrial unionism among revolutionary syndicalists elsewhere, such as in the United States among the Industrial Workers of the World, syndicalism in France tended to speak primarily for the interests of highly skilled workers in relatively small-scale industries. These were more often factory workers than self-employed artisans, and they sometimes achieved wider bonds of solidarity with less-skilled colleagues in the same neighborhoods or workshops. Nevertheless, such wider bonds were more the exception than the rule.[9]

These economic conditions, like the political conditions that had shaped prewar syndicalism, underwent certain changes in the wartime and immediate postwar period. The evolution of syndicalism must thus be examined not only in light of the political crises of war and revolution but also in terms of the growth of industrial concentration and the development of new technologies, the problems of inflation and postwar economic recessions, and the changing demographic composition of the labor force. This economic dimension of French trade unionism, partially explored elsewhere for the prewar years and again for the period since the 1930s, has been least examined for the wartime and immediate postwar era.[10] The nature of the changes in the wartime and postwar economy must first be described if one is to assess their political impact. Only then can one see if these changes necessitated a new political strategy, as the Communists and Socialists argued, or if the old syndicalist traditions were still relevant and viable after the war.

From such analysis, it can be shown that the survival and development of postwar syndicalism resulted in large part from the absence of vast economic or political transformations that would have made it truly outmoded. The war did accelerate the growth and concentration of French industry, the recruitment of new sources of labor, and the active participation of the government in the economy.[11] Some of these changes, however, had predated the war, while others were undone, or at least slowed, by the postwar "return to normalcy" and by the effects of a recession in 1921. Despite vast growth and technological change in some sectors, such as the automobile industry, others remained surprisingly stagnant or subject to the same fluctuations that had plagued the prewar economy. In general, the war caused more quantitative growth than it did structural changes. Neither the concentration of industry nor the recruitment of new groups of unskilled workers seriously challenged the predominance of skilled labor, on which the prewar syndicalist movement had been based.[12] Even the often cited "rationalization" of industry was more idea than reality, at least by the end of the postwar decade.[13] In this context, the old doctrines still appealed to those who dominated the unions, if perhaps not to the entire work force. Only with the onset of the Depression and the Popular Front would new economic pressures and party strategies create a mass base for the French labor movement; even then it was unclear how long this new phenomenon would endure.[14]

In the political realm as well, the war's impact should not be exaggerated. Although the war led to new discontents and new social and political conflicts, these did not decisively alter the labor movement after the war's end. Among some groups, the war led to greater moderation and willingness to collaborate with party or government leaders,[15] but this was true primarily among those who had already been moving toward reformism before 1914. Among other groups, who were instead radicalized by their wartime experience, postwar divisions and rivalries sometimes did more to enhance a revolutionary syndicalist outlook than to promote the Communist Party. Even the syndicalists did adapt to new circumstances, such as by recognizing the value of larger unions and more pragmatic philosophies, but they still refused to abandon their stress on union autonomy or accept the party leaders' pretensions to represent "the wave of the future." Indeed, the idea that the war had changed everything — that it was "the end of an era" — may be seen as part of the parties' own postwar propaganda, or as part of a "generational" myth of youthful revolt, which most historians have tended to echo rather than to analyze in its own right.[16]

To illustrate the survival of the syndicalist movement, and the nature of the political and economic forces that helped to shape it, it is instructive to examine the movement in two industrial communities, Limoges and Saint-Etienne. The early growth of trade unionism in both cities offers a fairly long historical perspective from which to examine what became of the movements later on. The two cities also represent contrasting political traditions on the left and a rich assortment of industrial and craft occupations. These features allow an examination of the roles played by leftist traditions and specific industrial conditions in the evolution of labor politics before and after the CGT schism. They also permit an assessment of how far national or international political issues became meaningful to local workers and unionists in their daily affairs.

Limoges is a classic example of a city with a well-organized but essentially moderate socialist movement. The city became known as a center of left-wing socialism and site of a pacifist movement that first questioned the party's politics of Sacred Union during World War I. However dramatic, these events contrasted sharply with the explosion of antiwar strikes, led by a small but highly militant syndicalist vanguard, in Saint-Etienne in 1917–18. This movement, the product of a long-standing history of anarchism and anarcho-syndicalism in the region, helped keep habits of prewar militancy alive well into the postwar era. It also revealed the weakness of moderate socialism in Saint-Etienne and the tendency of militant unionists to adopt extreme solutions rather than try to rally mass support.[17]

These contrasts continued to shape local unionism and politics in the years after the labor schism. Although the party split gave a majority to the Socialists in Limoges and to the Communists in Saint-Etienne, labor unionists in both cities quickly rallied to the new CGTU. Still, many quickly regretted the choice and turned instead to other options: autonomy, a third confederation, or a return to the old CGT. The strength of postwar syndicalism, even in Limoges, shows that it was not doomed by the evolution of wartime reformism, any more than communism meant the demise of revolutionary syndicalism in Saint-Etienne. The two cities may have diverged from the national patterns, but they were hardly unique cases of provincial particularism. As older industrial regions, with deeply implanted syndicalist traditions, they illustrated the obstacles, both economic and political, to the growth of new forms of Socialist or Communist unionism in postwar France.

The two cities also illustrate the contrasts that result from distinct patterns of social relations and industrial development. The strength and moderation of Limoges socialism were based in large part on the high degree of homogeneity and cohesion of its labor movement, where one major industry—porcelain manufacture—employed a large share of the city's work force and produced most of the local Socialist leaders. By contrast, the absence of such homogeneity in Saint-Etienne, with its wide variety of crafts and industries, hindered the growth of labor solidarity and led instead to a fragmented labor movement that ranged from extremism at its fringes to inertia and passivity among the bulk of the work force. These factors continued to shape labor politics in the two cities, even as technological and demographic changes began to modify the behavior of specific groups of workers. The local context provides a convenient setting in which to measure these economic and demographic changes as well as their effects on unionization, strike activity, and social relations with local employers and with rival segments of the working class.

The local context also demonstrates the continued importance of local differences in the French labor movement. These differences laid the basis for the syndicalists' stress on local autonomy and for their resistance to the centralization that Parisian — or Bolshevik — labor leaders sought to impose. In its preoccupation with unique local conditions, especially those of an economic or social nature, revolutionary syndicalism resembled the regionalist movement, as even spokesman Alfred Rosmer recognized in the 1920s.[18] Again, the experiences of Limoges and Saint-Etienne may be special cases, as older industrial regions whose particularism might be lost as the country continued to modernize. Nonetheless, such local and regional particularisms remain very much alive in France, even today.

To summarize, this study seeks to examine the syndicalist movement in action, as it evolved in response to changing economic and political conditions. It will begin by sketching the local profile of industries and workers and by introducing the diverse political currents of the labor movement before the war. From there, it will consider the war experience — labor strikes, the conditions of war production, and the emergence of international communism — and its effects on syndicalist theory and practice, in order to see how much syndicalism indeed changed with the times. The approach is essentially chronological, although the perspective will vary to include local as well as national events and economic as well as political developments. Underlying the chronology is an attempt to measure change and continuity, to weigh the effect of the war on French society, as seen through the prism of trade-union affairs.[19]

The study will also permit a reconsideration of the major literature on the origins of French communism. By looking at local affairs and at trade-union responses to Bolshevik doctrine, we can reassess the relative importance of outside ideological influences and indigenous conflicts that arose during and after the war.[20] In addition, by continuing the story through the end of the postwar decade, we can see how far the new doctrines created a genuine social impact. The local focus will also demonstrate that decisions made in Paris often failed to win local support.

The basic literature on French strikes will also receive careful attention. Again, the main intent is the same: to understand strikes as a political phenomenon and not just as a response to specific economic grievances.[21] The generalizations may nonetheless be modified by the study of strikes in specific localities and in different sectors of the major industries, which differed sharply in the degree of economic concentration and in the size or frequency of labor unrest. Closer scrutiny will reveal, for

example, the high incidence of strikes among mid-sized companies (neither the largest factories nor the smallest artisanal workshops)[22] and the
tendency for strikes to aim at single companies, with little regional or national coordination.[23] Postwar patterns show substantial continuity with
those from prewar days and seem more consistent with syndicalist than
with Communist strategy. Strike behavior also varied sharply according
to factional distinctions that led to differences in political strategies, in the
willingness to compromise, and in the desire to act independently or to
seek allies among rival groups.[24] These differences in aims and methods,
not just in organizational capacities, are part of the political meaning of
strikes and are best studied in their specific contexts rather than through
statistical averages that sometimes obscure as much as they reveal.

Above all, this study will attempt a reassessment of syndicalist theory
and practice. Although the literature is scanty, most authors seem to
share the view that the movement was little more than a *"syndicalisme de
métier,"* confined to a handful of artisans and doomed to extinction once
the artisan tradition disappeared.[25] Instead, the movement's appeal to
skilled workers in small or mid-sized factories (which remained the
norm, despite industrial concentration) enabled syndicalists to retain the
leadership of many unions and to continue to use them to defend their
special interests. If these interests sounded more "practical" than revolutionary in tone, that too had its roots in prewar practice, which was far
less devoted to "noise and impotence" than its critics often assume.[26]

In short, syndicalism was both more durable and less exotic than it has
appeared to historians and to contemporary observers. To explain its appeal, and to compare it to rival currents, this study will look beyond simple
ideologies to determine their actual impact and to see how the different
viewpoints were put into effect. Because these practices varied sharply according to specific economic and social contexts, they may seem to justify
the view that syndicalism was a "mongrel creed," or "a practice in search
of a theory," rather than the coherent product of a single thinker.[27] On
the other hand, these variations show the movement's relative flexibility,
as it adapted to changing conditions, and its ability to translate abstract
doctrines into practical programs that had meaning for average workers
and their everyday concerns.

It is, of course, difficult to write the history of "average workers," who
leave little documentation; this study thus necessarily focuses more on the
unionized minority than on the labor force as a whole. The larger context
is nonetheless apparent in the unions' efforts to expand their recruitment

and in the varying degrees of unionization and strike participation among the different groups of workers. By incorporating all these elements into a study of labor unionism in a specific geographic and temporal setting, this study tries to transcend—while not ignoring—the traditional labor historian's concern with ideas and institutions. Only by reintegrating the study of politics and ideology with the analysis of economic and sociological conditions can one hope to achieve a full understanding of labor history or of the historical reality of any social class.

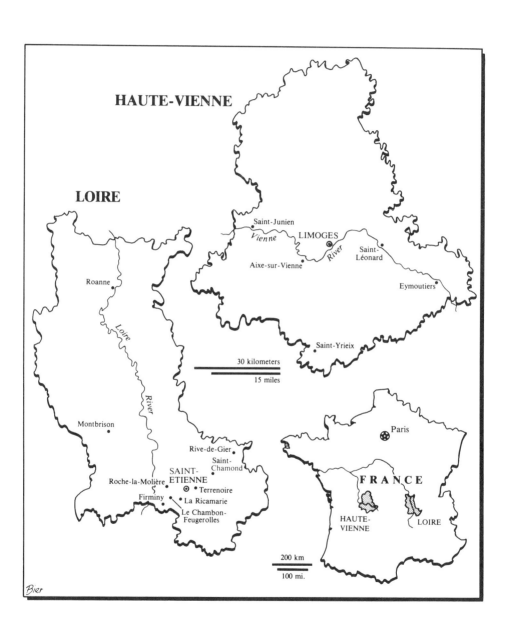

HAUTE-VIENNE

LOIRE

Saint-Junien
LIMOGES
Vienne River
Saint-Léonard
Aixe-sur-Vienne
Eymoutiers

Roanne

Loire

River

Saint-Yrieix

30 kilometers

15 miles

Montbrison

Rive-de-Gier
Saint-Chamond

SAINT-ETIENNE
Roche-la-Molière
Terrenoire
Firminy
La Ricamarie
Le Chambon-Feugerolles

Paris

FRANCE

HAUTE-VIENNE
LOIRE

200 km

100 mi.

Bier

Chapter 1

Limoges and Saint-Etienne: An Economic and Social Profile

The roots of the labor history of Limoges and Saint-Etienne in the early twentieth century must be sought in the economic and social transformations of the previous decades. Underlying the distinctive traditions of unionism and party politics in the two communities were major economic and social trends that shaped the industries and the populations from which the labor movements were to grow. In both communities, rapid industrial and urban growth in the nineteenth century underlay the precocious development of labor militancy and leftist politics. This rapid growth proved short-lived, however, and unable to dispel the relative economic backwardness of the larger region in which the two communities are located. Instead, the future labor history of the region was largely the outgrowth of an aging and fragmented industrial base, which modernized too slowly to keep up with more dynamic competitors at home and abroad.

The Cities and the Regions

Limoges and Saint-Etienne are located on the western and eastern fringes, respectively, of the mountainous Massif Central. Rugged climate and terrain accounted for much of the region's rural poverty and geographic isolation, as long as transportation and communication networks remained scarce and hard to build. The sparseness of local agriculture, in turn, set free a pool of surplus rural labor that turned the cities into centers of urban industrial expansion. Saint-Etienne also lies at the apex of a rich coal basin that has attracted labor and supplied fuel for other industrial activities, including artisanal metalworking and textile

weaving, first developed as cottage industries in the countryside to supplement the meager agriculture of the rocky terrain.

Limoges, capital of the department of the Haute-Vienne, is located in
the valley of the Vienne River. This location provided both a relatively
open plain for urban expansion and the pure waters and water power for
the growth of porcelain, leather, and paper industries. Beyond the plain
of Limoges is a hilly plateau that extends into the neighboring departments of Corrèze and Creuse. To supplement the region's agriculture
—classed in 1840 as among the least productive in the country—there
developed a variety of rural industries, including metal trades, kaolin
quarries, scattered paper and textile mills, and the making of chestnut
barrel staves: in sum, a set of small-scale enterprises as "archaic" as the
agriculture with which they coexisted.[1] In this region of primitive technology, the city of Limoges soon became a center of relative dynamism.
Other cities near Limoges, including Saint-Léonard and Saint-Yrieix,
grew primarily as urban satellites; only Saint-Junien, with its glove industry, attained some independent economic importance, which faded
quickly once that industry waned.

Unlike Limoges, Saint-Etienne has had several rivals for the center of
attention in its region. Today Saint-Etienne (capital of the Loire department) is the eighth largest city in France, but it long languished in the
economic and cultural shadow of its giant neighbor, Lyon (department
of the Rhône). Only the growth of its coal and steel industries helped the
Loire basin develop an independent economic identity distinct from that
of Lyon or the Loire's own textile center at Roanne. Even in the Loire
basin, Saint-Etienne shared the spotlight with such nearby cities as Firminy, Le Chambon-Feugerolles, and La Ricamarie in the Ondaine valley,
and Rive-de-Gier, Saint-Chamond, and Terrenoire in the Gier valley. Although these cities remained of secondary economic and political importance, they developed as partners rather than as satellites of Saint-
Etienne, and they often had distinct industrial strengths such as in heavy
metallurgy, which was relatively minor at Saint-Etienne itself.

Except for the fertile plains to the west, Saint-Etienne is surrounded
with mountainous land where, as in the Limousin, rural industry arose to
supplement marginal farming incomes. These cottage industries included
woodworking, small metallurgy (arms and hardware), and silk ribbon
weaving. Because these trades, unlike those in the Limousin, closely resembled their urban counterparts, they provided a pool of skilled labor

from which the cities could draw. The relative vitality of these cottage industries also slowed the rural exodus among artisans who could remain profitably in the countryside.[2]

The Growth of Industry

A key to understanding the attitudes and behavior of a city's workers is the type and structure of their occupations. These factors varied widely in Limoges and Saint-Etienne, where the principal industries ranged from luxury craft manufactures to such heavier industries as coal and steel. Even single industries included sharp contrasts in technological development, from small family workshops to larger factories employing several hundred workers at a time. This extreme variety prompted parallel contrasts in labor organization and blocked the cohesion that a common labor experience might have allowed.

Even today, the Limousin is known for its underdeveloped industry and its small establishments "anarchically dispersed" in the countryside.[3] Urban industries, although more highly developed than their rural counterparts, have remained no less traditionalist in outlook, slow to expand credit or marketing facilities, and dependent on high prices to compensate for the low-volume sales of luxury goods.[4] In the nineteenth and early twentieth centuries, the most modern of the region's industries was the famous porcelain industry, launched by Turgot in 1771 to make use of local kaolin supplies. The industry's rapid growth was owed primarily to the initiative of an outsider, the American David Haviland, who opened his own factory in 1842 to supply the china he had been importing into the United States. Haviland's widely copied idea was to improve efficiency by grouping the processes of manufacture and decoration under a single roof. After this one innovation, the industry resisted further mechanization or concentration and so had trouble competing with cheaper foreign production and keeping up with aggressive labor demands.[5]

The other principal Limoges industry was shoe manufacture, which grew slowly during the nineteenth century but surged ahead of porcelain in the 1920s, thanks to its wartime role as supplier of army boots. Ironically enough, the rapid growth did little to expand existing establishments but instead spurred the proliferation of small new companies, many of which were too marginal to survive postwar economic downturns. This fragmentation did as much to shape labor behavior as did the new ma-

chinery that replaced artisanal shoemaking with assembly-line production. In contrast, porcelain manufacture remained a more highly skilled profession even as its companies increased slowly in size.

Nearby Saint-Junien was the home of a wide range of leather industries, including glove manufacture and the tanning and dyeing trades to supply the leather for gloves and shoes. Although the tanning companies were relatively concentrated and mechanized, the glove industry was a classic case of a luxury trade practiced primarily in the home. As demand for luxury goods declined in the twentieth century, the glove industry faced heavy unemployment and the rise of a particularly bitter if erratic labor movement in Saint-Junien.[6]

In the countryside near Saint-Junien and Saint-Léonard were scattered many paper and cardboard factories, making use of the straw left over from the milling of rye grain. Although these industries were fairly concentrated by regional standards, their rural locations isolated workers from contacts with their urban comrades. This isolation, plus the high proportion of unskilled women and peasant employees, curbed the militancy that the industry's factory structure might otherwise have propelled.

Other secondary industries in Saint-Junien and Limoges included the manufacture of wool felt as a by-product of leather processing, a small-scale metals industry that produced light machinery for the porcelain and shoe factories, and the usual array of printing, construction, and public and private service industries, whose workers were sometimes active in the labor movement. The railroad workers would draw special attention in the postwar period. Nonetheless, the major industries, porcelain and shoe manufacture, set the context of economic activity and political behavior in which the various labor groups would interact.

Even more highly diversified than those in Limoges were the principal industries in Saint-Etienne and its environs. Though best known for its coal mines, the Loire basin was also the home of important textile and metals industries, including both highly traditional craft specialties and more modern factory trades. Even the coal mines displayed some of the Loire's endemic traditionalism. First developed as early as the Middle Ages, the coal industry was still splintered in a maze of tiny concessions and slow to adopt the new technology of its rival basins in the Nord and Pas-de-Calais. At their peak in the nineteenth century, the coal mines spurred both urban growth and labor militancy throughout the Loire basin; later on, the industry and its workers instead showed the same stagnation that had come to typify the artisanal sector in Saint-Etienne.[7]

While the availability of coal helped to launch modern steel production in the Loire in 1820, the large reserves of skilled labor meant that artisanal gun and hardware manufacture remained more important, first as cottage trades and then also as urban industries. This diversity long hindered the unionization of the region's metalworkers. The most traditional sector was Saint-Etienne's gunsmiths, similar in status to independent artisans although hired and supervised as workers by outside entrepreneurs. Even the newer cycle and auto trades borrowed many artisan techniques — and workers — from the older specialties. Large factories remained the exception, as small shops proliferated to produce parts rather than assemble entire machines under one roof. The steel industry likewise remained largely traditional in outlook and method, despite its vast expansion during World War I. Wartime profits appear to have been invested in land purchases, not in modern equipment. Later on, cheaper domestic and foreign competition forced a conversion to labor-intensive specialties, such as automotive and electrical parts and high-grade steel, to take advantage of local labor skills.[8]

Silk ribbon weaving, for a long time the largest industry in the Loire basin, might seem out of place in a region of mines and steel mills. Like metalworking, however, the textile industry owed its origins to the availability of labor and to the cultivation in cottage industries of artisanal attitudes and skills. Until recent decades the ribbon industry — known as *passementerie,* and its weavers as *passementiers* — retained the commercial and industrial structures of preceding centuries. Factories were virtually nonexistent; most of the work was done at home by weavers who owned their own looms but who were hired by entrepreneurs as in the old putting-out system. Some weavers hired journeymen to operate more looms than could be run by their own spouses and children. Although these weavers still called themselves workers rather than small entrepreneurs, especially for tax purposes, they were quite distinct from a proletarian labor force.[9]

Even in the twentieth century, when large factories began producing cheaper synthetic ribbons, mass production never supplanted the artisanal manufacturing typical of the Loire. Employers now set up their factories in isolated rural locations, in order to avoid the cities' higher wages and reputed labor unrest. With declining demand for high-priced silk ribbons, however, city weavers likewise faced stagnant wages and frequent bouts of unemployment, tempering whatever militancy they might have felt.[10]

Because of its coal supplies, the Loire basin also developed a sizable glassmaking industry, centered at Givors (in the Rhône department) and at Rive-de-Gier rather than at Saint-Etienne. Other local industries included printing, construction, transportation, and various services, whose workers were sometimes active in the labor movement, as at Limoges. Still, their behavior was shaped as much by local influences as by any universal characteristics of a given occupation. The combined factors of local geography and political traditions, plus the way labor groups interacted with one another, tell more about a city's labor history than can the sum of case studies of single labor groups.

Industrial Structure and Urban Demography

The industrialization of Limoges and Saint-Etienne was the main spur to their growth in population, as rural migrants flocked to the cities in search of jobs. From a modestly sized city in the eighteenth century, Limoges grew rapidly in the decade after 1840 to become one of the country's twenty-five largest cities by mid-century and then doubled in population by 1896. The Loire basin grew even more spectacularly, expanding between 1820 and 1870 at a rate three times the national average, while Saint-Etienne's own population more than tripled in size. By the late nineteenth century, however, both cities began to stagnate as much in population as in industrial and economic growth. After 1911, when the cities reached peak levels of approximately 92,000 (Limoges) and 149,000 (Saint-Etienne), a combination of wartime casualties, the modest birth rates of an aging population, and the scarcity of jobs for would-be rural migrants caused short-term *declines* in urban populations and irregular growth rates that continue to the present day.[11]

A stagnant population has been a problem for the entire Limousin region, where rural exodus has drained far more manpower than the region's own cities have absorbed. The region has also attracted few migrants from distant parts of the country or—until the 1960s—from abroad. Thus, while Limoges has owed its growth to the influx of rural workers, most have come from the same or neighboring departments, as shown in Figure 1 (see Appendix). This highly insulated regional population would shape the city's labor movement in decisive ways.

Although the Loire typically lost less of its population to emigration outside the region, it has been scarcely more successful in attracting outsiders, except for the many foreigners recruited during and after World

War I. Until then, most of Saint-Etienne's population was, like that of Limoges, native either to the city or to its immediate environs (see Figure 1). The region's modest rural exodus showed the vitality of rural industries that long kept artisans employed in the countryside. As a result, the city's newcomers included a larger share of unskilled peasants, unsuited to the demands of skilled factory jobs.

Lured by the demand for industrial labor, both cities' populations owed much of their livelihoods to industrial activity. In Saint-Etienne, an especially high proportion of that industrial population was actively employed, probably because so many wives and children worked in the family shops.[12] Even within the active population, of course, not all were wage-earning workers. Still, the bourgeoisie in both communities included more artisanal entrepreneurs than wealthy captains of industry, and distinctions often blurred between wage earners and *petits patrons*.[13]

Both cities had developed large working-class populations by the late nineteenth century. In Limoges, according to figures for 1881, workers and employees in industry, commerce, and related services totaled one-half of the active male population. In Saint-Etienne, by 1891, industrial workers of both sexes comprised nearly two-thirds of the active population; the total including shop and office employees was as much as three-fourths.[14] Nonetheless, in both cities, artisanal trades remained common even within major industries. Although it is difficult to distinguish artisanal from proletarian labor for separate measurement, evidence from individual industries can illustrate the scant degree of "proletarianization" that had occurred by the end of World War I.

In Limoges, the primacy of skilled labor is shown first by the distribution of workers among the city's major industries (see Figure 2). Together, shoe and porcelain manufacturing employed the vast majority of the city's industrial work force, with the porcelain industry well in the lead at the turn of the century and falling behind shoe manufacture only after the war.[15] In both industries, the most strictly artisanal specialties—that is, hand-painted porcelain decoration and non-mechanized shoemaking— were still quite common in prewar years but declined sharply thereafter, according to data sampled from the city's manuscript censuses of 1911, 1921, and 1931[16] (see Figure 3). In both cases the numbers rebounded during the 1920s but remained low in proportion to the total work force. Still, even other specialties remained highly skilled and non-proletarian in spirit, especially as the average size of enterprise remained quite small.

Among both porcelain and shoe workers, the vast majority worked in small factories, many with 5 or fewer employees. Companies with more than 500 employees were not unknown but remained highly uncommon, both before and after the war (see Figure 4). The number of smaller establishments did decline in both industries, while larger companies (with more than 20 employees) rose in number, both during the war period and (at least for shoes) after 1921.[17] In both industries, moreover, the largest companies were in Limoges rather than in outlying communities. Even for city workers, however, the preponderance of small establishments — and attendant problems of inefficiency and high unemployment — remained facts of life.[18]

As in Limoges, "proletarianization" was slow to occur in the industries of the Loire basin, defined as the districts of Saint-Etienne and Montbrison in the Loire department and the district of Yssingeaux in the nearby Haute-Loire. Throughout the basin, textiles alone employed approximately as many workers as mining and metalworking together, although at Saint-Etienne the metals industry grew predominant during and after World War I[19] (see Figure 5). Like the porcelain painters and shoemakers in Limoges, artisanal gunsmiths in Saint-Etienne declined sharply in number during the war decade and then rebounded only slightly in proportion to the larger work force. Meanwhile, at least prior to the 1930s, the textile industry remained essentially as artisanal as ever, especially since journeyman weavers were often able to open their own workshops[20] (see Figure 6).

The large number of independent weavers meant that most establishments had five or fewer employees. The total number of these tiny shops declined during the war period but then rose again in the 1920s, even as the industry's total employment decreased. Nor was there an appreciable increase in the number of larger companies (see Figure 7). Despite some shift from artisanal to factory weaving as synthetic textiles began to displace high-quality silk ribbons, factories in the 1920s still operated only about one-fourth of the total looms in the region. Moreover, unlike the Haute-Vienne's larger porcelain or shoe companies, most of the Loire's larger textile establishments were located in rural, not urban, domains.[21]

In the metals industry, the principal change was a shift from gun manufacture to cycle, automotive, and diverse small machine trades. These continued to need skilled and semiskilled workers, who far outnumbered the unskilled manual laborers in steel mills or heavy metallurgy, especially in Saint-Etienne proper, where few of the region's largest establishments were located (see Figure 6). In the city's machine trades, most auto parts companies and some producers of arms and cycles (such as Manu-france or the government-controlled Manufacture Nationale d'Armes) employed more than 1,000 workers each. Of the city's more than 230 manufacturers of cycle parts, in contrast, most had fewer than 50 — and sometimes fewer than 5 — employees; most gunsmiths still worked either in small workshops or *à façon* in their own homes.[22] In the metals indus-try generally, the number of tiny shops declined proportionally as larger shops (all those with more than 5 employees) became more numerous (see Figure 7). Except in heavy metallurgy, however, the process of con-centration remained modest throughout the postwar period and failed to alter significantly the structure of the industry as a whole.[23]

Even the coal mines did little to challenge the preeminence of small in-dustry in the Loire basin. Although the coal industry grew rapidly in the mid-nineteenth century, it leveled off by the next century except for a brief postwar surge. More so even than the steel mills, most of the mines were located outside the city of Saint-Etienne. Regardless of location, most miners were relatively highly skilled workers, although the number of unskilled manual laborers, as distinguished in the manuscript census, increased slowly between 1911 and 1921 (see Figure 6). Nor was large-scale organization a universal pattern in the region, ever since the failure in the 1850s of an attempted merger to create a single huge mining cor-poration. By the twentieth century, the basin had four large companies (including two at Saint-Etienne) that each employed more than 3,000 miners, but several others employed fewer than 500, and elsewhere in the department companies with under 100 or even under 20 workers were not unknown. During the war period, the total number of the smallest mines actually increased, while those in the intermediate ranks declined (see Figure 7). By the 1930s, economic difficulties forced the merger or shutdown of several ailing companies, and few but the largest companies survived. Nonetheless, the industry remained fragmented and inefficient until the nationalizations that followed World War II.[24]

Although glass manufacture was prominent elsewhere in the Loire basin and in the neighboring Rhône department, it was only a minor ac-tivity at Saint-Etienne. The city's glassworkers, engaged primarily in the production of table glassware, were employed in mid-sized companies of 100 to 150 workers each. Mechanization was further advanced at Givors and Rive-de-Gier, which specialized instead in bottles and windowglass, but even there the factories rarely exceeded 500 employees. While the number of larger establishments in the industry did increase during the war period, companies with 20 or fewer workers continued to exist (see Figure 7). Again, subsequent economic difficulties hit the smallest companies most heavily.[25] Overall, however, the processes of technological change and industrial concentration, while not absent in Saint-Etienne's major industries, did little to alter the pattern of small workshops and domestic manufacturing that coexisted beside the larger establishments well after the end of World War I.

In addition to company size and structure, factors of age, sex, and geographic origin can characterize an industrial labor force and illustrate its change in composition over time. These factors can also distinguish one labor group from another and indicate the homogeneity that might foster class consciousness within or among individual labor groups. Like the occupational details, these demographic factors appear in the cities' manuscript censuses, as sampled for the period 1911 to 1931.

A major trend shown in the census data was the growing proportion of women in the labor force. In the Haute-Vienne, women were especially numerous in both the Saint-Junien glove industry and the rural paper industry, but they also represented at least a third of the Limoges porcelain workers and a fourth of the shoe workers, the latter share increasing steadily as the industry expanded after the war[26] (see Figure 3). In Saint-Etienne, women outnumbered men in the textile industry, but they scarcely appeared in the coal mines and they held a small though increasing share in the various machine trades[27] (see Figure 6). Women were likewise a negligible quantity in the railroad industry of both cities[28] (see Figure 8). The latter industry merits special attention because of its relatively large labor force and active strike record before and after the war.

The growth of female employment paralleled changes in industrial structure as male-dominated artisanal professions gave way to less exclusive factory jobs. In both cities, women rarely entered the most elite artisanal specialties (see figures 3 and 6). In the textile industry, some women were self-employed weavers but most served as factory workers or auxiliary personnel. Men likewise dominated porcelain painting and artisanal shoemaking. The scarcity of wartime labor did open to women certain skilled trades, as in shoes, gloves, and metallurgy, although many of these jobs reverted to men after the war's end.[29] Still, most women were at least semiskilled factory workers, not unskilled manual laborers, so their role did not mean the "proletarianization" of the local labor force as a whole.

If growing female employment was often a sign of an industry's mechanization, the proportion of elderly workers was instead often an index of industrial stagnation or decline. Elderly workers were particularly numerous in the artisanal professions, where they could delay their retirements. In times of economic depression or slowdowns in hiring, young workers were also readier to avoid (or to quit) jobs in sluggish industries, while older workers stayed on the job out of inertia or from reluctance to forfeit past contributions to pension funds.[30]

Today the Haute-Vienne has an older than average labor force, as part of its general demographic stagnation.[31] In 1921 it had a large proportion of young workers under age twenty, but its intermediate age groups had been heavily hit by military casualties during the war. These effects were more muted in urban centers, where industrial workers were sometimes spared active military service. Overall, the industrial work force remained relatively elderly and showed little change since before 1914.[32]

Despite this overall stability, certain changes were visible within single industries. After the war, according to the sampled census data, the booming shoe and railroad industries employed growing numbers of younger workers, including young women. By contrast, the now stagnant porcelain industry lost its share of younger workers and barely held steady among those between thirty-five and fifty years of age (see Figure 3). Although these losses resulted in part from wartime casualties, which were greater in luxury trades than in defense-related industries, the effects were compounded by technological change. The porcelain painters displaced by mechanization had been relatively youthful, but the artisanal *cordonniers* had been far older than the factory shoe workers, even as early as 1911.

A high average age structure also characterized the Loire's laboring population. The pattern had already typified Saint-Etienne's work force in the late nineteenth century, although wartime casualties compounded the result. Even working women, while younger than the men, tended to be disproportionately elderly: a sign of stagnation in the industries where they worked (see Figure 6). In the textile industry, according to separate figures for the mid-1920s, an estimated 30 percent of Saint-Etienne's artisanal weavers were over age sixty and fewer than 4 percent were under thirty years of age. The industry's low wages also slowed the recruitment of younger workers, male or female. Among *ourdisseuses* (women who prepared the silk for the loom) by the mid-1920s, more than a third were over age fifty and fewer than a fifth were under twenty years of age.[33]

The metals industry attracted more young workers (including some

women), although the overall age structure had changed little by the end
of the postwar decade. Even artisanal gunsmiths remained relatively
youthful, despite a decline in their numbers. The industry's importance
in national defense probably helped it avoid heavy wartime casualties,
but recruitment leveled off after the end of the war. In contrast, the mines
and railroads—also spared extensive wartime losses—showed sharp
postwar downswings in age distribution as they recruited heavily among
younger workers, although among miners this trend was reversing by
1931 (see figures 6 and 8).

A final factor apparent in the census data was the geographic origins of
the labor force. While both cities attracted few newcomers from distant
regions, they drew heavily on peasant labor from the nearby countryside;
Saint-Etienne also recruited thousands of foreign workers during and after the war.[34] Within each city, geographic origins varied sharply from
one industry to another. Those occupations that required the most specialized skills typically employed the highest ratios of city-born workers,
while peasants and foreigners filled the jobs that local workers shunned.

In Limoges by the twentieth century, both the porcelain and the shoe
industries recruited mostly city-born workers (see Figure 3), but as of the
1890s many shoe workers had still come from elsewhere in the department. The sharpest differences were between artisanal shoemakers,
many of whom had learned their trade in a village workshop, and porcelain painters and decorators, nearly all of whom were born in the city,
where they were likelier to learn such a localized skill.[35] The decreased
role of artisans in both industries, in the course of the early twentieth
century, thus helped to make similar the geographic profiles of the two
groups of workers. In addition, during the war decade, both industries
gained slightly in the proportion of workers from outside the department
as overall geographic mobility increased.

As these examples suggest, certain industries drew large numbers of
rural workers if the required skills were not strictly local specialties. Like
the Limoges shoe industry, Saint-Etienne's industries typically recruited
not just unskilled peasants but also rural-born artisans experienced in
cottage weaving and metalworking trades. While artisanal ribbon weaving, like Limoges porcelain decoration, had the highest ratio of city-born
workers, other textile and metals trades employed rural migrants from
the zones where these cottage industries were practiced; migrants from
strictly agricultural zones worked instead in unskilled jobs in heavy metallurgy or in the coal mines.[36]

These patterns persisted well into the twentieth century (see Figure 6). Despite the progress of mechanization, the textile industry continued to employ relatively few rural migrants, as most of the factory silkworkers and auxiliary employees were wives or daughters of weavers in Saint-Etienne. In the metals industry, the high proportion of rural migrants that had characterized prewar artisanal gunsmiths continued among less skilled factory workers as rural and foreign labor multiplied after the war. Foreign workers became particularly numerous in heavy metallurgy, where they accounted for most of the postwar increase in employment. The coal mines likewise drew heavily on foreign labor as they became less attractive to native workers. Even among foreign workers, a sort of class system distinguished these two least favored industries: Italians and Spaniards monopolized the jobs in metallurgy while Poles and Moroccans were left to work in the mines.[37]

The influx of rural and foreign migrants affected both the workers' relations with employers and their own sense of solidarity. Migrants would be especially hard to organize in labor protests if they saw existing salaries as better than what they had left behind.[38] Many rural-born coal miners also continued to engage in part-time or seasonal farm labor, thereby helping to cushion against low wages or the threat of unemployment and prolonging their ties to a rural way of life.[39] Newcomers often lived in migrant ghettos, spoke *patois* or local dialects, and comprised a separate "culture"—one author called it a separate "race"—that adapted less readily to factory employment and to the institutions of urban politics.[40] These problems may have been eased by the narrow range of migration that let city and countryside preserve a common regional identity.[41] Nonetheless, only unusual political astuteness could forge these shared regional attitudes into a cohesive party or union campaign.

Still harder to assimilate were the foreign workers, especially those of non-Latin origin. Their isolation was compounded by the separate residential "colonies" that employers built to tie the immigrants to their new jobs. Despite these efforts, problems of high employee turnover, plus low productivity and exotic customs, continued to make foreign workers a less than satisfactory answer to the labor shortages that had spurred their recruitment. Native workers had fewer complaints about the foreign influx, as long as the tight labor market minimized job competition. Still, they rarely succeeded in drawing foreign workers into French unions or political associations, which could do little to handle the consular or legal problems addressed by the foreigners' own groups.[42]

Unlike the other main local industries, the railroad industries of Limoges and Saint-Etienne employed few city-born workers and a large number of newcomers from distant regions of France (see Figure 8). This pattern persisted after the war, although employment of local workers increased slightly. If the narrow range of recruitment in other industries helped to preserve a common regional culture, this wider sphere exposed the cities to new political strategies. The difference may explain in part the active role played by railroad workers in the postwar labor movement, especially in Limoges.[43]

Overall, it is difficult to assess the role of these geographic and demographic factors in the history of labor politics. Without detailed lists of unionists or strikers, there is no way to show that given groups of workers were more or less likely to take action. Nor should one assume a uniform pattern of behavior for given categories according to stereotypes that might portray artisans, or women, or elderly workers, or rural migrants as less radical or ready to organize. Such assumptions would fail especially to account for the frequent strikes and pacifist activities by wartime women. In general, when employed in the same occupations, women joined unions at rates comparable to those for men; the differences, for women and for migrants alike, may result in large part from the unskilled trades in which they were so often employed.[44]

Beyond differences according to skill level, it may also be possible to see differences in militancy according to the social composition of given cities or industries. Regardless of how an individual factor influenced behavior, the fact of social or demographic diversity within the work force would tend to obstruct the solidarity of the group. Even if women, or the elderly, or migrant workers were by themselves no less militant, their presence provided an element of disunity or potential rivalry that could distract their comrades from common goals. Homogeneity of any sort was sometimes an asset, such as among coal miners, whose high degree of rural origins added to the bonds of unity within the corporation; on the other hand, this very factor would further isolate the miners from their comrades in other trades.

Homogeneity was also weakened by the wide range of trades and specialties among the major industries. Even if a single subgroup with common experiences could achieve a high level of craft consciousness, such experiences might well fail to inspire solidarity throughout the industry, much less a genuine class consciousness among workers overall.

These factors help to explain not only the slow development of class consciousness and labor militancy among French workers generally but also important differences among local communities. In the two cases here considered, Limoges workers showed a relatively high degree of social cohesion, both within and among major industries, while Saint-Etienne workers were far more heterogeneous, even fragmented, in isolated or competing groups. These differences led to important distinctions in the two cities' labor movements, as succeeding chapters will illustrate. Such differences also underlay persistent trends of localism, or the desire for local autonomy, among workers whose material interests and cultural horizons long remained defined primarily in local terms.

If social and demographic factors helped to shape labor politics, it remains to assess how much these factors, or their political consequences, changed during the era of World War I. Even if they resulted from material conditions that no longer prevailed after a period of social or technological transformation, early political attitudes might well have remained influential, especially among older individuals who had come of age during a previous era. Such circumstances might account for perceived age differences among rival political groupings, or for the often assumed generational conflicts between labor radicals and moderates, or between Communists and syndicalists, after the end of the war.[45] But such claims would instead appear largely polemical, or without factual basis, if it could be shown that the conditions that had shaped earlier attitudes had not in fact been transformed as much as partisans assumed.

From the evidence so far presented, certain changes did alter the social and demographic composition of the work force during the World War I era. The most dramatic changes included the influx of foreign workers in the Loire basin and the larger role of women workers both there and in the Haute-Vienne. Neither change, however, vastly transformed the local work forces, as the same groups remained numerically predominant in each industry, even if to a lesser extent. Some change also took place in the age distributions of industrial workers. The influx of youth might have stimulated new ideas among Limoges shoe workers, Loire miners, and railroad workers from both areas, but the relative aging of Limoges porcelain workers and Loire weavers and metalworkers would add instead to the persistence of attitudes from the past.

In addition, these demographic changes paralleled changes in occupational and industrial structure, as factory workers—including women, foreigners, and younger Frenchmen—began to replace the older and typically male artisans of the previous era. Despite this shift to factory labor, however, most of the new workers were skilled or semiskilled, at least in the cities' major industries. There was so far no vast explosion of un-skilled manual labor that might have sustained a new form of mass unionism transcending the craft distinctions that had so far kept the French labor movement divided and weak. The same skilled workers who had long since dominated labor politics continued to prevail even after the end of World War I.[46]

This continuity was reinforced by the survival of artisanal attitudes, even as artisans assembled under the roofs of larger workshops. The slow growth of factory concentration did little to upset these patterns. Larger companies did become somewhat more numerous, in the decades before the Depression, but the change applied more to those with ten to twenty employees than to those at the higher end of the scale. Even the tiniest establishments, with under five employees, held virtually constant in the Limoges porcelain industry and rebounded sharply in the Loire metals and ribbon industries after a brief decline in the years prior to 1921. Indeed, among Saint-Etienne ribbon weavers, the 1920s were a time of artisanal renaissance, not decline, as the weavers fought to pre-serve the benefits of home manufacture against the new factory system, against harmful tax laws, and against the political battles of the CGT and the CGTU.[47]

These observations also apply to French industry generally during the early twentieth century. Whereas silk ribbon weaving was marginally less concentrated in the Loire than in other regions, the other principal indus-tries in both departments were in fact slightly more concentrated there than elsewhere, although these differences lessened after the war (see figures 4 and 7). In most French industries, the process of concentration so far meant little more than the disappearance of the tiniest companies, while large companies remained rare, and family enterprises that em-ployed no salaried workers actually multiplied. These patterns prevailed even during World War I, when high demand disguised inefficiency and few smaller companies were eliminated or absorbed.[48] Despite these figures, large companies, especially those at the top of the scale, often be-came larger still, while also employing an increased proportion of all French workers.[49] Nonetheless, because most changes affected only those industries that had already begun to modernize, there was little structural change in French industry — or in labor politics; the rank order of industries, by degree of concentration, remained much the same as before.[50]

As a result, the experiences of the Loire and the Haute-Vienne were by no means unique in France, even if they were also far from universal. As older economic regions, these communities missed the rapid growth begun elsewhere in the new century, but such growth was still the exception, not the rule. As older regions, they also preserved the patterns of unionism and leftist politics that had been shaped by earlier economic conditions. It remains to define these local patterns of labor politics and to see how well they survived the political and social upheavals of the era of World War I.

Chapter 2

Labor and the Left: The Prewar Setting

Symbolizing the reputations of Limoges and Saint-Etienne for left-wing militancy is the label, commonly affixed to each, of *une ville rouge*. In both cases the histories of trade-union and socialist activity date back at least to the Revolution of 1848.[1] More recently, Limoges was the site of the founding congress of the CGT in 1895 and of the framing of the Socialist Party's first wartime pacifist manifesto in 1915. Saint-Etienne, for its part, was the site of the founding congress in 1892 of the Bourse du Travail Federation, the first step toward the CGT's later merger, and the locus of a virulent general strike in 1918 aimed at forcing an end to the war.

Beneath these superficial similarities, however, lie fundamental differences in the structure and orientation of each city's labor movement and in its relationships with leftist politics. These contrasts, shaped in part by the structure of the cities' industries and by the demographic composition of their labor forces, must also be understood in the context of the cities' political histories and in particular the prevailing ideologies of the local leftist groups.

The role of ideology in labor history is the subject of much historical controversy, particularly among those who stress the economic preoccupations of most workers or their greater concern for conditions in the home or at the workplace than for the theoretical flights of fantasy in which politicians and intellectuals so often seemed to indulge.[2] The debate is especially relevant to the labor history of Limoges, with its strong Socialist Party, and of Saint-Etienne, with its highly visible anarchist movement. These ideologies never controlled the unions, for the latter charted their own courses according to their own perceptions of workers' interests. Nonetheless, the ideologies formed the context and shaped the contours of each city's labor movement: a broad leftist consensus in Limoges and a weak, fragmented leftist movement in Saint-Etienne. While the former joined most workers and many bourgeois Radicals in a heavily Proudhonian and pragmatic socialism, the latter failed to transcend craft rivalries or class tensions and ranged from anarchist extremism at its fringes to conservatism and inertia among the unorganized laboring mass.

The Socialist Traditions

The development of radical and socialist movements in both the Loire and Limousin regions was spurred, of course, by the growth of a sizable urban proletariat. Also important were the links between city and countryside and the peasantry's susceptibility to new political ideas. This process may explain why the otherwise "archaic" and rural Limousin was so precocious a center of socialist influence, and why even today the left, especially the Communist Party, remains important throughout the region. Limousin socialism, typically "sentimental" or humanitarian in style, stemmed from a rural utopian tradition that predated the rise of Marxist or proletarian socialism in France.[3]

The complementary growth of urban and rural leftist traditions in the Limoges region was enhanced by the process of seasonal migration, introducing peasant laborers to urban ideologies that they then brought back with them to the farms. Later on, urban Socialists would actively recruit rural voters by speaking *patois* and by translating collectivist principles into less drastic terms that the peasants could accept. The countryside also had its own reasons for rallying to socialism: small peasant proprietors predisposed to republican and democratic ideologies were further drawn, after an economic crisis in the late 1840s, to the promise of fiscal liberation from creditors even if not to the idea of land redistribution. This utopian, not revolutionary, rural tradition fit in well with the cities' own "associationist" form of socialism, rooted more in Proudhonian than in Marxist doctrine and attractive to broad segments of the Limousin middle class.[4]

Like the absence of large landowners in this region of small proprietorships, the absence of a powerful clergy also facilitated the growth of socialism and the early demise of royalist politics. Widespread "dechristianization" and anticlericalism freed the region from the authoritarian leadership of individual churchmen while it fostered the spread of leftist ideas. Per-

haps paradoxically, however, the decline of religious practice did not uproot the kind of primitive religiosity that nurtured a humanitarian or
para-religious form of socialism: another example of the dialectic of "ar-
chaism" and "modernity" so characteristic of the Limousin.[5]

A final influence on the spread of socialism was the factor of education, which enabled new political ideas to take root among skilled urban
workers but which might have retarded political development elsewhere
in a region long known for its high level of illiteracy and its dearth of
printed materials and schools.[6] Here again, Limousin Socialists succeeded remarkably in overcoming this apparent handicap. Of course, advances in education could not alone supply readers for party tracts or
for other written documents. Nonetheless, the Socialists soon learned the
art of oral propaganda, expressed in local dialect, and added party newspapers with both rural and urban editions once adequate readership was
assured.[7]

While Limousin socialism predated the growth of a large urban proletariat, even the early industrialization of the Saint-Etienne region was not
enough to nourish a strong socialist movement. Weavers and coal miners
in the Loire basin had been active in unions and strikes since the early
nineteenth century. Still, their successes did little to promote political
socialism, which remained weak, more petit-bourgeois than proletarian,
and divided among an array of competing sects.

As in the Limousin, the strength or weakness of socialism in the Lyon/
Saint-Etienne region depended as much on rural social and economic
structures as on urban patterns of industrial growth. Unlike the Limousin, the Lyonnais countryside was little touched by the radical currents of
the 1848 Revolution: these ideas appealed neither to small peasants
whose poverty was tempered by supplemental artisanal incomes nor to
landless peasants, in regions of larger proprietorships, where the influence of notables and clergy reinforced conservative beliefs.[8] Even in the
cities, where labor agitation flared repeatedly from the July Revolution in
1830 through the short-lived revolutionary Communes at Lyon and Saint-
Etienne in 1871, the republican and socialist movements made little
headway. Unrest erupted mostly among Lyon silkworkers and Saint-
Etienne ribbon weavers threatened with encroaching mechanization. Instead of rallying to leftist parties after 1871, these craftsmen embraced a
petit-bourgeois social conservatism that had little appeal for local factory
workers, who sought an active labor or socialist movement of their own.[9]

The weakness of the left in the Loire basin was also a result of its inability to win the middle-class support it attracted in Limoges. At Lyon and Saint-Etienne, intense labor agitation since the 1830s had strengthened the elites' arch-conservative biases and their hostility toward even the moderate left. Catholic influence also retarded the spread of socialism among certain labor groups as well as in bourgeois circles. Although socialism slowly gained a foothold, it remained an essentially conservative movement, closely tied to the autonomist politics of the sometime Loire deputy Aristide Briand.[10] Indeed, given the strength of social conservatism in the region, it is hardly surprising that disaffected fringe labor groups saw anarchism or anarcho-syndicalism as the only way to revolutionize local politics and to rouse the consciousness of the working class.

The contrasts between the Limousin and Loire forms of socialism reflected not only long-term political distinctions but also differing relations between leftist parties and the urban work force. Although industrial workers were not the only party members or voters, their concerns helped to strike the balance between revolutionary and reformist strategies and between political and economic goals. The early experiences of labor organization will help to explain the divergent character of party-union relations in the two communities: generally close cooperation in Limoges but mutual suspicion or rivalry in Saint-Etienne.

The Growth of Labor Organization in Limoges

The first modern trade union in Limoges was founded among porcelain painters in January 1870. The event, although incited by a visiting delegation from Sèvres, another center of porcelain manufacture, followed a history of early cooperative associations and strikes that began before the July Monarchy. The next few months of 1870 saw the birth of unions in other porcelain specialties and among shoemakers, cabinetmakers, weavers, and other groups, with a combined membership of nearly one-fourth of the city's 11,000 workers. Organized exclusively around craft specialties, these unions revealed their deliberate reformism in their choice of names, such as "L'Initiative" for the first porcelain union, and "Concorde," "Espérance," and "Progrès." While more combative in principle than the earlier mutual aid societies, these unions also condemned the strike tactic as harmful and proposed to settle conflicts "*à l'amiable.*"[11] Inspired by the First International, the new unions embraced its fundamental Proudhonian ideology and engaged in only five reported strikes in the years 1870–71.[12]

Despite their reformism, many unions were forced to disband in 1871 after a one-day Limoges Commune, and others survived only precariously for the next several years. Even after their official legalization in 1884, the unions remained weakened by unemployment until the economic upturn of the early 1890s, which prompted union reorganization, the creation of a local Bourse du Travail, and the emergence of the national CGT.[13] Throughout this period, although unionization spread to nearly every local industry, the ceramic workers remained at the forefront of the movement and defined its relations with the concurrently growing political left.

The porcelain workers owed their leadership in part to their elite status as highly skilled and relatively well paid workers and in part to the singularities of work in their industry. The low noise level in their workshops allowed ceramicists to discuss political or other subjects and even to hire readers to read aloud from popular literature or the local press, which soon included a union monthly of their own. The industry's relatively high concentration in a small number of companies also made it easier for a single militant to multiply converts where he worked.[14] Despite their receptivity to socialism, however, porcelain workers remained fundamentally reformist and reluctant to sacrifice craft privileges for the sake of industry-wide benefits. For example, only when the use of lithographed decals replaced costly hand-painted decoration did the elite decorators agree to join forces with their less skilled comrades and renounce the special privilege (in their eyes) of piecework pay.[15]

This decision came at the time of the Limousin's most explosive labor conflict, the porcelain workers' strike and lockout of April 1905. Sometimes seen as an example of the period's revolutionary syndicalism, the strike was less revolutionary in ideological content than in sheer passion and violence: one worker was killed when troops fired on a crowd. Although strikers protested (unsuccessfully) against the tightening discipline at larger factories such as Haviland, most workers remained more concerned with economic interests and opposed to the revolutionary rhetoric of the early CGT.[16] Thereafter, while the memory of 1905 still inspired revulsion at the use of armed force in labor conflicts, a new conciliatory spirit began to arise among both workers and employers, parallel to the waning of the "heroic era" elsewhere in France.[17]

In contrast to the emerging factory system in the porcelain industry, the Limoges shoe industry remained organized in tiny workshops that provided little opportunity for group discussion and collective spirit.

Often newcomers to the city, and lacking even a primary education, most shoe workers were unresponsive to the city's new movements on the left. The industry's elite — first the *cordonniers,* or artisanal shoe makers, and later the *coupeurs en chaussures,* who cut the leather pieces from the treated skins — were craftsmen opposed to mechanization and often more interested, if they unionized, in an anarchist or anarcho-syndicalist philosophy than in a mass collectivist program. The traditional radicalism of the craft's more self-conscious fringes never mobilized the bulk of the work force and remained more characteristic of nineteenth- than twentieth-century France.[18]

These attitudes hampered the growth of the shoe workers' union, which first appeared in March 1870, and of the national Leatherworkers' Federation, founded in 1902. Reflecting their craft biases and their distaste for industrial unionism, a majority of Limoges shoe workers opposed the inclusion of glove making (a major industry in nearby Saint-Junien) in the national federation, although the fusion was quickly adopted by the federation at large.[19] Nor did the glove industry, similarly fragmented in domestic workshops and plagued by low wages and high unemployment, prove receptive to any kind of socialist or union organization, although signs of anarchism and anarcho-syndicalism were apparent before and after the war.[20]

Labor organization in Saint-Junien proved especially difficult, not only among glove makers but also among workers in the dirtier and more dangerous leather-treatment and paper industries, which allowed little sense of pride in one's work. Weak unions and high unemployment made most strikes in these industries bitter protests against wage cuts or equally fruitless demands for recognition of the unions' right to exist.[21] In Limoges, by contrast, better economic and social conditions permitted stronger unions and milder ideologies to flourish, especially as anarchist shoe workers remained in the shadow of their colleagues in the larger and more prosperous porcelain industry.

The ceramicists' contagious reformism soon dominated the local Bourse du Travail and spurred its choice of a new secretary: Jean Rougerie, head of the shoe workers' union and member of the city's Socialist Party.[22] Rougerie's accession to leadership in 1906 reflected the new mood of conciliation that followed the shock of the previous year's strike and lockout. Few workers joined the general strike planned for May Day 1906, and the unions voted against the libertarian principles of the CGT's new Amiens Charter.[23] The conciliatory mood also extended to labor conflicts, as Rougerie counseled against wildcat strikes and as employers, enjoying a boom in demand for porcelain, granted wage increases to avert work stoppages and to lure scarce labor to their own doors. In this atmosphere, strikes became shorter if no less numerous, aimed at attainable economic goals instead of at futile issues of workshop discipline and mechanization, and hence part of a process of negotiation, not signs of irremediable class conflict.[24] This new mood also permitted the recovery and spread of socialism, from its defeat in the 1906 municipal elections to its conquest of the mayoralty in 1912 and of four of the department's five parliamentary mandates, with the highest percent Socialist vote in the country, in 1914.[25] This scale of victory, based on middle-class and peasant as well as proletarian backing, showed the widespread appeal of a reformist program that combined class compromise with support for legitimate labor demands.

The Growth of Labor Organization in Saint-Etienne

Unlike those at Limoges, Saint-Etienne's early labor unions contributed little to the growth of socialism and remained preoccupied with their own corporative interests. The textile industry proved especially conservative, despite a brief flicker of radicalism during the July Monarchy, sparked by the *canuts* of Lyon. While Lyon and Roanne later housed larger factories for silk and cotton weaving, Saint-Etienne and its environs remained sprinkled with tiny home workshops that made it difficult for unions or strikes to organize. In an industry buffeted by caprices of fashion and by recurrent crises of unemployment, most ribbon weavers preferred to work long hours to advance their individual security rather than put collective pressure on employers to improve working conditions for all.[26]

Also hampering solidarity was the ambiguous status of the *chefs d'atelier,* or independent ribbon weavers. Although classed juridically as workers, such as for tax purposes, they often employed journeyman labor and behaved in other respects like *petits patrons.* Their early unions focused less on demands for benefits than on professional functions including job placement, exchange of tools and loom parts, and verification of the weight and quality of the silk supplied by the *fabricants.*[27] These unions at first grouped *chefs* and journeymen together but then split apart after a major strike in the winter of 1899–1900 revealed deep conflicts of interest: the journeymen wanted to be paid by the day or hour, while the *chefs* preferred to pay only for the completed task, which often took several weeks.[28]

More interested in fighting the journeymen than in advancing their own demands for a uniform pay scale *(tarif)* from the employers, the *chefs d'atelier* soon organized in a "yellow" union that sided with employers against the "red" union of journeymen, which in turn joined the CGT and endorsed the revolutionary principles of class struggle and the general strike. While the former group allegedly dreamed of "social pacification," the latter insisted that no entente was possible between the workers' goal of winning "the highest wages possible" and the employers' will "to pay as little as possible."[29] Predictably enough, however, from the limited terms of this dispute, the journeymen's radicalism quickly faded once their salary demands were met. Disturbed by the libertarian tone of the Amiens Charter, which their federation as a whole likewise resisted, the journeymen soon quit the CGT and rejoined the *chefs* in a single union devoted mainly to enforcing the new *tarif*.[30] Only after the war did the expansion of factory weaving promote a new and exclusively "proletarian" union, which survived only briefly, as unionism failed to penetrate this heavily rural (and female) factory labor force.[31]

Loire miners were more readily unionized than were the weavers, thanks in part to the teamwork structure of mining labor that inspired solidarity without distinction according to status or specialty. But miners' unions remained both divided by locality and isolated from other labor groups, whose economic and political interests the miners seldom shared. Like other French miners, those in the Loire rarely joined in general strikes begun in other industries, and they tended to dismiss both socialism and anarchism as outside their own corporative concerns.[32]

In 1866 the Loire basin saw the birth of the nation's first modern miners' union, aimed both at improving wages and hours and at wresting control of a retirement pension fund from company hands. Promoted by members of the First International, the union soon grew to include half the basin's 10,000 miners, led a long and bloody strike in 1869, and also campaigned actively in that year's national elections. Although forced to disband when its leader, Michel Rondet, was arrested for his role in the Saint-Etienne Commune, the union later reemerged as a leading component in the new national mineworkers' federation that Rondet helped to found in 1884.[33] With Rondet as secretary, the federation soon adopted the same reformist stance that had come to prevail among the Loire's own miners. In its statutes, the federation included a list of immediate demands but no vision of social transformation as the ultimate goal.[34]

Rondet's reformism included the notion that workers should act through parliament to demand protective legislation instead of proceeding through direct action and the general strike. Rondet's influence remained particularly strong in his hometown, La Ricamarie, in the Ondaine valley, while Saint-Etienne miners gained a more revolutionary reputation for their readiness to strike in 1889 and 1907. Unions in the Loire and elsewhere also temporarily withdrew from the national federation in 1903, after miners in the Nord and Pas-de-Calais refused to join them in an attempted general strike.[35] Still, most local miners saw the general strike not as a revolutionary act but as a simple method of parliamentary pressure to win such benefits as retirement pensions and the eight-hour workday. Indeed, by demanding mere economic rights and not questioning the employers' right to a reasonable profit, the miners hoped to win enough public support to push the government to give in quickly, without forcing a fight to the end.[36]

Despite this basic consensus on strategy, Loire miners were divided both on tactics and by local loyalties, which discouraged region-wide solidarity. Separate unions existed for each of nearly a dozen local companies, including (until the unions later merged) the two for Saint-Etienne itself. Their scattered locations on the cities' fringes also kept the miners from close contacts with other unionists or with the Bourses du Travail. This isolation compounded the movement's insularity: even after their regional federation agreed to join the CGT in 1911, in recognition of its now tempered ideology, the local miners' unions stayed out of the Loire's Union Départementale—until it too mellowed after the failed strike wave of May 1918.[37]

The Saint-Etienne metalworkers lay midway in spirit between the corporatist coal miners and the individualist ribbon weavers. Often militant and strike-prone, metalworkers nonetheless resisted the miners' mass unionism and tended instead to espouse anarcho-syndicalism, a sign of their distrust for socialist reformism and their preference for small unions organized on craft lines. The metalworkers' spirit of craft exclusiveness, spurred in part by their myriad specialties and skill levels, can be seen in their distaste for industrial unionism, even after the founding of a unified national Metalworkers' Federation in 1909. Artisan gunsmiths, copper workers, and certain factory craftsmen (such as the *mouleurs*) retained separate unions alongside the one for the rest of the industry. Still another union formed at the state-owned Manufacture Nationale d'Armes, whose workers organized with other state employees in a national Union Fédérative des Travailleurs de l'Etat. Although nearly all these groups adhered to the prewar CGT, they professed divergent economic and philosophical aims.[38]

Least readily organized were the artisan gunsmiths, who worked in scattered domestic shops and enjoyed a nearly petit-bourgeois social status, like that of the ribbon weavers. Factory gunsmiths were scarcely more militant: their strikes rarely extended beyond a single establishment and remained mild in tone, as long as the industry enjoyed relative prosperity (until the 1930s) and above-average pay.[39] State employees at the Manufacture Nationale could choose either the conservative Amicale, a non-union association, or the CGT affiliate, whose statutes initially called for "collaboration" with the company directors for the peaceful settlement of disputes.[40] The principal metalworkers' union, which grouped members from the larger cycle and gun companies and from heavy metallurgy, did endorse the class struggle and included more anarchists and other "revolutionaries" than any other union in the city.[41] Still, it rarely drew more than a small fraction of the total work force, most of whom preferred "yellow" or independent unions or refrained from collective action of any kind.

Metalworkers were especially difficult to unionize at Saint-Etienne, where even factories were little more than clusters of highly specialized craftsmen. The bigger steel mills and machine shops were concentrated instead in surrounding communities, where unions sometimes grew larger and more militant than those at Saint-Etienne. The giant—and paternalistic—steel works at Firminy, Unieux, and Saint-Chamond escaped most labor unrest until the latter days of World War I. The town of Le Chambon-Feugerolles, in contrast, with its mix of artisanal file making and small-scale factory bolt making, developed an unusually cohesive labor community and experienced long and often violent strikes. The employers' readiness to unite against the unions rather than compromise also made these strikes a bitter struggle for union survival, like those at Saint-Junien (in the Haute-Vienne).[42]

These circumstances helped to produce one of the region's fiercest prewar conflicts, the metalworkers' strikes and lockout at Le Chambon in 1910–11. The movement, under anarchist leadership, included many acts of violence against employers and non-striking workers and symbolized the last gasp of the "heroic era" of the CGT.[43] After its failure forced many anarchists to leave the area, the atmosphere suddenly became more "tranquil" in the authorities' view; more accurately, the union movement simply collapsed. Unlike the case at Limoges, where the shock of violence ushered in an era of conciliation, matters at Le Chambon became quieter but more desperate: frightened workers joined "yellow" unions (which flowered dramatically) or quit the movement altogether, while militants came to see revolutionary agitation as the only way to keep a dying movement alive.[44] The events also launched the careers of two later Communist leaders, Pétrus Faure and Benoît Frachon, the latter a strike participant at the age of seventeen. Both traced their roots to the local anarchist and syndicalist movements, not to electoral socialism, although they came to renounce their early "nihilism" as "an ideal of youth."[45]

The Labor Movement in Economic and Social Perspective

The early history of labor militancy in the two communities prompts further analysis of the economic and social conditions that shaped these movements in the prewar decades. Factors including standards of living, demographic patterns in the work force, and the larger context of social class relations helped to determine both union size and strike intensity, which varied along both industrial and geographic lines.

According to most analysts, union recruitment and strike participation are highest in times of prosperity, when the prospects for wage gains are most promising and the risks are least that a worker might lose his job. For the immediate prewar years, however, there is some doubt as to whether strike militancy — especially of the revolutionary syndicalist variety — was triggered by increasing prosperity or instead by declining real wages, eroded by inflation.[46] It is probably true that relative prosperity after 1890 sustained the simultaneous flowering of trade unionism and leftist politics and enabled strikes to become part of the accepted negotiating process for keeping wages and prices in harmony. On the other hand, strikes often expressed workers' personal rancor toward the factory system, a mood that flared regardless of wage levels and that dampened only when unions admitted its futility and turned instead to more negotiable wage demands.[47] Pecuniary questions may also have sharpened unrest in times of short-term hardship, rendered all the more unbearable when conditions had been prospering over the longer term.

Economic prosperity at the turn of the century was at best uneven in the Limoges and Saint-Etienne industries, where wage levels varied sharply and unemployment loomed with frequent menace. Limoges porcelain workers often earned as much as eight francs per day but shoe workers (many of whom were women) trailed behind, at least prior to the industry's wartime boom.[48] In Saint-Etienne, with its lower than average living costs, most metalworkers and especially gunsmiths appear to have enjoyed steadily rising living standards after 1890. Miners' wages rose more slowly, however, and ribbon weavers faced both rampant unemployment and declines in nominal (not just real) wages—sometimes to less than two francs per day.[49]

These wide variations also affected union memberships. Wages alone, of course, were not the determining factor; despite marginal incomes, Loire miners were sometimes nearly 50 percent unionized, while better paid artisan gunsmiths were among the least unionized of all. Still, matters of economic security do help to explain why more than 60 percent of Limoges porcelain workers joined their union, compared to barely 3 percent of ribbon weavers in Saint-Etienne and its environs.[50] Perhaps surprisingly, the two Bourses du Travail drew comparable totals: approximately one-fourth of each work force, well above the national average. The Saint-Etienne total, though, included rival craft groups averse to industrial unionism, plus (until 1912) an array of independent unions hostile to the CGT.[51] Beyond these general totals, there are few reliable measures of union memberships in the prewar era. Sheer size was far less important, however, than the degree of cohesion or solidarity, a trait advanced in Limoges by the leadership of a single large porcelain union, plus the support of the Socialist Party, and retarded in Saint-Etienne by the proliferation of smaller unions and mutually hostile sects.

Working-class solidarity varied also according to social factors such as the demographic composition of the work force. Highest levels of unionization were achieved in industries where workers were primarily young men born in the city, precisely the profile of the porcelain workers of Limoges. A large proportion of elderly workers (such as among artisan shoemakers, gunsmiths, and ribbon weavers) or of rural or foreign immigrants (among miners or less skilled factory workers) might in part reflect lower wage levels that deterred recruitment of city-born youths. These lower wage levels would in turn impede unionization, as previously described. In addition to this economic factor, however, the presence of aged or immigrant workers also hindered unionization by reducing the shared interests or background that would promote solidarity. Later on, unskilled rural or foreign immigrants might form their own mass (often Communist) unions, but they were least likely to join prewar Socialist or syndicalist movements based on a tradition of skilled craftsmanship.[52]

The factor of female labor was a special problem, not only for women who had to balance family and professional responsibilities but also for men threatened by growing competition for their own jobs. Women workers were not necessarily less unionized or strike-prone than males employed in the same industries. Like the elderly or the rural immigrants, however, they usually held jobs in less prosperous sectors, as in textiles, where economic factors discouraged militancy.[53] Women's presence at the workplace was also a source of rivalry or dissension that hindered collective action against employers. When male-dominated unions opened their doors to women, the aim was usually to ensure women's support for men's strike demands. If men endorsed the demand for "equal pay for equal work," it was less to protect women's wages than to defend their own jobs from the competition of women workers available at lower cost.[54]

Perhaps in response to this sexual rivalry, women workers sometimes organized in independent unions, as in Saint-Etienne's textile industry. Many such unions were religious in inspiration and directed by the employers' wives. Feminine unions also arose at Limoges in the prewar porcelain industry and later among seamstresses and white-collar employees, who formed the core of the nascent Catholic confederation (CFTC).[55] Most of the city's women workers, however, preferred the mainstream CGT unions, which they joined at rates nearly equivalent to those for the men. In fact, women comprised some 20 percent of the city's prewar labor movement, while at Saint-Etienne too few women were employed outside the textile industry for their unionization to amount to much until after the start of the war.[56]

Like the female unions, Catholic and "yellow" or independent unions were often another element of working-class disunity. Neither variety drew much support in the dechristianized and leftist atmosphere of Limoges, except among some women and a few categories of male white-collar employees.[57] Catholic unions did grow amply among railroad workers, miners, weavers, and metalworkers in the Loire, which became an important center for the postwar CFTC. Later on, as these unions were further secularized, they often cooperated with CGT or Communist unions, as does today's CFDT.[58] More deeply divisive were the "yellow" unions, which preached class collaboration instead of class conflict and expressed open hostility to the CGT.

Named for their yellow insignia, in contrast to the red flag of socialism, "yellow" unions first appeared at Montceau-les-Mines (Saône-et-Loire) in 1899 and formed a national federation in 1904. A regional group arose at Saint-Etienne in 1907, promoted by the industrialists Georges Claudinon and Joseph Leflaive. The movement flourished especially through 1911, helped in part by reaction against the bitter strikes of metalworkers in Le Chambon-Feugerolles. Aimed by statute to defend "liberty and labor" from the CGT's "demagogic and revolutionary tyranny," these unions later came under close police surveillance as possible breeding grounds for fascism in the Loire.[59]

Beyond helping to organize "yellow" unions, Leflaive and other Loire captains of industry also joined together in patronal associations, such as the Comité des Forges and the Comité des Houillères. Intended both as public pressure groups and as defensive arms against labor agitation, these groups foreshadowed the postwar Unions Civiques, founded first at Lyon during the strike wave of early 1920.[60] Loire textile manufacturers were much less united, as were Limoges industrialists; the latter barely upheld the 1905 lockout and remained averse to other forms of joint action, whether to fight the unions or to win tariff protection and improve marketing techniques.[61]

The Loire's steel magnates were also active in right-wing politics. Leflaive himself, president of the departmental Comité des Forges, never held political office, but Jean Neyret, president of the Verdié steelworks at Firminy, was mayor of Saint-Etienne during World War I and active later in the conservative Republican Union. Georges Claudinon, head of the vast Claudinon steelworks at Le Chambon-Feugerolles, was likewise parliamentary deputy at the turn of the century and mayor of Le Chambon until 1919.[62] In 1910, as a symbol of his alleged conspiracy against striking metalworkers, the mayor's offices were set on fire and cheering crowds blocked firemen from extinguishing the flames.[63]

In this highly charged atmosphere, it is not surprising that labor relations were more hostile and more readily politicized in the Loire than in the Haute-Vienne. At Limoges, after the shock of the 1905 lockout, most strikes came to focus on readily negotiable wage issues, whereas at Le Chambon-Feugerolles (and at Saint-Junien) unions had to fight for the sheer right to exist. Because employers also commonly retaliated by dismissing strikers and suspected union leaders, Loire strikes remained small and far from unanimous, whereas Limoges strikes often achieved high rates of participation, even when not all workers were unionized.[64]

These observations are supported by strike statistics for the years 1912–14. Although the Loire, with its larger number of industrial workers, easily outpaced the Haute-Vienne in its totals of strikes, strike participants, and working-days lost, each strike was a relatively brief affair (see Figure 9). In both cases, strikes in major industries (except the textile industry, which had a long general strike in 1914) were even shorter and smaller than departmental averages for all industries or than averages for each industry throughout France (see figures 10 and 11). Miners and metalworkers thereby accounted for only slim percentages of the Loire's totals of strikers and working-days lost.[65] These small conflicts also had a relatively high rate of failure, especially in metallurgy, while the porcelain strikes, even when small, achieved a higher rate of success (see Figure 12).

Nonetheless, these results do not necessarily undermine the Loire's revolutionary syndicalist reputation; instead, they illustrate that the strength of syndicalist ideology cannot be measured by strike rates alone.[66] Among Loire miners, for whom syndicalist ideology was scarcely an issue, the small strikes show simply the modest goals and local interests that rarely extended beyond a single coal field. Among metalworkers, the syndicalist influence can be seen precisely in the prevalence of small unions, brief wildcat strikes, and insufficient solidarity—or strike funds —to make strikes an accepted part of the bargaining process for either side.

Labor and the Left: Socialism, Anarchism, and the CGT

The final gauge of syndicalist or socialist influence on the labor movement cannot be union recruitment or strike participation, however revealing, but the actual record of union relations with leftist parties. The net product of harmony or friction in day-to-day contacts, these relationships showed the practical side of trade-union ideologies, just as did tactical questions of how to unionize or when to go on strike. As in a circular process, the experience of cordial relations led most Limoges unionists to cooperate readily with the local Socialist Party, while Saint-Etienne unionists preferred to ignore the party or actively opposed it, whether from the right or from still further to the left.

The idea of close party-union cooperation in France is usually linked to Guesdist socialism, which called on trade unions to stress economic issues and defer to socialist parties for political leadership.[67] Guesdism, however, was never a clear-cut doctrine in Limoges, where the local branch of Guesde's Parti Ouvrier at the turn of the century also included Allemanists, independents, and even some Radicals in its ranks. Guesdists and Allemanists remained allied in municipal politics, against their Jauressian rivals, who included Millerandists and assorted Radicals.[68] Doctrinal distinctions paled before the knowledge that most local socialists, whatever their label, were industrial workers and trade-union members. Although custom discouraged any individual from holding union and political office concurrently, the rule was often observed in the breach.

Among its leaders the Guesdist group counted three future SFIO deputies: Adrien Pressemane, Jean Parvy, and Albert Chauly, all one-time officers of the porcelain workers' union. The group also included the ceramicist Edouard Treich, founding secretary of the Limoges Bourse du Travail, and Jean Rougerie, shoe workers' secretary and Bourse leader from the early years of the twentieth century until after World War I. The most notable Allemanist was Jacques Tillet, long-time head of the national porcelain workers' federation and early proponent of the general strike. The Jauressian group, less involved in the labor movement, included two future SFIO deputies, one of whom—Léon Betoulle—was also mayor of Limoges from 1912 until the end of the Third Republic.[69]

Best personifying the Limoges style of party-union cooperation was the Bourse secretary and Guesdist spokesman Jean Rougerie. It was he who prompted the Bourse's new conciliatory posture after the disastrous porcelain strike of 1905. He also led the vote against the Amiens Charter and in favor of active collaboration with the new SFIO.[70] Then, in 1912, Rougerie defied local custom and CGT statutes to take the post of municipal councillor, and during the war he deferred to party leadership in the pacifist movement rather than endorse syndicalist notions of "direct action" by unions alone.[71] Clearly a Socialist with trade-union functions, not a unionist who entered politics to advance syndicalist precepts,

Rougerie eventually came under attack for his all too moderate outlook, but until then he represented an effective balance of two apparently harmonious roles.[72]

Socialist deputy Adrien Pressemane began his career as a porcelain painter in Saint-Léonard, the district that first sent him to parliament on the eve of the war. Endowed with only a primary education and largely self-taught in political matters, Pressemane became a leading party leftist and wartime pacifist, while rejecting communism for its threat of outside interference in local and national affairs. Opposed to the Bolsheviks' conditions for admission to the new Communist International, Pressemane also denounced the principle of revolutionary defeatism, which seemed to negate popular patriotism and the possibility of revolution by popular enthusiasm once the revolutionary consciousness of the proletariat had been sufficiently aroused.[73] Local Communists later condemned Pressemane as an opportunist who had abandoned his proletarian origins for the sake of a parliamentary mandate, but his supporters credited him with preserving — despite his own theoretical temper — the party's contact with the aspirations of the common man.[74]

Less doctrinaire and even more popular with Limoges voters was mayor Léon Betoulle, who had entered politics in 1906 as the department's first Socialist deputy. A self-styled Jauressian, Betoulle favored pragmatic reformism in municipal politics and spoke in parliament for the interests of small proprietors in order to win their support for the SFIO.[75] During the war, he deferred to his comrades' pacifist initiatives only to preserve party unity on the local level.[76] His profound influence on the Limoges Socialist movement thus stood as a marked counterweight to Guesdist orthodoxy. True, Guesdists inspired the party's rejection of ministerialism and of local electoral alliances with the Radical bourgeoisie. Guesdists also sponsored the party's anticlerical and antimilitarist platforms and appealed most strongly for working-class and peasant support.[77] Still, their victories depended heavily on Betoulle's personal appeal as the department's leading vote-getter. With Betoulle's guidance, the local party filtered out much of its Marxist or revolutionary content and kept only the Guesdist principles of party organization, plus a vague leftism that attracted lower-class voters while not alienating the middle class.

Doctrinaire Guesdism was even less characteristic of the Saint-Etienne region. Officially born in Roanne, as a result of a split with Saint-Etienne's "possibilists," Guesdism won a sizable following in Roanne's cotton mills and in the larger factories in and around Lyon. But even there it coexisted — or blurred — with rival possibilist and anarchist tendencies, which came to dominate in the mines and workshops of the Loire basin. With little support among workers, the Guesdists recruited more heavily among local teachers, shopkeepers, and white-collar employees, quite contrary to the then current national trend.[78] This pattern persisted into the new SFIO. After Briand and his supporters quit the party in 1906, the Loire Federation inched leftward, while continuing to favor Radical alliances in local politics as needed to oust the right from power.[79] The strength of right-wing politics plus the leftists' own bourgeois biases combined to make Loire socialism a surprisingly conservative force.

Despite its heavily bourgeois composition, the Loire socialist movement did not altogether ignore workers' interests nor fail to attract working-class voters. Miners and ribbon weavers most often supported Briand and other independent socialists. A good example was the *passementiers'* leader Jules Ledin, who became Bourse secretary in the 1890s, then mayor and parliamentary deputy by 1906. An early Allemanist known for his "revolutionary" leanings at the time of the weavers' strike of 1899–1900, Ledin remained hostile to Guesdism but helped to form the Republican Socialist party with Briand in 1910. With the aid of its working-class supporters, this new party far surpassed the young SFIO in local members and voters through the legislative elections of 1914.[80]

Another favorite of Saint-Etienne workers was Antoine Durafour, a leading Radical-Socialist spokesman for the eight-hour day and retirement benefits for coal miners. First elected deputy in 1910 (as Ledin's successor), Durafour then became Minister of Labor in the leftist coalition government of 1925–26. More recently his son also became Minister of Labor and served for more than a decade as mayor of Saint-Etienne.[81] The senior Durafour's popularity may have stemmed less from his social reformism than from his readiness to do favors for his constituents. Said a Communist rival: "Write him on any question. Ask him for information on planting vegetables or for this or for that. Your answer will come by return mail and will give you complete satisfaction." Even that critic, however, found Durafour sincere and unwavering in his ideas, quite unlike the "ex-revolutionary" Briand.[82]

Of the SFIO's personalities, the best known was Ernest Lafont, mayor of Firminy and parliamentary deputy from the eve of the war through the mid-1920s. As a friend of organized labor and the CGT's local attorney,

Lafont was among Briand's most active critics for his suppression of the railroad strike of 1910.[83] Unlike the Guesdists, Lafont also believed that the bourgeois SFIO should defer to the unions as representatives of true socialism. His influence thus helped to account for the rather close prewar relations between local Socialists and the CGT.[84] After the SFIO schism, Lafont joined but then quickly left the new Communist Party and subsequently evolved toward the right, along with such "neo-Socialists" as Marcel Déat.[85] Nonetheless, before these ventures tarnished his reputation, Lafont enjoyed considerable prestige among Loire voters, and he retained his parliamentary mandate even during the conservative landslide of 1919.

Even if most Loire workers found bourgeois Radicals or Socialists aggressive enough to suit their own moderate tempers, there was an active minority for whom disappointment with Ledin or Briand only intensified the demand for a more independent and revolutionary union program. This fringe was an outgrowth of Saint-Etienne's long history of labor agitation, but it diverged in an anarcho-syndicalist direction when that militant rootstock failed to yield a labor movement that leaned far enough to the left. Most Loire unions were more anti-Guesdist than explicitly anarcho-syndicalist, a nuance illustrated by the founding at Saint-Etienne of Pelloutier's national Bourse du Travail Federation and by the early Allemanism of local Bourse secretary Ledin. Nonetheless, the tone contrasted sharply with the Limoges leaders' instinctive Guesdism, as shown when Bourse secretary Treich refused to join the infant Bourse federation and helped instead to form the as yet more moderate CGT.[86]

These differences also appeared in debates over the Amiens Charter, which codified the CGT's aversion to ties with leftist parties. The Limoges unions voted twenty-two to four *against* the terms of the charter, thereby rejecting the claim that close party ties would divide the unions from within. Even local Socialists could see both sides of the issue and reversed position several times in their own votes.[87] At Saint-Etienne, however, the prevailing anti-Guesdism was premised precisely on the fear that party ties would divide the workers, so many of whom voted with the center or the right. Loire unionists therefore favored the Amiens Charter more for its anti-Guesdist than its anarcho-syndicalist content; indeed, local anarchists rejected the charter as a passive and neutral schema unsuited to modern needs.[88]

Starting from surprisingly similar premises, Limoges and Saint-Etienne unionists thus came to sharply divergent conclusions, largely because of

the different political contexts in which they functioned. Like their Limoges comrades, most Saint-Etienne unionists accepted the principle of
overt political action: they put up only token resistance to the joint holding of union and political office, and they saw little reason to object to
municipal subsidies for Bourse expenses, at least when the city government was in leftist hands.[89] Their quarrel concerned not the fact but the
aims of political action, whether for revolution or for reform. Anarchists
did not demand strict abstention from politics, but they sought a more
truly revolutionary program, perhaps more revolutionary than possible
for a party with parliamentary pretensions, and certainly more extremist
than the local variety, bogged down as it was in the blandness of Briand.

Against this background, the role of anarcho-syndicalism in the prewar
labor movement can finally be examined. Anarcho-syndicalism marked of
course a compromise with "pure" anarchism by embracing unions both
as an alternative to individual action and as a means to convert the
masses to the revolutionary cause.[90] Not all anarchists equally accepted
this compromise, however. In Limoges, most anarchists stayed close to
their individualist origins, and anarcho-syndicalism remained little more
than a fringe current within the shoe workers' and a few other unions. In
Saint-Etienne, where anarchists were both more numerous and more
readily collectivized, they became a major force within the unions and an
ardent rival to Socialist—and later Communist—control.

Limoges was only a minor center of anarchism, either inside or outside
the unions. The entire department, according to police count in 1897,
comprised only 13 anarchists as against 271 in the Loire.[91] The doctrine
did appeal to artisanal shoe and glove makers threatened by mechanization, and it won some lasting influence in Saint-Junien, where no well entrenched socialist movement of any kind stood in its way.[92] In Limoges,
however, the shoe industry was too small, until after the war, to be much
of an anarchist hotbed, and most unions were at once too Guesdist to
give their rivals room for action and yet sufficiently independent, or
ouvriériste, to co-opt some of the libertarians' appeal.

By 1904 Limoges anarchists had sufficiently overcome their disdain for
formal organization to found a local "Groupe Communiste Anarchiste,"
as part of a loose federation of "collectivist" anarchists throughout
France. The group soon numbered some twenty members, including at
least a dozen trade unionists, several of whom headed the autonomous
unions after the war.[93] Nearly all members had working-class occupations, which ranged from ceramics (known more for involvement in so-

cialism) to diverse artisanal or commercial trades and unskilled day-labor as well. Although the group's putative leader, Jules Téty, was only fifteen years of age, most members were in their late twenties or thirties, according to reports on those present at meetings in 1910.[94] Those still active after the war were thus approaching middle age.

A surprising number of group members were migrants from outside the city. Téty was born in Saint-Léonard, and half of those for whom birth information is known were born outside the Haute-Vienne. This factor may correspond partly to occupation: most ceramicists, whatever their political persuasion, were born in Limoges, and many shoe workers, anarchist or otherwise, were born outside the city.[95] As a form of protest against modern industrialism and socialist politics, however, anarchism may have appealed especially strongly to workers not yet integrated into an urban milieu.

Once unionized, several anarchists rose to administrative positions at the Bourse du Travail. Examples included the tailors' and the shop clerks' delegates, both of whom remained active anarchists after 1918.[96] In both the Bourse and the unions, though, the anarchists remained only a weak minority element. Téty and others tried to create a more effective opposition group, known as the Jeunesses Syndicalistes. But the group, condemned by Bourse leaders as an anarchist "hotbed" *(foyer),* made little headway before it was interrupted by the outbreak of war.[97]

Despite these rivalries, the anarchists and Socialists had much in common, from their Proudhonian sympathies to their cooperation for political and economic reforms. Some self-styled "Young Syndicalists" were simply anti-Guesdist Socialists who later embraced more conventional reformism. An example was Marcel Vardelle, a reputed "Blanquist or Allemanist," who came to head the CGT at Limoges after the schism and held office as city councillor and parliamentary deputy for the SFIO.[98] The anarchists engaged in scant dangerous activity, and few other than Téty translated an avowed antimilitarism into overt nonsubmission to military duty during the war.[99]

Indeed, a sentimental antimilitarism pervaded both the labor and the socialist movements. At heart was no insurrectionalist conspiracy but just a repugnance, after the 1905 tragedy, toward the use of armed force against labor strikes.[100] Common goals made it natural for Socialists, anarchists, and reformist unionists at Limoges to collaborate in a Comité de Défense Sociale, to fight the three-year law, governmental repression, and the *"lois scélérates."*[101] Bourse leaders also objected when the CGT in Paris chose to act alone against the threat of war rather than join with Socialist allies for the sake of unanimity in the working class.[102] These urgent matters made factional rivalries seem especially sterile and the antipolitical rhetoric of the Amiens Charter to make little sense. Unions and politics were not separate spheres competing for a militant's attention but complementary parts of a larger campaign for libertarian social reform.

In the Lyonnais region, the absence of a strong socialist rival allowed anarchism to flourish both inside and outside the unions. Despite their visibility, however, anarchism and anarcho-syndicalism never lured more than a small fringe of workers from the competing charms of Briandism or simple inertia. Indeed, the enormity of the struggle to rouse working-class militancy may account for the movement's greater violence and extremism here than in Limoges. A sense of desperation could tempt militants to make a virtue of necessity, by insisting that tiny sects were better than mass, bureaucratized institutions and that sheer audacity could succeed where careful planning might fail.

While Limoges anarchism remained largely the preserve of individualist artisans, the Loire's movement appealed less to gunsmiths and ribbon weavers than to an intermediate rank of metalworkers employed in a variety of skilled factory trades. Insufficiently "proletarianized" for Guesdist socialism, these metalworkers were still prone to a collectivist strategy that, however contemptuous of "bourgeois politicians," was not antipolitical as such. Best known of the region's anarchists were the terrorist/assassin Ravachol, in the 1890s, and somewhat later, the individualist Sébastien Faure, founder of the national publication *Le Libertaire*. Most other anarchists readily joined unions and other associations. Those who hesitated, such as metalworker Benoît Liothier, did so mostly in fear of the unions' avowed political neutrality: "Syndicalism cannot be revolutionary if it cannot be political. . . . Whether we like it or not, the economic struggle is tied to the political struggle."[103] This did not mean a plea for parliamentary action instead of strikes or sabotage, but simply the recognition that revolution was a political act. This view may explain the group's latter attraction to Bolshevism and their refusal to join Faure's Anarchist Communist Federation, to which the Limoges group adhered.[104]

The social composition of the Loire anarchist movement can be analyzed not only through reports on members present at meetings but also through a detailed list of those anarchists subject to arrest in the event of mobilization for war. This list, similar to the Carnet B of other "dangerous" militants, identified 164 anarchists throughout the department, including 67 at Saint-Etienne.[105] Together, these sources show that most of the department's anarchists were industrial workers from the Saint-Etienne basin, although an important minority were merchants or café owners in Roanne (see Figure 13). Among industrial occupations, by far the most numerous were metalworkers, including a few artisan gunsmiths; coal miners and manual laborers also appeared, more often elsewhere in the Loire basin than at Saint-Etienne itself. Predictably, anarchism was weaker at Firminy and Unieux, where large mines and steelworks predominated, than in towns with a mixture of artisanal and skilled factory occupations, such as Rive-de-Gier, Saint-Chamond, and Le Chambon-Feugerolles[106] (see Figure 14). Thus anarchism appealed to precisely those workers in the mid-sized factories who might otherwise have rallied to Guesdism. This helps to explain the two movements' intense competition, whereas each had its own separate sphere of influence in Limoges.

As in Limoges, a high proportion of Loire anarchists were rural-born immigrants, again, probably because of their occupations (few were city-born weavers or gunsmiths) and the doctrine's appeal to those not yet integrated into an urban milieu[107] (see Figure 15). Also like their Limoges comrades, most Loire anarchists were experienced workers well beyond adolescence. A surprising number, in fact, were over age fifty, especially in the artisanal professions, but most were in their twenties and thirties, young enough to be free of residual influence from the movement's earlier, Proudhonian days[108] (see Figure 16).

Despite the high number of anarchist metalworkers, the doctrine never won more than a minority of the industry's total work force or even of its small unionized fraction. No anarchist rose to leadership of a major Saint-Etienne union in the prewar period, except Benoît Liothier, who headed the metalworkers' union briefly in 1910–11. Others who achieved high positions did so more on the strength of their personalities than on the basis of their ideological following; an example was the new Union Départementale's treasurer, Jean-Pierre Lescure (named in 1911), whose union of weavers was hardly an anarchist enclave.[109] Sometimes anarchists became union delegates to Bourse meetings, where they could voice their own personal opinions. Nevertheless, on strike votes or other issues reflecting the views of an entire union, anarchists remained strictly in the minority—as Liothier bitterly complained in 1914.[110]

This "crisis of syndicalism," as Liothier called it, was made all the more discouraging by the scant results of joint leftist programs such as the local Comité de Défense Sociale. Less fortunate (or less patient) than their Limoges counterparts, Saint-Etienne anarchists found their erstwhile allies unwilling to back rhetoric with action. In 1913, Socialists who supported the campaign against the three-year law on military service balked nonetheless at the anarchists' demand for disarmament; Bourse leaders likewise condemned the anarchists' distribution of tracts, which had led to several arrests, for discrediting the unions in the public eye.[111] In response, the anarchist-led Jeunesses Syndicalistes withdrew from the Bourse to free themselves for direct action, while their leaders, including Liothier, resumed the time-worn debate on the merits of joining unions that might never advance a revolutionary point of view.[112]

Loire anarchists thus attempted to combine a collectivist strategy with an enduring appetite for direct action. Local militants admired, even if they did not copy, the exploits of the assassin Ravachol and the tactics of the now-discredited *propagande par le fait*.[113] The romantic appeal of violence also spurred local anarchists in 1914 to cheer the news of Franz Ferdinand's assassination and to hope that the same fate would soon befall the president of the French Republic.[114] Later on, after a period of deceptive quiet, wartime anarchists and syndicalists launched an antiwar movement that far surpassed in violence and extremism anything organized by left-wing pacifists in Limoges.

Despite its small numbers and its uncertain role in the unions, the anarcho-syndicalist movement has rightly given the Loire a distinct "red" revolutionary coloration. Although the authorities and the right-wing politicians no doubt exaggerated its size and its danger, the movement did denote a potent challenge to labor reformism in prewar Saint-Etienne. In the context of a highly fragmented labor force, hostile class relations, and the absence of a unifying leftist tradition, anarcho-syndicalism represented a desperate option for a labor movement that ranged widely between extremism and inertia. It had less appeal for Limoges workers, who combined revolutionary theory with moderate practice to attract middle-class support. These contrasts were the product of distinct prewar conditions that had evolved steadily since the early nineteenth century. It remains to be seen how the labor movements would further respond to wartime and postwar changes, and how much anarcho-syndicalism—the legacy of the prewar "heroic era"—would continue to shape labor politics after 1918.

Chapter 3

The Mobilization of the Left:
The War Experience, 1914–17

World War I was as much a turning point in French labor history as in most other aspects of economic, social, political, and military affairs. That the war accelerated class conflict and radicalized labor and socialist movements throughout Europe is shown by the impact of two revolutions in Russia and the founding of Communist parties within a few years after the war's end. It is easier, however, to assume than to prove the scale of this "watershed," as in volumes that offer little explanation for their choice of 1914 as a starting or ending point. It is also unclear that the war transformed workers and unions as much as it did politicians and parties, perhaps because the economic and social pressures that could have reshaped labor history were eased, at least temporarily, by the "return to normalcy" with which the postwar era began.[1]

We need not minimize the war's impact on the French economy, on leftist politics, or on the relations among unions, parties, employers' associations, and the government. Once past the initial disruptions caused by the mobilization, the requirements of national defense spurred massive growth in mining and metallurgy and sparked the revival of trade unionism to defend labor from the particular hardships of the war. The union revival also rekindled controversy over the politics of "Sacred Union" that had at first promised labor support for the war effort. Perhaps most importantly, the government's increased role in the economy also pushed the unions toward greater centralization of decision making in Paris and toward closer ties with leftist parties for parliamentary reforms, as against the dogmas of local autonomy in the past. None of these changes, however, were irreversible. Once the war ended, and once new economic and political conflicts took the place of old ones, unionists and party leftists again debated ideologies and tactics for the new era. Were the old socialist or syndicalist principles indeed outmoded and in need of replacement by more "modern" — or Bolshevist — strategies? Many militants then (and some historians since then) made this argument, but for others the answer was much less clear.

Like their prewar settings, the wartime experiences of Limoges and Saint-Etienne show interesting contrasts, exemplified by the Limoges Socialists' early conversion to pacifism and by the Saint-Etienne syndicalists' role in mobilizing a potentially revolutionary general strike. These developments stemmed in part from specific wartime circumstances, including the Loire's importance in steel and munitions manufacturing, but had deeper roots in the patterns of labor militancy and party-union relations that had evolved since well before 1914. The local context also gave meaning to the abstract debates that divided Parisian labor leaders into opposing and often hostile factions. If these debates found lasting echoes in the provinces, it was because they struck familiar chords among local Socialists and syndicalists faced with daily decisions on how to cope with the economic and political problems raised by the war.

The Politics of War: Party-Union Relations and the Dilemmas of "Sacred Union," 1914–16

At the outbreak of war, French unionists faced two crucial decisions: first, of course, whether to rally to defend the nation; but just as urgently, whether — or how far — to coordinate their action with that of the leftist political parties. As a sign of their own growing reformism, most unionists quickly abandoned any thought of insurrection and joined the Socialists both in defense of workers' material interests and in support of the war. Neither decision came automatically, however, or survived unscathed the changing wartime circumstances. By the time the party began to question the war effort, the unions had their own reasons to rupture the "Sacred Union" and eventually to engage in far more revolutionary agitation than the usually staid Socialists had in mind.

The decision to support the war effort may have been conditional from the very beginning. Both the SFIO and the CGT national leaderships engaged in some preliminary wrangling, and even after their decisions there were isolated protest demonstrations in Paris and around the country. A general strike nearly broke out in Lyon before CGT leaders intervened. In Saint-Etienne no public meetings were held, but some groups did meet privately to discuss the mobilization. In Limoges there were at least three public meetings, under Bourse and Socialist auspices; the largest drew a crowd of well over 5,000 onlookers and participants.[2] These signs of unrest were enough to convince later leftists that their leaders had stifled the natural pacifism of the masses. But even Benoît Frachon, by then a Communist convert, called the idea of a general strike in 1914 a "utopian illusion" — like most *"fanfaronnades gauchistes."*[3]

Indeed, the reported episodes were mostly calm and orderly and quite devoid of insurrectionary implications. At the giant Limoges meeting, the closing resolution urged the authorities to do all in their power for peace, while it affirmed that only with the disappearance of capitalism could peace be definitively assured.[4] This balanced tone was far from accidental. In an official proclamation, praised by the prefect as a sign of "perfect union" with the government, the Socialist-led Municipal Council of Limoges called on all citizens "to defend the national soil and safeguard the Republic" without "judging events" — at least for the present, as implied the proviso: *"Nous verrons ensuite."*[5]

In their own public declarations, Saint-Etienne Socialists voiced no such ambivalence to temper their professed patriotic fervor and devotion to duty.[6] Not surprisingly, however, local anarchists expressed a somewhat different viewpoint. After learning of Franz Ferdinand's assassination — the audacity of which they admired and envied — the anarchists planned ways to put into action the antimilitarism and antipatriotism that they alone had professed in the past. As Benoît Liothier, the city's leading prewar anarchist, had carefully phrased it: "If you want to answer the call of mobilization, you need only *not* tear down the telegraph poles and cut the wires, *not* bomb the bridges and tunnels, *not* derail the trains. If on the other hand you don't want to depart, you've understood me. . . ."[7] Now Liothier and a half dozen others sought to evade the mobilization order and, according to police allegation, met clandestinely to manufacture arms and explosives and "to terrorize the region by acts of pillage."[8] Not long after these few incidents, however, all suspects had reported as ordered to their regiments. For the next two years at least, the situation remained tranquil, as anarchists did no more than defend their personal interests by seeking factory jobs to avoid service at the front.[9]

In both cities, the mobilization proceeded calmly with no public incidents to protest the troops' departures. In Limoges, the Socialist press did take note of tearful soldiers and weeping women and acknowledged the "sadness" and even "consternation" of the crowd. The report does contradict the usual images of "drunken patriotism" and "war fever," but it may reflect the antimilitarism of the local news editors more than true public sentiment.[10] And between "sadness" and active opposition a huge gap remained.

Like their Socialist and anarchist comrades, most unionists were resigned if not enthusiastic at the war's reality. In Paris, the CGT had been slower than the SFIO to rally behind the war effort, and when the shift came the syndicalist leader Pierre Monatte resigned in protest from the CGT's national committee. Three days later, however, the Limoges Bourse du Travail met to approve the CGT's new policy, with no mention of Monatte's opposition. Only Jules Téty, the young anarchist leader, spoke out against the Bourse decision; six months later he failed to appear for his induction and fled to Spain. In the meantime Téty had engaged in no reported antiwar activity.[11] His nonsubmission was thus more a private gesture than a public act of protest, of which there had been no other symptoms among Limoges leftists thus far.

In the Loire region there were more signs of antiwar opinion, as Monatte observed during a visit in January 1915. The Union Départementale at Lyon, which had tried to mount a general strike against the mobilization, now issued a manifesto that denounced "the dreadful slaughter" and called for international action to make "war against war."[12] In Saint-Etienne, however, the antiwar current was still confined to a few lone activists, primarily in the metalworkers' union. The group met in January to hear a reading of a pacifist tract written by Sébastien Faure, a local anarchist now living in Paris. As the police noted, the meeting was altogether "insignificant": only twenty persons attended, and no action was decided or discussed.[13]

This muted response to the mobilization resulted in part from the unions' disruption as members and leaders left for the trenches. In the Limoges Bourse du Travail, the number of dues-paying member unions dropped from 24 before the war to 16 by September and to 6 by December 1914.[14] Union memberships also dropped sharply: among Limoges lithographers, only 19 of the union's 58 members remained at work after the mobilization, and an additional 4 were unemployed.[15] Even in industries that eventually benefited from draft deferments, the short-term losses were staggering: the metalworkers' union at Le Chambon-Feugerolles dropped from 400 to 100 members just after the mobilization, while that at Saint-Etienne fell from a prewar level of several hundred to barely a dozen members as late as May 1916.[16]

Under these conditions, the unions could not hope to sustain more than rudimentary action. The Limoges lithographers expressly avoided anything so risky as a demand for a wage increase and concentrated instead on defensive measures, such as aiding families of soldiers and the unemployed.[17] The Saint-Etienne Bourse likewise met several times after the mobilization to arrange aid for needy families and proclaimed that for the war's duration "no economic or political issues" would be acknowledged or discussed.[18]

This weakness spurred the unions to defer to party leftists to articulate their response to the war. Immediately following the mobilization, national CGT leaders had admitted the need to "close ranks" *(reserrer les liens)* with the Socialist Party and had established a joint Comité d'Action to deal with such issues as living costs, food supply, and unemployment.[19] Even left-wing syndicalist Alphonse Merrheim, opposed in principle to any cooperation with the government, supported the organization and chaired a subcommittee on workers in the war industries to provide the government with information on private firms capable of producing for national defense.[20] Associated organizations in the provinces included the Comité d'Action du Prolétariat Organisé (CAPO) formed at Saint-Etienne in February 1916. This group—intended to serve the proletariat "in all its domains: political, syndical, or cooperative"—focused primarily on practical issues of assistance to families of soldiers and war prisoners, the supply and price of fuel and foodstuffs, and the operation of its own store.[21] The group's secretary, known to police as a moderate pacifist, soon quit his union and withdrew from all other political action to devote attention to the committee's material objectives.[22] These limited aims were so far sufficient to forestall more militant agitation, at least until the unions came back to life.

While there is no record of a comparable Comité d'Action in wartime Limoges, local unionists endorsed similar principles of cooperation with leftist parties. Bourse secretary Jean Rougerie, himself a Socialist, stated frankly that the weakened CGT could defend labor interests only by cooperating with government leaders—in return for their regulation of wages and food supplies—and with the SFIO.[23] Of course, cooperation with the party might include opposition to rather than support of the war effort, once the Socialists issued their own antiwar manifesto at Limoges in May 1915. But Rougerie, who signed that document in his capacity as party member and municipal councillor, expressly rejected the alternative of independent syndicalist action either in labor disputes or on the military question. Such agitation, he told fellow unionists, was mere "bluff and demagogy," and a dangerous prewar relic that could not serve workers' interests then or now.[24]

The Socialists' manifesto was drafted by Paul Faure, editor of the Haute-Vienne party newspaper and municipal councillor from the Dordogne. The manifesto, aimed at party leaders and at other member federations, urged them to press all belligerent governments to work toward a rapid and equitable peace. The party should "extend an open ear to all propositions for peace from any source, as long as the territorial integrity of Belgium and France shall be uncontested. . . ." Above all, the party should not condemn in advance the peace efforts of Socialists in neutral or belligerent countries by refusing to consider peace terms until German militarism were destroyed or the Slavic nationalities were liberated, as demanded by the partisans of the formula *"jusqu'au bout."*[25]

Although mild in phraseology, the text was a daring challenge to party and government policy, and it met some resistance even among local party leaders: Limoges mayor and deputy Léon Betoulle signed it only to avoid a local schism, as he feared the declaration would arouse unrest and possibly weaken national defense.[26] However daring, the document still represented the limits of antiwar action by a group that never voted to deny war credits or called for "peace at any price." In May 1916 the local Socialists did help to found *Le Populaire de Paris* (administered at Limoges), which became the principal voice of antiwar opinion within the national party. But they were soon outflanked on the left both by Monatte and his friends from the syndicalist journal *La Vie Ouvrière* and by the SFIO antipatriot Fernand Loriot, who was closer to the Leninist mold.[27]

While Parisian Socialists had initiated the wartime party-union collaboration, the bond was—as police expected—a "fragile marriage" likely to dissolve once the unionists' own antiwar sentiment revived.[28] In early 1916, Loriot of the left-wing Socialists and Merrheim of the national metalworkers' federation did organize the joint Committee for the Resumption of International Relations (CRRI) as a means to spread the ideas of the recent international conference at Zimmerwald and to work toward reestablishing relations among the European Socialist parties in order to hasten the end of the war. Within a short time, however, the organization ruptured between the moderate fraction led by Merrheim, who acclaimed Woodrow Wilson's "peace without victory" message, and the more radical Loriot fringe. When Merrheim quit the committee it passed to more purely Socialist leadership, while disgruntled left-wing syndicalists joined Raymond Péricat (of the building workers' federation) and Pierre Monatte in a separate Committee for the Defense of Syndicalism (CDS).[29] This syndicalist current, committed both to pacifism and to independence from party dictate, remained virtually nonexistent in Limoges but grew to ample proportions in the Loire.

From its bare beginnings in early 1915, the Loire's antiwar movement grew slowly among local anarchists and syndicalists and remained quite independent of the local Socialist Party. In late 1916, the anarchists resumed regular meetings to discuss and distribute Sébastien Faure's new weekly propaganda journal, whose title gave the group its name: "Amis de *Ce Qu'il Faut Dire.*"[30] The journal, intended for all pacifists regardless of label, aimed to create a *"union sacrée des pacifistes en face de celle des chauvins."*[31] Apart from their meetings, however, the group (approximately seven in number) engaged in no reported activities, alone or with others. Not until March 1917 did these "few partisans of pacifist doctrine" seem inclined "to emerge from the calm in which they had so far confined themselves," according to police reports, and show an interest in "Merrheim's" minority syndicalist movement.[32] The group then dissolved a few months later, even before Faure's journal was officially suppressed at the end of the year. Meanwhile, the anarchists also moved closer to the syndicalist movement, as prewar leader Benoît Liothier (who had decried unions as inherently reformist) dropped out of the group and was replaced by such new figures as Firminy metalworker Clovis Andrieu and Saint-Etienne typesetter Charles Flageollet, the latter elected UD secretary in May 1917.[33]

The Loire's pacifist current, first perceived among metalworkers who had met to discuss Sébastien Faure's anarchist pamphlet, was likewise showing the trace of contacts with Merrheim and the national metalworkers' federation, who founded their own pacifist journal, *L'Union des Métaux,* in May 1915. Within a year, a small antiwar committee began to meet at the Bourse du Travail, led by Bourse secretary Philippe Grégoire and by the local metalworkers' secretary, a suspected revolutionary and "friend of Merrheim" (a favorite police epithet), Laurent Torcieux.[34] The Bourse itself, however, remained otherwise aligned with Sacred Union politics: it refused to sign Merrheim's antiwar resolution (a text issued in 1915 proclaiming that "this war is not our war!"), and some unions continued to oppose all pacifist activities. By contrast, the

Bourse at Firminy did endorse the Merrheim resolution, as did the Union Départementale of the Loire (and that of the Haute-Vienne).[35] Soon the UD, under Flageollet's leadership, supplanted the Bourse as the head-quarters of local antiwar agitation, which quickly transcended the mild terms of Merrheim with which it had begun.

The growth of the anarchist and syndicalist currents owed little to the local Socialists, who themselves slowly adopted a moderate pacifist position. At their congress in July 1916, Loire Socialists hailed the initiatives of the international conferences at Zimmerwald and Kienthal and approved the resumption of relations with the German Social Democratic minority — over the objection of deputy Ernest Lafont, who insisted that the French must patiently await the end of "this war which we neither declared nor desired."[36] A year later, Lafont helped to found a new Socialist weekly, *La Flamme,* to rekindle "the fires of democracy" and to defend Wilsonian war aims from the twin threats of governmental intransigence and the "Kienthalian extremists" to his left.[37] In the latter group, the most prominent Loire partisan was the teachers' unionist Antoine Moulin, a later chief of the local Communist Party. Still, however extreme his political views, Moulin, like former teacher Fernand Loriot in Paris, was no more successful than Lafont in establishing close ties with left-wing syndicalists or in shaping their wartime strikes. Although they fought for the teachers' right to unionize, Moulin and Loriot remained suspect for their non-proletarian status and more committed to parliamentary than to direct action. The teachers' role in the later Communist Party likewise made it easy for syndicalists to spurn its alleged effort to serve as "pedagogues" to a movement deemed too immature to act on its own.[38]

This split in the pacifist ranks between rival Socialist and syndicalist factions paralleled that within the CRRI in Paris but contrasted sharply with the continued homogeneity of the left in the Haute-Vienne. That homogeneity reflected the Socialists' lasting ability, as trusted labor leaders, to rally the unions to their own moderate pacifist program. Unionists recognized but accepted the limits of the party's initiative and declined to pursue a direct action campaign of their own. Loire Socialists, by contrast, never won this support, perhaps in part because of the slower growth of their own pacifist awareness but also because of the syndicalists' deep-rooted mistrust of political socialism, even that of the party's extreme-left fringe. For this reason, the unionists' attitudes must be ex-

plained not only by the presence or absence of an acceptable socialist
movement with which to identify but also by the unions' own unique circumstances during the war.

The Material Dimension: Unionism in a War Economy, 1914–16

The changing tenor of French labor politics, midway through the war
years, was owed not just to the rebirth of pacifism but also to the intensi-
fication of labor grievances as the war ravaged the economy. Workers
concerned more with material than political issues were drawn increasingly into strikes and protests that crystallized their resentment against
the war. Of course, this resentment, however widespread across the
country, varied considerably with the circumstances of each locality and
each industry. By contrasting the wartime position of Haute-Vienne and
Loire workers, one can better understand why the latter developed a militant syndicalist strike movement while the former remained content with
the milder pacifism of the SFIO.

Industrial workers were not, of course, the only ones disadvantaged or
radicalized by wartime conditions. Front-line casualties were heaviest
among the peasants, who benefited least from draft deferments, although
some did stand to gain from rising food prices. Trench life also served—
as had migration and military service in an earlier era—to expose the
peasantry to new and sometimes extremist ideas. These circumstances
may help explain the paradox noted by one of Albert Thomas's informants: the left-wing Socialists' antiwar program found more support among
some peasants than among urban workers in the same region.[39] But even
exemption from military service did not quiet the workers' complaints
about long workdays, inflated living costs, and the sense of being exploited
—with government acquiescence—at the hands of "war profiteers."[40]

Wartime grievances were still slow to find expression, largely because
of the widespread disruption of industrial and union activity that followed the mobilization. An estimated 47 percent of factories, stores, and
offices closed down; production was virtually suspended; and unemployment among those exempt from military duty quickly rose to nearly two
million throughout the country, including twelve to fifteen thousand in
Limoges.[41] The temporary surplus of labor also allowed employers to cut
wages, sometimes by as much as 30 percent.[42] Only once it became apparent that the war would not end quickly did factories reopen to supply

goods essential to the war effort, with the help of new sources of labor to replace workers now at the front.

As might be expected, the least vital luxury industries, like Limoges porcelain and Saint-Etienne silks and ribbons, were the first to close down and the last to reopen during the war. These industries lost not only manpower but overseas markets for their exports, as well as access to coal or electricity to power the kilns or looms. As a result, employment in each industry dwindled to little more than half the prewar level. In the ribbon industry, still staffed largely by women, the problem was not a shortage but a surplus of labor, especially among women unable or unwilling to find alternate jobs in the mines and factories.[43] These problems, plus lower wages than in more prosperous industries, sharply affected the scope and success of labor militancy during the war.

While luxury industries suffered, industries vital to the war effort flourished once the first dislocations of mobilization had passed. With the war as the catalyst, the Limoges shoe industry doubled its work force by 1917 and tripled it by 1920 to become the city's largest postwar employer.[44] Even more spectacular was the growth of the Loire's mining and metallurgy, now that the industrial basins of northeastern France had fallen into German hands. The Loire's coal mines were back to prewar employment levels by 1915 and up another 50 percent by the end of 1917, although high turnover rates among foreign workers kept output below optimal levels.[45] Finally, the "war industries" of steel and munitions were vastly expanded as private manufacturers supplemented the state-owned establishments in filling military orders. In all, wartime employment in metallurgy rose by approximately two-thirds nationally and more than doubled—to a total of 108,000 in 825 separate companies—in the Loire.[46]

This growth depended on the influx of new sources of labor to replace workers now in the trenches. By early October 1914, evacuees from northern France and refugees from Belgium were seen arriving "by the thousands" to work in the mines and war industries of the Loire.[47] Several thousand Spaniards, Italians, and colonial Africans and Asians were also recruited for the region's industries, until foreign labor totaled more than a quarter of the Loire's miners and about 5 percent of its metalworkers; another 10 percent of the metalworkers were German and Alsatian prisoners of war.[48] Female employment also increased more than eight-fold in the nation's war industries, to comprise about a fourth of the total work force and nearly a third at Saint-Etienne, up from less than 10 percent before the war.[49] Women, pressed into service not just by

patriotic motives but by the conscription of men who had previously supported them, found jobs also in formerly male preserves like mining and
railroads. Still, the overall proportion of female labor in French industry
and commerce rose rather modestly from about 30 to 40 percent between
1914 and 1918.[50]

The most important new source of labor came from the recall of front-
line soldiers, beginning in early 1915. Within two years the mobilized
military workers comprised more than a third of the staff of the war industries nationally and nearly half the total in the Loire. These mobilized
workers were particularly numerous in the larger steel mills of the Loire
basin, while women filled the vacancies in the city's smaller machine
shops.[51] Partly for this reason, the conflicts triggered by the influx of military labor proved even more acute in areas so far little touched by labor
militancy, such as Saint-Chamond and Firminy, than in Saint-Etienne itself.

A principal result of this vast labor influx was rampant inflation, spurred
by the scarcity of fuel and foodstuffs and by the high average wages that
accelerated demand for goods. In France generally, prices rose by some
50 percent in the first two years of the war and then doubled again by the
end of 1919; the rates were even higher for the Loire region than for Limoges or the rest of the country[52] (see Figure 17). These increases were
partially compensated by the high wages among metalworkers, but incomes of coal miners and especially ribbon weavers rose more slowly if at
all. On the average, purchasing power eroded by approximately 15 percent between 1914 and 1916.[53] Workers who profited did so at the cost
of longer hours and the increased use of piecework wage scales; for
weavers, even these measures offered scant relief, as energy restrictions
limited the number of hours they could operate their looms.

Inflation in turn accelerated social changes in the work force by nar-
rowing the wage gap between skilled and unskilled labor. Employers
generally granted cost-of-living increases either at uniform rates for all
workers or at regressive rates, with the largest sums going to those at the
lowest end of the scale.[54] Skilled workers also faced a loss of control over
conditions at the workplace. The introduction of new machines, the
spread of Frederick W. Taylor's time-saving methods, and the influx of
less-skilled female and foreign workers not only freed more Frenchmen
for front-line service but also devalued the skills and lowered the pay
scales of those who remained at work.[55] This "dilution" of skilled labor,
in France and elsewhere, helps to explain the bursts of unrest among

wartime metallurgists just as among skilled workers in prewar industries faced with mechanization. These issues also showed that skilled workers had reason to fear for their futures, however privileged their higher wages and their security from military service made them otherwise appear.[56]

These changes were part of long-term economic and technological transformations not confined to the war period. The war surely won greater acceptance for new methods among reluctant employers, while it weakened opposition among labor militants and skilled workers, so many of whom had been reassigned to the front.[57] Wartime use of Taylorism or assembly-line techniques of mass production was less systematic than often assumed, however, even in the bigger automobile companies, and less responsible for increased productivity than was the simple addition of manpower and machines.[58] If these changes had immediate political consequence, it was less the "proletarianization" of France's "labor aristocracy" than the politicization of economic grievances. Skilled workers fought to retain their special privileges as they blamed the government for complacence — or complicity — in the efforts to maximize wartime production and to curb labor unrest.

The government's efforts were part of a larger patchwork of economic measures that included rationing, the subvention of vital industries, and the extension of control over the mines and railroads.[59] To handle its delicate tasks in the war industries, the government quickly named right-wing Socialist Albert Thomas to the new post, created in mid-1915, of Under Secretary of Artillery and Munitions within the War Ministry (later a separate Ministry of Armaments). Dismayed that the exploitation of mobilized labor allowed employers to earn colossal profits, Thomas insisted that the government guarantee the wages and other privileges of mobilized workers to compensate for necessary restrictions on their right to strike. For these purposes, Thomas organized a system of workshop delegates or shop stewards *(délégués d'atelier)* — similar to those already in use in the coal mines — to call employers' attention to labor grievances, and a network of regional mediation and arbitration boards to seek the peaceful settlement of conflicts.[60] The program of shop stewards was instituted by a total of 315 arms manufacturers, including 4 in the Loire and 2 in the Haute-Vienne.[61] The program lasted until it was discredited by the strikes in the spring of 1918.[62]

By defending the "social rights" of mobilized labor, Thomas sought and won the support of the more moderate wing of the trade-union movement. But militants further demanded the right of mobilized workers to take part in unions and strikes, a right that Thomas's measures were designed to supplant. These restrictions made the government, and Thomas, seem the ally of the employers against the workers, as did the threat that dissident workers would be removed from the factories and returned summarily to the trenches.[63] All these circumstances helped to provoke, by late 1916, the revival of unions and the rebirth of labor protest, led by the mobilized workers in the war industries, and most acute in areas where the war industries were concentrated, especially in the Loire.[64]

The union revival was launched in Saint-Etienne by the metalworkers' union secretary, Laurent Torcieux, a mobilized worker at the Manufacture Nationale d'Armes. In May 1916 Torcieux had lamented that the union movement had yet to give a "sign of life" since the mobilization.[65] That September, he began his campaign to reactivate the unions by publishing a letter of protest against the exploitation of the war industries' military personnel. Government regulations, sponsored by Albert Thomas, had promised these workers the "average and normal" wages paid to civilians. The system was nonetheless discriminatory, according to Torcieux, because it calculated "average" wages on the basis of the city's largest enterprises, which paid lower rates than the smaller companies and which employed a lesser portion of the total work force. In addition, mobilized workers were denied overtime pay supplements, because as soldiers they were considered to owe all their time to the state.[66] With these wage differentials, local employers—described by Merrheim as "arrogant, intransigent and feudalistic"—were able to pay "the lowest wages in the country."[67] In protest, mobilized workers demanded a new sliding scale *(barème)* to adjust wages in the war industries, the demand that would trigger a nationwide explosion of strikes in 1917.

Torcieux's own experiences showed how the special status of mobilized workers complicated the question of wartime militancy. Fearing reprisals, Torcieux signed his letter of protest with a pseudonym ("T. Lamant"), and by the end of 1916 he resigned as union secretary to take the more innocent title of "archivist." Meanwhile, the union leadership passed to his less vulnerable civilian successors.[68] Nonetheless, members still faced mounting restrictions on any activities that might threaten the nation's defense.

In theory, the unions remained free even in wartime to meet and discuss purely corporative issues. In Limoges, where the unions seemed safely moderate, only railroad employees (as mobilized workers) appear to have had to request prior authorizations for their meetings, which they readily obtained in all cases for which records exist.[69] In the Loire, however, the authorities refused to permit several meetings to discuss wages and inflation, issues well within the scope of corporative unionism but which might be dangerous if they led to a strike. The expected attendance of large numbers of mobilized workers was also deemed grounds to disallow a meeting.[70] Indeed, as the antiwar movement gained momentum, permits became the exception, not the rule. The authorities now saw corporative issues as a mere pretext for "criminal" propaganda, especially in the war industries; since the Minister of Armaments was sponsoring wage talks, unionists had no need to discuss the issue further among themselves.[71]

The resumption of strikes also showed the gradual revival of wartime labor militancy. In the last five months of 1914, strikes had virtually ceased throughout the nation, because of both the spirit of Sacred Union and the widespread disruption and high unemployment in industry (see Figure 9). Strikes resumed slowly in 1915, perhaps as a result of Merrheim's influence in the metalworkers' federation.[72] These strikes were still modest in size and in frequency, however, and metalworkers accounted for only one of the year's conflicts, with just 18 participants. The continued revival in 1916 did, nonetheless, include more metalworkers: they held fifty-four strikes, averaging 188 participants each.[73]

Similar patterns appeared on the local level. By national standards the Loire remained fairly militant, ranking fourth among the departments in strike frequency in 1916. These strikes were generally brief affairs, however, and not much larger or more frequent than the Haute-Vienne's, especially if figured in terms of the size of the labor force. Of the departmental totals, only a flurry of brief episodes occurred in Limoges and virtually none in the Saint-Etienne basin. Most activity took place instead in the textile mills of the Roanne area, or in the Saint-Junien glove industry—where a single long strike accounted for nearly all the working-days lost to strikes in the Haute-Vienne in 1916[74] (see figures 10 and 11).

In addition, most strikes in 1915–16 occurred as spontaneous responses to local grievances, with no coordination in timing or in chosen targets. Most disputes were simple demands for wage increases, still relatively easy to settle in the workers' favor and sometimes resolved without a strike at all. Union involvement was reported only in the case of the Saint-Junien glove workers.[75] In scale and format, these strikes bore little resemblance to the larger and more ambitiously planned actions, especially in the Loire, in 1917–18.

By the end of 1916, unions and strikes had barely begun to revive from their early wartime disorganization. Certain features of the later wave of protest were nonetheless apparent: the growing problems of wages and inflation, and the special grievances of mobilized workers in the war industries. So far, the campaign had focused almost exclusively on economic issues, and as in peacetime, it reflected less a state of misery or desperation than a state of general prosperity, which made long hours and high living costs all the harder to endure. Soon, however, these economic grievances merged with a generalized mood of war-weariness. Especially in the Loire, and especially among mobilized metalworkers, labor unrest quickly acquired a political connotation and fueled the pacifist agitation that erupted in late 1917.

From Economic to Antiwar Protest: The Crisis Year 1917

There is little question that 1917 was the most critical year of the war for French politics and society. Military difficulties led to mutinies in the armed forces, labor unrest exploded in larger and more frequent strikes, and left-wing Socialists and syndicalists raised serious challenges to the politics of Sacred Union.[76] Also during that year two revolutions occurred in Russia, with lasting influence on labor politics in France and throughout the world. Still, the connections among these various threads are hard to evaluate. Did they mean that France was on the verge of its own revolution? What revolutionary pressures were then building for later explosion, in 1918 or after the end of the war?

A valuable study has examined the French army mutinies, which crescendoed from April to July 1917 and continued to echo through January 1918. While army officials readily blamed the crisis on left-wing pacifist propaganda, or on the government for failure to control the situation, most outbursts instead resulted from general lassitude and the collapse of morale at the time of the failure of the spring offensive led by General Robert Nivelle. Incidents occurred almost solely in zones of combat, especially where attacks were least successful and where sacrifices seemed particularly vain. Divisions reported in contact with leftist groups had few if any cases of indiscipline; nor was there a clear pattern of outbreaks according to regional voting patterns, or by such personal characteristics as occupation, prior police record, or age.[77]

Pacifist doctrine did operate on the fringes of the movement, as did the influence of the Tsar's overthrow in March, but "the France of 1917 was not Russia."[78] Outside the army, the same conclusions can be drawn. Conditions at the front reinforced pacifist currents on the home front, but even those most pessimistic about France's military prospects failed to endorse a positive campaign for military defeat.[79] Militants who hailed the events in Russia rarely saw them as a model for French agitation, either to end the war or to overturn the capitalist system. The March Revolution could be read as a Jacobin-style defense effort, and even after November "the Russian Revolution" could be hailed uncritically by Bolshevist sympathizers and social democrats alike.[80] By 1918, some elements of Leninist insurrectionalism may have begun to penetrate France, but until then the extreme left grew from indigenous war-weariness, not from an international Bolshevik (or pro-German) conspiracy.

Most important for present purposes are the connections to be drawn between antiwar protest and the labor strikes of 1917. Minister of the Interior Jean-Louis Malvy declared at the time that the strikes were essentially economic, not pacifist, in motive, but most historians (as well as Malvy's critics) have proved more skeptical: whatever the initial cause, the strikes often turned into demonstrations against the war.[81] This connection, however, was neither universal nor altogether spontaneous. In the Haute-Vienne, where left-wing Socialists led the antiwar movement, most strikes remained strictly economic and quite modest in scale. By contrast, in the Loire, where the Socialists' actions were at best half-hearted, left-wing syndicalists quickly turned labor strikes into a vast antiwar movement of their own.

In the Loire, and in France generally, strike frequencies in 1917 more than doubled from those of the previous year; the Loire now ranked third among all the departments. In the Haute-Vienne, by contrast, the number of strikes declined from its already low figure for 1916 (see Figure 13). Many disputes in Limoges were settled without recourse to work stoppages, since employers were quick to make concessions.[82] Strikes that did occur achieved high rates of participation in the companies affected, but they were scattered throughout the department and among a diverse array of small industries. A general strike of shoe workers in

August did rally a large turnout, but the impetus came from Paris, where the national federation was demanding the *semaine anglaise* (half-day off on Saturdays) and a modest wage increase. Even then, the local union remained dormant, and secretary Rougerie (in his capacity as Bourse leader) had to address the demands to employers on his own.[83]

While these strikes showed little sign of union direction, much less an overt pacifist motivation, those in the Loire were now far better organized and likely to reveal syndicalist leadership. The latter strikes were longer and larger as well as more frequent: the number of working-days lost to strikes had risen by nearly 800 percent since 1916. As in previous years, the textile and other industries of the Roanne and Montbrison districts still accounted for more than half the departmental total, but this time the metals industries of the Saint-Etienne basin also came into the spotlight. Six large metallurgical strikes (all but one outside Saint-Etienne proper) accounted alone for more than a third of the total strikers and a sixth of the total working-days lost (see Figure 11). These strikes were somewhat shorter than average in duration, either because the mobilized metalworkers feared military reprisals, or because as political strikes directed at the Ministry of Armaments rather than at the employers, they served their purpose as well in brevity as in length. The strikes nonetheless achieved an unusually high rate of participation, averaging 20 percent even in large establishments and peaking in July with a reported turnout of all 3,500 workers at the Aciéries de Saint-Etienne.[84] Perhaps as a result, the strikes were more than usually successful, even in metallurgy, which had experienced a high rate of failure in the past (see Figure 12).

The strikes' high rates of participation and potent political impact were the result not just of the special grievances of the mobilized metalworkers but also of their ability to galvanize mass support. Many of the mobilized workers were assigned to the Loire from military depots elsewhere in the country. As such, their presence, and their frequently active roles in the labor movement, brought to the region new political ideas often distinct from the syndicalist traditions that had prevailed in the past. Their roles also allowed authorities to blame "outside agitators" for local disruptions.[85] Nonetheless, these new influences actually complemented, rather than contradicted, the region's prewar militant traditions. Indeed, the wartime strike waves showed the vigor of the Loire's own syndicalist currents, not the birth of a new revolutionary strategy, such as on Bolshevik lines.

Of the wartime leaders, the first to rise to local prominence was the metalworkers' secretary, Laurent Torcieux, mobilized at Saint-Etienne since 1915. Although a Loire native, Torcieux had worked in Paris from 1910 to 1912 after losing his job for taking part in the violent strikes at Le Chambon-Feugerolles; he then returned to Saint-Etienne and served as union secretary in 1913–14. During the war, Torcieux quickly came under suspicion as a "revolutionary" in contact with Alphonse Merrheim, but he remained of a relatively moderate persuasion and played little role in later strikes. He thus served mostly to promote the union reorganization on which other, more radical pacifists could build.[86]

Among these the most important was Clovis Andrieu, a Parisian syndicalist mobilized at the Holtzer steelworks at Unieux and soon elected secretary of the metalworkers in neighboring Firminy. As an outsider, Andrieu had hesitated at first to accept the office but succeeded quickly in securing his position, as shown by the mass strikes of late 1917 to protest attempts by the authorities to return him to the front. Andrieu also maintained his ties in Paris, first with Merrheim and then with more extreme left-wingers such as Raymond Péricat.[87] Still, however reviled by the authorities, Andrieu proved to be more pacifist than revolutionary, and less extremist than Péricat or his principal Loire contact, the anarchist typographer and Lyon native Charles Flageollet.

A still more prominent newcomer was the CGT's assistant secretary Georges Dumoulin. A native of northern France, Dumoulin was mobilized in 1917 as a coal miner in the Loire community of Roche-la-Molière. Before the war, Dumoulin had taken an active part in his union, where he had evolved from Guesdism to revolutionary syndicalism and had supported the Amiens Charter. Once in the Loire, however, he played a negligible role in local labor affairs. Although he claimed in his autobiography to have worked to organize and strengthen the union at Roche-la-Molière, these efforts left no trace in the public record, and his union took little part in strikes or antiwar protests. By virtue of his national reputation, Dumoulin did chair the antiwar congress held at Saint-Etienne in 1918. Nonetheless, like Merrheim, he remained a moderate in wartime politics and lost initiative in local matters to militants further to the left.[88]

However important these individual personalities may have been, their impact depended on their ability to adapt to local conditions and to win broader support as attention shifted from economic to political issues. Beginning with wage demands among mobilized metalworkers, a flurry of strikes occurred in January 1917 that threatened to paralyze the war industries of Paris and several provinces. In response, the government issued in April a new *barème,* or wage scale, to codify the minimum wages practiced in each region and to attempt to enforce them for military as well as civilian labor. The *barème* also raised wages wherever they had been lower than average, while ensuring that higher wages would not be reduced.[89] These advantages, however, left militant unionists still dissatisfied. Most gains were at the lowest wage rates and offered little benefit to more highly skilled workers, who stood even to lose production bonuses that some employers had previously offered.[90] A second revision in June 1917 still failed to avert a new wave of strikes that summer, which spread throughout the country and merged with the antiwar movement sponsored by Merrheim and the left wing of the CGT.

Perhaps not surprisingly, this agitation had little impact in Limoges, where only a handful of metalworkers were engaged in defense production and where all seemed to accept the new *barème* with equanimity.[91] In the Loire, however, discontent remained acute and readily politicized, aimed at the government as arbiter of wages and working conditions in the war industries. Militants also rejected the conciliatory efforts of Albert Thomas, whose network of mediation and arbitration boards seemed unable to get intransigent employers to apply the revised *barème.*[92] The new system of shop stewards *(délégués d'atelier),* whose appointments required employers' approval, also seemed destined to become a covert agency of the *patronat.* Workers insisted especially that the shop stewards be exempted from military responsibility so that they could not be threatened with punitive reassignment to the trenches. The dispute became still more heated when Thomas's successor, the industrialist Louis Loucheur—dubbed by unionists *"l'ami des patrons"*—refused to allow the new shop stewards the same protections accorded the existing delegates in the coal mines. Even before Loucheur's accession, however, Loire militants had condemned the system of shop stewards as a thinly veiled attempt by government and industry to sidestep the unions' control of their own affairs.[93]

The dispute over the shop stewards was also a sign that Loire militants were moving beyond the moderate positions of Merrheim and the national metalworkers' federation. As federal secretary, Merrheim had been a main spokesman for Thomas's system, and he lost credit with Loire left-wingers when he agreed to the stiff terms offered by Loucheur.[94] Despite Merrheim's counsel of calm and moderation, unrest persisted in the Loire and helped to unseat some local union leaders, whose moderate views no longer matched the prevailing mood.[95] In this way, the movement launched by militants "in contact with Merrheim" had now achieved a leftist momentum of its own.

The second phase of the movement saw the spread of unrest from the mobilized workers to other groups in the war industries, with the help of Clovis Andrieu in Saint-Chamond and Firminy. Andrieu sought especially to rally women and foreign workers to the growing unions, both to gain their support for wage demands and to lessen the competition that would free eligible Frenchmen for service at the front. Both groups, of course, had grievances of their own to draw them into the unions. Some women and foreign workers were already protesting spontaneously against low wages and dangerous working conditions; in Paris, the first big strikes of January 1917 had begun among women workers and then spread to the men.[96] Outside the labor movement, housewives staged angry incidents in the marketplaces to protest inflation and denounced both farmers and manufacturers as war profiteers.[97] Women also had strong emotional reasons to oppose a war that threatened the lives of their sons or husbands. At Saint-Junien (in the Haute-Vienne), a crowd of women held a peace demonstration in January 1917 that had no apparent link to labor issues or syndicalist protest of any sort.[98]

In the Loire, these combined emotional and practical issues drew women readily into organized antiwar agitation, where they could speak out without fear of reassignment to the trenches. In April 1917, new women's sections were formed in the metalworkers' unions at Saint-Chamond and Firminy, where women called for higher wages and shorter hours — and for peace, to the tune of the theme song *"Nous voulons nos poilus."*[99] Andrieu and other syndicalists also urged women to refuse work at reduced wages, or even, preferably, to stay home, as their presence in the factories promoted the war effort. His friend Raymond Péricat expressly blamed the prolongation of the war on women's "selfish" desires "to earn money to buy themselves jewelry and cosmetics" while "their sons, their husbands, their fiancés are being mowed down by machine-gun fire."[100] To these men, the campaign was thus much more explicitly pacifist than corporative or feminist in inspiration. Their professed concern for the plight of foreign workers was similar: some militants allegedly fomented agitation among the foreigners to make them undesirable replacements for Frenchmen eligible for service at the front.[101]

The agitation among female and foreign workers was only part of the larger movement to revive dormant unions for both economic and political purposes. From their weakened state just after the mobilization, unions grew spectacularly in 1917: the Saint-Chamond metalworkers' union reported 2,000 members in April and 4,000 in May, including some 800 women; other localities claimed similar gains, and the department-wide Union des Métaux may have had more than 20,000 members, more than half of whom were mobilized workers, by June or July.[102] Merrheim's national federation also soared to some 150,000 members, up from 25,000 before the war.[103] These figures were based on the unions' own estimations, but even if inflated they give some measure of the scale of growth. Unionization had also grown relative to the burgeoning labor force. Still, unions represented only a small minority of all industrial workers; the days of a truly mass union movement had not yet arrived.

The growth also extended beyond the metalworkers to other local labor groups. The railroad workers' union more than quadrupled to some 900 members, and the mining and construction unions also resumed activities.[104] By March 1918, the Union Départementale claimed a total of 25,000 members in the Loire.[105] There are few indications of just how this mammoth growth was accomplished, other than records of ever larger and more frequent public meetings, including some that reported attendance figures of 5,000 or more.[106] The growth, far surpassing prewar levels, was more than a simple recovery from the weakness that had followed the mobilization; it was a dramatic response to unique wartime circumstances, and it failed to occur in localities where circumstances differed, as in Limoges.[107]

While the Loire's unions revived, they also sought enhanced coordination throughout the department. The Bourse du Travail served only a single city, and in Saint-Etienne the Bourse proved unable to galvanize mass support. Until May 1917, the Bourse — and the UD — were headed by the moderate pacifist Philippe Grégoire, a musician with no base of power in an important union; he then resigned, in a dispute over management of the workers' cooperative, and was succeeded at the Bourse by a moderate Socialist from the teachers' union, Antoine Reynard, who opposed all militant action against the war.[108] To fill this power vacuum, the metalworkers' union in February 1917 founded a Comité Intercorporatif, first for the war industries and then to include all major unions throughout the department. This body soon became the Loire's foremost instrument of strike and antiwar activity, in close contact with the Parisian militants in the CDS.[109]

The first group to join with the metalworkers in the new committee was the construction workers, who were similarly subject to wartime regulation by the Armaments Ministry. Perhaps for this reason, these workers proved particularly militant, as exemplified in Paris by their leading spokesman, Raymond Péricat.[110] Less eager to join were the coal miners, who also stayed out of the Union Départementale until nearly the end of the war. The miners refused categorically to join with or even extend support to the striking metalworkers; they feared reprisals that might send them back to the trenches, and they resented the metalworkers' failure to support their own prewar strikes. Although they briefly joined the general strike to release Clovis Andrieu, their main goal was to win a wage increase; they continued as usual to stress corporative interests against political activism of any sort.[111]

As the strike movement gained in militancy, the government's natural desire to uphold wartime productivity became a concerted effort to dampen revolutionary enthusiasms before they became aroused. As long as economic issues seemed preeminent, the authorities willingly worked to revise the *barème* of wages and to monitor the cost of living for mobilized personnel.[112] But these conciliatory gestures, inadequate to halt the protest, may even have aggravated it, as claimed the Loire prefect, blaming Albert Thomas for leniency that "paralyzed the measures of prudent firmness" that had hitherto kept things quiet.[113] Evidently concurring, the government replaced Thomas at the Armaments Ministry as well as Malvy at the Ministry of the Interior, and even opened legal proceedings against the latter. Finally, the new government of Georges Clemenceau took power in November, expressly to revive the flagging war effort and to thwart the apparent "defeatist" threat.

In order to quell the labor agitation, the authorities employed paid informants to keep the munitions factories under surveillance; there were as many as forty such informants in the Loire.[114] The police also compiled lists of militants to be "purged" from the war industries and returned to the trenches. The idea of such punitive action was not a new one: as early as 1915, when left-wing syndicalists had begun to challenge the moderate CGT leadership, the Ministry of the Interior envisaged drafting Merrheim, Péricat, and other "impenitent revolutionaries" to keep them quiet.[115] In June 1917 the wave of strikes and their alleged

Bolshevik inspiration nearly led to Merrheim's arrest, had not Malvy (before his own downfall) intervened.[116] If Merrheim's influence had once cast suspicion on the Loire militants, their own agitation now conversely incriminated Merrheim, no matter how moderate his own actions might otherwise have appeared.

The list of militants to be removed from the factories included a few of the local anarchists and syndicalists *"de mauvais esprit"* who had been under surveillance since 1914. Most of the suspects were newcomers to the region, however, men whose very unfamiliarity made them easy to condemn as *"sans-patrie"* in the pay of Berlin.[117] The police also hoped that the unrest, so far the creation of a handful of leaders, would be easy to quell once these "outside agitators" were forced to depart; instead, at least for the moment, the attempted repression set off the largest and most widely supported strike that the region had yet seen.

The episode began in late November with demands for still another revision of the *barème* of wages, coupled with complaints at the threatened shortages of food and fuel for the coming winter. Clovis Andrieu of Firminy led the agitation, which he claimed expressed a simple refusal to endure wartime hardships when war profiteers were "pocketing millions" from the workers' own toil—and pressuring governments to prolong the war.[118] Merrheim now played the role of conciliator, urging Loire militants to wait while the federation negotiated wages with the new Armaments Minister Loucheur.[119] Yet by now the government, with Clemenceau at the helm, had apparently lost faith in the possibility of a negotiated settlement and decided instead to return Andrieu to the front.

On the news of Andrieu's forced departure, the Loire erupted in a mass general strike in his defense. From its start at the Holtzer steelworks in Unieux, the movement soon engulfed an estimated 100,000 to 200,000 strikers, including munitions workers at Roanne, Le Creusot, and Lyon.[120] The more moderate staffers at Saint-Etienne's Manufacture Nationale joined the strike belatedly, while miners declared only a one-day sympathy strike—over the objections of those who protested the movement's political overtones or recalled the metalworkers' failure to join with them in the past. The Manufacture Nationale was also forced to close its doors to protect the safety of workers who refused to join the strike. Despite these defections, however, the strike was large enough and potentially violent enough to require the transfer of troops from the front to assure order and to compensate for the shortage of police forces in the Loire.[121]

After ten days the government and the Loire's Comité Intercorporatif reached an agreement designed to protect the honor of both sides: it would be announced officially that Andrieu was only "on leave" from his factory duties and that the Ministry of War would now reopen the wage question.[122] This sudden switch to a conciliatory policy is difficult to evaluate: perhaps Clemenceau was showing signs of leniency, which Malvy's friends hoped might extend to the ousted minister;[123] or perhaps the cause was simply the change at the Loire prefecture, as the former prefect, a known "Clemenciste," left for Paris to take a post in Clemenceau's Ministry of War.[124] The authorities may in fact have concluded that the whole affair was a hasty miscalculation. In any case, they now had a clearer idea of the extent — and probable limits — of militant syndicalism in the Loire.

The success of the strike propelled the Loire to national prominence in the antiwar movement and prompted Péricat to choose Saint-Etienne as the site of the next year's left-wing syndicalist congress.[125] But not all strikers had acted from antiwar motives. Wage questions were still largely at issue, according to Merrheim's deputy secretary Marius Blanchard, who arranged the settlement: *"Tout se basait sur un barème."*[126] These concerns may indeed have prevailed among the miners, who joined only at the last minute, and among others who took part from the outset but then complained bitterly that the strike ended with no wage increase.[127] Most metalworkers probably acted for the stated aims of solidarity with Andrieu and the defense of syndicalist liberties. Only the most radical fringe, led by the new UD secretary Charles Flageollet, scorned the goal of simple solidarity and tried to mythologize the strike as the first phase of a revolutionary insurrection. In his assessment, strikers refused at first to accept the settlement because *"on voulait autre chose."*[128] Even Flageollet, however, had acknowledged the value of economic issues in broadening support for the strike.[129]

Most important, the episode revealed the new line of demarcation within the syndicalist movement, no longer between prowar and antiwar factions but between the moderate and extreme fringes of the pacifist left. This shift, already implied by Merrheim's growing moderation, was further accentuated by Andrieu himself. As in Merrheim's case, the authorities were slow to appreciate the nuances of Andrieu's position. Like those employers who sought to justify their own hard line by condemning the strikes as "seditious" and "criminal," the authorities professed to see signs of Leninist "defeatism" in any plan to send mobilized labor out on strike.[130] To Andrieu and his friends, however, the movement sought only a negotiated and just peace, not "peace at any price."[131] More properly termed pacifists than defeatists, most Loire militants shared the moderates' goals for ending the war and differed only in their acceptance of somewhat more violent means.

Andrieu's politics are hard to glean from the records, but, like Merrheim, he always stressed unionism and the defense of labor interests rather than revolutionary agitation. He was also enough of a patriot to agree that if the Germans refused a negotiated peace settlement, "we would return to offer our breasts to the country."[132] There may indeed have been signs of Leninist defeatism in the Loire strikes of 1918, as influenced by the still greater extremism of Charles Flageollet. Still, only a government obsessed with the danger of revolutionary contagion — or, as Andrieu claimed, out to "get" him for his hard line in the wage talks[133] — could have seen the specter of Bolshevism in the strikes of 1917.

The split in the pacifist ranks was also symbolized nationally by the CGT's national conference in late December at Clermont-Ferrand. At this conference, its first since the war's beginning, the CGT agreed to work for peace on the basis of a Zimmerwaldian platform, repudiated the politics of Sacred Union, and endorsed (without distinguishing between them) the principles of Woodrow Wilson and the Russian Revolution. This compromise resolution — said to be drafted by the Limoges Bourse secretary Jean Rougerie, who read it aloud to the assembly — neatly expressed Rougerie's own ambivalence: love for his country as "the flame of liberty in the world" and dismay that a democracy could refuse its warriors a say in defining the terms of peace.[134] The compromise won virtually unanimous support, rallying even the erstwhile left-wingers Merrheim and Péricat. Two lone voices dissented at Clermont: teachers' unionists Fernand Loriot and Marie Mayoux, who soon called openly for a CGT schism.[135] Outside the conference, the dissidents also found favor among left-wingers in the Loire, who denounced their own delegate, Bourse secretary Antoine Reynard, for voting his conscience at Clermont in violation of a supposed mandate from home.[136]

To be sure, the compromise required concessions on both sides. To the regret of reformist Auguste Keufer from the printers' federation, the Clermont resolution made no call for the return to France of Alsace and Lorraine.[137] However disappointing to extremists, the resolution marked the CGT's dramatic conversion to the pacifist movement, in a "centrist coalition" against both the right and the extreme left.[138] This orientation matched that of most Haute-Vienne unionists, who endorsed the Clermont compromise wholeheartedly.[139] Yet those in the Loire and elsewhere who had spurned such moderation in 1915 were scarcely more cordial to it at the end of 1917. These extremists, who had met provisionally at Saint-Etienne on the eve of the Clermont conference, began immediately thereafter to mobilize their forces in the southeast region with the help of the Parisian CDS.[140]

From the strikes of 1917 to the attempted insurrection of 1918, the Loire remained in the forefront of the country's syndicalist agitation. This special position reflects both the catalytic role of the mobilized workers in the wartime defense industries and the anarcho-syndicalist traditions deeply rooted in the conflicts of the past. As a sign of continuity, the wartime split of the CGT into left- and right-wing factions followed familiar occupational lines: most extremists were still in the smaller-scale metals, construction, and clothing industries while the moderates were in the mines, the railroads, the state-run utilities, and other large-scale enterprises.[141]

These links to the past should not minimize the wartime movement's innovations. In a region where unions and strikes, especially among metalworkers, had typically been small-scale if ardent in spirit, new forces were needed to galvanize the mass strikes of July to December 1917 and the threat, at least, of a mass insurrection the following year. New forces also help to explain how the huge steelworks at Saint-Chamond and Firminy, hardly renowned for prewar militancy, were scenes of wartime protests even larger and more violent than those at Le Chambon-Feugerolles or Saint-Etienne. New leaders also took charge of the wartime movement, while Benoît Liothier and other prewar anarchists remained on its fringes and upheld the prudent stance that they had assumed after the first days of August 1914. As a result, the links may seem quite tenuous between the prewar and the wartime — or postwar — movements of the left in the Loire.

In essence, the wartime movements represented a dramatic extension of prewar traditions, which had set the stage but then quickly ceded the spotlight to new ideas and new leaders. In this sense, the authorities were not altogether wrong to blame the unrest on "outside agitators," who may have won only scant local support for their most revolutionary aims. These outsiders nonetheless had an impact because they offered a strategy of mass organization that Loire militants might have dreamed of but had never brought to fruition, while they echoed the same syndicalist and antiwar principles that local militants had always espoused. These ambiguous links to the past also characterized the events of 1918, which combined some Leninist revolutionary theories with the syndicalist concepts of direct action by small but ardent minorities, ideas that had flourished in the Loire since well before 1914.

Chapter 4

May 1918: The Climax of Revolutionary Syndicalism in the Loire

By 1918 the wave of unrest that had peaked the previous year began to recede sharply, both as economic grievances found partial satisfaction and as German military advances silenced some critics of "Sacred Union" politics. Despite — or perhaps in part because of — this new mood of moderation, however, militant syndicalists redoubled their efforts to launch a general strike movement that might force an end to the war. The strike coincided with a congress of left-wing syndicalists that convened at Saint-Etienne in May 1918. The congress was national in scope, led by Raymond Péricat and his Committee for the Defense of Syndicalism (CDS), and the strikes found some echoes throughout the country, especially in the war industries of Bourges and Paris. Still, as in 1917, the Loire remained in the forefront of the strike movement and determined even to act alone if Péricat and the CDS should back down.

For the Loire, the events of May 1918 were important not just as the climax of antiwar agitation but as the occasion for a factional dispute over syndicalist strategy that foreshadowed the future labor schism. Militants disenchanted with the moderate pacifism of the CGT's new majority, as defined at the conference at Clermont-Ferrand the previous December, now prepared to sacrifice labor unity and national discipline for the sake of a revolutionary gesture, no matter how local and how limited its support. The tactic of the general strike — especially controversial in wartime — confirmed their rupture with less militant Socialist pacifists and also with moderate unionists, who had come to reject "direct action" in favor of parliamentary action in concert with the political left. For these reasons, the May events have become the centerpiece of the Loire's revolutionary syndicalist mythology — in much the same way as other events fifty years later came to symbolize a rebirth of syndicalism and student radicalism in contemporary France.[1]

From Mass Strike to Revolutionary Strike

To build their strike movement, militants needed to maintain or extend the mass support that had peaked in the strike for Andrieu's defense the previous autumn, as well as to shift the movement leftward toward a more distinctly revolutionary program. Not surprisingly, however, these goals proved contradictory: as the movement turned leftward, it lost rather than gained mass support. The majority of workers remained committed at most to economic considerations, or to solidarity with Andrieu; many erstwhile left-wingers, including Merrheim and his local supporters, defected from the movement along the way.

The mass strike for Andrieu seemed to have given the Loire a historic role to play as detonator of a French working-class uprising. As Andrieu himself put it, "The Loire must be capable of propelling the CGT toward an insurrectionalist movement."[2] To broaden and coordinate support throughout the region, Loire delegates first met with Péricat and other CDS leaders in Paris and then toured the heavily industrial southeast region in late January to conduct propaganda meetings in Lyon, Dijon, Valence, Nîmes, Bourges, and Alais.[3] Two months later an interdepartmental congress at Saint-Etienne convened delegates from the entire region, including Vienne, Grenoble, Clermont-Ferrand, and Marseille.[4]

Vienne was now a major center of pacifist activity. In June 1917 its Bourse du Travail had issued an antiwar resolution that demanded a "peace without victory" as the only form of a "just peace with the consent of all Peoples." Still more dramatically, Bourse secretary Emile Miglioretti, of the textile workers' union, now called on workers to "take to the streets" in a truly "revolutionary" movement: his appeal seemed excessive—or at least too impatient—even to militants in the Loire.[5] In Lyon, meanwhile, the tide of militancy had already ebbed somewhat. While the Union Départementale was a CDS affiliate, the Bourse du Travail was not: it voted a resolution approving only the compromise peace terms of the Clermont conference, and even the UD secretary spoke out against a strike on May Day, although in later votes he apparently "kept his reservations to himself."[6]

The Loire's own support for an antiwar movement was also far from unanimous. In Roanne, unionists at the Arsenal voted to approve the pacifist initiatives of their comrades in the Loire basin, but other workers in the city remained more sympathetic to Socialist than to syndicalist leadership.[7] Even in the Loire basin, the antiwar movement was still dominated by the Comité Intercorporatif of the war industries and was increasingly resented by other unionists who complained that their own economic grievances were being ignored.[8] Saint-Etienne also lagged behind Andrieu's Firminy in antiwar fervor. Still refractory were the coal miners and the civilian employees at the Manufacture Nationale, whose corporatism, militants feared, might lead them to "betray" the movement.[9] Least likely to join in were the weavers and the railroad workers, whose unions remained weak and exclusively economic in focus until well after the end of the war.[10]

The toughest obstacle to the growth of a radical antiwar movement was the metalworkers' own weak political commitment. Alphonse Merrheim's moderate viewpoints remained ascendant, as implied by the crowds of up to 6,000 who came to hear him speak about the goal of a *"paix des Peuples"* and the need to remain disciplined and calm.[11] Merrheim also urged local leaders to proceed slowly and to offer satisfaction to those still concerned with wage issues. Although Loire militants publicly rejected that advice, most privately recognized its value: Andrieu likewise emphasized the issue of the new tax on wages, and others echoed Merrheim's appeals to avoid violent confrontation.[12] UD secretary Charles Flageollet liked to perorate about revolution "in the Russian manner," in which rioters would "massacre half the millionaires and seize their wealth." But Andrieu had little tolerance for such "excessive language" *(propos inconsidérés).*[13] Still more moderate was the union secretary at the Manufacture Nationale, Auguste Lebraly, who dismissed Flageollet contemptuously as *"un haricot"* (a bean), a pun on the militant's name.[14]

Caught between Merrheim's and Flageollet's contrary influences, workers in the Loire may not yet have been ready for revolution, but they were, as Merrheim observed uneasily, "white-hot" *(chauffés à blanc).* Even the police foresaw an inevitable conflagration unless the government moved quickly to permit contacts between Allied and German Socialists and to declare Allied war aims.[15] In late winter, two immediate issues threatened to spark an explosion: charges that the labor unrest was the product of German "espionage," and plans to recall the younger age-groups *("jeunes classes")* of mobilized workers for duty at the front.

The so-called *affaire d'espionnage* began in late February when the arrest of certain German café operators in Saint-Etienne aroused suspicion that they were spies responsible for the upsurge of labor unrest in the region.[16] Militants quickly protested the attempt to discredit the movement by the spread of these "calumnies," which they blamed on a wide range of culprits: the "bourgeois and reactionary press" in Paris; the Clemenceau government for allegedly encouraging the accusatory press releases; and the right-wing Socialist deputy Pierre Renaudel for allegedly using the rumors to sway party opinion to his own side.[17] The Bourse at Saint-Etienne further denied "any political influence whatsoever" in its corporative efforts, and even those who admitted a political bias expressly denied any foreign ties (except perhaps to Woodrow Wilson) and reiterated their commitment to pacifist, not defeatist, aims.[18] These themes, expressed at a series of propaganda meetings throughout the department, failed nonetheless to spark great public enthusiasm: attendance peaked at approximately 1,200 participants, far from the 5,000 or more at meetings the previous December or, more recently, during Merrheim's visits. As the authorities explained, the majority of workers were now "tired of all the meetings," not personally touched by the rumors and innuendos, and still unmoved by the campaign for peace. Nonetheless, despite these "good signs for the future," the affair marked the start of "a new period of agitation" that eventually took its toll.[19]

Less remote to most workers' interests than the "espionage affair" was the increase in military departures for the trenches. Through the spring of 1918, as German attacks depleted France's military manpower, the French authorities sought to supply fresh troops from among younger mobilized workers and young civilians not previously inducted. In the Loire, a total of 1,151 workers from these "young classes" were to be withdrawn from the war industries and replaced with older workers or— according to rumor—with Americans, the latter alleged to have struck a secret deal that promised them safe jobs in the rear while Frenchmen assumed the added burdens of the front.[20] Dramatized by these controversies, the troop departures sparked a series of demonstrations: women gathered in the streets and at the train stations, where they tugged on the soldiers' coats and cried out, *"Ne partez pas! restez! à bas la guerre!"*[21] According to the military authorities, the demonstrations were too large to be spontaneous, and Andrieu and other syndicalists were observed contributing to the unrest.[22]

Although the protests were in part political in inspiration, the main motive was the more immediate concern for one's own life or that of a loved one, which leaders feared if publicized might discredit the peace movement. As militants realized, soldiers risking their own lives were unlikely to sympathize with workers' desires to avoid front-line service any more than with the wage demands that had preoccupied most workers in the past.[23] For this reason, left-wing Socialist Paul Faure tried to defend the later strike in Paris by calculating that the small number of mobilized workers subject to the recall represented only a minuscule proportion (one in thirty-six) of the strike's total participants.[24] However sincere Faure's argument, the suspicion remained that most workers were far less concerned with peace than with their own lives and livelihoods, and far less militant than the leaders who sought to mobilize their unrest.

The Limits of Radicalism

Despite the increase since late 1916 in economic dissatisfaction and political awareness, a revolutionary insurrection was still far from imminent. Even economic self-interest aroused less unrest than in 1917, as inflation slowed enough to keep wages and prices temporarily in line.[25] In the Loire and the Haute-Vienne, as in France generally, both the scope and the frequency of strike activity declined sharply in 1918 (see Figure 9).

In the Loire, most of this decline came after the failure of the May strike movement; the months January through April saw as many strikes (twelve) as any four-month period of 1917.[26] These early strikes were nonetheless scattered in a broad array of towns and specialties, especially in the textile trades of the Roanne and Montbrison districts (see Figure 11). Except for the May general strike, only four strikes occurred in metallurgy and all were outside Saint-Etienne. These strikes were also particularly small-scale episodes. Although the departmental average of working-days lost per strike (approximately 2,000) was slightly above the national average, more than half the total were tallied during a single long weavers' strike; the metalworkers' conflicts (again, excluding the May general strike) averaged fewer than 500 working-days lost each.[27] Whatever the impact of the wartime syndicalist resurgence, it had not served to make Loire strikes either longer or larger in scope.

In addition to economic conditions, changing military circumstances also helped to moderate labor activity. Germany's harsh treatment of Russia at Brest-Litovsk made most workers skeptical of the chances for a negotiated peace settlement and unwilling to accept what Socialist deputy Adrien Pressemane called *"une paix à la russe."*[28] The heightened German offensive prompted leftists in both Saint-Etienne and Limoges, as elsewhere in the country, to transcend sectarian differences and join with Pressemane when he urged, *"Sauvons la France d'abord!"*[29]

In the political sphere, moderate Socialists of all persuasions joined in "Comités de Gauche" to fight both the perceived danger of counterrevolution at home and the military threat abroad. At Saint-Etienne the Radical-Socialists and the League of the Rights of Man formed one of the first such groups, headed by Benjamin Ledin, editor of the mildly pacifist *La Flamme.* Tensions persisted between the Socialist faction, which endorsed Wilsonian peace terms, and the Radical-Socialists and some Briandists, who found these aims too "extremist" for their taste.[30] Still, however extreme in some eyes, these aims were modest indeed compared to those of the syndicalist movement's left wing.

Although the CGT showed a parallel evolution toward the center, sectarian differences remained acute. At Saint-Etienne, the Bourse du Travail joined the local republican-Socialist coalition but did not send speakers to meetings or otherwise take an active role.[31] Firminy's metalworkers, still more intransigent, refused any alliance with republicans who failed to support the demand for an armistice on all fronts.[32] With similar vigor, Andrieu denounced Merrheim for joining such a coalition in Paris, and the CGT National Committee refused to allow its general secretary, Léon Jouhaux, to join the coalition in the CGT's name.[33] Here the issue of peace became linked to the question of party-union relations, as syndicalists remained wary of the Socialists' parliamentary methods. France's military ordeal may have reaffirmed the moderation of Jouhaux and Merrheim, but it sharpened dissent on the extreme left. From a mere two votes at the Clermont conference in December 1917, the CGT minority burgeoned into a full-grown radical pacifist movement, with deep roots in the war industries of the Loire.

The military issue continued to divide centrists from extremists as they debated such tactical questions as the desirability of an immediate confederal congress or a May Day general strike. Among the resolutions of the Clermont conference was that a full-scale congress—the first since the war's beginning—be held during the spring of 1918. As a loyal supporter of Sacred Union, Jouhaux felt that the fierce German offensive and the bombardments of Paris made a national congress or other antiwar demonstration unthinkable.[34] Merrheim concurred, adding that pressure for peace at this time might provoke Japanese intervention at Russian expense. With Merrheim's approval, the metalworkers' federation also agreed to postpone all antiwar protest until the military picture had improved.[35]

While Merrheim rallied to the idea of Sacred Union, Raymond Péricat, a professed "antipatriot," repeated his refusal to sacrifice "a millimeter of skin" to reclaim Alsace-Lorraine or to save France. He also found it absurd for the ostensibly pacifist and politically neutral CGT to "preoccupy" itself with "the fluctuations of the front." After all, he argued, if each side waited until it was in the best military position, there would never be any move toward peace.[36] As Péricat realized, however, he was only "preaching in the desert." At least in Paris, most workers seemed to agree with Jouhaux and Merrheim. Paris had never been considered "ripe" for a movement, and now the bombardments reduced pacifist sentiment to a new low.[37]

The problem, leftists said, was that moderates wished not just to gain time for the war effort, but in effect to keep adjourning a congress *"aux calendes grecques."*[38] Thus it now seemed necessary to force the CGT's hand. To discuss this issue, Péricat's supporters in the southeast region convened an interdepartmental congress in late March in Saint-Etienne. Delegates debated especially when and how to organize a national congress and whether the leftists, grouped in the CDS, should hold the congress on their own if the CGT refused.

The issue here was not just peace but discipline within the central labor hierarchy. Moderates at Saint-Etienne, led by Bourse secretary Antoine Reynard, insisted that the minority had no right to "substitute" itself for the CGT leadership; in fact, Reynard claimed, the interdepartmental congress was itself an unauthorized "national" gathering because it drew delegates from Paris and other places outside the Southeast.[39] Here again, Merrheim confirmed his newfound centrism when he agreed that the CDS must not proceed on its own if the CGT withheld its sponsorship. As a sign of his disapproval, he even planned for a rival congress of the metalworkers' federation to be held in Paris on the same days as the projected CDS congress at Saint-Etienne.[40]

Over Merrheim's and Reynard's objections, the interdepartmental congress voted thirty-five to nineteen to demand a national congress and to ask the CDS to organize it if the CGT refused. Nonetheless, according to police informants, enough moderates had walked out in disgust after the morning session that their ballots, if cast, would have turned the vote around.[41] Merrheim's influence may also have caused the CDS's change in plans to avoid further charges of bad faith. Instead of a full confederal congress, the CDS now planned to convene only a national minoritarian congress, for study rather than for action, and then to pass on its conclusions to the CGT at large. In theory, at least, the congress would also admit majoritarians who wished to attend, in order to rule out charges of schism.[42] This arrangement, even if self-contradictory, was an apt compromise for such fence-sitters as Georges Dumoulin, who had backed the CDS motion at the interdepartmental congress as the delegate for the miners of Roche-la-Molière. In May, as the presiding officer at the CDS congress, Dumoulin could insist legalistically that the session was mandated only to plan minority strategy for the forthcoming confederal congress (held in July) and thus had no business voting an immediate general strike.[43]

Dumoulin's logic notwithstanding, the strike question was at the very heart of the CDS program. At the regional congress, the debate on when to convene the national congress hinged on plans to hold a one-day strike on May Day. Reynard and Merrheim argued that a congress would take time to organize and should itself be delayed until May Day at the earliest. But the victorious motion, sponsored by left-wingers Andrieu and Flageollet, called for the congress to be held before the end of April, in time to plan for the May Day strike.[44] Ironically enough, when the CGT refused to act and the CDS was forced to proceed alone, Péricat himself found it necessary—over the Loire's objections—to postpone the congress until the third week in May.[45] As Reynard remarked acidly, the left-wingers were now forced to accept from the CDS the delay that they would not tolerate from the CGT leadership.[46] Still, it was far from clear that the CGT would have agreed to a congress even by the later date. Two days before the May congress opened, the CGT finally announced plans for the July confederal congress and called on all loyalists to boycott the rival CDS congress at Saint-Etienne.[47]

More than a question of legitimacy or timing, the strike issue raised larger problems of syndicalist strategy that threatened to rupture the CGT's left-wing minority from within. Like the patriots who opposed a strike at such a time of "national anguish," Merrheim feared that a strike would backfire because most workers would refuse to participate. Even in the Loire, he said, many workers were hostile to the antiwar agitation; among weavers, only the women were "revolutionary," and "we can scarcely count on them."[48] Péricat, meanwhile, had been the main proponent of a huge May Day strike movement: not just an antiwar demonstration, he had specified, nor even a one-day work stoppage, but the prelude to a general insurrection against the war.[49] When the time came, however, even the CDS divided on the issue, and Péricat himself advocated a one-day strike at most, so as not to jeopardize plans for the now-delayed minoritarian congress. He explained his decision in terms not so different from Merrheim's: "It would be absurd to call a general and compulsory work stoppage and not be followed. That would play right into the confederal majority's hands."[50]

This evidence of CDS hesitation posed the strike issue in entirely new terms in the Loire. Left-wing syndicalists, led by Andrieu and Flageollet, had voted at the March congress to follow the CDS if the CGT refused to organize the strike and the national congress. But what if the CDS itself defaulted? Local militants had discussed but so far rejected the idea of organizing their own local action, and Andrieu remained adamant against any move by the Loire alone. Flageollet, however, had no qualms about such a limited, local gesture. In fact, he called on the Saint-Etienne arrondissement to go it alone in case the Union Départementale should back down.[51]

In their plans for May Day, neither the UD nor the CDS in fact defaulted. The question of the Loire's acting alone remained nonetheless at issue throughout the May movement and best distinguished Flageollet's radicalism from the more cautious views of Péricat and most unionists in the Loire. Following Merrheim, a succession of Loire moderates had begun to back down on various issues: first, the secretary of the Saint-Etienne metalworkers' union, Jean-Baptiste Barlet, resigned his post when extremists attacked him for echoing Merrheim's appeals for calm and moderation.[52] Next, the assistant UD secretary, Marius Jean Bonnefond, who had joined in the attacks on Barlet, refused nonetheless to support the UD's vote for the May Day strike.[53] Finally, Flageollet's closest allies, Péricat and Andrieu, prepared to retreat if the campaign failed to get wider backing. More sensitive than he to the need for a mass, unified movement, they hesitated to proceed without the planning and organization that would promise success.

The question, then, was not so much how to organize a strike or a congress but rather whether the time was ripe for a large-scale movement. According to Merrheim, the lack of mass support outside the Loire would —and did—doom the movement to failure.[54] Flageollet, however, hoped instead that the Loire's own dynamism would be contagious in Paris and throughout France. Flageollet also refused to doubt the enthusiasm of the local strikers; he worried only that "if we get them out [on May Day] we might have trouble getting them to come back."[55] Although he fully recognized the virtues of a mass, nationwide strike movement, he preferred to overlook them rather than back down.

As critics predicted, the May Day strike misfired nearly everywhere. A handful of national federations endorsed the movement, including the ceramics and clothing workers, plus certain subgroups of metals and construction workers, but not the latter two federations as a whole.[56] Despite the support of the ceramics federation (headquartered in Limoges), the Union Départementale of the Haute-Vienne opposed the movement, as did the UDs of the Rhône and the Paris region.[57] In the Loire, the UD voted (over some opposition) to support the movement, but the Saint-Etienne Bourse du Travail, led by Antoine Reynard, refused to go along.[58]

The strike itself gained some following at Bourges but otherwise remained confined to the Loire, where turnouts were still at best uneven. Militants claimed more than 30,000 participants at Saint-Etienne alone, and good results also in the usual locales of Firminy and Le Chambon-Feugerolles, but acknowledged the scant response at Saint-Chamond and Rive-de-Gier.[59] Again as usual, the miners showed little enthusiasm for the movement, despite Dumoulin's personal endorsement, and the employees at the Manufacture Nationale refused to stay off work unless the army authorized the holiday (as for Easter Monday) or—at the very least—the CGT itself issued the order to strike.[60]

Despite its meager following, the strike nonetheless had immediate repercussions. After the new shift failed to appear at the Verdié steelworks in Firminy, three furnaces were extinguished, their contents ruined, and several workers dismissed or sent back to their depots as punishment for their alleged "sabotage." When Andrieu and other union leaders could not avert the sanctions for what they termed only a "regrettable" mishap, the union responded by calling a general strike. Even Minister of Armaments Loucheur stepped in to urge the company to drop the sanctions. But the company's director, who was then also Saint-Etienne's mayor, threatened to close the steelworks rather than back down.[61]

It was this conflict, not an upsurge of antiwar fervor, that set loose the massive strike wave to engulf Firminy and the entire Loire basin. The strike did have some political content: anger at the company for punishing workers it considered "bad elements" and dismay at the recall of the "young classes" for service at the front.[62] Even now, however, most workers remained preoccupied with simple corporative issues. As Flageollet himself was forced to acknowledge, events in Firminy were moving too fast for most workers, there or elsewhere, to keep up.[63]

One problem was that the strikers had been told to await the signal from the CDS congress (scheduled to open May 19 at Saint-Etienne) before launching into action. On the news of the Firminy outbreak, an estimated 200,000 Parisians abruptly joined the movement; as Flageollet exulted, *"il y'a de l'éléctricité dans l'air."*[64] Strikers elsewhere in the Loire seemed, conversely, to be waiting for assurances of support in Paris before ratifying their own strike declaration. Finally, on the eve of the minoritarian congress, the strike was announced simultaneously in Firminy, Le Chambon-Feugerolles, and Saint-Etienne.[65]

This timing made the strike seem to force the hand of the congress delegates, who by voting a general strike of the nation's war industries were only confirming a *fait accompli*.[66] Viewed another way, however, the strike's abrupt start was less a sign of unbridled enthusiasm, or the masses getting ahead of the leaders, than simply a failure of coordination between the transient grievances at Firminy and the larger campaign against the war. In fact, by the time the Saint-Etienne congress opened, the brief strike in Paris had virtually ended.[67] This may explain the large number of abstentions in the vote at the congress: the Parisian delegates could not "decently" vote a general strike resolution (or so a police informant argued) when the Parisian strikers were nearly all back at work.[68]

The vote at the congress was 114 to 4 — with 60 abstentions — in favor of a general strike of the war industries. Despite the vote, the strike was far from general: it spread to Bourges and Nevers but attracted little support in Lyon and virtually none outside the Southeast.[69] Even in the Loire, the strike remained largely confined to the metalworkers of Firminy, Unieux, and Le Chambon-Feugerolles, while it barely touched Saint-Chamond and was scarcely more effective at Saint-Etienne. When the union at the city's Manufacture Nationale voted, belatedly, to participate, only some 20 percent of the work force actually joined in. The miners again called only a one-day solidarity strike, and in most companies the majority of miners remained at work.[70]

In all, the movement's rhetoric far exceeded actual performance. Flageollet himself was anxious to maintain calm and discipline, although others hoped to create violent incidents for their own sake. At a crowded meeting at the Bourse du Travail in Saint-Chamond, one speaker proclaimed that "it is better to die on a barricade than in a trench." A second speaker lauded the example of women in Italy who had thrown themselves in front of trains to block the departures of their husbands to the front. The same individual also called for violent measures against the *"jaunes"* (non-striking workers) and soon was arrested for leading just such a campaign. A third speaker at the Saint-Chamond meeting proposed the use of bombs and grenades, industrial sabotage, and the cutting of telephone and telegraph lines. Yet when he asked for volunteers to join him, none responded.[71] Nor were many such incidents actually reported. There were occasional cut telephone wires, some disturbances at the departures of mobilized workers, and a few "violations of the right to work" *(entraves à la liberté du travail).*[72] Still, most days passed, especially at Saint-Etienne, in relative calm.[73]

The calmness of the rank and file contrasted sharply with the militancy of some leaders, such as one who called for *"l'action directe des minorités agissantes."*[74] This contrast encouraged the authorities to believe that only a tiny fringe of "outside agitators" sustained the movement, without support from the "ninety percent" of the populace who were "sane and serious" and wanted only to work. According to this analysis, the average worker joined the movement only out of solidarity or fear of reprisals and would be happy to see the end of a situation he deplored as anti-French.[75] As if to confirm these suspicions, an independent union of metalworkers at Firminy wrote to Paris to express its "profound dismay" at this "revolutionary intrigue" that it deemed "intolerable" at a time of national crisis. The union assured the government that "any repressive measure to block this rush to riot and revolution would be welcomed by the majority of the population."[76]

Thereby encouraged, the local authorities sent to Paris a list of principal strike leaders and recommended, "The sanction is simple: the immediate arrest of all."[77] The arrests began within a day. The most prominent targets were Péricat in Paris and Loire leaders Flageollet and Andrieu. A total of approximately fifty militants, most of them mobilized workers, were sent to Clermont-Ferrand for military indictment; another seventy-three were removed from the factories and sent back to their depots; and the Bourse du Travail at Saint-Etienne was closed and occupied by troops.[78] As a result, the movement subsided almost immediately; by May 28, although 20 percent of the workers were still on strike at Firminy, work had returned virtually to normal at Saint-Etienne.[79] To survive such repression, the Union Départementale had taken the precaution of naming alternate leaders. Merrheim had also argued that a movement with mass support could not be crushed simply by arrests at the top.[80] The quick impact of the arrests thus supported the authorities'—and Merrheim's—suspicions that indeed the time for a mass insurrection had not been ripe.

The arrests not only decapitated the strike movement but crippled the Loire unions for some time, at least until militants were freed in an amnesty the following winter. In the meantime, unions fell into the hands of moderate or majoritarian leaders, and memberships often declined to a fraction of their former size.[81] Some of the effect was durable: Firminy would not again be the left-wing center that it had been, so briefly and so spectacularly, during the war. Indeed, the government had done more to strengthen its position than if it had simply stopped the May movement before it had begun.

For this reason, the episode may have been the result of deliberate government provocation.[82] It is hard to explain otherwise why the government, with ample knowledge of the movement's illegal intentions, had granted authorization—despite the prefect's contrary advice—to such blatantly pacifist gatherings as the minoritarian congress at Saint-Etienne.[83] The government's apparent aim was for the strikers to dig their own grave. By letting the movement overextend itself and alienate the moderate segments of the rank and file, the authorities would gain a free hand to exact the sanctions that labor solidarity had prevented in Andrieu's case in 1917. That strike's very limits also permitted the hope that any danger of insurrection could be thwarted before it got out of hand. The government's strategy was nonetheless risky, as it triggered resentments that would push future minoritarians ever further leftward. Still, in the short run, the perceived threat of revolution was neatly sidestepped. Later problems could be tackled after the end of the war.

The Politics of Revolution and Schism

The modest reality of the strike movement makes it clear that France was not, in 1918, on the verge of revolution. Nonetheless, the strike was both a major factor in future labor politics and a revealing index of revolutionary opinion in the Loire and throughout the country. It is time, then, to step back from the rush of events and see just what the movement meant to its participants. Of course, their goals were often ambiguous or contradictory, and they engendered disputes that divided radicals one from another as much as leftists from the center or the right.

Arrested strikers were charged mostly with "desertion" or "abandoning their posts," or—as in the case of Flageollet, who had a medical exemption from military service—the related crime of "provocation" of these illegal acts.[84] Beyond these charges, the authorities aimed to use the strike as proof of the "revolutionary" and "defeatist" goals that they had long attributed to syndicalism in the Loire. As in the past, despite its militancy and its potential for violence, the movement remained more simply pacifist than defeatist or revolutionary. This time, however, the movement did contain some new extremist elements, not just in its challenge to national defense but in its tactic of direct action by militant minorities, ready to proceed without mass support.

In the authorities' eyes, any pacifist action implied revolution in wartime. Moreover, by their strategy of direct action, the syndicalists, unlike the Socialists, expressly refused to concentrate on shaping public opinion by pacifist rhetoric, international party congresses, or the like. Still, the syndicalists never fully clarified the aims of their own strike: an immediate armistice? a revolutionary seizure of power? or simply a gesture of sympathy in behalf of a just peace?

Probably the boldest statement of purpose was a remark attributed to Andrieu that "since the government is incapable of ending the war, we must end it by force."[85] This kind of statement should not, however, be taken at face value. Since Andrieu did not intend to overthrow the government, the use of "force" could only mean pressure on the government to take steps it would otherwise avoid. What kind of steps? The Loire strike committee demanded an immediate armistice followed by peace negotiations in which the Socialist International would participate.[86] The CDS leadership, however, apparently disagreed. At the minoritarian congress in May, Péricat and Dumoulin reportedly stated that the strike aimed only to force the government to declare its war aims and to grant the CGT the authority (and the passports) to attend an international labor conference.[87] These more modest goals—plus some economic issues—were apparently all that interested the Parisian strikers, who thus returned to work after winning a few *"bonnes paroles"* from Clemenceau.[88] In fact, as one militant in Paris admitted, the economic motives alone were publicized at the beginning; only after the strike was well underway would the leaders "declare" it a revolutionary action against the war.[89]

With its goals unclear, it was also uncertain how long the strike would have to last to achieve them. The Parisian strike, meant just for "demon-strative" purposes, could be brought to a quick conclusion.[90] Péricat wanted a longer but still limited movement: "As soon as the maximum is reached," he said, "we'll try to cut it [the strike] off so that it won't have a chance to disintegrate on its own."[91] Flageollet, on the other hand, planned more than a symbolic gesture: he wanted the strike to paralyze war production for at least three weeks, so as to make it impossible to continue the fighting.[92] The demand for an immediate armistice also im-plied that the strike would persist until an armistice was declared.

Even the Loire strike committee remained vague on this last issue. In a letter to the prefect, the committee complained that the government had not yet "responded" to its demands for peace, and it vowed to continue the strike until the government made a "satisfactory response"—whatever that might be.[93] This new terminology suggests that the strikers, aware that the movement had passed its "maximum," were belatedly taking Péricat's advice to find a graceful way out. Still, despite Merrheim's bar-gaining efforts, the Loire refused to accept terms similar to those that had settled the Parisian strike.

A further question is whether the strike's aims were truly "defeatist." Péricat claimed not to care about France's military fate, but Andrieu agreed to fight for his country if Germany rejected a negotiated peace set-tlement.[94] He and his friends in the Loire also rejected the terminology of "peace at any price," a phrase attributed at least once to Péricat.[95] The resolution of the Saint-Etienne minoritarian congress expressly called "not for peace at any price, but for peace *tout court,* honorably achieved by the international action of workers." The Loire strike committee like-wise coupled its demand for an armistice with a word of acclaim for the peace terms of Woodrow Wilson, whose plea for "no annexations" meant that Germany must liberate *"le sol français."*[96] Even Flageollet spoke of peace as the goal, and of revolution as the method "if necessary" to achieve that end.[97] None welcomed the prospect of military defeat as a means toward revolution. Nonetheless, to a government haunted by the specter of the Russian Revolution, these distinctions were all too easily overlooked.

To justify their charges of "defeatism," the authorities read a myriad of seditious aims into the Loire strike movement: "The class struggle was drummed into the minds of the workers; the factories were said to belong to them; bank robberies would furnish the necessary funds; food stores would be raided for their supplies; etc., etc. Thus [the police concluded] we find at the very base of the movement all the ideas of Russian Bolshevism."[98]

Continuing their summary of the strike movement, the police acknowledged that "taken individually, the members of the Comité Intercorporatif did not agree completely with these ideas." When speaking of peace, for example, the militants did not — a surprising disclaimer — accept the idea of peace at any price. Still, their private scruples did not stop them as a group from disseminating "hardcore revolutionary and defeatist ideas" to the public. Obviously, then, their action was "guided by . . . a *mot d'ordre* that they received from outside."[99]

What was the source of this outside guidance? Not just the CDS in Paris, but rather a foreign influence, transmitted through the alleged antipatriots Pierre Monatte and Henri Guilbeaux. The conclusion, though admittedly hard to prove, struck the police as inescapable: Flageollet's activities were rooted in German direction and even German pay.[100]

These insinuations of German guidance had been a favorite theme of the movement's opponents, outside or inside organized labor, at least since the strikes of May 1917.[101] The claim made it all the easier to dismiss the movement as anti-French and harmful to the workers' own interests. It also helped to explain why many workers welcomed government measures to purge this menace from within their ranks. Essentially, according to this argument, the CDS was a schismatic organization, serving just as the patronal scheme of "divide and conquer" to sow discord within the working class.[102]

By this tortuous process of reasoning, the police may nonetheless have hit upon the most crucial aspect of the May strike movement: its role in the eventual CGT schism. The specter of schism had haunted the labor movement at least since the conference at Clermont the previous December, when a last-ditch unity resolution had temporarily exorcised the demon. The ghost formally reappeared at the minoritarian congress in May and was hard to ignore from then on.

At that congress, certain moderates, including Georges Dumoulin, had hoped to avoid the appearance of schism by seeing the event as just a planning session for the forthcoming confederal congress, not as an overt challenge to the CGT leadership. Dumoulin's evasiveness, however, drew a quick retort from Marie Mayoux, a left-wing teacher from Angoulême, who was about to enter prison on charges of "defeatist" propaganda. The very purpose of the congress, she insisted, was to say clearly, do we or do we not want a schism. When even Péricat answered no, Mayoux taunted: "Our sheer presence here is evidence of a schism. You refuse to face the truth. If you accept the fact of schism but not the word, you are not men."[103]

Mayoux's was the only voice at the congress for schism, and even she rallied finally to a unanimous resolution for unity to show that the split was not to come from the minority side. Nevertheless, the incident revealed that for Mayoux, unity was not an absolute value. She and Fernand Loriot, also of the teachers' federation, had been the only voters against the unity resolution at Clermont; even Péricat had compromised for unity's sake. Now Péricat, angered by Mayoux's taunting, burst out with a tirade against "women in general and women teachers in particular": they were not and never had been workers, and they came into "our" movement with "a total inability to understand the needs and aspirations" — i.e., for unity — "of the working class."[104]

The question of schism was once again banished at the CGT confederal congress held finally in July. In part because the German offensive had not yet abated, most erstwhile radicals rallied to a compromise resolution that pledged support for Wilsonian pacifism and that indirectly condemned Péricat and the CDS.[105] The vote nonetheless followed heated debate, especially within the metalworkers' federation, on Merrheim's role in the recent strikes. The question of "confidence in Merrheim" showed how far the extreme left had moved beyond and against his tepid radicalism, especially in the Loire.

The May strikes placed Merrheim in an admittedly delicate position. While he disavowed the CDS congress, he wished to take control of and help to settle the strikes that had erupted in Paris and the Loire. Yet this was hard to do, Merrheim acknowledged, without provoking "insinuations" that the federation sought "the division and disintegration of the movement."[106] When Merrheim's deputy secretary Marius Blanchard visited the Loire, a crowd of 2,000 stormed him with insults, forced him to seek refuge inside the Bourse du Travail, and let him leave safely only when Flageollet and others came to his rescue two hours later. As a result, hard-line majoritarians within the federation now accused the Loire militants of "criminal" behavior toward the working class.[107]

In return, the Loire leaders accused the federation of betrayal. While Merrheim did later defend the strikers from charges of defeatism or conspiracy with the enemy, he and Blanchard refused to endorse an expression of "sympathy" for the arrest victims, including Péricat and Flageollet, because these were not members of the metalworkers' federation.[108] This narrow view of labor solidarity deepened the left-wingers' contempt for Merrheim's entire wartime record. Suspicious of his new "governmental methods," Loire militants now claimed that Merrheim, "originally a majoritarian," had joined the left wing only out of "hurt pride" when the government had moved to Bordeaux in the early stages of the war.[109]

Not all Loire syndicalists joined this campaign of vilification. At the federal congress in July, the Loire metalworkers' new secretary, Louis Soubeyrand, was sufficiently swayed by Merrheim's explanations that he abstained rather than vote no-confidence in the federation's recent actions, and his vote received the nearly unanimous approval of the 800 unionists who later met at Saint-Etienne to hear Soubeyrand's report.[110] Although first described as a "notorious revolutionary" who had somehow managed to avoid arrest during the strike movement, Soubeyrand now seemed to the authorities to have posed initially as a left-winger mostly so as not to lose local support.[111] The union's former secretary, Barlet, who had long since broken with the extremists, now echoed Merrheim's complaint that their violent tactics had "almost killed" the labor movement in the Loire.[112] Indeed, whatever the merits of each side's position, the conflict clearly threatened the future of labor unity, as mutual recriminations persisted well beyond the end of the war.[113]

Merrheim later attributed the dispute to a "misunderstanding" of his peace program. The Loire strikers, he argued, simply failed to realize the fallacy of their demand for an armistice: unlike a declaration of war aims, an armistice required the compliance of enemy powers, where unfortunately the pacifist movement was not yet so well developed as in France.[114] Flageollet, however, perceived the conflict in different terms: Merrheim was simply unwilling to take the action needed to put his own pacifism into effect.[115] It was the question of tactics, more than goals, that divided Merrheim from the bulk of the Loire strikers, themselves pacifists and not revolutionary defeatists. To Merrheim, a general strike in wartime was unacceptable not so much because it threatened national defense but because it would alienate the mass of the workers and thus compromise the unity of the working class.

This conflict also consummated Georges Dumoulin's evolution from left to center. Unlike Merrheim, Dumoulin had endorsed the May Day work stoppage and had attended (in fact presided at) the minoritarian congress at Saint-Etienne. Nonetheless, he later claimed to have already had private doubts about these two actions, both of which he supported publicly so as not to lose all influence in the left-wing camp.[116] At the May congress, he spoke out against the general strike resolution, but from the purely procedural basis of CGT discipline. Later on, he backed Merrheim's view that a strike, even if conducted in "good faith," was inappropriate when the country was in the grip of a German attack. With this latest assessment, Dumoulin rallied to the new centrist majority at the CGT confederal congress in July 1918.[117]

As in Merrheim's case, this evolution was slow to convince the authorities, who continued to distrust Dumoulin as an "outside agitator" with "occult" influences in the Loire. For example, the prefect attributed to Dumoulin's "maneuvers" the disturbing news that the local miners' unions, after years of hesitation, were now finally to join the Union Départementale.[118] Despite public concern, this belated rapprochement — like that of the miners to the CGT in 1911 — was less a sign of the miners' own newfound radicalism than a mark of the organization's increased temperance, as a result of the disastrous strikes. Nonetheless, the prefect did have a hint of an insight when he described Dumoulin as no true moderate but merely "clever" and "practical" enough to "dissimulate . . . the violence of his own sentiments." The mine leader had opposed the decisions of the May congress "for the simple reason that he deemed them doomed to failure; he would not hesitate to support a movement that he considered likely to succeed."[119]

Of course, such caution could itself signify moderation (or pessimism), especially if by underestimating the masses' revolutionary fervor one always denied that the time for action was ripe.[120] Still more decisive, however, was the commitment to working-class unity. It was this final consideration, which Péricat and Andrieu shared with Merrheim and Dumoulin, that made them reject or at least question the Loire strike movement, because by alienating the more moderate tempers it risked hopelessly dividing the working class.

Of the principal Loire militants, only Flageollet appeared willing to condone a labor schism, such as that heralded at the May congress by the teacher Marie Mayoux. Flageollet did not expressly devalue labor unity: like most syndicalists, he would have seen the need for unity as a main argument against collaboration with the Socialist Party. In the strike movement he sought to attract as much support as possible, both inside and outside the department, but only on strict syndicalist terms. He refused to pander to workers' economic preoccupations; he called openly for revolution; and he remained undaunted at the thought that the Loire, or even Saint-Etienne, might have to act alone.

Unlike most of his colleagues, Flageollet seemed to believe in the virtues of a minority movement no matter how tiny, a movement that by its very audacity could disdain mass support. This view bears remarkable resemblance to Leninism, in its quest for revolution by a small core of enthusiasts unwilling to curry mass favor at the cost of ideological purity. If there was a Leninist tinge to the Loire's strike movement, it was not in any insurrectionalist or "defeatist" ambition, which remained alien even to Flageollet. The real issue was no longer war or revolution, but the commitment to preserve labor unity; not "peace at any price" but "unity at any price."

This Leninist dimension to the strike movement leads to two related conclusions. First, it helps to account for why syndicalists, including those in the Loire, were to be among the earliest (if most fleeting) converts to Bolshevism, which they saw as a variant of their own strategy of "direct action" by *"minorités agissantes."*[121] As long as the substance of Leninism remained obscure, syndicalists could seek to imitate Bolshevik structures like the *soviets,* which were said to embody syndicalist virtues of decentralization or to resemble anarchist associations of free producers.[122] Still, as pseudo-Leninists, these militants remained true to the Loire's basic syndicalist traditions. Perhaps the failure of the May 1918 strikes might lead to further strategic revisions in the future, as militants abandoned anarchism for the leadership of an organized political left.[123] So far, however, the syndicalists retained their mystique of direct action by small revolutionary bodies that preserved their local autonomy against the all too moderate leadership of the central confederation. Whatever the postwar era might bring, the wartime experiences of party-union collaboration and the government's growing encroachments in the economic realm had left the prewar syndicalist dogmas remarkably intact.

The dynamics of Leninism also help to explain the course of the later labor schism, which took quite distinct forms in the SFIO and in the CGT. These differences were already foreshadowed in late 1918, when the factional division in the unions lay between a tiny left-wing fringe and a vast centrist majority, and that within the party was between two more nearly equal camps. The simplest explanation of this contrast is that while the Socialists still disputed the question of wartime pacifism, the

CGT—from the start less committed to "Sacred Union"—had now, since its conference at Clermont, rallied almost unanimously to the pacifist position.[124] In fact, however, to the left of this vast pacifist majority still lay a radical fringe that rejected both mild pacifism and all its correlates including, on the one hand, collaboration with governments and socialist parties in peace negotiations and, on the other, commitment to labor unity as against the direct action of an audacious minority unwilling to compromise for the sake of mass support.

Indeed, for the centrist CGT majority, the question of peace was now less at issue than the question of syndicalist tactics: in rejecting a general strike in wartime, the CGT centrists began to sound much like ordinary Socialists, however pacifist their ultimate goals. Thus the syndicalist minority emerged as the first distinctly left-wing faction—as befit their precocious conversion to Leninism—and they defined their differences, and eventual split, with the CGT majority on issues quite distinct from those that would divide left and right within the SFIO.

Syndicalists and Socialists in 1918

The strikes of May 1918 had important repercussions not only in the unions but also within the Socialist Party, despite its lack of direct involvement and its general distrust of independent syndicalist action against the war. Even Fernand Loriot, the party's most outspoken left-winger, never adopted Leninist defeatism and refused to endorse the strike tactics of Péricat and the CDS.[125] Among moderates, both the Loire and the Haute-Vienne Socialists stopped short at Zimmerwaldian pacifism and rejected the left-wing syndicalist alternative. Still, the tone of debate differed in the two communities, according both to long-standing patterns of party-union relations and to the immediate impact of the strike, which ravaged the Loire but left the Haute-Vienne virtually unscathed.

While the Loire unions gathered steam for the strike explosion, those in the Haute-Vienne were no longer even considered "minoritarian," now that the term denoted membership in the CDS.[126] Left-wing syndicalists, based in the war industries of Paris and the Loire basin, could expect little support in a department that produced few munitions and employed few mobilized workers on leave from the trenches. Most local unionists, like Bourse secretary Jean Rougerie, had long since joined

Merrheim in his moderate but forthright pacifist movement. These one-time "minoritarians" now had to decide, as had Merrheim, what attitude to take toward the unfolding events in the Loire.

When the question of a proposed general strike first arose, on the eve of the conference at Clermont, Limoges unionists had voted simply to continue the pacifist tactics that they had adopted in 1915.[127] As long as Limoges remained far from the scene of conflict, this bland confirmation of business as usual never had to succumb to the pressure of rapidly changing events. At both Limoges and Saint-Junien, union leaders endorsed the CGT's ban on May Day strikes or demonstrations, and the day proved, in the prefect's words, "particularly calm, and absolutely without incident."[128] Still, the unions reserved the right to act in defense of their professional interests; thus, on the eve of Saint-Etienne's minoritarian congress, the Limoges lithographers met to discuss a demand for a cost-of-living wage increase.[129]

Rougerie also managed to keep an open mind about events in the Loire. When the CGT leather workers' federation held its national congress in May, Rougerie helped to sponsor a resolution of sympathy for the minoritarian congress at Saint-Etienne. The resolution, passed by a large majority, took the place of a stronger statement that would have added sympathy to "all our comrades who are victims of governmental repression."[130] Rougerie later explained that even the milder gesture had not been his own idea, but he nonetheless endorsed it, perhaps—like Dumoulin—to avoid losing all influence in the minoritarian camp.[131] This compromise deftly avoided the bitterness that ravaged the metalworkers' federation when Merrheim disavowed the minoritarian congress and refused any gesture of aid or sympathy to the victims of the strike.

As Rougerie noted happily, his federation was moving away from what he termed the "bluff and demagogy" of prewar days and toward the reasoned pacifism expressed at Clermont in December 1917.[132] He might have added that his federation, unlike Merrheim's, had the grace or the fortune to do so without first enduring the trauma of a syndicalist general strike. Thus Rougerie and the Limoges unions came to symbolize the CGT's new centrist compromise, without the shadow of schism that clouded Merrheim's own evolution toward the center; that may explain why Limoges was initially chosen as the site for the July confederal congress, until it became apparent that the city lacked sufficient housing for all the delegates.[133] At that congress, ultimately held in Paris, Rougerie unhesitatingly voted confidence in Jouhaux's leadership since the Clermont conference.[134] Of course, this gesture of unity only postponed the inexorable process of schism, in Limoges and in the national CGT alike.

The new centrism of the Limoges unions also cemented their cordial relations with the local Socialist Party. Continuing their wartime collaboration, Bourse and party leaders now planned for joint postwar activities to deal with peacemaking, inflation, and the campaign for the eight-hour day.[135] As the unions seemed to lose any trace of hostility to party politics, the party reciprocated by remaining closely attuned to working-class sentiments. A prime example was the Socialists' balanced response to the antiwar strikes in the Loire.

These strikes clearly exceeded the moderate aims of the Limoges Socialist leaders. Despite his own pacifist leanings, parliamentary deputy Adrien Pressemane had refused to attend the Zimmerwald conference for fear of launching a schism, and he continued to vote war credits for fear of letting his country, which had "suffered enough under the yoke of bourgeois supremacy," be "crushed" in turn "under the invader's boot."[136] Without directly approving the strikes, Limoges Socialists still deplored the arrests of the strikers and stoutly defended participants from charges either of exclusive self-interest or, more grave, of guidance by "an enemy hand." Instead, affirmed Paul Faure and *Le Populaire du Centre,* the strikers were motivated solely by their "noble dream of peace," and by their devotion to "the welfare of the nation" and "the proletarian cause."[137] This vote of confidence contrasted sharply with the party's response on the strikers' home turf.

The Loire Socialists failed not only to approve the strike movement but even, it seemed, to acknowledge its existence. Ernest Lafont, the Socialist deputy and local CGT attorney, had always shown some ambivalence: he had protested the authorities' ban on certain union meetings, but perhaps only as a *pro forma* gesture since it was issued, the prefect noted, several months after the fact.[138] Later on, Lafont and his colleagues spoke out to defend Andrieu from charges of "defeatism" or German influence but without directly approving the strike in December, and the party journal *La Flamme* published only two brief (and heavily censored) references to the antiwar strike in May 1918. Instead, the paper highlighted the wage demands of the weavers and the railroad workers, groups that took no part in the May events and that openly supported the party's own moderate programs.[139] The paper likewise ignored the metalworkers' demands for an immediate armistice to publish instead an appeal by railroad unionist (and SFIO municipal councillor) Marcellin

Guillot of Firminy, who called for republicans and Socialists to "invite" the government to set up a League of Nations and work for a durable peace.[140]

The Socialists' preference for conventional politics did not necessarily mean abdication of the pacifist movement. Although they joined a republican coalition for national defense at the height of the German offensive, they remained on the left of the new group and approved the votes of those deputies who refused to grant war credits.[141] In practice, however, the Loire Socialists proved more concerned with curbing the syndicalists' excesses than with promoting the efforts of Merrheim or Pressemane. Political socialism, one militant complained, would continue to lag behind syndicalist direct action unless it could "escape the torpor" in which it was currently bogged down.[142]

The SFIO's virtual unanimity against the syndicalist strike tactic did not fully bridge earlier differences on national defense or later quarrels over adhesion to the Communist International. Growing hostility to *"jusqu'au bout"* patriotism—especially now that the tide of battle had turned in France's favor—helped replace the old by a new leftist majority in two crucial party votes in July and October 1918.[143] Still, this shift hardly meant that the party became more extremist than the CGT, where Merrheim and Dumoulin joined with Jouhaux to extend the old majority; instead, the changes simply brought the party and union majorities in line with one another in a common stance of mild pacifism and parliamentary reformism. Only a small syndicalist fringe remained committed to the "bluff and demagogy" of direct action and the revolutionary general strike.

Despite changing circumstances in the immediate postwar era, the present alignments proved a prescient prediction of the patterns of the future labor schism. While the party debated rival forms of political action, unionists split between those who accepted political action of some sort and those who preferred the direct action preached by the CGT before 1914. If the war was a turning point in this tactical debate on revolutionary syndicalism, the pivot was during the events of May 1918, a critical moment in labor politics even if not, as it turned out, for the nation's internal or external security. The strike movement was both the climax of old-style revolutionary syndicalism and the trauma that confirmed the new "governmental" tactics of the CGT majority after the war. This evolution did not, however, mean the death of revolutionary syndicalism. It may virtually have died in the Haute-Vienne, where its demise was already foreshadowed by prewar patterns of party-union relations. But it remained alive in the Loire, where from a small fringe in late 1918 it would grow to a larger faction after 1920 by building on the memories and myths of the drama of May 1918.

Chapter 5

Revolutionary Strategy in Transition: The Dilemmas of Mass Unionism, 1918–19

With the end of World War I, France faced both the resurgence of social conflicts postponed for the war's duration and the rise of new problems that quickly punctured the popular elation felt at the military victory. The conversion to a peacetime economy brought problems of industrial demobilization, unemployment, and rampant inflation, all of which led many workers to question the military sacrifices that had failed to guarantee their standard of living. At the time of the armistice, unions and leftist parties were still weakened by the war's dislocations and especially by the repercussions of the antiwar strikes of May 1918. Once their organizations revived, however, leftists launched into a new phase of agitation, climaxing both in strike waves in 1919 and 1920 and in the growth of a French Communist Party and a Communist wing of the CGT.

The rise of Communist influence both in the unions and among political leftists marked a certain recognition that the methods of prewar and wartime militancy had shown their bankruptcy and were unsuited to the postwar era. Neither the politics of Sacred Union nor the attempted revolutionary strike wave of 1918 had successfully protected working-class interests or ended the war on terms that ensured a just and lasting peace. Opposing factions, of course, interpreted differently the lessons of the wartime experience: moderates resolved to strengthen their ties with the Socialist Party and to negotiate their differences with government and industrial leaders, while left-wingers turned instead to Soviet Russia for a model of a more revolutionary party and union strategy.[1] Not all leftists agreed, however, that the traditions of prewar syndicalism were truly outmoded. Some hoped to assimilate certain Leninist tactics with the syndicalist strategies of direct action that they had espoused in the past.

The support for a syndicalist alternative was slim indeed in the aftermath of the May 1918 strike failure. Ex-minoritarians, including Alphonse Merrheim and his provincial supporters, rallied to the "centrist coalition" represented by CGT general secretary Léon Jouhaux. This *ralliement* also implied an endorsement of the CGT's nascent postwar program, which stressed union recruitment and corporative benefits while deferring to party leaders for more explicitly political goals. Even much of the remnant minority endorsed this new postwar strategy, but their endorsement was only a temporary response to circumstantial weakness. No permanent shift to a new form of mass unionism occurred to repudiate the old concepts of direct action, minority agitation, and trade-union autonomy. Once the unions began to revive, left-wing leaders would seek to turn them once again toward the revolutionary purposes that they had temporarily forsworn.

The New Corporatism: Labor and the Postwar Economy

The first signs of a new shift in trade-union strategy appeared prior to the armistice but after the defeat of the recent antiwar strike movement. As a result of the strike's spectacular failure, most workers either quit their unions or focused attention on those corporative, economic issues that the left wing had seemed to abandon in favor of political or revolutionary goals. Militants also began to plan for the new economic problems that would arise during and after the military demobilization. These issues, including taxation, social legislation, and the nationalization of vital industries, had implicit political connotations in that they involved government action in the postwar economy. So far, however, most unionists preferred to avoid political controversies and to concentrate instead on rebuilding their unions and obtaining economic reforms.

Although this new corporatism prevailed similarly throughout most of the French labor movement, it marked a more startling — and more temporary — shift in the heavily political Loire unions, while it simply expressed "business as usual" in Limoges. In the Loire, where the May strike failure had had its sharpest impact, the arrests of leaders and the disillusionment of union members caused a crisis of recruitment that spared the more stable Limoges unions. By October, the Saint-Etienne metalworkers' union was down from several thousand to less than 700 members, so that it found even simple wage demands to be out of the question.[2] Other unions, similarly weakened and resolutely cautious, avoided all but the wage or hours issues that best promised to win back members alienated by the revolutionary agitation of the past.

The union crisis also weakened the left-wing faction in its struggle to unseat the old majority. With the arrest of Charles Flageollet, the Loire's Union Départementale came into the hands of Saint-Etienne's moderate Bourse secretary, Antoine Reynard. On Reynard's instigation, the UD voted by a margin of twenty-two to seven to "abandon political battles and egotistical campaigns" so as to devote attention to purely economic issues, especially the fight against high living costs.[3] Throughout the department, the metalworkers' unions also impressed authorities with their unexpected moderation and caution. After the metalworkers' federal congress, most local unionists approved the decision of their delegate, Louis Soubeyrand, to abstain rather than vote with the left to condemn Merrheim for his role in the May strike movement. Although Soubeyrand continued to call himself a minoritarian, the authorities saw this as a mere gesture of solidarity with his local colleagues in order to retain their support as he shifted slowly toward more corporative terrain.[4]

This new corporative attitude thus extended well into the minority camp, at least among those who had avoided arrest in the wake of the May strikes. Even after the minority resumed leadership of the Bourse and the UD, by early 1919, the new secretaries Laurent Torcieux and Jean-Baptiste Frécon followed cautious policies that belied the aggressiveness that Torcieux, at least, had shown in wartime. Both repudiated ties with the Parisian Committee for the Defense of Syndicalism (CDS), now discredited by the May 1918 strike failure, and both sought to keep the departmental Comité Intercorporatif (the Loire's antiwar nerve-center) from intervening in Bourse or UD affairs.[5] Although committed to corporative action, the two were not deliberately antipolitical: both were party members who approved *ad hoc* collaboration with the moderate SFIO.[6] So far, then, the issue was not a debate for or against syndicalist doctrine but a simpler matter of political preference, a choice of allies to assume the political functions that the unions were too weak to pursue independently. As left-wing metals unionists likewise acknowledged, the adoption of *"une politique ouvrière"* was indispensable, *"puisque la politique domine tout."*[7]

Although cut off from routine union business, the Loire's Comité Intercorporatif continued to represent the most ardent syndicalists in the department. In August 1918, the Comité had set forth its goals as the definition of war aims and the acquisition of passports for international labor conferences, as well as the improvement of labor's economic position.[8] Once the armistice forestalled the peace question, however, the Comité shifted attention to other issues, including the demand for amnesty for the strikers arrested in May 1918.

The question of amnesty was a recurrent theme of labor protest, seen for example in the strike to free Andrieu in December 1917 and in the strikes of 1920 to defend unionists threatened with dismissal from their jobs. The issue was of obvious political import, not only in its target (the government) but also in its implications for labor factionalism. Although both wings favored amnesty, the arrested strikers themselves were usually minoritarians, who now condemned the majority leadership for insufficient vigilance in their defense. Militant metalworkers reacted especially angrily when their national secretaries Merrheim and Blanchard hesitated to express "sympathy" with the arrested strikers, and when Blanchard argued lamely that the strikers were better off going to prison than getting transferred to the front.[9]

The amnesty issue also clouded party-union relations, when unionists complained that the SFIO, along with its wartime Radical allies, too readily abandoned the cause of the imprisoned strikers.[10] Despite these political aspects, however, the issue rallied support — more so than other political matters — mostly because it touched the lives and livelihoods of the arrested strikers in a manner similar to the material issues that otherwise preoccupied most unionists at this time. Like the majority, the left wing realized the need to focus on issues of self-interest that would help rebuild the weakened unions, even if only to prepare for more overt political action in the future. Indeed, the authorities sensed this double motive; they noted, for example, that if those who now waxed so enthusiastic on wage questions had not let themselves be distracted by revolutionary pipedreams, they might have long since won a wage increase.[11] Most workers nonetheless ignored or accepted this political undercurrent as they looked to the unions to satisfy their immediate economic needs.

The unions' new corporatism stemmed not only from the recent strike failure but also from the need to prepare for changed economic circumstances as the war neared conclusion. Old issues of inflation and unemployment joined with new issues of the eight-hour day, government tax policy, and the nationalization of the mines and railroads, once the conversion to a peacetime economy got underway. As in wartime, circumstances after the war varied widely from one industry or locality to another, but they revealed a persistent legacy of prewar economic problems that endured despite later fluctuations and that foreshadowed economic crises in 1921 — and in 1929.

In industries hardest hit by the wartime mobilization, the end of the war brought eventual but incomplete recovery. The porcelain industry in Limoges was troubled anew by cheaper foreign (now especially Japanese and American) competition and by rising costs associated with fuel shortages and the eight-hour day.[12] The textile industry in the Loire also faced higher costs and declining sales volumes, which it countered by shifting from quality silk ribbons toward cheaper synthetics and elastics, manufactured largely in the countryside where wages remained relatively low.[13] Despite these signs of incipient "proletarianization," the two industries remained heavily artisan-dominated and tradition-bound, subject to repeated economic crises that clouded their brief periods of prosperity before and after the recession of 1921.

In the Limoges shoe industry, the war had vastly expanded demand and productivity but had done so mainly by causing small, new companies to proliferate, many of which proved too marginal to survive postwar economic contractions. Like porcelain and textiles, the shoe industry remained stalled awkwardly in the transition from artisanal to "proletarian" manufacture, and its workers were hard hit by wage fluctuations and unemployment throughout the 1920s.[14] The Loire metals industry also had grown to mammoth proportions in wartime but likewise faced a crisis with the decline in postwar demand. Fuel shortages and high transportation costs, plus competition from the restored northern and eastern regions of the country, threatened the survival of the Loire's heavy metallurgy and hastened a shift to newer specialties that made better use of local supplies of skilled labor. The production of handguns and cycles prospered temporarily, and there was even talk of converting the state-owned arsenal into a sewing machine plant. As in the Limoges shoe industry, however, too many small and inefficient companies (825 in war production alone) had flourished during the war and were now ill equipped to endure repeated economic crises. Even the larger manufacturers remained shortsighted, according to critics, and unwilling or unable to invest their vast wartime profits in postwar renovations that might improve their chances for survival.[15] This fragmented and stagnant condition, though perhaps extreme by national standards, throws doubt on contrasting generalizations based on the experiences of a few large and dynamic companies such as Renault.[16]

The Loire coal mines also faced renewed problems of low productivity — said to be lower in 1919 than in 1912 — plus high transportation costs and cheaper domestic and foreign competition, once they lost their wartime advantage of a secure location far from the trenches. Many of the region's coal fields now joined the category of *"mines à condition difficile,"* which sought aid from national employers' associations and were forced eventually to fall back on the state. Although unemployment was rarely a problem, labor scarcity was all the more critical now that workers sought easier and more profitable jobs in other industries. Foreign workers, with their high turnover and poor labor skills, helped only partially to fill the vacuum. The labor shortage did help miners attain high wages, but these in turn made it far too difficult (as employers complained) for mines in the Loire to compete.[17]

The source of these problems was inevitably hard to pinpoint, but workers and employers routinely blamed one another, either for neglecting overdue renovations or for demanding excessive wage or hours benefits that multiplied production costs.[18] As most workers recognized, wage increases were at best a temporary solution, because they fueled the inflation with which they were meant to keep pace.[19] Still, workers argued, greedy employers compounded the problem by raising prices even higher than their cost increases warranted and by imposing wage cuts in times of recession rather than accepting lower profits, trimming costs in other areas, or using market innovations to boost sales. Therefore, pending more fundamental social reorganization, "the war of wages" would remain the crux of the proletariat's struggle against the bourgeoisie.[20]

Against this background, unionists launched a new wage campaign that extended from the fall of 1918 through the spring of 1920. To support its demand for a 40 percent wage increase, the Loire's Comité Intercorporatif cited local food prices that had more than tripled between 1914 and August 1918.[21] In fact, according to national figures, the latest increase was somewhat slower than in the peak war years, and prices actually dropped slightly in the summer of 1919, only to rise sharply again in 1920.[22] Nonetheless, food prices remained particularly acute, with local shortages caused by a temporary transport crisis. Prices also remained well above the national average in the southeastern region, including the Loire; even in Limoges, they stayed well ahead of local wage levels.[23] Such inflation had social and psychological as well as economic repercussions. As during the war, flat-rate wage increases narrowed the gap between skilled and unskilled workers; the narrowest wage differential coincided with the peak of the inflationary spiral, although the later recession restored the balance somewhat after 1921.[24] Perhaps more enduringly, workers lost the "stabilizing, conservative habits" that led them in normal times to frame limited wage demands. Instead, rapid inflation triggered "a spiraling of expectations and demands" and a sharpening of class conflict if these demands were not fulfilled.[25]

Another serious problem was unemployment, especially as demobilized soldiers found it difficult to return to old jobs or to find new ones. In Paris, the number of unemployed on the city's rosters rose from 1,300 to 15,000 between January and May 1919.[26] In the Loire, the situation was eased by the return of wartime mobilized workers to their original places of residence. In Limoges, however, the problem was acute enough for a special group of *"démobilisés chômeurs"* to be founded in February 1919; this later became the local branch of the Société des Anciens Combattants, which remained politically active on the left throughout the 1920s.[27] More jobs became available as women resigned voluntarily in return for generous bonuses. Still, although the problem was under control by the end of 1919 (until the 1921 recession), short-term unemployment persisted as long as the transport crisis and the shortage of raw materials delayed postwar industrial recovery. Such unemployment further narrowed the wage gap between skilled and unskilled workers, as each would receive the same subsistence income on the dole.[28]

Perhaps because of its brevity, the unemployment problem aroused less public attention in 1919 than in 1921 or later. Nonetheless, the problem was potentially disastrous for the labor movement, because most unemployed workers quit or failed to join the unions and because competition for scarce jobs weakened labor solidarity and destroyed the effectiveness of strikes.[29] Voluntary cutbacks in female and foreign employment did help to ease rivalries within the labor movement, now that unionists stressed "equal pay for equal work" rather than demand outright that highly paid jobs be reserved for French males.[30] Beyond these palliatives, militants sought to attack the problem at the root by preventing overproduction through such methods as eliminating piecework pay scales and instituting the eight-hour day.

The campaign against piecework pay had begun before 1914 but then stalled when employers and the government upheld the device as a means to stimulate wartime productivity. Although some skilled workers and "yellow" unionists saw a benefit in piecework wages, most unions dismissed such boons as illusory, since employers would lower piece rates to keep wages at subsistence levels. Thus workers had to join together to demand comparable pay for less work, thereby also curbing unemployment by leaving more work for others to do.[31] The eight-hour day would have a similar effect. If instituted with hourly wage increases, the shorter workday would maintain incomes and also decrease overproduction — that is, as long as workers were not lured into working overtime by the hope (again illusory) of increasing their total take-home pay.[32]

The limitation of working hours was the CGT's principal demand in 1919 and the main issue in that year's planned May Day demonstration. To forestall a larger outburst (and also to ease tensions aroused by the recent acquittal of Jean Jaurès's assassin), the government hastily passed the eight-hour-day law on the eve of the May Day strike. Predictably enough, the extreme left immediately denounced the act as a gesture of government co-optation.[33] Even moderates, however, soon lost their initial enthusiasm when the law proved uneven in application and difficult to enforce. A wave of strikes in May and June 1919, including many wildcat strikes without CGT sponsorship, protested these economic problems as well as such political issues as the terms of the new peace treaty, intervention in Soviet Russia, the slow rate of military demobilization, and the refusal to grant full amnesty for wartime political crimes.[34]

Like wage increases, the eight-hour day proved controversial in part because of its economic consequences, which employers — and some "yellow" or independent unionists — blamed for the hardships facing postwar French industry.[35] The matter further raised the controversial political issue of labor relations with the state. The issue was not a new one, especially as the war had vastly expanded the state's role in the French economy. Similar issues were raised by the proposed new tax on wages, first instituted in 1917 to help defray wartime expenses but now planned as a permanent feature of the tax system. Some workers, again the "yellow" unionists and also the Loire weavers, accepted the new tax under certain conditions: as long as temporary cost-of-living supplements were not taxed as income, and, for the Loire group, as long as weavers were taxed as workers rather than as independent entrepreneurs.[36] Most workers and their unions, however, were unconditionally opposed to the tax on workers when it was the industrialists who had made their fortunes as war profiteers.[37]

In this case, the tax represented a clear evil emanating from the state, and one that syndicalists might oppose unambiguously. But what if the government offered help rather than hindrance? Should the unions "collaborate" with the government to obtain favorable legislation or the mediation of labor-management conflicts, rather than insist on seizing all gains through "direct action" without party or government intervention? These questions emerged especially clearly in the debates on the so-called Minimum Program that the CGT adopted in December 1918.

The Minimum Program opened with a ritual greeting to the revolutionary regimes of Russia and Central Europe, but then quickly turned attention to needed reforms within the existing system, such as the guarantee of constitutional liberties and the eight-hour workday.[38] Despite its modest tone, however, even its framers viewed these goals as a "minimum," not a total statement of purpose, so that the document at first rallied both majority and minority support. In the Loire, left-wing unionists agreed to postpone attempts to turn general secretary Jouhaux out of office so as not to jeopardize his ongoing programs.[39] Still, the gulf between the two camps soon widened as leftists resumed the old rhetoric of direct action and the general strike.[40]

As a sign of the CGT's changed orientation, the Minimum Program asked for a seat at the Paris Peace Conference and for an international Labor Charter, mandating the eight-hour day and other rights of labor, to be written into the Versailles Treaty.[41] By applying the eight-hour day in all countries, the Labor Charter would incidentally avoid those economic disadvantages that "yellow" unionists later attributed to France's having acted on its own.[42] Use of this tactic, however, further indicated the CGT's deference to new reformist institutions, such as the International Labor Office, to be directed by the right-wing Socialist Albert Thomas. This new policy conflicted sharply with the CGT's old strategies of direct action and class struggle as the principal weapons of social change.

For the CGT, the eight-hour day would also be part of a larger program of industrial modernization to pay for the shorter working hours and to overcome what Jouhaux saw as "patronal inertia."[43] Such efforts would not, however, be enough to rescue every industry: the mines and railroads, above all, should instead be nationalized because they were too vital (or too vulnerable) to remain in private hands. With the precedent of state action in wartime, the demand for nationalization became a widespread issue in 1919 and especially during the general strike of May 1920. Railroad federation secretary Marcel Bidegaray strongly backed the effort, as did Socialist Albert Thomas, who sponsored the proposed law and argued that the war had proven that "only state control could make the railroads a useful tool."[44] Other leftists remained unconvinced. To them, state control might prove no better for workers than private management and no closer to the goal of true "socialism." Among its advocates, the Radical-Socialists, in fact, hailed nationalization as a means toward "general prosperity" to benefit all citizens, and not as a truly "revolutionary" goal.[45]

These new concepts of state intervention were especially welcomed by the CGT's Auguste Keufer, now a member of a governmental board (headed by Albert Thomas) to study the problem of industrial unemployment. Even before the war Keufer had emerged as one of the labor movement's rare true reformists, dedicated to the preservation of the capitalist system and not its revolutionary overthrow.[46] Now he explicitly endorsed the idea of "class collaboration," to him "the only method able to assure the productivity that everyone urgently demands, and able at the same time to respect the freedom of opinion of all members of the working class." Going further, he appealed for compulsory arbitration of labor disputes, not to rule out the right to strike (which would still prevail in extreme circumstances) but to promote union negotiation with employers and collaboration with the government for the twin goals of "general prosperity" and "social peace."[47]

Keufer's apparent rejection of the time-honored canon of the class struggle seemed heretical not only to minoritarians but also to most reformists in the labor movement.[48] Others, however, who retained the old terminology came surprisingly close to Keufer's own views. At the CGT's national congress in Lyon, in September 1919, Limoges Bourse secretary Jean Rougerie denied that it was "class collaboration" to "negotiate as equals" with the employers or the government; the worst offense would be to refuse to act and thereby achieve nothing at all.[49] A year earlier, Saint-Etienne's Bourse and UD secretary Antoine Reynard had even redefined "the class struggle" as no longer a desperate war by the proletariat against the bourgeois system; instead, it was now "a process of collaboration aimed to oblige the capitalist class to make concessions to the working class." Reynard also defined labor's goals as *"sociétaire"* rather than strictly socialist, in that they sought "not the destruction, but the conquest of Capital" and the preservation of national prosperity, on which workers' welfare ultimately depended.[50] But these views, if not so alien to most Limoges unionists, probably helped defeat Reynard in the Bourse and UD elections at Saint-Etienne, where left-wingers now spurned the reformist heresies of the postwar CGT.

The CGT's new program also implied a heightened willingness to collaborate with leftist political parties. Both Rougerie and Reynard were SFIO members who openly advocated joint action as the best way to wrest economic concessions from the state. Just as during the war, however, the impetus for such collaboration came more from the party than from the unions; Rougerie himself spoke as a party member and not as Bourse secretary when he argued that "the political party of the working class has the duty to put into effect the program of the CGT."[51] Still, Rougerie also thought — again as in wartime — that the CGT's reliance on party leadership for political action left it freer to devote its own energies to its preeminently corporative interests.[52] As Merrheim likewise acknowledged, the strength and unity of labor's government and industrial opponents forced the movement to give up "direct action" for the sake of a unified left.[53]

Such collaboration also presupposed a certain harmony of outlook between the two branches of the labor movement. In the past, the CGT had scorned the SFIO as insufficiently revolutionary, but now, like the party's reformist wing, the CGT had begun to question not only the idea of class struggle but the idea of revolution itself. Saint-Etienne's Reynard went perhaps the furthest in this direction when he wrote that "all revolutionary methods" — or alternately "all violent and rapid methods" — "will fail and will end in reaction."[54] Still, the CGT's general secretary Léon Jouhaux, who sought to preserve the concept of revolution, did so only by redefining it: it was no longer "a catastrophic act" but only "the long process of evolution which, little by little, penetrates the system . . . and which, at the very center of a regime, constitutes the new organism."[55]

Similar terminology appeared in the SFIO's own postwar program, when Léon Blum defined social revolution — which must still be the final goal, since the war had proved the impotence of capitalist society — as "neither more nor less than the substitution of one system of property for another." In a thinly veiled reference to Soviet Russia, Blum denied that a forceful proletarian seizure of power was necessarily the Revolution; only the radical transformation of property relations was "in itself and by itself the Revolution," even if it should be accomplished by legal and peaceful means.[56] Blum actually found the CGT's Minimum Program to have swung too far away from revolution, now that it stressed the eight-hour day and simple nationalization of industry rather than the "dictatorship of the proletariat."[57] Still, the similarity of Blum's and Jouhaux's conceptions allowed the Limoges SFIO deputy (and former porcelain unionist) Jean Parvy to praise the CGT's Minimum Program as an admirable expression of "revolutionary realism" and "realistic revolutionism."[58] Indeed, the document sounded so much like the party's own program because the unions, having learned the lessons of wartime, had "moved closer to Jauressian reformism and away from the insurrectionalism of the heroic age."[59]

The CGT's acceptance of closer relations with the government and with leftist parties thus implied a far-reaching revision of the principles of revolutionary syndicalism that had prevailed, at least in theory, in the prewar era. An early and explicit recognition of this change was an essay by CGT assistant secretary Georges Dumoulin in June 1918. Already Dumoulin had begun the march from prewar syndicalism to corporative reformism, a journey marked by his ambivalence toward the May strike movement and by his defense of Jouhaux at the CGT's national congress in July. In this essay, Dumoulin wrote as a minoritarian to uphold syndicalist "passion and ardor" and to reject class collaboration — or participation in Keufer's governmental committees — which would "chain" workers to the capitalist system. Still, he condemned no less sharply the CGT's prewar policy of "noise and impotence." In recognition of the lessons of wartime, he argued, the CGT must introduce "order" into union policy — and must also charge higher dues. The effect would be both to challenge the majority's dominance by adopting its own methods and to create a more potent trade unionism on the English model, even including an equivalent labor party. The movement's strength would lie in funds and in manpower, not in an illusory "myth" of the general strike.[60]

As Dumoulin's essay suggested, the issues for postwar unionists concerned less the dilemma of revolution vs. reformism than the choice between prewar tactics of syndicalist neutrality and the newer options of government action and leftist party alliances. This does not mean, as Annie Kriegel has suggested, that both CGT factions were united on the issue of revolution and divided only on the advisability of "immediate" action, especially with the guidance of international Bolshevism.[61] Majoritarians like Jouhaux and Reynard, who continued to mouth the phrases of "revolution" and "class struggle," had muted their content to the point that revolution became the mere evolutionary accumulation of gradual reforms. Minoritarians, however, not only demanded a more truly revolutionary program but also argued in favor of political goals and refused to defer to the party for revolutionary leadership in their behalf.[62] Those who had temporarily accepted simple corporatism did so only in response to the May 1918 strike failure and in view of the postwar economic problems that the crippled unions could not resolve independently. They quickly resumed a more political and revolutionary posture once the weakened unions began to revive.

The Acceleration of Militancy: Unions and Strikes in 1919

The union revival and the left's return to a militant, aggressive position were well underway by the spring of 1919. In both the Loire and the Haute-Vienne, and throughout France generally, union memberships reached unprecedented levels, strikes multiplied in size and frequency, and left-wing factions grew at the expense of the moderates' strength in both the Socialist Party and the CGT. These combined events raised the specter of mass revolution that France had only barely escaped during wartime. Now, led by the newly formed Third International, a "red menace" seemed ready to engulf the whole of the civilized world.[63]

The simultaneous growth and sharp leftward shift in the labor movement have led historians and contemporary observers to look for a causal connection between the two developments. The new recruits seemed to differ from the older "generation" of union and party members either in the degree of their revolutionary commitment or, at least, in their readiness to accept a political definition of union goals. Age alone cannot explain these differences, despite a tendency to assume that radicalism recedes with advancing years.[64] Still, the new "generation" may have shared some collective political outlook, drawn from their experiences in wartime or from the changes in their industrial environment, that differentiated them from older groups.[65]

The war decade did mark some structural changes in the labor force, as sketched here in Chapter 1 for Limoges and Saint-Etienne. A shift from artisan to semiskilled or unskilled factory occupations might suggest a parallel shift from anarcho-syndicalism toward newer trade-union programs with a corporative or political emphasis. The shift might also mean that younger workers, concentrated in the factory occupations, would be less likely to choose anarchism than would older artisans, whatever the mellowing effects of middle age. The postwar work force also included a large number of women. Whatever their "natural" response to revolutionary agitation, these women also commonly worked in trades, like ceramics or weaving, with a corporative, not syndicalist, tradition. The same applies to the many new rural and foreign immigrants, who rarely came from anarchist backgrounds and who usually worked as unskilled laborers in the factories and mines.[66]

These patterns of slow but steady "proletarianization" may seem to justify the new corporative unionism that both Georges Dumoulin and his Communist counterparts were beginning to advocate for ideological reasons. There is no proof, though, that these demographic changes similarly affected union memberships, which cannot be subjected to the same kind of statistical analysis as that for the labor force at large. Summary data by industrial federation suggest, in fact, that most of the postwar membership growth occurred in those industries that had been the CGT's traditional centers of strength, not in the newer industries, like metallurgy and transportation, that had grown most rapidly during the war.[67] This growth—unlike that in 1936, after more intense industrial change and under new political circumstances[68]—would reaffirm old patterns, not establish new kinds of labor ideologies. Moreover, any demographic or doctrinal shift in the unions during their expansion in 1919 to 1920 might well be undone by the subsequent downturn in 1921. If the new recruits seemed to promise a new form of unionism, abruptly torn from its traditions of direct action and minority agitation, they did not remain in the movement long enough to unseat the old syndicalist leaders or to provide a reliable source of mass support.

Union growth in 1919 to early 1920 included both the expansion of union memberships and the founding of new or reorganized unions in industries unrepresented in the later war years. Although overall figures are at best approximate, and often inflated for political reasons, estimates show that the CGT nearly doubled between 1913 and 1918, doubled again by early 1919, and nearly doubled a third time by early 1920, to a total of more than 1.6 million members.[69] Rates of growth varied sharply, of course, from one industry or locality to another. The metalworkers' federation had more than quadrupled between 1913 and 1918, but then it leveled off, or perhaps even declined somewhat, before growing once again in early 1920. The railroad federation also grew far less sharply after 1918 than during the war, when many of its unions were founded for the first time.[70] On the local level, UD memberships in 1919 were estimated at 19,500 in the Haute-Vienne and at 15,000 in the Loire, where recovery from the May 1918 debacle was not yet complete.[71]

Data on individual unions are particularly scattered but sometimes revealing. The Saint-Etienne metalworkers reported an increase from 700 to 1,500 members in the last three months of 1918, while the construction workers' membership rose from 200 to 700 during the course of the following year.[72] In Limoges, porcelain unionists claimed to have tripled their membership, to some 3,200 members, after a long and widely supported campaign for increased wages.[73] Since this union had already been quite large in 1914, however, its postwar growth was more a matter of recovery than a sign of unforeseen strength. More remarkable was the growth in the shoe workers' union, from a mere 255 members in 1914 to some 3,450 members in January 1920, as a result of the industry's vast wartime expansion.[74] The railroad union, first founded in 1917, more than doubled between 1918 and January 1920 to include virtually all of the industry's 1,800 local employees.[75] Still, in both the shoe and the railroad industries, the upsurge was more dramatic than durable. While the porcelain union faced future crises with relative stability, the shoe and railroad unions were decimated either by strike failure in May 1920 or by economic recession and political schism in 1921.[76]

The appearance of new unions was another important though not always lasting sign of the postwar syndicalist resurgence. In Limoges, 8 new CGT unions were created in 1919 in industries not previously represented; 4 more unions were officially reconstituted after wartime inactivity; in addition, a variety of new Catholic and independent unions, particularly among women workers and commercial employees, joined together in a departmental branch of the new CFTC founded nationally in 1919. A new Union Locale—a city-wide association or Bourse without the building— was also created at Saint-Junien. By the start of 1920, a total of 48 unions were UD members, including 33 in the Limoges Bourse, compared to 41 and 24 respectively, before the war.[77] Similarly, in Saint-Etienne at least 5 new CGT unions were created in 1919, including a "red" union of factory textile workers to rival the old "yellow" union of *chefs d'atelier*. Several Catholic unions were also established among miners and metalworkers as well as among commercial employees. New unions also emerged elsewhere in the department, so that the UD grew from approximately 70 unions in early 1919 to 121 unions in early 1920, of which 32 were members of the Saint-Etienne Bourse du Travail.[78]

In some cases, however, these new unions were ephemeral creations that failed to survive beyond infancy. While all the new postwar unions in Limoges still existed five years later, either in their original forms, as part of larger unions, or under a new name as a result of the labor schism, at least eight of the Loire's new unions had dissolved by 1925.[79] Several, in fact, seem to have been formed for deliberate political motives by left-wing militants eager to add a new vote to their own camp.[80] This strategy was not unique to the Loire; the national teachers' federation likewise divided regional unions into separate bodies for each department in order to give the federation (and its leftist supporters) more votes in the CGT.[81] In the Loire, at least, these short-lived phenomena suggested that corporative self-defense was often a weaker motive for unionization than was political ideology.

The campaign for union growth in the Loire began suddenly in early 1919 with the return of those militants, including Andrieu and Flageollet, who had been arrested after the strikes of May 1918. It was Andrieu, for example, who now insisted that the eight-hour day be obtained through "direct action," not through government legislation or by proclamation of the Paris Peace Conference.[82] In meetings throughout the department, Andrieu and his friends also denounced the CGT majority for its betrayal of the May 1918 strike movement and for its reformist postwar program, when what was needed was not mere wage increases but the total "suppression of the wage system."[83] These militants did not ignore economic issues, but they stressed their political implications—especially in the cases of the eight-hour day and the tax on wages—and sought to use these issues to rally the workers toward a larger campaign against the government and against the CGT majority.[84] The tone of their arguments was more expressly revolutionary than was the pacifist line Andrieu had taken in 1917–18.

In addition to creating new unions, left-wingers also tried to shift the alignment of existing unions that still backed the old majority. For example, the Bourse's new minoritarian secretary, Jean-Baptiste Frécon, revoked the special discount on dues that his predecessor Reynard had offered to lure the large (and reformist) coal miners' union into the Bourse du Travail. This step was easily justified as a means of restoring lost income in order to forestall a return to a municipal Bourse subsidy. Yet if the miners should refuse to pay and instead quit the Bourse, the move would enable left-wingers to create a dissident union that, although far smaller, would add a vote to their own camp.[85] In fact, the dispute was settled short of a schism, but it showed how factional rivalry sometimes seemed more important than labor unity or mass support.

Despite ardent efforts, the minority was scarcely more successful in finding new sources of support than in rallying older groups like the coal miners. Thus far, most unions remained in the hands of leaders who, even if "minoritarian," were nonetheless loyal to the CGT. At most meetings, listeners ignored the flamboyant rhetoric of Andrieu or Flageollet, who sometimes had to force their way to the rostrum in order to speak.[86] Although these men had attained considerable prestige during the war years, they failed to regain their position — or Flageollet his UD office — after their return from prison. Within a few months, Andrieu was sufficiently disheartened to plan to leave for Lyon, in search of greener pastures, although he then postponed his departure until late 1920.[87] As results showed, the wartime movement had depended too heavily on "outside agitators" like Andrieu to rebound easily when these outsiders dispersed after the armistice. In the Saint-Etienne metalworkers' union, a center of wartime activism, the demobilization of its wartime labor force meant the departure of twelve of the twenty-one members of its Conseil Syndical.[88]

The record of strike activity in 1919 also showed much ambiguity between the goals of mass, corporative unionism and the political aims of a militant minority. In terms of size, frequency, and duration, strike activity throughout France in 1919 far exceeded even the peak wartime levels of 1917–18. The movement engulfed both the Loire and the hitherto quiescent Haute-Vienne (see Figure 9). These strikes, most observers have argued, showed not only the response to economic grievances but also the revolutionary spontaneity of the masses of workers: exhausted by the war, exhilarated by the Russian Revolution, and ready even to exceed their leaders in their enthusiasm for direct action.[89] A closer look at the strike data suggests instead that the strikers, even if defiant of CGT leadership in Paris, were acting less from sheer spontaneity than in accord with local militants, like those in the Loire, who were promoting unrest to serve sectarian interests. Nor were the strikes, however large, truly general, as the vast majority of workers still did not take part.

Special attention has been paid to the strikes of metalworkers, who in the Loire and in Paris were typically the most radical and readily mobilized for political aspirations. In fact, however, while metalworkers nationally were still the most strike-prone, the biggest increase in total strike participation came among miners, whose goals remained highly corporative: shorter workdays, higher wages, and better retirement benefits[90] (see Figure 11).

On the regional level, the strikes hit a wide variety of industries and localities. Still highly strike-prone were the Loire's rural textile workers; by contrast, the Limoges porcelain industry and the Loire mining and metals industries (except for a single long steel strike in Firminy) accounted for only small fractions of the departmental totals of strikes and working-days lost (see figures 10–11). This time the strikes did show greater coordination both in their timing (in months May through July) and in their issues (wage increases and the application of the eight-hour workday).[91] However spontaneous the workers' enthusiasm, the strikes capped a campaign of agitation that minoritarian leaders, such as Andrieu and Flageollet, had been conducting since the early spring.[92]

Unrest first ignited during the annual May Day demonstrations, which reached particularly violent levels in Paris; as a result in part of police intervention, there were several deaths and nearly 600 injuries.[93] This violence, despite the CGT's calls for moderation, helped to justify the claims of mass spontaneity getting beyond the leaders' control. Still, the crowds' ideals were far from consistently revolutionary: May Day marchers mixed chants of "*Vive* Wilson!" with their revolutionary slogans and renditions of the "Internationale."[94]

Nor should one conclude the masses' revolutionary spontaneity from the strike wave in May and June that protested the uneven application of the new eight-hour-day law. Although disavowed by the CGT and by Merrheim's federation of metalworkers, the strikes received support and guidance from left-wing leaders, both in the Parisian CDS and in the Loire's Comité Intercorporatif, which had been newly reorganized to combat the tepid leadership of the local Union Départementale.[95] These left-wingers intended the strikes to combine economic with political (if not explicitly revolutionary) demands, such as for amnesty for political prisoners and for an end to intervention in Soviet Russia. As Pierre Monatte described it, the strategy was to move "from discontent to discontent, from strike to strike, from a semi-economic and semi-political strike to a purely political strike," with revolution as the ultimate goal.[96]

These revolutionary aims help to explain why CGT moderates disavowed the strike movement, although they were not above trying to appeal to the same political issues in their own protest demonstration scheduled for July 21. As in 1918, however, the CGT leaders distrusted the May–June strike movement, and canceled the planned July demonstration, because of their sense that the time for a mass insurrection had not yet come.[97] Explained Merrheim, "My greatest regret is to have seen a revolutionary situation in France without having found a revolutionary spirit in the working class."[98] Merrheim also claimed that he and his federation were right to ignore the political issues raised by the strike movement, because these were supported not by disciplined unionists but only by "non-unionized crowds" or even *"agents provocateurs."*[99] His allies concurred that scarcely one in thirty among the Parisian strikers was properly unionized; thus the emphasis should be on recruitment, even of those who had not yet achieved revolutionary consciousness, so as to avoid the prewar fallacy of a *"syndicalisme de bluff"* based on the action of *"minorités squelettiques."*[100]

In response, left-wingers again accused the moderates of ignoring, or even holding back, the masses' revolutionary momentum by disavowing current strikes and by supporting reformist legislation—including the eight-hour-day law—that co-opted the workers' grievances. In fact, however, left-wingers showed scarcely more faith in the masses' readiness for revolution. The Loire's Clovis Andrieu recognized that the moderates' endless "preparations" just disguised their own lack of revolutionary commitment. To show that the time was ripe, though, he claimed only that even if the masses were not ready to act, *"Nous, minoritaires, sommes prêts."*[101]

As in 1918, Andrieu and his friends thus professed little concern for the goal of mass organization and instead preferred to act from a minority initiative. Andrieu continued to hope that economic grievances would rally support for a larger movement; he called, for example, for a general strike to seize the factories by force and install a communist system if the eight-hour day were not applied to the workers' satisfaction by the deadline of June 1.[102] Still, he showed scant regret when the UD rejected his proposal: only twelve unions voted with him, including the tiny metals and construction workers' unions, against fifteen negative votes and sixteen abstentions.[103] This lack of mass fervor, even on his home turf, did not alter his conviction that the movement's failure was due principally to the CGT's, and Merrheim's, sabotage.

Of course, even left-wing leaders recognized that they could not alone create a mass strike movement where popular support was nonexistent. In fact, labor unrest remained acute in the Loire, though short of revolutionary in its intentions, because of economic dissatisfaction plus the hostile tenor of social class relations. The prefect himself complained that the bourgeoisie's taste for luxury and self-indulgence "demoralized" and "excited envy" among the workers, who chafed under their own low wages and high living costs.[104] Similarly troublesome was the high failure rate of local strikes in 1919 and early 1920, compared to their greater success in the Haute-Vienne and in France generally[105] (see Figure 12). This record made it easier for Limoges Bourse secretaries Bonnet and Rougerie to remain conciliatory and obedient to CGT leadership and to hold onto their posts, despite nascent opposition, at least through the spring of 1920.[106] In the Loire, moderate leftists Frécon and Torcieux quickly unseated the "class collaborationist" Reynard at the Bourse and UD helms but faced in turn mounting pressure from their own left.[107]

These contrasts showed that the comparable moderation of the two local labor movements was but a fleeting result of postwar circumstance. In the Haute-Vienne, labor politics changed little from prewar traditions, but in the Loire the left's moderation contradicted prewar and wartime patterns and proved vulnerable to the new pressures that mounted after the war's end. Haute-Vienne moderates profited from their large, stable unions and from the relatively secure Socialist Party to maintain a strategy of consensus, with close cooperation of union and party leaders; Loire militants had to make do with weaker, often ephemeral unions and with a party that failed to protect working-class interests or attract mass labor support. These contrasts also showed that the two labor movements cannot be defined, as one author has attempted, by the simple ratio of Socialist Party to trade-union members: lower than average in the Loire, with its revolutionary syndicalist traditions, while more than twice the national average in the Haute-Vienne.[108] In fact, the Loire had surprisingly few unionists relative to its large industrial population. The movement's weakness, not its strength, led militants to adopt the intemperate rhetoric of revolutionary syndicalism as a strategy of minority agitation that could do without mass support.

For these reasons, Loire militants continued to measure their success in terms not of union size but of the number of union posts they controlled and votes they commanded in Bourse and CGT elections. These tactics may have aggravated the problem of union weakness, but on their own terms proved remarkably successful: the left wing grew steadily in union votes if not in mass enthusiasm from 1919 through the CGT schism at the end of 1921. This growth hinged on the moderates' failure to satisfy workers' economic grievances and to resolve bitter political controversies. Indeed, the Socialists' poor showing in the 1919 legislative elections, both in the Loire and in France generally, deepened the syndicalists' contempt and their determination to take political issues into their own hands, while the party's victories in the Haute-Vienne slowed the unions' further radicalization at least until after the middle of the next year.

Unions and Politics: To the Elections of November 1919

French unions in 1919 showed a growth in political awareness parallel to their growing memberships and their heightened self-confidence. No longer did unionists need to concentrate strictly on corporative issues and defer to party leaders to express their political concerns. In part, this political emphasis stemmed as in wartime from the government's role in the economy, now that the perceived failure of its economic programs discredited both the government and those who spoke for parliamentary reformism in place of syndicalist "direct action." In addition, new political issues, which ranged from amnesty for political prisoners to foreign relations with postwar Germany and Soviet Russia, further radicalized the unions and influenced their roles in the legislative elections of November 1919.

The question of amnesty had quickly rallied left-wing unionists—who comprised the bulk of the arrestees—against the government and the reformist faction, both accused of insufficient vigilance in defense of the prisoners.[109] Within a short time, however, the leftists found a less self-interested and more strictly "political" issue to publicize: the problem of peace negotiations, dramatized by the arrival of Woodrow Wilson in France in late December 1918. In honor of the American president's arrival, and as a means of pacifist propaganda that was still otherwise illegal, unionists throughout the country held meetings and demonstrations organized jointly with the Socialist Party. Just as in wartime, support for "the Wilson-Trotsky program" joined moderates and radicals, Socialists and syndicalists, in a democratic campaign for peace that transcended factional boundaries.[110] The troubled course of the peace negotiations quickly shattered this sense of unity, however, by setting Wilson clearly against Lenin as opposite poles of a leftist movement that only the myth of Jaurès (as Léon Blum had envisioned) might reunite.[111]

Support for Wilson caused little controversy among Limoges unionists, who had readily accepted wartime leftist alliances and the goal of moderate pacifism. In December, when the Socialist Party hailed Wilson's arrival in Paris, the Bourse agreed without discussion to join a parade in his honor that would culminate at the American Consulate in Limoges.[112] In Saint-Etienne, however, only the reformists, including the leaders of the railroad workers' union, greeted Wilson's program, the Fourteen Points, and the proposed League of Nations with unmixed enthusiasm. The embittered Charles Flageollet, recently returned from prison, instead quibbled that Wilson was, after all, "a bourgeois."[113] As for joint action in his honor, the Loire Socialists welcomed the prospect warmly as "the true sacred union." The more skeptical UD leaders, in contrast, accepted such collaboration only as a fleeting exception to the rule of syndicalist autonomy.[114]

These doubts grew with the publication of the Versailles Treaty. Within the Socialist Party, some critics just lamented Wilson's "honorable defeat" at the conference table, while others condemned his efforts as "bourgeois" and bankrupt from the start.[115] Most Loire and Haute-Vienne Socialists adopted the former, less hostile position.[116] Syndicalist dissidents instead took a hard line against both Wilson and his defenders within the SFIO.

The peace terms with Germany were but one of a growing set of grievances against Woodrow Wilson and his moderate allies. Left-wingers also blamed Wilson for failing to stop — or perhaps even supporting — Allied intervention in Soviet Russia. Moderate leftists likewise condemned the intervention, but they disagreed with extremists over the extent of Wilson's responsibility and over the methods to protest the action.[117] The conflict came to a head over plans for a joint Anglo-French general strike on July 21 to demand withdrawal from Russia as well as immediate military demobilization and amnesty.

The CGT leaders' initial support for the demonstration showed that they did not object on principle to such a "political" movement as long as they remained at its helm; in fact, they had used the planned July strike as an excuse to oppose the May Day work stoppage, which had had similar political aims. But when, as in May 1918, it became clear that most workers — exhausted by the earlier strikes — would fail to join the planned demonstration, the CGT leadership voted to cancel the venture. The French leaders also refused to act once British unionists withdrew their support.[118] However justified, the cancellation outraged the minoritarians and made them more determined than ever to unseat the majority leadership of the CGT.

In Limoges, most unionists were disappointed but willing to accept the cancellation and willing to approve their delegate Léon Bonnet (the assis-

tant Bourse secretary), who had joined in the CGT's vote.[119] The Socialist editors of *Le Populaire du Centre* defended the cancellation on the
grounds that parliament instead could resolve the issues, now that "the
peoples' representatives" had finally "emerged from their torpor" and begun to act against the government's "intransigence."[120] Their hopes were
inspired by the onset of a brief ministerial crisis — perhaps deliberately
engineered — that seemed to promise the fall of Clemenceau.[121] Moderate
unionists likewise deferred to party leadership and parliamentary action.
Argued Bourse secretary Rougerie: "The masses come to us more for
their corporative revendications than for their general aspirations." The
unions must therefore leave to others the task of *"la révolution sociale."*[122]

For the first time in recent years, however, a dissident current began to
appear in the Haute-Vienne labor movement. The Union Locale at Saint-
Junien refused to cancel its plan for the demonstration, and more than
half the city's workers took part.[123] Left-wingers in Bonnet's ceramics
union also denounced the cancellation, and Louis Bert resigned in protest
from his posts as secretary of the railroad workers' union and delegate to
his federation's central committee.[124] Bert, leader of his union's left-wing
faction, had tried to force his colleagues to take part in the demonstration and even sought to pressure the railroad company, by a separate
strike if necessary, to dismiss all non-strikers from their jobs.[125] A Socialist Party member, and credited with both intelligence and political ambition, Bert later rose to head the Limoges Bourse (after May 1920) and
helped to found the nascent Communist Party in the Haute-Vienne.[126]

In Saint-Etienne, UD secretary Frécon had abstained rather than vote,
as had Bonnet, to cancel the movement, but his reticence did not silence
local controversy. Although the UD itself later voted by a wide margin
(ninety to seventeen, with eight abstentions) to approve the cancellation,
there remained a hostile leftist current, especially in the metalworkers'
union and in the Comité Intercorporatif.[127] Ironically enough, these
same leftists had at first hesitated to endorse the planned strike, because
of its support by moderates preoccupied mostly with economic questions
as defined in the CGT's Minimum Program.[128] While seeking to raise
larger political issues, these left-wingers refused to defer to or even ally
with the Socialists as the workers' political spokesmen. Whether by "direct action" or by alliance with a nascent Community Party, left-wing
syndicalists were determined to make the unions again the vehicle of social revolution, not of mere corporative reform.

The political debates of 1919 thus had quite different impacts in the two localities. Although the debates helped to draw together the moderate Socialists and trade unionists in both departments, they further alienated some future Communists in Limoges and a larger number of left-wing syndicalists in Saint-Etienne. By the time of the CGT's national congress, held at Lyon in September, even the Loire miners' unions had turned against the reformists' Minimum Program and voted to oust general secretary Léon Jouhaux. In fact, for the first time since late 1918, the Loire "minority" now outnumbered the "majority"—by a vote of twenty-six to seventeen—thus reversing the balance of forces that still prevailed among unions in the Haute-Vienne and elsewhere in France.[129] This shift did not guarantee that the Loire would support the drive toward schism that some extremists now openly advocated; nor did it prove that the masses of Loire workers had likewise converted to the cause of revolution. Left-wing leader Clovis Andrieu still proclaimed, at the Lyon congress, that the minority could if necessary make the revolution on its own.[130] Nonetheless, extreme leftists could hope at least to seize control of the union movement (with or without a schism), even if they might never rally the proletariat as a whole.

The tensions in the labor movement between parliamentarianism and direct action and between gradualism and immediate revolution reached a climax during the electoral campaigns of autumn 1919. For the Socialists the results were a bitter disappointment, especially compared to the gains anticipated from years of wartime and postwar unrest. Overall, the party won thirty-five fewer seats in parliament than in the 1914 elections, to yield the largest conservative majority since the start of the Third Republic. In the Haute-Vienne the Socialists gained a seat, for a clean sweep by all five of their candidates, despite a small decrease in total votes since 1914. But in the Loire, where the vote actually rose slightly, the party only retained its one seat—that of Ernest Lafont in Firminy—and lost in other districts to two Radical-Socialists and five *"réactionnaires."*[131]

These failures forced the left to reevaluate its election tactics and to reconsider its entire strategy, given that the time for mass revolution had clearly not yet arrived. Only part of the blame could be attributed to the new electoral system, a form of proportional representation, which most benefited the "reactionary" candidates. The greater problem, as one Saint-Etienne party leader admitted, was the apparent "indifference or ignorance of the popular masses."[132] On the positive side, the Loire Socialist Federation had in the past year more than doubled in size, to some 1,500 members, and had recently launched its own weekly newspaper,

Le Peuple de la Loire.[133] The party's strength, however, was still modest in urban as well as rural areas and diminished further by the legacy of divisions on the left. Thus the Socialists had to look again at the benefits of electoral alliances, which they had foregone in this election to comply with the party's national platform. Such alliances might have no use in the Haute-Vienne, where the Radicals were the Socialists' principal rivals, but the party program did permit compacts in extreme cases, where needed to defeat well-entrenched conservatives like those in the Loire.[134]

The relative weakness of labor support for the Loire Socialist Party is suggested by the geographic distribution of the election results, although the occupational status of individual voters cannot be identified. The Haute-Vienne Socialists, while not without appeal among the peasantry, gained most of their votes in the urban centers where workers were concentrated, especially in Limoges. For example, in the legislative elections, the party lost in the heavily rural arrondissements of Saint-Yrieix and Bellac, and won by a narrow margin in the arrondissement of Rochechouart, although it did obtain better results in the districts' main cities, including Saint-Junien. Likewise in the municipal elections, held two weeks later, the Socialists won majorities in twelve additional towns in the Limoges arrondissement (of a total of twenty-eight new Socialist-led municipalities throughout the department), and the entire party slate won in an uncontested election in the city of Limoges. This concentrated appeal in the most populous districts paradoxically benefited the party under the terms of the new electoral system, in which total votes counted for more than did the breadth of geographic support.[135]

In the Loire, by contrast, the party lacked such concentrated appeal in the key urban centers of Saint-Etienne and Roanne, which contributed less than one-third of its total votes. Except in Firminy, Lafont's constituency, the party also proved weaker in urban areas than did the Radical-Socialists: the latter won 44 percent of the vote in Saint-Etienne as against less than 20 percent for the SFIO.[136] Many voters may also have split their tickets between the two parties, as implied by the gap in votes earned by the SFIO's most and least popular candidates.[137] Even in Saint-Etienne's municipal elections, in which the two parties together won a clean sweep, the Socialists held only fourteen of the thirty-six slots on the joint leftist ticket, a good sign of the Radicals' greater electoral strength.[138]

The Socialists' weak appeal among working-class voters is also suggested by the unions' response to the elections. Even in Limoges, several unions refused to discuss the campaign, much less to contribute funds to the Socialists, in part out of resentment at the party's apparent eagerness to exploit workers' grievances for the sake of partisan advantage.[139] In both departments, only the railroad workers were considered die-hard SFIO supporters, convinced that their future hinged on a Socialist victory and that all problems could be solved by *"le bulletin rouge."*[140] Party rhetoric seemed especially empty after the election results showed that votes alone could not guarantee the workers' welfare, much less "save the Russian Revolution" from imperialist assault.[141] Still, in the Haute-Vienne, the main question was how deep was the unions' commitment to a Socialist victory. In the Loire, rival options ranged from conservatism or independent socialism to the anarchist movement, whose members vowed to abstain from and to sabotage all election campaigns.[142]

The elections of 1919 thus marked a critical point in party-union relations, particularly in the Loire. Despite the unions' new concern for political questions, they showed little sign of improved relations with the Socialist Party. Except in the party's traditional strongholds, such as among coal miners and railroad workers, few unionists ran for political office, and the UD maintained its strictures against party candidates holding union posts.[143] Individuals who sought to break the rule met ample hostility, as in the case of Clovis Andrieu, whose alleged electoral ambitions were blamed for much of his loss in popularity after 1918.[144] Even in the Haute-Vienne, however, it was becoming more difficult to hold party and union mandates concurrently. Socialist deputies Pressemane and Parvy, who had begun their careers as union officials, faced charges of opportunism as they rose in the party hierarchy. Bourse secretaries Rougerie and Bonnet did run successfully for the municipal council, but they received the fewest votes on the SFIO slate.[145]

Despite these tensions, the elections did tighten the bonds between the SFIO and the moderate wing of the union movement. Even in Saint-Etienne, the joint Socialist-Radical victory in the municipal elections led the Bourse to approve a new subsidy from the city, as long as there were no strings attached.[146] In a larger sense, the rapprochement indicated a new harmony of purpose, as both groups came to value parliamentary reformism and slow preparations to build mass support. On both grounds, however, the linkage antagonized left-wingers, whether they took seriously the CGT's traditional political neutrality or whether they, far from neutral, simply wanted a more revolutionary — or more successful — party with which to ally.

The conflict between rival Socialist and Communist political currents would prove most decisive in the Haute-Vienne labor movement, where minority unionists objected more to the CGT's moderation than to its latent ties with leftist politicians. But in the Loire the situation remained far more complex. While some dissidents soon rallied to communism, others remained suspicious of any form of party action. This choice was postponed for the moment, but it returned with a vengeance after the attempted May 1920 general strike.

These strategic choices were further complicated by the prospect that mass revolutionary fervor might already have passed its maximum. In the Loire, the electoral disappointments seemed finally to shatter the region's image as *"un foyer révolutionnaire."*[147] While moderate Socialists opted for an alliance with the Radicals, extremists preferred to look leftward, toward a Communist Party that would maintain ideological rigor even at the cost of mass support. From a syndicalist perspective, however, these two options soon proved all too similar, as both parties worked through parliament to influence public policy and agreed to postpone the revolution for the sake of winning votes. Nonetheless, at least for the moment, syndicalists could take their Leninism literally and look to communism not for a new strategy of mass labor politics but for a refurbished tactic of direct action, led by a militant vanguard who refused to compromise for the sake of mass support.

Chapter 6

May 1920: Mass Unionism on Trial

In May 1920 the French labor movement launched a general strike that climaxed the postwar growth of left-wing radicalism and raised at least the specter of social revolution under Moscow's leadership. Better organized and more extensive than the Loire's antiwar strikes of 1918 or the seemingly spontaneous labor conflicts of 1919, this strike became a veritable test of strength against the employers and the government: in their eyes, a "civic battle of the Marne."[1] In fact, the clash displayed less the left's strengths than its weaknesses: the loss of mass fervor, spent in earlier confrontations, and the new strength of conservative forces as postwar stabilization began to take root. Still, the event is important in the labor history of the era, both to explain the conflicts and schisms that followed and to show how far the union movement paralleled—or diverged from—the evolution of the political left.[2]

The strike of May 1920 was the culmination of the new program of mass, corporative unionism developed jointly by left- and right-wing unionists since the end of the war. Its new features can be shown by contrasting its goals and its tactics with those of the strike movement of May 1918. Whereas both strikes professed to aim toward the ultimate goal of revolution, the first sought an immediate end to the military conflict while the second sought a longer-term structural change in the economy through nationalization of the mines and railroads. In methods, as part of its challenge to wartime notions of national defense and Sacred Union, the first strike openly disavowed the need for the mass support or organizational discipline that it could not, under wartime circumstances, hope to obtain. The second strike, by aiming at a goal shared even by moderate leftists, instead deliberately sought to blur factional differences and to gain mass support and the centralized direction of the national CGT.[3]

The two movements also differed sharply in their impact on labor history. The failure of the first strike led to a centrist resurgence in both the CGT and the Socialist Party, that is, a determination in both camps to stress corporative issues and mass recruitment before embarking again on such a dangerous venture. The second strike may be seen as a testing ground for just these ideas of mass recruitment and corporative organization. Nonetheless (and all too predictably), the effort failed. In light of this failure, left-wing dissidents — whose loyalty to large-scale organization had been at best conditional — chose now to desert the movement or to resume the ideas of local autonomy and minority agitation that they had temporarily forsworn.

For these reasons, the May 1920 strike movement was a prelude to the later labor schisms. Still, the point is not, as others have argued, that the strike failure rallied a new labor generation to Bolshevism and away from the "spontaneous" strategies of the immediate postwar years.[4] These labor strategies were far from truly spontaneous, as left-wing leaders carefully weighed the alternative benefits of mass organization and the revolutionary commitment of a small but active minority. If the strike failure led some on the political left to choose communism, it caused left-wing syndicalists to distrust a mass, centralized labor movement of any political persuasion. These latter dissidents were the ones who launched the CGT schism at the end of 1921. The ideal of mass unionism, rendered suspect as thousands of workers deserted their unions after the strike failure, became all the more unworkable when an economic crisis in 1921 further decimated union memberships. Left-wing unionists may have temporarily allied with the Communists against their reformist CGT opponents, but they never embraced the Communists' idea of mass, centralized unionism, which they saw as partly to blame for the failure of the May 1920 general strike.

The Ideal of Mass Unionism

The strikes of May 1920 capped a series of conflicts that began in January with a walkout by railroad workers in Périgueux, a city on the Paris-Orléans (PO) railway line, which extends southwest from Paris. From there the agitation spread to the Paris-Lyon-Méditerrannée (PLM) railroad workers, in the southeastern region, and finally to the entire national federation.[5] Although the strikes at first concerned simple corporative issues of workshop regulations and the application of the eight-hour workday, the events took on a more revolutionary tone as demands extended to the nationalization of the railroads and as left-wing unionists vowed to act even without the assent of moderates in their own federation or in the CGT. The May general strike, an avowedly political or revolutionary act and not a simple corporative conflict, thus accelerated the rupture between extremist and moderate factions even while it professed to speak for the working class as a whole.

The role of the railroad workers in the 1920 strike movement may be contrasted with that of the metalworkers in the antiwar strikes of 1918. The railroad federation was now in the vanguard of the left-wing labor movement, but its militancy was closer to communism than to the anarcho-syndicalism that had flourished among metalworkers before and during the war. Later CGTU secretary Gaston Monmousseau, now a leader of his federation's left wing, expressly called for a modernized "revolutionary syndicalism" with closer ties to leftist parties.[6] Indeed, his views implied the unions' later Bolshevization, but these were views that not all current unionists endorsed.

Several factors explain why the railroad industry was an appropriate context for a mass strike movement. Like the coal miners, and unlike artisanal craftsmen, railroad workers were commonly organized in large-scale industrial unions that stressed solidarity across professional boundaries and tight coordination on a nationwide basis. These workers were further radicalized by the war experience, which had led to state regulation of their industry and state restrictions on their right to organize and strike. The war also accelerated demographic changes in the industry's work force: young recruits flocked to the industry to replace the foreign (especially Belgian) and military workers employed during the hostilities; nationwide recruitment also brought a new mix of workers to each community, along with new ideas and ideologies, much as the influx of military workers had helped to politicize the war industries in the Loire.[7]

These factors help to account for the sharp postwar growth in railroad unionism—from some 80,000 members in 1917 to nearly 300,000 in 1919;[8] the sharp leftward shift in the federation's politics; and the movement's ability to spark support among other labor groups. This "spark-plug" effect, again like that of the wartime metalworkers, was intensified by the popularity of the railroad workers' goal of nationalization of their vital industry. The demand, introduced in the CGT's postwar Minimum

Program, would help to ease the transport crisis that was causing shortages of raw materials and high unemployment in all industries, hurting
workers and also cutting the profits of the bourgeoisie. The demand was
thus able to appeal at once to left-wing Socialists committed to collectivi-
zation and to moderates and Radicals preoccupied with "the general interest."[9] Still, this broadly based consensus was no more lasting than it
had been in wartime, not just because the movement failed but because it
had arisen from conditions in the railroad industry that did not apply to
French labor at large.

The railroad workers' movement epitomized the "new" unionism, a
deft blend of corporatism with politics, which represented the best hope
in France for a mass labor movement with nationwide coordination and
effective leadership. The nationalization issue was a way to acknowledge
—and to gain from—the state's growing role in the economy as well as
from the unions' own collaborative action with the political left. As
shown during and after the 1919 elections, the railroad workers were
committed participants in the political process and supporters of the
Socialist Party—or later the Communist Party—in order to win corporative advantages.[10] They also repeatedly deferred to the leaders of their
central federation or confederation, rather than insist on exercising local
initiative in independent or wildcat strikes. These patterns appear both in
the politics of the local Limoges and Saint-Etienne unions and in the campaigns for a nationwide general strike that gained momentum after 1919.

The special nature of railroad unionism is well illustrated in the Saint-
Etienne context. During the war, like other local unions, the railroad
union had grown markedly in size—from 190 to 912 members between
1915 and 1917—but it had adhered strictly to corporative activity and
played no role in the antiwar strikes of May 1918. Its two main leaders,
Pierre Chovet and Marcellin Guillot, named to the central committee of
the new national federation (founded in 1917), were both Socialist Party
members who remained most concerned with a cost-of-living wage increase then pending before the Senate, and who deferred to the party—or
to Woodrow Wilson—to express their views on the questions of war and
peace.[11]

Despite their wartime moderation, Loire railroad workers took part
eagerly, at an estimated rate of 93 percent, in a one-minute strike of the
PLM line in January 1919. Soon afterward, however, the Saint-Etienne
union came out against a planned May Day strike for the immediate institution of the eight-hour workday, which Chovet argued could not for

technical reasons be applied *"du jour au lendemain."* Only a slim majority endorsed the proposed July 21 (1919) protest strike, over Chovet's own objections, and most concurred with its eventual cancellation by the CGT. Still, the union, although considered unlikely to launch a strike on its own initiative, was expected to obey any federal or confederal strike order with solidarity and discipline.[12]

Like its Loire counterpart, the Limoges railroad union remained quiescent in wartime but showed new signs of militancy after the war. Its wartime meetings, subject to military approval, were routinely authorized and devoted strictly to professional questions. Nonetheless, the union doubled in size, until it encompassed virtually all the industry's local work force. As a PO union it took no part in the one-minute PLM strike in January 1919, but the group did favor a nationwide railroad strike to demand higher wages and the eight-hour workday. Although considered no more likely than their Loire comrades to launch such a strike on their own initiative, the Limoges unionists were expected to join a general strike with great enthusiasm, with or without the blessing of the CGT.[13]

Despite their increased militancy, these railroad workers remained squarely in the Limoges tradition of corporative and Socialist action. At a meeting in March 1919 to discuss the planned strike, Limoges workers spurned the pro-Bolshevik harangues of two delegates from Périgueux, who called on the workers "to rise up *en masse* to impose their will." Instead, local workers welcomed the moderate appeals of their own Socialist deputy, Adrien Pressemane, who argued that their large and well-organized federation could win the point through mass political pressure and without extremism or violence.[14] This faith in mass action remained the hallmark of Limoges unionism at least until the end of the May 1920 strike movement. Indeed, the widespread support for the strike in Limoges shows how well it fit accepted patterns of mass strike strategy without yielding to syndicalist adventurism, which would have won little local support.

Given the discipline but relative inertia of both local unions, it took an outside initiative to spur them to action. The initiative came first from Périgueux, which remained a Communist stronghold in the 1920s even as Communist unionism weakened in Limoges. A regional junction on the PO railway line, Périgueux was the scene of the strike in January 1920 that eventually triggered the explosion in May. This strike, although begun over simple corporative grievances, achieved notoriety because of the strikers' willingness to act independently without the prior agreement of their national federation, accused of dragging out fruitless negotiations for more than a year.[15] When the movement spread, Limoges workers joined in nearly unanimously, but more from solidarity and their own job dissatisfaction than from any revolutionary inspiration.[16] Limoges unionists also supported the Périgueux strike leader, Emile Olivier, in his rise to leadership of the PO sector at its congress in April 1920. Still, they did seek to veto the sector's call for immediate action, preferring instead to reorganize and prepare for a future campaign. However "minoritarian" in political sympathy, Limoges unionists hesitated to launch a premature and probably fruitless May Day movement, and they refused to back any strike that might fail to win majority participation and at least the federation's endorsement, if not the approval of the CGT.[17]

After the PO strike in January 1920, the agitation spread to the PLM sector. The movement, begun at Villeneuve-Saint-Georges, again addressed simple corporative grievances while also showing the strikers' willingness to act independently without their federation's prior approval. Although many unions, including that of Limoges, again took part for reasons of solidarity, Saint-Etienne's leader Chovet instead condemned the PLM sector's "dictatorial" tactics and called for obedience to the moderate leadership of the federation and the CGT.[18] Clearly, the Limoges union had evolved further to the left than had its Saint-Etienne counterpart. Both stressed, nonetheless, the need for central coordination and the virtues of mass unionism against the habits of local initiative and the tactics of a minority syndicalist strike.

This emphasis on centralization and coordination continued to characterize the national federation even as it came under minoritarian leadership. (Left-wing syndicalist Gaston Monmousseau was named federal secretary during the railroad workers' national congress in April.) Moderates later complained that the federation's strike call had superseded CGT initiative and presented the central committee with a *fait accompli*. In fact, however, the federation's new directors had made substantial concessions to win the support of the CGT majority. In the closing resolution of its congress in April, the federation agreed to coordinate its strike plans with a CGT decision to call a May Day work stoppage. Thus the federation was, in effect, submitting its plans to the CGT for approval.[19] In response, the CGT decided only reluctantly to support the strike, which it regarded as ill timed and poorly organized, and then proved unwilling to see it spread to the rest of France's industrial work force. These hesitations aroused much left-wing anger and dissatisfaction. Still, the minority had no intention of going it alone, as it had envisioned doing in May 1918.

The leftists' deference to CGT leadership resulted in part from their fear that the situation was not ripe for revolution and that spontaneous adventurism would do more harm than good. As shown by their inclusion of corporative as well as more political demands in the April strike resolution, the railroad militants were aware that the masses, although minoritarian in sympathy, might not in fact be ready to overturn the capitalist system.[20] Like the CGT's Georges Dumoulin, who visited Saint-Etienne in March, these cautious left-wingers seemed to acknowledge that revolutions must be allowed to ripen and could not be decreed from above.[21] Nor did federal secretary Gaston Monmousseau expect the general strike in fact to usher in the revolution; instead, it would simply restore the revolutionary momentum that had been lost since the days of Sacred Union and since the CGT's cancellation of the strike plans the previous July.[22] Once underway, striking miners and railroad workers urgently demanded the solidarity of other federations, even without CGT approval. In the planning stages, however, these groups had instead stressed obedience to the CGT so that they would not risk being left to go it alone.[23]

The minority also rejected the prospect, accepted by some extremists in 1918, of an independent local initiative launched with only scant hope of spreading the contagion. Again, the CGT's national leaders were the most adamant in favor of centralized organization and discipline: Merrheim, for example, lamented the destructive tendency of regional groups to defy decisions made in Paris; Dumoulin, in fact, later called for the abolition of the Unions Départementales.[24] In response, Loire minoritarians insisted that it was the UDs' job to make the decisions, and the CGT's to execute them, not the reverse.[25] Still, during the strike, most local unions acceded to national discipline by awaiting the CGT's order to join the work stoppage and then obeying its command to return to work.

The Making of a General Strike

Even where minoritarian in theory, most unions proved quite moderate and disciplined in practice, both in the planning and in the conduct of the May 1920 strike movement. The spread of the strike from the railroad workers to other labor groups showed a willingness to endorse the former's goal of nationalization and their methods of mass, coordinated protest. Although this endorsement later sparked renewed controversy, most workers now seemed hopeful that a mass movement would prove more effective than the isolated, spontaneous strikes of the past.

In Limoges, where union leaders had sought to veto a strike for fear that it would fail to gain widespread participation, an estimated 70 percent of railroad workers in fact joined in the May Day work stoppage, although participation was minimal elsewhere in the department, even at Saint-Junien. After May Day, the strike continued to draw approximately 50 to 60 percent of the railroad workers, with little day-to-day variation. Even the announced dismissals of striking workers failed to cause noticeable defections, as strikers became all the more determined to maintain solidarity.[26] Still, enough workers remained on the job to assure continued, though reduced, train service. Opponents also created an independent union of railroad workers that accused the *"chambardeurs"* (agitators) of perverting the unions' legitimate professional function in order "to destroy society and bring bloody revolution." Formed in mid-May, this Syndicat Indépendant quickly grew to more than 450 members, an ominous sign of dissension in a local labor movement that had so far survived the tests of war and revolution remarkably intact.[27]

In view of their long hesitation, the Limoges railroad workers' final decision to support the strike appears to have come from their sense of solidarity, not from genuine revolutionary fervor. The dissident independent unionists accused the strikers of more incendiary aims, but even the authorities remained impressed by the strikers' determination to remain disciplined and calm. As the strike began to spread to other industries, there was some impatience to join in without the CGT's instructions, but the Bourse du Travail leaders insisted firmly on strict obedience to the CGT.[28]

The CGT's plan was to organize the strike in successive waves, which a journalist dubbed *"vagues d'assaut."* The first contingent of strikers was to include groups such as miners and dockers, who, like the railroad workers, supplied raw materials for industry, without which the economy would be crippled and forced to shut down. Hence, it would be counterproductive for manufacturing workers to enter the movement prematurely, because their action would lessen the impact of the railroad strike by reducing the industries' need for raw materials.[29] Loire Communist Benoît Frachon later denounced the tactic as a deliberate attempt to sabotage the strike by isolating the strikers in combat, but there was little sign of criticism of the tactic at the time.[30]

By May 9, several manufacturing unions in Limoges had become impatient enough to disregard the CGT's instructions. Yet these unions were acting more from solidarity with the striking railroad workers than from revolutionary spontaneity or distaste for central coordination. The first to join in were the metals and construction workers, but by May 14 many of these were already returning to work. New groups followed but likewise held out for only a few days.[31] Neither the shoe nor the porcelain union—each headed by one of the Bourse's own moderate leaders—joined the strike movement. The latter union, in fact, had at first planned to take part but then decided against it, perhaps because its members had recently completed a series of successful wage strikes, begun the previous year, and had managed to settle their grievances without a work stoppage earlier that spring. Instead, the union contributed a sum of 35,000 francs to the local strike fund.[32] Although all unions seemed to sympathize with the striking railroad workers, they showed no interest in a comparably long and arduous battle of their own.

Still, while their own determination may have wavered, the mass of unionists at Limoges balked at the CGT's order to end the strike. Moreover, when Bourse secretaries Rougerie and Bonnet continued to call for obedience to CGT directives, unionists replaced them with more ardent leaders, railroad worker Louis Bert and typographer Etienne Rivet.[33] Meanwhile, the railroad federation vowed to continue the strike, and local railroad unionists led the attacks against Rougerie's and Bonnet's past leadership. Bert's election as Bourse secretary also marked his rise to prominence beyond his own union and throughout the city's labor movement, from there to local and national politics as well.

This shift in Bourse leadership is the clearest sign at Limoges of the heightened militancy that followed the May strike and that would precipitate the Socialist and CGT schisms. Nonetheless, Bert's background as railroad activist and party organizer meant that the ideas of mass unionism that underlay the May movement continued to prevail in Limoges even after the failure of the strike. Since 1919, Bert had drawn attention as an ambitious and outspoken leader: assistant head of his union; Socialist Party member; proponent of the Third International; and leading critic of the moderates who then headed the CGT, the national railroad federation, and the local Bourse du Travail.[34] His accession to the post of Bourse secretary showed the unions' new sympathy for left-wing or Communist doctrines while they continued to support close alliance with the political left.

Conversely, the lack of such habits of cooperation in the Loire made it difficult for the Saint-Etienne railroad union to rally support for the May strike movement. As in Limoges, and for similar reasons of solidarity, the Saint-Etienne union quickly shifted from reluctance to launch a strike without CGT approval to ardent support for the strike once it began. Like Bert in Limoges, Saint-Etienne union secretary Pierre Chovet also denounced local moderates who sought to keep the strike from spreading, such as UD secretary Jean-Baptiste Frécon. Later on, Chovet also joined the Communist Party; unlike Bert, though, he failed in his bid to become UD secretary when Frécon resigned.[35] However similar their unions and their own political outlooks, these men obtained far different receptions on their home turf, as a result of the strike's conduct and the long-term syndicalist traditions in the Loire.

The main striking groups in the Loire were the railroad workers and the coal miners, both called into action according to the CGT's strategy of *"vagues d'assaut."* It is ironic to see these two traditionally moderate unions now behaving like a militant avant-garde. Still, the strike was just the sort of movement to rally these two groups. Both groups endorsed the strike's goal of nationalization as a non-revolutionary means of "industrial reorganization." Both also expressed similar values of trade-union solidarity when they urged the CGT to generalize the movement so that strikers would not lose interest and back down.[36] Indeed, more than 75 percent of the Loire's coal miners reportedly took part in the movement, although a large (but unspecified) number of railroad workers remained on the job.[37] The threat of arrests and dismissals also gave both groups a personal reason, apart from politics, to continue the strike after the CGT's back-to-work order. In fact, however, the strike lasted only twenty-four hours beyond the federation's own deadline of May 24.[38]

While the strike's special features gave the miners and railroad workers a certain leftist coloration, other local groups expressed quite different sentiments. As usual, the ribbon weavers remained immune to the agitation; although they had contemplated a strike for a wage increase in February, they seemed far more concerned with opposing a new law to tax them as independent entrepreneurs.[39] Most other unions had also backed Frécon's vote in the CGT's National Committee to support only a strike with CGT sponsorship.[40] Meanwhile, however, the metalworkers' union and other smaller groups were agitating for a more genuinely revolutionary movement. These groups, and especially their anarchist members, wanted the strike to address issues other than the reformist goal of nationalization. Once the May strike began, they also demanded more "audacity and action" (not mere speeches), urged other unions to join the movement, and blasted moderates for recommending an early end to the strike.[41]

It is ironic to see similarities in the attempts by miners and railroad workers on the one hand and anarchist metalworkers on the other hand to extend the strike without CGT authorization. But their motives for defiance were very different: personal interest and trade-union solidarity in the former case, and a taste for violence and independent action — at least on the rhetorical level — in the latter. Even among metalworkers, fresh from the ordeals of May 1918, only a handful supported such extremism in practice. Union secretary Théodor Dieu spoke out boldly for independent action in the privacy of union or Bourse meetings but hesitated to do so in public for fear of losing support.[42] Finally, on the decision of their national federation, the metalworkers did join the strike, but with negligible results. As CGT strategists would have predicted, the employers were quite happy to cease production now that the transport strike had caused raw materials to be in short supply.[43]

As in the Haute-Vienne, the strike's failure in the Loire led to an eventual shift in UD leadership. Frécon's moderation lost him the support of those who had hoped to defy the CGT. Still, the miners and railroad workers did not follow up their attacks on Frécon with the ouster of their own moderate leaders. Instead, the miners blamed the strike failure on the extremists of the railroad federation, accused of acting "abruptly and without preparation"; the railroad workers regretted the many defections in their own industry, although these they blamed on Frécon for what they deemed his false reports of low strike participation on other railway lines.[44] Some in his union accused the CGT and the federation of betraying the minority, but secretary Chovet — who admitted his own doubts about the strike — quickly resumed a conciliatory stance toward the moderates, who were back in command of the federation after the arrest of left-winger Gaston Monmousseau. At the next federal congress in September, moreover, the union refused to take a clear position: it voted only to rebuild membership in the now-weakened federation by focusing on *"action purement syndicaliste."*[45]

The union leaders in the Loire thus held back from the brink of extremism, while their Haute-Vienne counterparts began a headlong rush to the left. As candidate for the post of UD secretary, Chovet offered no real alternative to the politics of his predecessor, Frécon. Chovet's posi-

tion as municipal councillor also made him ineligible for union office unless the UD statutes were revised.[46] More problematically, Chovet represented a political current that appealed only to the more moderate of the
Loire's left-wing unionists. Although this current remained so far in the
majority, it failed to satisfy the more militant anarchist wing, especially
among metalworkers, whose continued push toward extremism led finally to the schism in the CGT.

The Repercussions of "Class Warfare"

Despite the mild tone of a movement that sought mass support and
tried to transcend factional differences, the May 1920 strike had profound impact both on class relations and on subsequent labor politics.
Violent incidents and disorders were in fact infrequent, but frightened conservatives nonetheless perceived the strike as an implicit revolutionary
threat. In both Limoges and Saint-Etienne, and in many communities
throughout the country, local chambers of commerce joined with the
prefectures to form volunteer auxiliaries — called Unions Civiques — to
assure the functioning of vital transport and telegraph services. These
groups claimed to acknowledge "the right to strike" for legitimate "professional" (non-political) purposes, but they opposed the "abuse" of such
rights by public servants and the threat that strikers posed to non-strikers'
"right to work." Moreover, especially in the Loire where disorders were
predicted, conservatives spoke openly of the need to organize against the
dangers of "Bolshevism" and "anarchy."[47]

In expectation of violence, the Loire prefect had called for supplemental troops to control "the syndicalist and revolutionary elements" who
"predominated" in the region. No such provisions seem to have been
made, or requested, at Limoges.[48] During the strike, although police
reports mentioned no actual disturbances, some ten militants at Saint-
Etienne were arrested, apparently for the implicit threat these "revolutionaries" posed to the regime.[49] In fact, the Loire prefect was himself accused by the extreme right of harboring "quasi-Bolshevist" or "Malvyist"
sympathies, because of his alleged failure to assure order and "the right
to work" during the conflict.[50] At least the authorities, however antirevolutionary their own perspective, accurately saw the danger less in the
strike itself than in the extremist currents, outside the striking miners'
and railroad workers' unions, that would gain force later on.

While the actual record of strike behavior differed little in the two communities, the tone of public response was rather more hostile in the Loire than in the Haute-Vienne. In both communities, sanctions against striking workers aroused much bitterness. In addition to the many strikers who received fines or pay reductions, a total of 122 railroad workers in Limoges and 82 in Saint-Etienne lost their jobs; their grievances remained at issue for several years and played a role in the general elections of 1924.[51] Beyond these sanctions, the arrests and the fear of violence in the Loire implied a higher than usual degree of class tension, aggravated by what the prefect saw as the insensitivity and the taste for ostentatious luxury on the part of the local bourgeoisie.[52] This difference helps to explain the local contrasts in the strike's political repercussions. While the strike at Limoges radicalized the unions and tightened links to the new Communist Party, it did not break the unions' habit of working within the political system. At Saint-Etienne, the strike gave moderates a chance to test the merits of mass political unionism, but its failure convinced extremists to resume old patterns and old hatreds developed since before the war.

These contrasts deepened in the months after the strike ended. In Limoges, Bert and Rivet still faced opposition from Bourse moderates who made their position increasingly precarious. Discontented railroad unionists blamed Bert for leading them into the May debacle and for provoking, by his extremism, the loss of more than half the union's membership and the creation of the rival Syndicat Indépendant. Although the union remained "minoritarian" in CGT politics, it became once again so preoccupied with corporative interests and stronger recruitment as to be far more "extremist" in word than in deed.[53]

At the Bourse du Travail, which likewise voted with the left in confederal politics, it was also unclear how deep the minoritarian current ran. The shoe workers' union now sided firmly with the left, but the porcelain union—that "bastion of reformism," said its critics—voted support of the CGT at the next Bourse meeting and simply failed to attend the vote at the UD.[54] Both unions also faced sharp membership losses, which rose to one-third among ceramicists and more than two-thirds among shoe workers.[55] (Nationwide, the CGT's losses, including the effects of the 1921 recession, totaled about half its pre-strike membership.)[56] In recognition of the need to recruit new members, the ceramicists reelected secretary Bonnet, whose role in a wage strike that autumn further strengthened his position against the minoritarians.[57] Although deposed as Bourse leaders, Bonnet and Rougerie also retained the confidence of the

Socialist Party and *Le Populaire du Centre,* which still had substantial prestige among local workers. At union meetings held on the eve of the Orléans confederal congress in September, Socialist speakers won more acclaim than did advocates of extremism. A regional gathering of left-wing unionists even concluded, remarkably, with cries of tribute to a local Socialist deputy, Albert Chauly.[58]

The Socialists' continued influence marked the limits of change that the May strike had caused in the Limoges labor movement. In the Socialists' view, the strike only proved the merits of Guesdism and the need for party-union cooperation. The Socialists likewise reaffirmed their commitment to labor unity by rejecting conditional adhesion to the new Third International if that would require internal schism and, in Paul Faure's words, a "declaration of war" against the CGT.[59] Despite the leftward trends at the Limoges Bourse and unions, these enduring Socialist principles remained of overwhelming popular appeal.

The commitment to labor unity did come into question elsewhere in the department when the Union Locale at Saint-Junien threatened to quit the CGT in frustration at its continued majoritarian politics.[60] Saint-Junien later had stronger Communist and CGTU movements than did Limoges, but this early desire for schism probably rose instead from the anarcho-syndicalist currents that had also been lively here since before the war. Even Louis Bert urged his Saint-Junien colleagues to reconsider, if only to assure their vote at the Orléans confederal congress on behalf of the minoritarian faction. In view of the popular outrage at the threatened schism, the Saint-Junien unions finally agreed to back down.[61]

Thus Bert's own politics, while firmly minoritarian, remained consistent with long-established local patterns. In the coming months, Bert grew increasingly hostile to the Socialist Party because of its continued loyalty to Rougerie and its aversion to the Third International. Until the process of Bolshevization cooled his own ardor for the Communist Party, however, Bert would agree simply to trade his Socialist for Communist allegiances, with no doubt that unions and parties shared a common goal: "the suppression of the *salariat.*"[62] Not all local unionists agreed with Bert's assessment, but most did see the choice as between two party programs, not between party politics and union autonomy. Faced with this choice, many did opt for the Communist Party. Still, their decision hinged not on the results of the strike but on the conditions and traditions of labor politics in Limoges.

In the Loire after May 1920, unionists divided not according to political persuasion but according to their willingness to accept party-union connections. As in Limoges, there were assorted new right-wing labor currents, including "yellow" or independent miners' and railroad workers' unions, which endorsed simple corporatism or loose ties with moderate or Radical parties.[63] More important was the growth of a new left-wing current, which included anarchists or anarcho-communists increasingly alienated from simple trade unionism and political reformism. These dissidents now dismissed the unions as inherently reformist, corrupted by their corporatism, their zeal for recruitment, and their ties to Socialist "politicians" who "manipulate" the unions for their own ends.[64] These complaints, echoing those of prewar anarchists, were amplified by the experiences of May 1920. Some anarchists who had drifted provisionally into the trade-union orbit now began to drift back outward; others who stayed did so only on the gamble that they would succeed in imposing the extremism and schism that they saw necessary to regenerate the unions as a true revolutionary force.

As in Limoges, the strike failure caused sharp declines in union membership and a renewed commitment to corporative programs and recruitment efforts. In Saint-Etienne's railroad union, down within two months to about one-third of its pre-strike membership, moderates attended first to the plight of unemployed former strikers, for whom secretary Chovet, as municipal councillor, was sometimes able to get jobs with the city.[65] Chovet retreated so far from his brief fling with militancy that he even justified "class collaboration" as sometimes necessary for corporative victories, an attitude which his union now almost unanimously approved.[66] However calculated to bring the masses back to their unions, these developments nonetheless angered extremists who thought mass support unnecessary. In the metalworkers' union, down by late fall to forty paid members and still declining, secretary Dieu proclaimed that if only the leaders were committed to revolution, *"la masse bête"* would follow suit.[67]

These extremists were no happier with developments in the Union Départementale. Although Chovet's political office had ruled out his candidacy for UD secretary, the victorious candidate Henri Lorduron was likewise a Socialist Party member whose politics differed little from those of Chovet or former secretary Frécon. Lorduron was a long-time activist in the construction workers' union, which he had helped to engage in the wartime strike movements, but he maintained close ties with the Socialist Party and never embraced the anarchistic extremism of other strikers during the war.[68] Local anarchists, who had at first voted to abolish all paid UD offices, supported instead the candidacy of metalworker Emile Arnaud, described by contemporaries as a *"libertaire-communiste."*[69] In frustration at Lorduron's victory and at the UD's persistent reformism, the metalworkers' secretary Dieu quit his post on the UD Executive Committee and then left Saint-Etienne by the end of the year.[70]

Under Lorduron's leadership, the UD proved indeed to be more minoritarian in word than in action. It refused to take part in a regional conference of left-wing unions on the eve of the Orléans confederal congress, in marked contrast to its activism before the CGT congresses of December 1917 and May 1918. Even the Haute-Vienne UD helped to organize its own left-wing regional conference, although not all local unionists may have approved.[71] Of Loire unions, only the metalworkers — that bastion of anarcho-syndicalism — voted to participate in the preliminary conference.[72] Most local unions, including several formerly tied to the majority, did vote with the left at the Orléans congress. Still, because the delegates were chosen at meetings with only a few members present, even this switch was no proof of a dramatic change of heart.[73]

The fact that both the Loire and the Haute-Vienne voted with the minority at Orléans, and by a margin of more than two-thirds of their member unions, was still a significant sign at a time when the left won only a fourth of the CGT's total votes.[74] In both departments, however, the minority's victory was at best uncertain. In the Haute-Vienne, Bert still faced opposition from his moderate Socialist rivals; in the Loire, Lorduron faced an even more serious challenge from the anarcho-syndicalist fringe to his left. Both leaders, and both movements, turned eventually toward communism and labor schism, but neither saw them as alternatives to a syndicalist movement deemed ineffectual because of its experiences during or after the war. For Bert and for Lorduron, Bolshevism would rescue the unions from their subservience to Socialist reformism. Even the Loire's anarcho-syndicalists, who likewise turned to Bolshevism, saw it as the best guarantee of a truly revolutionary form of syndicalism to replace the mass, corporative unionism that seemed otherwise to prevail.

The events of May 1920 thus threw into doubt not the tactics of spontaneous strikes, embraced by revolutionary syndicalists, but the strategies of mass, coordinated unionism these left-wingers, cowed by the effects of the 1918 strike failure, had cautiously adopted. In the view of Pierre Monatte, a leading "Communist-syndicalist" in Paris, the left wing may have imposed the timing of the strike on the CGT but was forced to accept the moderates' goals and methods; hence, the failure was theirs, not the left's own.[75] After the failure, which ravaged the unions' strength and membership, some syndicalists turned, with Monatte, to Bolshevism, but only as a means of restoring the unions' lost prewar grandeur. Instead of large, mass unions, led by a strong Communist Party, syndicalists resurrected the idea of a small, vigorous avant-garde. This was the idea associated with Lenin since the heady days of the Russian Revolution. Yet what syndicalists sought in Leninism proved quite different from what they found.

Chapter 7

Misalliance: Syndicalists and Communists in 1920–21

By late 1920, the momentum toward labor schism in France appeared virtually unstoppable. In December, the Congress of Tours formalized the split in the SFIO and the formation of a Communist Party adherent to the Third International. At the same time, left-wing unionists despaired at the meager results of the confederal congress at Orléans and organized their own dissident factions within the CGT. These groups, called Comités Syndicalistes Révolutionnaires (CSRs), aimed only to strengthen the CGT minority, not to provoke an immediate schism. But their actions —and the majority's reactions—made continued unity all but impossible. Although the groups espoused the ideas of syndicalist autonomy, as first prescribed in the Amiens Charter, they endorsed nonetheless the unions' adhesion to Moscow's new Profintern or Red Syndicalist International (ISR).

These two sets of events—in the party and the unions respectively— were of course not unrelated. As most authors have argued, the party split offered a model for disgruntled unionists to copy in their own movement; the Communists helped to organize the CGT minority and played a role in the union schism; and the issues of adhesion to international communism were in both cases much the same.[1] Still, the union split did not follow automatically or reflect an identical set of motives. Although the Communists sought to dominate the union movement, left-wing unionists did not share comparable enthusiasm for the Communist Party. Their show of concern for union autonomy was more than the *pro forma* gesture that some observers (then and later) have thought it to be. Even the provocation of union schism—against the will of the Communists, who preferred to maintain unity so as to win over the unions (and the working class) in their entirety—expressed a kind of syndicalist impatience, a preference for small, avant-garde agents of revolution, an idea akin to Leninism in some aspects but distinct from the greater caution of the Communist movement by 1921.

The union schism thus marked a resurgence of syndicalist ideology thought dead or outmoded in the heyday of mass, corporative unionism that had followed the end of the war and that had helped to initiate the general strike of May 1920. With the strike failure, and the subsequent weakness of the union movement, syndicalists hoped to make a virtue out of necessity: to make their unions, though small, the paragons of revolutionary fervor that they had been (or had seemed) in prewar days. Unlike their party colleagues, these unionists saw in Bolshevism not a substitute for revolutionary syndicalism but a way to make the unions more truly revolutionary, by tearing them away from Socialist reformism without binding them to a rival party that would also ignore their distinct revolutionary capabilities. Although few in number, these hybrid "anarcho-Communists" and "Communist-syndicalists" played a decisive role in the labor history of the period, because they—not their strict Communist counterparts—were to trigger the CGT schism and set the political course of the early CGTU.

The Anarchists and the "Ultra-Left"

The labor movement's early enthusiasm for Bolshevism must be set in the context both of changing anarchist and syndicalist theories and of the generalized appeal of Bolshevism across the spectrum of the postwar French left. Widespread confusion about the true meaning of Bolshevism made it easy for divergent groups to rally to the world's first successful modern revolutionary movement and to find what they wanted in Leninist doctrine, much as diverse leftists had rallied indiscriminately to Wilsonianism during the war.[2] Later attacks on the Bolshevik regime by antirevolutionists outside and inside Russian territory made it all the more urgent for leftists to affirm their solidarity with the Russian program, whether or not it was literally applicable to France. This solidarity was easily misread by the authorities, who labeled "Bolshevist" any allegedly revolutionary occurrence, including a planned demonstration to honor Wilson's arrival in France in December 1918.[3] Still, even militants who denied they were Bolshevists saw a certain logic in Bolshevik principles. In the Loire, former strike leader Clovis Andrieu explained the spread of Bolshevism as the simple product of "capitalist rapacity" and of government inability to resolve the postwar economic crisis.[4] In Limoges, future Bourse secretary Louis Bert adopted Albert Thomas's and Léon Blum's phraseology, although not their conclusions, when he proclaimed that since "one must choose," he chose the Third International.[5]

It may have been some instinctive anarchist sentiment that kept these militants from closer affiliation with the cause of Bolshevism. Both Bert and Andrieu had early ties with the anarchist movement and later broke off from the Communist unions, the latter to join the CGTSR.[6] But anarchists likewise had found some elements of early Bolshevism attractive. Many who accepted the idea of joining groups or unions saw the Russian *"soviets"* as useful models of syndicalist organization. In his pamphlet *Le Soviet* (1919), Loire anarchist André Lorulot reserved the right to criticize the Russians' establishment of a forcible "dictatorship" but praised nonetheless their system of "direct democracy" as a version of Proudhon's concept of "authority from below."[7] Going further, Lorulot once even affirmed that "in a period of revolution a certain degree of dictatorship is necessary," an idea he no doubt still held in 1919.[8]

In addition, and more important for the history of the labor movement, the anarchists were drawn to the Leninist idea of schism: the notion that a small band of activists could be more effective than a mass movement forced to compromise its principles in order to broaden its support. In 1918, this idea had rallied anarchists to the antiwar strike movement, whose defeatist overtones had made mass participation all but unthinkable.[9] Later on, even as anarchists shied away from the Bolshevik dictatorship, the idea of schism continued to dominate the French "ultra-left."

The term "ultra-left," applied today to the various factions to the left of the Communist Party, first signified an anarcho-Bolshevist movement launched in Paris in 1919, a year before the modern PCF's formation. The movement's founder was Raymond Péricat, veteran leader of the May 1918 strikes and of the minoritarian Comité de Défense Syndicaliste (CDS). Péricat's anarchistic "Parti Communiste" sought to trigger a deeper political schism and to rally the left wing of the SFIO. He also spoke out for a CGT schism, on the occasions of the confederal congresses at Lyon in 1919 and at Orléans in 1920, and he quit the CGT in 1921 to form an autonomous movement around the Marseille construction workers' union.[10] His tiny party proved ephemeral and his activities "an almost ludicrous example of the divisive tendencies in the French working-class movement."[11] Still, they had important echoes, especially in the provinces, where militants incorporated his ideas into the new Communist Party (SFIC) and into the left wing of the CGT. Far from dying out, or falling victim to "successive" syndicalist or communist alternatives, this "ultra-left" continued to influence later movements even though it lost its formal, institutional bases of support.[12]

Early signs of an anarcho-Bolshevist tendency appeared in provincial groups, the "Amis de *La Vague,*" named for the weekly journal that they helped to distribute. Such groups were formed in both Limoges and Saint-Etienne in early 1919. In Limoges, the group's leaders were Louis Bert and Léonard Gros, the latter an architectural draftsman who, like Bert, was a prominent "libertarian" Socialist and a founder of the later Communist Party.[13] In Saint-Etienne, the group included a variety of anarchists and other leftists, most notably the "revolutionary Socialist" (and later Communist) teacher Antoine Moulin.[14]

The groups forged links almost immediately to the new Third International. After contacting left-wing Socialist Fernand Loriot in Paris, Moulin's group formed a local section of the Committee for the Third International, which grew from fourteen to twenty-seven members (approximately one-half the size of the "Amis de *La Vague,*" which still existed) by the end of 1919.[15] Although the Limoges body dissolved quickly, before the founding of a new Communist group the following April, the Saint-Etienne section lasted until its merger with a new local group, also founded in 1920, called the Ruche Communiste. This latter group showed its anarchist overtones when it renounced electoral politics (in partial reaction against Moulin's controversial Senate candidacy), formally resigned from the Socialist Party, and joined other anarchists and syndicalists in the local CSR.[16] Meanwhile, "pure" anarchists, organized in a separate group (the "Amis des journaux *Le Libertaire* et *La Mêlée*"), had distrusted "politicians" like Moulin from the beginning and had loudly denounced anarchist participation in the trade unions. Nonetheless, they followed the others in voting to join the Third International.[17]

The split with the Socialists did not in itself denote anarchist or "ultra-left" tendencies. Limoges left-wingers Gros and Bert attacked the party for its persistent reformism but did not question its political function; Gros further saw the problem as a conflict of generations, because *"les aînés négligent beaucoup trop les jeunes."*[18] Yet in the Loire, it was the anarchists who first rallied to Bolshevism, and who exerted the "invisible pressure" (in the authorities' terms) behind the Socialists' own shift to-

ward the Third International.[19] Even then, the anarchists remained suspicious of the party, as long as its electoralism and bourgeois composition continued essentially unchanged.

Labor Politics and the SFIO Schism

Although it first appeared as a fringe "ultra-left" current, the trend toward adhesion to the Third International soon grew among left-wing Socialists and climaxed in the party schism at the Congress of Tours. The
new Communist Party failed to gain a majority of Haute-Vienne Socialists, even though it did win the support of most left-wing unionists in the
region. In the Loire, the party quickly won a provisional majority, but
the moderate temper of most former Socialists led them to quit the new
party within a few years. These developments, of obvious importance for
the labor movement, served less to provoke a parallel CGT schism than
to deepen labor's distrust of the political left.

In both departments, the move toward communism was at best slow
and erratic. At the SFIO National Congress at Strasbourg, in February
1920, both departmental federations voted with the party center on a
motion to "reconstruct" the old International on a more revolutionary
basis (not simply to preserve the old International or to replace it with a
new one), thus aiming to restore the unity of the left.[20] While the Loire
group's position continued to evolve between February and December,
the Haute-Vienne group remained resolutely centrist in the hope of
avoiding a schism at the party congress at Tours.

The SFIO centrists objected not so much to the principle of a new International as to the necessity of accepting foreign conditions for admission (the famous Twenty-One Conditions), especially those that would
destroy party unity. In Limoges, leading Socialists Adrien Pressemane
and Paul Faure remained convinced left-wingers in party strategy, but
they refused to impose a split in a party or a community where the desire
for unity had always been unusually strong. Local moderates even offered to join the new International if the party could do so *tous ensemble et sans conditions!* It might be foolish (they felt) to join the International, but if so, "let's commit the *bêtise* all together," to maintain party
unity "at any price."[21]

However committed to party unity, the Haute-Vienne federation did
not in fact switch its vote to avoid a schism. Nor did the SFIO loyalists
have all the arguments for unity on their own side. Supporters of the

Third International also tried to avoid a schism by finding common grounds for the adhesion of all party members. As a Limoges spokesman argued, Moscow's conditions for admission were needed to avoid "the indiscipline that had caused the ruin of the Second International." In his view, discipline was not intolerance but simply a kind of democratic centralism: *"l'observance absolue des règles générales librement acceptées."*[22]

As the same spokesman continued, the worst sign of indiscipline was the refusal to compromise party sovereignty for the sake of international solidarity. Indeed, while vaunting their faith in local and national unity, Haute-Vienne Socialists denied that any one international strategy could apply to all national conditions: in Pressemane's phrase, Bolshevik methods "cannot be ours." In lieu of the Third International, Pressemane envisioned a "purely French" socialism without foreign domination.[23] Although he voted to reconstruct the Second International, he might well have preferred to have no International at all.

While defending national traditions against a common international strategy, Limoges Socialists seem also to have valued local autonomy against the threat of a highly centralized party apparatus. Whether it came as a foreign import or as a part of the French bureaucratic tradition, centralization violated their wish to preserve local freedom of action to make decisions as they saw fit. Thus, many early Communists quit the party to protest its attempts to impose outside doctrines and leaders on local branches, while many left-wing unionists likewise abandoned the early CGTU.[24] This spirit of localism and independence may have stemmed from a latent anarchist mentality;[25] if so, it bore little resemblance to anarchist currents in the Loire. Instead, it remained primarily a corporatist gesture of hostility to party domination, while accepting *ad hoc* cooperation with the political left.

Although Haute-Vienne Socialists retained much influence in the region's labor movement, despite the party and union schisms, Loire Socialists remained far more distant from the unions, even as both movements evolved toward adhesion to the Third International. At the Strasbourg congress, Loire delegate Ferdinand Faure had violated a leftist mandate from home by voting the Longuet motion for "reconstruction" of the old International rather than the Loriot motion for immediate adhesion to Moscow; his aim, he said, was to maintain party unity. Local left-wingers, including Antoine Moulin, denounced Faure's vote and called for an immediate schism to end prolonged delay on the issue. Nonetheless, the vast majority of Saint-Etienne and Loire party members approved Faure's vote and long resisted the pressure to move further to the left.[26]

By late summer, however, Reconstructionists throughout the country began to change their message. On their return from a mission in Russia, French delegates Marcel Cachin and L.-O. Frossard now approved the International, on the grounds that Lenin had made sufficient concessions to preserve French unity and party traditions. Ex-Reconstructionist Daniel Renoult made similar arguments, though defending "the legitimate role of national sentiment"; his plea was reprinted in Saint-Etienne's Socialist weekly, *Le Peuple de la Loire*.[27] The experiences of Loire deputy Ernest Lafont, expelled from Russia as an alleged "imperialist agent," probably set back temporarily the cause of adhesion in the department.[28] Nonetheless, on the eve of the Tours congress, the Loire federation voted unanimously to approve the Cachin-Frossard motion to join the International. Even those who had disagreed in preliminary votes of their sections now rallied to maintain party unity, relieved that such unity would not exclude the known "reformists" Lafont and Ferdinand Faure.[29]

Despite their different votes on the issue of adhesion, both the Haute-Vienne and the Loire Socialists claimed to wish above all to preserve party unity. Ironically enough, in the Loire, these same professions of unity served to justify several later party schisms: in 1923, the formation of the so-called Union Socialiste-Communiste, and in 1930, the creation of the Parti d'Unité Prolétarienne.[30] However genuine their ideals, Loire Socialists remained unable to put them into practice without repeated schism and political fragmentation. Like centrists elsewhere, who joined the new International without fully embracing Bolshevik principles, Loire Socialists only postponed until later the conflicts that their ambivalence seemed to ensure.

The definitive party schism took place in January 1921, as the departmental federations voted in response to the results of the recent Tours congress. In the Haute-Vienne, most elected officials remained in the old party, although a few aspiring politicians did join the new one, perhaps to break the SFIO's virtual monopoly on electoral mandates in the department.[31] The Communist Party also recruited heavily in rural areas, including the cantons of Eymoutiers and Saint-Junien, while Limoges workers remained surprisingly faithful to the SFIO.[32] The Communists disputed this fidelity, which they claimed applied only to the municipal employees, scorned as "henchmen" *(seides)* of the Socialist mayor. Meanwhile, they vaunted their own ties to the masses, in contrast to the old party's electoralism and parliamentary "sinecures."[33] In turn, however, the Socialists derided the new Communist recruits as youngsters impatient for revolution and lacking the experience of mature party veterans.[34] In fact, although all these claims had some validity, the two parties remained remarkably similar in social composition, at least until the process of Bolshevization further dissolved the new party's ties to the past.[35]

The Haute-Vienne's new Communist federation was little more than a fringe organization, ranked twenty-ninth in size throughout the country (in late 1921) and less than half as large as the party in the neighboring and heavily rural Dordogne. It included no more than 1,000 members, compared to 4,500 in the Socialist federation before Tours.[36] The group's small size, and the Socialists' enduring appeal in the department, pushed the new federation to establish an identity separate from that of its rivals, who traditionally followed a leftist political line. This may explain why local Communists likewise chose a distinctly left-wing orientation, whether on issues of national strategy or on relations with the Third International. Additionally, the very fact that most local centrists had stayed in the Socialist Party meant that local Communists were relatively far to the left from the very beginning, unlike those in the Loire. Ironically enough, however, this ideological choice strained relations with local syndicalists, whom party leaders thought insufficiently "leftist"; thus unionists Louis Bert and Léonard Beaubelicout (the latter was then UD secretary) quit the party along with renegade party secretary L.-O. Frossard in early 1923.[37] Until then, most left-wing unionists in Limoges still saw their Communist Party affiliation as quite compatible with revolutionary syndicalist principles, and as the best cure for the reformism that had infected the party and the unions alike since 1914.

In the Loire, where the new party rallied even centrists Ferdinand Faure and Ernest Lafont, there were few signs of the SFIO schism except at Roanne. There a group of twenty-two dissidents—fewer than one-tenth of the old Roanne section—created a rival SFIO federation that eventually attracted a diverse group of Radicals and Radical-Socialists from Saint-Etienne.[38] In the Communist Party, the inclusion of nearly all the old Socialists made the new federation, with an estimated 2,200 members, the ninth largest in the country.[39] Even with incessant propaganda, however, the party proved unable to extend much beyond the traditional Socialist enclaves; nor could it recruit the worker and peasant memberships that the Haute-Vienne federation more successfully attracted.[40] At Saint-Etienne, the party section was in fact smaller than its Limoges counterpart and included more teachers and other public employees than the artisans or factory workers who comprised most of the city's large working-class population.[41] Without a strong Socialist rival, the party also felt little pressure to adopt a left-wing program that might have drawn more working-class support.

The party's centrism and bourgeois composition also affected its relations with the local trade unions. Ernest Lafont was known for his non-Guesdist respect for trade-union autonomy; his later Socialist-Communist Union, founded in 1923, did attract the sympathy of some dissident trade unionists opposed to the Bolshevization of the CGTU.[42] Until that time, however, the relations among anarchists, syndicalists, and Communists were quite strained, especially within the left wing of the trade-union movement. Hard-liners hostile to the old Socialist Party proved no less hostile to the new party's recycled socialism, in thin Communist disguise.

The party schism thus affected the unions as much by exacerbating old conflicts over party-union relations as by hastening a rupture between the unions' revolutionary and reformist factions. Once a new Communist Party existed, some left-wing unionists felt able to abandon old syndicalist rules of autonomy (premised on the absence of a truly revolutionary party with which to ally), but others doubted the new party's revolutionary credentials or still insisted that the unions could—and must—make the revolution on their own. As a compromise, a hybrid "Communist-syndicalist" faction urged the unions to form what one member called "circumstantial accords" with the new party, while still stressing their own preeminence in the revolutionary movement. This faction would reject, that is, Trotsky's claim that the unions were mere "auxiliaries" while the party was the *"avant-garde directrice"* of the working class.[43] The "Communist-syndicalists" also recognized some need for new tactics but insisted that the movement remain "faithful to itself" and to the living traditions of the Amiens Charter.[44] This group, led in Paris by Pierre Monatte and his friends at the journal *La Vie Ouvrière,* found strong provincial echoes in the Haute-Vienne and especially in the Loire.

In 1919 Monatte and his friends had described the Russian Revolution as "a revolution of syndicalist character." Their journal *La Vie Ouvrière,* relaunched in April 1919 after a wartime interruption, echoed the anarchists' claim that the *soviets* were a Russian version of the French *syndicats* and adopted English unionist Tom Mann's slogan that "Bolshevism, Spartacism, Syndicalism all mean the same thing under different names."[45]

This "hybrid" doctrine may have marked a drastic change from its purer, less politicized prewar version, but it also showed how far syndicalism could adopt a vaguely Bolshevist profile and still emerge not so much altered as revitalized and reaffirmed.[46] Indeed, while championing the Third International and deploring the CGT's wartime reformism, Monatte insisted that the war had served to validate, not destroy, the unions' prewar ideals and traditions. "Although the war did teach us new things, it did not teach us that we were wrong to fight at once against capitalism and against the State, or that our concept of revolution based on the trade union was an illusion."[47] Monatte's group also scoffed at the CGT majority for professing allegiance to the Amiens Chapter while accepting ties to the Socialist Party and membership in the International Labor Organization at Geneva.[48] Soon their own devotion to union autonomy would be severely challenged by their adhesion to Moscow, but it was more than mere empty rhetoric. As its author agreed, the Amiens Charter was not a "dead letter" but a "living idea," fully able to survive and grow in the modern world.[49]

The issue of union relations with the international Communist movement was formally raised at the CGT's confederal congress at Orléans in September 1920. Discussion was occasioned by the recent Second World Congress of the Communist International and its plans to create a trade-union branch, the Profintern, officially established in 1921.[50] Although the timing—shortly after the May strike failure—was more than coincidental, unionists seemed far more concerned with planning the future than with settling the blame for the past. The May strike failure may have convinced party leaders of the need for Bolshevik methods, and for union deference to party leadership, but it had less direct impact on unionists themselves.

The issue of party-union relations had become increasingly controversial among both Loire and Haute-Vienne unionists. Even in Limoges, unionists had begun to resent the party's blatant electoral preoccupations. Railroad unionists, until then the party's most ardent electoral supporters, now questioned its interpretation of the May strike failure: that the unions should cast aside their outmoded syndicalist prejudices and form *"une armée homogène."*[51] Louis Bert, the new Bourse secretary, also resented the party's defense of his predecessors Bonnet and Rougerie, ousted for their alleged mishandling of the May strike. Still, though he claimed to endorse revolutionary syndicalist terminology, Bert objected less to the principle of party politics than to the reformism of the SFIO.

After the Orléans congress, the Union Locale at Saint-Junien was the first labor group in the department formally to endorse the Third International.[52] Louis Bert worked to mobilize local opinion further by arguing that only close links to Moscow could transform professional unions into agents of revolution. Left-wing unionists—often the same individuals as left-wing party members—thus used political reasons to justify their acceptance of Bolshevism. In Bert's view, unionists had the duty to open their doors to party militants for propagation of those communist principles that all true revolutionaries shared. The unions must not "under pretext of distinguishing between the 'political struggle' and the 'economic struggle' " be allowed "to wander aimlessly in a reformist policy of class collaboration."[53] The only real distinction, to Bert, was between reformist and revolutionary syndicalism, not between "anarcho-syndicalism" and "socialo-syndicalism," terms which for all practical purposes had ceased to exist.[54]

This argument, a classic statement of the Communist Party's own union policy, is noteworthy mainly for its ready acceptance among leading Limoges unionists. In a new weekly journal established to disseminate this political viewpoint, Bert vowed to uphold the true spirit of the Amiens Charter, which was under attack, he said, not by his own group but by the reformists of the SFIO and CGT.[55] The unions, he added, would battle exclusively in "the economic sector," while "cooperating with the Socialist Party [SFIC] for the conquest of political power and the formation of the proletarian State."[56] Hence, communism would complement, not contradict, revolutionary syndicalism by helping the unions to emerge from their reformist lethargy. As a final sign of its confidence in party-union harmony, the journal merged in 1921 with the new regional Communist Party newspaper, which remained the organ of the early CGTU. This joint affiliation, the syndicalists argued, would allow them "to preserve [their] full autonomy" while "fusing [their] program of action" with that of the new PCF.[57]

The Haute-Vienne syndicalists thus saw the Communist Party as a cure for political reformism and a legitimate ally of revolutionary unionists willing to update the Amiens Charter. Since it was now necessary to choose one International or the other, they opted "for Moscow and a program of action, against Amsterdam and inaction."[58] Those who might have hesitated to accept the Bolshevik conditions for admission to the Comintern found no such objection to entry, without conditions, into the Profintern, or Trade-Union International. They also denounced strict libertarians, who stressed the party's supposed "authoritarian" dangers, as tacit allies of "the social traitors" and "the counter-revolutionary syndicalists," far more dangerous to the unity and vigor of the working class.[59]

While Haute-Vienne unionists temporarily suppressed their libertarian instincts, Loire unionists felt those instincts surface, as debates on the Third International got underway. The UD leadership moved cautiously toward adhesion, which they feared would divide the unions, even if they agreed that without some political collaboration the unions could never make the revolution alone.[60] Among the first to rally to the International was the local teachers' union, led by left-wing Socialist Antoine Moulin. But this was a group that other unionists distrusted for its "political" tendencies, its non-proletarian status, and its apparent eagerness for schism in defiance of the need for labor unity.[61] When the UD also endorsed the Third International, in mid-1921, its belated decision may have hurt more than helped its reputation among anarchists for revolutionary zeal.[62]

These anarchists questioned both the Socialists' electoral preoccupations and the unions' ties to a political party that was revolutionary in name only. Those already wary of the party's electoral maneuvers in 1919 further resented the Socialists' calls, after the May 1920 strike failure, to abandon revolutionary insurrectionalism and place all hopes in *"le bulletin rouge."*[63] Local anarchists, scarcely impressed with the party's slow evolution leftward, now denounced Parisian convert Marcel Cachin as a "liar"; even adhesion to the Third International would not, they said, change the party's "bourgeois" identity and its inclination to pass over "to the other side of the barricade."[64]

Outside anarchist circles, most unionists were less hostile to *ad hoc* party-union cooperation. Despite some misgivings, the unions had joined with the party to sponsor May Day meetings and demonstrations in mid-1920, to call for the nationalization of the mines and railroads, and to protest against alleged threats of war later that year.[65] During the UD elections in July, however, unionists accused party leaders of trying to install their own candidate, municipal councillor (and former railroad secretary) Pierre Chovet, in violation of UD statutes against joint holding of union and party office.[66] The victorious candidate, Henri Lorduron, was also a party member. His opponent Emile Arnaud, the "libertarian-

Communist" candidate, in turn won election as Bourse secretary at Saint-Etienne, succeeding party member Laurent Torcieux, early the next year.[67]

These elections revealed the growing rift between the Socialist and anarchist wings of the Loire's labor movement. While the former wing shifted toward greater stress on corporative action, mass organization, and party alliances, the latter group decried precisely those changes — and the need to charge higher union dues.[68] Always ambivalent about trade-unionism on principle, even those anarchists who joined the unions did so only on condition that the unions adhere to a revolutionary program. During the war, the pacifist strike movements had temporarily convinced the anarchists of the unions' revolutionary potential. But after the war, when the unions resumed a corporative focus, former strike leader Charles Flageollet reissued the old anarchist arguments against unions and union members, who, he said, were by definition "politicians." The only meaningful strikes, Flageollet added, followed the Italian example by seizing machines and factories; simple wage questions were no longer *"à l'ordre du jour."*[69]

Flageollet had personal grounds for his bitterness against the labor movement. After his imprisonment for his wartime strike activities, he had failed to regain his post as UD secretary, and he apparently never forgave the unions for this slight.[70] Another anarchist, the printer Eugène Soullier, began with greater confidence in union action, but he soon grew frustrated at his own union's reformism and at its habit of passing resolutions without acting on them.[71] Finally, the metalworkers' secretary Théodor Dieu, not a member of the anarchist group or a fan of its "obstructionist" methods, likewise despaired at his union's lost revolutionary fervor. Along with the anarchists, he denounced the use of paid full-time officers, a practice that led to dependence on municipal subsidies and dimmed the unions' revolutionary élan.[72] As the UD languished under Lorduron's tepid leadership, and as his own union dwindled to fewer than forty members, Dieu resigned his office and finally quit the region altogether, reportedly to work in the city of Roubaix.[73]

For these left-wingers, the only way to restore the unions' vigor lay in a new institution formed in late 1920, the Comités Syndicalistes Révolutionnaires (CSRs). Led at the start by the Parisian Pierre Monatte, the CSRs intended first to organize the CGT's minority faction, defeated at the Orléans confederal congress, and to prepare for an eventual victory at the next year's congress at Lille.[74] In addition, the CSRs aimed to revitalize the unions, although the degree and direction of proposed changes remained unclear. This blurring of goals was magnified by the blurred composition of the groups, which were to include left-wing unionists of all colorations against their common reformist rivals. Where these left-wing subgroups were already in conflict, the CSRs became the battleground, destined—as the Loire authorities predicted—to wind up destroying themselves from within.[75]

The Limoges CSR, headed by Bourse secretary Louis Bert, brought together all syndicalists who also favored the nascent Communist Party. Its leading members were the railroad workers, always the mainstay of Socialist or Communist unionism in the department. In other industries, although the union secretaries refused to join the new organization, an estimated 30 percent of the porcelain workers and 20 percent of the shoe workers had become members by January 1921.[76] For such workers, party sympathies and union memberships were no more contradictory now than in the heyday of Socialist unionism before or during World War I.

Such was of course not the case in the more turbulent Loire context. Left-wing labor leaders Lorduron and Torcieux hesitated to join the CSR, which they saw as a source of division within the union movement.[77] In all, the Saint-Etienne section had only thirty-nine members by the end of 1920 and sixty members by mid-1921.[78] Only the city's leather workers' union, with its handful of members, joined as a group, although suburban unions of miners, metalworkers, and construction workers did join sister organizations elsewhere in the department.[79] While the railroad workers had expressed some interest in joining, the teachers and metalworkers—once leading left-wingers—refused to adhere. The metalworkers' new secretary, anarchist Jean Seigne, was regional CSR director and a prime spokesman for adhesion. Most members, however, feared that the move, by advancing the prospect of schism, would cause the collapse of a union that was already near dissolution by the winter of 1920–21.[80]

The CSRs thus attracted first those unionists most favorable to Communist alliances and to adhesion to the Third International. In addition, however, they rallied a diverse group of anarcho-syndicalists whose ties to the union movement, or to the nascent Communist Party, were tenuous at best. This faction gained temporary ascendancy even within the

CSR central committee, once the anarchist Pierre Besnard succeeded Monatte as secretary,[81] and it proved especially influential in the Loire.

The two factions sometimes debated the very merits of Bolshevik revolutionary theory. Communists argued that it was idle to criticize the Bolshevik "dictatorship" in favor of democracy; the real choice, to them, lay between bourgeois dictatorship and proletarian dictatorship, the latter of which, at least, had "democracy" as the final goal.[82] But anarchists who had once sympathized with Bolshevism now began to see even the Third Republic as preferable to the tightening "yoke of Bolshevik oppression."[83] The CSR leaders in Saint-Etienne, while endorsing the Trade-Union International, also reserved the right to criticize the Soviet dictatorship and to proclaim as their goal "the complete emancipation of the individual."[84] These debates might seem to be routine disagreements among ideological rivals, but they were important signs that the early anarcho-Communist alliance was now breaking down.

More than by distant events in Soviet Russia, local anarchists were dismayed by the evolution of party-union relations in France, especially since the formation of the Communist Party. The new party saw the unions as the natural terrain for its own propaganda, and as the vehicle for winning over the working class to its cause. By a technique called *"noyautage,"* a form of infiltration, the party would expand from a "kernel" or "nucleus" *(noyau)* of support inside the union and eventually take over the entire organization. As part of this strategy, all party members (in appropriate jobs) would be required to unionize and to obey party orders on union activities.[85] To some anarchists, the prospect of Communist control was so distressing that they vowed, in the event of a CGT split, to remain neutral rather than join the Communist camp.[86]

Of course, the anarchists' own views were far from genuinely neutral. Like prewar anarchists, who had scorned the Amiens Charter as an excuse for flabby neutrality, postwar anarchists may have argued the need for union autonomy only so far as it suited their political ends.[87] A main goal was to win control of the CSRs in order to combat the influence of the Communist Party. Indeed, Pierre Monatte later claimed that it was while he and his friends were in prison for their role in the general strike of May 1920 that the anarchists gained ascendancy in the CGT's minority camp, a position they retained for several months in the early CGTU.[88]

The anarchists' role in the CSRs was limited by the rule that only regular union members could join the organization. Thus the Loire's Charles

Flageollet, who disdained the unions, also urged his comrades to boycott the CSR.[89] But the metalworker Jean Seigne instead quit the anarchist group to devote full time to the new organization, and the typographer Eugène Soullier held off quitting his union just to have the right to join the CSR. Both rose to top CSR positions in the department but were scorned by "pure" anarchists as traitors who had sold out to the trade-union movement.[90] Even the authorities found that the membership rule, which UD secretary Lorduron insisted on applying strictly in the Loire, reduced the CSRs to meaningless revolutionary verbiage. As the police phrased it: *"il faut paraître révolutionnaire sans l'être, tout en l'étant."*[91]

The rule was a legalism designed to avert a rupture with the CGT leadership. As in May 1918, at the time of the minoritarian congress, the more cautious left-wingers sought to preserve the fiction that they were acting solely under the CGT's authority, rather than aiming to subvert the institution from within.[92] This very caution showed the limits of the group's revolutionary intentions. Indeed, the CSRs' Communist-syndicalist faction struck a tenuous — and ultimately unsuccessful — balance between the most blatant partisans of the Third International and its most die-hard opponents. Their battles proved especially bitter in the Loire.

The balance was difficult enough to maintain in the abstract. Pierre Monatte thought it sufficient to refuse to join the Communist Party — he stayed out until 1923 — even while he supported adhesion to the Trade-Union International.[93] Others, including the Loire's Henri Lorduron and Emile Arnaud, joined the new party, or came into it from the old SFIO, while preserving a certain moral distance. Still, their positions were almost untenable in the face of day-to-day decisions. As Bourse secretary, Arnaud refused the anarchist-led CSR a meeting room at Bourse headquarters, arguing that Bourse statutes forbade the recognition of such a "political" grouping. By this action, Arnaud lost his libertarian credentials and seemed to anarchists to have drifted alarmingly close to the Communist camp.[94]

Later on, both men broke with the Communist Party and resumed their ties with the syndicalist movement, in response to the unions' threatened "Bolshevization." The progression from "ultra-left" to communism was thus reversed, or indeed it had not been definitive from the start. Instead, once strict neutrality ceased to be a viable option, these advocates of union independence agreed to a succession of political alliances, depending on which one then seemed the lesser evil. Thus Lorduron and Arnaud sided first with both Communists and anarchists against the CGT reformists, and then with one ally against the other, as the fragile left-wing coalition began to break down.

Toward the CGT Schism

Although the conflicts among left-wing rivals continued to rage after the CGT schism, they also played a big role in hastening that rupture. Moderate unionists, like those in the party, remained reluctant to consummate the break with the right-wing faction. Nonetheless, a small but vocal group of anarchists and other extremists forced the issue by seeing schism as a desirable end in itself. By late 1921, after the minority's failure to unseat their rivals at the Lille confederal congress, even the Loire's Henri Lorduron recognized that the time for schism had arrived.[95] Still, only the left wing's prodding, plus the majority's immobility, could explain how the idea spread from a tiny fringe to the bulk of the CGT minority, which now comprised nearly half the body's total membership.

At first sight, the competition among rival Communist, anarchist, and reformist factions seemed to make the trade-union schism virtually inevitable. All that remained was for each group to choose its new affiliation, now that, as the Haute-Vienne prefect observed uneasily, *"la scission s'accentue."*[96] Despite the traditional ideal of labor unity, Limoges Bourse secretary Louis Bert now found unity impossible "except among identical elements, with the same affinities."[97] The emergence of new parties forced a choice between the Second and Third Internationals, or, more broadly, between communist doctrine and the preservation of the capitalist system. As Parisian Communist Amédée Dunois agreed, the choice meant that unionists "can no longer be neutral," no longer deny ideological differences to preserve the harmony of interests that had sustained syndicalist unity in the past.[98]

Even the Communists, however, hesitated to impose on the unions the same process of schism that they had just carried out, sometimes reluctantly, in the Socialist Party. Now that world revolution no longer seemed imminent, the Communists had adopted a "united front" strategy, calling for at least temporary leftist alliances. Dunois himself, an early advocate of this new strategy, denied that the party split forced the trade-union rupture, which he blamed instead on the majority's intolerance.[99] Lenin also had tried to lure reluctant Socialists into the new party by claiming not to want a union schism, or what Paul Faure had called "a declaration of war" against the CGT.[100]

These arguments, of course, had their own partisan content. Leninists regarded union schism as no more than a symptom of ultra-left "infantilism," which must now, after the purge of right-wing reformism, be battled and eliminated in its turn.[101] In addition, the party still hoped to win control of the entire labor movement, rather than just of its left-wing faction. Thus the strategy of *"noyautage,"* or infiltration, became a substitute for schism and a step toward future victory, much as were Lenin's new pragmatic policies in the economic and diplomatic spheres.

In this sense, union schism was a major tactical error, a "disaster" as French Communist Alfred Rosmer called it. The left-wing camp was already close to victory — or perhaps even slightly outnumbered the old majority, Rosmer claimed — but would lose many supporters when it came time to quit the CGT.[102] (Thus the leftists later sought to avoid blame for the schism by naming their dissident organization the CGTU — for "Unitaire.") Beyond these practical issues, Rosmer professed to see the preservation of unity, a mere question of opportunity for a party, as a matter of principle for the trade unions.[103] This principled stance was further typified by Pierre Monatte, as well as by some of his Communist-syndicalist friends in the Haute-Vienne and the Loire.

In Monatte's view, schism would make a union "no more than a political grouping." Unity alone gave the unions a revolutionary capacity and a mass base of support that no partisan fraction could hope to attain.[104] For this reason, Monatte opposed schism to the very end, cast one of the few negative votes at the Congress of Paris (December 1921), and even quit the direction of *La Vie Ouvrière* when Monmousseau and other colleagues refused to support him.[105] Most others acknowledged by this time that the CSRs and the vote to join the Profintern had created a moral schism in the labor movement, to which they must be resigned if not enthusiastic. Even Louis Bert, for whom the strength of Socialist reformism in Limoges made prolonged unity all but impossible, had urged his Saint-Junien colleagues to avoid a premature rupture in 1920. The UD had also persistently voted against schism through the summer of 1921.[106] In the Loire, most unionists had likewise stopped short at schism ever since it first threatened seriously during the antiwar strikes of May 1918.[107]

While the Communists and the Communist-syndicalists hesitated, however, the anarchist faction expressed a positive desire for schism, which they preferred both to Socialist reformism and to prolonged inaction under Communist leadership. Although most left-wing unionists aimed to win control of the unions, anarchists wanted only to hasten the revolution, with or without the unions, to which their loyalty remained conditional at best. Since 1918, taking seriously Lenin's idea of revolution by a vanguard of activists, anarchists had grown impatient with those unionists who hesitated to act for fear of provoking a schism or losing the support of the masses.[108] Now, as schism beckoned, these extremists hoped to precipitate the rupture in order to purge the unions of weak elements that could only hold the revolution back.

This aim was especially apparent among anarchists and anarcho-syndicalists grouped in the CSR in the Loire. Because Monatte intended the organization only to mobilize the CGT minority, not to trigger the schism, Loire militants condemned the CSR as a wretched "half-measure" that failed to offer an escape from the majority's domination.[109] Once in anarchist hands, the local group called openly for schism and attacked Monatte and the CSR's Central Committee for sliding too close to the Communist Party. The group also urged (unsuccessfully) that non-unionists be allowed to join it and thus become an independent revolutionary agent outside the CGT's control.[110]

Similar views gained ascendancy in the national organization in May 1921, when Pierre Besnard succeeded Monatte as secretary of the CSR's Central Committee. Monatte later described Besnard as "the stereotypical utopian," doctrinaire, isolated, and bent on building his own personal organization — *"sa maison à lui."*[111] This temperament no doubt helps to explain Besnard's later work in founding the fragmentary CGTSR ("Syndicaliste Révolutionnaire") once the CGTU had come under Communist domination.[112] Before then, Besnard — a railroad unionist in Paris — became best known for sponsoring a secret accord, signed in February 1921, with seventeen of his anarcho-syndicalist comrades. This secret "Pacte," not publicized until more than a year later, expressed the group's determination to preserve syndicalist autonomy and to win over the CSR and the CGT to their own libertarian views. These aims were to be pursued "by every means" including schism, which seemed increasingly urgent once the Communists and Communist-syndicalists drew closer together and threatened to win control of the minority camp.[113]

However committed to syndicalist independence, the anarchists also had plans to remold the unions in their own image. In particular, they wished to accent the traditions of federalism or local autonomy as against the pervasive centralism of the Communist Party and the CGT alike. The movement's nuclei were to be the local CSRs, like cells in the Communist Party's later structure. These cells would then be grouped in departmental and regional clusters to serve as organs of administration; the organ of action remained the local *comité* itself. As a final guarantee of local initiative, the industrial branches of the Central Committee (one each for mining, metallurgy, etc.) were to have their seats in the provinces rather than in Paris, to avoid being too easily subdued by government surveillance or co-opted by parliamentary temptations.[114] These measures reaffirmed the anarcho-syndicalists' libertarian aims, even in temporary alliance with the Communist faction, and maximized their influence in local strongholds such as the Loire.

For the Communist-syndicalists as well, the CSRs had larger strategic aims beyond the defeat of the reformist opposition. Indeed, Monatte, their founder, hoped the groups would survive as "active minorities" even if the left wing emerged victorious at the CGT's Lille congress in July 1921. In Monatte's view, the goal was to "revitalize" the union movement and to highlight its unique revolutionary capacities.[115] Unlike the anarchists, he felt that these aims could and must be accomplished without schism; hence, he still clung to the prewar Charter of Amiens. Nonetheless, he welcomed party ties, although not party leadership, to "revitalize" the unions. The question thus remained: how valid were the terms of the Amiens Charter? Were they rendered outmoded by the war and the Russian Revolution? Had they already, in fact, been proved inadequate before 1914?

For Monatte, the greatest need was for close relations between the unions and the workshops in order to overcome the workers' aloofness toward their unions, still a special problem in France. Toward that end, the CSRs were to evolve into a network of factory committees *("comités d'atelier")*.[116] These new organizations, as elaborated by Monatte and others, were to complement, not supplant, the existing trade-union system. Still, they implied some dissatisfaction with the way unions functioned — at least then, and perhaps always — in France.

As Monatte acknowledged, the prewar French unions had failed to rally the masses. Even the reformist unions were no more widely organized, though somewhat larger in sheer numbers, than those with revolutionary tendencies. In their own defense, French syndicalists typically retorted that they had the *quality* while British and German unions had mere *quantity* of membership, but this was in fact false, Monatte said, as the weakness of wartime labor had shown.[117]

In short, Monatte rejected the argument that French unionism had benefited from its reliance on a small revolutionary vanguard or "active minority." That was, in fact, why Monatte opposed a schism: it would sacrifice quantity, or mass membership, without necessarily improving quality, or revolutionary zeal. Meanwhile, the anarchists approved the schism precisely because they still believed in the supposed virtue of quality over quantity. Indeed, however newly smitten by Communist methods, Monatte's Communist-syndicalists had remained true to syndicalist goals, while anarchists had kept the old libertarian methods but altered the goals: they sought to make small size a virtual end in itself.

Whatever their aims, the anarchists did wield an influence in postwar labor politics that far surpassed their numbers. Never more than an active minority within the left wing of the unions, they still triggered a schism that momentarily thrust them into the leadership of the new CGTU. Their efforts were aided, but not caused, by the prior split in the Socialist Party. Although they did not act alone, they precipitated a process in which the majority's intransigence and the left wing's impatience together ruptured a movement whose moral unity had long since ceased to exist.

The role of this small group of extremists was further accentuated by the shrinking size of the unions' memberships. Already weakened by the failure of the May 1920 strike movement, the unions lost additional members unwilling to endorse the Communist or anarchist doctrines that many leaders espoused. An added factor that weakened the unions was the deepening economic recession, which began in late 1920. This recession further piqued extremists' impatience with mass unionism, whether Socialist or Communist in format, and thus hastened the schism in the smaller but still more strident labor movement at the end of 1921.

Chapter 8

Unionism in Crisis: The Economic Recession of 1921

It was no accident that the CGT schism occurred in the winter of 1921–22, on the heels of a year-long economic recession. This economic crisis, although far shorter and less severe than the Great Depression of the subsequent decade, has been unduly neglected, both as an episode in economic history and as a critical event in labor politics.[1] Even if social reforms did temper large-scale misery or unrest (as again in the 1930s), the crisis was no less decisive in shaping factional squabbles and strategic debates. Among its effects, the recession further weakened a labor movement already undermined by the May 1920 strike failure, and it helped to discredit the mass, parliamentary tactics urged by CGT reformists and Communists alike. It thus hastened the schism among ultra-leftists, whose influence (if not their numbers) increased in the smaller unions and whose thirst for "direct action" became all the more acute.

The political impact of the crisis was in part the result of the weakening of unionization and strike activity. These weaknesses were not in themselves surprising, given the throngs of unemployed workers ready to replace union members or strikers at their jobs. The effect on union politics or ideology was nonetheless harder to predict. One might expect weakened unions to be more defensive and less militant, just as it was commonly assumed that the rapidly growing unions of 1919–20 would move sharply to the left.[2] In fact, in both cases, the effect was quite the opposite. While the growing unions recruited masses of workers with unsure revolutionary commitments, the weakened unions lost these tepid recruits at the first signs of crisis and retained those die-hards who saw in ardent protest the only way to make their presence felt.

The crisis also had different impacts in different sectors of the economy and among different groups of workers. It hit the hardest in those industries that had expanded most sharply (and most precariously) during the war years, such as the shoe industry in Limoges and the steel industries in Saint-Etienne. In so doing, the recession helped to "turn back the clock" in economic terms, showing that the wartime advances in productivity or in the scale of enterprise had been more apparent than real. Similarly, the crisis most touched those workers who might have been tempted to adopt new labor strategies to match their new economic situation. Those who had chosen reformist or corporative strategies since before the war were not likely to change their minds now, whereas those who had begun to shift from syndicalism to communism often halted the process or actually shifted into reverse.

The recession of 1921 thus served, much as the political disputes of the same year, to accelerate the conflicts within the CGT's left-wing minority. While it hastened the schism, it did so at the expense of Communists and reformists alike, since their strategies seemed equally unable to resolve the crisis or to rally the workers to political action in pursuit of economic goals. These circumstances, like those in prewar France, magnified the appeal of a syndicalist alternative. While it too underwent certain postwar modifications, the syndicalist option showed a continued taste for small, avant-garde "active minorities" and for local autonomy, as alternatives to the centralization and mass unionism that both the Communists and the CGT reformists preferred.

The Economics of the Postwar Recession

The economic crisis of late 1920 to 1921 was an international phenomenon, the cumulative product of wartime inflation, postwar reconversion, and the disruption of trade. The crisis appears to have begun in Japan in February 1920; it then spread to the United States and from there to Europe, where it hit France by June of the year. The first sign of trouble was a sharp decline in consumer spending, as inflation and speculative price increases led consumers to postpone nonessential purchases in the hope that prices would soon drop back down. The resulting *"mévente"* did spark price reductions, especially in the wholesale market, as well as trigger a series of factory closings, employee layoffs, and wage reductions for those still at work. Meanwhile, however, high taxes and transportation costs seem to have kept the consumer from enjoying comparable reductions in food prices and retail living costs.[3]

Although sometimes termed a crisis of "overproduction," the episode might better be called a crisis of "underconsumption," as total industrial productivity remained below prewar levels until 1924.[4] Certain industries that had expanded unusually rapidly in wartime now had either to adjust their output or to find new markets, a difficult task in a world of trade barriers and lower-class impoverishment. Luxury manufactures, in which France still specialized, were particularly hurt by the deferral of consumer spending, as well as by the vagaries of fashion and by competition from cheaper foreign goods.

For these reasons, the textile and leather industries in the Loire and Haute-Vienne regions and throughout the country were especially hard hit by the recession. In both industries, the high cost of labor and raw materials added to the inadequacy of marketing practices and the inefficiency of small-scale operations to show the basic vulnerability that underlay the recession's transient effects.[5] Likewise, in other Loire industries, gun and hardware manufacture remained small-scale and inefficient, while even larger steel mills and coal mines faced dwindling demand and intense competition from suppliers abroad or in northern France and Lorraine, the latter region now restored to French hands.[6] In contrast, the Limoges porcelain industry, in slow decline since before the war, managed to weather the postwar crisis without special difficulty.[7] Nonetheless, the crisis showed the latent weaknesses of all France's older industries, and older industrial regions, as long as new structures and new methods failed to intervene.

When sales began to plummet, employers commonly responded by cutting wages to reduce production costs, especially in labor-intensive industries. Cuts ranged from 10 to 15 percent among Loire miners and ribbon weavers and Limoges shoe and clothing workers, although the ceramicists' wages appear to have been spared.[8] These measures enraged most workers and brought no clear economic benefit, for they depressed purchasing power and thereby further reduced consumer demand. Recent studies suggest that wages in fact fell less sharply than retail prices, which declined in this period by an average of 22 percent. (Living costs in the Loire are charted here in Figure 18.)[9] Even if accurate, however, this comparison did little to appease most workers, who felt that wages had long since lagged behind rampant inflation.[10] Any advantage would also apply only to full-time workers, not to the thousands with shortened work weeks or to the unemployed. The wage cuts also hurt most those who could least afford them, thereby restoring in part the wage differentials eroded by wartime gains offered at flat rates for skilled and unskilled workers.[11] Those with skilled jobs and strong unions could more easily refuse to accept a threatened wage cut without the threat of unemployment that faced the mass of unskilled workers and made them unable to defend their interests through unions or strikes.

The problem of unemployment was especially difficult for the French to handle because it had rarely occurred since the mid-nineteenth century. Brief bouts of unemployment had followed the wartime mobilization and the postwar demobilization, but in general, French industries instead faced labor shortages, compounded by wartime casualties and the slowing birth rate, and only partially filled by the influx of female and foreign labor supplies.[12] Now, however, the attempts to cut back production caused widespread layoffs and factory closings. While the availability of substitute farm jobs had masked the problem through the summer of 1920, the crisis hit with a vengeance in the autumn and early winter and lasted throughout most of the following year.[13]

Overall, unemployment in 1921 hit an estimated 2.6 percent of the total active population; departmental quotients were lower for the Haute-Vienne but even higher for the Loire. These rates were little more than half those reached during the Great Depression but were approximately twice those in 1920 or during most of the rest of the decade, except for a brief crisis in 1927.[14] The percentages would have been higher still if figured just among industrial workers and employees, and they varied sharply from one industry or locality to another. Especially hard hit were the shoe and clothing industries, which represented a large proportion of the total work force in Limoges. By January 1921, more than half the city's 8,000 shoe workers were laid off, while another quarter worked only part-time; nearly 2,000 were still unemployed at the end of the year.[15] In the textile industry of the Loire and the Haute-Loire some 70 to 90 percent of the looms were reportedly inactive; some 75 percent of glassworkers at Rive-de-Gier were also unemployed. Few miners or metalworkers lost their jobs, as unsold stock instead was allowed to accumulate, but these workers did face the wage cuts and other hardships that afflicted the region's economy as a whole.[16]

Even within a given industry, not all workers were equally subject to employment cutbacks. While native Frenchmen frequently complained about job competition from women and foreign workers, in fact the latter groups were usually the first to lose their jobs when a crisis arose.[17] Unemployment was especially high among female weavers and shoe workers, both in sheer numbers and in proportion to the industries' total active population for each sex.[18] Indeed, the large numbers of women normally employed in these occupations may be linked to their willingness to accept the industries' low prevailing wages. Nonetheless, in these and other industries, men were newly afflicted by a problem that had previously touched mostly women, except for the demobilized war veterans who had faced brief delays in resuming their old jobs.[19] The new experience probably explains the male unionists' sudden preoccupation with an unemployment problem that had been easier to ignore in the past.

Other factors that affected unemployment were job specialty and the structure of enterprise. In Limoges, as the prefect assured the national authorities, the layoffs touched few "professional" shoe workers from prewar days.[20] Despite this attempt to play down the seriousness of the crisis, however, the real implication was that in a rapidly expanded industry, those most vulnerable were the semiskilled newcomers, not the skilled veterans who remained numerous in the industry and a dominant force in the trade unions. This pattern can be seen in the unemployment statistics for the shoe industry. As might be expected, the smaller companies did lay off larger percentages of their staffs[21] (see Figure 19). Yet most of these smaller establishments were not artisanal workshops but small factories (with from six to twenty employees) that had been launched during the war and staffed by the semiskilled newcomers who were now the first to lose their jobs. Moreover, despite the percentages, the larger *number* of layoffs occurred in the bigger companies, which comprised a greater portion of the normal work force. The crisis thus served not to accelerate the industry's concentration but in fact to slow it, especially as larger companies permanently cut back their staffs, while smaller firms survived the crisis and limped on (if they did not prosper) through the rest of the decade.[22]

The same pattern probably applied to the Loire metals industry, although it cannot be verified by company-level unemployment statistics.[23] In the textile industry, factory workers did remain more active, by producing synthetic textiles and elastics, than did the artisanal ribbon weavers, who faced the sharpest loss in demand for their goods.[24] Nonetheless, after the crisis the industry experienced an artisanal renaissance, as most weavers reopened their workshops and resolved to protect their long-standing skills and traditions.[25] The process of proletarianization was also slowed, as in other industries, by the reduced employment of less-skilled women or foreign workers so long as jobs remained scarce. These results echoed the effects of the wage cuts in restoring a balance between skilled and unskilled workers. The former may not have won back their prewar position as a so-called labor aristocracy, but they did widen the gap that had been narrowed by technical and financial changes during and after the war.

These economic patterns also influenced the course of labor politics during and after the recession. Parallel to the layoffs, the biggest losses in potential union membership occurred in the larger companies, whereas fewer skilled artisans lost their jobs or their inclination to unionize. Even in the Loire textile industry, where the weavers' union was badly hurt by the crisis, it survived until better times, whereas the new "red" union of factory workers disappeared.[26] In most unions, as memberships dwindled, the shock of crisis served to sharpen the militancy of remaining unionists, with their artisanal skills and their syndicalist traditions. Conversely, the crisis dulled the mass unionization of the less-skilled factory workers whom the Communist Party sought to recruit.

The Response to the Crisis: Unionization and Strikes

Beyond the economic reality of the crisis, still more significant was how it was perceived by union members and militants and how it affected the course of the labor movement. A common argument among unionists was that the wave of wage cuts and factory layoffs constituted a "plot" or "blackmail" by employers to extort longer working hours for the same low incomes and thus to dismantle the eight-hour day. Perhaps, some militants also argued, the crisis was also deliberately timed to exploit the May strike failure and subsequent factional squabbles, which made it all the more difficult for the unions to stand firm against "the patronal offensive."[27] It is hardly likely that the employers did bring on the crisis intentionally, but they may nonetheless have coordinated their responses in order to minimize the risk of labor strikes or other protests. In any case, as some militants also acknowledged, the employers seemed far more united, in patronal unions and associations, than were the workers and their representatives, for whom the crisis could hardly have come at a worse time.[28]

Perhaps surprisingly, not all organized workers even opposed the principle of reduced wages. Some "independent" (or "yellow") unionists found that "reasonable" wage cuts might be a legitimate way to improve French industry's competitive position. The same group, which had previously denounced the eight-hour-day law as harmful if applied in France exclusively, now also welcomed modifications of that law to permit workers to earn overtime pay.[29] (Proponents of this argument conveniently forgot that any benefit would be canceled by a lowered hourly wage.) Except for this conservative fringe, most unionists refused to assume the burden of lower costs to boost sales volumes, when employers might instead modernize their methods and equipment or accept lower profits for themselves.[30] Indeed, as the Loire ribbon weavers insisted, even in the unlikely event that the capitalists cut prices by the same margin as the wage cuts, their rate of earnings would still increase (while the raw total remained the same).[31]

Most unionists also regarded past wage gains as now beyond negotiation as *"positions acquises."* For example, the unions had insisted since 1919 that the eight-hour day be applied with no reductions in daily income, and also that cost-of-living supplements be defined as wage increases in order to make them harder to cancel if and when living costs declined.[32] The perception that living costs were not in fact declining made wage cuts all the less tolerable, especially since wages seemed always to trail behind, not to cause, any price increases. In one writer's view, the rumored *"vague de baisse"* was merely a *"blague de baisse,"* with reductions visible only in workers' pay envelopes.[33] Moreover, any possible benefit from wage reductions would be more than canceled by the drop in buying power; instead, many argued, wages should be increased to stimulate demand for surplus goods.[34]

Despite their nearly universal opposition to wage cuts, however, workers and unions proved little able to prevent such reductions. In the Limoges shoe industry, unionists first voted by more than a three to one margin to reject a 10 percent cutback, but they soon changed their minds out of fear that any protest or delay might provoke still larger pay cuts, as already experienced in one large factory after the failure of an attempted strike.[35] Similarly, the Loire coal miners proposed only a smaller reduction rather than reject the idea altogether.[36] Among ribbon weavers, those in Saint-Etienne wished to stand firm, but they were outvoted by those in rural districts, where unemployment was especially intense.

Soon the weavers began to undercut even the lowered pay scale, as desperation for work at any price caused union discipline to break down.[37]

As this case illustrated, the fear of unemployment was far graver to most workers than the prospects, however grim, of reduced wages. The two problems were of course closely linked: as militants perceived it, layoffs were part of the "plot" by employers to smash the unions, slash wages, and sabotage the eight-hour day.[38] Whatever the plan, loss of a job did make most workers far too insecure to be able to protest. As one militant phrased it, "One cannot walk off the job when one has no job."[39] Unemployment also undermined labor solidarity by making workers desperate enough to accept pay cuts, to work as strikebreakers, and in general to fight one another for scarce jobs rather than to unite successfully against the bourgeoisie. Attempts multiplied to restrict the employment of foreign workers and the training of new apprentices.[40] Workers also found it difficult to refuse to work supplementary hours, even if this denied jobs to others or aggravated the overproduction that Marxists still saw as the fundamental capitalist disease.[41]

The effect of the economic crisis was thus to weaken the labor movement, both by draining away union memberships and by minimizing strike effectiveness. Overall, the CGT lost more than half its 1.6 million members between early 1920 and late 1921; comparable declines occurred in the UDs of the Haute-Vienne and the Loire.[42] Some unions showed even sharper losses: the Loire miners' federation, a highly corporative body, lost only about one-fourth of its 5,200 members, but Saint-Etienne's precarious metalworkers' union, which had boasted 1,500 members at the end of the war, sank to a reported low of 14 members before it revived somewhat under new leadership in late 1921.[43] Some of these losses were no doubt linked to the effects of the May 1920 strike failure, although reports were too incomplete or infrequent to reveal the timing and probable source of the declines. In the case of the Limoges shoe union, however, figures do show a drop from 3,400 to 1,000 members over the course of 1920, as a result of both the May events and the first stages of the economic crisis, and then a further drop to 500 members as the crisis continued through the fall of 1921.[44]

As established unions were shrinking, some marginal unions disappeared altogether. In the Loire, where many former unions had existed only on paper, UD membership declined from a reported 121 unions in early 1920 to 98 unions at the end of the next year, and the authorities regarded even this latter figure as inflated beyond reality.[45] Among the losses were four small metals and construction workers' unions in the Firminy area, plus the recently formed union of factory silk workers at Saint-Etienne.[46] Even in the Haute-Vienne, where most unions proved more durable, the UD lost 7 of its 48 member unions. As an example, the construction union in Limoges, faced with a wage cut and with high unemployment, ceased to exist between 1922 and 1924.[47]

As unions weakened, strike activity in 1921 also reached a nadir. Strike frequency nationwide fell to approximately one-fourth of the previous year's total, and the numbers dropped still more sharply to a mere ten strikes in the Loire and five in the Haute-Vienne (see Figure 9). Most of these were small-scale affairs that involved a single company and lasted no more than a few days, or even several hours. Rare exceptions, such as a month-long strike of paper workers in the Haute-Vienne and a one-day general strike of coal miners in the Loire plus twenty-two other departments, meant that remaining cases accounted for even fewer of the already low totals of strike participants and working-days lost.[48]

Although the strikes affected a diverse array of industries, some industries were conspicuous by their absence (see figures 10–11). No strikes were reported among Haute-Vienne shoe or glove workers, despite the wage cuts imposed.[49] The Loire metallurgical strikes (three in the Saint-Etienne basin, plus one in Roanne) touched mostly a small group of bolt-makers, not the steelworkers or the cycle and gun makers who had been relatively strike-prone in the past. Even the Limoges porcelain industry, spared the worst hardships of the crisis, had only one small strike as compared to the larger movements of previous years, including a conflict among twenty-five companies in October 1920. This time, moreover, the union's moderation was not the mark of cordiality or past successes, because the October movement had met sharp patronal resistance and had failed to win most of its demands.[50·]

In this and later cases, the employers' intransigence resulted in part from the surplus of unsold stock, which made them willing (if not eager) to suspend production. Such intransigence, plus labor disunity, explains the high failure rate of strikes during the recession: approximately two-thirds of the year's strikes in the Loire and Haute-Vienne (half of those in France nationally) failed to yield even a compromise solution, compared to only one-fourth (locally and nationally) for the years 1917 through 1920 (see Figure 12). Of the rare local exceptions, a surprising two (one in each department) achieved wage *increases,* but most strikes were futile attempts to resist wage cuts or to protest the firing of workers who had been dismissed, in all probability, for leading a labor dispute.[51] Such defensive acts are characteristically doomed to failure. Indeed, given the weak unions and the dismal economic context, it may be more surprising that strikes succeeded—or occurred—at all.[52]

Toward the Schism: New Controversies on the Left

Much of the response to the recession was virtually unanimous across all factions of the labor movement. Whether Communist or Socialist, "revolutionary" or reformist, most workers shared a common resentment of their employers or the public authorities and a common inability to do much to improve their fate. Despite these parallels, major differences existed and grew among the factions, especially between Communists and syndicalists, as they debated strategies and tactics appropriate in a time of economic disarray.

With their ability to strike at a low ebb, unionists faced a choice between two main alternatives. Either they could maintain a strict defensive posture to minimize hardships and preserve the unions until their prospects brightened, or they could adopt more aggressive means, such as the forceful occupation of the factories, on the model of earlier experiments in Italy.[53] According to the latter tactic, workers faced with layoffs would simply refuse to leave the factories and instead assume the management of the industries for themselves. The idea was an extension of the argument that the employers had contrived the unemployment crisis for their own benefit and could not be trusted to operate the factories in the general interest. Only a handful of militants, mostly anarchists and anarcho-syndicalists, endorsed such tactics in a desperate enthusiasm for direct action. Nonetheless, the idea offered a distinct alternative to conventional tactics, whether Communist or reformist, which seemed equally ineffectual in syndicalist eyes.

The idea of seizing the factories by force was sponsored in part by Auguste Herclet, secretary of the textile workers' union at Vienne (Isère). In January 1921, Herclet proposed the tactic in a circular to nearby unions in the southeastern region, thereby opening debate on the issue among syndicalists in the Loire. While Lyon militants apparently approved Herclet's initiative, those in the Loire responded much less favorably. Most enthusiastic were the anarchists, including Jean Seigne and his fellow metalworkers; anarchist Charles Flageollet had also proposed similar tactics in the past. Those closer to the Communist Party, such as Bourse and UD leaders Arnaud and Lorduron, called instead for rebuilding the unions before launching such a venture.[54] Yet even Arnaud—who quit the party in 1922 to protest its role in the CGTU—switched then to a more vigorous stance, for sabotage if necessary to defend the eight-hour workday.[55] In Limoges, the Communist-led CSR did endorse the principle of factory seizures; the gesture sparked no immediate controversy between the unions' Communist and syndicalist wings.[56]

The proposed tactic was a classic example of syndicalist direct action. It was designed to substitute for conventional strikes, which Herclet insisted were "impossible" in times of unemployment and which even in better times were now too familiar to arouse any "fear" among the bourgeoisie.[57] Since parties and parliaments could likewise offer no cure for unemployment, the tactic would be conducted by the revolutionary CSRs acting alone. The tactic would also rely on local or regional initiative in order to circumvent the passivity of centralized leaderships, as Herclet explained both in his circular and at a regional conference held in March.[58] Nor was the idea mere empty rhetoric, one of countless resolutions that, as Loire anarchists had complained, the unions liked to pass but never followed. In April, textile unionists at Vienne did briefly occupy the factories to protest a threatened wage cut, and secretary Herclet was arrested for his role in the episode. As Herclet reported, however, the seizures lasted only a few hours or at most a full day; by evening the protests had ended. More like a mere "demonstration" than a step toward insurrection, the act aimed simply to teach employers "a lesson" and to inspire workers toward further action later on.[59]

As an alternative to strikes, the tactic retained the distant goal of total social revolution. Indeed, Herclet substituted the phrase *"la Grande Occupation Générale pour la Révolution"* for the conventional concept of the general strike.[60] The eventual goal was "workers' control" of industry, to be achieved once the workers permanently replaced the capitalist managers. A more immediate goal, however, was mere participation in management by means of workshop committees, or *"comités d'atelier."* These committees, Herclet admitted, did not differ greatly from those proposed by the reformist Alphonse Merrheim, or even those organized by Socialist Minister Albert Thomas during the war. Both programs would allow workers and employers to meet together to discuss wages and hours, hiring and firing, and workshop regulations. Both would also permit enough scrutiny of daily operations for workers to see how, without cutting wages, productivity might be heightened and costs trimmed. A main difference was that syndicalists wanted a role in other managerial questions, such as quality control, prices, and investments, that did not directly concern workers now but that would train them for later responsibilities once they assumed control of the entire economy. A second difference was that syndicalists planned to proceed by force if necessary and not rely on patronal consent.[61]

The concepts of workers' control and workshop committees also resembled the idea of *soviets* in Communist strategy. Communist-syndicalists Gaston Monmousseau and Pierre Monatte endorsed similar methods, and Herclet himself later became "a full-fledged Leninist."[62] Indeed, the syndicalists' strategy implied a willingness to try new tactics and institutions, in recognition that old-fashioned unionism might no longer suffice. As such, the issue appears to mark a phase in the abandonment of the Amiens Charter; if so, the change still resulted from the economic crisis of 1921 and not the strike failure of May 1920, which syndicalists denied had put their own strategies and methods to the test.[63] Instead, the syndicalists were determined to renovate their program without adopting Communist methods, without agreeing that party strategy alone was effective and up-to-date.

In view of these qualifications, the uniqueness of the syndicalists' own economic program should not be exaggerated. Like reformists, they welcomed short-term benefits within the capitalist system, as long as these did not strengthen the regime and weaken the workers' zeal for revolution.[64] Like the Communists, the syndicalists also searched for new ways to mobilize the masses who were unaroused by union activities in the past.[65] Still, the issue of factory seizures showed the syndicalists' impatience with their rivals' stress on organization and planning for the future, now that economic difficulties doomed immediate action to probable failure. Among Communists, this caution was marked in international terms by Lenin's New Economic Policy, by his distrust for "infantile" ultra-leftism, and by the Comintern's general efforts to take stock for future action now that the first wave of revolutionary agitation had passed.

In the view of some syndicalists, the party's current outlook went beyond defensiveness to outright inertia. With surprising enthusiasm, the party endorsed a variety of reforms or, as Limoges Communists preferred to call them, "immediate gains."[66] To preserve appearances, party members sought to clothe these reforms in revolutionary verbiage, by insisting, for example, that the eight-hour-day law was a "revolutionary" achievement, not an attempt by the Chamber to forestall a larger confrontation. Still, to protect this achievement, the party did little but urge the government to enforce the law.[67] In response, the Loire's dissident Communist Emile Arnaud called for sabotage, and not mere words, to defend the shortened workday, while he also speculated that "the spread of misery" might hasten the revolution. He seems not, however, to have concluded that material reforms might do more harm than good.[68] Other anarchists and syndicalists sought to outdistance the Communists by demanding instead a six-hour day.[69]

Even when the party took a harder line, it backed its words with little action. Party leaders did denounce the government's new tax on wages, but it took the syndicalists, led by Monmousseau and Herclet, to organize a *"grève de l'impôt,"* in which the unions collected the tax bills and returned them to the authorities unpaid.[70] In the Loire, the UD attempted such a strike, but by the end of 1921 only the anarchist-led unions of leather workers and textile dyers had joined it.[71] Although they may not have opposed the tactic, the Communists gave it little priority; they chose instead to work through parliament or to publish angry articles in *L'Humanité.*[72]

Despite these limits, it should not be inferred that Communist policy had become simple reformism, just like that of the CGT majority. Party members did come out squarely against the tax on wages, which the CGT rejected only "as currently applied."[73] They likewise scorned the CGT's response to threatened wage cuts—when the miners' union proposed only a smaller reduction—as a typical majoritarian "reform."[74] More fundamentally, the Communists saw their own reforms as steps toward an ultimate revolution, while true reformists sought only "class collaboration" and "social peace."[75] Indéed, these terms were sometimes voiced by CGT spokesmen—the Haute-Vienne's Marcel Vardelle and the Parisian Hyacinthe Dubreuil—but were more commonly heard from the independent unions or the Church-oriented CFTC.[76]

Nor did the Communists maintain their reformism once the economic crisis had ended. Later on, after Bolshevization, the party staunchly denounced the proposed "rationalization" of the economy, which some reformists accepted, as the worst proof of their support for class collaboration and their willingness to strengthen the capitalist regime.[77] In the short run, however, the party's line was more defensive than aggressive, and content to compete with reformists by claiming to offer the best reforms. The aim was to advance its political interests, and to recruit party members and left-wing unionists, while biding its time until resuming the offensive. This rivalry was especially acute where reformists still held ample influence, such as in the Haute-Vienne or among coal miners in the Loire.

Political priorities may indeed have overshadowed the economic crisis. At its national congress in December, the party failed even to discuss industrial policy and filled its agenda instead with issues of agricultural policy, national defense, electoral strategy, and—above all—relations with the trade unions.[78] This inaction was sure to frustrate the syndicalists, who were already dismayed by the party's attempts to infiltrate the unions and eventually to seize control. At least in its current guise, Communist policy did not seem to substantiate the claim that a sufficiently revolutionary party now existed to lead the unions. These tensions widened the gulf between syndicalists and Communists just as the CGT schism approached.

The economic crisis thus hastened the schism while it altered the balance among the CGT's left-wing factions. In sheer numerical terms, the crisis probably weakened the anarchist movement: in the Loire, the scarcity of jobs—especially in metallurgy—reportedly forced many anarchists to leave the region.[79] Nonetheless, those who remained in the weakened unions now preferred "direct action" to prolonged inertia and favored a schism to purge those "counterrevolutionaries" who might hold the unions back. These shifts do not appear in the votes at CGT congresses, which measure only the relative size of the majority and minority factions, but they can be detected in union debates and especially in the growing sentiment for a schism that even the Communists sought to avoid.

The votes also give a misleading view of the size of the factions. Without proportional representation, which Loire unionists still rejected, a small union could swing the vote leftward, even as large unions remained aligned with the center or the right.[80] By July 1921, at the CGT's Lille congress, the left had won more than 700 new votes, nearly enough to overturn the old majority, but more the result of switched votes in smaller unions than of any real gain in mass support.[81] Here again, the economic crisis played a key role as it sharpened the militancy of smaller unions. Such militants may also have wished to provoke the schism while their influence was at a peak, before it waned with the return of economic prosperity and larger-scale unionization. Launched when union membership was at a nadir, the schism expressed the goals not of most workers, in or outside the unions, but of a small revolutionary avant-garde.

Chapter 9

A Schism of Desperation: The Birth of the CGTU

Triggered both by strike failure and by a year-long economic crisis, the labor schism at the end of 1921 was a gesture not of strength but of profound weakness. As membership losses magnified the role of the minority camp, and as extremists turned to violent methods to compensate for their lack of numbers, so the now-threatened majority chose to risk a schism rather than lose control of the whole CGT. The schism itself further weakened the movement by forcing a choice between rival confederations and by alienating members who thought partisan disputes irrelevant or dangerous to their own material interests. The new CGTU claimed to promote "unity" against the divisive influence of Socialist politics, but it soon found itself sharply divided internally once the loss of a common reformist opponent allowed the fragile left-wing alliance to break down.

Although conflicts among anarchists, syndicalists, and Communists had precipitated the schism, the actual rupture occurred between the reformist majority, which had barely survived the Lille congress in July, and the combined forces of the left-wing minority, organized in the CSRs. The latter groups comprised in embryonic form the new left-wing confederation as it took shape between the fall of 1921 and the CGTU's first congress, held at Saint-Etienne in June 1922. By that time, with the process of schism finally consummated in the local unions and in the departmental and industrial federations, both the balance of forces and the general composition of the rival bodies had become quite apparent. The left had won clear control not only of the Loire and the Haute-Vienne labor movements but also, at last, of the majority of French unions, especially as union memberships reached a nadir in 1922.

The process of schism showed the depth of local antagonisms that pitted one union faction against another. Still, despite these antagonisms, and despite the quick victory of the left, it was clear that most unionists had rallied to the new organization for reasons other than sheer enthusiasm for the Communist Party or the Third International. Special circumstances—such as local strikes, the power of local personalities, or even the weight of a "bandwagon" effect—counted for more, in the unionists' choices, than did the abstract polemics of national or international leaders, whatever their partisan philosophy. Those who joined the CGTU favored revolutionary over reformist programs but often failed to agree on party-union relations, an issue that the debates of 1921 had left unresolved. Nonetheless, by the time of the Saint-Etienne congress, opinion had begun to crystallize on the issue and conflicts had hardened within the new CGTU.

"The Crime of Exclusions and Schism": *Toward the* Congrès Unitaire

By late 1921 a trade-union schism was all but inevitable, however reluctant the two sides may have been to precipitate the rupture. Since the previous winter, left-wingers had threatened a schism if they failed at Lille to overturn the reformist majority, and the CGT's nervous leaders had in turn sought to punish the left by expelling those unions that joined the dissident CSRs. These expulsions enabled left-wingers to blame the right wing for the "criminal" schism that jeopardized the ideal of syndicalist unity and that risked further weakening the unions against the economic crisis and the apparent capitalist offensive. In response, the majority retorted that the dissidents "excluded themselves" by the very act of joining an organization that violated CGT statutes and that aimed to "destroy" the unions by subordinating them to the Communist Party and the Profintern or ISR.[1]

There is some irony in the majority's professions of outrage at the prospect of ties to the Communist Party. Although Guesdist unionists saw no conflict in their own party membership, they bitterly opposed the right of Socialist (later Communist) Party secretary Frossard to address the CGT congress at Orléans, a right that the anarchists, paradoxically, demanded for themselves.[2] Socialists, likewise, had been urging the unions toward closer ties with their own party, especially after the strike failure in May 1920, but they now took a strict "hands-off" position, if only to distance themselves from the Communist strategy of *noyautage*.[3] In response, left-wingers sneered that their rivals' lip-service to trade-union autonomy was just a ruse in the fight against communism and revolution.[4] The same argument warned anarcho-syndicalists not to fall into the reformists' trap before the schism was consummated, while it also foreshadowed later epithets like "anarcho-reformism" that condemned all the party's enemies in a single breath.[5] Still, beneath the polemics, both Communists and reformists had the same goal: to win over the mass of undecided unionists who, as controversy raged, might conceivably lean either way.

The CGT's campaign against the left-wing opposition climaxed in the move to expel the CSRs' member unions. These sanctions, victims claimed, showed not only the majority's intolerance of dissent but, worse, the CGT's desire to curry official favor so as to escape charges of subversion and a court-ordered dissolution after the May 1920 general strike.[6] The expulsions, proposed but voted down at the Orléans congress, were formally endorsed by the CGT's National Committee at meetings in November 1920 and February 1921. The decision, which was not immediately carried out, reaffirmed the left-wingers' determination to avoid a schism at least until after the Lille congress, which, they said, alone could ratify the plans of the National Committee.[7] Their hopes for victory faded, however, when the committee advanced the date of the congress, allegedly to prevent the opposition from organizing in time.[8]

More than abstract polemics, the issue of exclusion crystallized local opinion for or against the CGT majority. A natural sense of solidarity rallied support for the sanctions' victims, even among those hitherto ambivalent toward the CSRs. In the Loire, which enforced the rule that the CSRs include only full-fledged union members and no outside anarchist or Communist "politicians," the UD voted nonetheless to allow those expelled from the CGT to maintain their local affiliations; this vote was hailed by left-wingers elsewhere as a step closer to schism.[9] In the Haute-Vienne, in a rare spirit of vengeance, the UD further resolved to expel one reformist union for each revolutionary union excluded by the CGT.[10]

While there is no record of which Haute-Vienne unions faced expulsion, those in the Loire included the construction and leather workers' unions at Saint-Etienne, plus a union of municipal employees and three coal miners' unions in nearby towns of the Loire basin. The wave of sanctions aroused the UD, which had abstained on the issue in February, to vote a protest in October against this "criminal" and "divisive" act. Even the Firminy miners' union, although still aligned with the majority, abstained rather than defend the expulsions. Only the teachers' delegate voted approval, much to the professed astonishment of his colleagues.[11] After the vote, cynical police observers attributed the leaders' careful stance to their desire to stay in power, not to a sincere wish to avoid schism.[12] Nonetheless, a genuine desire for unity, shared by nearly all but the anarchist faction, seemed more important to most unionists than did the polemics that threatened to divide the working class.

The depth of this sentiment allowed the minority to gain sympathy by posing as saviors of unity even while both sides advanced closer to schism. The left could blame the majority not only for the expulsions but for preferring a schism to the threat of losing their posts. Leftists liked to point out, for example, that Georges Dumoulin—who claimed to have sacrificed his own revolutionary convictions in 1918 for the sake of labor unity—now sponsored the CGT's program of exclusions, and that he refused to rule out a schism if the Lille congress approved adhesion to Moscow.[13] Leftists also accused their rivals of precipitating a schism in order to establish new unions and federations where they had already lost their old majority. In the railroad federation, for example, when the two sides contested the vote at their national congress, left-wingers elected their own new secretary, Pierre Sémard, and forcibly seized the federation's headquarters; they then complained bitterly when CGT officers refused to investigate the conflict and immediately recognized the reformist leadership.[14] In turn, the CGT's National Committee voted to allow moderate wings from expelled unions to form separate groups and rejoin the confederation, thereby also adding their votes to the majoritarian camp. Such steps had already been taken by a group of Saint-Etienne construction workers, led by a local member of the Republican Socialist Party.[15] These actions blurred responsibility for a schism that neither side professed to welcome but that both seemed unwilling to prevent.

In their stated outrage at the threatened schism, left-wingers convened a special *Congrès Unitaire* at Paris in December. At this congress, delegates even offered to withdraw from the CSRs, in order to avoid a schism —or to ensure that the blame for a split still fell to the majority camp.[16] Some hardliners had initially opposed such a withdrawal as a "tactical error" or capitulation that might still fail to preserve unity. But even the most conciliatory—with the notable exception of Pierre Monatte—recognized at last that the time for a schism had come.[17]

The congress itself, held in defiance of CGT statutes, was an admission, if not another cause, of the schism. Left-winger Gaston Monmousseau had tried to assure those present that they could not *all* be expelled from the CGT; exclusions could occur only *"par grignotage"* (in small bites) or the proletariat would protest.[18] Minoritarians also called on the *majority* to attend the congress, to preserve the appearance of legality, just as during the antiwar congress at Saint-Etienne in May 1918. Some majoritarians may indeed have done so, because nearly 200 more unions were represented at Paris than had voted with the left at the Lille congress. These unions also joined in voting for the final resolution at Paris, which passed unanimously except for two votes.[19] If these gains are added to the left's tally, they give it at last an absolute majority of the unions, including victories in nine UDs and one industrial federation that had sided with the moderates at Lille.[20]

Despite these gains, there were also cases of previously minoritarian unions that did not attend the Paris congress, perhaps because they did not wish to consummate the schism or risk the threat of exclusion. An example was the Limoges porcelain union, the "bastion of reformism" that had finally switched to the minority only on the eve of the Lille congress. (This union did, however, join the CGTU.)[21] Nor did all unions that attended the Paris congress adhere later on to the new confederation. Still, the balance of forces in December was quite revealing: the left dominated forty-eight of ninety-two departmental unions and seventeen of forty-three federations, as compared to the forty-two UDs and fourteen federations that later joined the CGTU.[22]

Nonetheless, votes at congresses and later adhesions, however important in their own right, were not always reliable measures of the opinion of the union membership, much less of the mass of workers the unions represented. At best, union votes spoke only for the portion of workers who attended the union meetings, not for those who stayed at home or — worse — walked out of a meeting before the vote or quit the union altogether. In the Loire, the UD's vote to attend the Paris congress caused special controversy. Majoritarians later protested that the UD executive committee had made the decision on its own and then had presented the hastily convened general assembly — which alone could authorize the move — with a *fait accompli*. At the assembly, UD delegates were also said to have voted solely on their personal initiative without prior mandates from their unions.[23] Those unions that opposed the vote and refused to attend the congress later joined the reconstituted CGT in the department. Not all those represented at the congress may have intended to quit the CGT, however, and some may even—as reformists later claimed—have participated *"à leur insu."*[24]

Similar controversies concerned the votes within the UDs and industrial federations. In the railroad federation, which ruptured early, left-wingers had complained that even with a slight edge at the last national congress, they could not win control of the key federal offices; these were named by regional bureaus, most of which were still in majoritarian hands.[25] Leftists also contested their narrow loss at the metalworkers' federal congress, where Alphonse Merrheim had been reelected "by the defection of a handful of delegates," or simply by his personal charisma, despite the left-wing sentiment that member unions soon showed at Lille.[26] At the porcelain workers' federal congress, national secretary Jacques Tillet was reelected by a comfortable margin, but the vote on political orientation was evenly split; left-wingers further claimed that their own votes stood for the larger unions and hence a majority of union members.[27] Thus the left wing claimed a moral victory even in marginal federations, while the moderates held firm in few major industrial federations other than those for transports and mines.[28]

If the minority may indeed have been underrepresented in some federations, it was probably overrepresented in the departmental unions. Most UDs gave an equal vote to all member unions, regardless of size. Even the heavily reformist UD du Nord would have swung to the left at the Lille congress had it not been for the local rule of proportional representation.[29] In the Haute-Vienne and the Loire, where the large porcelain workers' and most miners' unions were now aligned with the minority, the voting system no longer made much of a difference. In other UDs, however, the left's hold was tenuous at best. Member unions varied widely in size, more so in UDs than in most federations, so that votes here were especially misleading. In fact, of the nine UDs newly won over between the Lille and the Paris congresses, six failed to join the CGTU. In addition, the more recent converts seem to have been those in which the number of member unions had most grown since 1918—probably those with phantom unions deliberately created to give the left wing some extra votes.[30]

If the voting system helped to inflate the minority's growth at the national congresses, it also deepened the frustration at their failure to unseat the old majority. Once the system appeared to work to their disadvantage, leftists concluded that only a schism could break the right's unfair domination. Especially unfair, they contended, was the equal representation of UDs and federations on the CGT's National Committee, when federations were the "bastions of reformism" while UDs were far "closer in spirit" to the mass of unionists and "better expressed their will."[31] Indeed, the left was much stronger in the UDs than in the federations, but this had little to do with the will of the masses. Despite its slight majority of union votes, the left remained concentrated in the smaller unions, heavily anarcho-syndicalist in orientation, and infused with the UDs' spirit of local autonomy.[32] It also gained far more from frustration at the CGT's rules and regulations than from positive sympathy for the Communist Party. These traits appeared both in the process of schism, as it progressed after the congress at Paris, and in the factional squabbles that still raged within the new CGTU.

"A Salutary Purge": The Schism is Consummated

Even after the congress at Paris, the CGT schism was still not official. As left-wingers defined it, the CGT *"unitaire"*—the last word an adjective, not yet part of a new name—was still only a provisional liaison among unions that wished their unity to be preserved.[33] These unions had offered to withdraw from the CSRs in return for a promise that the CGT would hold an emergency congress early in the new year. Not until the CGT refused, and moved to expel all unions represented at the Paris congress, did leftists draft a new set of statutes and plan a constituent congress to open at Saint-Etienne in June.[34] Additionally, it was unclear what the balance of forces would be after the UDs and federations consummated the rupture. By the time of the Saint-Etienne congress, the new body claimed to outweigh the CGT's remnants by a margin of 350,000 to 250,000 members. Any victory, though, referred just to the flattened total of union memberships and would not last once unionization rebounded in 1923.[35]

After months of debate on heady ideological issues, the actual rupture came as individual unions decided from which body to purchase membership cards and stamps for the new year. Unlike the party schism, which occurred from the top downward, the union split seemed thereby to develop from the bottom up.[36] Not all unions, in fact, immediately succumbed to the pressure of schism. Limoges lithographers, frequent critics of the Communist Party's "intolerance," voted to remain in the CGT but then quickly moved on to a more urgent matter: limiting the in-

flux of new apprentices into the struggling trade. A minority disapproved
of remaining in the CGT but agreed to obey the decision, apparently recognizing that their small union, with some fifty members, could not survive if ruptured in two.[37] The dispute was more heated in the typesetters'
union. An initial vote favored the CGT, but left-wingers demanded inclusion of another seventeen ballots from members denied a vote because
they were too far behind in their payment of dues. As the conflict raged,
CGT loyalists walked out of the meeting in protest; the decision to join
the CGTU was thus made only by those remaining, while the opposition
set up its own affiliate with the CGT.[38]

In the Loire, the picture was further clouded when several unions
adopted a position of neutrality while waiting for matters to clarify or for
their federations to decide the issue for them. Even Saint-Etienne's metalworkers, despite their usual left-wing orientation, voted in a general assembly to buy their cards and stamps from both confederations; later on,
it was the union's executive council that voted to take stamps just from
the CGTU.[39] The UD leadership had also tried to maintain "autonomy"
until the first CGTU congress, in an effort to preserve local unity. Finally, a choice became necessary as the CGT refused to sell stamps to groups
that also ordered them from the opposition.[40] Neither side ultimately
had much patience for this professed neutrality, which seemed to stem
from indecision and not from a sincere desire to preserve unity. Said one
Bourse delegate, "For us, a union that remains neutral does not exist."[41]

The process of schism revealed that both sides usually preferred to
consummate the rupture rather than maintain a façade of unity or remain
in groups dominated by the opposition. Throughout the country, rival
unions and industrial and departmental federations were formed quickly
by those factions unwilling to follow majority rule. These decisions let
the *"Unitaires"* again blame reformists for the schism, especially where
most unions had voted to join the left-wing body, as in the Haute-Vienne
and the Loire. The issue was blurred, however, in cases where the national federation remained aligned with the old majority. For example,
among Limoges porcelain workers, the leader of the reconstituted CGT
union could argue, with some sincerity, that the blame lay not with his
own group but with the left-wingers, who had refused to take their cards
and stamps from the legally constituted federation in the CGT.[42]

Even *Unitaires* who had deplored the idea of rival unions in the same
trade or city soon proved equally anxious for schism when their own side
failed to win a majority. Left-wing miners set up a rival union at Firminy,

where the CGT remained ascendant, even while they condemned the opposition for forming its own unions elsewhere in the Loire.[43] Indeed, left-wingers may have triggered the initial split in the regional coal miners' union by expelling four leading reformists who had protested the results of previous internal elections.[44] Whatever the miners' commitment to corporative unity, partisan rivalries, if not deeper ideological differences, made a schism seem impossible to avoid.

In simplest terms, the schism occurred because both sides wanted it. Although they accepted no responsibility, both sides welcomed the split as a "salutary" measure to "purge" the movement of unhealthy elements. For the reformists, the schism completed the process, begun by the expulsions, of helping the CGT "consolidate itself morally" and healing the fissures caused, they said, by left-wing agitators.[45] Leftists in turn hailed the chance to "rid syndicalism of all the parasites that exploit it" and to strengthen unity and discipline, now that only "the serious and active elements are in our ranks."[46]

Even the Communists, who had long resisted a schism, soon agreed that the move, although "imposed by the reformists," was nonetheless "a great benefit" for the left.[47] Loire Communists in fact required party members to push for schism rather than stay in a CGT affiliate, although this rule contradicted the party's earlier pronouncements and its emerging doctrine of the "united front."[48] The Parisian Pierre Monatte did stay in the CGT, with the rest of his union, but his choice was later used against him as proof of a "petit-bourgeois" deviation.[49] This experience belied Monatte's previous claims that the reformists—or the anarcho-syndicalists—were alone to blame for the schism.[50] Indeed, as rival *Unitaires* began to attack one another, reformists nodded smugly that these recriminations vindicated the CGT.[51]

This reluctance to endorse, or sometimes even to consummate, the schism raises the question of why it occurred, especially among local unionists who may not have felt the urgency proclaimed by Parisian or Soviet ideologues. Local circumstances must have been especially influential in accounting for why the coal miners in the Loire and the porcelain and shoe workers in Limoges rallied to the left while their federations remained in the old CGT. In some cases, local unionists mouthed the rhetoric of national congresses and press editorials. Still, they based their decisions on local conflicts, local personalities, or a desire for local unity that sometimes outweighed the petty squabbles that threatened to drive them apart.

The case of the Loire construction workers' union, the first to proceed to a schism, showed how a local dispute took on ideological overtones but might well have sparked a rupture on its own. Since 1920, an air of scandal had touched UD and union secretary Henri Lorduron, accused of taking bribes from employers outside the Loire to foment local strikes that would free workers for those regions afflicted by a shortage of labor.[52] The implication that the strikes served no purpose for the workers had its own indirect partisan content, but the charges — which were never proven — gave dissidents a substantive reason to distrust Lorduron and his friends in the new CGTU.

In most cases, a left-wing leadership could practically guarantee that a union would join the new organization. In both departments, where the left had already won control of most local unions, members may simply have endorsed a virtual *fait accompli.* Among Saint-Etienne metalworkers, whose executive council reversed the general assembly's vote for neutrality, the membership could have disavowed the decision had it been sufficiently unpopular. Nonetheless, the procedure belied the assumption that the schism arose from the initiative of the rank and file. Even if not imposed from Paris, it seemed indeed imposed by local leaders, who made it, as the Limoges authorities charged, the act of the *syndicats,* not the *syndiqués.*[53]

Opponents also liked to point out that, with a few key exceptions, the groups that quit the CGT were mostly the small ones, those with "no more than a few hundred members."[54] True, the CGT owed much of its relative strength after the schism to its hold on a few large federations, including those for textiles and mining; but in turn, the CGTU controlled the large federations of metals and construction workers, railroad workers, and public service employees, and also claimed the support of the miners in "all the principal centers," including Alsace and Lorraine, the Nord, and the Loire (except for Firminy).[55] The old CGT proved so weak throughout the Loire basin that the reconstituted UD, first planned at Firminy, was headquartered instead at Roanne, also site of the rump Socialist federation. The UD included only nineteen unions, as against sixty-six in the CGTU, and it returned to Saint-Etienne only in 1927 when dissident *Unitaires* began to rejoin the CGT.[56]

The CGTU also gained broad support in Limoges, without the help of a large-scale Communist movement. Under Socialist leadership, the city council tried to dismiss the CGTU as an artificial and lifeless creation, and canceled the old Bourse's subsidy, while city councillor Marcel Var-

delle became secretary of the reconstituted CGT. Even though the new
Bourse received no subsidy, the city's evident favoritism allowed left-
wingers to denounce the new body in turn as a "phantom," "composed
uniquely of politicians," and hardly as faithful as it pretended to the
terms of the Amiens Charter.[57]

Further proof of the left's strength at Limoges came as all the city's major unions adhered to the new confederation. The nine unions that initially formed the reconstituted CGT were all in minor occupations and
ranged in size from 37 members in the union of pharmaceutical workers
to 187 members in the union of employees at the state-run Manufacture
des Tabacs.[58] In addition, the UD was said to have inflated its membership with twenty-six rural sections of *"cultivateurs,"* a key leader of
which was no farmer but an employee at *Le Populaire du Centre*.[59] Soon
other unions were formed among dissident ceramicists, shoe workers,
railroad workers, and typographers. Still, their leaders, including Vardelle, were not "workers" but city officials and other public employees
who, leftists claimed, had been active in their industries only "a long, a
very long time ago."[60]

In general, as *Unitaires* realized, the reorganized CGT attracted a large
share of white-collar employees. In both the Haute-Vienne and the Loire,
the unions of municipal and postal employees were among the few to
stay in the CGT. The influx of state *fonctionnaires,* especially after 1926
when their federation gave up its autonomy, compensated the CGT's earlier loss of working-class memberships and helped to confirm its political
moderation. In turn, the CGTU also drew strong minorities of teachers,
postal workers, and office workers, while it won a majority of railroad
employees. Indeed, the proportion of service employees nationwide was
nearly identical in the two confederations, and it continued to grow
through the late 1920s as recruitment among them stabilized and that of
industrial workers declined.[61]

The relative balance of forces between the two organizations may be
shown not only in the different trades that joined one or the other confederation but also in the membership levels in each trade once the individual unions had split. Of the major Loire and Haute-Vienne labor groups,
all but the metallurgists and the railroad workers sustained CGT unions
that were genuine alternatives to those of the CGTU[62] (see Figure 20).
Thus, the CGTU did not monopolize the cities' labor movements, but
neither body had yet achieved mass unionization of the scale reached
after 1936. Indeed, total unionization remained modest at best after the

schism, especially as those disgruntled by partisan politics abandoned unions altogether or joined independent or Catholic unions outside either CGT.[63]

Within given industries, it is hard to determine whether rival unions represented real sociological distinctions within the work force. Because its memberships generally remained more stable, the CGT may have drawn more of the highly skilled workers, but there is little evidence to support this inference directly.[64] In the Limoges shoe industry, a small group of skilled craftsmen were the first to seek the reconstitution of a CGT union. Still, the gesture failed for many months to reach fruition, and the new union won scant support in any category until after the subsequent split of the CGTU.[65] In the Loire coal mines, claimed one observer, the CGTU was stronger in the larger companies and the CGT stronger in the smaller companies; in fact, however, the Firminy mines, where the CGT flourished, were among the largest in the department.[66] In the long run, Communists hoped to make the larger industrial establishments, especially in metallurgy, the bastion of their new unionism. But these companies long resisted any form of unionization, while the smaller companies remained rife with anarcho-syndicalism, just as before the war.[67]

So far, then, the two confederations differed more in ideological than in sociological makeup. The choice of affiliation had come after partisan squabbles, amplified by local personalities, while the rank and file remained comparatively silent. Still, these quarrels articulated local interests, not just the noisy bombast of party leaders in Paris. Even where union leaders seemed to dictate the choices, those leaders had come to power during conflicts that made doctrinal distinctions meaningful in local terms. For example, the Limoges porcelain union had switched from reformist to left-wing leadership a few months after a major strike failure in October 1920.[68] Among Loire coal miners, who made the switch just after the CGT schism, the preceding wave of wage cuts had turned unionists against those whom left-wingers denounced as a gang of traitors who had given in without a proper fight.[69] These disputes expressed genuine policy differences between the two organizations, which seemed to verify the CGTU's claim to represent *"syndicalisme de lutte de classe,"* while the CGT stood merely for *"syndicalisme d'intérêt général."*[70]

Later on, sociological distinctions would deepen further, as the CGTU went through "Bolshevization" and sought greater proletarian recruitment. It then lost some of its skilled industrial or white-collar members, who opted instead for autonomy or for a return to the CGT. These conflicts also focused at first on practical issues, such as adhesion to the Profintern and relations with the Communist Party. As conflicts progressed, the disputes revealed deeper differences between these erstwhile allies in the new CGTU.

"Syndicalism in Danger":
The CGTU Congress at Saint-Etienne

In the months immediately after the CGT schism, the anarchists and syndicalists who had provoked the rupture were also the provisional leaders of the new organization. Because the *"Congrès Unitaire"* at Paris had not even acknowledged the formal founding of a new body, it postponed to a later congress the tasks of adopting statutes, electing officials, and declaring its political orientation. This congress was scheduled at Saint-Etienne, perhaps in the hope that the city's anarcho-syndicalist ambiance would strengthen the hand of the provisional CGTU Bureau. Instead, the congress marked an important Communist victory and the first stage in the movement's Bolshevization. Just as importantly, it marked the growth of a lively syndicalist opposition, which linked dissident Communists and left-wing unionists who were dismayed by changes both in the party and in the CGTU.

The factional conflicts that plagued the nascent organization had begun well before the schism to threaten the fragile anarchist-Communist alliance. Until the schism, party leaders had exhorted their allies not to "overdramatize" these differences or to confuse "the real issue": in the common fight against the reformists, the motto was *"Pas d'équivoque!"*[71] Conflicts crystallized, though, once the schism dispatched the common reformist enemy and once the party further clarified its own trade-union program. In response, angry syndicalists first abandoned the party and eventually quit the CGTU.

The first step toward framing a trade-union policy was the party's acceptance of the Comintern's Twenty-One Conditions, which required close union ties and the formation inside the unions of a Communist *"noyau"* (kernel) or militant vanguard. These instructions had until then remained largely a dead letter, resisted both by the party's own syndicalist faction and by those party centrists, like secretary Frossard, who refused to defer totally to Moscow's lead. Frossard was also a pragmatist, eager for a compromise to preserve the widest range of support in the unions just as in the party. Nonetheless, once the imminent schism shut out other distractions, and after the Third Comintern Congress challenged the party's revolutionary credentials, party leaders placed the trade-union question at the top of their agenda for the national congress at Marseille in December 1921. In his report to the congress, left-winger Amédée Dunois insisted that the unions were in no way "self-sufficient" and that the party must combat their "federalist, individualist and libertarian deviations."[72] This report may be seen as an effort to impose discipline on errant party members in the unions as the first step toward winning control over non-party members in the CGTU.

Although Dunois's report called only for party-union "coordination," not "subordination" or total loss of independence, it still aroused intense opposition both outside and inside the party. CSR national secretary Pierre Besnard, a leading libertarian syndicalist, launched a long-term campaign to defend the principles of federalism, thereby earning the epithet "anti-Communist" from Dunois's friends.[73] A group of Parisian syndicalists—joined by Louis Bert, until then the party's most ardent defender in the Limoges unions—also drafted a counter-motion to deny the party's role as the unions' "vanguard" and its right to interfere in their daily affairs.[74] The Haute-Vienne Communist Federation did vote to support Dunois's motion, but with a proviso that rejected any subordination of the unions to party dictate.[75] Loire Communists Ernest Lafont and Ferdinand Faure likewise feared that the motion would hinder their efforts to win trust in a traditionally hostile union atmosphere.[76]

Dissidents also quarreled with the Comintern's "united-front" strategy, similarly announced in December 1921.[77] This strategy, which sought renewed ties with Socialists and with reformist unionists, seemed to conflict with the reality of the schism, although, in fact, the Comintern had never favored the CGT split. While the strategy aimed to win mass support by restoring working-class unity, Frossard and his Loire supporters feared that the masses would be confused by the party's zigzags and compromises. The strategy threatened especially to weaken ties with the nascent CGTU, with which these Communists wished to cooperate, rather than go over its head to restore ties with workers still in the old CGT.[78]

Like the changes in union strategy, the united-front tactic proved more controversial as an issue of party discipline than of revolutionary doctrine. Thus the party's leftists were more ready to accept the compromise, and the tighter links to Moscow, than were those on the center or the right. This may explain why the French party was one of the policy's most intense opponents, even though it was hardly the most left-wing of Comintern groups.[79] Among its supporters, left-winger Paul Bouthonnier, new regional secretary for the Haute-Vienne, claimed that once the policy had passed the Comintern, the French party should not even debate it; however, he also found no ideological objections, as long as the schism had purged the reformists and condemned their "unpardonable errors."[80] Now that the job was done, he and other leftists agreed, it was time for new tactics — even electoral blocs and ministerial participation — to ensure the defeat of the bourgeoisie.[81]

Despite such shifts, according to proponents, the united-front tactic would not negate the schism by restoring organizational ties with reformist leaders; instead, it sought only the support of the masses to create a united front "from below." The party's images were openly aggressive: the masses would be "plucked" like chicken feathers from the reformist organisms; their leaders would be "swallow[ed]" by the left, who would "grimace" and "detest" the taste.[82] Unlike party leaders, unionists valued instead the tactic's potential for labor unity, which some workers were achieving in action over the heads of their own leaders. In that hope, the Communist-syndicalist Gaston Monmousseau grudgingly endorsed the new tactic, while Pierre Monatte, who had tried so hard to avoid a schism, quickly pledged his support.[83] Still, unity alone was not enough to quiet the doubts of those confused by the zigzag or unwilling to defer to Moscow's leadership. Thus, most Loire and Haute-Vienne union leaders remained firmly opposed to the new tactic, even if they did not immediately break with the Communist Party on these grounds.[84]

The syndicalists' response was temporarily blurred by the party's own indecision. While the party ratified the Dunois motion on union policy and began to debate the united-front tactic, it also elected a new group of centrists to its central committee, including the Loire's Ferdinand Faure. (In protest, Dunois and fellow leftists resigned.)[85] This new leadership left future union relations highly uncertain. Some syndicalists even twitted the party for presuming to direct the unions when it still was far from "revolutionary" in its own right.[86] Monmousseau professed to steer a neutral course between rival party factions on the grounds that these disputes concerned party members alone and would cause unnecessary divisions among the workers.[87] However precarious such neutrality, most unionists remained cordial to the party as long as it hesitated to apply Moscow's dictates and seemed to defend the unions' right to independence. Still, maybe Merrheim was right when he said that the party was playing a "double game" by promising the unions autonomy only until it was strong enough to take them over.[88] These debates foreshadowed the growing controversies of the future, especially during and after the CGTU's congress at Saint-Etienne.

More urgent than theoretical issues of party-union relations was the practical question of adhesion to the Profintern or Trade-Union International. This issue had also arisen well before the CGT schism but had been postponed, not resolved, at the congress at Lille. Shortly before that congress had opened, the Profintern had published its new statutes, triggering protests among unionists otherwise willing to accept an alliance with Moscow as a gesture of "proletarian unity" and as a means to revolutionize the unions. As a result, support for adhesion was much less vocal at Lille than at the Orléans congress in 1920, and the anarchosyndicalist current rose to temporary ascendancy. Even Pierre Monatte, the leading Communist-syndicalist spokesman, recognized the merit of some of these objections, although he called the conflict a "momentary halt" rather than a real setback to the progress of Communist unionism in France.[89]

Most troublesome was the prospect of "organic liaison" between the Profintern and the Third International, causing critics to fear that French unions would lose their traditional autonomy. The threat of union subordination to party dictate had appeared ever since the Comintern had issued its Twenty-One Conditions. Indeed, the decision to form the separate Trade-Union International can be seen as a compromise to appease the CGT's mistrust.[90] Still, the new body would have close ties, and some joint officials, with the Comintern and with the Soviet government. These ties were sustained in the resolution voted at the Profintern's first congress; the text was signed even by France's own delegates, although they were roundly criticized by syndicalists at home.[91] Despite these results, Frossard and Monatte still stressed the prospects for compromise — for cooperation without subordination, or a "moral" but not "organic" liaison. Frossard also denied that a strong labor movement could be dominated by the party: "Only the weak run a risk of subordination to the strong."[92] Party leaders further promised that their own intent was to respect the French unions' autonomy, while Communist-syndicalists affirmed that, despite all objections, France must rally to *"Moscou quand même!"*[93] Nonetheless, just as one faction drew closer to Moscow, another faction withdrew ever further, convinced that even "conditional" adhesion was too sharp an affront to the time-honored syndicalist traditions of France.

Most noteworthy in the latter faction was Pierre Besnard, the railroad unionist and current CSR general secretary. As a leading libertarian syndicalist, Besnard was a frequent spokesman on such issues as "workers' control" and the need for a genuinely revolutionary trade-union program. These views were compatible with, if not identical to, those of the Communist Party, and Besnard often published them in the party's newspaper *L'Humanité*. Not until the debates over the party's union policy did opponents perceive the extent of his "deviation" from orthodoxy.[94] Still, he had never wavered, as did the Communist-syndicalists, in his faith that the Amiens Charter needed no updating: that syndicalism was and would remain "self-sufficient" without the need for party ties.[95] Besnard agreed that the Amsterdam International was bankrupt, but he refused to accept the Moscow International as the only alternative. Instead, he helped to found and then headed a rival anarcho-syndicalist league at Berlin, the International Workingman's Association, or AIT. This new group was an example of the same taste for schism that had led Besnard to draft the "Pacte" in 1921 and to form the CGTSR in 1926. It also had more positive pretensions: to resurrect the idea of the First International, that "the emancipation of the workers will be achieved by the workers themselves."[96]

As head of the provisional CGTU Bureau, Besnard drafted a resolution opposed to membership in any international organization that compromised syndicalist autonomy by its ties to a political party. (In Besnard's view, the AIT would be no such violation, since the anarchists were not a "political" grouping; the Communists, and many reformists, predictably disagreed.)[97] At the Saint-Etienne congress, Besnard's motion received only 406 votes, against 743 for the rival Monmousseau motion, which called for conditional adhesion to Moscow. Since the PCF's Frossard and the ISR's Lozovsky, both present at the congress, seemed ready to compromise on the issue of "organic liaison," most unionists found Monmousseau's motion an adequate guarantee of syndicalist autonomy.[98] The Besnard motion did win support in some unlikely places, including many unions in the Haute-Vienne.

The Haute-Vienne unions had repeatedly endorsed conditional adhesion to Moscow on the grounds that adhesion, as secretary Bert maintained, served to complete, not contradict, the Amiens Charter.[99] To these unionists the dangers of Socialist reformism, a real influence in the region, were of more pressing concern than the threat of union ties to party politics, which most unionists had readily accepted in the past. But as if shifting gears, once the labor schism had apparently resolved the first problem, local unionists turned instead to the second question and no longer accepted its easy answers. Unions that only weeks before had approved "conditional adhesion" now backed the Besnard resolution by a vote of twenty-seven to one and condemned the one contrary ballot (from the typesetters' union) as a "betrayal" of syndicalist autonomy.[100] Most surprising was the shift among Limoges railroad workers: at their national congress, Louis Bert led the opposition to Monmousseau, although the federation finally approved adhesion by a margin of three to two.[101] Others in Limoges who would have accepted adhesion demanded extra precautions; for example, the porcelain unionists insisted that the Profintern's headquarters be transferred from Moscow.[102] These contrary votes showed how far the once cordial syndicalist-Communist alliance had already crumbled in Limoges.

The Loire's votes also showed signs of changes. Despite their traditional mistrust of the Communist Party, Loire unions supported the Monmousseau motion by a vote of thirty to twenty-three. Individual votes were rather predictable: the Saint-Etienne metals and construction unions voted for the Besnard resolution, while the Loire's miners, railroad workers, and teachers—and the metalworkers at Firminy and Le Chambon-Feugerolles—voted with Monmousseau.[103] But the Saint-Etienne metalworkers had also previously approved the Profintern, at the time of the Lille congress.[104] As in the Haute-Vienne, these votes revealed new alignments in the party and union movements, as the Communists lost strength in some sectors while they seemed to be gaining support in other industries and regions in France.

Besides debating adhesion to the Profintern, the CGTU also had to adopt a new set of statutes. One problem was whether to include as a primary goal "the disappearance of the State." Again, Monmousseau represented the Communist-syndicalist viewpoint, while Besnard argued the libertarian position. In part, the conflict echoed earlier disputes on the nature of the Soviet system and the merits of a proletarian dictatorship. The battle flared again during the first session of the CGTU's National Committee, prior to the Saint-Etienne congress, when a resolution "against governmental authoritarianism" was interpreted by Besnard and the anarchists to apply to Soviet Russia as well as to bourgeois regimes.[105]

In response, party sympathizer Monatte denounced the idea that the Soviet system could be viewed as a government "like any other," and he also took the opportunity to remind Besnard and his friends that they were only "the provisional leaders" of the CGTU and should not overstep their bounds.[106] Monmousseau was even more outspoken, claiming that "the dictatorship of the proletariat is nothing more than the permanent experience of syndicalism in action."[107] Although he did not go quite so far in his own alternate set of statutes, he dismissed the anarchists' proposed language as dangerously "tendentious" because it ignored the potential necessity of a "provisional proletarian State."[108] In other words, as party secretary Frossard candidly phrased it, the CGTU must declare its "total solidarity" with Soviet Russia, "with its faults and even its crimes, if any, just as with its accomplishments."[109]

Other statutory provisions concerned the issue of federalism or centralization in the CGTU's internal structure. Here again, Besnard argued the libertarian viewpoint when he termed federalism just as necessary after the revolution as was the unions' "functional autonomy" in prerevolutionary days.[110] The debate focused on the provisional Bureau's proposal to replace departmental with regional unions (URs), while also phasing out the role of nationwide industrial federations, which had always been the bastion of reformism in the CGT.[111] Anarcho-syndicalists also urged the transfer of federal headquarters from Paris to Lyon, in the case of the metalworkers' federation, to escape the centralizing effects of national politics, although this proposal was quickly overruled.[112]

This time, however, the Communists' own positions were highly ambiguous. One party member had scorned Besnard's federalist campaign as a matter of form without revolutionary content—it could not help to overthrow the capitalist system—and therefore a proof of his "anti-Communist" bias.[113] But a Communist-syndicalist, Pierre Sémard (then secretary of the railroad workers' federation), had made his own pleas for federalism against centralization, if only to target the centralized CGT. (Meanwhile, he also called for the formation of intersyndical Unions Locales, with close party ties.)[114] Monatte and his friends even claimed that the proposed URs would lead to *greater,* not lesser, centralization—a "paradoxical authoritarianism" on the anarchists' part—and therefore defended the existing structure. To justify their own paradoxical plea for the status quo, the group argued that now (since the schism) the unions' revolutionary fervor would restore the proper balance and prevent the federations' reformism from getting out of hand.[115]

Although they claimed to defend federalism, the Communists also argued that it, too, could be authoritarian if imposed by the anarchists. Monmousseau further quoted the prewar syndicalist Fernand Pelloutier: "If centralization is good for the ruling class, why isn't it also good for the workers?"[116] These comments revealed new similarities between Communist unionism and the CGT's own centralized structure, now that the Communists had turned from battling the reformists to winning control over the CGTU. Later on, the CGTU did in fact replace the UDs with URs as part of its process of Bolshevization. By that time, the move (which did not eliminate the old federations) only furthered the CGTU's centralization, as Monatte had warned, and weakened the traditional roles of the Bourses and UDs.[117]

While Besnard's faction sought certain changes to enhance federalism or decentralization, Monmousseau's faction sought other provisions, such as proportional representation, reeligibility of union officials, and permission to hold party and union office concurrently. So far, the group had to compromise on the first two, although these were instituted in the CGTU by 1927.[118] Despite these limitations, the vote at Saint-Etienne marked a major victory for the Communist-syndicalist faction. Monmousseau and three allies were elected to the CGTU Bureau, and his statutes were approved by a margin of 779 to 391.[119] The result was less clear a victory for the Communist Party, given Monmousseau's own cautious position, but Frossard did set a precedent by meeting separately at Saint-Etienne with those delegates who were also party members. This gesture outraged the syndicalists but encouraged the Communists as a sign of still closer party-union ties.[120]

The vote on statutes gave Monmousseau an even larger victory than had the vote on the Profintern. The Loire voted identically on both resolutions, but the Haute-Vienne reduced its support for the Besnard option to a margin of only eighteen to ten, down from twenty-seven to one.[121] The difference may have resulted in part from the fact that the Monmousseau statutes were easier to accept as the status quo: several desired changes had been postponed, and the change to concurrent holding of party and union offices was already practiced in many areas, including the Haute-Vienne. The contrast also suggests, however, that the Haute-Vienne's vote—for Besnard and against the Profintern—did not mean an absolute endorsement of his views on federalism and libertarian democracy. Instead, the Haute-Vienne unions sought to steer a middle course, while those in the Loire were more strictly polarized between the Communist-syndicalist and the anarcho-syndicalist camps.

This impression is sustained by the record of votes by individual unions. Among the principal Limoges labor groups, the railroad workers and the ceramicists endorsed both Besnard resolutions, but the shoe workers preferred the statutes drafted by Monmousseau. In this union, usually known for its anarchist orientation, there was indeed an "anti-statist" faction that later joined Besnard's revolutionary syndicalist CGTSR. So far, this faction was outnumbered by supporters of union secretary André Brissaud, who defended the need for the "centralization" of all "proletarian forces" against the *"Bloc Réactionnaire."*[122] Still, even this group wavered on adhesion to the Profintern. In 1923 Brissaud quit the Communist Party and then sided with Besnard at the next CGTU congress; by the end of 1924, he had led his union out of the CGTU and into autonomy.[123] Thus his carefully struck intermediate posture was highly precarious and subject to imminent collapse.

The results of the Saint-Etienne congress helped to accelerate this breakdown by arousing new fears of the CGTU's Bolshevization. A wide range of unionists, including many with scant ties to the anarchist movement, now joined with Besnard in a new Comité de Défense Syndicaliste (CDS) designed to "save" syndicalism from the Communist threat.[124] Other revolutionary syndicalists, including Monmousseau and Monatte, instead drew closer to the Communist Party, which Monatte finally joined a year later. Monatte also claimed to find no reason for concern when he asked rhetorically, after the June congress, "Did syndicalism die at Saint-Etienne?" If there was a danger, it was said to come instead from Besnard and the anarchist faction.[125] Many, however, disagreed with this claim, including unionists and some party members in both the Loire and the Haute-Vienne.

The growth of an anti-Bolshevist current was especially significant at Limoges, where it affected unionists who had previously accepted party ties with little question. Except among Limoges shoe workers and Saint-Junien glove workers, few condemned the Communist Party, or the Soviet Union, from a specifically anarchist perspective.[126] Even party members, however, found it hard to accept the new orders from Moscow. Louis Bert, now in Paris to serve on his federation's national committee, had already disputed the party's Marseille resolution on the trade-union question, and he continued to side with Besnard until he eventually quit the CGTU and returned to the CGT.[127] Bert's successor as UD secretary was railroad unionist Léonard Beaubelicout, also treasurer of the local Communist Party. Critics found him a mediocre figure who accumulated more than his share of offices when their incumbents left the region for employment elsewhere.[128] Nonetheless, he was a committed unionist who resisted party interference. As controversy grew, he quit his party post in October 1922, and the next January he was expelled from the party altogether, along with general secretary Frossard.[129]

Despite these changes, Beaubelicout managed to hold on at the UD until July, when the party assigned his successor.[130] Even then, the party's victory was superficial, as leading local unions began to quit the CGTU for autonomy. Still, like Bert and Beaubelicout, most dissidents would have accepted some ties to a flexible Communist Party, one that respected both union autonomy and local control.

The loss of local control over the Communist Party was accentuated when its regional headquarters were moved from Limoges to Périgueux, in nearby Dordogne. The move was inspired in part by the party's chronic weakness and the wave of departures of local party officials. Nonetheless, it placed the party in the hands of hard-line leftists, led by Périgueux's mayor Paul Bouthonnier, who had no patience for the centrists' "indiscipline," moderate politics, or relative respect for trade-union autonomy.[131] Even after its headquarters were returned to Limoges, the party continued to send in leaders from outside the region.[132] These changes made the process of "Bolshevization" denote outside interference, just as unwelcome whatever the source: Moscow, Paris, or anywhere beyond the Haute-Vienne.

Unlike Limoges, Saint-Etienne did have a strong anarchist tradition that magnified anti-Communist sentiment after the CGTU congress. Many local anarchists were not even members of the new confederation, even though leftists had hoped to attract them by giving them truly revolutionary unions to join.[133] Among those who had joined, whether before or after the schism, many concluded after the June congress that their main task was to fight against "Bolshevization," and that this could be done best from outside, not inside, the CGTU. Some switched to specifically federalist organizations, attached to the Berlin International, and eventually took part in Besnard's CGTSR.[134] Even outside the CGTU, however, they could still join the CDS, which, unlike the old CSR, welcomed non-union members.[135] This distinction reflected in part Besnard's own ambivalence toward trade unionism, plus his impatience with the old legalisms—and the fear of schism—that had tied his hands in the factional struggles before 1922.

Not all the Loire's anarchists were quite so intransigent. The metal-workers' secretary, Jean Seigne, remained active in the union movement, although anarchist die-hards denounced him as an *"arriviste."*[136] Some young anarchists formed a group of "Jeunesses Syndicalistes," to work for changes in the labor movement, such as the abolition of paid full-time officers. But when Bourse secretary Emile Arnaud found the group too polemical (or perhaps too much of a threat to his own salary), and moved to dissolve it, the youngsters then formed a "Jeunesse Libertaire" outside of and hostile to trade unionism.[137] The episode further demonstrated the rift between the anarchist and Communist currents, each a comparable political force that sought to control the unions for its own purposes. Even anarchist sympathizers like Seigne and Arnaud, the latter once the "libertarians' " candidate for UD secretary, faced narrowed options as they sought to define an independent trade unionism between opposite, but equally perilous, extremes.

Meanwhile, Arnaud had also quit the Communist Party to protest the revised CGTU statutes that would allow elected party officials to hold union positions.[138] Others soon followed: UD secretary Henri Lorduron, who had joined Besnard's CDS even though he had agreed to accept conditional adhesion to the Profintern, quit the party in January 1923, along with general secretary Frossard.[139] Like Beaubelicout in Limoges, Lorduron managed to hang on as UD secretary, although in late 1924 he lost to the Communist candidate, and later CGTU national secretary, Benoît Frachon.[140] Still, he refused to follow Besnard into the CGTSR or his Limoges colleagues into autonomy; instead, he stayed in the CGTU to preserve unity, a goal he had also expressed at the congress in 1922.[141]

Again, like Bert and Beaubelicout, Lorduron represented a perilous compromise, hostile to Bolshevized communism but not to all forms of party-union ties. After quitting the party, he and fellow dissidents joined to form local sections of Frossard's "Socialist-Communist Union," or USC, which also claimed to promote leftist unity and which gained particular strength in the Loire.[142] The syndicalists' nascent alliance with dissident Communists may seem even more paradoxical than their earlier ties to Moscow. The goal then had been to revolutionize the unions; now the unions' revolutionary purity seemed far less crucial than their autonomy from outside interference. Whatever their own political preferences, syndicalists saw less of a threat to their independence from party dissidents or centrists than from the pro-Moscow faction on the left.

It is hard to judge how sincere the party centrists were in their defense of trade-union autonomy. Both Frossard and his Loire supporters, led by Ferdinand Faure and Ernest Lafont, had attacked the party's line at the Marseille congress as impracticable, not theoretically distasteful. Then, at the next year's party congress, they approved a joint center-left resolution substantially accepting Moscow's dictates, even if not quite as fully as the left wished.[143] Ernest Lafont did call himself a "revolutionary syndicalist," and his opposition to party interference in the unions was acknowledged even by reformists in Limoges. But Ferdinand Faure, by reputation a Guesdist, was no advocate of a hands-off policy toward the unions, and Frossard, by reputation a Jauressian, had moved away from his mentor's ideas of *"libre entente"* with the unions and toward a willingness to supervise (if not control) his party's trade-union members, as evidenced by his activities at the congress at Saint-Etienne.[144]

Later on, the three sought and won considerable support from the syndicalists as they published the latter's correspondence in their own party newspapers and joined in attacks against the process of Bolshevization. Their cynical critics, both Communist and anarchist, easily scorned such efforts as mere "opportunism," aimed at winning electoral support.[145] In Alfred Rosmer's words, *"le syndicalisme de Lafont"* was no more than a prewar relic that the supposed enthusiast had "carefully set aside" for the sake of wartime Sacred Union and had now conveniently picked up again, "altogether intact," for the simple purpose of fighting the Communist Party.[146] Still, whatever the motive, these gestures impressed syndicalists eager to combine political action with respect for union autonomy — and local autonomy — in an updated version of the Charter of Amiens.

Chapter 10

After 1922: Syndicalists vs. Communists

At the end of 1922, despite the Communist Party's partial victories at the Saint-Etienne congress, the CGTU remained heavily syndicalist in structure, aims, and social composition. The same lack of proportional representation that had helped to accelerate the growth of the minority wing before the schism now continued to magnify the syndicalist faction, which remained entrenched especially in smaller unions like that of metalworkers in the Loire. The party did begin to make inroads in the larger unions, like those of Loire miners, but even these proved surprisingly resistant to the strategies and methods of Communist unionism, at least until the time of the Popular Front.

The strength of this resistance to communism and to the process of Bolshevization is easily overlooked when one traces the CGTU's organizational history. From their partial victories at the Saint-Etienne congress, the Communists won further victories at the Bourges congress in November 1923, meanwhile consolidating their hold on most regional CGTU branches, including the UDs of the Haute-Vienne and the Loire, by the end of 1924. From then on, the party sought and won control over most union activities, subordinating strikes to political motives and gaining formal recognition of its supreme authority at the CGTU congress at Paris in September 1929. These victories only intensified the resistance of their opposition, however, as syndicalists either left the CGTU for autonomy, rallied to a third organization, or organized their forces as a dissident minority to fight the Communists from within the CGTU. Although these choices reflected important differences in strategy and in outlook, they shared a common purpose: to find an alternative both to Bolshevization and to the reformist socialism of the old CGT.

The course of these factional battles reveals not only the depth of the ideological conflicts that ruptured the unity of the French trade-union movement but also the continued importance of the syndicalist alternative, even after the upheavals of the Russian Revolution and World War I. While conditions had surely changed enough to forestall a simple return to prewar syndicalist "bluff and demagogy," as one reformist termed it,[1] they did not necessarily mandate a shift to Communist unionism, however ardently the party or the Comintern sought to present its program as the only viable solution for the postwar world. The record of the syndicalist movement in the mid- to late 1920s shows both how far it was able to adapt to altered circumstances and how far it sought to remain true to its prewar goals and methods. If the movement continued to find support, at least in certain regions and certain industries, it was precisely because it continued to fill a perceived need of many workers, unsatisfied by the centralization and the partisan politics of both the CGTU and the CGT.

The Syndicalist Alternative

The emergence of a coherent syndicalist movement in the 1920s is difficult to trace, because of the absence of a unified syndicalist organization after the Communists won control of the CGTU. In both organizational and doctrinal terms, postwar syndicalism seemed to critics to be "a practice in search of a theory"; as of 1929, the movement was still said to have "not yet found its way."[2] Whatever unity the movement possessed seemed to stem more from a common enmity toward the existing party-dominated labor organizations, rather than from a clear alternative program or ideology. Still, from these disparate sources grew a surprisingly well integrated current, which sought a movement at once more truly "revolutionary" and more responsive to workers' material needs.

The genesis of the syndicalist opposition can best be understood in the context of the Bolshevization of the party and the trade-union organizations.[3] Within the CGTU, an anti-Bolshevik opposition had arisen almost immediately after the new organization's founding congress at Saint-Etienne in June 1922. Conflict accelerated during 1923 as the party began to use new methods, including factory committees and joint action committees, designed to impose tighter coordination on trade-union activities. Some syndicalists welcomed these initiatives: Pierre Monatte finally joined the party, which he had at first found too remote from labor interests. Others rallied instead to the opposition, and even Monatte was expelled from (or quit) the party by the end of 1924.[4]

Another controversial issue was the CGTU's adhesion to the Profintern, which was ratified in March 1923. Only a small faction, led by Pierre Besnard and his "Comité de Défense Syndicaliste" (CDS), still opposed such adhesion and urged joining instead the anarchistic Berlin International, or AIT.[5] But others who had favored conditional adhesion, based on respect for syndicalist autonomy, found these guarantees negated by the party's new tactics of "organic liaison," or institutionalized party-union collaboration. This new opposition, assembled in the "Groupes Syndicalistes Révolutionnaires" (GSRs), included many who had voted with the Monmousseau faction at the Saint-Etienne congress. Two of its leaders, Madeleine Guillot and Léopold Cazals, were in fact members of the confederal bureau elected with Monmousseau in 1922.[6]

Both opposition groups were overwhelmingly defeated at the CGTU's congress at Bourges in November 1923; together, the two groups received barely one-fourth of the total votes. The GSRs may have been discredited in part by their apparent ties to the more unrelenting oppositionism of the CDS and the anarchists.[7] In fact, however, the two groups never fused, despite their common rejection of the Communist Party's leadership. Either way, they continued to represent substantial segments of labor opinion, even in the Haute-Vienne (where the UD was now under Communist leadership), and especially in the Loire, where the dissident Communist Henri Lorduron was temporarily still in charge.[8]

The Communists' command of the CGTU leadership was thus no guarantee of support throughout the union movement. Their victories at regional or national congresses could paradoxically be exaggerated by the absence of proportional representation, thereby underweighting the large opposition unions, such as those in the Haute-Vienne. Although dissident UD secretary Léonard Beaubelicout lost his post in July 1923, the opposition still controlled the large porcelain and shoe workers' unions, which soon quit the CGTU for autonomy. Limoges then became the nation's main bastion of autonomous unionism until the reunification of 1936. In addition, beginning in 1924, a handful of smaller unions, such as the clothing workers' and the bakers' unions, quit the CGTU to rejoin the CGT, as did dissident railroad unionist Louis Bert.[9]

The Communists' victory, although later, was somewhat more secure in the Loire, where the party had dominated most of the large coal miners' unions since the schism and then won control of the Saint-

Etienne metalworkers' union in August 1923.[10] As in the Haute-Vienne, a number of unions quit the CGTU shortly thereafter, but these included mainly the modestly sized unions of teachers and municipal employees, which rejoined the CGT, and the tiny groups of cabinet makers and metal polishers, most of whom eventually joined the CGTSR.[11] Still, despite its small size, the local CGTSR became one of the new organization's principal branches in the country. In addition, a variety of other dissidents, including the defeated UD secretary Henri Lorduron, chose to remain inside the CGTU in order to fight Bolshevization from within. This group, which continued to dominate the Saint-Etienne Bourse, quickly aligned with the dissident "Ligue Syndicaliste" of Parisians Pierre Monatte and Maurice Chambelland, once they too had quit the Communist Party, and with the Ligue's journal, *La Révolution Prolétarienne*.[12] Some of this group even continued as party members, but their support was at best conditional. The metalworkers' union at Le Chambon-Feugerolles, formerly a stronghold of Communist influence, nearly quit the CGTU in 1929 when local mayor Pétrus Faure was expelled from the party. (The union then backed down, but went ahead in December 1931.)[13] The Loire mineworkers' secretary Pierre Arnaud and his supporters also quit the party in late 1929, and then in 1933 the union withdrew from the CGTU to rejoin the CGT.[14]

As these developments suggest, there were three strands of "revolutionary syndicalism" that emerged during the course of the 1920s: first, the Ligue Syndicaliste, the remnant minority wing of the CGTU, which preferred to fight from within rather than quit that organization; second, the autonomous unions, which left the CGTU and then refused to adhere to any confederation; and third, the CGTSR, the dissident confederation formed by those who sought more than mere autonomy but rejected the politics of either established group. All three were often called "anarcho-syndicalist" by their reformist and Communist rivals, who intended the term as an insult.[15] Only one strictly merited that label: the third group, the CGTSR, which included many known anarchists or libertarians and which adhered to the anarchistic Berlin International (AIT).[16] The other two groups, rightly enough, rejected the appelation: the Ligue Syndicaliste (Monatte's group) still accepted communism in theory, if not in its Bolshevik practice; the autonomists, who stressed their corporative rather than political intentions, accepted only the label *"syndicalistes purs."*[17]

Among the three, the autonomists and the minority syndicalists were probably the most similar. Both groups rejoined the CGT by 1936, while the CGTSR remained independent. Despite this distinction, however, the CGTSR also showed important parallels to the other groups. Like the minority syndicalists, or "Communist-syndicalists," to use Monatte's term, the CGTSR was willing to be overtly "political," even if the two groups differed on the sort of politics to which the unions should adhere. Like the autonomists, the CGTSR shared a libertarian perspective; in fact, the new group recruited mostly from among the autonomists and was itself descended from an earlier "federation of autonomous unions" founded in 1924.[18] The CGTSR and the autonomists also shared the stated goal of continuing the CGT's prewar syndicalist traditions as expressed in the Amiens Charter, while the Communist-syndicalists accepted some form of party allegiance as a means to bring the prewar labor movement up to date.[19] All three groups, finally, avowed consciously a "revolutionary" commitment, even though they spent less time discussing goals than methods and sometimes omitted the very word "revolution" from their programs—as did the text of the Amiens Charter itself.[20] In all these respects, the three groups shared a common syndicalist tradition, born of reverence for federalist and neutralist principles of union organization, although now in varying degrees of modern dress.

Communist Unionism in the Era of Bolshevization

The growth of the syndicalist opposition was complicated not only by the variety of organizational options but also by its links to the troubled course of the Communist Party. Since late 1922 a tacit alliance had emerged between syndicalists and dissident Communists who shared a dislike for the Bolshevization that threatened both branches of the labor movement. This alignment was somewhat blurred by the centrist politics of most early Communist dissidents; most syndicalists were instead ultra-leftists, including those, like Pierre Monatte, who joined the party only after the "purge" of general secretary Frossard and his centrist supporters in January 1923. Nonetheless, once Monatte and his friends quit the party, they quickly joined forces with syndicalist dissidents from across the party's spectrum. This unlikely marriage may have justified the party's scornful talk of left- and right-wing "opportunists," or "anarcho-reformists."[21] But it also revealed a deeper desire for an independent and unified syndicalist movement that could transcend party or factional lines.

Among the unlikely marriage partners were syndicalists who had quit the party just when Monatte was ready to join it. This group included the Loire and Haute-Vienne UD secretaries Lorduron and Beaubelicout, plus leading figures in the Limoges shoe workers' union, in the Saint-Etienne unions of teachers and of workers at the state-run armaments plant, and in the railroad workers' unions in both cities. Many of these dissidents also joined Frossard's new Socialist-Communist Union, which had its main centers in Paris and the Loire.[22] Although the new party was formed primarily for electoral reasons, in time for the next year's legislative elections, it also sought to act as an "intermediary" between the two established Marxist parties and thereby help to restore "proletarian unity," a goal dear to most syndicalists as well. Those who joined this or any party were by no means strict anarcho-syndicalists, but they could sympathize with the party's promise to respect union independence and resist Bolshevization. As one party militant put it, "We are all more or less individualists and *libertaires*."[23]

Later developments further demonstrated the links between the syndicalist and dissident Communist currents. Even the Trotskyist movement, in which the Parisian Alfred Rosmer became active, may have gained some support among revolutionary syndicalists, although Trotsky himself had little sympathy for the idea of union independence.[24] The movement did seek to rally a wide segment of "left-opportunists" and appears to have had greater than average followings in the syndicalist centers of Limoges, Saint-Etienne, and Lyon.[25] The Frossard group failed to win a secure foothold and in 1927 rejoined the Socialist Party, again mostly in view of the next year's legislative elections, although the groups justified the move by claiming that "partial" unity was better than none.[26] Some who refused to follow Frossard's lead joined instead with Loire deputy Pétrus Faure, expelled from the party in 1929 for violating its new "class against class" electoral tactics, to form a separate "Parti d'Unité Prolétarienne" (PUP). This small group, another peculiar attempt to restore "unity" by way of schism, claimed representatives in thirty-eight departments, including the Haute-Vienne, but remained concentrated primarily in Paris and the Loire.[27] Still, it gained support among local unionists, including Saint-Etienne mineworkers' secretary Pierre Arnaud, who rejected the Communists' "class against class" tactics as imposed in the unions and in strike actions.[28] The party controversy also had links to the trade-union movement in Limoges: one ousted party member tried to draw the union of shop clerks from the CGTU into autonomy, and another became head of the porcelain workers' union in the CGT.[29]

The nature of the syndicalist opposition was blurred not only by its ties to dissident Communists from opposite ends of the party spectrum but also by the Comintern's sudden switch in 1927 from the tactics of "united front" to those of "class against class."[30] Those who opposed one tactic might be expected to applaud the other, rather than join forces with its opponents. In fact, however, Stalin's knack of adopting the gist of his rivals' programs meant that even party leftists could oppose the Comintern's "turn to the left" after 1927. Furthermore, from the syndicalists' viewpoint, party strategy showed a remarkable constancy despite the switch in tactics, a constancy that lent cohesion to the syndicalists' own anti-Bolshevik campaign.

The basic premise of the "class against class" tactic was that reformist organizations like the CGT and the Socialist Party were the workers' natural enemies, because they held out false hope of reform and so helped to sustain the capitalist system. Thus the Communists vowed to wage war against the reformists and all their allies, from bourgeois Radicals to "opportunists" within the Communist camp. The new tactic, designed by Stalin to discredit the right-wing opposition at home and to justify the turn against the NEP in the Soviet economy, also served to quench a glimmer of opportunism in France, which in orthodox eyes seemed to have flickered briefly in 1926–27, after the first wave of Bolshevization had receded.[31] As such, the change only renewed the tide of Bolshevization, as the emphasis shifted from organizational issues (especially the establishment of factory cells) to strategic problems, including electoral tactics and the conduct of strikes.

In both spheres, party strategy now renounced the pursuit of formal alliances with reformist organizations — the old tactic of seeking to restore labor unity "from above." But it did not abandon the opposite tactic of seeking unity "from below," by luring the masses away from their leaders and into the Communist camp.[32] Indeed, the new strategy might be read as an intensified version, not an abrogation, of the previous "united-front" strategy, which had emphasized the latter variant ever since its inception in 1922.[33] The new tactic could be openly aggressive, even destructive, at least in the short run; the immediate goal, as a Limoges Communist phrased it, was to weaken the rival camp by "nibbling away" at its sources of support.[34] Still, this was little different from earlier united-front tactics, characterized by Treint as a process of "plucking the [Socialist] chicken."[35] In both cases, or so critics felt, the goal was a "disguised offensive" against the reformists, a means of stealing their recruits rather than building new support among the masses or achieving a genuine reunification of the left.[36]

The party's constancy in aims and methods was apparent even in electoral strategy, where the switch to "class against class" tactics had the most immediate impact. In both the 1924 and the 1928 legislative elections, the party offered to form a "Bloc Ouvrier et Paysan" with the Socialists but refused to support any alliance with the Radicals, and thus ran its own candidates rather than join in a "Cartel des Gauches." This rivalry was carried further in the later elections, when the Communists sometimes backed Radicals or conservatives against the Socialist Party. Beyond that, the principal difference lay in the refusal to support the Socialists even on the second round, when the latter's chances were now seriously in doubt.[37]

The decision was not an easy one for party leaders who feared that voters might not understand the hard-line tactic. Thus, claimed opponents, the Loire Communists did not speak openly about it in campaign meetings but "prudently . . . kept the most hermetical silence."[38] Nor did all Communist voters go along with the switch: an estimated 40 to 45 percent of the party's first-ballot voters throughout the country deserted the party on the second round.[39] Nonetheless, and perhaps as the result of a recent economic crisis, the party showed a substantial increase in popularity. Meanwhile, the Socialists lost heavily, relinquishing all five seats (including one to the Communists) in the Haute-Vienne and five of the Cartel's eight seats (none to the Communists) in the Loire.[40]

The results must be attributed in part to the Socialists' own declining voter appeal, after years of Cartel impotency, and after a campaign that, in the Haute-Vienne, saw new and less charismatic personalities rest on their predecessors' laurels and fail even to attend campaign meetings.[41] The Socialists' weakness in the Loire was also magnified by their division into two rival groups.[42] Whatever the Communists' share of responsibility, from pursuing their hard-line tactic, not all later dissidents — not Loire syndicalist Pierre Arnaud, for example — spoke out against the policy at the time. Even one who did, candidate Pétrus Faure, had shown no similar scruples about maintaining a separate candidacy in the elections of 1924.[43]

In union strategy, the switch to "class against class" tactics also marked a mere ripple in the party's larger plan of Bolshevization. One example was the decision to create new Communist unions to rival existing CGT or autonomous organizations, rather than try to subvert the organizations from within.[44] As a result of this new policy, and on the initiative of the party's regional authorities, new CGTU unions were formed in 1928 among Limoges porcelain and shoe workers.[45] The move was a direct reversal of the earlier decision to maintain a "united front" inside the autonomous unions when they had quit the CGTU at the end of 1924.[46] Still, the shift had been anticipated well before the Comintern's "turn to the left": the possibility was raised in October 1926 as a response to the increasingly close collaboration of the autonomous unions with their CGT counterparts.[47] In fact, in mid-1924, the party had likewise sponsored a new CGTU union of bakers when the autonomous union rejoined the CGT.[48] Thus, the "class against class" tactics only reinforced an option that had sometimes been exercised even in the heyday of the "united front."

Nor did the shift mean a thorough overhaul of the party's strike strategy. The key aim was now to control and manipulate strikes, both to rally workers to the unions and to win political support for the party at election time. This did mark a change in the party's attitude toward strikes from an initial tendency to dismiss them as an anarcho-syndicalist aberration. Again, however, the transition had begun several years earlier, with the onset of Bolshevization, as a means to enhance the coordination of party and union activity on all fronts.[49] The Comintern's "turn to the left" made its strike aims more overt, and more controversial to party dissidents, while it sought to build on the earlier momentum. These points can be illustrated by comparing the Communist-led strike of Loire coal miners in the winter of 1928–29 with an earlier, and similarly unsuccessful, Communist-led strike of Loire metalworkers in the spring of 1924.

The strike of 1928–29 was an example of the party's attempt to call larger and more frequent strikes as a means to demonstrate and promote the "radicalization" of the masses. Like the new electoral tactics, this strike activity was to mark the start of a new "pre-revolutionary" period, with more intense social and political conflicts, and the end of the era of "capitalist stabilization" that had prevailed since 1921.[50] Still, if the party's enthusiasm for strikes had grown, and its rationale had altered to suit the tone of the Comintern's new leftist program, the political motives were not that different from those expressed earlier in the decade. As in 1924, the goal was to "unmask" the reformist "traitors" and thereby to develop "the political consciousness of the trade-union leaders."[51] This aim took precedence over winning mass support by satisfying workers' economic desires; as one party manifesto stated, "the battle for beefsteak is historically out of date."[52] Economic demands were valued mostly as a means to arouse combativeness toward later political upheavals.[53] By coordinating or controlling strikes toward political ends, the party could also combat both the habit of local, spontaneous outbursts and the newer trends of reformism or opportunism that seemed to have contaminated the movement ever since the era of the united front.[54]

The party's methods in the strike of 1928–29 included the demand for an across-the-board wage increase (five francs per day) for all miners, regardless of category;[55] the attempt to call a national strike despite signs of regional opposition to such a movement;[56] and the attempt to supplant local union authority by forming Communist cells, which would include workers from outside the industry in question, so that party control of the strike would be assured.[57] As an example of the "united front from below," non-unionists were encouraged to take part in the strike committees.[58] This tactic, however, could be read as a means to seize initiative away from union leaders rather than as a way of broadening support for the strike.[59] Above all, in the eyes of its syndicalist critics, party interference in union activity meant a disregard for workers' economic interests, a misreading of local economic conditions, and an exaggeration of the masses' revolutionary fervor. As long as "radicalization" was not yet a reality, the party's tactics were a "senseless" "invention" that "sabotaged" the movement by "disgusting" the workers and keeping the unions weak.[60] Indeed, critics said, the Communists themselves had become the rabid strikers they once had condemned for anarcho-syndicalist excesses. It was now the Communists who were the *"gréviculteurs,"* who practiced "bluff and demagogy" by calling strikes just as readily *"comme on se dit bonjour."*[61]

As a political gesture, the strike of 1928–29 aimed above all to justify Comintern tactics and to mobilize workers' revolutionary fervor, regardless of the strike's practical outcome. The strike may also have been intended to rally support for the party in municipal elections (the legislative campaign had already passed) and in elections for the union posts of *délégués mineurs.*[62] This political motive had also been apparent in the metalworkers' strike of 1924, held on the eve of that year's legislative elections. The party had attempted to disguise those aims by canceling the planned parliamentary candidacy of the local strike leader. Nonetheless, it had welcomed the opportunity to condemn the Socialists for their "treasonous" Cartel with the Radicals, as well as to discredit the rival

USC by denouncing its role in helping UD secretary Lorduron alone win
an acquittal when he and thirty-four other militants were arrested for
their role in the strike.[63] As a political gesture, the strike of 1924 was far
from the revolutionary climax wished for by local anarchists, who had
voiced regret at the failure to make use of "pistols and dynamite."[64] Still,
however moderate its tone and conventional its electoral purpose, the
strike had clearly aimed to strengthen the party's role in the trade unions,
as mandated by the Comintern's Bolshevization campaign.

In other respects, too, the strike of 1924 had revealed some of the same
party tactics that were to be accentuated later on in the decade. As in
1928–29, the strike committe had been composed exclusively of Communist Party members, perhaps to supplant the authority of a union in
which non-Communists still held the majority.[65] Again, the expressed
aim had been to win an across-the-board wage increase for all industrial
workers, this time of six francs per day.[66] The strike had begun as a simple wage dispute among a single group of specialists, but party leaders
quickly sought to extend it throughout the region, without, syndicalists
said, taking into account the vast differences among the special interests
of the varied groups of Loire metalworkers.[67] These very differences,
party leaders would argue, made their role essential to supply cohesion
and discipline.[68] But in calling a strike with no assurance that it would be
followed, complained the syndicalists, the party's actions hurt the unions
by alienating "the rare unionists who were so hard to recruit."[69]

As these examples illustrate, the grounds for syndicalist dissent against
Bolshevik strategy remained quite as constant as the strategy itself. One
issue was the very idea, first announced in 1924, of uniform wage increases for all industrial workers, regardless of rank or occupation.[70]
The party was not alone in making such a recommendation; the CGTSR
further envisioned a uniform wage for all workers, leveled upward to the
rates for the most highly skilled.[71] In the party's case, at least, the professed aim was to win the support of the least privileged groups of workers, who benefited least from a percentage gain applied to all wage
levels.[72] Skilled workers, though, who formed the bulk of union memberships in all organizations, had reason to object to such a system. The
issue concerned dissidents in the Haute-Vienne, notably at Saint-Junien,
as well as those in the Loire, although in each case they couched their
complaints in the less self-interested language of opposition to the Communists' arbitrary and inflexible demands.[73]

A second issue was the party's efforts, also constant since 1924, to gain control of the CGTU's strike strategy to ensure that all outbursts fit the party's own political interests. At first, efforts focused on curbing local or spontaneous outbursts, in order to favor larger national or international strikes under centralized leadership.[74] Again, such coordination was not unwelcome to all the party's opponents; those Communist-syndicalists who broke with the party continued to echo its call for "no partial strikes." The problem arose when the party and the CGTU returned to the tactic of partial strikes, as part of their new campaign of "radicalization" and perhaps on Moscow's initiative.[75] The change led mine unionist Arnaud to criticize the party for breaking its own rules by launching as a national strike a movement that promised to gain only local and limited following.[76] The very question of support now seemed to be of secondary concern to a party that stressed building political consciousness rather than winning over the masses by a broad program of economic reforms.

Finally, dissidents felt that the party's theme of "radicalization" was exaggerated if not altogether fictitious. Strikes were in fact proliferating, after a downturn during the 1927 recession, but these were not necessarily for "revolutionary" aims, and memberships in the CGTU and the Communist Party were both nearing all time lows.[77] Indeed, the party's strategy may have rested on a misreading, deliberate or not, of the economic and social mood of the end of the decade. Although new conditions doubtless existed, such as the technical "rationalization" of industry and the financial difficulties that followed the stabilization of the franc, there was no reason, syndicalists claimed, to assume that the end of the capitalist system was at hand.[78]

With these arguments, the syndicalists were open to attack from the left as "disguised reformists," whose "demoralizing defeatism" allegedly postponed the revolution by weakening the masses' will to fight.[79] The attack echoed that made by earlier left-wingers in 1917–20, during another phase of potentially revolutionary unrest.[80] Some Communists themselves, however, soon contested the theory of "radicalization," which the party softened after 1930. Although the "class against class" orientation remained, the party and the CGTU now sought "to conquer the masses" by becoming their representatives for their *"revendications les plus petites."*[81] Whether in acknowledgment of economic realities or in a simple retreat from sectarian excesses, the Comintern and the French party displayed early signs of what would later become the Popular Front program. Even the onset of the Great Depression had failed to launch the "revolutionary period" that Communists had claimed to envision since their strategic turn to the left.[82]

As a result of these disputes, and before the party's next tactical zigzag, the strike of 1928–29 and the larger issues of Comintern strategy triggered a new round of party purges and resignations. The circumstances were not all identical: Pierre Arnaud had defended party tactics in the parliamentary elections and then broke with the party over the issues surrounding the unsuccessful strike.[83] Pétrus Faure, who had opposed the electoral strategy (and was criticized for benefiting on the second round from Socialist withdrawals in his favor), was finally expelled for backing down in the plans for an antimilitarist and pro-Soviet demonstration on August 1, 1929, when authorities declared the demonstration illegal.[84] Still, despite these different beginnings, both came to oppose the party's ultra-revolutionary orientation, and both joined the new PUP, formed at the end of the next year.[85]

In addition, both men seem to have harbored distrust for the party ever since the onset of Bolshevization. Pétrus Faure had actually opposed joining the Comintern back in 1920; he went along with the party's decision, he later claimed, only to preserve unity and discipline.[86] Arnaud then resisted the party's call for his union to take part in, or provide financial aid to, the metalworkers' strike in 1924.[87] In fact, Arnaud's ambivalence toward party leadership, as shown by his occasional support for the opposing UD faction, suggests that he might have broken with the party earlier had it not been for the miners' initially successful strike record.[88] As usual, the miners' own corporative interests took precedence over partisan aims.

The strike strategy was only one of several means by which the party sought to create closer ties to the labor unions. Another method was the establishment of joint action committees *(comités d'action),* begun in early 1923, to link together all "revolutionaries" against such dangers as the Ruhr occupation or imperialist wars in Syria and Morocco. Although in some ways a logical continuation of wartime party-union collaboration, and acceptable on an *ad hoc* if not permanent basis, the committees were clearly intended to remain under the party's own supervision. The postwar action committees also proved unable to attract groups other than those already controlled by the party: the CGTU unions and the Communists' veterans organization, the ARAC.[89] In the Loire, anarchist groups had taken part initially but then withdrew to set up their own separate organization when the party won control of the local UD Unitaire.[90]

Among unionists, the issue also proved controversial; dissidents charged that the groups were an "immoral coalition," no better than the ties binding the CGT to the Socialist Party. These objections were soon voted down at the CGTU's Bourges congress in late 1923. Nonetheless, the whole idea of union participation in political activities remained open to question. Pierre Arnaud, on the verge of quitting the party, claimed to regret having failed to urge the miners *not* to join in the party's recent antimilitarist demonstration, because the arrests and repression that followed did the unions more harm than good.[91]

The party's political preoccupations may also have discouraged unionists from joining the party in the first place. One study of Communist recruitment suggests that those who joined the party at the height of its antimilitarist activity (1925–29) tended more often to be youngsters aroused by the problem of military service than older militants with years of trade-union experience. In other words, the usual pattern in those years was to join the party first, and only then (if at all) to join a union, rather than the reverse, the latter common before 1924 and again the norm by 1930 when the party began to place more emphasis on economic questions of trade-union concern.[92]

Even more direct interference in union affairs was threatened by the party's trade-union commissions *(commissions syndicales)* and factory committees *(comités d'usine)*, both taking shape by the end of 1923. The first were party agencies designed to coordinate members' activities within the unions and to compete with rival currents for unionists' favor; the second were union groups, although formed on the party's initiative, intended to facilitate contact with workers on the shop floor. Such measures may have been needed to organize workers on a factory basis, rather than by neighborhood unions or party sections; they would also help to "educate" non-unionized party members to the realities of working-class life. Above all, they would serve, as did the across-the-board wage demands begun in 1924, to mobilize support from workers still indifferent to party activities. For these reasons, even the later dissident Pierre Monatte hailed the new measures as a needed means toward the party's proletarianization and refuted the "imaginary danger" envisioned by the opposition.[93] Such opposition was particularly acute among Loire and Haute-Vienne syndicalists, and among the minority GSRs at the Bourges congress. In contrast, the CGTU leadership found the new measures no threat to the unions' "organizational autonomy," that is, to the letter if not the spirit of the rule against "organic liaison."[94] Moreover, as one Haute-Vienne Communist explained it, the party had the right to organize as it saw fit, inside or outside the unions; this was no violation of union autonomy since the unions could choose freely among the Communist and rival party lines.[95]

Such reasoning was less helpful in justifying the nascent factory committees, where the party was not organizing its own forces within the unions but seeking, or so syndicalists complained, to supplant the unions altogether. Some syndicalists still endorsed the idea in principle, as a step toward "workers' control" of the factories, but they insisted that the unions remain in control of all decisions and regretted the party's attempts to interfere.[96] Meanwhile, one party delegate suggested quite a different plan: that the factory committees be set up by party members "disguised" as unionists—presumably to mislead the workers as well as the employers.[97] Even if not deliberately deceptive, the groups would aim to include all workers, regardless of union membership, and hence serve as "the veritable united front from below."[98] Again, there was little opposition in the CGTU leadership but much more among syndicalists in both the Haute-Vienne and the Loire. The issue added fuel to the protests by the UD secretary in Limoges, on the eve of his resignation from office; by the shoe workers' secretary, as he prepared to bring his union into autonomy; by non-Communist metalworkers in the Loire, who fought against the party's eventual control of the local union movement; and by the coal miners' secretary in Saint-Etienne, after the strike that prompted his defection from the Communist camp.[99]

Spurred perhaps by the inefficacy of the unions' factory committees, the party moved in late 1924 toward its own reorganization into a network of factory "cells." These cells, to be organized at the workplace, would supplant earlier local party sections organized by neighborhood or *quartier*. They would also be linked hierarchically to the party's departmental, regional, and national administration in order to facilitate the execution of decisions made by the central command. In fact, in part because of the party's inability to penetrate the larger factories, only a small percentage of the new cells were established on an industrial rather than a geographic basis.[100] Where they did arise, they seemed to compete with local unions, whose members, one recalled, "could not understand why the Communists met separately to discuss their own affairs."[101]

The new system also aroused opposition from local Communists who feared the loss of local autonomy. Although Monatte had at first approved the party reorganization in the hope of strengthening the unions, he also insisted that the cells retain the right to elect leaders and representatives on their own.[102] The contrary was all too common in Limoges, where the shortage of local personnel had long resulted in a perceived "invasion" by outside leaders. Limoges Communists further attacked the cell system as inappropriate to local conditions that varied widely from place to place.[103] Similar grievances were voiced in the Loire, although local leadership was not directly the issue. Thus, Pétrus Faure cited the inadequacy of the cell system as one reason for the failure of the miners' strike in 1928, and for his own decision to quit the party and form the less highly centralized PUP.[104]

These party dissidents found natural grounds for sympathy with syndicalist dissidents, who faced their own loss of local autonomy. While the party worked out its new "cellular" structure, the CGTU likewise adopted further centralization by mid-1926, as regional URs replaced older departmental UDs. In most cases, regional secretaries were direct party appointees, often with few ties to the locality they represented. Indeed, one of the purposes may have been to override those UDs still remaining in non-Communist hands.[105] The party further justified the shift by the need for greater centralization to combat a highly organized employer class, as well as by the frequent scarcity of qualified local officials. Nonetheless, the change was a rude shock to local biases, and it seemed to hinder the work of the local unions.[106] To both its party and its union critics, "Bolshevization" thus meant the loss of local autonomy to outside interference, whether from Paris or from the Communist International.

The CGT and the Appeal of "Unity of Action"

The tightening hold of the Communist Party on the left wing of the labor movement meant that most syndicalists defined their attitudes in terms of opposition to Bolshevization. Some even carried their anticommunism so far as to rejoin the old CGT. For most syndicalists, however, the CGT was at best the lesser of two evils. In many ways, it represented much the same partisanship and centralization that they now found repugnant in the CGTU.

Not surprisingly, the CGT cheered the news of the CGTU's internal dissension as proof of its own superior wisdom since the earlier schism.

To win back the dissidents, and to further its campaign against Bolshevization, the CGT along with the Socialist Party adopted much of the rhetoric of "syndicalist autonomy" and claimed to defend the Amiens Charter, however inconsistent the claims may have been with the SFIO's Guesdist traditions and with the CGT's own record since 1914.[107] Just as predictably, this change of heart incurred the skepticism of the Communist Party, which saw only the partisan motives of both the SFIO and the new dissident fractions, the USC and the PUP. As one Communist sneered, the Socialists did not need their own special trade-union commissions, because their ties to the CGT were already so deeply entrenched.[108]

Despite its newfound syndicalist rhetoric, the CGT was indeed forging closer ties with the Socialist Party and adopting an openly reformist social program. In an extreme version of this new orientation, former CGT assistant secretary Georges Dumoulin urged the creation of a British-style labor party, to bring the unions to parliamentarianism, ministerial collaboration, and even class collaboration, as needed for constructive social reforms.[109] Few in the CGT initially endorsed this proposal — with such notable exceptions as the Federation of State Employees and the Haute-Vienne's UD secretary, Marcel Vardelle, who was also a municipal councillor and later parliamentary deputy for the Socialist Party.[110] Still, while renewing its vows to respect the Amiens Charter, the CGT clearly recognized, much as did the Communist Party, the need for some sort of party-union linkage. If their method differed from that of the Bolsheviks, it was in their professed commitment to open and official party action rather than to the "occult" maneuvers of the new-style "Blanquists" in their "secret cells."[111] Even general secretary Léon Jouhaux, who preferred to see himself as a *"socialiste de conception, d'esprit"* rather than as a *"socialiste de parti,"* defended the CGT's party ties as the only choice against the forces of political reaction. No longer, he said, could the CGT reject all parliamentary politics in favor of direct action in the professional sector. Instead, he sought to exercise a *"politique de présence,"* for representation "wherever working-class interests are discussed."[112] As such, the Amiens Charter was effectively, if not admittedly, laid to rest.

In its new defense of party-union ties, the CGT voiced the hope that the left's parliamentary majority would give the unions a better chance of influencing new legislation. In turn, as the Haute-Vienne's Vardelle insisted, the party should base its own action on the revised Minimum Program of the CGT. Paradoxically enough, left-wing Socialists, including others in the Haute-Vienne who were disillusioned with Cartel politics, urged instead that the party have its own separate platform now that the CGT's program was so reformist that even the Radicals had adopted it for themselves.[113] Not all unionists welcomed the Radicals' support, which seemed simple electoral maneuvering from a party "incapable of having its own program."[114] Nonetheless, the ironic turnabout from pre-war days, when unionists had been the ones to resist the Socialists' re-formism, was added proof of just how much the postwar CGT had changed.

The CGT's new reformism could be seen not only in its acceptance of parliamentary action but also in its willingness to compromise on practical issues rather than take a diehard and probably ineffectual stance of opposition. As on the wage tax issue just after war, so on the proposed "rationalization" or reorganization of industry toward the end of the decade, the CGT—unlike the CGTU or the Communists, or even the left-wing Socialists—chose to accept the inevitable, while seeking reforms or adjustments to limit the new policies' ill effects.[115] Again unlike its rivals, the CGT was willing to accept so-called compulsory conciliation, although not arbitration, as a way of promoting negotiated settlements of conflicts while not abdicating the right to strike.[116] This new conciliatory attitude, evident also in the unions' acceptance of compromise wage settlements, may have been mostly defensive in motive, given the weakened state of the unions and the uncertain economy, and it yielded at best a modest record of achievement.[117] Still, whatever its results, the new orientation was a far cry from the CGT's prewar "noise and impotence," as denounced by Dumoulin, as well as from the CGTU's current status as *"gréviculteurs."*[118]

To enhance its effectiveness and to promote the goal of labor unity, the CGT also approved practical "unity of action" with the CGTU and the autonomous unions while exploring prospects for the eventual reunification of the labor movement as a whole. Like the Communists, most CGT leaders were mainly interested in their own partisan advantage. Thus, while the Communists demanded unity by way of a national congress, empowered to create a new organization according to the will of the delegates, the CGT leaders insisted that unity be restored only within the old confederation, and that the blame for the schism be placed squarely with the syndicalist and Communist camps.[119] Still, a centrist faction, led nationally by Georges Dumoulin and Pierre Monatte—and joined by Maurice Chambelland of the CGTU's syndicalist camp—favored a more far-reaching compromise and sponsored a new campaign for unity that began in 1930.[120] Their group, known as the "Comité des 22" from the number of its original sponsors, rallied syndicalist supporters from both confederations across the country. In the Loire, cited by Monatte as the movement's key departmental stronghold, the campaign's leaders were the teachers' unionist Urbain Thévenon (CGT) and the miners' Pierre Arnaud while he was still in the CGTU.[121] In the Haute-Vienne, the campaign also won support from about one-third of the teachers' union (CGT), but the autonomists and the "Unitaires" (except for one CGTU teacher) were conspicuously absent.[122] UD secretary Vardelle (CGT) did not join the campaign but did act as a *"franc-tireur"* in favor of unity because, as he put it, the CGT could not "fly" properly without its left "wing."[123]

Despite their hostility to the Communist Party, Vardelle and Dumoulin perceived a certain common orientation that might ease the way toward eventual reunification. Like the Communists, the CGT leaders recognized the need for national and even international organization, and hence scorned the autonomists' more restricted horizons.[124] While paying lip-service to the Amiens Charter, they also denounced the autonomists and other syndicalists for alleged "anarchist" or "libertarian" prejudices, which sought to impose a *"dictature désguisée."*[125] The Loire branch of the CGT may have been more sympathetic to the principle of union autonomy, especially as it recruited more ex-Unitaires who had quit the CGTU on that basis.[126] Neither confederation, however, saw postwar syndicalism as more than a vestige of the "unhealthy and sterile individualism peculiar to the Latin races," a "disease" that might finally be "cured" by adopting the British model of party-union relations or by restoring the unity of the CGT.[127]

This shared contempt left syndicalists with little room to maneuver. Even those who preferred the CGT to the Communist unions hardly wished to embrace the old Guesdist reformism that they had rejected back in 1922. Like the autonomists who spurned both major confederations as too highly political, most syndicalists refused to submit to an overt partisan philosophy. Some may indeed have endorsed an anarchist ideal that critics termed quite as doctrinaire, even "dictatorial," as those of their rivals. Rather than merely abstain in the legislative elections, for example, a Limoges shoe worker on the verge of quitting the CGTU headed a "libertarian" or "abstentionist" list in the elections of 1924.[128] Others found it possible to join splinter groups like the USC or the PUP, or to permit, as the Loire's Pierre Arnaud had phrased it, "circumstantial ties" with the PCF.[129] To this extent, they did not achieve the ideal of "pure syndicalism," or strict political neutrality, that some may have envisioned. Still, they refused to make their unions a mere arm of the political struggle, or to adopt the bureaucratic structures—and high dues— that the Socialist and Communist programs alike seemed to require.[130]

Most syndicalists disliked the CGT's social reformism even more than its partisan politics. Like the Communists, the syndicalists saw the CGT's acceptance of "compulsory conciliation" or negotiated settlements as an abdication of the class struggle, worthy only of *"jaunes"* or *"alliés du patronat."*[131] Most syndicalists also denounced the CGT for accepting rationalization of industry; the CGTSR claimed to accept it, but only if it yielded the six-hour day.[132] If they found the Communist Party abhorrent politically, these syndicalists still shared its revolutionary fervor. They similarly hoped for the eventual radicalization of the masses, even if they thought that the time had not yet come for the "perpetual agitation" led by the party since 1928.[133]

Nonetheless, the same syndicalists who had once flirted with communism for the sake of revolutionary vigor now flirted with reformism for the sake of union autonomy. The shift implied just how much their priorities had changed. Or maybe the point was that they had always welcomed corporative benefits, if these could be harmonized with a revolutionary philosophy; the problem arose when the party's dogmatic "revolutionism" seemed to conflict with its corporative aims. In fact, in their zeal to win corporative benefits, the syndicalists may have partially merited the party's contempt as "anarcho-reformists." They preferred a "pure" syndicalism to partisan politics precisely in order to maximize their material interests, to concentrate on higher wages and better working conditions without being distracted by irrelevant concerns. This reformism applied less to those closest to the anarchists, including the Limoges shoe workers and some Loire metalworkers, than to the miners and ceramicists who had stressed corporative benefits since long before the CGT schism.[134] But even the shoe workers now disavowed the image as rabid strikers that they felt had been part of the prewar syndicalist mythology.[135] This newly pragmatic or constructive orientation helped the syndicalists to form fruitful ties with their CGT counterparts in order to achieve "unity of action" in strikes and negotiations for economic gains.

Like the CGT and the Communist Party, most syndicalists agreed on

the ultimate goal of labor unity, even if they disagreed with their rivals—
and with each other—on the means or the price they were willing to pay.
Strict anarchists, of course, were as contemptuous of the "chimera" of
unity as of the very idea of union organization; they openly applauded
the labor schism, which most others deplored as "criminal"—even if
those others had done little to stop it at the time.[136] Unlike the anarchists, Communist-syndicalists postponed their departure from the
CGTU as long as they thought possible; some, like the Loire's Henri
Lorduron, would have preferred to rejoin the CGT than to see a third
group emerge.[137] Well before actually joining the CGT, and while still
criticizing its lack of revolutionary fervor, Pierre Arnaud had welcomed
the possibility of joint action with the reformists in preference to the
Communists' "ultra-revolutionary" but impotent stance.[138] Others who
stayed in the CGTU resisted unity with a CGT that seemed committed to
class collaboration. Still, they hoped that the course of negotiations
might make the CGTU less sectarian or the CGT more willing to accept
unification on revolutionary terms.[139]

Even those who opted for autonomy claimed that their move would
help, not hurt, the cause of unity, since true unity could be achieved only
without the interference of political parties. Rather than rejoin either existing confederation, the autonomists called on the other factions to join
with *them*.[140] (To this claim the Communists retorted, "Unity by way of
autonomy is like curing an illness by way of suicide.")[141] Of the main
syndicalist groups, the CGTSR was the least willing to compromise for
the sake of unity; its members scorned the autonomists' zeal for practical
"unity of action" and refused to take part in the reunified CGT after
1936.[142] Some extremists in the CGTSR, true to their anarchist leanings,
spurned unity as "the castration of syndicalism" and claimed to prefer action by revolutionary "elites" or "active minorities" to that of "the blind,
servile, traditionalist, superstitious, and bestial masses."[143] Most of the
group, however, endorsed labor unity as an ideal, if it could be based on
political independence and a genuinely revolutionary platform.[144] Indeed, these were the preconditions for unity that syndicalists had posed
since the time of the Amiens Charter.

For most syndicalists, the goal of unity reflected a deep concern for
workers' interests on the local level, far removed from the national issues
that had triggered the schism or that would hasten the merger, which
they accepted without enthusiasm, in 1936. As ardent localists, the Limoges autonomists denied that they wished to be "isolated" from a larger

network, but they rejected the CGT's stress on national and international organization as ignoring the local and material issues that were most workers' primary concern.[145] Those most interested in anarchist theory explored the ideas of federalism and decentralization; others seemed as if subconsciously to feel that a federalist system was more responsive to local interests and to the desire to control one's own affairs.[146] In short, anarchist theory seemed at most to reinforce a sense of localism that most syndicalists had reached on other, more practical grounds.

This same sense of pragmatism, and the desire for unity, led most syndicalists to recognize the value of large-scale union organization. As the Limoges shoe workers' secretary argued, shortly before his union declared its autonomy, real action required more than the "skeletal" structure that they had had in the past.[147] These unionists cheered autonomy as the promise of stronger, not weaker, unions, unhampered by the partisan politics that had apparently discouraged union recruitment since the labor schism.[148] However cautious in forming alliances, or in accepting compromise for the sake of mass membership, they were hardly devoted to the syndicalist myth—also distrusted by the Communist Party—of *"minorités agissantes."*[149]

From this survey of syndicalist ideology as it evolved during the postwar decade, there emerges a fairly clear and coherent set of theoretical principles. While the movement grew in response to, and absorbed a diverse set of remnants from, its two major rivals, syndicalism comprised a positive alternative rather than just the sum of negative views of the opposing camps. Its main goals were a politically neutralist, federalist, and eventually reunified labor movement, which would best defend both the corporative and the revolutionary interests of the workers, including those who had quit or refused to join the existing and heavily politicized labor unions. While the degree or kind of political activism varied widely, from anarchism to dissident communism, most syndicalists preferred to leave their politics at the doorstep and to engage solely, inside union headquarters, in *"syndicalisme pur."*

For these syndicalists, the old motives for trade-union autonomy were still just as relevant as in prewar days. True, there was now a party that, unlike the prewar SFIO, was sufficiently "revolutionary" to claim the workers' partnership. Still, revolutionary credentials alone were not enough; syndicalists further demanded the right to oversee the revolutionary process, because they knew it would leave its stamp on post-revolutionary society. Thus, they insisted on the need for mass support, not just a dictatorial seizure of power; they also called on trade unions to serve as bases both for worker control of the factories and for an alternative political system to replace the Bolshevik goal of a proletarian State. These issues were not mere ideological phantoms but genuine matters of conscience, especially to those who had not rejected Communist unionism from the start but had once envisioned a workable compromise between conflicting sets of values. Now that they rejected its methods, these syndicalists refused to follow the party's lead when it claimed that it alone was a genuine force for revolution, or that the only issue of the day was "to defend the Revolution."[150] Like their prewar antecedents, who had stressed the methods of direct action perhaps even more than its ultimate goals, they refused to place, in effect, *"la Révolution au dessus de tout."*[151]

Postwar syndicalists also demanded recognition as revolutionaries in their own right. Against Bolshevik charges of "infantilism," they insisted that they were sufficiently "mature" to achieve a revolution on their own.[152] The phraseology was of course a reference to the prewar Amiens Charter. While Communists openly dismissed the charter as outdated, and CGT leaders paid lip-service but abandoned its terms in practice, syndicalists repeatedly affirmed their fidelity to the principles that had guided the movement in its "heroic" years.[153] To them, these principles were no "false sentimentality" or youthful illusion to be cast aside in the bright light of Bolshevik realism.[154] Syndicalists themselves acknowledged the need for some tactical adjustments to win mass support among factory workers and to challenge the capitalist system.[155] Nonetheless, they insisted that the capacity for change only proved the charter's vitality as a guide to the future, not a vestige of the past.

Approved changes might include "circumstantial ties" with leftist parties or practical "unity of action" with reformist unions. Other innovations were the method of "factory committees" and the goal of "workers' control," admissible as long as the unions, not the Communist Party, remained in charge. Finally, syndicalists recognized the dangers of prewar "myths" such as the value of constant agitation to arouse workers' revolutionary fervor or the virtue of small bands of militants to launch the revolution without mass support. Most of these changes were also endorsed by the Socialist and Communist parties. Where syndicalists differed was in their insistence that such changes involved no fundamental departure from prewar traditions and required no further adoption of the centralized bureaucracies and partisan politics that their rivals espoused.

In short, syndicalism represented an intermediate alternative both between anarchist individualism and close ties to political organization and between strict fidelity to aging traditions and a self-conscious "modernity" that demanded highly centralized institutions to bring the labor movement up to date. It remains, nonetheless, to consider how far these ideas, however coherent on paper, corresponded to the realities of the postwar decade. How many workers, and which groups, actually supported these ideas of revolutionary syndicalism? Did those who espoused them actually carry them out in practice in their union activities and strikes?

Chapter 11

Syndicalism in Action: The Dilemmas of Labor Unity

An attempt to measure both union membership and strike activity is needed to show that postwar syndicalism was more than a mere "cause without rebels."[1] Even more than in prewar years, the movement's strength was partially dissipated by its dispersion into myriad smaller factions; taken together, these groups were still far outnumbered by the dominant factions of the CGTU and the CGT. Still, the movement found substantial support in certain industries and in certain localities, including the Haute-Vienne and the Loire. Even in these areas, the movement failed to win a majority of unionized workers, much less of the entire work force, but it long proved a genuine alternative to the Socialist- and Communist-led organizations. None of these, after all, became a true "mass" movement, at least until the massive growth that accompanied the Popular Front in 1936.

Competing Constituencies: Sources of Syndicalist and Communist Support

The weakness of all factions reflected in part their ideological rivalries, since each group seemed more concerned with luring support away from the opposition than with seeking new sources of strength among the not yet mobilized masses. Indeed, total unionization remained stagnant throughout the 1920s, and far lower than in the immediate postwar years, while both confederations lost support among industrial workers and filled their rosters with large numbers of service employees and *fonctionnaires*.[2] The CGT also profited from the CGTU's internal disputes, even though the CGTU, unlike the Communist Party, actually grew in numbers during the years of hottest dissension and lost support only after 1926.[3] Nor did all dissidents join rival organizations, whatever the actions of their leaders; instead, they may have remained unorganized but aligned with former comrades in union elections or during a strike.[4] In fact, although CGTU membership remained highly volatile, it may have fluctuated more from economic conditions or fear of repression than from ideological rivalries.[5] Still, even if Bolshevization did not hurt CGTU membership, it did not help it. Critics found the CGTU to have become a "syndicalism of eunuchs"; even its partisans recognized that the organization was a tightly knit "vanguard of the proletariat" rather than a mass movement in its own right.[6] These were among the reasons cited for the eventual policy shift toward "the conquest of the masses" and away from the sectarian excesses of "class against class."[7]

As the CGTU "Bolshevized," the size of its syndicalist minority diminished but was difficult to measure precisely. From a vote of 391 out of 1,189 at the congress of 1922, the Besnard faction won only 208 of 1,271 votes in 1923 (another 145 votes supported the GSR); the combined dissident forces totaled only 22 of 1,365 votes in 1925 and 60 of 2,055 votes in 1927.[8] By the time of the latter congress, the CGTU had instituted a form of proportional representation according to union size, but the tallies still ignored the syndicalist minorities within a given union since a single union could not split its vote. In addition, syndicalists had begun to join outside organizations, such as the autonomous unions or the CGTSR, but these did not publish national membership figures.[9] Nor was there much evidence of the size of the Ligue Syndicaliste, organized by Maurice Chambelland and Pierre Monatte, beyond the scornful reference by a Communist rival to this "minuscule group."[10] One can nonetheless assume that, as a group organized around a newspaper, the Ligue Syndicaliste attracted only a narrow circle of militants and theoreticians, rather like Monatte's earlier group of supporters of the journal *La Vie Ouvrière*.[11] Except for these groups, the best measure of syndicalist support within the two confederations may be the 1,500 signers of the unity proclamation issued by the "Comité des 22" in 1930–31.[12] But this campaign for unity quickly fizzled once the two confederations vetoed its program at their congresses in the fall of 1931.[13]

On a departmental level, the data are far more revealing although still inconclusive. Even UDs with strong syndicalist influence in 1922–23 were won over to the Communists by 1925.[14] In the Loire, the victorious Communists echoed their CGT predecessors before the schism when they dismissed the opposition as mere "skeletal organizations created for voting purposes alone."[15] CGTU leaders also minimized the rupture of 1924–25, by claiming to have lost only a handful of minor unions with a small total membership.[16] Such claims again understated the importance of syndicalist minorities that stayed in the CGTU and the size of some unions that quit for autonomy, particularly in Limoges.

The strength of the Haute-Vienne syndicalist movement after 1925 is especially noteworthy, given the UD's early conversion to the CGTU majority. At the Bourges congress in 1923, of a total of twenty-two Haute-Vienne unions represented, only six voted for the Besnard faction and one for the GSR. Thus, several that had voted with Besnard in 1922 had now switched, including the railroad union at Limoges and the textile and other unions at Saint-Junien.[17] In response to this switch, few railroad unionists seem to have followed dissident leader Louis Bert, now in Paris to head the Paris-Orléans sector, when he rejoined the CGT in early 1924; the CGT's local union remained small, while the CGTU's grew steadily until the end of the decade when it outnumbered its rival by nearly four to one[18] (see Figure 20). Nor did many Saint-Junien unionists appear to follow syndicalist leader Henri Gaillard when he broke with the Communist Party to protest its partisanship and inflexible tactics. Despite Gaillard's defection, the unions remained aligned with the CGTU, and most voters continued to support the city's Communist mayor, although he lost his bid for a parliamentary mandate in 1928.[19]

Still, the Communists' gains in these sectors were compensated by losses elsewhere in the department. At the Bourges congress, the Limoges shoe and clothing workers' unions, which had split their vote on the two resolutions at the earlier congress, now sided resolutely with the Besnard faction. Others, including the ceramicists and the municipal employees, remained aligned with the minority, just as they had been in 1922. Only one group, the postal employees, part of the national federation led by GSR stalwart Joseph Lartigue, chose the GSR option of endorsing the Profintern while opposing Bolshevization.[20] Even the other votes represented an intermediate position, however, not the anarchistic fanaticism usually associated with Besnard and his later CGTSR.[21]

Among these dissidents, several unions soon quit the CGTU for autonomy. Despite the Communists' ridicule, the Limoges autonomists won not only the small tailors', bakers', and furniture makers' unions, but also the large porcelain and shoe workers' unions, with estimated memberships of 1,200 and 500, respectively, at the time of their departure from the CGTU. These autonomous unions remained the largest in their two industries at least until the end of the decade, somewhat surpassing their CGT rivals and far larger than the small Communist unions re-established in 1928[22] (see Figure 20). Although the autonomous unions did not attract as many new members as their leaders might have anticipated, neither did they lose members fearful that autonomy would deprive them of needed networks of union or party support. Not until the 1930s was there much of a move back to the CGT or toward a third confederation. Even then, the CGTSR drew little support outside the shoe industry, and most autonomists found a loose local association plus *ad hoc* cooperation with other union groups enough to satisfy their essentially local concerns.[23]

For the Loire, unlike the Haute-Vienne, the Bourges congress marked an upturn in support for the syndicalist minority. Especially noteworthy was the local support for the GSR faction (seventeen of sixty-three votes); combined with the Besnard faction (twenty-six votes) the syndicalists won a temporary majority in the Loire. Although this victory was short-lived, the Loire was one of only twelve UDs to have achieved it; among them, only four others had seen an increase in syndicalist support since 1922.[24] These increases included primarily the former "Communist-syndicalists" who now joined the GSR to protest Bolshevization; there were few additions to the support for Besnard.

Notable switches in the Loire included the unions of teachers, postal employees, and municipal employees, all typical GSR supporters, plus the miners at Saint-Etienne and the miners and railroad workers at Terrenoire, although other regional unions in the two latter occupations continued to vote with the CGTU majority. Unions faithful at both congresses to the Besnard faction included those in the Saint-Etienne shoe, glass, and construction industries; only the metalworkers' union, recently won over to the Communist faction, switched its vote from Besnard to the majority between 1922 and 1923.[25] In this case, the Besnard faction did include mostly small unions, highly anarcho-syndicalist in character; the GSR faction included larger unions that soon rejoined the CGT or became, like the miners, a durable opposition within the CGTU.

However traumatic, the split in the CGTU in early 1925 still meant less of a loss for the Loire than for the Haute-Vienne. Even the teachers' and municipal employees' unions, which soon rejoined the CGT, included only some 130 and 400 members, respectively. Together with eight other dissident unions, the defectors comprised fewer than 1,000 unionists in all.[26] The local CGTSR drew more support here than in Limoges, with an estimated 500 members by the late 1930s, but so far it included mostly the small cabinet makers', textile dyers', and metal polishers' unions, with rarely more than a few dozen members each.[27] As autonomous unionism gained little support in the region, the old CGT proved the principal beneficiary of anti-Communist dissidence. By 1928, after the UD moved its headquarters back from Roanne to Saint-Etienne, the CGT outnumbered the autonomists in the department by twenty unions to ten.[28] Still, even though they failed to win control of many unions, or to maintain these unions in autonomy, the syndicalists remained a substantial minority faction within both the CGTU and the CGT.

The disparity between syndicalist support and the number of unions in which the group held a majority had been apparent since the time of the Communists' victory in the UD in late 1924. On the eve of Frachon's election, reports had estimated the syndicalist faction to comprise two-thirds or more of total UD memberships, although it controlled only about one-half the total unions. Thus, Frachon's victory became possible as soon as he could win a few more union votes, even without a majority of all the members; this was an ironic result in view of the Communists' proclaimed commitment to proportional representation and their scorn for the syndicalists' own alleged reliance on the votes of small unions that lacked mass support.[29]

The growth of a syndicalist opposition was especially noteworthy among the Loire's coal miners, where there had been signs of resistance to Communist leadership since well before the union quit the CGTU in 1933. The records do not show how local miners voted on Frachon's election, but the group had supported his opponent Lorduron in 1923, voted with the GSR at the Bourges congress, and then opposed—as too partisan a gesture—Frachon's call to take part in the metalworkers' general strike in early 1924.[30] An early leader of this dissident current was Léon Mahistre, who also served as Bourse secretary at Saint-Etienne from 1923 to 1927, a term spanning Frachon's election at the UD and ending only when the Bourse, which by then included only CGT and autonomous unions, returned to confederal hands.[31] Later on, Mahistre was joined by union secretary Pierre Arnaud, who broke with the Communist Party after the strike failure during the winter of 1928–29; when he did so, a large number of fellow miners reportedly followed suit.[32] The defections from the CGTU to the CGT in early 1933 also included the miners' unions at La Ricamarie and Le Chambon-Feugerolles, once Communist strongholds; an exception was the union at Firminy, which remained pro-Communist, perhaps precisely because of the strong position of the CGT and the Socialist Party in that area.[33] After these defections, the party helped to organize a new CGTU union among the miners, but it rallied only a few hundred members as against some 1,500 in the revitalized CGT.[34]

Among the miners, syndicalism denoted less a conscious quest for union autonomy than a desire to subordinate partisan politics to their own corporative advantage. Even those who preferred communism to socialism had happily accepted the Socialists' reform program before the war and hoped to benefit now from the Communists' electoral strength in the region. Similarly, the miners recognized the utility of a strong national federation in order to engage in nationwide strikes and to exert pressure on both the employers and the government. For all these reasons, the miners long endured the CGTU, and then rejoined the CGT—which in national terms far outranked its Communist rival[35]—rather than remain in autonomy. Even then, the miners maintained a typically syndicalist, or intermediate, position. With Chambelland's Ligue Syndicaliste, Arnaud and his friends sought to restore trade-union unity, rather than just resurrect the old confederation.[36] They likewise continued to resist the trends of partisanship and centralization that dominated the reunified CGT.[37]

Like the miners, the Loire's teachers also preferred the old CGT to prolonged autonomy. Even the Communist faction that reestablished its own union in 1925 had offered to avoid a schism if the then autonomous union would rejoin the old confederation; the case was quite the opposite from that of the Limoges Communists, who seemed to accept autonomy but not the prospect of ties to the CGT.[38] The difference points in part to the acute rivalry between revolutionaries and reformists in Limoges; in Saint-Etienne this rivalry was outweighed by the recognition, among teachers and miners, that party ties and nationwide organization were needed to defend the groups' economic and political interests. Still, even after the reunification of 1936, the Loire teachers' union continued to be a principal opponent of the CGT's partisanship and centralization, whether under Socialist or Communist auspices. Before then, either within the CGT or as a main component of the CGTU's syndicalist opposition, the teachers in the Loire and elsewhere stressed the goal of syndicalist autonomy within the limits of their own corporative needs.[39]

As these examples suggest, the choice among competing trade-union ideologies followed certain industrial or occupational distinctions. Groups with long-standing corporative traditions tended to choose one or another syndicalist option, either by declaring their autonomy or by remaining a minority faction within the CGTU. That choice in turn reflected how much the group wished to rely on legislative action or felt the need for nationwide organization against a unified *patronat*. The same groups might choose the CGT, if it succeeded in maintaining its corporative traditions and its loose, though cordial, party ties. Such was the case in Limoges among sizable groups of porcelain and shoe workers, as well as among growing numbers of miners and teachers in the Loire.

Among the syndicalists, a third faction included those with more strictly artisanal traditions who joined or sympathized with the CGTSR.[40] In these cases, corporative bargaining seemed less important than a residual anarchist mentality, which called for revolutionary activism to compensate for the lack of mass support. This faction represented only a small part of the syndicalist total in either department, even among Limoges shoe workers and Loire metalworkers, heretofore relatively "anarchistic" local groups. Both industries were still among the least transformed technologically and hence could respond to the same conditions and attitudes that had traditionally fostered anarcho-syndicalism.[41] Other artisans, such as Loire weavers and gunsmiths, remained just as immune to postwar syndicalism as to prewar political currents.[42] The assumption that syndicalism was an artisanal phenomenon, and thus unable to survive technological changes, may be accurate for the CGTSR component but not for the movement as a whole.

The syndicalist movement appealed, in fact, to two quite distinct constituencies. One included highly skilled artisans and factory workers who had always been the mainstay of French syndicalism; the other was a more purely corporative sector, including miners, teachers, and other service employees, who accepted political unionism without wishing to be dominated by partisan politics. These groups overlapped the two main confederations and thus eagerly sought reunification—or autonomy—to restore the vigor they felt had been lost since 1922. These groups also comprised both main types of attitudes—corporative and revolutionary—that had dominated the prewar syndicalist movement and had shaped its major ideological controversies. The main group not included was the mass of unskilled manual workers that the Communist Party tried, without much success, to recruit.

Ever since the party and union schisms, the Communists had claimed to be the only true representatives of working-class interests. This claim was furthered by the "purge" of intellectuals and other centrists from the party in early 1923. From then on, the party sought to strengthen contact with the mass of workers through such new agencies as factory cells and workshop committees, while it also sought to "proletarianize" its own administrative hierarchy and electoral candidacies. Still, these efforts did not guarantee a real change in the party's social composition. As the Loire's new "Socialist-Communist" (USC) leaders taunted, their rivals could do no better in 1924 than to head their legislative list with that "Socialist to the marrow," Pétrus Faure.[43] Other dissidents later claimed that the Loire party was led not by workers but by "a handful of pedagogues" who "impose their will on the unions."[44] Some of these were former teachers dismissed from their jobs because of Communist activities and now in need of paid party positions.[45] Workers still suspected, however, that a lack of proletarian consciousness made the teachers prone to excessive sectarianism; the complaint echoed that heard from moderates fearful of schism at the Saint-Etienne congress in 1918.[46]

Indeed, although the Communists and the CGTU were hardly alone in this respect, they continued to draw many of their officers and members from the service sector. By the party's own reckoning, approximately 25 percent of its members were state-employed workers or *petits fonctionnaires* (some 50 percent were industrial workers), and the proportions had scarcely changed between 1923 and 1934.[47] The formation of party cells by occupational category did little to alter the pattern, especially when such cells remained outnumbered by older neighborhood groupings, and many cell members were simple *rattachés* not employed in the industry in question.[48] In local terms, only the Limoges railroad workers and the Loire railroad workers and state-employed gunsmiths formed occupational cells that, with some ten to fifteen members in each, were more than a dead letter.[49] At least in private congresses, the party also admitted its failure to take root in the Loire's largest steel mills, coal mines, or other leading establishments.[50] Such vast industrial terrains may have represented the party's "future," as Alfred Rosmer claimed in 1922, but they were not yet present reality, at least before 1936.[51]

The weakness of Communist unionism was especially remarkable among those groups usually considered the CGTU's major strongholds. In Limoges, of the three major labor groups, the railroad workers had traditionally been the most ardent Socialist supporters and were now the most firmly committed to the CGTU. Nonetheless, while they did form a Communist Party cell, its dozen members were a tiny fraction of the CGTU union's 500 to 800 adherents.[52] Even the union secretary refused to join, a refusal that did not prevent him, despite various conflicts with the CGTU leadership, from holding on to his post through the CGT reunification of 1936.[53] Despite this low party membership, authorities estimated that as many as one-fourth of the railroad workers voted for the party in the 1928 elections, as against approximately one-sixth of registered voters (or one-fifth of votes cast) throughout the department. Even this result, however, was attributed more to generalized discontent, especially over wage issues, than to support for Communist politics as such.[54]

Communist influence also proved surprisingly weak among the Loire's industrial workers, even among those who, unlike the miners, did not quit the CGTU. In Saint-Etienne's railroad industry, where the CGTU far outnumbered the CGT and remained pro-Communist in orientation, a large minority of voting unionists opposed the party ties that the CGTU had ratified at its national congress in 1929.[55] Among the city's metalworkers, where the party had won control of the union in August 1923, the victory had come more by a fluke than by any real power; as union membership was rising, on the eve of a general strike movement, the party was able to outvote the divided opposition, and then to hang on to its victory as dissidents quit the union after the failure of the strike.[56] As long as the union remained small, with rarely more than 200 to 300 members, the party could play a major political role even without the underpinnings of mass support. The movement failed to penetrate the larger factories, or to rally the masses of unskilled metalworkers, but these remained highly resistant to unionization of any sort.

Although Communist unionism gained no widespread support among skilled workers with the oldest corporative traditions or among the masses of proletarian laborers, it did appeal to certain groups whose interests were less well protected by the established labor organizations. In the Limoges porcelain industry, for example, the *"hommes du four"* — or furnace loaders — were the core elements of the reconstituted Communist union formed after the autonomists quit the CGTU.[57] In Saint-Etienne's mining and metallurgy, the Communists also recruited fairly heavily among foreign workers, who were the first to be fired in times of unemployment and who were often paid less than the prevailing wage.[58] Communism was also said to appeal to native miners whose peasant backgrounds left them less touched by the city's anarchist traditions, and

whose lack of education left them more easily swayed by the party's demagogic propaganda, or so the authorities argued.[59] For similar reasons,
the party often drew greater support among agrarian workers, or in rural
communities, than in urban industrial sectors with long traditions of corporatism or Socialist reform.[60]

This geographic distinction was particularly dramatic in the Limousin
region, where Communist electoral strength was consistently higher in
rural areas than in Limoges.[61] Nearly two-thirds of the department's
Communist membership after 1924 likewise came from outside the city;
while some of these were undoubtedly industrial workers, approximately
one-half of the regional total were peasants, according to the party's own
report for 1929.[62] In certain rural communities, party support may have
been less the result of Communist doctrine than of the personal charisma
of individual leaders, such as Jules Fraisseix, mayor of Eymoutiers, who
was elected parliamentary deputy in 1928.[63] The limits of doctrinal orthodoxy were also shown in the purges after that year's elections, which
affected several leading party members from outside Limoges.[64] Among
industrial cities, the only one to sustain a large-scale CGTU or Communist Party was Saint-Junien, a prewar center of syndicalist militancy but
not a traditional Socialist stronghold.[65] Both the factor of individual
leadership and the absence of rival political traditions thus helped the
Communists gain some support in new sectors rather than just drain support from the SFIO.

In the Loire, although the Communist Party won little support in rural
areas, it proved more successful in certain smaller cities than in Saint-
Etienne. Its main center of strength was in Le Chambon-Feugerolles, a
community of metalworkers with unique traditions of labor solidarity
and home of the Loire's most prominent Communist leader, UD secretary Benoît Frachon.[66] Even here, Frachon's influence was rivaled by that
of mayor Pétrus Faure (elected in 1925), whose exclusion from the party
in 1929 seems to have triggered the local metalworkers' decision to quit
the CGTU.[67] As in Saint-Junien, the city's prewar militancy may have
helped to prepare the terrain for a later Communist implantation. In the
short run, however, the two movements seem to have met more as rivals
for the same local constituencies than as successive "generations" of revolutionary campaigns.

As these observations suggest, the Communists showed a strong resemblance to their syndicalist rivals. Both groups owed their importance
more to their ardent militancy than to the force of numbers, and both ap-

pealed to militants who took revolutionary ideas seriously, rather than to those concerned solely with corporative reforms. Both movements, furthermore, became implanted more easily in medium-sized factories than in the largest steel mills or the smallest artisanal workshops, where a sense of "team spirit" would be harder to arouse. These similarities help to explain how individuals or groups made the transition from one movement to another. They also suggest that the transition was prompted by a political decision, rather than by an awareness of far-reaching economic changes; only later might "the masses" catch up to this revolutionary avant-garde.

Given these basic similarities, it is difficult to distinguish the competing constituencies according to neat sociological or economic criteria. If the most disadvantaged groups tended to prefer Communist to other forms of unionization, they also were among the least readily unionized, so that their numbers made little impact on the CGTU's total membership. Differences among industries also seemed to hinge more on political traditions of corporatism or solidarity than on strict socioeconomic distinctions. Still, these traditions may have grown in part from identifiable socioeconomic roots.

Economic factors to consider include wage levels and general levels of prosperity in the postwar decade. Relative prosperity continued to favor the Limoges porcelain workers, for example, who were able to obtain frequent wage increases. By contrast, the shoe industry faced continual economic difficulties even before the wave of layoffs in 1927 or the onset of the Great Depression after 1929.[68] These differences in prosperity (or in the perceived benefits of reformism) help to explain the porcelain workers' support for the CGT or for a highly corporative autonomous union, while among shoe workers the CGT remained weaker and many erstwhile autonomists soon joined the CGTSR. Still, these differences distinguished one syndicalist variant from another, rather than either one from a version of Communist unionism or from a durable constituency of the CGT.

In the Loire, coal miners similarly enjoyed rather high levels of prosperity through the late 1920s, as a shortage of labor kept wage levels relatively high. More serious problems of unemployment and periodic wage cuts plagued certain sectors of the metals industry, which had never fully recovered from the sudden contraction of demand that followed the end of the war.[69] These differences do help to explain how miners maintained relatively high and stable rates of unionization, while metalworkers endured far lower and more precarious rates, subject to general economic conditions that rose or fell. Again, however, these distinctions do not have neat political implications. In neither group did the Communists gain a durable foothold, although in each group the "syndicalist" opposition assumed a different form.

These examples may not, of course, justify a generalization for all industries or regions in the 1920s, or in any other period. They seem nonetheless to suggest that prosperous groups did not choose Communist unionism but instead favored the CGTU minority wing, corporative autonomy, or the CGT. Meanwhile, the less prosperous groups also spurned Communist unionism in favor of anarcho-syndicalism or remained non-unionized altogether. Put another way, the Communists exerted a negative attraction for the most highly skilled or privileged workers, but little positive attraction for the less privileged groups that might be rallied instead. As such, Communist unionism did not (or not yet) represent a distinct socioeconomic constituency, or anything more than a simple political choice.

Beyond short-term economic fluctuations, the labor movement was also shaped by longer-term structural factors, such as variant levels of industrial concentration, which influenced levels of unionization and solidarity. According to one study, high levels of concentration and solidarity were correlated with support for the CGTU majority (at least until 1925), while lower levels were correlated with support for the "anarcho-syndicalist" (Besnard) faction or for the "revolutionary syndicalist" GSR.[70] The first category included, however, such "high-solidarity" groups as the miners who accepted the Communist Party only on sufferance or who broke with it later in the decade. Moreover, the study also points out that these "high-solidarity" groups were the same ones that had enjoyed this distinction in the prewar era.[71] Thus, whatever its novelty, the party did not yet rally new groups hitherto isolated from trade-unionism or syndicalism. No real structural changes in fact altered the French labor movement until 1936.[72]

The same study of CGTU voting patterns also suggests the durable role of political traditions, especially on the local level. According to data for the Bourges congress, the "revolutionary syndicalist" (GSR) faction tended to comprise unions from previously majoritarian federations but minoritarian UDs.[73] These would include unions, like some in the Loire and the Haute-Vienne, with strong corporative traditions but with a dislike for Socialist reformism on political grounds. Moreover, these political choices were rooted in events of the wartime or immediate postwar

years, rather than in "new" developments that occurred only after the
CGT schism. As the same study shows, the anarchist and revolutionary
syndicalist factions usually included the earliest converts to the CGT minority (from 1918–19), while the CGTU's Communist faction comprised
the later leftist converts (from 1920–21).[74] Even this result could imply
that Communist unionism was a "new" or late-appearing political phenomenon; instead, those groups last to rally to the left were often simply
those—with higher solidarity and larger unions—in which gradual shifts
in opinion took longest to be felt.

The slow growth of Communist unionism also belied the party's expectation that economic changes by the end of the decade would create a
constituency that had so far been lacking. In the Loire, party leaders
claimed that their growth was virtually guaranteed by the course of capitalist concentration, now that artisanry and small manufacturing were
"about to disappear."[75] As industrial rationalization progressed, and as
the era of capitalist stabilization neared its end, economic crises would
radicalize the masses and bring on the collapse of the capitalist system.
The flaw in this reasoning, however, was not only the relative passivity
of the work force but also the slow pace of economic change, at least until the Great Depression hit with its full impact after 1929.

The phenomenon of "rationalization" was in fact more a goal (or a
threat) than an actual occurrence. The idea received substantial attention
in the labor and industrial press, especially by 1927. Still, there were few
signs that new technology was being applied, even in the nation's largest
mines and factories, much less in the smaller industries of the Loire and
the Haute-Vienne. The most common new technique was a method of
"chronométrage," or the time measurement of tasks, coupled with piecework pay scales to stimulate productivity.[76] Employers also sought to
lower costs by reducing manpower, and sometimes wages, but they rarely invested in new machinery or new assembly-line procedures.[77] Even
the Bedaux system, a variant of Taylorization, was not introduced in the
Loire until the mid-1930s, and then it was usually defeated by labor
strikes.[78]

One reason for this slowness was the lack of enthusiasm for change on
the part of smaller entrepreneurs, who perceived rationalization as a
threat to the French tradition of small business. Most were more interested in recovering from the war than in planning for the future. Such
employers, including many in Limoges and the Loire, agreed at most to

join together in patronal associations to resist labor strikes and to demand governmental concessions;[79] they still saw in small size an advantage in flexibility that greater concentration would negate.[80] The appeal of independent artisanal activity also remained surprisingly strong among Saint-Etienne weavers and gunsmiths, whose numbers declined in times of crisis but rebounded thereafter, if only to ensure a labor surplus when the next crisis threatened.[81] Even the Communists' own observers had to admit that as many as half the Loire's metalworkers were in small or mid-sized companies of fewer than 400 workers.[82] While the other half were considered likely prospects for party influence, that was a hope for the future, not a mark of present success.

The brief recession of 1927, which popularized "rationalization" as a way to survive future crises, still did little to set the process in motion. The crisis hit especially hard in luxury export industries, such as porcelain, shoes, and textiles, which had previously benefited from the French franc's low exchange rate.[83] These companies, however, were the least well suited to technological modifications and usually just waited for better times. Mechanization was also difficult to introduce in the Loire's coal mines because of their geological peculiarities; thus, employers did little to improve their competitive posture, relying instead on appeals for tariff protection or other government intervention on their behalf.[84] Heavy metallurgy was less affected by the crisis, especially in the Loire, where government orders for military equipment continued to be filled.[85] Despite numerous layoffs, most targets were foreign workers or "undesirables" such as labor activists; others usually found temporary jobs in other companies and were available to resume their posts once industry recovered in 1928.[86] Employers also sought to hold on to skilled workers by keeping them occupied at least part-time, rather than cut their staffs or close their doors entirely.[87] Overall, the crisis provided little incentive for the concentration of labor as a means to enhance efficiency or to ensure survival. As in 1921, the larger companies were often as badly hurt as the smaller ones, and some were finally forced to shut down permanently once the Great Depression got underway.[88]

The analogy to 1921 also applies to the political impact of the later crisis. Most workers still tended to avoid union membership or strike activity—dangerous risks in times of high unemployment—even if some militants may have been pushed toward the more radical language of "class against class." Whatever the rhetoric, the fact of resistance proved all too difficult, as the Communists themselves seemed to acknowledge by awaiting the end of the crisis before multiplying their calls to action.[89] By that time, moderates again argued the benefits of economic reformism, while denying the Communists' claims that the recovery was only transitory.[90] The same division of opinion persisted after the start of the Great Depression, which could be seen not as the death throes of the capitalist system but as yet another cyclical crisis to be endured.[91]

For all these reasons, the Communists' hopes for the radicalization of the masses proved little more than a revolutionary pipe dream. The party failed to win mass support among the unskilled factory workers so far little drawn to any form of unionization, and it also failed to "nibble away" at its rivals' strength among the skilled workers who still dominated the labor movement in most regions of France. The failure must be read as an error of economic analysis (if intended seriously) as well as of political strategy. Despite the premises of the "class against class" theory, French society was not (or not yet) polarized between a large unskilled proletariat and a small bourgeois elite.[92]

Above all, the theory exaggerated or misread the consequences of technological change and industrial concentration. These changes may have meant the shutdown of artisanal workshops but not the phasing out of mid-sized factories, in which skilled labor remained a scarce but highly valued commodity.[93] The wage gap between skilled and unskilled workers also tended to widen, not to narrow, partly as a consequence of inflation, now that the unskilled were too numerous and too weakly organized to bargain effectively for constant wage gains.[94] Most skilled workers remained staunch opponents of the Communists' "leveling" tactics, including demands for uniform wage gains at all ranks of the labor hierarchy.[95] Those who still opted to support the party's program were acting not from historical necessity but from a simple political choice.

If economic position did not guarantee the party a new labor constituency, the party hoped to win recruits according to age distinctions or other social criteria. As part of this campaign, the Communists claimed to represent a new "generation" of labor militants, a youthful "vanguard" to replace the elders who had been dominant—and who then lost their credibility—before and during the war. This claim echoed that of other revolutionary groups, left and right, in an age when "generational" ideas were especially fashionable.[96] Like its social composition, however, the party's age structure was at best ambiguous. Party leaders often seemed in fact to distrust the youngsters' "infantile" ultra-leftism (to use Lenin's term), just as they distrusted the "trade-union consciousness" of the untutored workers.[97] Militants who traced their roots to an anarchist inspiration now dismissed their early illusions as an *"idéal de jeunesse."*[98]

According to the few statistics available, communism did seem to appeal to a younger age group than did either the Socialist or the syndicalist alternative. At the time of the new party's formation, nearly all its national leaders were under forty years of age.[99] This relative youth continued through the 1920s, as the *"vieille maison"* (Léon Blum's own term for the SFIO) retained the loyalty of the older parliamentary deputies and skilled workers from the prewar labor movement, and the new party recruited younger militants, often without trade-union experience.[100] The patterns seem also to fit the available regional data. In the southwestern region, around Limoges, the party estimated in 1929 that approximately one-half its members were less than twenty-five years old; most party officials there and in the Loire were under thirty when they obtained their posts.[101] In contrast, most noted anarchists and revolutionary syndicalists in both regions were in their thirties or older.[102] The difference allowed the party to make a virtue of its declining membership as it purged the elders who, it said, most resisted the course of Bolshevization.[103] Thus, party militants could stress their own youthful allure and dismiss their rivals as aging relics of "an old, sentimental, romantic doctrine": little different, perhaps, from the aging hippies of the post-Vietnam generation. They may still have worn fashionably long hair, but they no longer threw bombs or otherwise showed themselves to be "unmitigated enemies of the bourgeoisie."[104]

Despite the propaganda value of such claims, however, it is hard to infer political choices from simple age categories. Young recruits had been falsely assumed to have pushed the labor movement leftward in the years 1919–20;[105] there is similar reason to doubt that most youngsters were radicals later on in the decade, even if many radicals were in fact young. Any age difference between Communists and rival groups could be explained in part by occupational distinctions. As shown in sample data from the cities' manuscript censuses, the postwar mining, metals, and railroad industries attracted a younger labor force than did the leading artisanal occupations in Limoges and Saint-Etienne.[106] If these groups then also rallied (at least partially) to communism, the process was the result of a variety of economic and political factors, not simple age considerations. If older ideas were sometimes espoused by older individuals, they likely came out of "older" industries or geographic sectors, which had seen the least technological change.

Furthermore, Communists who were "young" in the early 1920s were no longer so youthful by a decade later. Hence, any "generational" dynamic could operate as much against them as against their ideological rivals—as indeed seemed to be the case in 1968.[107] The factor of generationalism may have played more of a role in the CGT in the mid-1930s, when a sudden influx of new (and perhaps younger) militants, without syndicalist backgrounds, opened the door to Communist influence.[108] In the interim, however, there was more competition between established factions—and a shift back and forth of individual personalities—than a mobilization of new recruits.

Beyond the reality of age distinctions was the sense, promoted by self-serving propaganda, that the Communist Party represented "new men" uncontaminated by past ideologies and errors. This idea was advanced as the party purged earlier generations of wartime reformists, postwar syndicalists, and Frossardian centrists, and then continued in the course of Bolshevization to zigzag between left and right. Still, the very idea of a "zigzag" implies something other than constant renewal; eventually some of the doctrines (if not the individuals) once purged might regain legitimacy, as conditions further evolved.

The zigzags also showed the party's own ambivalence toward the idea of revolution as a generational conflict. Its youthful emphasis was most dramatic during the Comintern's "third period," when various representatives from Communist youth organizations were elevated to leadership roles. In France, two former Young Communist leaders, Henri Barbé and Pierre Célor, became members of a joint party secretariat, and its *de facto* leaders when colleagues Maurice Thorez and Benoît Frachon were jailed for their roles in antimilitarist demonstrations in 1929.[109] Both the youthful consciousness and the doctrinaire tendencies of the "Barbé-Célor group," as it became known, allowed critics inside and outside the party to blame these "young anarcho-communists" for the excesses of the "class against class" line: these were merely an expression of "the sectarianism inherent to the young."[110] Later on, once Thorez emerged from prison (in 1930) and Barbé and Célor were removed from their posts (in 1931), the ensuing *"tournant"* in party strategy meant a retreat both from ultra-leftism and from youthful impetuosity. From then on, the youth groups were to serve as simple training grounds, not as the party's revolutionary vanguard. As it became further Bolshevized and bureaucratized, on the Stalinist model, the party had also, in effect, "come of age."[111]

As a countercurrent to the Barbé-Célor group, Thorez and Frachon represented a pragmatic outlook that was drawn from the same chronological "generation" but that expressed their own beginnings in trade-union, not political, activities.[112] The contrast suggests that union activists were less susceptible to youthful sectarianism and helped to engineer the *"tournant"* of the early 1930s, to win the mass support that trade-union struggles required. The implication is further sustained by the pattern of party recruitment after 1929, when experienced unionists once again joined the party, rather than leave it in the hands of the untried youth who had joined it primarily for political and antiwar aims.[113] The point is not new that daily struggles over bread-and-butter issues may have bred a less dogmatic "trade-union consciousness." But the role of such ideas in the party and the CGTU weakens the Communists' claim to have been a revolutionary vanguard that had left old-fashioned syndicalism behind.

The Communists were not alone in their ambiguous use of generational propaganda. Among syndicalists, Pierre Monatte had expressed the fear that the war might make prewar ideas "the old school," thus making him, at age thirty-five, an old man before his time.[114] Still, he was just as concerned to portray his movement as sufficiently "mature" not to need the tutelage of a party avant-garde.[115] Above all, syndicalists sought to demonstrate the continued vitality of their doctrine in the context of social conditions that remained not so different from those in the prewar era. Whatever their success in recruiting members from new occupations or younger age groups, syndicalists did show their strength by the practical results of their tactics, which proved relatively successful in labor-management negotiations and in strikes.

Strike Activity: "Unity of Action" and Practical Results

If syndicalism remained a viable alternative to Socialist or Communist forms of unionism throughout the postwar decade, it was in part because of its relatively successful strike record. This record illustrates the degree to which syndicalists put their distinctive ideology into practice, and how far they based their opposition to rival movements on pragmatic as well as doctrinal grounds. The record also demonstrates the strengths and limits of the attempts at practical "unity of action" among the rival factions. Through their actions, the syndicalists showed a considerable pragmatism and willingness to compromise for practical benefits, even while they promoted a federalist and politically neutral program against the centralization and political partisanship that they perceived in the CGTU and the CGT.

In general terms, the years 1922 through 1930 were a time of relatively modest strike activity. In France as a whole, average yearly rates for strike frequency, participation, and duration equaled or exceeded those for the immediate prewar and wartime periods, although they trailed far behind those for the unusually militant years 1919 and 1920 (see Figure 9). Within the nine-year period, all three rates remained fairly constant, although frequency rose slightly while size and intensity, or numbers of strikers and working-days lost, somewhat declined.[116] These figures suggest a tendency to return to the strike patterns of the prewar era, with a relatively high number of small-scale conflicts, despite attempts by the CGT or the Communist Party to coordinate activities in larger-scale general strikes. As total strikers and working-days lost declined in number, the average *length* of strikes—in terms of days lost *per striker*—did rise slightly, nearly matching the rates for the immediate postwar period. This change may have been a sign of increased militancy, or of greater difficulty in gaining a victory, as well as of greater concentration of effort in a few longer conflicts.[117] Nevertheless, however well organized, these strikes were no indication that an era of "mass action" was underway.

These national patterns were generally paralleled in the Loire, where strikes in the 1920s were somewhat larger but no more frequent than those in the years 1912–14. In contrast to the national pattern, strikes after 1925 were also shorter in length than those in the prewar period, a sign that any greater cohesion or militancy in these later years may have been more apparent than real.[118] In general, although the Loire's strikes remained larger and more intense than the French national average, local workers seemed neither particularly strike-prone nor especially able to coordinate their efforts in large-scale general strikes.

These weaknesses appear especially in the Loire's two major industries, mining and metallurgy. Like both industries nationally, the Loire's metals industry showed sharp fluctuations in its strike activity, according to fluctuating economic conditions throughout the period, while the mining industry had a steadier but still relatively modest record of strikes (see Figure 11). In both industries, strikes were often larger but rarely much longer than the small, brief outbursts of the prewar period: except for rare general strikes, as among metalworkers in 1924 or miners in 1928, most strikes remained confined to a single shop or specialty and rarely lasted more than a few days. The principal exception was among metal-workers at Le Chambon-Feugerolles, where strikes were somewhat larg-er and usually much longer than average. Still, this difference seems to have resulted less from the local Communist Party's initiative than from economic conditions and habits of solidarity that the Communists were able to exploit.[119]

In the Haute-Vienne, strikes did prove longer than the yearly averages for the Loire or those for the nation, but they were still relatively small and infrequent, compared both to patterns elsewhere and to local pat-terns in earlier periods. In particular, annual strike frequency fell quite sharply in the years immediately following 1924, as a result perhaps of the exodus of major unions from the CGTU. This change was especially notable in the porcelain industry, where strike frequencies had until then been relatively stable, rather than fluctuating sharply as in the Loire metals industry. The decline was also visible, though less acutely, in the Haute-Vienne shoe industry (see Figure 10). In both industries, strike fre-quencies rebounded in 1929–30, along with similar results nationwide in those years.

In both Limoges industries, strikes also tended to become longer as the decade continued, but remained rather modest in size and smaller on av-erage than those for the department as a whole. General strikes were still quite the exception, with or without the influence of the CGTU. In con-trast, strikes in nearby Saint-Junien were often both larger and longer than average, but again this fact should be attributed more to preexisting conditions than to the direct influence of union or party leadership.[120] As in the Loire's Le Chambon-Feugerolles, the Communists proved better able to exploit favorable local conditions than to alter those conditions, or labor attitudes, that obstructed the party's aims.

One factor in these geographic variations was the size and structure of local industries. As other analysts have shown, most strikes tended to oc-cur in larger companies, which also yielded the largest number of strike participants, especially in the years after World War I.[121] This trend is sometimes seen as evidence of the social consequences of industrial con-centration: the growth of industrial unionism (of the Socialist or Com-munist variety) and the demise of revolutionary syndicalism, with its sup-posed base in artisanal or craft occupations.[122] Still, the data are far from conclusive, especially if one examines strike participation by company size within the same industries, rather than just across occupational lines.

As might be expected, the majority of strikers in the Loire mining industry came indeed from companies with more than 500 workers. This development marked quite a change from the prewar pattern, although it was less prominent by the end of the 1920s than earlier in the decade. Overall participation in strikes (as a percentage of employees in affected companies) also rose dramatically after the war, but likewise tapered off later on in the 1920s. Nor did the largest companies always have the highest participation rates, although their share had grown substantially since the prewar years (see Figure 21).

In cases where industrial concentration was less pronounced, smaller companies contributed a larger share of strike activity. Among Loire metalworkers, strikes were clustered in the largest companies only during World War I, for reasons discussed here in Chapter 3. Overall participation rates fluctuated sharply but remained highest in the small or mid-sized companies, especially those with fewer than 100 workers (see Figure 21). In larger companies, strikes were often confined to a single craft or specialty, although turnouts within the group were sometimes quite high.

These patterns also typified the postwar industries in the Haute-Vienne, although wartime and prewar strikes were too infrequent for meaningful comparison (see Figure 22). In both the porcelain and the shoe industries, companies with fewer than 500 workers had the most strikes, the most strikers, and the highest participation rates, even if craft-based strikes in larger companies often had proportionately high turnouts as well. As in other industries, the evidence points to a continuation of basic strike patterns rather than to a dramatic change as a result of industrial concentration. As companies grew in size, their strikes grew correspondingly larger and sometimes also more frequent, but no more able to rally the mass of their work force, who also remained largely immune to unionization and political influences. Even in the larger factories, there is no evidence that unskilled workers became the leading strike participants, although the exact identity of strikers is impossible to define.

These results uphold the view that industrial concentration did not clearly favor the growth of labor militancy, or of a new labor strategy designed to serve the interests of a new factory constituency. Even when their strikes were more frequent, workers in the largest companies were not as able to ensure large turnouts or to organize their strikes effectively toward successful ends.[123] Just as significant, however, is the evidence that the bulk of strikes occurred in the mid-sized factories, not in the smallest workshops, as critics of old-time syndicalist theory might suppose. Neither artisans nor unskilled factory laborers, these French strikers could endorse the modern syndicalist theories that seemed aptly suited to their needs.

The basic continuities in strike behavior are also evident in the record of strike outcomes. In France generally, the percentage of strikes that failed to reach even a compromise settlement declined somewhat after the economic crisis of 1921–22, except during the next crisis years 1927 and 1930, but still exceeded those of the wartime and immediate postwar periods[124] (see Figure 12). These results more likely stemmed from the persistence of unfavorable economic conditions or from the lack of unity in the labor movement than from weaknesses in any one group's strike strategy. Still, the results did show the new CGTU to be unable to overcome the problems that had blocked strike effectiveness in the past.

In the Loire, the postwar strike record (except for 1921) was actually quite favorable, compared both to national averages and to local records for earlier periods. These favorable results, however, reflect more the successes in the local textile industry than the experiences in metallurgy or the coal mines. Nationwide, strikes in mining and in metallurgy had higher than average failure rates, but the Loire's postwar rates for these industries were often higher still than the national averages, as well as higher than local rates for earlier years (see Figure 12). Moreover, the failures included the two largest strikes: those of metalworkers in 1924 and of miners in 1928–29. These results may account for the widespread disillusionment with Communist unionism in the Loire, even if they were not dramatic enough to cause these unions to break immediately with the local CGTU.

Unlike the Loire, the Haute-Vienne had a rather unfavorable strike record in the early 1920s: the failure rate was both higher than in previous years and higher than the national average, a startling result for a regional labor movement that had usually enjoyed a notable record of success. Moreover, these failure rates were especially high in the shoe and porcelain industries, even though these industries did not now suffer abnormal failure rates in France as a whole. Just as important, however, the percentage of failures dropped sharply in both industries, and in the department generally, in the six years after 1924 (see Figure 12). The implication is that the unfavorable strike record may have helped to trigger the unions' move out of the CGTU and into autonomy, and that the move strengthened the unions' effectiveness in local strikes.

The connection between strike results and political orientation is highly conjectural and was rarely acknowledged openly by the unionists. Nor would impressions of success be based simply on raw percentages; a compromise might seem more negative than positive, depending on the circumstances, and a huge victory, with valued benefits, might more than compensate for earlier defeats. Among miners, for example, two successful general strikes in 1923 gave the impression of a high overall success rate, apparently enough to compensate for the ill effects of the labor schisms, the recent economic crisis, and three smaller strike failures that year.[125] This result, however, also sustains the impression that Loire miners approved the CGTU only as long as it proved effective. Indeed, there is reason to believe that most unionists took such results into consideration, and that pragmatic interests helped to guide choices among competing ideological camps.

The clearest instance of such a choice occurred among Limoges building workers, whose union quit the CGTU and rejoined the CGT just after a strike failure in the late spring of 1925.[126] The local transit workers' union nearly did the same after a strike failure; the decision was forestalled only because the union secretary favored remaining in the CGTU, even though he had recently quit the Communist Party.[127] Among local autonomists, the shoe workers blamed the CGTU's sectarianism for low union recruitment, if not for strike failures, and expressed the hope that autonomy would attract new members alienated by both major confederations.[128] The union did not, in fact, grow appreciably, but it did hold its own into the 1930s, despite the onset of the Depression.[129] The Loire miners' unions in turn showed a sharp decline in membership after the strike failure of 1928–29, and then a slight rebound after the miners quit the CGTU to rejoin the CGT.[130] These fluctuations are quite common in French trade unionism and hence difficult to attribute to a given set of policies, but they do suggest that the CGTU's image as "rabid strikers" was more harmful than helpful, even among erstwhile "revolutionary syndicalists." In contrast, the autonomists and even the CGT reformists seemed to enhance their support with the claim that their own strikes were better planned, if fewer in number, and launched only after conciliatory efforts had been tried.[131]

Union behavior was reflected not only in strike statistics but also in attempts to establish joint action with rival unions toward the fulfillment of common interests. These efforts showed both the strengths and the limits of the ideal of syndicalist unity, as promoted by those who most regretted the earlier schism or sought to overcome its damaging effects.[132] Early efforts at joint action included a series of strikes in the Loire mining industry, beginning in late 1922. In these cases, the CGTU, which controlled most of the local miners' unions, sought CGT collaboration but initiated the strikes on its own. Their cooperation, however, was hindered by the CGT's greater willingness to compromise with management and its refusal to endorse the strike initiative; this refusal was also backed by local members, as shown by the light turnout of strikers in the CGT's local strongholds, Firminy and Roche-la-Molière.[133] The same divisions recurred in the attempted general strike of 1928–29, when as a result of the CGT's lack of support the strike drew only some 50 to 60 percent of the region's miners, as against an estimated participation of 90 percent of miners in the department of the Gard.[134] These results also let the CGTU take credit for the successes and blame the CGT for the failures, a stance likelier to promote partisanship than harmony on the two sides.[135]

Somewhat greater success resulted from early efforts at "unity of action" in Limoges. In June 1922 the CGT and CGTU porcelain workers' unions joined in a strike to limit the number of apprentices to be trained in the industry. Nonetheless, as in the Loire, the CGT showed a greater willingness to compromise for smaller gains. When the strike failed, the two unions exchanged angry recriminations: the CGTU accused its opponents of "treason" or "cowardice," while the CGT blamed its rivals for "inept" and "disorganized" handling of the affair, which, it said, caused many unionists to abandon the movement or to rejoin the moderate camp.[136]

Despite these early difficulties, the attempts at "unity of action" gathered momentum later in the decade, especially as syndicalists began to quit the CGTU for autonomy. In Saint-Etienne, the autonomists found a natural partnership with the CGT, once it moved its departmental headquarters back from Roanne in 1927. The two factions joined together in the local Bourse du Travail, which they agreed would house only one union for each industrial group or specialty. Meanwhile, they denied admission to the Communist unions, which instead formed a rival Union Locale Unitaire.[137] Two autonomous unions, in fact, continued on as

Bourse members, even after the CGT's reunification, as did one CGTSR union; another was barred from joining only because it duplicated a group already in the organization.[138] Prior to reunification, the autonomists and the CGT also maintained cordial relations with those minority syndicalists who preferred to stay in the CGTU, such as the coal miners (until 1933) and many metalworkers. Arnaud's miners, for example, tried to establish a united front with the local CGT in 1930–31, before their ultimate merger. The attempt was not actually consummated, because it was opposed by the CGT and by the CGTU's Communist leaders, and because conditions at the start of the Depression were not favorable for a strike.[139] Still, it showed the syndicalists' efforts to serve as intermediary and to work for unity among the various partisan groups.

This intermediate role was especially well illustrated by the Limoges autonomists, who intensified local efforts at unity of action in the porcelain and shoe industries after 1924. As joint action in strikes and contract negotiations became further routinized, the porcelain unions even issued joint communiqués signed only by "the secretaries" of "the corporation."[140] This habit of cooperation was nevertheless complicated by the founding of new Communist unions in both industries in early 1928. At first the Communist unions, both tiny groups, typically stood on the sidelines, issued their own strident demands, and condemned as "treason" the settlements reached by the "anarcho-reformists."[141] The autonomists in turn denounced the new unions as "bankrupt" and "fragmentary" bands *(groupuscules),* whose "perpetual agitation" threatened to sabotage the hard-earned victories that the two allies had won.[142] After about 1930, however, the tone began to change, as the autonomists drifted closer to the Communists and played, as observers put it, a "balancing game" between the two rival camps.[143]

The shift was especially dramatic among shoe unionists, some of whom now rejected their own former secretary's moderation (he soon rejoined the CGT) and moved instead toward the newly formed CGTSR.[144] Although these militants still found the Communists abhorrent politically, they shared their revolutionary fervor; for example, in a strike over a workers' dismissal for violation of the union contract, the autonomists joined the Communists in scorning all such contracts as mere "scraps of paper" and denouncing those (mainly CGT loyalists) who respected such contracts as *"jaunes."*[145] Autonomists in the porcelain industry did not take part in the CGTSR, but they still became increasingly hostile toward the CGT; they especially resented its heightened appeals for "integral unity," on its own terms, and its new critique of *ad hoc* cooperation as a mere "pantomime" or "charade."[146]

Despite these differences, it was clear that *ad hoc* unity found support because, or so far as, it proved fruitful in local actions, whether or not it fulfilled the political goals of the national organizations. The earliest efforts and the most fruitful results were among the most corporative labor groups, including the coal miners and the porcelain workers, who were likeliest to value material benefits over partisan advantage. Cooperation was also easiest when the groups shared similar skill levels and wage expectations, as was often the case among the autonomists or minority syndicalists and the CGT.[147] Meanwhile, the Communist Party appealed more to the interests of the least skilled workers, even if these did not join the party or the CGTU in large numbers. Although the party espoused its own version of labor "unity," it usually rejected the compromises favored by other groups.

The record of joint action was also influenced by economic conditions that affected entire industries. The same economic difficulties that would hinder unionization or strike activity also discouraged joint action among rival factions, as long as the results of such cooperation did not seem promising enough to overcome natural distaste. For this reason, there are few traces of joint action among Loire metalworkers (except insofar as minority syndicalists remained in the CGTU rather than opt for autonomy) and a more troubled record of joint action among shoe workers than among porcelain workers in Limoges. Nonetheless, even those skeptical of joint action seemed to base their position on practical grounds rather than on strict doctrinal considerations or partisan concerns.

To detect these "pragmatic" or "constructive" aspects of the postwar syndicalist movement may seem to confirm the idea that the syndicalists, like the Socialists or the Communists, had finally abandoned their prewar habits in recognition that these were no longer suited to modern realities. Such an argument, however, would reduce the essence of syndicalism to mere rabid revolutionism, or "noise and impotence" (as Dumoulin called it), with no more positive methods or goals. Instead, one can define a postwar syndicalist current that sought practical benefits while adhering to traditional syndicalist values of local autonomy and independence from partisan politics, and that resisted compromise for the sake of mass participation even while recognizing the utility of large-scale membership. Indeed, the idea of a "constructive" syndicalism, if applied as well to the prewar era, might help to resolve the apparent paradox of a movement all too easily dismissed as "a cause without rebels." If any proponent of constructive action is defined as a "non-syndicalist," no wonder there are few left to include in the syndicalists' ranks.

In addition to historians looking for the origins of "modern" forms of trade unionism, militants themselves have been all too eager to claim that their own faction represented "the wave of the future." These claims, whether by Socialists or by Communists, are much more significant as partisan propaganda than as an apt reflection of "the modern world." At least in the 1920s, there were neither mass unions, mass strikes, nor the economic conditions that might have helped to sustain them. Despite the war experience and the temporary postwar influx of new recruits, the labor movement in the 1920s remained not unlike, in composition or in strike behavior, the labor movement before 1914.

Beyond the schism itself, the major changes were the formation of a new Communist Party and its process of Bolshevization. However important, these changes were still based more on the political decisions of a minority—from Paris or from Moscow—than on the will of a mass movement with widespread local support. Despite its alleged commitment to labor unity and its search for new, more flexible methods, the party long proved unresponsive to variant local conditions and unable to win the support of the "proletarian masses" that it claimed to represent. After 1936, with a "new generation" of leaders and masses, the labor movement may finally have entered the long-anticipated "modern era." Nonetheless, recent events—from the strikes of 1968 to the ebbs and flows of the Communist Party—suggest that even today, the "syndicalist legacy" is far from dead.

Conclusion

World War I and the Russian Revolution marked an era of political and social upheaval in France and in most other European countries. Political conflicts over national defense plus social conflicts over industrial organization and labor relations served to radicalize the labor movement and interfered with the growth of reformism that had seemed all but inevitable in 1914. The example of revolution in Russia and the formation of a Communist Party in France launched a new type of French trade unionism that contrasted sharply with prewar syndicalist traditions. Still, despite the urgings of Communist — and Socialist — leaders, many unionists continued to endorse the principles of direct action and syndicalist autonomy. Although their numbers were limited, the syndicalists remained influential in various industrial and geographic contexts, while their Socialist and Communist rivals were no more successful in rallying mass support.

This study has examined the evolution of wartime and postwar trade unionism in two French localities in order to determine the nature of support for the syndicalist movement and the reasons for its continued survival. Two contrasting environments both produced fairly large syndicalist factions in the 1920s: the relatively moderate and well-organized labor movement of Limoges and the more extremist but highly fragmented labor movement of Saint-Etienne. In Limoges, the principal political influence was the Socialist Party, but most trade unionists either joined the Communist opposition or later quit the CGTU for autonomy; their defections only slowly replenished the ranks of the old CGT. In Saint-Etienne, the Communist Party temporarily dominated leftist politics but failed to overcome traditional syndicalist hostility to its own brand of reformism and its interference in union activities. Even those sectors normally among the party's strongholds, like mining and metallurgy, remained highly resistant to Communist unionism and were drawn instead to the revolutionary syndicalist CGTSR or to the minority opposition within the CGTU.

The case of Limoges shows the strengths and limits of Socialist reformism as a formative influence in trade-union politics. The close cooperation of prewar and wartime unionists and party leaders might imply that the Socialists' electoral and political strength would carry over to the postwar CGT. Instead, local unionists showed their acceptance of political unionism but their rejection of Socialist reformism when they joined the Communist Party and the CGTU. Still, those who quit both organizations to adopt a position of autonomy proved eager to cooperate with their former rivals. This cooperation was facilitated in part by the local Socialists' relative leftism, their working-class roots, and their traditional support for the principle of trade-union autonomy. Thus the region's prewar habits of cooperation without subordination continued to shape party-union relations in the postwar years and encouraged widespread support of, if not participation in, the CGT.

The case of Saint-Etienne shows instead the continued influence of prewar habits of anarcho-syndicalism and distrust for any leftist party. Despite the relative strength of trade unionism and syndicalist militancy in the region, neither the prewar Socialist nor the postwar Communist Party won widespread working-class support. Unionists who temporarily rallied to the new party, as a means to revolutionize their own organizations, were quickly disenchanted by its continued bourgeois composition and its pretensions to take charge of the unions when its own revolutionary credentials were at best uncertain. Even when the Communist Party did become more highly "proletarianized," it failed to convert the highly skilled craftsmen away from anarcho-syndicalism or to rally the mass of unskilled factory laborers who had resisted all forms of unionization in the past.

The parallel emergence of postwar syndicalist currents in both localities suggests certain common characteristics, despite the evident contrasts. Both cities were part of "older" industrial regions, with deeply embedded political traditions and a highly skilled labor force. These special features were perhaps less characteristic of other parts of the country where Socialist or Communist unionism did prove more successful. But these were hardly lone cases, and hardly identical one to the other: despite the incipient parallels the contrasts remained sharp. The syndicalist options themselves were quite distinct, with less anarchist influence in Limoges than in Saint-Etienne. Those who accepted *ad hoc* party allies made different choices—the Communists in the latter case, and the Socialists in the former—even while they renounced permanent ties.

These geographic differences were also at least as great as those among the various industries. Within the same city, common patterns developed: both the shoe and porcelain workers' unions in Limoges opted for autonomy, while Saint-Etienne's miners and metalworkers both expressed their ambivalence toward the CGTU. Nor did these unions regularly follow the patterns set by their national federations, either at the time of the CGT schism or in later conflicts among the CGTU's rival factions. Their local particularism echoed their earlier insistence that strikes be determined by local decision rather than according to a national or international timetable. Indeed, as others have concluded from the study of strike statistics, regional differences reflected distinct political attitudes and not just different patterns of industrial organization.[1] These regional differences, shown in levels of unionization as well as in strike frequencies or participation rates, have also remained relatively constant over time, despite the impact of technological change and political upheaval in the early twentieth century. This combination of continuity over time with diversity by geographic or industrial sector points in turn to several conclusions about the nature of postwar unionism and labor politics and about the difficulties of building a mass labor movement that could appeal to all groups.

The local emphasis shows first of all the limits of the appeal of Socialist or Communist unionism. Even if union leaderships inclined toward one or the other alternative, the rank and file did not necessarily follow suit. Their reluctance stemmed both from suspicion of central bureaucracies and from practical concern for bread-and-butter issues, which might best be handled by local leaders in tune with local needs. The point is not, however, to argue that ideas and ideologies were irrelevant to the everyday concerns of average workers. Although "the masses" are hard to know, given the limits of the historical record, there is evidence that syndicalist ideas (like those of rival factions) did have significant rank-and-file support.

It is also clear that Socialist and syndicalist traditions alike blocked the implantation of postwar communism, which developed more readily in rural areas and among unskilled workers than in sectors with deeply entrenched patterns of union or party behavior. Socialism might have led more directly to communism in areas where party-union ties were more rigid than in Limoges, whose unionists and workers instead enjoyed a dominant position in the local party. Continued collaboration of syndicalists and CGT loyalists was possible, but only in common opposition to the CGTU and the Communist Party. Autonomists in Limoges tried to create a compromise form of unionism that would collaborate with leftist parties, but only on its own terms.

The example of autonomous unionism was one of a variety of syndicalist options, which ranged from the CGTSR at its most sectarian to the CGTU minority at its most willing to cooperate with leftist politics. All reflected different choices but shared a common distrust for party domination and a common desire for the unions to take the lead in revolutionary strategy. Most were willing to compromise to some degree with the reality of national and international organization (even the CGTSR joined the anarchistic Berlin International), with the need for large unions and with the workers' desires for material improvements, although these were not to be supreme ends in themselves. Syndicalists also recognized the need for effective leadership, especially on the local level. The strikes of 1919–20, in particular, were not "spontaneous" except in their frequent disregard for the instructions of a central bureaucracy. Syndicalists also accepted *ad hoc* alliances either with the CGTU against the CGT, or vice versa, according to which seemed the most serious danger at the time.

These examples show how far the syndicalists had felt the impact of the war and the Russian Revolution. Like their Socialist and Communist rivals, the syndicalists tried to adapt to changed circumstances and to develop a pragmatic program to replace their prewar "noise and impotence," but they refused to see party-led union movements as the only workable solution. Not all their own answers were in fact equally viable or pragmatic. The highly sectarian CGTSR, like the fragmentary PUP, was a far-fetched attempt to achieve labor "unity" by yet another schism. The autonomists likewise underestimated the need for wider networks and government pressure groups, when they emphasized local groupings to exert "direct action" on local employers. The Communists, too, were far from pragmatic in their submission to Bolshevik dictate or in their attempts to impose uniform strategies on widely variant local conditions.

Nor did their strategic "zigzags" attract or keep the mass support that party leaders reputedly sought.

The Communists' own record illustrates the "love-hate" relationship between the French labor movement and the new Bolshevik phenomenon. However ambivalent the response of party leaders in Paris, the greatest resistance to Bolshevik implantation occurred among unionists in the provinces, who judged the new program according to its applicability to local conditions and its successes or failures in local strikes. Even when the party readily won control of the union organizations, on a local or national level, it often lost control of union members, so many of whom joined rival groups or quit the movement altogether. Nor was the choice of Communist unionism much more than a political decision by committed activists. Although it tried to create its own distinct proletarian constituency, the party still appealed mostly to the same groups of skilled workers and white-collar employees who supported the rival Socialist or syndicalist movements. Thus the debates among rival ideologies were still essentially confined to narrow labor elites rather than broadly extended throughout the working class.

Despite its failure, so far, to build a new social or economic constituency, the party did represent a new ideology and practice. As such, it was much more than just an extreme form of socialism, able simply to win the support of all those who habitually voted for or aligned with the group furthest to the left. In fact, the issue on which Communist politics hinged was not even the question of revolution, or extreme-left orientation, but the question of discipline and control by a centralized bureaucracy in Paris or in Moscow. This issue was dramatized by the continuities in the process of Bolshevization, despite the tactical "zigzags" after 1924. In turn, the issue for syndicalists was not revolution, as it had seemed in 1917–20, but union independence or autonomy. The various factions divided according to their views of union strategy, not by the degree of their orientation to the left.

As a result, the union schism was far more complex than the rupture that had created the Communist Party. Even unionists who demanded a truly revolutionary program failed to agree on how that program should be executed, or on which groups to turn to for support. Some of these conflicts were not yet apparent by the time of the CGT split at the end of 1921, when the syndicalists still mouthed the rhetoric of the Communist Party and joined in its critique of the highly skilled and privileged workers who remained in the old organization. The syndicalists, however, quickly abandoned their own proletarian rhetoric and consolidated their position in the smaller unions and troubled industries that had always been their principal strongholds. As such, they were often better able to cooperate with CGT reformists, when these shared their sociological makeup, than with the self-consciously (if exaggeratedly) "proletarian" unionists of the CGTU.

The syndicalists' base in the smaller unions was in part an accident of the labor movement's organization and statutes. These unions were easiest to convert to the left with a few votes, and then likeliest to demand that their votes be weighted equally with those of the larger unions rather than slighted in a system of proportional representation. The smaller unions were also those with the least hope for a massive recruitment that might, through sheer force of numbers, bring pressure for change on the government or the employers. Generally speaking, the smallest unions were also those in industries where industrial concentration had made relatively little progress. Still, this pattern did not make syndicalism a mark of industrial "backwardness" or a twentieth-century anachronism. Instead, it was associated more with the process of transformation than with the absence of change. Thus, it did not occur among the highly skilled artisans of the early nineteenth century—or later on among Saint-Etienne's artisanal silk weavers, who continued to work under much the same conditions. Instead, it arose among skilled factory workers faced with the loss of the special privileges and high wages that they had enjoyed in the past.

The survival of syndicalism in the postwar period was a sign that the conditions that had promoted it were not yet superseded. In political terms, the war hastened the conversion of some groups to the left but not necessarily to the Communist Party, especially if these were small groups where only the votes of a few individuals had triggered the shift. Nor did the failure of earlier revolutionary programs necessarily mandate support for the new party. The syndicalists blamed the postwar strike failures not on their own strategy but on the CGT's social reformism and attempts at mass unionization, and hence remained suspicious of the Communists' own version of mass unionism after 1921. The postwar "revolutionary failure" and political stabilization may have magnified the Communists' orthodoxy, as Robert Wohl has contended,[2] but it also minimized their appeal to many workers, who scorned the party's stress on long-range reorganization in favor of short-term syndicalist outbursts or sullen inaction. The same sense of frustration with which syndicalists dismissed the Socialists in 1921 was just as readily aimed at the Communists themselves after 1924.

Weak unionism and syndicalist frustration also reflected the economic effects of the postwar stabilization. Unlike a large-scale depression that might have furthered technological change by destroying the most inefficient industrial sectors, the recessions of 1921 and 1927 served only to weaken these industries and keep them vulnerable to economic hardships for the rest of the decade. These circumstances, in turn, weakened the unions but let them still recruit among these less efficient and more vulnerable sectors, where syndicalist tactics retained their familiar appeal. Although industrial concentration and new technologies did occur in certain sectors, and increased the number of unskilled workers, these changes were slow to transform union memberships or to cause a shift to new union strategies, as long as unions competed for the same skilled minorities rather than rally the less-skilled masses who resisted any form of unionization. The decline of artisanal specialties, insofar as it occurred, did not mean the demise of the syndicalist movement, which had long since broadened its appeal beyond the handful of skilled craftsmen who had reputedly constituted its "active minorities" during the "heroic years" before World War I.[3]

The nature of economic and social conditions in postwar France, and their continuity from the prewar era, thus explain much of the parallel continuity of French syndicalist doctrine. It would, of course, be simplistic to link labor strategies too closely to economic conditions, especially in the short term. Working-class attitudes may be said either to retain considerable autonomy from economic fluctuations or at least to demonstrate some inertia, which lets them respond to economic changes only after a delay or time lag of greater or lesser degree.[4] Nor should historians be so preoccupied with the limits of labor radicalism to overlook its extent, or to exaggerate the continued influence of traditional ideologies, especially those of a reformist nature.[5] Still, postwar unionists were not simply reluctant to endorse a given revolutionary strategy; they proposed a practical alternative to combat it. Syndicalists who rejected Communist leadership were not living in the past but had a distinct vision of the future, wherein practical reformism could be combined with revolutionary goals.

There is also a partisan edge to some arguments that "objective conditions" were not ripe for a Communist victory.[6] The claim allows one to avoid the less flattering assumption that Bolshevik doctrine was an alien import unsuited to native soil.[7] It also permits the hope that later structural changes would at last create the basis for Communist success, an assumption that is far from proven by the record of the 1930s or of the period since World War II.[8] Whatever its objective handicaps, the Communist Party must bear its own share of responsibility, especially for the negative results of its ultra-revolutionary strategies. These results might, of course, not be deemed a "failure" if the goal was not mass support but a party of disciplined cadres.[9] Even on its own terms, however, the party failed to uproot a syndicalist opposition that retained a substantial positive appeal.

As these debates illustrate, the problem for labor historians is still to determine the interconnections between class and politics, or between skill or salary differentials within the work force and factional divisions on the left.[10] There is surely no mechanistic correspondence, but one can nonetheless show circumstances in which workers do act as a class and others where they fail to do so, according both to the economic exigencies of the moment and to the strategic aims of leaders who may set particularist interests ahead of those of the larger group. The period of World War I was one of relatively high class solidarity, which bridged the economic and philosophical gap between skilled and unskilled workers and led the former to act more as a revolutionary vanguard than as a "labor aristocracy" defending their own craft privileges.[11] But their efforts collapsed with the end of the war.[12] The point is not, however, that this collapse left a revolutionary void into which Communist unionism rushed to enter.[13] That vacancy existed where Socialist and syndicalist currents had never developed, but not in areas where they flourished—if mostly as spokesmen for skilled labor—both before and after the war.

More than a problem in the economic roots of political behavior, the study of postwar syndicalism is finally an exercise in the problem of historical continuity. For historians of the early twentieth century, it is easy to exaggerate the political and economic consequences of World War I. The developments that changed the shape of French trade unionism—the proletarianization of the work force, the growth of reformism, and the emergence of new forms of party-union collaboration—predated the outbreak of hostilities and remained unfinished long after the peace treaty was signed. The war years were not "the end of an era" but rather an intermediate phase in a larger transformation that continued at least into the 1930s.[14] Labor historians who debate whether to place the turning point in 1918, in 1920, or in 1924 have in mind the germination of new labor strategies but not their growth or implantation, which occurred only much later on.[15]

It is tempting to place that turning point in the 1930s. The massive scale of economic hardship during the Great Depression brought both an increased government role in the economy and the flowering of new left-wing doctrines that finally did rally mass support. The decade also introduced new forms of strike activity, including brief but immense labor stoppages aimed mostly at political targets.[16] Nonetheless, these changes reflected external political developments—the Comintern's strategic about-face and the rise of Nazism in Germany—as much as internal social or economic realities.[17] The strength or unity of the new labor movement also did not last much beyond the demise of the Popular Front in 1938.[18] Even today, it is unclear whether the bases exist for a durable, unified, mass labor movement that can transcend France's anarcho-syndicalist heritage without becoming a simple appendage of the political left.

The special character of French trade unionism is sometimes explained by the ambivalence toward authority in a highly centralized political culture, or by the taste for extremism and violence commonly attributed to a "Latin" or Mediterranean personality. Economic considerations may be more to the point, as anarchism and revolutionary syndicalism have arisen especially in areas of uneven industrial development, where workers are caught in the transition from an artisanal economy and are disinclined to organize in large-scale unions or parties to defend their interests as a class. More characteristic of France than economic "backwardness," however, is the diversity of its economic structures, both in different regions and in different economic sectors. These differences may have narrowed in the 1920s but continued to exist. The point is not that "modernization" had not occurred but that it had failed to produce uniformity, failed, that is, to eliminate the geographic or industrial variations and the skill or salary differentials that typically divide one labor group from another. Indeed, any revolutionary ideology that expects such uniformity may be justly doomed to failure. The "failure of the revolution" in modern France is not the failure of a given set of tactics but the failure of an ideology that does not take such variations into account.

Note on Sources

The sources for this study include a wide variety of descriptive and statistical materials from private as well as public collections in France. The single most important category encompasses the police and prefectoral reports to the Ministries of Interior and Labor, available in the departmental and national archives. The collections open to scholars include most documents through 1940 (with the exception of certain confidential materials), now that the fifty-year access rule has essentially been lifted.[1] This ready access to documents now makes the twentieth century as attractive a subject for labor history as the late nineteenth century, which has so far received the most attention.

The police reports contain detailed information on the day-to-day activities and attitudes of the various local party and union organizations. While such reports must always be used carefully, with an eye for possible distortion or counterrevolutionary bias, they were nonetheless designed to give Paris an accurate view of local affairs. A greater potential difficulty lies in their frequent reliance on the use of paid informants, whose own motives and accuracy may be suspect. The police were, however, in a position to screen the evidence before they passed it on.[2]

The most important variable in the reports' quality was not basic accuracy or perceptiveness in their preparation but rather the energy or determination with which they were researched. For reasons that are not entirely clear, but that probably depended on the local authorities' readiness to perceive in leftist activities a revolutionary danger, Saint-Etienne engaged in much more energetic surveillance and much heavier use of paid informants than did Limoges.[3] The Limoges police, responding primarily to ministerial requests for information, offered more sporadic coverage of labor activity. They also offered less confidential information or insight, since they culled their data most often from public meetings, leaflets, and the press. The Saint-Etienne police were much more thorough in their surveillance of the more "dangerous" anarchist or Communist groups and the more strike-prone or shrill-voiced unions. Still, they tended, quite as their Limoges counterparts, to ignore the more moderate or routine tendencies within the labor movement. Therefore, despite its richness, the police documentation alone cannot provide a complete or balanced picture of the labor movement as a whole.

Occasional prefectoral overviews of local public opinion help in part to correct this imbalance. A further corrective may be found in private documents from trade-union or party archives, offering alternative points of view. While the diverse hazards of time, war, and housecleaning have taken their toll on the availability of such private archives, certain registers of union meetings and debates can nonetheless be found at the local Bourses du Travail.[4] In addition, some interviews with local figures and their families, rare privileges in view of the fading memories or simple absence of individuals old enough to have been active in the 1920s, have provided valuable insights lacking in the conventional documentation.[5] The local party and union press remains, of course, a vast and readily accessible source for accounts of day-to-day events and issues.[6]

In addition to this category of narrative or descriptive sources is a mass of quantitative data that serves as underpinning for the accounts of political and union activities described above. Although no precise membership figures are available in local party or union documents, the police data give some indications of relative organizational strength. Detailed election reports identify working-class and other candidates and evaluate voter sympathy. Strike reports describe each incident of strike activity and may be compared to the summaries published by the Labor Ministry, which indicate strike frequency, duration, worker participation, and result, for each industry, each locality, and each year.[7]

The manuscript strike reports, unlike the published statistics for the interwar years, also provide data on the number of local enterprises and the total size of the labor force in the affected industry, the salary levels before and after the strike, and the details of the strikers' demands. Other information concerning wage and price levels, unemployment, and the general structure and operation of the local industries may also be found in the police and prefectoral reports. Private business archives unfortunately are scarce or are closed to scholars, except for the massive documentation from the now-nationalized mining industry available at the departmental archives in Saint-Etienne.[8] Most of the administrative and financial data contained in such business records would lie, however, outside the scope of the present study.

The absence of business archives is especially regrettable, because they alone would provide detailed information on the identity and work behavior of individual employees. Companies in Limoges and Saint-Etienne contacted for purposes of this study lacked any such comprehensive personnel files and could at best provide periodic pay lists with employees' names.[9] Although these lists of names might be helpful to estimate job turnover within each company, they gave insufficient information to permit positive identification with individuals named in other sources. Thus, for example, it is not possible to know from the pay lists that a worker at the Haviland porcelain company who practiced a certain specialty or who lost his job at the time of a strike or a recession was the same individual named in police reports as a leader of the porcelain union — even if the name might be the same.

In the absence of usable personnel files, the analysis of the composition of the labor force must be based primarily on the manuscript census, which cites occupation, sex, and place and date of birth. Sample data from the censuses of each city provide the basis for analysis of the labor force in the major industries in 1921 and 1931 and the changes in its composition since 1911.[10] The decline of artisanal employment as industries mechanized and the accompanying changes in the age and sex distributions and geographic origins of the work force help to explain changes in the political behavior of the major labor groups during and after the war. The census data can also be compared to data in the police reports on the union and party leadership. The rank and file of these organizations, however, must remain anonymous, since there are no membership lists to provide similar identification or description. The statistical data alone can thus provide no conclusive correlations between the social characteristics of the labor force and the size or orientation of a union or party; nevertheless, the census data can suggest fruitful hypotheses to be evaluated with the help of qualitative data from the other sources.

The Manuscript Census: Note on Methodology

The manuscript census for a French city records the name, date and place of birth, and occupation (if any) of each city resident.[1] This information provides the basis for the published summaries of the departmental and national populations. Except for recent years, however, no published summaries of such population data are available on the municipal level. The volumes of the manuscript census list totals of the city population, divided by canton, and sometimes divided into rough age groups. Nonetheless, for further information the researcher is obliged to tally the data himself.

In order to keep the numbers manageable, this study has relied on samples from the total census data. The arrangement of the census by alphabetical order of the street names provides a ready technique for sampling, free of any intrinsic bias. The technique used in this study was to record all workers (in the industries chosen for study[2]) who were listed on one of a given number of pages from the census. This method was simpler than selecting one out of a number of names on each page. The technique also provided a sample of the entire population rather than just a proportion of the workers in each industry. The totals can therefore be used to indicate the relative size of the labor forces in each industry in each city.

The samples measure the labor force in one-eighth of the population of Limoges and one-twenty-fourth of the population of Saint-Etienne. The size of the sample was chosen to provide a large enough number of cases in each occupational category—approximately 100 or more cases—for the results to be statistically significant. While decimal samples are more common than fractional samples, one-tenth seemed too small for Limoges. The one-eighth sample instead chosen for Limoges would in turn have been too large for Saint-Etienne. To reduce the sample while keeping it proportional to that of Limoges, it seemed appropriate to reduce the dimension to one-third that of Limoges, or one-twenty-fourth of the Saint-Etienne population.

For Limoges, only the canton "Nord" was chosen for study, in order to limit the size of the sample. This canton was the most characteristically "urban" and the only one of the city's four cantons defined as within the city limits until after 1901. All four cantons were used in the Saint-Etienne study, however, as all were equally part of the city's identity, and each had its own most characteristic industries that might have been misrepresented if only one canton were used. These differences in the size of the two cities' samples do not affect the reliability of the results, as long as it is remembered that the samples reveal proportions rather than the absolute size of each component group.

As in any use of sampling techniques, even an unbiased sample may not yield totals that reflect perfectly the "real" census totals. The chance for error is especially great as the categories are broken down into component elements that may contain only a few cases.[3] As a check on the reliability of the sample data, however, it is possible to compare the sizes of the labor force of each group in the sample with the totals derived from other sources. To do this, one must first adjust the sample totals to compensate for their proportion of the total city population.

In the case of Saint-Etienne, the sample totals (cited in Figure 6) can be extrapolated to reflect the total city population merely by multiplying the samples by twenty-four.[4] In the case of Limoges, however, the sample totals (cited in Figure 3) reflect only a single canton, which accounted for about one-half (43 to 44 percent) of the city's total population. Thus the totals need to be multiplied by sixteen, rather than by eight, to reflect the population of the city as a whole.[5]

In the case of Saint-Etienne, the correspondence between the two sets of figures is quite striking:

Industry	Census Extrapolations			Other Estimates		
					Early	*Late*
	1911	*1921*	*1931*	*1891*	*1920s*	*1920s*
Textiles	5,760	7,368	7,440	11,500	8,000	8,800
Metals	6,984	12,216	14,928	5,400	15,000	17,400
Mines	5,760	9,096	8,376	4,500	8,000	10,400
Railroads	1,464	2,256	2,760	1,100	3,000	3,500

Only the figures for the textile industry in the prewar era are noticeably out of line. This discrepancy can probably be attributed in large part to changes between 1891 and 1911, during which time the textile industry was declining while other industries continued to grow.[6] In the case of Limoges, the two sets of figures appear less well matched:

Industry	Census Extrapolations			Other Estimates		
					Early	Late
	1911	*1921*	*1931*	*1905*	*1920s*	*1920s*
Porcelain	4,768	3,232	2,816	10,500	6,000	6,000
Shoes	1,648	3,424	4,368	2,000	7,500	6,900
Railroads	1,696	2,160	2,064	?	2,500	2,100

Although the figures do give similar proportions of porcelain to shoe workers, the census samples seem to account for only about half the totals estimated in other sources. It is likely, however, that those estimates referred to the entire department rather than just to the city.[7] While sampling error may account for further distortion, the accuracy of the proportions suggests that the sample totals are sufficiently reliable for the analysis in this study.

The original samples for Saint-Etienne also included glassworkers, but too few were recorded for analysis. In all likelihood, the small numbers were not the result of sampling error; rather, they reflected the small size of the industry at Saint-Etienne. If the total of 9 glassworkers in the 1911 sample and the 7 each in the 1921 and 1931 samples are extrapolated to reflect the entire city population, they would imply totals of 216 glassworkers in 1911 and 168 in 1921 and in 1931. These totals are not far from those estimated in other sources. Although there were nearly 600 glassworkers in the city in the mid-1920s, the industry had declined sharply during the war and was hard hit by economic crisis in 1921 and again after 1929.[8]

Some of the discrepancy in the sizes of the samples may be the result of difficulties in identifying workers and specialties from the information recorded in the census. Only those individuals identifiable as workers in the industries chosen for study were included in the samples. (In the case of the railroad industry, white-collar employees were also included because it was not possible to distinguish them from workers.) In most cases it was a simple matter to identify workers and their industries, even where the census cited the specific trade rather than the industrial label. But some individuals had to be omitted, where no reasonable guess as to their occupation was possible. For example, *"mouleurs"* and *"tourneurs,"* trades in both the porcelain and the metals industries, were omitted from the Limoges samples unless the census specified *"—sur porcelaine."* *"Coupeurs"* (cutters) were similarly omitted unless the census specified *"—en chaussures."* In Saint-Etienne, there were fewer cases where occupation was in doubt. Nonetheless, except for the 1931 census, where the document specified otherwise, those few individuals labeled *"patrons"* were omitted from the samples, although they may indeed have been artisans rather than *fabricants*.

Another problem was the identification of the place of birth of each individual. In some cases, where only the name of the commune was recorded, it was not possible to identify its location in a department or region. Such "unknown" cases numbered only 7 out of 1,632 in the Limoges samples (plus 15 cases where no birthplace was recorded), but 62 out of 3,547 (1.7 percent) in the samples for Saint-Etienne. That figure was kept within reasonable bounds by the decision to assign, whenever possible, a probable departmental location—with preference for the one closest, in ambiguous cases—to places with doubtful spelling or identification. This decision can be justified by the fact that the census taker's omission of the name of the department implied that the commune was familiar or nearby. (Distant birthplaces were usually identified by department alone.) It may be assumed, finally, that unidentified birthplaces were all outside Limoges or Saint-Etienne. Thus, the proportion born in the city should be calculated as a percentage of the total, rather than just as a percentage of the known data.

The "birthplace code" used in the tables in the appendix defines workers' origins as belonging to one of several locations or regions. These categories are self-explanatory except for that labeled "neighbor departments." This label refers to those departments literally bordering on the Haute-Vienne or the Loire, whose proximity facilitated migration to the cities.[9] In the case of Saint-Etienne, however, those born in the neighboring department of the Haute-Loire are considered part of the department itself because of their proximity and economic ties to the Loire basin. The arrondissement of Yssingeaux (Haute-Loire) is often defined as part of the Saint-Etienne economic region because it engaged in many of the same textile and hardware trades and supplied much peasant labor for the coal mines.[10] Including these workers as migrants from neighboring departments would exaggerate the city's attraction for newcomers from outside the city's immediate zone.

A final remark may be in order concerning the handling and interpretation of this body of census data. The process of counting and cross-tabulating the data might have been readily computerized but was instead done entirely by hand. In the absence of more elaborate technology, no attempt was made to calculate correlation coefficients or other statistical measures except for the obvious device of percents. But there is no point calculating mathematical correlations between one demographic attribute and another; simple cross-tabulations are sufficient to show relationships between sex and geographic origins, for example, or between artisanal specialization and age. More elaborate methods might be appropriate to show correlations between these attributes and rates of unionization, for example, if better data on union membership were available. At present, the census data can suggest reasons for continuity or change in labor behavior but cannot show mathematically that such patterns indeed had sociological or demographic roots.

Appendix: Tables and Graphs

Figure 1. Geographic Origins of Limoges and Saint-Etienne
Populations, 1911

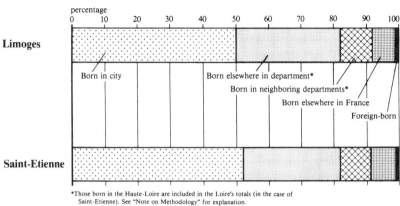

*Those born in the Haute-Loire are included in the Loire's totals (in the case of
Saint-Etienne). See "Note on Methodology" for explanation.

Sources: Larivière, *La population du Limousin,* 2:480, 590; Schnetzler, "L'origine de la
population de Saint-Etienne," in *Les villes du Massif Central,* p. 50.

Figure 2. Estimated Industrial Employment in Limoges, Early 1920s

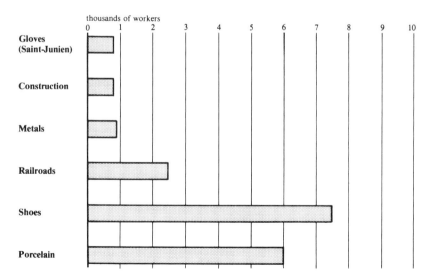

Sources: Diverse; see ch. 1, n. 15.

Figure 3. Workers in Limoges Industries, 1911 to 1931 (Sample Data)

	Porcelain Industry			Shoe Industry		
	1911	1921	1931	1911	1921	1931
Total sample	298	202	176	103	214	273
Male	172	136	92	78	158	126
Female	126	66	84	25	56	147
*Total no. artisans**	58	17	24	55	3	50
Male	46	12	19	55	3	47
Female	12	5	5	–	–	3
No. aged under 20	44	23	13	20	59	28
Male [artisans]	20 [5]	14 [1]	6 [–]	13 [6]	40 [1]	10 [5]
Female [artisans]	24 [1]	9 [–]	7 [2]	7 [–]	19 [–]	18 [–]
No. aged 20 to 34	136	65	45	37	72	134
Male [artisans]	79 [22]	35 [5]	19 [3]	24 [17]	49 [1]	60 [14]
Female [artisans]	57 [6]	30 [2]	26 [1]	13 [–]	23 [–]	74 [1]
No. aged 35 to 49	64	72	65	30	51	69
Male [artisans]	39 [9]	52 [2]	34 [7]	27 [19]	41 [1]	29 [14]
Female [artisans]	25 [4]	20 [2]	31 [–]	3 [–]	10 [–]	40 [1]
No. aged 50 to 64	42	33	38	12	25	36
Male [artisans]	24 [7]	28 [2]	19 [4]	10 [10]	21 [–]	21 [10]
Female [artisans]	18 [1]	5 [1]	19 [2]	2 [–]	4 [–]	15 [1]
No. aged 65 or over	12	9	15	4	5	6
Male [artisans]	10 [3]	7 [2]	14 [5]	4 [3]	5 [–]	6 [4]
Female [artisans]	2 [–]	2 [–]	1 [–]	–	–	–

No. born in city					
210	133	124	69	137	164
Male [artisans] 116 [40]	85 [7]	67 [19]	47 [31]	93 [2]	78 [30]
Female [artisans] 94 [10]	48 [4]	57 [4]	22 [–]	44 [–]	86 [–]
No. born in dept.					
68	44	44	24	48	68
Male [artisans] 45 [5]	32 [2]	20 [1]	22 [16]	39 [1]	33 [11]
Female [artisans] 23 [1]	12 [1]	24 [1]	2 [–]	9 [–]	35 [1]
No. born in neighbor depts.					
12	10	4	7	16	25
Male [artisans] 7 [1]	9 [1]	2 [–]	6 [5]	13 [–]	7 [3]
Female [artisans] 5 [–]	1 [–]	2 [–]	1 [–]	3 [–]	18 [1]
No. born elsewhere in France					
8	3	2	3	6	14
Male [artisans] 4 [–]	1 [–]	1 [–]	3 [3]	6 [–]	6 [3]
Female [artisans] 4 [1]	2 [–]	1 [–]	– [–]	6 [–]	8 [1]
No. foreign-born					
–	1	2	–	3	2
Male [artisans] –	1 [1]	2 [–]	–	3 [–]	2 [–]
Female [artisans] –	– [–]	–	–	–	–

*"Artisans" include painters and decorators in the porcelain industry and shoemakers (*cordonniers*) in the shoe industry.

Source: Sample data from the manuscript census.

Note: Differences between sample totals and totals by age or birthplace reflect cases where information is unknown.

Figure 4. Size and Structure of Haute-Vienne Industries, 1906 to 1931

Porcelain Industry

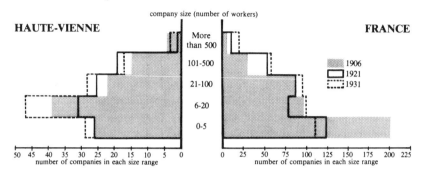

Shoe Industry

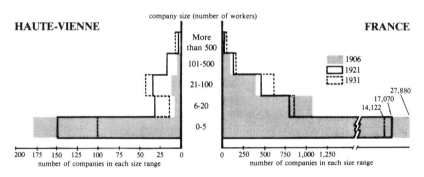

Source: *Résultats statistiques du recensement,* 1906, 1921, and 1931.

Figure 5. Estimated Industrial Employment in Saint-Etienne
and Loire Basin, Early 1920s

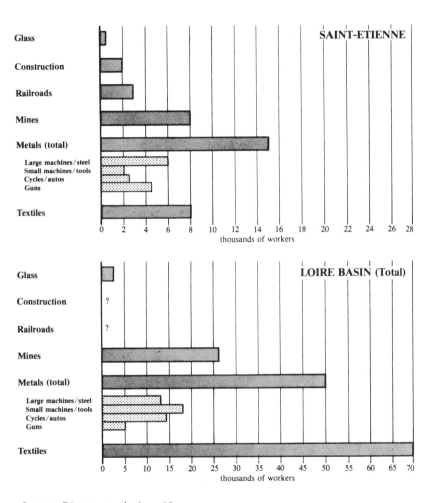

Sources: Diverse; see ch. 1, n. 19.

Figure 6. Workers in Saint-Etienne Industries, 1911 to 1931 (Sample Data)

	Textile Industry			Metals Industry			Mining Industry		
	1911	1921	1931	1911	1921	1931	1911	1921	1931
Total sample	240	307	310	291	509	622	240	379	349
Male	86	89	102	287	473	557	240	373	344
Female	154	218	208	4	36	65	—	6	5
*Total no. artisans**	116	149	101	75	46	85	—	—	—
Male	74	87	60	75	46	84	—	—	—
Female	42	62	41	—	—	1	—	—	—
Total no. manual laborers	—	—	—	19	67	27	10	25	23
No. aged under 20	19	44	30	33	60	55	13	32	15
Male [artisans]	—	5 [5]	3 [1]	31 [8]	51 [4]	45 [10]	13	30	14
Female [artisans]	19 [2]	39 [13]	27	2	9	10	—	2	1
No. aged 20 to 34	88	83	73	109	189	231	86	151	138
Male [artisans]	15 [11]	13 [12]	13 [6]	107 [21]	171 [20]	197 [31]	86	150	137
Female [artisans]	73 [21]	70 [20]	60 [12]	2	18	17	—	1	1
No. aged 35 to 49	77	88	74	83	152	197	94	136	120
Male [artisans]	36 [34]	25 [24]	23 [14]	83 [17]	143 [14]	180 [26]	94	134	118
Female [artisans]	41 [10]	63 [18]	51 [14]	—	9	3	—	2	2
No. aged 50 to 64	40	71	105	56	90	114	40	51	66
Male [artisans]	24 [20]	36 [36]	46 [29]	56 [16]	90 [7]	111 [12]	40	51	65
Female [artisans]	16 [7]	35 [10]	59 [12]	—	—	1	—	—	—
No. aged 65 or over	16	21	28	9	18	25	7	8	10
Male [artisans]	11 [9]	10 [10]	17 [10]	9 [3]	18 [1]	24 [5]	7	8	10
Female [artisans]	5 [2]	11 [1]	11 [3]	—	—	1	—	—	—

No. born in city	165	212	205	139	246	336	95	97	111
Male [artisans]	62 [52]	67 [42]	69 [43]	136 [41]	226 [28]	301 [48]	95	96	107
Female [artisans]	103 [28]	145 [28]	136 [23]	3	20	35 [1]	—	1	4
*No. born in dept.***	61	81	84	95	147	182	100	128	88
Male [artisans]	22 [20]	18 [14]	25 [16]	94 [18]	136 [12]	164 [22]	100	125	88
Female [artisans]	39 [12]	63 [16]	59 [15]	1	11	3	—	3	—
*No. born in neighbor depts.***	8	6	12	22	27	33	25	13	25
Male [artisans]	1 [1]	1 [1]	4	22 [3]	25 [2]	30 [3]	25	13	25
Female [artisans]	7 [2]	5 [1]	8 [1]	—	2	3	—	—	—
No. born elsewhere in France	4	2	8	23	26	37	14	22	8
Male [artisans]	1 [1]	1	4 [1]	23 [8]	25 [1]	32 [8]	14	20	8
Female [artisans]	3	1	4 [2]	—	1	5	—	2	—
No. foreign-born	—	—	1	4	43	34	1	105	117
Male [artisans]	—	—	—	4 [2]	42 [1]	30 [3]	1	105	116
Female [artisans]	—	—	1	—	1	4	—	—	1

*"Artisans" include weavers in the textile industry and gunsmiths in the metals industry.
**Those born in the Haute-Loire are included in the Loire's totals. See "Note on Methodology" for explanation.

Source: Sample data from the manuscript census.

Note: Differences between sample totals and totals by age or birthplace reflect cases where information is unknown.

Figure 7. Size and Structure of Loire Industries, 1906 to 1931

Silk Ribbon Weaving

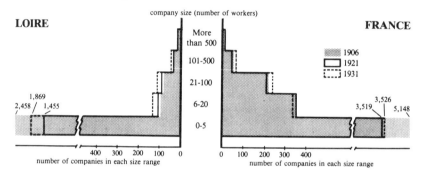

Metals Industry

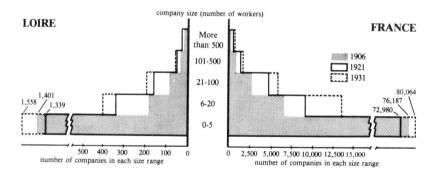

Mining Industry

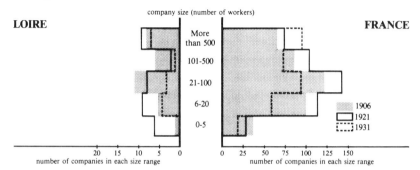

Glass Industry

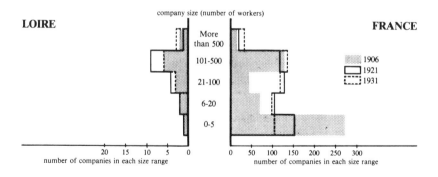

Source: *Résultats statistiques du recensement,* 1906, 1921, and 1931.

Figure 8. Railroad Workers in Limoges and Saint-Etienne, 1911 to 1931
(Sample Data)

	Limoges			Saint-Etienne		
	1911	1921	1931	1911	1921	1931
Total sample	106	135	129	61	94	115
Male	105	132	126	61	93	114
Female	1	3	3	—	1	1
No. aged under 20	—	10	—	—	2	2
Male		9			2	2
Female		1			—	—
No. aged 20 to 34	44	53	36	22	39	51
Male	44	51	34	22	39	50
Female	—	2	2	—	—	1
No. aged 35 to 49	37	48	73	24	34	40
Male	36	48	72	24	34	40
Female	1	—	1	—	—	—
No. aged 50 to 64	22	17	20	15	19	20
Male	22	17	20	15	18	20
Female	—	—	—	—	1	—
No. aged 65 or over	2	4	—	—	—	2
Male	2	4				2
Female	—	—				—
No. born in city	7	19	19	19	32	32
Male	7	16	19	19	32	32
Female	—	3	—	—	—	—
No. born in dept.	38	51	53	27	34	60
Male	38	51	53	27	34	60
Female	—	—	—	—	—	—
No. born in neighbor depts.	38	36	36	11	9	14
Male	37	36	34	11	9	13
Female	1	—	2	—	—	1
No. born elsewhere in France	22	23	21	2	17	9
Male	22	23	20	2	16	9
Female	—	—	1	—	1	—
No. foreign-born	—	—	—	—	—	—
Male						
Female						

Source: Sample data from the manuscript census.

Note: Differences between sample totals and totals by age or birthplace reflect cases where information is unknown.

Figure 9. Size and Frequency of Strikes, 1912–30

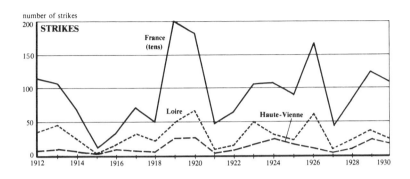

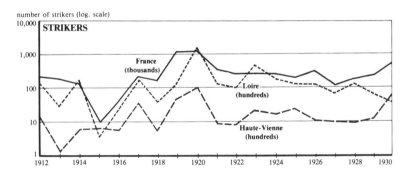

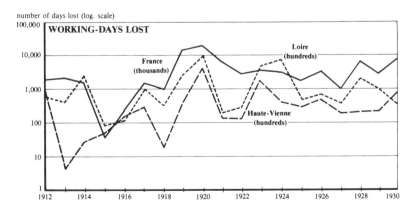

Source: *Statistique des grèves*, 1912–30.

Note: These graphs are intended to show patterns of change over time; there is no fixed proportionality between the figures for the two departments and those for France as a whole.

Figure 10. Strikes in Haute-Vienne Industries, 1912–30

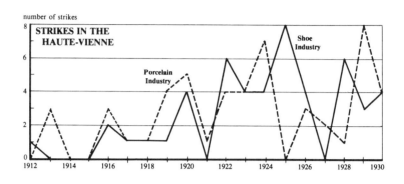

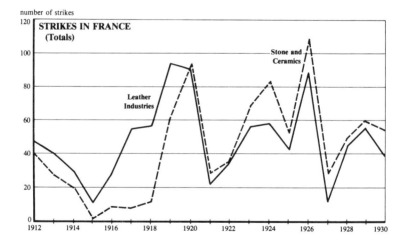

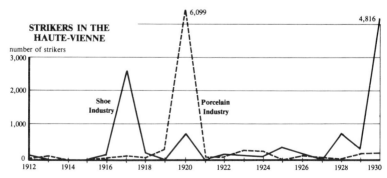

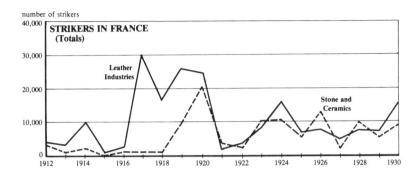

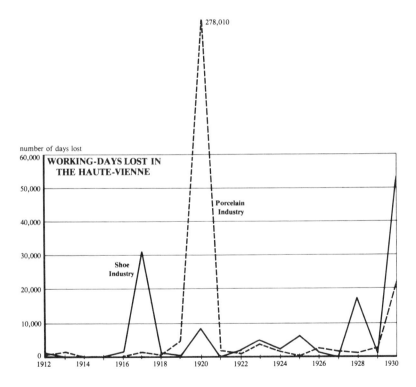

Source: *Statistique des grèves,* 1912–30.

Note: Total working-days lost are not reported per industry for France as a whole after 1914.

Figure 11. Strikes in Loire Industries, 1912–30

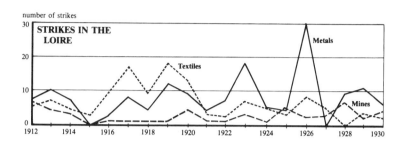

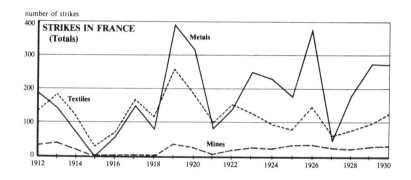

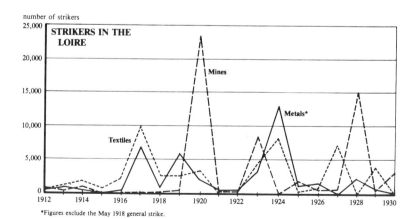

*Figures exclude the May 1918 general strike.

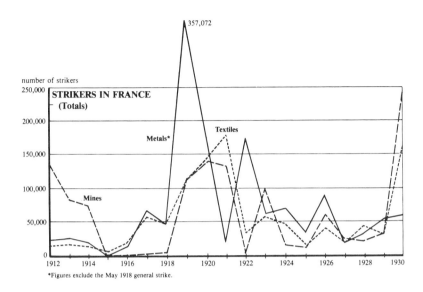

357,072

number of strikers

STRIKERS IN FRANCE (Totals)

Metals*

Textiles

Mines

*Figures exclude the May 1918 general strike.

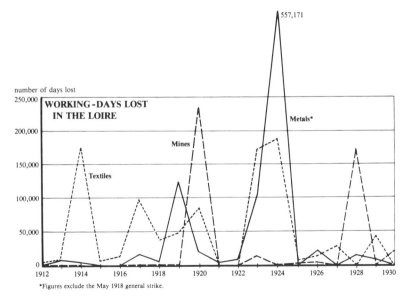

557,171

number of days lost

WORKING-DAYS LOST IN THE LOIRE

Metals*

Mines

Textiles

*Figures exclude the May 1918 general strike.

Source: *Statistique des grèves*, 1912–30.

Note: Total working-days lost are not reported per industry for France as a whole after 1914.

Figure 12. Results of Strikes, 1912–30
(Failures as Percent of Total Strikes)

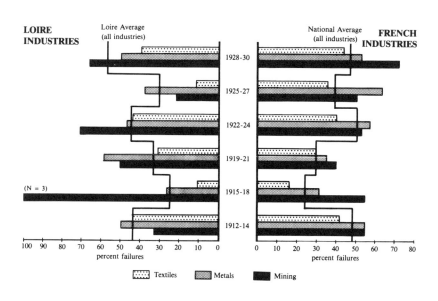

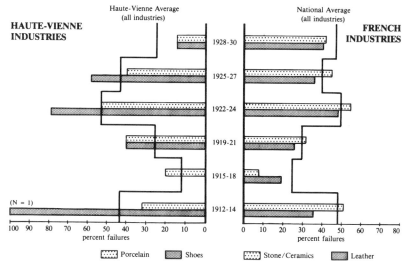

Source: *Statistique des grèves*, 1912–30.

Note: "Failures" are strikes that failed to reach even a compromise solution.

Figure 13. Anarchists in the Loire, by Occupation, 1914

Occupation	Saint-Etienne Activists	Departmental List			
		Saint-Etienne	Saint-Etienne Suburbs	Roanne and Montbrison	Dept. Total
Factory metalworkers	10	17	21	5	43
Gunsmiths	4	10	—	—	10
Weavers	3	9	2	11	22
Other artisanal trades					
Construction	1	5	7	—	12
Wood	2	2	1	—	3
Glass	1	—	2	—	2
Shoes	1	1	—	2	3
Tailors	1	1	2	—	3
Dyers	—	1	8	—	9
Other	—	4	4	1	9
Total	6	14	24	3	41
Miners	—	1	9	—	10
Typesetters	1	2	—	—	2
Commerce	—	6	6	8	20
Manual laborers	—	5	4	4	13
Housewives	—	3	—	—	3
Unknown	2	—	—	—	—
Grand Total	26	67	66	31	164

Sources: For Saint-Etienne activists: ADL 19 M 33–37, reports on anarchist meetings, naming those present, 1913–14; M 432, Anarchistes et antimilitaristes, rayés, décédés ou disparus, 1911–20. For Departmental List: 19 M 37, Etat nominatif des anarchistes inscrits dans le département de la Loire (1914).

Figure 14. Anarchists in the Saint-Etienne Basin,
by City of Residence and by Occupation, 1914

City of Residence	Metal-workers	Weavers and Other Artisans	Miners	Commerce	Other	Total
Saint-Chamond/ Izieux	5	17	1	—	3	26
Rive-de-Gier	3	3	4	1	—	11
Le Chambon-Feugerolles	8	1	—	1	—	10
Firminy/Unieux	1	1	—	2	—	4
Total	17	22	5	4	3	51

Source: ADL 19 M 37, Etat nominatif des anarchistes inscrits dans le département de la Loire (1914).

Figure 15. Geographic Origins of Saint-Etienne Anarchists, 1914

Birthplace	Metal-workers	Gun-smiths	Weavers	Other Artisans	Other	Total
Saint-Etienne Activists						
City	3	2	2	3	2	12
Arrondissement	3	—	1	—	—	4
Dept. and neighbors	2	2	—	2	—	6
Other France	—	—	—	—	—	—
Foreign	—	—	—	—	—	—
Unknown	2	—	—	1	1	4
Total	10	4	3	6	3	26
Departmental List (Saint-Etienne)						
City	4	6	7	5	10	32
Arrondissement	5	1	1	2	2	11
Dept. and neighbors	3	3	1	7	3	17
Other France	4	—	—	—	1	5
Foreign	1	—	—	—	1	2
Total	17	10	9	14	17	67

Sources: For Saint-Etienne activists: ADL 19 M 33-37, reports on anarchist meetings, naming those present, 1913–14; M 432, Anarchistes et antimilitaristes, rayés, décédés ou disparus, 1911–20. For Departmental List: 19 M 37, Etat nominatif des anarchistes inscrits dans le département de la Loire (1914).

Figure 16. Age Distribution of Loire Anarchists, by Occupation, 1914

Age Group	Metal-workers	Gun-smiths	Weavers	Other Artisans	Other	Total
			Saint-Etienne Activists			
50 and over	—	—	—	—	—	—
35 to 49	—	1	2	3	—	6
20 to 34	8	3	1	3	—	15
Under 20	—	—	—	—	—	—
Unknown	2	—	—	—	3	5
Total	10	4	3	6	3	26
		Departmental List (Saint-Etienne)				
65 and over	—	—	—	—	—	—
50 to 64	2	1	1	—	3	7
35 to 49	5	4	7	6	5	27
20 to 34	10	5	1	6	9	31
Under 20	—	—	—	2	—	2
Total	17	10	9	14	17	67
			Departmental Totals			
65 and over	1	—	—	3	1	5
50 to 64	12	1	5	8	13	39
35 to 49	11	4	14	18	21	68
20 to 34	19	5	3	10	12	49
Under 20	—	—	—	2	1	3
Total	43	10	22	41	48	164

Sources: For Saint-Etienne activists: ADL 19 M 33–37, reports on anarchist meetings, naming those present, 1913–14; M 432, Anarchistes et antimilitaristes, rayés, décédés ou disparus, 1911–20. For Departmental List: 19 M 37, Etat nominatif des anarchistes inscrits dans le département de la Loire (1914).

Figure 17. Cost-of-Living Indices, Regional and National, 1911–19

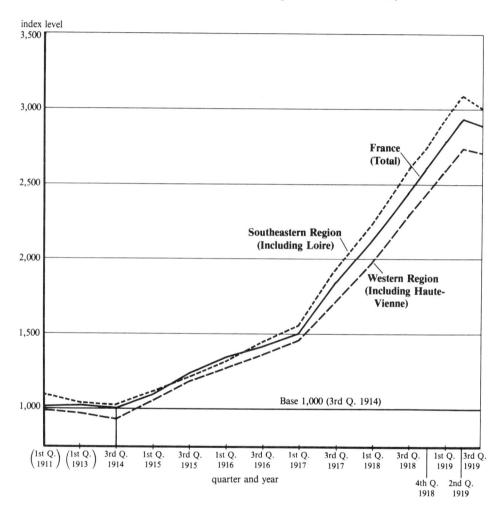

Source: *Bulletin du Ministère du Travail et de la Prévoyance Sociale,* nos. 11–12 (Nov.– Dec. 1919), p. 548.

Figure 18. Cost-of-Living Index, Loire, 1920–30

Sources: ADL M 640 and 640 bis, reports for 1920–29; M 452, reports for 1929–30.
Note: Broken lines are estimates for unavailable information.

Figure 19. Unemployment in the Limoges Shoe Industry, 1921:
Averages by Company Size

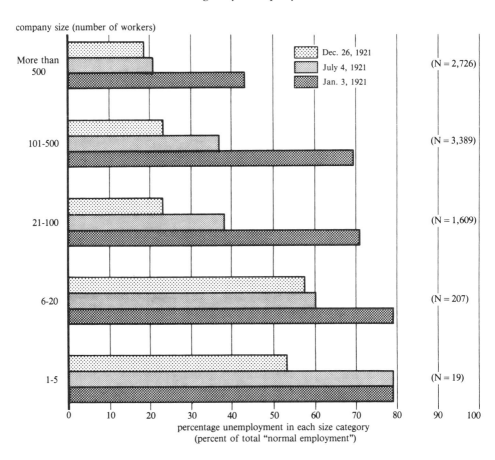

Source: ADHV 10 M 64, weekly reports on unemployment in the Limoges shoe industry,
(These reports give the "normal" size of each company and the number of workers actually
employed at each date.)

Figure 20. Unionization in Limoges and Loire Industries, 1921–30

Industry	1921 (Totals)	1922		1924		1927			1930		
		CGT	CGTU	CGT	CGTU	CGT	Autonomists	CGTU	CGT	Autonomists	CGTU
Limoges Industries											
Porcelain	2,550	817	1,100	800	1,200	1,100	1,280	—	1,200	900	100
Shoes	1,000	—	500	60	500	400	950	—	550	650	250
Railroads	1,300	500	500	100	500	160	—	700	250	—	800
Loire Industries											
Mines											
Saint-Etienne	?	100	500	?	?	600	—	1,500	200	—	700
Firminy	?	900	150	?	?	?	—	?	800	—	300
Loire (total)	4,000	1,000	3,000	?		?	—	?	1,000	—	1,000
Metals											
Saint-Etienne	140	?	240	?		84	—	215	40	—	200
Loire (total)	?	?	?	?		?	—	800	?	—	700
Railroads											
(Saint-Etienne)	?	?	?	?		62	—	1,100	160	—	800

Sources: Diverse; see ch. 9, n. 62.

Figure 21. Strike Participation by Company Size, Loire Industries, 1912–30

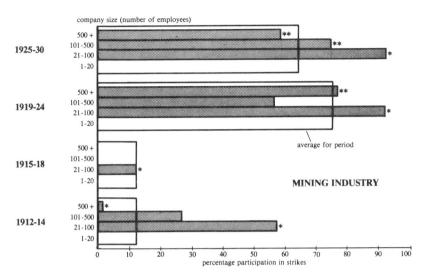

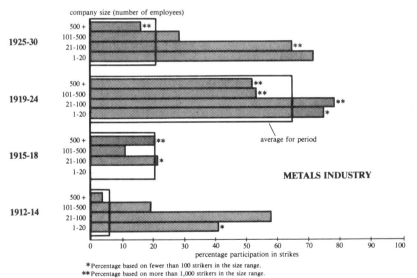

*Percentage based on fewer than 100 strikers in the size range.
**Percentage based on more than 1,000 strikers in the size range.

Source: *Statistique des grèves,* 1912–30.

Note: Participation rates are calculated on the basis of total employment in affected companies. Period averages are calculated according to the actual numbers of strikers in each category. Strikes of more than one company are classed according to the average size of the companies involved.

Figure 22. Strike Participation by Company Size,
Haute-Vienne Industries, 1912–30

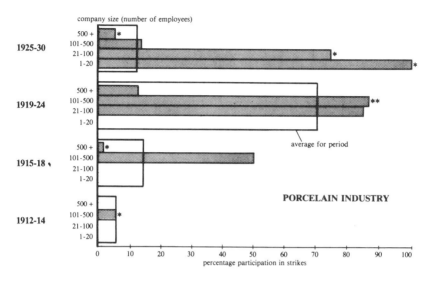

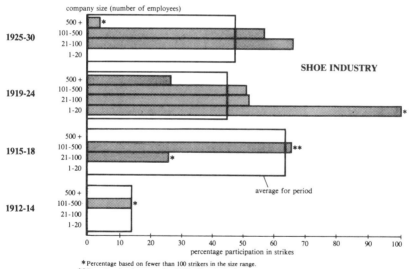

*Percentage based on fewer than 100 strikers in the size range.
**Percentage based on more than 1,000 strikers in the size range.

Source: *Statistique des grèves,* 1912–30.

Note: Participation rates are calculated on the basis of total employment in affected companies. Period averages are calculated according to the actual numbers of strikers in each category. Strikes of more than one company are classed according to the average size of the
companies involved.

Abbreviations Used in the Notes

NEWSPAPER SOURCES

Bataille Synd. Lim.	*La Bataille Syndicaliste Limousine*
Bull. C.	*Bulletin Communiste*
Bull. CCL	*Bulletin de la Chambre de Commerce de Limoges*
Bull. CCSE	*Bulletin de la Chambre de Commerce de Saint-Etienne*
Bull. Synd. Typos	*Bulletin du Syndicat des Typos, Imprimeurs et partis similaires de Limoges*
C. Rouge	*Le Centre Rouge*
Céram. Lim.	*Le Céramiste Limousin*
Combat Synd.	*Le Combat Syndicaliste*
Cri (Loire)	*Le Cri du Peuple* (Loire)
Cri (Paris)	*Le Cri du Peuple* (Paris)
L'Hum.	*L'Humanité*
Indép. O.	*L'Indépendance Ouvrière*
Mineur U.	*Le Mineur Unitaire*
O. Céram.	*L'Ouvrier Céramiste*
O. Chaussures	*L'Ouvrier en Chaussures Limousin*
Petit Lim.	*Le Petit Limousin*
Peuple L.	*Le Peuple de la Loire*
Pop. (Paris)	*Le Populaire de Paris*
Pop. C.	*Le Populaire du Centre*
Prol. C.	*Le Prolétaire du Centre*
RP	*La Révolution Prolétarienne*
R. Peuple	*Le Réveil du Peuple*
R. Tiss.	*Le Réveil des Tisseurs*
Trav. C-O	*Le Travailleur du Centre-Ouest*
Trav. S-S	*Le Travailleur du Sous-Sol*
Trib. R.	*La Tribune Républicaine*
Trib. SMUL	*La Tribune Syndicaliste des Mineurs Unitaires de la Loire*
VO	*La Vie Ouvrière*

SCHOLARLY JOURNALS

AHR	*American Historical Review*
Actes CNSS	*Actes du Congrès National des Sociétés Savantes*
Annales: ESC	*Annales: Economies, Sociétés, Civilisations*
Cahiers IMT	*Cahiers (d'Histoire) de l'Institut Maurice Thorez*
FHS	*French Historical Studies*
ILWCH	*International Labor and Working Class History*
IRSH	*International Review of Social History*
JCH	*Journal of Contemporary History*
JMH	*Journal of Modern History*
JSH	*Journal of Social History*
M. Social	*Le Mouvement Social*
Proc. WSFH	*Proceedings of the Western Society for French History*
RFSP	*Revue Française des Sciences Politiques*
RHES	*Revue d'Histoire Economique et Sociale*
RHMC	*Revue d'Histoire Moderne et Contemporaine*

ARCHIVES AND LIBRARIES

ADHV	Archives Départementales de la Haute-Vienne, at Limoges
ADL	Archives Départementales de la Loire, at Saint-Etienne
AM	Archives Municipales; used here only for Limoges
AN	Archives Nationales, in Paris
BM	Bibliothèque Municipale; used here only for Roanne
BN	Bibliothèque Nationale, in Paris

Notes

Introduction

1. On the political schism, see Annie Kriegel, *Aux origines du communisme français, 1914–1920: Contribution à l'histoire du mouvement ouvrier français,* 2 vols. (Paris, 1964); Robert Wohl, *French Communism in the Making, 1914–1924* (Stanford, 1966); Jean Charles, "Le temps des scissions," in *Histoire du réformisme en France depuis 1920,* by Daniel Blum et al., 2 vols. (Paris, 1976), 1:1–45; and Jean-Louis Robert, "Les origines du P.C.F.," in *Le P.C.F., étapes et problèmes,* by Roger Bourderon et al. (Paris, 1981), pp. 13–39. On the trade-union schism, see also Maurice Labi, *La grande division des travailleurs: Première scission de la C.G.T. (1914–1921)* (Paris, 1964); and Jean Charles, "A propos de la scission syndicale de 1921," in *Mélanges d'histoire sociale offerts à Jean Maitron* (Paris, 1976), pp. 59–74. There is no general history of the internal conflicts within the CGTU that led to the second trade-union schism in 1924–25; some of the events, however, are surveyed in Jean Maitron's *Le mouvement anarchiste en France,* 2 vols. (Paris, 1975), 1:56–72.

2. This is the argument of Kriegel, *Aux origines,* 1:348–53 and 2:724–54.

3. Compare Vicard in *Le Réveil* (SFIO, Saint-Etienne), 10 Mar. 1929; and Gaston Monmousseau, *Le syndicalisme devant la révolution* (Paris, 1922), pp. 3–6.

4. Peter N. Stearns, *Revolutionary Syndicalism and French Labor: A Cause without Rebels* (New Brunswick, N.J., 1971).

5. See F. F. Ridley, *Revolutionary Syndicalism in France: The Direct Action of Its Time* (Cambridge, 1970); and Henri Dubief, *Le syndicalisme révolutionnaire* (Paris, 1969).

6. Compare Edward Shorter and Charles Tilly, *Strikes in France, 1830–1968* (London, 1974), pp. 28–44, 165–73, 181–84, 343–45.

7. For general views of this problem, see Charles F. Sabel, *Work and Politics: The Division of Labor in Industry* (Cambridge, 1982); Peter N. Stearns, "The Unskilled and Industrialization: A Transformation of Consciousness," *Archiv für*

Sozialgeschichte 16 (1976): 249–82; and Jacques Rancière, "The Myth of the Artisan: Critical Reflections on a Category of Social History," *ILWCH*, no. 24 (1983), pp. 1–16, plus commentaries, pp. 17–25.

8. On corporatism and reformism, see Martin Fine, "Toward Corporatism: The Movement for Capital-Labor Collaboration in France, 1914–1936" (Ph.D. diss., Univ. of Wisconsin, 1971). On craft divisions in the labor movement, see Bernard H. Moss, *The Origins of the French Labor Movement: The Socialism of Skilled Workers, 1830–1914* (Berkeley, 1976).

9. On solidarity between artisans and industrial workers, see Michael P. Hanagan, *The Logic of Solidarity: Artisans and Industrial Workers in Three French Towns, 1871–1914* (Urbana, Ill., 1980). Other works on syndicalism and industrial unionism, especially from an international perspective, are listed in the bibliography.

10. On the prewar period, see Joan Wallach Scott, *The Glassworkers of Carmaux: French Craftsmen and Political Action in a Nineteenth-Century City* (Cambridge, Mass., 1974); Rolande Trempé, *Les mineurs de Carmaux, 1848–1914,* 2 vols. (Paris, 1971); Yves Lequin, *Les ouvriers de la région lyonnaise (1848–1914),* 2 vols. (Lyon, 1977); and Michelle Perrot, *Les ouvriers en grève: France, 1871–1890,* 2 vols. (Paris, 1974). On the 1930s–40s, see Antoine Prost, *La C.G.T. à l'époque du Front Populaire: Essai de description numérique* (Paris, 1964); Denise Fauvel-Rouif, ed., *Mouvements ouvriers et dépression économique, 1929–1939* (Assen, 1966); and Michel Collinet, *L'ouvrier français: L'esprit du syndicalisme* (Paris, 1951). On the wartime and early interwar periods, see Patrick Fridenson, ed., *1914–1918: L'autre front* (Paris, 1977); James E. Cronin, "Labor Insurgency and Class Formation: Comparative Perspectives on the Crisis of 1917–1920 in Europe," *Social Science History* 4 (1980): 125–52; Annie Kriegel, *La croissance de la C.G.T., 1918–1921: Essai statistique* (Paris, 1966); Jean-Louis Robert, "Les luttes ouvrières en France pendant la première guerre mondiale," *Cahiers IMT,* n.s., no. 23 (1977), pp. 28–65; and Robert, *La scission syndicale de 1921: Essai de reconnaissance des formes* (Paris, 1980).

11. On the wartime and postwar economies, see Gerd Hardach, *The First World War, 1914–1918* (Berkeley, 1977); Alfred Sauvy, *Histoire économique de la France entre les deux guerres,* 4 vols. (Paris, 1965–75); Claude Fohlen, *La France de l'Entre-Deux-Guerres (1917–1939),* 2nd ed. (Paris, 1972); Tom Kemp, *The French Economy 1913–1939: The History of a Decline* (London, 1972); and Martin Wolfe, "French Interwar Stagnation Revisited," in *From the Ancien Régime to the Popular Front: Essays in the History of Modern France in Honor of Shepard B. Clough,* ed. Charles K. Warner (New York, 1969), pp. 159–80.

12. M. Cahen, "La concentration des établissements en France de 1896 à 1936," *Etudes et Conjonctures* 9 (1954): 840–81; François Caron and Jean Bouvier, "Structure des firmes, emprise de l'état," in *Histoire économique et sociale de la France,* ed. Fernand Braudel and Ernest Labrousse, 4 vols. (Paris, 1979–80), vol. 4, pt. 2, pp. 770–73; and Robert, *Scission syndicale,* pp. 33–38, 164–65.

13. Compare Judith A. Merkle, *Management and Ideology: The Legacy of the*

International Scientific Management Movement (Berkeley, 1980), pp. 148–71; and Yves-Claude Lequin, "La rationalisation du capitalisme français: A-t-elle eu lieu dans les années vingt?" *Cahiers IMT,* n.s., no. 31 (1979), pp. 115–36.

14. Compare Prost, *La C.G.T.,* chs. 3–4. The present author is currently exploring the problems of the 1930s in a further study of Limoges and Saint-Etienne.

15. Compare Fine, "Toward Corporatism," passim.

16. Compare Robert Wohl, *The Generation of 1914* (Cambridge, Mass., 1979). In his study of the PCF, Wohl does see 1924, if not 1920, as the end of an era; see *French Communism,* especially pp. 42–43, 433–54. Kriegel sees 1920 as the "dénouement," while Charles, Robert, and Fine place the turning point during the war itself. Kriegel, *Aux origines,* especially 2:757–58; Charles, "Temps des scissions," pp. 8–14, 27–28; Robert, "Origines du P.C.F.," pp. 28, 34–39; Robert, *Scission syndicale,* pp. 177–79; Fine, "Toward Corporatism," pp. 1–3.

17. The basic histories of socialism in Limoges and of trade unionism in Saint-Etienne are surveyed in Jean Lenoble et al., *Etudes sur la vie politique et les forces électorales en Limousin (1871–1973): La Gauche au pouvoir depuis un siècle* (Limoges, 1978); P. Héritier et al., *150 ans de luttes ouvrières dans le bassin stéphanois* (Saint-Etienne, 1979); and Pétrus Faure, *Histoire du mouvement ouvrier dans le département de la Loire* (Saint-Etienne, 1956).

18. Cited in Christian Gras, *Alfred Rosmer et le mouvement révolutionnaire international* (Paris, 1971), p. 36.

19. Compare Arno J. Mayer, *The Persistence of the Old Regime: Europe to the Great War* (New York, 1981), especially Preface and Introduction; Charles S. Maier, *Recasting Bourgeois Europe: Stabilization in France, Germany, and Italy in the Decade after World War I* (Princeton, 1975); Maier, "The Two Postwar Eras and the Conditions for Stability," *AHR* 86 (1981): 327–67.

20. In addition to the works by Kriegel, Wohl, Charles, and Robert cited above, see Maurice Moissonnier, "Octobre et le mouvement ouvrier de la région lyonnaise," *Cahiers IMT,* o.s., nos. 7–8 (1967), pp. 37–47; and Moissonnier et al., "Naissance du P.C.F. et traditions ouvrières (Débat)," *Cahiers IMT,* n.s., no. 3 (1973), pp. 152–82.

21. Compare Shorter and Tilly, *Strikes in France;* Hugues Lagrange, "La dynamique des grèves," *RFSP* 29 (1979): 665–92; and Claude Durand and Pierre Dubois, *La grève: Enquête sociologique* (Paris, 1975). For contrasts to Britain, see James E. Cronin, *Industrial Conflict in Modern Britain* (Totowa, N.J., 1979).

22. Compare Shorter and Tilly, *Strikes in France,* pp. 227–35 (the authors do not distinguish here between small shops and mid-sized factories of fewer than 500 employees); and Lagrange, "Dynamique des grèves," pp. 690–91. On the political militancy of workers in mid-sized factories, see Claude Willard, *Le mouvement socialiste en France (1893–1905): Les Guesdistes* (Paris, 1965), pp. 317–18.

23. Compare Shorter and Tilly, *Strikes in France,* pp. 269–71, 343–46.

24. Compare Lagrange, "Dynamique des grèves," pp. 690–91; Shorter and Tilly, *Strikes in France,* pp. 92–93, 172; Yves Lequin, "Classe ouvrière et idéologie dans la région lyonnaise à la fin du XIXe siècle," *M. Social,* no. 69

(1969), pp. 3–20 (Shorter and Tilly cite this essay as support for their claim that ideologies meant little to rank-and-file workers); and Bertrand Badie, *Stratégie de la grève: Pour une approche fonctionnaliste du Parti communiste français* (Paris, 1976).

25. The term is Lagrange's, in "Dynamique des grèves," p. 690; see also Robert, *Scission syndicale,* pp. 179–82.

26. The term is that of CGT reformist Georges Dumoulin, in "Les syndicalistes français et la guerre" (June 1919), in *Cahiers du Travail* [1921], and reprinted in Alfred Rosmer, *Le mouvement ouvrier pendant la guerre,* 2 vols. (Paris, 1936–56), 1:523–42; the quoted phrase is from p. 540. Compare the view of syndicalist Pierre Monatte in *VO,* 5 Aug. 1913, reprinted in his *La lutte syndicale,* ed. Colette Chambelland (Paris, 1976), pp. 119–20.

27. Racamond in *VO,* 12 May 1922; and Joseph A. Schumpeter, cited in Wohl, *French Communism,* p. 27.

Chapter 1. Limoges and Saint-Etienne

1. The "archaic" qualities of the Limousin's agriculture and rural industry are described by Alain Corbin in *Archaïsme et modernité en Limousin au XIXe siècle, 1845–1880,* 2 vols. (Paris, 1975), esp. 1:21–42. Despite the time limits of Corbin's study, many of his observations apply also to the twentieth century. See Jean-Pierre Larivière, *L'industrie à Limoges et dans la vallée limousine de la Vienne* (Paris, 1968).

2. A general survey of Saint-Etienne's geography and economic development is Maxime Perrin, *Saint-Etienne et sa région économique: Un type de la vie industrielle en France* (Tours, 1937). For the entire Lyon region, see Lequin, *Ouvriers de la région lyonnaise,* vol. 1, chs. 1–2.

3. "Les villes françaises: Limoges," *Notes et Etudes Documentaires,* 10 Apr. 1970, p. 12.

4. Larivière, *Industrie à Limoges,* pp. 12–18, 25–30. On individual industries, see also Serge Reynaud, "L'industrie de la porcelaine en Haute-Vienne," Limoges, 1971 (mimeographed); Reynaud, "L'industrie de la chaussure en Haute-Vienne," Limoges, 1970 (mimeographed); and Michel Posselle, "Face à l'économie moderne, une industrie traditionnelle: La porcelaine de Limoges" (Mémoire de stage, Ecole Nationale d'Administration, Dec. 1961).

5. Larivière, *Industrie à Limoges,* pp. 70–121.

6. On Saint-Junien, see especially Georges Gaudy, *La ville rouge* (Paris, 1925).

7. On the mining industry in the Loire, see Perrin, *Saint-Etienne,* pp. 68–79; L.-J. Gras, *Histoire économique générale des mines de la Loire,* 2 vols. (Saint-Etienne, 1922); Pierre Guillaume, "Les mines de la Loire après la première guerre mondiale," *Histoire des Entreprises,* no. 5 (1960), pp. 21–39. On mining elsewhere, see Trempé, *Mineurs de Carmaux.*

8. Perrin, *Saint-Etienne,* pp. 245–46; Marcel Arbogast, *L'industrie des armes à Saint-Etienne* (Saint-Etienne, 1937), pp. 154–68; André Vant, "L'industrie du cycle dans la région stéphanoise," *Revue de Géographie de Lyon* 49 (1974): 155–84; Claude Beaud, "La première guerre mondiale et les mutations d'une en-

treprise métallurgique de la Loire: Les établissements Jacob Holtzer," *Bulletin du Centre d'Histoire Economique et Sociale de la Région Lyonnaise,* no. 2 (1975), pp. 1–29.

9. Henri Guitton, *L'industrie des rubans de soie en France* (Paris, 1928), esp. pp. 215–20. The weavers' views on tax and other issues are presented in their own monthly, *Le Réveil des Tisseurs,* beginning in Sept. 1898. The weavers' ambiguous social status and special interests are also described in Steven M. Zdatny, "The Origins of the Artisanal Movement in France, 1919–1925," *Proc. WSFH* 9 (1981): 284–92.

10. Perrin, *Saint-Etienne,* pp. 276–77; Guitton, *Rubans,* pp. 5–49, 164–97, 230–31. On economic problems in the prewar ribbon industry, see also Henri de Boissieu, "La rubanerie stéphanoise," in *Le mouvement économique et social dans la région lyonnaise,* ed. Paul Pic and Justin Godart, 2 vols. (Lyon, 1902), 1:69–126; and Gabriel Clerc, *Passementiers stéphanois en 1912: La crise du ruban* (Saint-Etienne, 1912), esp. pp. 1–9.

11. Population growth in the two cities, plus Clermont-Ferrand, is compared in Pierre Estienne, *Villes du Massif Central* (Paris, 1963), esp. the graph on p. 38. Other local demographic studies include G. Callon, "Le mouvement de la population dans le département de la Haute-Vienne au cours de la période 1821–1920 et depuis la fin de cette période," pts. 1 and 2, *Revue Scientifique du Limousin,* no. 356 (1929), pp. 33–48, and no. 357 (1930), pp. 13–26; Jean-Pierre Larivière, *La population du Limousin,* 2 vols. (Lille, 1975); J. Schnetzler, "Un demi-siècle d'évolution démographique (1820–1876)," *Etudes Foréziennes* 1 (1968): 157–89; Schnetzler, "L'évolution démographique de la région de Saint-Etienne de 1876 à 1946," *Etudes Foréziennes* 4 (1971): 157–95; and Schnetzler, "L'origine de la population de Saint-Etienne," in *Les villes du Massif Central,* ed. Université de Saint Etienne (Saint-Etienne, 1971), pp. 50–70. The larger problems of demographic stagnation and rural exodus are examined in Pierre Merlin, *L'exode rural* (Paris, 1971).

12. Maurice Robert, "La société limousine, 1870–1914," Limoges, 1971 (mimeographed), p. 27; Corbin, *Archaïsme et modernité,* 1:584; ADL 54 M 8, Classement de la population par profession, Saint-Etienne, 1891.

13. Larivière, *Industrie à Limoges,* pp. 12–13; Corbin, *Archaïsme et modernité,* 1:226–40; Perrin, *Saint-Etienne,* pp. 417, 432–33; David M. Gordon, *Merchants and Capitalists: Industrialization and Provincial Politics in Mid-Nineteenth-Century France* (University, Ala., 1985).

14. Corbin, *Archaïsme et modernité,* 1:584, 588; ADL 54 M 8, Classement de la population, 1891.

15. Estimates for the porcelain and shoe industries are in "Les villes françaises: Limoges," p. 12; Reynaud, "Porcelaine," pp. 7–8; Reynaud, "Chaussure," pp. 2–3. Other figures are drawn from scattered strike reports for 1920–22 in ADHV 10 M 99, 10 M 100, 10 M 112, 10 M 136, and 10 M 146. The published census for this period gives no employment figures for individual cities.

16. Département de la Haute-Vienne, Arrondissement de Limoges, Liste nominative des habitants de la commune de Limoges, canton du Nord, Dénombrement(s) de 1911, 1921, 1931. The census of 1911 was chosen for comparison

to show changes since the prewar period; it was used in preference to earlier pre-war censuses because those documents, in the case of Saint-Etienne, did not specify place of birth. The single canton of Limoges-Nord was used because it corresponded most closely to the urban center of Limoges. Sampling procedures for this study are described in a separate "Note on Methodology."

Instead of the manuscript census, some historians have used marriage records to study the composition and recruitment of the labor force. See Lequin, *Ouvriers de la région lyonnaise,* vol. 1, ch. 5; D. Tenand, "Les origines de la classe ouvrière stéphanoise" (Mémoire de maîtrise, Lyon II, 1972); and Roger Boutaud, "Les ouvriers porcelainiers de Limoges de 1884 à 1905" (Mémoire de maîtrise, Poitiers, 1970). Such records focus, however, on young people of marriageable age and thus give a distorted image of a city's total population. On methodologi-cal problems in the use of marriage records, see Jean Merley, "La contribution de la Haute-Loire à la formation de la population stéphanoise au milieu du XIXe siè-cle," *Cahiers de la Haute-Loire* 2 (1966): 165–80.

17. Department-level data on company size are from the published censuses: Ministère du Travail, Statistique Générale de la France, *Résultats statistiques du recensement général de la population,* 1906, 1921, and 1931 (Paris, 1908–35). The 1906 census was used instead of that for 1911, which recorded no company data.

18. Data on company size in Limoges are in ADHV 10 M 136, Fabricants de la porcelaine, Limoges, 14 Oct. 1920; and 10 M 64, Fabricants de la chaussure, Limoges, Dec. 1920. The connection between company size and unemployment is further discussed here in ch. 8, concerning the recession of 1921.

19. The geographic extent of the Loire basin is defined according to the usages by Schnetzler in "Evolution démographique (1820–1876)"; by Perrin in *Saint-Etienne;* and by the local Chamber of Commerce in its annual reports in *Bull. CCSE,* 1921–36. Employment estimates for the Loire basin are from these re-ports and from the works of Perrin, Schnetzler, Guitton, and Gras; municipal figures are from strike reports for 1920–25 in ADL M 1066, M 1068, 92 M 257, 92 M 261, 93 M 103, and AN F7 13895.

20. Sample data from the manuscript censuses: Département de la Loire, Ar-rondissement de Saint-Etienne, Liste nominative des habitants de la commune de Saint-Etienne, Dénombrement(s) de 1911, 1921, 1931. Unlike the data for Limoges, those for Saint-Etienne are drawn from all four cantons of the com-mune. For further explanation, see the "Note on Methodology."

21. Guitton, *Rubans,* ch. 4; *R. Tiss.,* July 1905 and Sept. 1908.

22. Various statistics on company size in the metals industry are in ADL M 1066 and M 1068, reports for 1920–26; Vant, "Cycle," pp. 155–61; M. Devun, "L'industrie du cycle à Saint-Etienne," *Revue de Géographie Alpine* 35 (1947): 21, 39; and Arbogast, *Armes,* pp. 169–75. The city's cycle parts manufacturers, as well as the multitude of other metalworking establishments, are listed in the *Annuaire Administratif, Commercial, Industriel, et Statistique du Département de la Loire,* 1925.

23. *Recensement,* 1906, 1921, and 1931. Even in heavy metallurgy, where

most companies exceeded 100 employees, five of the ten new companies formed in the Loire in the 1920s had fewer than 10 employees.

24. Ibid., for departmental figures; for the Loire basin alone, figures are from ADL Houillères, carton 2480, dossier 1920, Notes, 3 June 1920; M 1068, report of 12 Oct. 1925; and Perrin, *Saint-Etienne,* p. 102, for 1935. On the unsuccessful merger, see Perrin, *Saint-Etienne,* pp. 75–79, or Pierre Guillaume, *La Compagnie des Mines de la Loire, 1846–1854* (Paris, 1966). On postwar problems, see Guillaume, "Mines de la Loire," pp. 30–39.

25. On the glass industry, see L.-J. Gras, *Histoire des eaux minérales du Forez, suivie de notes historiques sur l'industrie de la verrerie en Forez et en Jarez* (Saint-Etienne, 1923), pp. 220–30; annual reports in the *Bull. CCSE,* 1925–32; reports in ADL M 1068, 1924–25; and M 1066, dossier on "Chômage dans les verreries." The small number of glassworkers at Saint-Etienne made it impossible to use the samples from the manuscript censuses to analyze the industry's labor force; only nine glassworkers appeared in the sample for 1911 and seven each in the samples for 1921 and 1931. On glassworkers elsewhere, see Scott, *Glassworkers of Carmaux.*

26. The expanded role of women is also apparent in the published census data, which show women holding an even larger share of total jobs (41 percent in porcelain and 48 percent in shoes) in 1921. (The departmental figures were 40 percent and 54 percent, respectively, in 1931.) These figures, however, include employees as well as factory workers and thus exaggerate the role of women in industrial occupations. On women's employment see also Boutaud, "Ouvriers porcelainiers," pp. 7–8; Larivière, *Industrie à Limoges,* pp. 49–51; and Madeleine Guilbert, *Les fonctions des femmes dans l'industrie* (Paris, 1966), esp. pp. 42–44.

27. Figures on female employment at Saint-Etienne are also available in AN F7 13525, 11 Jan. 1927; by then, women represented 62 percent of employment in textiles, 23 percent in metals, and 8 percent in the coal mines. Despite their role in textiles, women's total employment in the Loire was lower than the national average (27 percent as against 32 percent), both because of the department's small agricultural work force and because of the high concentration of male labor in heavy industry. Conversely, women represented a high of 39 percent of the total (agricultural plus industrial) labor force in the Haute-Vienne, according to the published census for 1921. On female labor in the Loire, see also Tenand, "Classe ouvrière stéphanoise," pp. 61–66; Rosa Jozefowicz, "Le travail des femmes et des enfants dans la région stéphanoise de 1850 à 1914" (Mémoire de maîtrise, Lyon II, 1961); and figures in ADL 54 M 8, Classement de la population, 1891. Women workers were less uncommon in other coal basins of the country where there were fewer other employment opportunities comparable to the Loire's textile industry. See Trempé, *Mineurs de Carmaux,* 1:134.

28. According to the published census, women comprised 8.2 percent of railroad workers and employees both in the Haute-Vienne and in the Loire in 1921, and even lower proportions in 1931.

29. During the war, female employment in the metals industry at Saint-Etienne rose to a peak of 30 percent. Statistics (1917) in ADL M 1066; see discussion in ch.

3 of this study. For trends in other industries, see also Larivière, *Industrie à Limoges,* p. 51; Guilbert, *Fonctions des femmes,* p. 61; and Yvonne Delatour, "Le travail des femmes pendant la première guerre mondiale et ses conséquences sur l'évolution de leur rôle dans la société," *Francia,* Band 2 (1974), pp. 482–501.

30. Larivière, *Industrie à Limoges,* pp. 52–53; Trempé, *Mineurs de Carmaux,* 1:141–47; Scott, *Glassworkers of Carmaux,* p. 77.

31. Larivière, *Population du Limousin,* 1:122–87; "Les villes françaises: Limoges," p. 12; Posselle, "Porcelaine de Limoges," pp. 6–9.

32. These observations apply both to the totals of the three industries sampled from the manuscript census and to the city's overall population, as recorded in the census summary tables. (No age data are recorded for the city collectively in the census of 1931.) Compared to the city, the department in 1921 had smaller proportions of young adults (aged twenty to thirty-nine) and larger proportions of elderly and children (aged over sixty or under twenty), perhaps as a consequence of the war. These differences, if translated to the working populations, suggest larger contrasts between urban and rural patterns than just the fact that city young people were likely to remain longer in school.

33. Data for the mid-1920s are from Guitton, *Rubans,* pp. 237–39. In 1891, by contrast, the textile industry had been relatively youthful as compared to other local trades, because the industry then had not yet passed its prime. Data for 1891 in ADL 54 M 8.

34. On geographic recruitment to the two cities, see Larivière, *Population du Limousin,* esp. 2:481, 589–98; Schnetzler, "Evolution démographique, 1876 à 1946," pp. 188–93; and Schnetzler in *Villes du Massif Central,* ed. Université de Saint-Etienne, p. 50. For the nineteenth century, see also Corbin, *Archaïsme et modernité,* 1:583; and Lequin, *Ouvriers de la région lyonnaise,* vol. 1, ch. 5.

35. Data for 1891 are sampled from the Liste nominative for Limoges, according to the same procedures as for the samples for 1911 to 1931. (These results cannot be compared to data for Saint-Etienne, whose census for that year did not indicate geographic origins.) According to the sample, 42 percent of shoe workers and 66 percent of porcelain workers were born in the city; most of the rest were from elsewhere in the Haute-Vienne. Among artisanal shoemakers, who comprised four-fifths of the shoe industry's total in 1891, virtually the same proportion were born in the city as for the shoe industry generally. But among artisanal porcelain painters, who comprised only a fourth of that industry's total, 91 percent were born in the city of Limoges. Similar results for the 1880s, obtained from a study of marriage records, are described in Boutaud, "Ouvriers porcelainiers," pp. 4–8.

36. These patterns are described for the early nineteenth century in Tenand, "Classe ouvrière stéphanoise," pp. 70–84, and for the later nineteenth century in Lequin, *Ouvriers de la région lyonnaise,* vol. 1, ch. 5. Lequin's use of marriage records also provides data on the profession of the father, to distinguish peasant migrants from those with artisanal backgrounds.

37. Among sampled workers in heavy metallurgy (workers employed in the city's four largest producers of steel and heavy machinery, as identified by the cen-

sus taker's notation of place of employment), there were no foreigners in 1911 and 34 foreigners in 1921. The latter figure more than accounted for the increase in total number from 77 in 1911 to 105 in 1921. Conversely, the sample figure of 87 heavy metallurgists in 1931 included only 13 foreigners, a sign of the industry's decreasing demand for labor by that time.

On foreign workers generally, the census samples are not large or representative enough to permit correlations of occupation with individual nationalities. Statistics that do offer such cross-tabulations are for the Loire as a whole, in AN F7 13518, Tableau numérique des travailleurs étrangers par nationalités et par professions (Loire), 6 Mar. 1925. According to these figures, Italians and Spaniards each comprised some 30 percent of the nearly 11,000 foreign workers in metallurgy; Poles and Moroccans, each about 10 percent of the foreign work force in metallurgy, comprised some 20 percent and 40 percent, respectively, of the more than 9,000 foreign workers in the mines. (A similar report for Limoges is in ADHV 4 M 201, report of 20 Apr. 1925, which identified most of the city's 500 foreign workers as Spaniards employed as day-laborers in the city's construction industry.) Further statistics on foreign labor in the Loire's coal mines are in ADL Houillères, carton 823, *Rapports de l'Ingénieur en Chef,* Houillères de Montrambert et de la Béraudière, 1920–25; and in Malika Rachidi, "La population minière immigrée à Saint-Etienne de 1920 à 1940" (Mémoire de maîtrise, Saint-Etienne, 1973). On foreign labor in the Loire's war industries, see statistics (1917) in AN F7 13356 and F22 292, and discussion here in ch. 3.

38. See the remarks by Théo Argence at a metalworkers' congress (CGTU) in 1922, cited in Collinet, *Esprit du syndicalisme,* pp. 53–54; and observations in *RP,* 10 May 1932, cited by R. Dufraisse, "Le mouvement ouvrier français 'rouge' devant la grande dépression économique de 1929 à 1933," in *Mouvements ouvriers,* ed. Fauvel-Rouif, p. 167.

39. ADL 93 M 25, 8 Oct. 1912; see also Lequin, *Ouvriers de la région lyonnaise,* 1:38–39; and Trempé, *Mineurs de Carmaux,* 1:190–96, 215, 248–53. The same was true among some manual laborers in Limoges, according to Boutaud, "Ouvriers porcelainiers," p. 9. A general study of worker-peasant alternation of activities is Yves Le Balle, *L'ouvrier paysan en Lorraine mosellane* (Paris, 1958).

40. M. Desmoulins, quoted in Georges-Emmanuel Clancier, *La vie quotidienne en Limousin au XIXe siècle* (Paris, 1976), pp. 230–31; see also Elinor Accampo, "Entre la classe sociale et la cité: Identité et intégration chez les ouvriers de Saint-Chamond, 1815–1880," *M. Social,* no. 118 (1982), pp. 39–59; Eugen Weber, *Peasants into Frenchmen: The Modernization of Rural France, 1870–1914* (Stanford, 1976), pp. 281, 288–90; Shorter and Tilly, *Strikes in France,* pp. 271–76; and, on contemporary rural migrants, Alain Touraine and Orietta Ragazzi, *Ouvriers d'origine agricole* (Paris, 1961).

41. John M. Merriman, "Incident at the Statue of the Virgin Mary: The Conflict of Old and New in Nineteenth-Century Limoges," in *Consciousness and Class Experience in Nineteenth-Century Europe,* ed. Merriman (New York, 1979), p. 135. On short-distance migration, see also Mary Lynn McDougall,

"Consciousness and Community: The Workers of Lyon, 1830–1850," _JSH_ 12 (1978): 137–38.

42. ADHV 4 M 201, 27 Oct. 1924 and 17–22 Apr. 1925; AN F7 13518, 6 Mar. 1925; ADL Houillères, carton 823, _Rapports de l'Ingénieur en Chef, 1923_, pp. 1–3, and 1925, pp. 1–3; Guillaume, "Mines de la Loire," pp. 28–29; Jean-Charles Bonnet, "Les travailleurs étrangers dans la Loire sous la IIIᵉ République," _Cahiers d' Histoire_ 16 (1971): 77–79; Bonnet, "Histoire de la main-d'oeuvre étrangère dans l'agglomération stéphanoise" (D.E.S., Lyon, 1960), pp. 147–52. Other works on foreign labor, citing similar problems in France generally, are listed in the bibliography.

43. On the railroad workers, who played a critical role in the general strike of May 1920, see Kriegel, _Aux origines,_ 1:359–76 ("Pourquoi les cheminots").

44. On women, see especially Madeleine Guilbert, _Les femmes et l'organisation syndicale avant 1914_ (Paris, 1967), pp. 28–34; and Guilbert, _Fonctions des femmes,_ pp. 42–54. On rural migrants, see also Stearns, "Unskilled and Industrialization," pp. 253–68; and, for non-French examples, Diane Koenker, _Moscow Workers and the 1917 Revolution_ (Princeton, 1981), pp. 44–53; and E. J. Hobsbawm, "Peasants and Rural Migrants in Politics," in _Politics of Conformity in Latin America,_ ed. Claudio Veliz (New York, 1967), pp. 45–65. As Koenker points out, residential patterns that promoted contacts off the job may have had as much to do with labor solidarity as geographic origins or skill levels; see also Hanagan, _Logic of Solidarity,_ pp. 98–106, 149, 195–99; and McDougall, "Consciousness and Community," pp. 134–37.

45. On the questions of aging and generational conflicts in the French labor movement, see Wohl, _Generation of 1914,_ ch. 6; Wohl, _French Communism,_ pp. 428–32, 442, 453; Kriegel, _Aux origines,_ 1:238–47, and 2:827–43 passim; Kriegel, _Croissance de la C.G.T.,_ pp. 165–77; Kriegel, _The French Communists: Profile of a People_ (Chicago, 1972), pp. 47–59, 98–135; Prost, _La C.G.T.,_ pp. 156–61; also R[obert] F. Wheeler, "German Labor and the Comintern: A Problem of Generations?" _JSH_ 7 (1974): 304–21.

46. For the nineteenth century, see Moss, _Origins of French Labor;_ and Hanagan, _Logic of Solidarity,_ ch. 1. On the twentieth century, see also Collinet, _Esprit du syndicalisme;_ Prost, _La C.G.T.;_ and Sabel, _Work and Politics,_ ch. 4.

47. On the artisanal "renaissance," see Guitton, _Rubans,_ pp. 198–253; Zdatny, "Artisanal Movement," pp. 284–92; and the postwar issues of _R. Tiss._

48. Sauvy, _Histoire économique,_ 1:231–32; Robert, "Luttes ouvrières," p. 35.

49. Caron and Bouvier, "Structure des firmes," in _Histoire économique et sociale,_ ed. Braudel and Labrousse, vol. 4, pt. 2, pp. 770–73; and Cahen, "Concentration des établissements," pp. 840–81. Information on the proportion of workers in each size rank, rather than just the number of companies in each group, is available only on the national and not on the departmental level.

50. Cahen, "Concentration des établissements," pp. 877–81; Jean-Louis Robert and Michel Chavance, "L'évolution de la syndicalisation en France de 1914 à 1921: L'emploi de l'analyse factorielle des correspondances," _Annales: ESC_ 29 (1974): 1099, 1104–7; and Robert, _Scission syndicale,_ pp. 33–38, 164–65.

Chapter 2. Labor and the Left

1. The general history of the prewar labor movement in Limoges may be traced in Corbin, *Archaïsme et modernité,* vol. 2; Lenoble et al., *La Gauche au pouvoir;* Pierre Cousteix, "Le mouvement ouvrier limousin de 1870 à 1939," *L'Actualité de l'Histoire,* nos. 20–21 (1957), pp. 27–96; and Antoine Perrier [A. Pittle], *Une esquisse du mouvement ouvrier à Limoges depuis le XIXᵉ siècle* (Angoulême, 1929).

On Saint-Etienne and its environs, see Lequin, *Ouvriers de la région lyonnaise,* vol. 2; Lequin, "Classe ouvrière et idéologie," pp. 3–20; Héritier et al., *Luttes ouvrières;* Hanagan, *Logic of Solidarity;* Faure, *Mouvement ouvrier;* and Janet Jacobs, "A Community of French Workers: Social Life and Labour Conflicts in the Stéphanois Region, 1890–1914" (Ph.D. diss., Oxford Univ., 1973).

2. Compare Ridley, *Revolutionary Syndicalism;* Stearns, *Revolutionary Syndicalism;* and Moss, *Origins of French Labor.*

3. Corbin, *Archaïsme et modernité,* 2:790–94, 824–43. On the rural Limousin today, see Philippe Gratton, "Le communisme rural en Corrèze," *M. Social,* no. 67 (1969), pp. 123–45; and Lenoble et al., *La Gauche au pouvoir,* pp. 147–70.

4. Antoine Perrier, "Esquisse d'une sociologie du mouvement socialiste dans la Haute-Vienne et en Limousin," *Actes du 87ᵉ CNSS,* Poitiers, 1962 (Section histoire moderne et contemporaine), pp. 380–84; Corbin, *Archaïsme et modernité,* 1:535–52; 2:758–90, 824–52, 911–16. On the appeal of socialism to small peasant proprietors, see also André Siegfried, *Tableau politique de la France de l'Ouest sous la Troisième République* (Paris, 1964), pp. 370–80; and Tony Judt, *Socialism in Provence, 1871–1914: A Study in the Origins of the Modern French Left* (London, 1979).

5. Corbin, *Archaïsme et modernité,* 1:619–20, 661–62, 693; Pierre Cousteix, "Le catholicisme social en Haute-Vienne sous la IIIᵉ République," *Information Historique,* 16ᵉ année (1954), pp. 100–101. On regional differences in religious practice, see also Gabriel Le Bras, *Etudes de sociologie réligieuse: Sociologie de la pratique réligieuse dans les campagnes françaises* (Paris, 1955), pp. 235, 267–75.

6. Corbin, *Archaïsme et modernité,* 1:321–417.

7. Guy Decouty, "Introduction à l'étude de l'évolution de l'opinion politique dans le département de la Haute-Vienne" (Thèse, Institut d'Etudes Politiques, Paris, 1950), pp. 189–92, 365–66.

8. See especially Gilbert Garrier, *Paysans du Beaujolais et du Lyonnais, 1800–1970,* 2 vols. (Grenoble, 1973), 1:213, 317–27, 685–87.

9. Robert J. Bezucha, *The Lyon Uprising of 1834: Social and Political Conflict in the Early July Monarchy* (Cambridge, Mass., 1974), esp. pp. 73, 193–94; Maurice Moissonnier, "La province et la Commune," and Julian Archer, "The Crowd in the Lyon Commune," *IRSH* 17 (1972): 152–82, 183–88; Lequin, *Ouvriers de la région lyonnaise,* vol. 2, ch. 3.

10. Lequin, *Ouvriers de la région lyonnaise,* vol. 2, chs. 4–5; Le Bras, *Sociologie réligieuse,* p. 325; and Pierre de Pressac, *Les forces historiques de la France: La tradition dans l'orientation politique des provinces* (Paris, 1928), pp. 113–16.

11. Statutes of "L'Initiative," quoted in Cousteix, "Mouvement ouvrier limousin," p. 32. On early trade unionism in Limoges, see also Corbin, *Archaïsme et modernité,* 1:318–19, 535–49; and André Pompon, *Les ouvriers porcelainiers de Limoges: Etude d'économie sociale* (Paris, 1910), pp. 84–85.

12. Cousteix, "Mouvement ouvrier limousin," pp. 31–32; Corbin, *Archaïsme et modernité,* 1:547–49.

13. Cousteix, "Mouvement ouvrier limousin," pp. 33–39, 51–58.

14. Antoine Perrier, "Une industrie limousine: la porcelaine. La crise économique vue d'un centre porcelainier," *Revue du Centre-Ouest de la France,* Mar. 1937, pp. 17–18. An intermediate level of concentration was probably better suited to both socialism and trade unionism than was a vast factory structure; see Willard, *Les Guesdistes,* pp. 317–18, and Shorter and Tilly, *Strikes in France,* pp. 227–35.

15. Cousteix, "Mouvement ouvrier limousin," pp. 65, 75; Boutaud, "Ouvriers porcelainiers," p. 74.

16. Geneviève Désiré-Vuillemin, "Une grève révolutionnaire: Les porcelainiers de Limoges en avril 1905," *Annales du Midi* 83 (1971): 32–34, 50, 74–76; Martial Desmoulins (anarchist shoe worker), letters to Michel Laguionie (assistant UD secretary of the Force Ouvrière at Limoges), personal files of Michel Laguionie, Limoges, 26 Feb. 1974.

17. ADHV 10 M 192, 23 Sept. 1907 and 20 Jan. 1908; Geneviève Désiré-Vuillemin, "Les grèves dans la région de Limoges de 1905 à 1914," *Annales du Midi* 85 (1973): 51–52, 80–82.

18. Desmoulins letters, 14 Oct. 1972 and 3 May 1974; Cousteix, "Mouvement ouvrier limousin," pp. 29–30, 59, 65, 75–76; and E. J. Hobsbawm and Joan Wallach Scott, "Political Shoemakers," *Past and Present,* no. 89 (1980), esp. pp. 111–13. According to the latter authors (p. 97), readers were often hired in larger shoe factories, as in Limoges porcelain firms, but this does not seem to have applied to the small shoe companies of Limoges. On labor militancy among leather workers, see also Perrot, *Ouvriers en grève,* 1:389–95.

19. Syndicat des ouvriers et ouvrières en Chaussures de Limoges, Procès-verbaux de l'Assemblée Générale et du Conseil Syndical (Archives of the Syndicat CGT de la Chaussure, Limoges), meetings of 10 Sept. and 2 Dec. 1909; compare the arguments in favor of industrial unionism by Jean Rougerie (shoe workers' secretary) at the Bourse du Travail de Limoges, Procès-verbaux des délibérations de la Commission Administrative et du Comité Général (Archives of the Syndicat CGT de la Chaussure, Limoges), meeting of 10 Sept. 1906.

20. Cousteix, "Mouvement ouvrier limousin," p. 56; Cousteix, "Influence des doctrines anarchistes en Haute-Vienne sous la IIIᵉ République," *L'Actualité de l'Histoire,* no. 13 (1955), pp. 32–33.

21. Cousteix, "Mouvement ouvrier limousin," pp. 60–64, 70–73; Désiré-Vuillemin, "Les grèves," pp. 62–63; Gaudy, *Ville rouge,* chs. 13–14.

22. Rougerie's assistant at the Bourse by 1910 was Léon Bonnet, secretary of the porcelain workers since 1909 and also member of the SFIO. Biographical sketches of the two are in Jean Maitron, ed., *Dictionnaire biographique du*

mouvement ouvrier français, pt. 3 (vols. 10–15), "De la Commune à la Grande Guerre (1871–1914)" (Paris, 1972–77), 15:97 (Rougerie) and 10:331 (Bonnet).

23. Bourse, Limoges, 10 Sept. 1906; Synd. Chaussures, Limoges, 27 Sept. and 29 Nov. 1906. Exceptions to the vote on the Amiens Charter were the typographers and the porcelain workers, who supported it (the latter against the vote of their own federation); the porcelain *painters* and the shoe workers voted with the majority at Limoges.

24. AN F7 12734, 31 Mar. 1907; Désiré-Vuillemin, "Les grèves," pp. 66–80. On general trends in French strikes, compare Perrot, *Ouvriers en grève,* 1:69–70; Shorter and Tilly, *Strikes in France,* pp. 28–45, 66–67; and Peter N. Stearns, "Measuring the Evolution of Strike Movements," *IRSH* 19 (1974): 1–27. Changing patterns of strike activity are further discussed later in this chapter.

25. Lenoble et al., *La Gauche au pouvoir,* pp. 56–73.

26. On economic and social conditions in the ribbon industry, see Clerc, *Crise du ruban,* pp. 103, 192–94; and Guitton, *Rubans,* pp. 50–83. On labor militancy among textile workers, see also Perrot, *Ouvriers en grève,* 1:352–66.

27. ADL 93 M 3, Statutes of the Chambre syndicale des Passementiers, Veloutiers, et Caoutchoutiers de la Ville de Saint-Etienne et de la Banlieue, 5 July 1874.

28. J. Lorcin, "Un essai de stratigraphie sociale: Chefs d'atelier et compagnons dans la grève des passementiers de Saint-Etienne en 1900," *Cahiers d'Histoire* 13 (1968): 179–92; Guitton, *Rubans,* pp. 84–85. Early signs of antagonism between the *chefs* and the *compagnons* are reported in ADL 93 M 3, 30 May 1880 and 9 Dec. 1888. On the origins and outcome of the strike, see also *R. Tiss.,* Sept. 1898 to Aug. 1900.

29. *R. Tiss.,* May 1901 (quoted passage); also Dec. 1901, Apr. 1903, and June 1904.

30. On the Amiens Charter and the CGT: *R. Tiss.,* Oct. 1906; ADL 93 M 58, 24 Aug. and 10 Sept. 1912; 93 M 69, 25 Mar. 1912. On the *tarif:* ADL 93 M 45, 23–24 Aug. and 13 Sept. 1909; 93 M 3, 17 Feb. to 4 July 1911; *R. Tiss.,* Aug. to Dec. 1912, and June 1914; Guitton, *Rubans,* pp. 97–99.

31. *R. Tiss.,* July 1905 and July 1919; ADL 93 M 3, 25 Oct. 1919; Guitton, *Rubans,* pp. 120, 230–31.

32. On mining unionism in the Loire and in France, see Gras, *Mines,* 2:508–89 passim; Trempé, *Mineurs de Carmaux,* vol. 2, pts. 3–4; Trempé, "Le réformisme des mineurs français à la fin du XIXe siècle," *M. Social,* no. 65 (1968), pp. 93–107; C. Bartuel and H. Rullière, *La mine et les mineurs* (Paris, 1923); and Perrot, *Ouvriers en grève,* 1:366–76.

33. Lequin, *Ouvriers de la région lyonnaise,* 2:200–202, 263–66; Gras, *Mines,* 2:529–65, 752–73, 783–92; Bartuel and Rullière, *Mine et mineurs,* pp. 432–46, 467–82, 505–7.

34. Héritier et al., *Luttes ouvrières,* p. 90.

35. ADL 93 M 52, Etat des syndicats professionnels, 1 Jan. 1894; 93 M 30, 6 Oct. 1890; 93 M 31, 22 Feb. 1903; Lequin, *Ouvriers de la région lyonnaise,* 2:266–71, 323–25; Gras, *Mines,* 2:827–31; Bartuel and Rullière, *Mine et mineurs,* pp. 491–98, 507–13. To compare the politics of other French miners,

see also Trempé, "Réformisme des mineurs," pp. 93–94; Trempé, *Mineurs de Carmaux,* 2:628, 819–23; and Leo Loubère, "Coal Miners, Strikes, and Politics in the Lower Languedoc, 1880–1914," *JSH* 2 (1968): 25–50.

36. Bartuel and Rullière, *Mine et mineurs,* pp. 447–52. Casimir Bartuel, named secretary of the national miners' federation in 1911, was also a member of the Parti Socialiste Français (non-SFIO) from Saint-Etienne. On the issue of the general strike, see also Trempé, "Réformisme des mineurs," pp. 95–97.

37. ADL 93 M 25, May to Nov. 1911, and 20 May 1913; 93 M 31, 19 Oct. 1911; 93 M 54, 10 Mar. 1912; 93 M 27, 26 Dec. 1912. On the miners' decision in 1911, see also Bartuel and Rullière, *Mine et mineurs,* p. 514. On the miners' switch in 1918: AN F7 12994, 14 Aug. 1918.

38. ADL 93 M 8, 21 Dec. 1913; L.-J. Gras, *Histoire économique de la métallurgie de la Loire, suivie d'une notice sur la construction mécanique et l'industrie des cycles et automobiles dans la région stéphanoise* (Saint-Etienne, 1908), pp. 85–89. On obstacles to industrial unionism, especially in the metals industry, see also Collinet, *Esprit du syndicalisme,* pp. 24, 31. On metalworkers' strikes, see also Perrot, *Ouvriers en grève,* 1:384–89.

39. Arbogast, *Armes,* pp. 177–79; Gras, *Métallurgie,* p. 85.

40. ADL 93 M 57, 8 Dec. 1906; 93 M 19, Statutes of the Syndicat des ouvriers de la Manufacture Nationale d'Armes de Saint-Etienne, 1900.

41. ADL 93 M 52, Rapport sur les syndicats professionnels, 1890; 93 M 8, 8 Dec. 1911 and 6 Mar. 1912. The role of anarchism in the union movement is further discussed later in this chapter.

42. On prewar Firminy, Unieux, and Saint-Chamond: ADL 93 M 11, 29 Mar. 1911 and 22 Apr. 1913; 93 M 13, 15 Oct. 1912 and 3 Jan. 1914; and Accampo, "Identité et intégration," pp. 40–42. On Le Chambon: 93 M 14, extract from *Le Nouvelliste,* 21 Apr. 1912; and Pétrus Faure, *Le Chambon Rouge: Histoire des organisations ouvrières et des grèves au Chambon-Feugerolles* (Le Chambon-Feugerolles, 1929), pp. 36, 50–52, 83–98. The contrasts between Le Chambon and the other local communities are stressed in Jean-Paul Martin, "Une culture militante à l'époque du syndicalisme révolutionnaire: Les métallurgistes de l'Ondaine," *Cahiers d'Histoire* 27 (1982): 315–17; and Hanagan, *Logic of Solidarity,* esp. chs. 5 (on Saint-Chamond) and 6 (on Le Chambon). On the role of community cohesion in support of strike activity, see also Shorter and Tilly, *Strikes in France,* pp. 267–83; and Perrot, *Ouvriers en grève,* 2:520–40.

43. Faure, *Mouvement ouvrier,* pp. 306–35; Faure, *Chambon Rouge,* pp. 50–98; Hanagan, *Logic of Solidarity,* pp. 167–72; Héritier et al., *Luttes ouvrières,* pp. 131–37.

44. ADL 93 M 8, 8 Dec. 1911, 2–8 Dec. 1912, and 6 Apr. to 8 Sept. 1913; 93 M 14, report of 31 Dec. 1911, and extract from *Le Nouvelliste,* 21 Apr. 1912.

45. Pétrus Faure, *Un témoin raconte . . .* (Saint-Etienne, 1962), p. 42; Benoît Frachon, *Pour la CGT: Mémoires de lutte, 1902–1939* (Paris, 1981), pp. 21–25, 40–41; and Claude Willard, ed., "Souvenirs de Benoît Frachon. A l'appel d'Octobre: Premiers pas d'un militant ouvrier de l'anarcho-syndicalisme au com-

munisme," *Cahiers IMT,* o.s., no. 5 (1967), p. 64. Faure was Communist mayor of Le Chambon beginning in 1925; he left the party in 1929. Frachon was head of the Loire's CGTU once it came under Communist domination, and he later became national secretary of the reunified CGT after 1936. Their activities are further discussed here in chs. 10–11.

46. See especially Jean-Marie Flonneau, "Crise de vie chère et mouvement syndical, 1910–1914," *M. Social,* no. 72 (1970), pp. 49–81; and, on the Loire region, Hanagan, *Logic of Solidarity,* pp. 72–80, and Lequin, *Ouvriers de la région lyonnaise,* 2:111–13. The influence of economic conditions on unions and strikes is also discussed generally in the previously cited works of Shorter and Tilly, Stearns, and Perrot, and in Michelle Perrot, "Grèves, grévistes, et conjoncture: Vieux problème, travaux neufs," *M. Social,* no. 63 (1968), pp. 109–24; and Robert Goetz-Girey, *Le mouvement des grèves en France, 1919–1962* (Paris, 1965), pp. 129–40, 151–63.

47. Lequin, *Ouvriers de la région lyonnaise,* 2:135–56; Hanagan, *Logic of Solidarity,* pp. 65–68; Shorter and Tilly, *Strikes in France,* pp. 66–75, 174–93, 227–33, 284–305, 343–45; Stearns, *Revolutionary Syndicalism,* pp. 27–28, 53–67, 73–102; Perrot, "Grèves et conjoncture," pp. 116–18; Goetz-Girey, *Mouvement des grèves,* pp. 146–50.

48. Corbin, *Archaïsme et modernité,* 1:317–18, 595–96; 2:1037–38; Cousteix, "Mouvement ouvrier limousin," pp. 70–72; and Yves Sabourdy, "Approche des conditions de la scission de 1920 dans le mouvement socialiste de la Haute-Vienne" (Mémoire de maîtrise, Paris I, 1971), pp. 131–32. There are also scattered reports on food prices in Limoges in ADHV 6 M 393 (for 1911–40) and 6 M 398 (for 1914–38).

49. Hanagan, *Logic of Solidarity,* pp. 68–80; Lequin, *Ouvriers de la région lyonnaise,* 2:22–39, 60–93; Arbogast, *Armes,* pp. 177–79; Gras, *Métallurgie,* pp. 364–65; Gras, *Mines,* 2:812, 854; Clerc, *Crise du ruban,* pp. 50–96; Guitton, *Rubans,* pp. 169–76. There is also a table on industrial wages in Saint-Etienne in 1889 in ADL 56 M 10.

50. Scattered estimates of unionization in the Loire are in Gras, *Mines,* 2:564, 586–87; Gras, *Métallurgie,* p. 85; and Arbogast, *Armes,* pp. 177–79. Estimates for the Haute-Vienne are in Gaston Ducray, *Le travail porcelainier en Limousin* (Angers, 1904), pp. 140–41; and Francine Bourdelle, "Evolution du syndicalisme ouvrier à Limoges, 1870–1905" (Mémoire de maîtrise, Limoges, 1973), appendices 5, 8, and 12. In addition, there are membership figures on unions in the two Bourses du Travail in AN F7 13605 (Saint-Etienne, 1907), in AN F7 13622 (Limoges, 1911), and in Ministère du Travail, Direction du Travail, *Annuaire des syndicats professionels industriels, commerciaux et agricoles déclarés conformément à la loi du 21 mars 1884 en France et aux colonies,* 18ᵉ année, 1912 (Paris, 1921).

51. Bourse membership figures are from the *Annuaire des syndicats professionnels,* pp. 318–25, 803; estimates of the size of the work forces are from ch. 1 of this study. The average rate of unionization for all French wage-earners before the war was approximately 10 percent (1 million out of 9.4 million workers or

11.4 million workers and employees), including Catholic and independent unions as well as the CGT. *Annuaire des syndicats professionnels* (1912), p. xxxix; *Annuaire Statistique* 34 (1914–15): 12–15.

52. On the demographic profile of the work force, see ch. 1 of this study. On the unionization of skilled workers, see Moss, *Origins of French Labor,* chs. 5–6; Hanagan, *Logic of Solidarity,* ch. 1; Collinet, *Esprit du syndicalisme,* pp. 23–63; and compare Stearns, "Unskilled and Industrialization," pp. 253–68.

53. See Guilbert, *Fonctions des femmes,* pp. 42–54; Guilbert, *Les femmes,* pp. 28–34; and Perrot, *Ouvriers en grève,* 1:318–30.

54. Guilbert, *Les femmes,* pp. 185–202; Marilyn J. Boxer, "Foyer or Factory? Working Class Women in Nineteenth Century France," *Proc. WSFH* 2 (1974): 192–203; and, on Britain, Harold Smith, "The Issue of 'Equal Pay for Equal Work' in Great Britain, 1914–19," *Societas* 3 (1978): 40, 44–45. The issues of female labor and unionization are also noted locally in Cousteix, "Mouvement ouvrier limousin," pp. 59, 63–64, 80; Bourdelle, "Syndicalisme ouvrier à Limoges," pp. 98–99, 109, 127–30; and, for Saint-Etienne, in R. *Tiss.,* June 1904, Dec. 1906, and Nov. 1907.

55. *Annuaire des syndicats professionnels* (1912), pp. 314–25, 802–5; ADL 93 M 3, reports of 10–13 Apr. 1912; Jean Pralong (former UD secretary of the CFTC at Saint-Etienne), interview, 5 Feb. 1975; and, on the postwar feminine unions in the Limoges CFTC, ADHV 10 M 166–67, lists of new unions created in 1920–30.

56. Bourdelle, "Syndicalisme ouvrier à Limoges," p. 99. According to her figures for the porcelain industry in 1905, women comprised 40 percent of the labor force and 30 percent of union membership.

57. In addition to the feminine unions, there were a railroad workers' union (founded in May 1920) and a few employees' unions in the CFTC. ADHV 10 M 146, 3 June 1920; 10 M 147, 1 Apr. 1926; 10 M 166–67, lists of new unions created in 1920–30; 10 M 188, reports of Oct. 1929 and Mar. 1930. On Catholic unionism, see also Cousteix, "Catholicisme social," pp. 103–6.

58. ADL 93 M 52, "L'organisation ouvrière," 1913; 93 M 72, May–Nov. 1913, and June 1919 to June 1922; M 540, dossier on "CFTC," reports of 10 Dec. 1921 and 8 Sept. 1922; M 1068, 3 Aug. 1925; AN F22 73–74, lists of unions dissolved from 1914 to 1935. On Catholic unionism, see also Lequin, *Ouvriers de la région lyonnaise,* 2:337–42, 346–47; Héritier et al., *Luttes ouvrières,* chs. 12–13 and 15–16 on the CFTC, and chs. 19–21 on the CFDT (the latter no longer "Chrétien" but "Démocratique"); and Pierre Delon, *Le syndicalisme chrétien en France* (Paris, 1961).

59. ADL 93 M 71, report of 19 Dec. 1907, including text of a poster; and extracts from *La Loire* and *Le Nouvelliste,* Aug. 1912 to Jan. 1913; 93 M 14, extract from *Le Nouvelliste,* 21 Apr. 1912; 93 M 52, "L'organisation ouvrière," 1913; Lequin, *Ouvriers de la région lyonnaise,* 2:342–46. The postwar politics of the "yellow" union movement are cited in ADL M 541, dossier on "Fascisme," reports of 19–28 Dec. 1925. The monthly *L'Indépendance Ouvrière* also chronicled the activities and attitudes of the "independent" unions in Lyon and the southeastern region for 1903–14 and 1918–29. On "yellow" unionism generally,

see also the volumes by Pierre Biétry (founder of the national federation): *Les Jaunes de France et la question ouvrière* (Paris, 1907), and *Le socialisme et les Jaunes* (Paris, 1906); and George L. Mosse, "The French Right and the Working Classes: 'Les Jaunes,' " *JCH* 7 (1972): 185–208.

60. ADL 93 M 52, 11 Jan. 1894; 93 M 8, 11 Jan. to 1 July 1911; Gras, *Métallurgie*, pp. 80–83; and Guillaume, "Mines de la Loire," pp. 30–36. On wartime and postwar patronal unionism, see also ADL Houillères, cartons 2278 and 2480, notes, Comité des Houillères de la Loire, 1917–1930; and, on the "Unions Civiques," M.-J. Millevoye, "Une page d'histoire contemporaine lyonnaise: Les grèves révolutionnaires de 1920," *Mémoires de l'Académie des Sciences, Belles-Lettres et Arts de Lyon. Sciences et Lettres,* 3ᵉ Série, t. 18 (1924), pp. 103–30. On patronal unionism generally, see also Perrot, *Ouvriers en grève,* 2:659–90; Georges Lefranc, *Les organisations patronales en France, du passé au présent* (Paris, 1976); and Peter N. Stearns, "Against the Strike Threat: Employer Policy toward Labor Agitation in France, 1900–1914," *JMH* 40 (1968): 474–500.

61. Guitton, *Rubans,* esp. p. 96; Clerc, *Crise du ruban,* pp. 122–26, 136–38, 153–62; Larivière, *Industrie à Limoges,* pp. 72–73, 79, 89; Posselle, "Porcelaine de Limoges," pp. 9–10.

62. ADL M 541, dossier on "Fascisme," report of 19 Dec. 1925; Gras, *Métallurgie,* p. 349; Pétrus Faure, *Histoire de la métallurgie au Chambon-Feugerolles* (Le Chambon-Feugerolles, 1931), pp. 10, 32.

63. Héritier et al., *Luttes ouvrières,* pp. 134–35.

64. Hanagan, *Logic of Solidarity,* esp. p. 167; Faure, *Chambon Rouge,* pp. 36–37, 70, 83, 96; Arbogast, *Armes,* p. 179; Gaudy, *Ville rouge,* chs. 13–14; Ducray, *Travail porcelainier,* pp. 140–41; Desmoulins letters, 3 May 1974.

65. Ministère du Travail, Direction du Travail, *Statistique des grèves et des recours à la conciliation et à l'arbitrage,* 1912–14 (Paris, 1913–19). For the three years combined, the Loire miners' strikes accounted for 3.3 percent of the Loire's total strikers and 0.8 percent of working-days lost; the metalworkers accounted for 3.4 percent and 2.2 percent of these totals, respectively. On the low strike rates of Loire metalworkers, see also Christian Gras, "La Fédération des Métaux en 1913–1914 et l'évolution du syndicalisme révolutionnaire français," *M. Social,* no. 77 (1971), p. 91.

66. Compare Stearns, *Revolutionary Syndicalism,* p. 96 (the author cites "the supposed syndicalism of the miners around Saint-Etienne"), and Jacques Julliard, "Théorie syndicaliste révolutionnaire et pratique gréviste," *M. Social,* no. 65 (1968), pp. 55–69.

67. See especially Willard, *Les Guesdistes,* pp. 46–50, 345–60.

68. Ibid., pp. 105, 282–83, 510–11; Cousteix, "Mouvement ouvrier limousin," pp. 42–46; Bernard Bobe, "Contribution à l'histoire de l'idée socialiste durant la Seconde Internationale: Essai sur le département de la Haute-Vienne" (D.E.S., Paris, 1969), pp. 12–14, 19.

69. Bobe, "Idée socialiste," pp. 12–14, 29–31; Cousteix, "Mouvement ouvrier limousin," pp. 44–46, 53, 61–63; Cousteix, "Doctrines anarchistes," p. 27.

70. Bourse, Limoges, 10 Sept. 1906.

71. At the time of Rougerie's election in 1912, some local controversy was reported at a meeting of the lithographers' union, but none in the Bourse's own records. Chambre Syndicale des ouvriers Imprimeurs-Lithographes, Limoges, Procès-verbaux des séances du Comité Syndical et des Assemblées Générales (Archives of the Syndicat CGT du Livre, Limoges), meeting of 10 Aug. 1912. On Rougerie's wartime views, see Bourse, Limoges, 11 Aug. 1915, and 30 May and 5 July 1918; and Synd. Chaussures, Limoges, 11 July 1918.

72. Rougerie's later politics are discussed here in chs. 5–6; see also the biographical sketch in Maitron, *Dictionnaire biographique,* 15:97.

73. On Pressemane: Cousteix, "Mouvement ouvrier limousin," pp. 47, 84; Lenoble et al., *La Gauche au pouvoir,* pp. 73, 76–77, 86; and Sabourdy, "Conditions de la scission," pp. 191–200 passim.

74. For the Communists' views of Pressemane: *C. Rouge,* 8 Jan. 1921; *Prol. C.,* 12–19 Feb. 1922; and Docteur [Jules] Fraisseix, *Au long de ma route: Propos anecdotiques d'un militant limousin* (Limoges, 1946), pp. 59–60. There is also a biographical sketch in Maitron, *Dictionnaire biographique,* 14:311–13.

75. On Betoulle: Cousteix, "Mouvement ouvrier limousin," pp. 48–49; Lenoble et al., *La Gauche au pouvoir,* p. 72; Decouty, "Opinion politique," pp. 277–81; Roger Penot, "Comment Limoges vota socialiste en 1912, 'Betoullistes' contre 'Goujadistes,' " *Limousin Magazine,* Dec. 1974, pp. 10–13; and Maitron, *Dictionnaire biographique,* 10:289–91.

76. AN F7 13023, 22 June to 25 Sept. 1915.

77. Willard, *Les Guesdistes,* pp. 579–81, 588–92; Lenoble et al., *La Gauche au pouvoir,* pp. 53–54, 75–78, 95–106; Cousteix, "Mouvement ouvrier limousin," pp. 48–51, 68. See also Donald Noel Baker, "The Politics of Socialist Protest in France: The Left Wing of the Socialist Party, 1921–39," *JMH* 43 (1971), esp. pp. 10–11.

78. Willard, *Les Guesdistes,* esp. p. 508. The Guesdist and rival movements in the Lyon region are further described in Willard, pp. 85, 269–82, 316–25, 398–402, 506–8; Lequin, "Classe ouvrière et idéologie," pp. 5–6, 12–18; and Lequin, *Ouvriers de la région lyonnaise,* 2:224–42, 280–90, 301–4. On the stronger Guesdist influence among miners in the Nord, see Robert Parsons Baker, "A Regional Study of Working-Class Organization in France: Socialism in the Nord, 1870–1924" (Ph.D. diss., Stanford Univ., 1966), ch. 6.

79. Willard, *Les Guesdistes,* pp. 578n, 584; Lequin, "Classe ouvrière et idéologie," pp. 6, 18; Lequin, *Ouvriers de la région lyonnaise,* 2:348–51. On the Socialists' electoral strategy, see also *Peuple L.,* Nov. 1919, and *Réveil,* Feb. to May 1928.

80. On Ledin: ADL 93 M 56, 17 Feb. 1887, 8 Nov. 1893, and 23 May 1894; 93 M 57, June 1895 to Oct. 1896; Héritier et al., *Luttes ouvrières,* pp. 121–29; Lequin, *Ouvriers de la région lyonnaise,* 2:350–51, 362–64; and Maitron, *Dictionnaire biographique,* 13:242–43.

81. On Durafour: Gras, *Mines,* 2:567; *La Flamme,* 29 Nov. 1919; *Peuple L.,* May 1920, Apr.–May 1924, and 23 Aug. 1925; and François Ménard, *Antoine Durafour, 1876–1932* (Saint-Etienne, 1976).

82. *Le Bloc Ouvrier et Paysan* (PC, Loire), 3 May 1924.

83. Ernest Lafont, "L'aventurier contre la loi: L'étranglement de la grève des cheminots" (Paris, 1910), pamphlet, cited in entry for Lafont in Maitron, *Dictionnaire biographique,* 13:173.

84. On Lafont: Lequin, *Ouvriers de la région lyonnaise,* 2:351–52, 363; Wohl, *French Communism,* p. 31.

85. Daniel Ligou, *Histoire du socialisme en France, 1871–1961* (Paris, 1962), pp. 393–94; Maitron, *Dictionnaire biographique,* 13:172–73. Lafont's political shifts in the 1920s are also detailed in *Peuple L.,* esp. 1–28 Jan. 1923 and 31 July 1927.

86. On the Saint-Etienne Bourse: ADL 93 M 57, 4 July 1895; and Héritier et al., *Luttes ouvrières,* pp. 98–102, 125–27, 137–40. On the Limoges Bourse: Bourdelle, "Syndicalisme ouvrier à Limoges," pp. 60, 73, 78–83, 130–44 passim; and Cousteix, "Mouvement ouvrier limousin," pp. 61–62. On Treich: Maitron, *Dictionnaire biographique,* 15:247–48. On the Bourse Federation and the early CGT, see also Georges Lefranc, *Le mouvement syndical sous la Troisième République* (Paris, 1967), pp. 64–84.

87. Bourse, Limoges, 10 Sept. 1906; Synd. Chaussures, Limoges, 27 Sept. and 29 Nov. 1906; Bobe, "Idée socialiste," pp. 63–66. Bobe also notes the Socialists' division on the question of the general strike; not all were such "orthodox" Guesdists as to reject this syndicalist principle.

88. ADL 19 M 36, 3 Oct. 1913; 19 M 37, 31 Jan. 1914.

89. On Saint-Etienne: ADL 93 M 52, 25 Oct. 1907; 93 M 58, 9 Aug. to 10 Sept. 1912; 93 M 69, 25 Oct. to 23 Dec. 1911. On Limoges: Synd. Chaussures, Limoges, 27 Sept. 1906; Synd. Imprimeurs-Lithographes, Limoges, 10 Aug. 1912; AN F7 13622, 30 Sept. 1911; and ADHV 10 M 151, Notice sur la Bourse du Travail, Exercice 1919. The Limoges Bourse canceled its subsidy in 1911 but resumed it in 1912.

90. See especially Maitron, *Mouvement anarchiste,* 1:265–330.

91. AN F7 13053, report on "L'anarchisme en France," Sept. 1897, pp. 29–32. Maitron also cites figures for 1893–94, in *Mouvement anarchiste,* 1:128–29.

92. Cousteix, "Doctrines anarchistes," pp. 26–33; Desmoulins letters, 10 Sept. and 18 Dec. 1972, 3–9 Mar. 1973, 26 Feb. 1974. Several Saint-Junien anarchists, reported as active before the war, are cited in ADHV 4 M 316, 24 May 1923 and 10 June 1924.

93. AN F7 13057, report on anarchism in Limoges, 1913; F7 13053, report on "Anarchistes français, groupes communistes et individualistes," May 1914; Michel Laguionie, "Le groupe Sébastien-Faure, Limoges," draft article in Laguionie's personal files, Limoges; and Maitron, *Mouvement anarchiste,* 1:448–51. Data on individual members are in AN F7 13053, dossier on "Révolutionnaires principaux en province," 1911; ADHV 4 M 316, 13 Sept. 1910, 17 May 1923, and 30 Nov. 1936; 10 M 189, dossier on "CGTSR," reports of 1933–36; and Desmoulins letter (to Adrien Perrissaguet, anarcho-syndicalist shoe worker at Limoges), 12 Apr. 1970.

94. Age data are in ADHV 4 M 316, 13 Sept. 1910. Also on Téty: 4 M 316, 30 June 1913; AN F7 13053, individual report on Jules Téty, 1911.

95. ADHV 4 M 316, 13 Sept. 1910 and 17 May 1923; individual reports on militants, Apr.–May 1923. The question of place of birth among Limoges workers is examined here in ch. 1.

96. André Lansade and Michel Darsouze, cited at Bourse, Limoges, 9 Feb. 1911, and in ADHV 4 M 316, 17 May 1923 and 1 June 1935.

97. Bourse, Limoges, 1905 to 1920, lists of delegates present; Desmoulins letters, 14 Jan. and 3 Mar. 1973, and 22 Mar. 1974.

98. Desmoulins letters, 14 Jan. 1972; ADHV 10 M 151, report on the Limoges, 25 Sept. 1908, 17 Aug. and 4 Dec. 1912; Synd. Imprimeurs-Litho-15:286–87. Vardelle was first cousin of the striker (Camille Vardelle) shot and killed by troops during the porcelain strike of 1905.

99. Bourse, Limoges, 9 Dec. 1914; AN F7 13053, individual report on Jules Téty, Oct. 1915; Desmoulins letters, 13 Apr. 1972 and 18 Dec. 1973; Maitron, *Dictionnaire biographique,* 15:14.

100. ADHV 10 M 192, 23 July 1907 and 20 Jan. 1908; Synd. Chaussures, Limoges, 25 Sept. 1908, 17 Aug. and 4 Dec. 1912; Synd. Imprimeurs-Lithographes, Limoges, 13 Sept. 1912; Cousteix, "Mouvement ouvrier limousin," p. 68.

101. ADHV 10 M 193, 12 Nov. 1911; AN F7 13053, report on "Groupements anarchistes et révolutionnaires, province," Apr. 1912.

102. Bourse, Limoges, 17 Aug. 1912.

103. ADL 19 M 37, 31 Jan. 1914.

104. General information on the Loire anarchist movement is in AN F7 13053, report on "Anarchistes français, groupes communistes et individualistes," May 1914. The anarchists' debates on joining unions or the national anarchist federation are reported in ADL 93 M 56–57 for 1890–96; 93 M 54 and 93 M 69 for 1911–12; and 19 M 35–37 for 1913–14. The activities of Sébastien Faure and Ravachol are described in Maitron, *Mouvement anarchiste,* 1:131–32, 161–63, 213–27, 448–51, 2:80–87; and Maitron, *Dictionnaire biographique,* 12:174–76, 15:9–10. The competing appeals of anarchism and Guesdism in the Loire are discussed in Maitron, *Mouvement anarchiste,* 1:88–90, 111–32; Willard, *Les Guesdistes,* pp. 198–99, 317–18; and Lequin, *Ouvriers de la région lyonnaise,* 2:240–42, 281–86.

105. ADL 19 M 37, Etat nominatif des anarchistes inscrits dans le département de la Loire, 1914; 19 M 33–37, reports on anarchists' meetings, 1913–14; M 432, dossier on "Anarchistes et antimilitaristes, rayés, décédés ou disparus, 1911–1920" (includes files on individuals active in the movement before their removal from the list). According to the departmental list, in addition to the sixty-seven anarchists residing in Saint-Etienne, there were sixty-six in the other towns of the Loire basin, twenty-five in the Roanne area, and six in the Montbrison area. These totals contrast with those cited by Maitron for the 1890s, when there appeared to be more anarchists in Roanne than in Saint-Etienne. *Mouvement anarchiste* (1955 ed.), 1:424–25 (the 1975 edition omits this information). On the Carnet B, see Jean-Jacques Becker, *Le Carnet B: Les pouvoirs publics et l'antimilitarisme avant la guerre de 1914* (Paris, 1973).

106. See also Hanagan, *Logic of Solidarity,* pp. 192–94; and Martin, "Culture militante," pp. 315–17.

107. One should note the high ratio of city origins among the few anarchist weavers and gunsmiths, and the low ratio—even lower than the average for this industry generally—among the anarchist metalworkers other than gunsmiths. The geographic origins of Saint-Etienne workers are examined in ch. 1 of this study.

108. In the short list of Saint-Etienne activists, fifteen were aged twenty to thirty-four, and six were aged thirty-five to forty-nine. Ages of five were unknown.

109. Maitron, *Dictionnaire biographique,* 13:298 (on Liothier); ADL 93 M 8, 8 Dec. 1911 and 6 Mar. 1912; 93 M 57, 23–27 Apr. 1901, and 24 Feb. and 16 Mar. 1911; 93 M 69, 23 Dec. 1911 to 25 Mar. 1912.

110. ADL 93 M 57, 22–30 Sept. 1903; 93 M 69, 25 Oct. to 23 Dec. 1911; 93 M 8, 17 Apr. and 2 Dec. 1912; 19 M 37, 31 Jan. 1914.

111. ADL 19 M 33, 27 Apr. 1913; 19 M 35, 2 Apr. 1913; 19 M 34, 19 Oct. 1913; AN F7 13057, 15 June 1914. On the SFIO and the three-year law, see also Lequin, *Ouvriers de la région lyonnaise,* 2:359–61.

112. ADL 19 M 34, 25 July 1913; 93 M 54, 13 Oct. 1913; 19 M 36, 16 Jan. 1914; 19 M 37, 31 Jan. 1914.

113. ADL 93 M 56, 29 Dec. 1893. For expressing their approval of Ravachol at a Bourse meeting, these anarchists saw their union (the Hommes de Peine) expelled from the organization—a clear sign of Bourse hostility at this time.

114. ADL 19 M 36, 3 July 1914.

Chapter 3. *The Mobilization of the Left*

1. On World War I and the postwar era, see Kriegel, *Aux origines;* Wohl, *French Communism;* Wohl, *Generation of 1914;* Fine, "Toward Corporatism"; and Maier, *Recasting Bourgeois Europe.* Other works that touch on the problem of continuity and change include Cronin, "Labor Insurgency," pp. 125–52; Robert, "Luttes ouvrières," pp. 28–65; and Fridenson, ed., *L'autre front.* Books that end more abruptly in 1914 include Moss, *Origins of French Labor,* and Harvey Mitchell and Peter N. Stearns, *Workers and Protest: The European Labor Movement, the Working Classes and the Origins of Social Democracy, 1890–1914* (Itasca, Ill., 1971); in the latter, see especially the introduction by Robert Wohl, pp. 1–11.

2. *Pop. C.,* 31 July 1914; AN F7 12934, 31 July 1914; F7 12936, 4 Aug. 1914; F7 13372, report on pacifist propaganda, 1914–18, pt. 1, p. 6.

3. Frachon, *Pour la CGT,* pp. 57–58. On the response to the mobilization, see also Jean-Jacques Becker, *1914: Comment les Français sont entrés dans la guerre* (Paris, 1977), pp. 149–56; and Annie Kriegel and Jean-Jacques Becker, *1914: La guerre et le mouvement ouvrier français* (Paris, 1964), pp. 94–105.

4. Becker, *1914,* pp. 163, 170n; *Pop. C.,* 31 July 1914.

5. AN F7 12939, 2 Aug. 1914.

6. AN F7 12936, 4 Aug. 1914.

7. Report of 10 Nov. 1912, cited in AN F7 13384, "Les projets de sabotage de la mobilisation (Juillet 1914)." On the response to the assassination of Franz Ferdinand: ADL 19 M 36, 3 July 1914.

8. ADL 19 M 38, 1–20 Aug. 1914. According to Becker, these cases of nonsubmission were the only ones in France that openly avowed antimilitarist motives, as expressed in testimony before the military tribunals. *1914,* pp. 351–52.

9. ADL 19 M 38, 18 Aug., 9 Nov., and 4 Dec. 1914. Monthly reports for 1915 and 1916 record "no meetings" and "no unfavorable remarks" for anarchists under surveillance in the region.

10. AN F7 12936, 4 Aug. 1914; *Pop. C.,* 4 Aug. 1914; Becker, *1914,* pp. 326–27. Becker does cite the more enthusiastic tone of the conservative local daily, *Le Courrier du Centre.*

11. Bourse, Limoges, 9 Dec. 1914; ADHV R 261, dossier on Jules Téty; Desmoulins letters, 13 Apr. and 27 Aug. 1972, 18 Dec. 1973. Desmoulins, also an anarchist, was with Téty in Spain, along with a group of French, Spanish, Italian, and Russian fugitives.

12. Text of manifesto reprinted in Rosmer, *Mouvement ouvrier,* 1:509, and discussed on p. 215 of the volume. On Lyon, see also Moissonnier, "Octobre," pp. 38–39, and Edmond Pelé, "Le mouvement ouvrier lyonnais pendant la première guerre mondiale, 1914–1918" (Mémoire de maîtrise, Lyon, 1970).

13. ADL 93 M 8, 25 Jan. 1915. On Faure's tract, "Pour la Paix," see also AN F7 13372, report on pacifist propaganda, pt. 2, entry for Dec. 1914. The Bourse at Saint-Etienne revealed no signs of antiwar opinion in minutes of its monthly meetings, from Sept. 1914 until Dec. 1915, when a reference to Merrheim first appeared. Bourse du Travail, Saint-Etienne, Procès-verbaux des délibérations du Conseil d'Administration (Archives of the Union Locale CGT, Saint-Etienne).

14. Bourse, Limoges, 7 Apr. 1917, report on financial situation for the period 1 Jan. 1914 to 31 Mar. 1917.

15. Synd. Imprimeurs-Lithographes, Limoges, 21 Nov. 1914.

16. ADL 93 M 14, 14 Jan. 1914 and 20 Nov. 1917; 93 M 8, 8 Dec. 1911 to 8 Dec. 1913, and 15 May 1916.

17. Synd. Imprimeurs-Lithographes, Limoges, 27 July 1916.

18. ADL 10 M 166, 9 Sept. 1914; Bourse, Saint-Etienne, 19 Sept. and 3 Oct. 1914.

19. AN F7 13574, 31 July 1914; F7 13571, 18 Dec. 1914; see also John Horne, "Le Comité d'Action (CGT-PS) et l'origine du réformisme syndical du temps de guerre," *M. Social,* no. 122 (1983), pp. 33–60.

20. Horne, "Comité d'Action," p. 46; Nicholas Papayanis, "Collaboration and Pacifism in France during World War I," *Francia,* Band 5 (1977), pp. 441, 444–45.

21. Comité d'Action du Prolétariat Organisé de Saint-Etienne, *Rapport Général du Comité d'Action, présenté à l'Assemblée Générale du 24 janvier 1917,* papers of the late Urbain Thévenon (personal files of Michelle Zancarini, Saint-Etienne); ADL 93 M 58, 20 Apr. 1916; 10 M 172, 29 Apr. 1916; AN F7 12994, 30 Apr. 1918; ADL 10 M 183, 27 Oct. 1919.

22. ADL 10 M 176, 2 Aug. 1917; AN F7 12994, 6 Aug. 1917; ADL 93 M 103, 20 Nov. 1917.

23. Bourse, Limoges, 11 Aug. 1915.

24. Quoted passage in Synd. Chaussures, Limoges, 11 July 1918; see also Bourse, Limoges, 11 Aug. 1915 and 14 Dec. 1917; and AN F7 13023, text of Circulaire Minoritaire of the Fédération SFIO de la Haute-Vienne (with signatories), 15 May 1915, attached to report of 24 June 1915.

25. AN F7 13023, Circulaire Minoritaire, 15 May 1915. The text of the manifesto is also reprinted in Rosmer, *Mouvement ouvrier,* 1:292–96.

26. AN F7 13023, 22 June to 25 Sept. 1915.

27. On the Limoges Socialists, compare Rosmer, *Mouvement ouvrier,* 1:296–97 (the author calls this group minoritarians *"à mi-chemin"*), and Lenoble et al., *La Gauche au pouvoir,* pp. 76–79. On Monatte and Loriot, see Kriegel, *Aux origines,* 1:77–80, 122–32, 279–80; Wohl, *French Communism,* pp. 59–82 passim; and *Syndicalisme révolutionnaire et communisme: Les archives de Pierre Monatte, 1914–1924* (Paris, 1968), ed. Colette Chambelland and Jean Maitron, chs. 1–4. The "Vie Ouvrière" group remained active even though the journal suspended publication from 1914 to 1919.

28. AN F7 13571, 4 Feb. 1915. The Comité d'Action reportedly continued to meet through at least May 1917.

29. Kriegel, *Aux origines,* 1:97–142; Wohl, *French Communism,* pp. 69, 80–82; Papayanis, "Collaboration and Pacifism," pp. 428–34, 439.

30. ADL 19 M 38, 13–29 Sept. 1916.

31. AN F7 13372, report on pacifist propaganda, pt. 2, entries for 3 Apr. 1916 (quoted passage) and Jan. 1917.

32. ADL 19 M 38, 5 Mar. 1917. A second report, dated 10 Mar., further qualified these remarks by claiming that the anarchist movement at Saint-Etienne remained as small and inconsequential as ever, although the movement was somewhat larger and livelier at Firminy.

33. ADL 19 M 38, 13–29 Sept. 1916; 93 M 55, 10 Apr. 1917. On the suppression of Faure's journal: AN F7 13372, report on pacifist propaganda, pt. 2, entries for July to Dec. 1917. The roles of Andrieu and Flageollet in the wartime syndicalist movement are further discussed below and in ch. 4.

34. ADL 10 M 172, 21 Apr. 1916; 93 M 8, 15 May and 9 June 1916; 93 M 69, 29 May 1916; 93 M 55, 23 Aug. 1916; 93 M 58, 29 Aug. and 27 Nov. 1916.

35. ADL 10 M 171, text of Merrheim resolution (with signatories), 15 Aug. 1915; 10 M 173, 18 Oct. 1916. (These issues are not reported in the Bourse's own minutes.) The Merrheim resolution is also printed in *L'Union des Métaux,* May–Dec. 1915, p. 16. It was supported by twenty-seven UDs or Federations, as against eighty-one votes for a Jouhaux resolution and ten abstentions.

36. ADL 10 M 172, 29 Apr. 1916; 10 M 173, 3–31 July 1916.

37. *La Flamme,* especially 22 Sept. and 20 Oct. 1917.

38. On Moulin in the SFIO: ADL 10 M 179, 30 July 1918; AN F7 12995, 21 Mar. 1920. On Moulin in the Loire teachers' union: ADL 93 M 97, 27 May 1911 to 24 Oct. 1912, and 9 Feb. 1918. The teachers' unions nationwide were a major force of antiwar activism, as reported in AN F7 13575, 21 Apr. and

17 May 1916; in F7 13372, report on pacifist propaganda, pt. 4; and in François Bernard et al., *Le syndicalisme dans l'enseignement: Histoire de la Fédération de l'Enseignement des origines à l'unification de 1935*, 3 vols. (Grenoble, 1966 [orig. ed. 1938]), 2:52–82. The signs of syndicalist hostility toward teachers in the labor movement and in the later CP are discussed in chs. 4 and 11 of this study.

39. Cited in Philippe Bernard, *La fin d'un monde, 1914–1929* (Paris, 1975), pp. 78–79; the reference is to peasants in the Allier and industrial workers in Montluçon and Moulins. For the incidence of wartime casualties among the peasantry, see Michel Huber, *La population de la France pendant la guerre* (Paris, 1931), p. 423; for the economics of food prices and the social impact of trench life, see Gordon Wright, *Rural Revolution in France* (Stanford, 1964), pp. 28–31. Parallels between migration and military service are suggested in Weber, *Peasants into Frenchmen*, pp. 288–90, 297–98.

40. ADL 14 M 15, 3 Nov. 1917. According to Gilbert Hatry, wartime profits at Renault were high but, because of taxes, counted for only a small part of the company's booming gross income. Hatry also describes working conditions at Renault, which likely had more direct impact on labor attitudes, especially if annual profits were not publicized. *Renault, Usine de Guerre, 1914–1918* (Paris, 1978), pp. 156–58, 88–95.

41. Arthur Fontaine, *French Industry during the War* (New Haven, 1926), pp. 22–25; William Oualid and Charles Picquenard, *Salaires et tarifs. Conventions collectives et grèves. La politique du Ministère de l'Armement et du Ministère du Travail* (Paris, 1928), pp. 4–11; and, on the Haute-Vienne, AN F7 12939, 4–25 Aug. 1914. There is also a dossier on the "Lutte contre le chômage au début de la guerre de 1914" in F22 542.

42. Oualid and Picquenard, *Salaires et tarifs*, p. 12; Sabourdy, "Conditions de la scission," p. 95.

43. ADL 91 M 5, 17 May 1915; ADHV 10 M 135, 30 Nov. 1916. See ch. 1 for prewar figures. For general observations, see also Guitton, *Rubans*, pp. 125–34, 264–69; Larivière, *Industrie à Limoges*, pp. 70, 78–79; and Fontaine, *French Industry*, p. 61.

44. ADHV 10 M 113, 22 Aug. 1917 and 7 Feb. 1920. For the leather industries generally, see Fontaine, *French Industry*, p. 61. While the shoe industry flourished, the luxury glove industry withered; data for Saint-Junien are in ADHV 10 M 119, 3 Aug. 1915 to 30 Nov. 1916.

45. Gras, *Mines*, 2:869–71; Bonnet, "Main-d'oeuvre étrangère," pp. 31–47. The economic importance of the occupied northeastern zones, which had supplied 75 percent of France's coal, 81 percent of her pig iron, and 63 percent of her steel, is discussed in Fontaine, *French Industry*, pp. 16–21.

46. AN F7 13356, Liste numérique, par département, des établissements militaires, usines et ateliers privés travaillant pour la défense nationale, Jan. 1917; ADL M 1066, Statistique des établissements de l'industrie privée travaillant pour la défense nationale et du personnel global qu'elles occupent (Loire, 1917). According to these sets of figures, the Loire ranked first among all French departments (excluding the Seine) in both the number of workers and the number of companies engaged in wartime national defense; note that the average company

size thus remained small. There were also some 2,000 workers in the war industries in the Haute-Vienne. For general information, see also Jean-William Dereymez, "Les usines de guerre (1914–1918) et le cas de la Saône-et-Loire," *Cahiers d'Histoire* 26 (1981): 150–81; and Gerd Hardach, "La mobilisation industrielle en 1914–1918: Production, planification et idéologie," in *L'autre front,* ed. Fridenson, pp. 84–86, 100–2.

47. AN F7 12936, 6 Oct. 1914.

48. On the miners: AN F7 14607, 3 Dec. 1917. On the metalworkers: the tables in F7 13356 specify foreign workers but not war prisoners; the tables in ADL M 1066 specify both categories but only for the companies outside Saint-Etienne. In the nation at large in 1917, foreign labor comprised 8.9 percent of the total employment in the war industries, and war prisoners 1.8 percent, according to totals in AN F22 292, Rapport sur la situation de la main-d'oeuvre au 1 Mai 1917. On the use of war prisoners and foreign labor, see also Fontaine, *French Industry,* pp. 40–42, 50–52; B. Nogaro and Lucien Weil, *La main-d'oeuvre étrangère et coloniale pendant la guerre* (Paris, n.d.); and Jean Vidalenc, "La main-d'oeuvre étrangère en France et la première guerre mondiale," *Francia,* Band 2 (1974), pp. 524–50.

49. On the Loire: ADL M 2023, Enquête sur la main-d'oeuvre féminine, 19 Oct. 1916; M 1066, Statistique des établissements, 1917. On France overall: AN F22 292, Situation de la main-d'oeuvre, May 1917; Fontaine, *French Industry,* pp. 42–46; and Mathilde Dubesset et al., "Les munitionnettes de la Seine," in *L'autre front,* ed. Fridenson, pp. 209–16; the tables in F7 13356 do not distinguish women workers.

50. Jean-Louis Robert, "La CGT et la famille ouvrière, 1914–1918: Première approche," *M. Social,* no. 116 (1981), pp. 51–53; see also Yvonne Delatour, "Le travail des femmes pendant la première guerre mondiale et ses conséquences sur l'évolution de leur rôle dans la société," *Francia,* Band 2 (1974), pp. 482–501.

51. ADL M 1066, Statistique des établissements, 1917; AN F22 292, Situation de la main-d'oeuvre, May 1917; see also Fontaine, *French Industry,* pp. 31–34. The tables in M 1066 indicate female and military labor by company for each of the towns in the Loire basin. On the relative proportions of female, foreign, and mobilized labor in other French regions, see also Dereymez, "Usines de guerre," pp. 165–71.

52. ADL 10 M 168, 15 Sept. 1915; AN F7 12994, 7 Sept. 1918; cost-of-living table by region for 1911–19 in the *Bulletin du Ministère du Travail,* nos. 11–12 (1919), p. 548. For general observations, see also Henri Gerest, "Problèmes posés par le ravitaillement d'une population ouvrière pendant la Grande Guerre: Le cas de l'agglomération stéphanoise en 1917–1918," *Actes du 98ᵉ CNSS,* Saint-Etienne, 1973 (Section histoire moderne), 2:253–70; and Sabourdy, "Conditions de la scission," pp. 131–32.

53. ADL 10 M 168, 15 Sept. 1915; Guitton, *Rubans,* pp. 170–72; Gras, *Mines,* 2:879–80; Sabourdy, "Conditions de la scission," pp. 131–32; Oualid and Picquenard, *Salaires et tarifs,* pp. 20–21.

54. Robert, "Luttes ouvrières," pp. 42–43; Cronin, "Labor Insurgency," pp. 140–41; also K. G. J. C. Knowles and D. J. Robertson, "Differences between

the Wages of Skilled and Unskilled Workers, 1880–1950," *Bulletin of Oxford Univ. Institute of Statistics* 13 (1951): 110–14.

55. Jean-Paul de Gaudemar, *La mobilisation générale* (Paris, 1979), pp. 183–90, 204–6; Bernard Waites, "The Effects of the First World War on the Economic and Social Structure of the English Working Class," *Journal of Scottish Labour History Society* 10 (1978): 6–8, 18–19; and Fontaine, *French Industry,* pp. 93–94, 289–90.

56. On Taylorism and mechanization, see Fontaine, *French Industry,* esp. pp. 93–94, 289–90; Aimée Moutet, "Les origines du système de Taylor en France: Le point de vue patronal (1907–1914)," *M. Social,* no. 93 (1975), pp. 3–49; Yves-Claude Lequin, "Le Taylorisme avant 1914: Réponse technique et idéologique aux exigences du monopolisme," *Cahiers IMT,* n.s., no. 16 (1976), pp. 14–37; and Michel Collinet, *Essai sur la condition ouvrière (1900–1950)* (Paris, 1951), esp. pp. 65–75. On the response of the labor movement in France and elsewhere, see Cronin, "Labor Insurgency," pp. 137–41; Carmen J. Sirianni, "Workers' Control in the Era of World War I: A Comparative Analysis of the European Experience," *Theory and Society* 9 (1980): 29–88; James Hinton, *The First Shop Stewards' Movement* (London, 1973); David Montgomery, "The 'New Unionism' and the Transformation of Workers' Consciousness in America, 1909–22," *JSH* 7 (1974): 509–29; and, more generally, Collinet, *Esprit du syndicalisme,* pp. 30–53; Moss, *Origins of French Labor,* chs. 5–6; Hanagan, *Logic of Solidarity,* pp. 13–20; and Scott, *Glassworkers of Carmaux,* ch. 4.

57. Gaudemar, *La mobilisation générale,* pp. 204–6.

58. Robert, "Luttes ouvrières," pp. 34–35; Lequin, "Rationalisation," pp. 116–17.

59. On government policies, see Hardach, "Mobilisation industrielle," in *L'autre front,* ed. Fridenson, pp. 81–109; Hardach, *First World War,* chs. 4–6; Kemp, *French Economy,* ch. 3; and Jean-Baptiste Duroselle, *La France et les Français, 1914–1920* (Paris, 1972), ch. 5.

60. Oualid and Picquenard, *Salaires et tarifs,* pp. 35–39, 131–35; Ministère du Travail, Direction du Travail, *Règlement amiable des conflits collectifs du travail* (Paris, 1924), pp. 60–74. The new institutions are also discussed in Hardach, "Mobilisation industrielle"; Alain Hennebicque, "Albert Thomas et le régime des usines de guerre, 1915–1917"; and Gilbert Hatry, "Les délégués d'atelier aux usines Renault," all in *L'autre front,* ed. Fridenson, pp. 89–100, 111–44, and 222–27; Madeleine Rebérioux and Patrick Fridenson, "Albert Thomas, pivot du réformisme français," *M. Social,* no. 87 (1974), pp. 85–97; and Martin Fine, "Albert Thomas: A Reformer's Vision of Modernization, 1914–1932," *JCH* 12 (1977): 548–49.

61. Ministère du Travail, *Règlement amiable des conflits,* p. 64.

62. Ibid., p. 72; Fine, "Albert Thomas," p. 549.

63. Oualid and Picquenard, *Salaires et tarifs,* pp. 420–22; Roger Picard, *Le mouvement syndical durant la guerre* (Paris, 1926), pp. 118–25; Hatry, "Délégués d'atelier," in *L'autre front,* ed. Fridenson, pp. 228–35; Papayanis, "Collaboration and Pacifism," pp. 441, 446–49. On the views of the independent or "yellow" unions, see also *L'Indépendance Ouvrière* (Lyon), Jan. 1918.

64. Oualid and Picquenard, *Salaires et tarifs,* pp. 343–53; Picard, *Mouvement syndical,* pp. 109–13; Max Gallo, "Quelques aspects de la mentalité et du comportement ouvriers dans les usines de guerre, 1914–1918," *M. Social,* no. 56 (1966), pp. 3–33; R. Huard, "Aspects du mouvement ouvrier gardois pendant la guerre de 1914–18: Les grèves de 1917," *Annales du Midi* 80 (1968): 305–18; Gérard Raffaelli, "Les mouvements pacifistes dans les usines d'armement de la région de Saint-Etienne (1914–1918)," *Actes du 98ᵉ CNSS,* Saint-Etienne, 1973 (Section histoire moderne), 2:221–37; and Michelle [Zancarini] and Gérard Raffaelli, "Introduction bibliographique, méthodologique et biographique à l'étude de l'évolution économique et sociale du département de la Loire, 1914–1920: Le mouvement ouvrier contre la guerre" (Mémoire de maîtrise, Paris-Nanterre, 1969).

65. ADL 93 M 8, 15 May 1916.

66. ADL 93 M 8, cover letter from Torcieux to Director of *Tribune Républicaine* (Saint-Etienne), Sept. 1916; 93 M 9 (misfiled), draft article "Dans la métallurgie"; 10 M 169, extract from *Journal Officiel,* 25 Feb. 1915.

67. Cited (with no precise reference) in Raffaelli, "Mouvements pacifistes," p. 232.

68. ADL 93 M 9, draft article "Dans la métallurgie"; 93 M 8, cover letter from Torcieux to Director of *Tribune Républicaine,* and report of 22 Dec. 1916; 93 M 11 (misfiled), letter from Saint-Etienne metalworkers' union to Loire Prefect, 3 Apr. 1917.

69. ADHV R 258, 4 Nov. 1917 and 5 July 1919; 10 M 194, requests for authorizations, Mar.–Oct. 1919. Authorizations for meetings were no longer necessary once the "state of siege" was lifted in Oct. 1919.

70. ADL 93 M 68, 16 Dec. 1915; 93 M 55, report of 26 Dec. 1915, and letter from Loire Prefect to CGT delegate, 26 Dec. 1915; 93 M 40, letter from Saint-Etienne railroad workers' union to Loire Prefect, 29 Feb. 1916, and report of 7 Mar. 1916; 93 M 8, 24 Dec. 1916.

71. ADL 93 M 55, reports of 14 May and 23 Aug. 1916; telegrams from Interior Ministry to all Prefects, 2 June, 21 July, and 6 Sept. 1916.

72. See Bernard, *La fin d'un monde,* p. 34.

73. *Statistique des grèves,* 1915–18; see also Oualid and Picquenard, *Salaires et tarifs,* pp. 24, 337–43, and Picard, *Mouvement syndical,* pp. 104–13.

74. Oualid and Picquenard, *Salaires et tarifs,* p. 24; *Statistique des grèves,* 1915–16.

75. *Statistique des grèves,* 1915–16.

76. On public opinion and the crisis of 1917, see especially Pierre Renouvin, "L'opinion publique en France pendant la guerre, 1914–1918," *Revue d'Histoire Diplomatique* 84 (1970): 289–336; and "Colloque sur l'année 1917" (special issue), ed. Renouvin, *RHMC* 15 (Jan.–Mar. 1968).

77. Guy Pedroncini, *Les mutineries de 1917* (Paris, 1967), esp. pt. 1, ch. 3, and pt. 2, chs. 1–2.

78. Ibid., p. 310.

79. Jean-Louis Robert, "Une analyse d'implication: L'évolution du groupe des Temps Nouveaux en 1915," *M. Social,* no. 122 (1983), pp. 61–74; Fred Kupfer-

man, "L'opinion française et le défaitisme pendant la Grande Guerre," *Relations Internationales*, no. 2 (1974), pp. 91–100. On the history of the neologism "defeatism" and the various meanings attached to the term, see also Catherine Slater, *Defeatists and their Enemies: Political Invective in France, 1914–1918* (London, 1981), esp. pt. 2.

80. See, for example, *Pop*. (Paris), 16–22 Apr. and 22 Dec. 1917, and 2 Feb. 1918; *L'Hum.*, 17–24 Mar. 1917 and 6 Jan. 1918; and the texts of CGT and SFIO resolutions, reprinted in *L'Hum.*, 27 Dec. 1917 and 30 July 1918. On the response to the Russian Revolution, see also Annie Kriegel, "L'opinion publique française et la Révolution russe," in *La Révolution d'Octobre et le Mouvement ouvrier européen*, by Victor Fay et al. (Paris, 1967), pp. 75–104; Ioannis Sinanoglou, "Frenchmen, Their Revolutionary Heritage, and the Russian Revolution," *International History Review* 2 (1980): 566–84; and Moissonnier, "Octobre," pp. 39–42.

81. AN F7 13349, report on antimilitarism during the war, conclusions; compare Wohl, *French Communism*, pp. 89, 104; Kriegel, *Aux origines*, 1:162; Picard, *Mouvement syndical*, pp. 114–15; Moissonnier, "Octobre," pp. 39–43; and Huard, "Grèves de 1917," pp. 305–18.

82. ADHV 10 M 22, 5–6 June 1917; AN F7 13369, 23 July 1917; compare Sabourdy, "Conditions de la scission," pp. 100–101, and Cousteix, "Mouvement ouvrier limousin," p. 81.

83. ADHV 10 M 113, 22 Aug. to 15 Sept. 1917. According to the minutes of the Synd. Chaussures, Limoges, no wartime meetings were held until 16 Jan. 1918. The meeting of 8 May 1918 further reported that some of the workers' demands of Aug. 1917 had been postponed until the next year.

84. ADL M 1066, 26–27 July 1917; 92 M 240, 8 Aug. 1917; *Statistique des grèves*, 1917. The average duration of the metallurgical strikes was only 2.3 working-days lost per striker, as against a departmental average of 6.3 and a national average of 7.3 working-days lost per striker. These figures exclude, however, the giant solidarity strike in Dec. 1917, which had overt political motives; see discussion below.

85. ADL M 1066, 8–9 May and 6 June 1917; 92 M 247, 25–30 May 1918; AN F7 12994, 22 Apr. 1918; see also Raffaelli, "Mouvements pacifistes," pp. 224–25, 234–35, and Gallo, "Usines de guerre," pp. 17–18. None of these sources indicate the proportion of mobilized workers who came from outside the region; that information cannot be determined except in individual cases. One source does estimate that 20.2 percent of the male workers and 14.9 percent of the female workers in the war industries had habitual residence outside Saint-Etienne, but not all of these were military personnel. AN F22 593, dossier on "Mésures contre la vie chère," Enquête sur la main-d'oeuvre occupée dans les usines de guerre, Saint-Etienne, Mar. 1917. (The purpose of this inquiry was to compare living costs for temporary and permanent city residents.)

86. ADL 93 M 8, 2 Mar. 1913 to 27 Feb. 1914, and 25 Jan. 1915 to 16 June 1917; 93 M 55, 23 Aug. 1916; see also the brief biographical sketch of Torcieux in Maitron, *Dictionnaire biographique*, 15:240. Torcieux later served as Bourse

secretary in 1919–21 and then as secretary of the municipal employees' union (CGT) in the mid-1920s. 93 M 58, letter from Saint-Etienne Bourse to Loire Prefect, 21 Jan. 1919; *Peuple L.,* 4 Apr. 1926.

87. ADL 93 M 13, reports of 30 Jan. and 2 Feb. 1917; text of letter from Andrieu to Merrheim, 22 Jan. 1917; letter from metalworkers' union at Firminy to Loire Prefect, 11 Apr. 1917; 92 M 240, 20 Oct. 1917; 14 M 15, 12 Aug. to 29 Dec. 1917; AN F7 12994, reports of 6 Jan. to 22 Apr. 1918, and text of letter from Andrieu to Péricat, 13 Apr. 1918. There is also a biographical sketch of Andrieu in Maitron, *Dictionnaire biographique,* 17:155–58.

88. Georges Dumoulin, *Carnets de route: Quarante années de vie militante* (Lille, [1938]), pp. 85, 91; on his general politics, see Dumoulin, "Syndicalistes français"; and Peter M. Arum, "Du syndicalisme révolutionnaire au réformisme: Georges Dumoulin (1903–1923)," *M. Social,* no. 87 (1974), pp. 35–62. The police dossier on the miners' union at Roche-la-Molière, ADL 93 M 27, contains no information on Dumoulin's activities. His role in the strike movement of 1918 is discussed in ch. 4 of this study.

89. ADL M 1066, report on "Salaires dans les usines de guerre"; and Tarif des salaires horaires et des majorations applicables dans l'arrondissement de Saint-Etienne (Loire), 30 Apr. 1917.

90. ADL M 1066, 23 Apr. to 11 May 1917; 93 M 19, 25 May 1917; M 2023, 27 May 1917.

91. AN F7 13356, Liste numérique des établissements militaires, Jan. 1917; F7 13369, 23 July 1917.

92. ADL M 1066, 3 June 1917.

93. AN F7 12994, 4 Aug. to 12 Nov. 1917; ADL M 2023, 22 Sept. 1917; 93 M 8, 3 Oct. 1917; *Union des Métaux,* May–Dec. 1917, p. 2; see also Gallo, "Usines de guerre," pp. 22–23; and Hatry, "Délégués d'atelier," in *L'autre front,* ed. Fridenson, pp. 223–27.

94. AN F7 13575, 13 Feb. 1917; *L'Hum.,* 12 Sept. 1917; ADL 93 M 8, 3 Oct. 1917; on Merrheim, see also Papayanis, "Collaboration and Pacifism," p. 447.

95. ADL M 1066, 3 June 1917.

96. ADL 14 M 15, 14 Apr. 1917; 92 M 240, 13 Apr. to 1 Aug. 1917; see also Dubesset et al., "Munitionnettes," in *L'autre front,* ed. Fridenson, pp. 209–16; Delatour, "Travail des femmes," pp. 486–90; and Vidalenc, "Main-d'oeuvre étrangère," pp. 535–36.

97. ADL 93 M 68, 16 Dec. 1915; 93 M 55, 26 Dec. 1915. The poster announcing the meeting at the Bourse at Firminy specifically invited *"les ménagères"* to attend.

98. AN F7 13023, 6 Jan. 1917.

99. ADL 93 M 13, report of 18 June 1917 (with text of song, distributed at the meeting); 92 M 240, 15 Apr. 1917; M 1066, 25 Apr. 1917; 14 M 15, 19 Dec. 1917; M 2033, 22 Mar. and 3 Apr. 1918; and AN F7 12994, 3–11 Feb. 1918.

100. Péricat at meetings in Paris in 1916–17, quoted in Robert, "Famille

ouvrière," p. 62; on Andrieu, see AN F7 12994, 10 Sept. 1917; ADL 92 M 240, 29 Oct. 1917; 14 M 15, 1 Oct. 1917 and 21 Apr. 1918; 93 M 13, 15 Mar. 1918; M 2033, 3–28 Apr. 1918.

101. ADL M 1066, 1–3 June 1917; see also Gallo, "Usines de guerre," pp. 16–18.

102. ADL 14 M 15, 6 Apr. 1917; 93 M 11, 4 May 1917; M 1066, 6 May and 3 June 1917; M 2023, 27 May 1917; 93 M 19, 25 May 1917; 93 M 12, 6 Oct. 1917; 93 M 14, 20 Nov. 1917.

103. *Union des Métaux,* May–Dec. 1917, p. 1; AN F7 13372, report on pacifist propaganda, pt. 1, entry for 4 Nov. 1917; on the prewar period, see Gras, "Fédération des Métaux," p. 86.

104. ADL 93 M 40, 4 Nov. 1916 and 15 Sept. 1917; 93 M 25, 2 July 1917; 93 M 81, 30 Apr. and 27 June 1917; M 1066, 27–28 Apr. 1917; 14 M 15, 3 May 1917.

105. ADL 92 M 249, 25 Mar. 1918.

106. AN F7 13891, 28 Nov. 1917; F7 14607, 4 Feb. 1918. Before the Andrieu strike in December, attendance at meetings in the summer and fall had peaked at 2,000 to 2,500. See, for example, ADL 93 M 8, 1 July and 3 Sept. 1917.

107. Few comparable figures on union size are available for wartime Limoges. Bourse records do show, however, that the number of dues-paying member unions, which had dropped to six just after the mobilization, was up to only seven in March 1917. These included the unions in the struggling porcelain and printing industries, but not in the flourishing shoe industry; the latter union did not resume activity until Jan. 1918. Bourse, Limoges, 7 Apr. 1917; Synd. Imprimeurs-Lithographes, Limoges, 4 Aug. 1915 (the minutes list the unions rejoining the Bourse at that time); Synd. Chaussures, Limoges, 16 Jan. 1918.

108. On Grégoire: ADL 93 M 58, 27 Jan. and 22 Feb. 1913, 27 Nov. 1916, and 25 May 1917; 93 M 69, 11 Feb. 1915 and 29 May 1916. On Reynard: ADL 10 M 176, 2 Aug. 1917; 92 M 250, 11 Jan. to 25 May 1918; AN F7 12994, 23–29 June 1918; ADL 93 M 69, 27 Aug. 1918. On both, see also Bourse, Saint-Etienne, 19 Sept. 1914 and 18–23 May 1917.

109. ADL 92 M 240, report of 20 Oct. 1917, and extract from *Tribune Républicaine,* 12 Dec. 1917; AN F7 12994, report of 15 Jan. 1918; text of letter from Comité Intercorporatif to union secretaries, Loire, 15 Jan. 1918; text of Rapport Moral, 24 Mar. 1918.

110. On Péricat: AN F7 13086, 31 May and 1 June 1915; F7 13574, 15 Dec. 1915; F7 13575, 17 May and 12 Sept. 1916; F7 13576, 17 Apr. 1918; F7 13372, report on pacifist propaganda, pt. 1, entries for Nov. 1915, 11 Oct. 1917, and 23–25 Dec. 1917. Péricat's activities are also discussed in Kriegel, *Aux origines,* 1:160, 207–10. The antiwar movement in the Lyon construction industry is discussed in Pelé, "Mouvement ouvrier lyonnais," pp. 50, 154. Economic aspects of the labor movement in the construction industry are discussed in Abel Chatelain, "La main-d'oeuvre dans l'industrie française du bâtiment aux XIXe et XXe siècles," *Revue de l'Enseignement Technique,* no. 101 (1956), pp. 35–42.

111. ADL M 1066, 5 June 1917; AN F7 14607, 30 Nov. 1917 and 4 Feb.

1918; F7 12994, reports of 19 Dec. 1917 to 30 Jan. 1918, and 4 Aug. 1918; and extract (by G. Dumoulin) from *Le Syndicaliste* (UD Loire), 20 Jan. 1918. On the miners' own corporative grievances: ADL 93 M 28, 22 May 1917; and 93 M 25, 2 July and 29 Dec. 1917, and 24 June 1918.

112. ADL M 1066, report on "Salaires dans les usines de guerre"; and AN F22 593, dossier on "Mésures contre la vie chère," 1917–18.

113. ADL 92 M 240, 23 Apr. 1917.

114. AN F7 13356, report on "Surveillance dans les usines de guerre" (c. 1917). Only four departments other than the Loire reported the use of informants: Savoie (nine), Calvados (sixteen), Seine-Inférieure (eighteen), and Doubs (twenty-six).

115. AN F7 13086, 1 June 1915.

116. Wohl, *French Communism*, pp. 87–88.

117. ADL M 1066, 25 Apr. to 9 May 1917; AN F7 12994, 6 Aug. 1917; see also ADL 92 M 247, 25–30 May 1918. A total of seventeen names were listed of mobilized workers to be returned to the trenches. Of these, three were *"anarchistes inscrits"* (under surveillance in the Loire since before the war, and hence permanent residents of the region), while nine were identified as newcomers to the region. The list of *"anarchistes inscrits"* in the Loire in 1914 is in ADL 19 M 37.

118. ADL 14 M 15, 3 Nov. 1917; on related economic issues, AN F7 12994, 17–21 Oct. 1917; ADL 93 M 14, 28 Oct. and 20 Nov. 1917; 93 M 13, 25 Nov. 1917; *Flamme*, 20 Oct. to 1 Dec. 1917.

119. AN F7 12994, 11 Nov. 1917.

120. ADL 14 M 15, reports of 3–23 Dec. 1917, including Andrieu's own claim of 210,000 participants; lower estimates are by H. Raitzon, of the Saint-Chamond metalworkers, in a letter (intercepted) to the journal *Ce Qu'il Faut Dire*, 8 Dec. 1917, in AN F7 12994; and by André Beaugitte, *Le Chemin de Cocherel* (Paris, 1960), p. 79. (This book is an anecdotal biography of Aristide Briand.)

121. ADL 14 M 15, 30 Nov. to 3 Dec. 1917; AN F7 14607, 30 Nov. to 8 Dec. 1917; F7 13891, 27 Nov. to 18 Dec. 1917.

122. AN F7 14607 and ADL 14 M 15, reports of 6 Dec. 1917.

123. Beaugitte, *Chemin de Cocherel*, pp. 86–91.

124. The new prefect was credited with the settlement by Secretary Barlet of the Saint-Etienne metalworkers' union: AN F7 12994, 14 Dec. 1917. On the former prefect's departure for Paris, see Beaugitte, *Chemin de Cocherel*, pp. 77–79.

125. AN F7 12994, report of 17 Jan. 1918, and text of letter from Péricat to Flageollet, 9 Apr. 1918. The syndicalist congress is discussed here in ch. 4.

126. Blanchard at the Clermont conference, in CGT, *Compte-rendu de la Conférence Extraordinaire, tenue à Clermont-Ferrand les 23, 24, 25 décembre 1917* (Paris, n.d.), p. 84.

127. ADL 14 M 15, 30 Nov. 1917; 92 M 241, 19 Dec. 1917; AN F7 12994, 19 Dec. 1917 to 15 Jan. 1918.

128. Flageollet at the Clermont conference, in CGT, *Conférence Extraor-*

dinaire, 1917, p. 84; see also ADL 14 M 15, 1–23 Dec. 1917; 93 M 44, 26–27 Dec. 1917; AN F7 12994, reports of 29 Dec. 1917 and 14 Jan. 1918, and extract from *Le Syndicaliste,* 20 Jan. 1918.

129. AN F7 14607, 1 Dec. 1917. This combination of motives was also later acknowledged by Communist leader Benoît Frachon, who had served during the war at an arsenal near Nevers. Frachon, *Pour la CGT,* p. 64.

130. On the employers' views: AN F7 12994, telegram from Director of the Aciéries et Forges de Firminy (Verdié) to Armaments Minister, 24 Aug. 1917. On the authorities' views: ADL 93 M 13, 2 Feb. and 25 Nov. 1917; M 1066, 8 May 1917; 92 M 240, 20 Oct. 1917; AN F7 12994, 24 Oct. 1917 to 14 Jan. 1918; F7 14607, 4 Feb. 1918. On the meanings of the term "defeatism," see also Slater, *Defeatists and Their Enemies,* pp. 58–84, 105–6; and Kupferman, "Défaitisme," pp. 91–100.

131. AN F7 13891, 3–4 Dec. 1917; ADL 14 M 15, 3 Nov. to 29 Dec. 1917; 93 M 13, 25 Nov. 1917; 92 M 247, 3 Mar. 1918. See also the terms of a peace resolution by the Bourse at Vienne (Isère), 7 June 1917, in ADL 14 M 15; and the terms of a defense of Andrieu in *La Flamme,* 29 Dec. 1917. The issues of pacifism and defeatism in the strikes of 1918 are discussed in ch. 4.

132. Cited (with no precise reference) in Jean Nicot and Philippe Schillinger, "L'opinion publique et les grèves de la Loire, Mai 1918," *Actes du 98ᵉ CNSS,* Saint-Etienne, 1973 (Section histoire moderne), 2:250. On Merrheim, see Papayanis, "Collaboration and Pacifism," pp. 440–51.

133. ADL 14 M 15, 23–29 Dec. 1917; AN F7 12994, 31 Dec. 1917.

134. Rougerie at the Clermont conference, in CGT, *Conférence Extraordinaire, 1917,* pp. 62–65; also text of majority resolution, p. 155. On the Clermont conference see also AN F7 13372, report on pacifist propaganda, pt. 1, entry for 23–25 Dec. 1917; Wohl, *French Communism,* pp. 103–4; Kriegel, *Aux origines,* 1:205–6; and Labi, *Grande division des travailleurs,* pp. 80–89.

135. The text of the minority motion is in CGT, *Conférence Extraordinaire, 1917,* p. 154. On Loriot, Mayoux, and the question of schism, see ADL 92 M 250, Compte-rendu of minoritarian congress, Saint-Etienne, 19–20 May 1918; and discussion here in ch. 4.

136. ADL 92 M 250, 11 Jan. 1918. Reynaud's mandate was to vote for those positions previously held only by the minority, which in effect he did. Bourse, Saint-Etienne, 16 Dec. 1917.

137. Cited in AN F7 13372, report on pacifist propaganda, pt. 1, entry for 23–25 Dec. 1917.

138. The term "centrist coalition" *(rassemblement centriste)* is Kriegel's, in *Aux origines,* 1:204–33.

139. Bourse, Limoges, 14 Dec. 1917.

140. ADL 93 M 55, text of letter from Flageollet to "Camarades secrétaires des Fédérations, Unions Départementales, et Bourses du Travail minoritaires," 6 Dec. 1917, with report of 18 Dec. 1917; 93 M 58, 22 Dec. 1917; 93 M 44, 25 Dec. 1917; AN F7 12994, 13 Jan. to 9 Feb. 1918.

141. Observed by Dubreuilh of the Seine in his pamphlet "La vraie cassure"

(1917), cited in AN F7 13372, report on pacifist propaganda, pt. 1, entry for Oct. 1917; see also Raffaelli, "Mouvements pacifistes," pp. 223–24, 235–36.

Chapter 4. *May 1918: The Climax of Revolutionary Syndicalism in the Loire*

1. Despite their importance, the events of May 1918 have received relatively little historical attention. For brief discussions see Kriegel, *Aux origines,* 1:212–14; Wohl, *French Communism,* pp. 103–5; and Héritier et al., *Luttes ouvrières,* pp. 146–48. Four works establish the context but present little on the strikes or related events themselves: Gallo, "Usines de guerre," pp. 3–33; Dereymez, "Usines de guerre," pp. 150–81; Raffaelli, "Mouvements pacifistes," pp. 221–37; and [Zancarini and] Raffaelli, "Mouvement ouvrier." One study focuses on public opinion as expressed in letters seized by the *"contrôle postal"*: Nicot and Schillinger, "Grèves de la Loire," pp. 239–52.

2. AN F7 12994, 4 Feb. 1918; see also report of 17 Jan. 1918 and text of letter from Péricat to Flageollet, 9 Apr. 1918.

3. ADL 93 M 58, 22 Dec. 1917; AN F7 12994, 13 Jan. to 9 Feb. 1918; ADL 92 M 250, summary report on interdepartmental congress, Saint-Etienne, 24–25 Mar. 1918. One report in the Loire's file is from the police at Bourges and another is from the prefect of the Gard. The delegates' visits are also discussed briefly by Huard in "Grèves de 1917," pp. 316–17, and by Moissonnier in "Octobre," p. 44.

4. AN F7 12994, list of delegates to interdepartmental congress, Saint-Etienne, 24–25 Mar. 1918.

5. ADL 14 M 15, resolution of Bourse at Vienne (Isère), 7 June 1917; 92 M 250, 24–25 Mar. 1918.

6. AN F7 13372, report on pacifist propaganda, pt. 1, entry for 21 Jan. 1918; F7 12994, reports of 13–14 Feb. 1918, and resolution of Bourse at Lyon, 17 Feb., in *Le Syndicaliste* (Loire), 5 Mar. 1918; ADL 92 M 250, report on votes at minoritarian congress, Saint-Etienne, 20 May 1918; and (on Miglioretti), Pelé, "Mouvement ouvrier lyonnais," pp. 206, 214. The Lyon antiwar movement in 1918 is also discussed in Jean-Luc Pinol, "Origines et débuts du communisme à Lyon, 1918–1923" (Mémoire de maîtrise, Lyon, 1972), pp. 114–24; and in Moissonnier, "Octobre," pp. 43–45.

7. AN F7 13372, report on pacifist propaganda, pt. 1, entry for 1 Mar. 1918; F7 12994, 25–28 Apr. 1918.

8. AN F7 12994, 15 Jan. 1918.

9. AN F7 12994, 29 Jan. to 22 Apr. 1918; ADL 92 M 250, 24–25 Mar. 1918; 92 M 249, 25 Mar. 1918; 92 M 247, 15 May 1918.

10. ADL 93 M 40, 31 Dec. 1917 and 4 Mar. 1918; 93 M 3, letter from weavers' union to Loire Prefect (requesting authorization for a meeting), Jan. 1918; *Flamme,* 6 Apr. 1918 ("Chez les cheminots") and 1 June 1918 ("Chez les tisseurs").

11. AN F7 12994, 20 Jan. to 12 Feb. 1918; F7 14607, 18 Feb. 1918;

Flamme, 26 Jan. 1918; *Syndicaliste,* 5 Feb. 1918.

    12. AN F7 12994, reports of 13 Jan. to 21 Mar. 1918; open letter from Comité Intercorporatif (Loire) to union secretaries, 15 Jan. 1918; Rapport Moral of CI, 24 Mar. 1918; ADL 93 M 13, 15 Mar. 1918; 92 M 250, 24–25 Mar. 1918.

    13. Cited (with no precise reference) in [Zancarini and] Raffaelli, "Mouvement ouvrier," biographical entry on Flageollet. On the two militants, see also AN F7 12994, 5 Mar. 1919.

    14. ADL 92 M 247, 15 May 1918.

    15. AN F7 12994, 11–22 Feb. 1918.

    16. The details of the police inquiry are in AN F7 14607, 23 Feb. 1918. There is a brief discussion of related "espionage affairs" in Kriegel, *Aux origines,* 1:196.

    17. *Trib. R.* (Saint-Etienne), 23 Feb. 1918 (with excerpts from the Paris press); AN F7 12994, text of open letter from UD and CI to Pierre Renaudel (Var deputy), 26 Feb. 1918; ADL 92 M 247, text of open letter from Firminy metalworkers' union to all French parliamentary deputies, n.d. Renaudel published a response to the UD Loire in *L'Hum.,* 17 Mar. 1918.

    18. Bourse, Saint-Etienne, 1 Mar. 1918; ADL 93 M 69, text of circular from UD and CI to union secretaries, 25 Feb. 1918; letter from UD and CI to Loire Prefect, 26 Feb. 1918; report of 27 Feb. 1918; 92 M 247, 3–4 Mar. 1918; 92 M 250, 3–10 Mar. 1918; AN F7 13372, report on pacifist propaganda, pt. 1, entry for 12 Mar. 1918.

    19. ADL 93 M 69, 27 Feb. 1918; 92 M 250, 3–12 Mar. 1918; AN F7 14607, 12 Mar. 1918.

    20. ADL 92 M 247, 11 May 1918; 14 M 15, 19–22 May 1918; AN F7 13775, 23 May 1918; *Pop. C.,* 17 May 1918 ("La relève dans les usines de guerre"). The rumors (declared to be false) of American workers displacing French soldiers in the factories are discussed by Yves-Henri Nouailhat in "L'opinion à l'égard des Américains à Saint-Nazaire en 1917," *RHMC* 15 (1968): 101.

    21. AN F7 12994, 4–23 Feb. 1918. Similar demonstrations occurred in May: ADL 92 M 247, 12 May 1918; 14 M 15, 20–23 May 1918.

    22. AN F7 14607, 4 Feb. 1918; F7 12994, 23 Feb. 1918.

    23. AN F7 12994, 13 Jan. 1918; F7 14607, 4 Feb. 1918; ADL 92 M 247, 18–20 May 1918.

    24. *Pop. C.,* 30 May 1918 ("Politique ouvrière," by Paul Faure).

    25. Statistics on inflation are available in the *Bulletin du Ministère du Travail,* nos. 11–12 (1919), p. 548, and are summarized in Figure 17, p. 304. According to these figures, the rate of increase in prices in the first quarter of 1918 had slowed to 15 percent nationally (slightly higher in the southeastern and western regions), down from 19 percent nationally (and as much as 25 percent in the southeast) in the third quarter of 1917. This reprieve did not last beyond the end of 1918; nor did the table of prices compiled by the CI Loire (in AN F7 12994, 7 Sept. 1918) show a parallel slowdown in the rate of inflation, which fails to appear when the figures are averaged over periods of longer than three months.

    26. *Statistique des grèves,* 1915–18. The Loire's strikes for each four-month period in 1918 numbered 12, 4, and 3, respectively; those for 1917 numbered 8, 12, and 12, respectively. (The Haute-Vienne had too few strikes in these years to

periodize meaningfully.) In France at large, there were 154 strikes in Jan.–April 1918, as against 158 in Sept.–Dec. 1917 and 450 in May–Aug. 1917.

27. *Statistique des grèves,* 1918. Of the Haute-Vienne's five strikes, one each occurred in the Limoges porcelain and shoe industries, two in other Limoges industries, and one among iron miners elsewhere in the department. None was a particularly long or large-scale affair.

28. Pressemane in Chamber, 29 Mar., cited in *L'Hum.,* 30 Mar. 1918; Loire opinion in AN F7 12994, 1 Mar. 1918. For similar views, see also Nicot and Schillinger, "Grèves de la Loire," p. 248.

29. Pressemane in Chamber, 29 Mar., cited in *Flamme,* 6 Apr. 1918; similar views are expressed in *Flamme,* 30 Mar. 1918; *Pop. C.,* 25 Mar. and 1 Apr. 1918; ADL 10 M 178, 2 Apr. 1918.

30. *Flamme,* 9 Feb. to 6 Apr. 1918; AN F7 12994, 5–15 Feb. 1918; F7 14607, 12 Mar. 1918; ADL 10 M 177, 13 Feb. and 11 Mar. 1918; 10 M 178, 25 Apr. and 24 June 1918.

31. AN F7 12994, 15 Feb. 1918.

32. AN F7 12994, 21 Mar. 1918.

33. ADL 92 M 249, 25 Mar. 1918; AN F7 13576, 8 Mar. 1918. On the national Entente Républicaine, founded 4 Apr., see also *L'Hum.,* 6–7 Apr. 1918.

34. AN F7 12994, 8 Apr. 1918; F7 13576, 19 Apr. 1918; text of CGT Manifesto for 1 May, in *L'Hum.,* 23 Apr., and in *Pop. C.,* 24 Apr. 1918.

35. ADL 92 M 250, 24–25 Mar. 1918; AN F7 12994, 26 Mar. 1918; F7 13576, 19 Apr. 1918; F7 13372, report on pacifist propaganda, pt. 1, entry for 21 Apr. 1918; *L'Hum.,* 30 Apr. 1918.

36. AN F7 13372, report on pacifist propaganda, pt. 1, entry for 3 Apr. 1918; ADL 92 M 250, text of letter from Péricat to Flageollet, n.d., with report of 15 Apr. 1918. On Péricat's "antipatriotism," compare a similar statement in Oct. 1916, cited in Papayanis, "Collaboration and Pacifism," p. 432.

37. ADL 92 M 250, text of letter from Péricat to Flageollet, n.d., with report of 15 Apr. 1918; and, on labor sentiment in Paris: AN F7 12994, 13 Feb., 21 Mar., and 20 Apr. 1918; ADL 92 M 250, 24–25 Mar. 1918; 14 M 15, 21 May 1918; AN F7 13576, Note, 21 May 1918 ("La situation ouvrière"); ADL 93 M 13, 10 Oct. 1918.

38. ADL 92 M 250, 24–25 Mar. 1918.

39. ADL 92 M 250, 12 Mar. 1918.

40. ADL 92 M 250, 24 Mar. and 30 Apr. 1918; 92 M 247, text of circular by metalworkers' federation, n.d.; also *L'Hum.,* 14 May 1918 ("Pour l'unité ouvrière"). Apparently the plans for such a federal congress were not carried out. Instead, a federal congress was held in conjunction with the confederal congress in Paris in July. AN F7 13771, summary report on metalworkers' congress, 10–13 July 1918; *Union des Métaux,* Sept. 1918.

41. ADL 92 M 250, 25 Mar. 1918. A total of seventy-nine mandates were represented at the congress; thus, twenty-five did not vote.

42. ADL 92 M 247, text of tract by UD and CI Loire, n.d., with report of 15 May 1918. On this question see also Kriegel, *Aux origines,* 1:210–11. Kriegel states that the majoritarians were not to attend, but in fact Antoine Reynard of

the Bourse at Saint-Etienne was there as a delegate. ADL 92 M 250, 20 May 1918.

It should be recalled that the terms "majority" and "minority" refer to the relative size of these factions in the national party or union organizations. These terms, roughly equivalent to right- and left-wing, or to moderate and extremist, throughout most of the war period, took on new meanings by the end of 1918 when the relative size of the factions changed. Thereafter, it would become common to refer to the "ex-majority" and "ex-minority," especially in the SFIO, to keep these alignments clear. Note also that "minoritarians," or left-wingers, in the national organizations were sometimes in the majority in local groups, especially in the Loire and the Haute-Vienne; hence, such terms are best applied to the national bodies alone.

43. ADL 92 M 249, 25 Mar. 1918; 92 M 250, 24–25 Mar. and 19–20 May 1918. For similar arguments, see H. Lorduron in *VO*, 24 Sept. 1920 and 23 Dec. 1921 ("Quelques souvenirs"). Dumoulin's politics and his role at the CDS congress are further discussed below.

44. ADL 92 M 250, 25 Mar. 1918; AN F7 12994, 26 Mar. 1918.

45. AN F7 12994, texts of letters from Péricat to Flageollet, from Andrieu to Péricat, and from Flageollet to Péricat, 9–13 Apr. 1918; F7 13372, report on pacifist propaganda, pt. 1, entry for 19 Apr. 1918. The UD Isère also protested the postponement of the minoritarian congress.

46. ADL 92 M 250, 14 Apr. 1918.

47. *L'Hum.*, 17 May 1918; similar item in the issue for 20 May 1918.

48. AN F7 12994, 26 Mar. 1918; F7 13576, 19 Apr. 1918.

49. AN F7 13372, report on pacifist propaganda, pt. 1, entry for 21 Jan. 1918.

50. AN F7 12994, text of letter from Péricat to Flageollet, 9 Apr. 1918; ADL 92 M 250, text of letter from Péricat to Flageollet, n.d., with report of 15 Apr. 1918; AN F7 13372, report on pacifist propaganda, pt. 1, entry for 19 Apr. 1918.

51. AN F7 12994, 29 Jan. and 9 Apr. 1918; ADL 93 M 69, 4–14 Apr. 1918; AN F7 13372, report on pacifist propaganda, pt. 1, entry for 15 Apr. 1918.

52. AN F7 12994, reports of 7–27 Feb. and 16 Apr. 1918; and text of letter from Barlet to Merrheim, 1 June 1918. Barlet had been among the anarchists under surveillance in the Loire in 1914, as listed in ADL 19 M 37.

53. AN F7 12994, 27 Feb. and 20 Apr. 1918; ADL 92 M 250, 24–25 Mar. and 14 Apr. 1918. Bonnefond had also been among the anarchists under surveillance in the Loire in 1914, as listed in ADL 19 M 37.

54. AN F7 12994, 26 Mar. 1918; F7 13771, 10–13 July 1918.

55. ADL 93 M 69, 4 Apr. 1918; AN F7 12994, text of letter from Flageollet to Péricat, 12 Apr. 1918.

56. *L'Hum.*, 30 Apr. 1918.

57. ADHV 1 M 180, 24 Apr. 1918; AN F7 12994, 20 Apr. 1918; ADL 92 M 250, 27 Apr. 1918; Moissonnier, "Octobre," p. 45. Among the Haute-Vienne unions, it is unclear whether the porcelain workers endorsed the movement, since the votes are not recorded for each group.

58. AN F7 12994, 20–22 Apr. 1918; ADL 14 M 15, 30 Apr. 1918.

59. ADL 14 M 15, 2 May 1918; 92 M 250, reports of 2 May 1918; text of letter from Flageollet to Bécirard (UD Rhône), 5 May, with report of 8 May 1918; text of letter from Henri Raitzon (Saint-Chamond) to "the anarchist Einfalt" (Paris), 1 May, with report of 11 May 1918; AN F7 12994, 11–12 May 1918; F7 13576, 21 May 1918.

60. ADL 92 M 249, 25 Mar. 1918; AN F7 12994, 12–22 Apr. 1918; ADL 92 M 250, 27 Apr. 1918.

61. AN F7 12994, 3–9 May 1918; ADL 92 M 247, 9–12 May 1918.

62. ADL 92 M 247, report of 12 May, and undated telegram (c. 16 May), 1918.

63. AN F7 12994, 15 May 1918.

64. ADL 92 M 247 and AN F7 12994, 16 May 1918. The Parisians may in fact have started the strike, according to Hatry, "Délégués d'atelier," in *L'autre front,* ed. Fridenson, pp. 231–32.

65. ADL 92 M 247, 15–18 May 1918; AN F7 12994, 18 May 1918.

66. Compare Kriegel, *Aux origines,* 1:211 n. 2.

67. *L'Hum.,* 19 May 1918; see also Jean-Paul Brunet, *Saint-Denis, la ville rouge: Socialisme et communisme en banlieue ouvrière, 1890–1939* (Paris, 1980), pp. 179–83.

68. ADL 92 M 250, 19–20 May 1918.

69. ADL 92 M 250, 20 May 1918; 14 M 15, 21 May 1918; AN F7 12994, 21 May 1918; F7 13775, 23 May 1918; F7 13576, Note, 21 May 1918 ("La situation ouvrière").

70. ADL 92 M 247, undated telegram (c. 21 May 1918); AN F7 12994, 21–28 May 1918; F7 13775, 22 Aug. 1918.

71. ADL 92 M 247, reports of 20–21 May, and official record of police inquiry, 21 May 1918.

72. ADL 92 M 247, letter from the Director of the Aciéries et Forges de Firminy (Verdié) to the Contrôleur de la Main-d'Oeuvre Militaire at Firminy, 21 May 1918; official records of police inquiries, 21 May 1918; telegram, 23 May 1918; 14 M 15, 23 May 1918.

73. ADL 92 M 247, 21–25 May 1918. Compare the discussion by Robert Wohl, who, citing a Moscow author (1936), reports: "The workers seized control of factories and entire municipalities. Soldiers sent to suppress the strikes fraternized with the strikers" (*French Communism,* p. 104). None of this appears in fact to have been the case. On the attitudes of the soldiers, see also Nicot and Schillinger, "Grèves de la Loire," p. 245.

74. AN F7 12994, 24 May 1918.

75. ADL 92 M 247, 15–30 May 1918; AN F7 12994, 20 May 1918. For similar views, see Nicot and Schillinger, "Grèves de la Loire," pp. 245–46.

76. AN F7 12994, letter from the Independent Union of Metalworkers, Firminy, to the War Ministry, 17 May 1918. On independent unionism during the war, see also *L'Indépendance Ouvrière* (Lyon), Jan. to Sept. 1918; and on the prewar period, ch. 2 of this study.

77. ADL 92 M 247, 25 May 1918.

78. AN F7 12994, report of 26 May 1918, and Liste des ouvriers mobilisés rayés de l'effectif industriel à la suite des mouvements ouvriers du Bassin de la Loire et laissés à la disposition de l'Autorité Militaire, n.d.; ADL 92 M 247, Individus poursuivis à l'occasion des incidents du mouvement du bassin de Saint-Etienne et en prévision du Conseil de Guerre, list dated 27 May 1918.

79. ADL 92 M 247, 22–25 May 1918; AN F7 12994, 26–28 May 1918.

80. AN F7 12994, 25 Apr. 1918; ADL 92 M 250, 24–25 Mar. 1918.

81. AN F7 12994, text of letter from Barlet to Merrheim, 1 June, and reports of 29 June, 2 Sept., and 19 Nov. 1918; ADL 93 M 9, 22 Dec. 1918. The militants' return to the Loire is described in AN F7 12994, 5 Mar. 1919, and discussed here in ch. 5.

82. This argument is suggested in Kriegel, *Aux origines,* 1:217–19, and Wohl, *French Communism,* p. 105. Moissonnier, however, disagrees; as a Marxist, he rejects the idea of police initiative, which implies to him "a deliberate minimizing of the role of the working class" and of its own revolutionary leaders. "Octobre," p. 45. On the use of police as *agents provocateurs* in prewar labor conflicts, see also A. Fryar Calhoun, "The Politics of Internal Order: French Government and Revolutionary Labor, 1898–1914" (Ph.D. diss., Princeton Univ., 1973), pp. 127–28.

83. AN F7 12994, 9 Apr. 1918; ADL 92 M 250, 19 Mar. and 12 May 1918.

84. ADL 92 M 247, Individus poursuivis, list dated 27 May 1918. The list indicates the categories of alleged crimes and notes the military status of each individual arrested.

85. Statement dated 1 May 1918, cited (with no precise reference) in Kriegel, *Aux origines,* 1:213.

86. ADL 92 M 247, letter from the Loire strike committee to the Loire Prefect, 23 May, and report of 21 May 1918.

87. ADL 92 M 250, report of 19–20 May 1918 (citing informant's conversations with Péricat and Dumoulin); AN F7 12994, text of letter from Merrheim to Blanchard (at Saint-Etienne), 23 May, and Note, 28 May 1918. The Loire strike leaders did sometimes appear to use the two statements of purpose interchangeably: for example, two statements by Henri Raitzon (metalworkers' secretary at Saint-Chamond), in ADL 14 M 15, 21–22 May 1918.

88. *L'Hum.,* 19 May 1918; comments in Brunet, *Saint-Denis,* pp. 182–83.

89. AN F7 13372, report on pacifist propaganda, pt. 1, entry for 19 May 1918.

90. *L'Hum.,* 19 May 1918.

91. ADL 92 M 250, report of 19–20 May 1918 (informant's conversation with Péricat).

92. AN F7 12994, 16 May 1918.

93. ADL 92 M 247, letter from the Loire strike committee to the Loire Prefect, 23 May 1918.

94. On Péricat: AN F7 13372, report on pacifist propaganda, pt. 1, entry for 3 Apr. 1918; ADL 92 M 250, text of letter from Péricat to Flageollet, n.d., with report of 15 Apr. 1918. On Andrieu: passage cited (with no precise reference) in

Nicot and Schillinger, "Grèves de la Loire," p. 250. These passages are quoted above (n. 36) and in ch. 3 (n. 132), respectively.

95. On the Loire militants: AN F7 13372, report on pacifist propaganda, pt. 1, entry for 12 Mar. 1918. On Péricat: statement in "late March," cited (with no precise reference) in Kriegel, *Aux origines,* 1:213.

96. ADL 92 M 250, resolution at minoritarian congress, Saint-Etienne, 20 May 1918; 92 M 247, 21 May 1918; 93 M 66, 22 May 1918.

97. AN F7 13372, report on pacifist propaganda, pt. 1, entry for 3 Mar. 1918.

98. ADL 92 M 247, 30 May 1918. The closest real approximation to this vision of revolution is Flageollet's remark cited in n. 13 above.

99. Ibid.

100. Ibid. Similar charges were leveled against Péricat, as reported in *L'Hum.,* 30 May 1918. Guilbeaux's activities are described in AN F7 13086, 11 Sept. 1917, and in Kriegel, *Aux origines,* 1:198–202, 214–18.

101. ADL M 1066, 3 May 1917; 92 M 247, 3 Mar. and 15–22 May 1918; Nicot and Schillinger, "Grèves de la Loire," p. 245; see also the discussion of the "espionage affair" above.

102. ADL 92 M 247, 15–30 May 1918; AN F7 12994, letter from the Independent Union of Metalworkers, Firminy, to the War Ministry, 17 May 1918.

103. ADL 92 M 250, 19–20 May 1918.

104. Ibid. The text of the resolution voted at the minoritarian congress is also in this dossier. On the Clermont conference, see ch. 3 of this study.

105. AN F7 13372, report on pacifist propaganda, pt. 1, entry for 18 July 1918; see also Wohl, *French Communism,* p. 108, and Kriegel, *Aux origines,* 1:220–22. The vote on the resolution was 908 to 253, with 46 abstentions.

106. *L'Hum.,* 19 May 1918; AN F7 13576, 21 May 1918; F7 12994, text of letter from Merrheim to Blanchard (at Saint-Etienne), 23 May 1918. On Merrheim's role in the strike movement, see also Nicholas Papayanis, "Masses révolutionnaires et directions réformistes: Les tensions au cours des grèves des métallurgistes français en 1919," *M. Social,* no. 93 (1975), pp. 66–70.

107. AN F7 12994, 22–28 May 1918.

108. AN F7 13771, 11 July 1918; Wohl, *French Communism,* p. 105.

109. AN F7 13771, 11 July 1918; ADL 93 M 9, 29 June 1918.

110. AN F7 13771, 13 July 1918; *Union des Métaux,* Sept. 1918 ("Deux congrès," and summary report on metalworkers' congress); ADL 14 M 15, 14 Aug. 1918; 93 M 11, 1 Sept. 1918; 93 M 46, 30 Sept. and 1 Oct. 1918.

111. AN F7 12994, 29 June 1918; ADL 93 M 9, 3 July 1918; 93 M 13, 14 Aug. 1918; 93 M 11, 1 Sept. 1918.

112. AN F7 12994, report of 16 Apr., and text of letter from Barlet to Merrheim, 1 June 1918.

113. AN F7 13771, 12–14 July 1918; F7 12994, texts of letters from L. Blanc and Blaise Brunet (Saint-Etienne) to Merrheim, 2–9 June 1918; ADL 93 M 13, 14 Aug. and 10 Oct. 1918; 93 M 9, 1 Oct. 1918; *Union des Métaux,* 28 Feb. 1919 ("Déclaration du Comité National Fédéral des Métaux"); and Fédération

des Ouvriers sur Métaux, 4ᵉ Congrès National, *Rapport Moral et Compte-rendu du Congrès Extraordinaire,* tenu à Lyon, les 10, 11, 12, et 13 septembre 1919 (Paris, 1919).

114. AN F7 12994, text of letter from Merrheim to Blanchard (at Saint-Etienne), 23 May, and Note, 28 May 1918.

115. ADL 92 M 250, text of letter from Flageollet to Bécirard (UD Rhône), 5 May, with report of 8 May 1918. Pierre Monatte described Merrheim in similar terms at the Lyon CGT congress in 1919, cited in *VO,* 24 Sept. 1919; also cited in Wohl, *French Communism,* p. 108.

116. Dumoulin, *Carnets de route,* pp. 93–94. See also Dumoulin's letter to Monatte, 22 Apr. 1918, in *Archives de Monatte,* ed. Chambelland and Maitron, p. 257. Monatte, who encouraged Dumoulin's public support of the strike movement, may have agreed with his private misgivings. See Bernard et al., *Syndicalisme dans l'enseignement,* 2:81.

117. ADL 92 M 250, 19–20 May 1918; Dumoulin at CGT congress, July 1918, cited in Bernard et al., *Syndicalisme dans l'enseignement,* 2:81. On Dumoulin's *ralliement* to the new majority, with some differences as to its precise timing, compare Kriegel, *Aux origines,* 1:230–31; and Arum, "Georges Dumoulin," p. 43.

118. ADL 92 M 247, 30 May 1918; AN F7 12994, 14 Aug. 1918.

119. AN F7 12994, 14 Aug. 1918. On the miners in 1911, see ch. 2.

120. Compare remarks by Monatte and Andrieu at the Lyon CGT congress (1919), cited in *VO,* 24 Sept., and *Peuple L.,* 10 Oct. 1919; and similar arguments by Wohl in *French Communism,* p. 109, and Papayanis in "Masses révolutionnaires," pp. 71–72. Kriegel, however, rejects such arguments: *Aux origines,* 1:229–30.

121. AN F7 12994, 24 May 1918. The syndicalists' conversion to Bolshevism is discussed here in ch. 7.

122. ADL 92 M 250, 11 Jan. 1918; AN F7 12994, 30 Jan. 1918; see also pamphlet *Le Soviet* (1919) by Loire anarchist André Roulot [Lorulot], in F7 12994.

123. See Frachon, *Pour la CGT,* pp. 69, 74; Moissonnier, "Octobre," pp. 44–47; and Kriegel, *Aux origines,* esp. 1:215–17.

124. The SFIO's evolution is further discussed below. See also Kriegel, *Aux origines,* 1:220–33; and Wohl, *French Communism,* pp. 105–10.

125. Wohl, *French Communism,* pp. 105, 112; see also Loriot's speech and resolution at the SFIO's July National Council, in *Pop.* (Paris), 30 July and 2 Aug. 1918.

126. AN F7 12994, 14 Feb. 1918.

127. Bourse, Limoges, 14 Dec. 1917. There was no delegate from the Haute-Vienne at the Saint-Etienne conference of minoritarians that preceded the Clermont conference. List of delegates in ADL 93 M 58, 22 Dec. 1917.

128. ADHV 1 M 180, 24 Apr. to 1 May 1918.

129. Synd. Imprimeurs-Lithographes, Limoges, 18 May 1918.

130. AN F7 13697, 21 May 1918; *L'Hum.,* 21 May 1918.

131. Synd. Chaussures, Limoges, 11 July 1918.

132. Ibid., 8 May and 11 July 1918; also summary of federal congress's closing resolution in *Pop. C.,* 22 May 1918.

133. Bourse, Limoges, 20 June and 5 July 1918.

134. Ibid., 5 July 1918; also report on the CGT congress in *Pop. C.,* 17 July 1918.

135. Bourse, Limoges, 30 May, 5 July, and 11 Dec. 1918, and 22 Apr. 1919; also *Pop. C.,* 30 Apr. and 2 May 1919.

136. Quoted passage in AN F7 13372, report on pacifist propaganda, pt. 3, entry for 20 Oct. 1918; a similar statement was issued in Chamber, 29 Mar., reported in *L'Hum.,* 30 Mar. 1918. On Zimmerwald, see Wohl, *French Communism,* p. 64.

137. *Pop. C.,* 11 Mar. 1918 ("Patriotisme ouvrier"); 30 May 1918 ("Politique ouvrière," by Paul Faure); and 2 June 1918 ("Politique de répression").

138. ADL 93 M 55, text of letter from Ernest Lafont to the Interior Ministry, 24 July, and report of 23 Aug. 1916.

139. Lafont in Chamber, cited in *Pop. C.,* 11 Mar. 1918 ("Patriotisme ouvrier"); *Flamme,* 29 Dec. 1917 ("Chronique régionale"); 4 May 1918 ("Le Premier Mai chez nous"); 18 May 1918 ("Saint-Etienne et la guerre"); 6 Apr. and 20–27 July 1918 ("Chez les cheminots"); and 1 June and 13 July 1918 ("Chez les tisseurs").

140. *Flamme,* 30 Mar. 1918 ("La guerre et la paix," by M. Guillot). Unlike other Firminy unionists, Guillot was also active in the Loire's Comité de Gauche (Ligue de Défense Républicaine) formed in Feb. 1918: AN F7 12994, 21 Mar. 1918; ADL 10 M 178, 25 Apr. 1918.

141. ADL 10 M 177, 13 Feb. and 11 Mar. 1918; 10 M 178, 24 June 1918; *Flamme,* 23 Mar. 1918.

142. *Flamme,* 25 May 1918 ("A l'oeuvre," by L. Michel, of SFIO Roanne).

143. On the SFIO National Council in July: *L'Hum.,* 30 July, and *Pop.* (Paris), 31 July and 2 Aug. 1918. On the party's National Congress in October: *L'Hum.* and *Pop.,* 11 Oct. 1918. The votes in July were 1544 for the resolution by (ex-)minoritarian Jean Longuet, 1172 for the resolution by (ex-)majoritarian Pierre Renaudel, and 152 for the resolution by extreme-leftist Fernand Loriot. In October the votes were 1528 for Longuet, 1212 for Renaudel, and 181 for a centrist resolution by Léon Blum. On these votes, see also Kriegel, *Aux origines,* 1:232–33; and Wohl, *French Communism,* pp. 106–10.

Chapter 5. Revolutionary Strategy in Transition

1. The question of conversion to communism is discussed here mainly in ch. 6. See also Kriegel, *Aux origines,* 1:235–353; Wohl, *French Communism,* pp. 114–207; Robert, "Origines du P.C.F.," pp. 13–39; and, on the moderate faction, Fine, "Toward Corporatism," pp. 51–84.

2. AN F7 12994, 2 Sept. 1918; ADL 93 M 9, 7 Oct. to 31 Dec. 1918. The exact membership of the wartime metalworkers' unions is uncertain, but in mid-

1917 the Saint-Chamond union reported 4,000 members and the department-wide Union des Métaux more than 20,000 members. ADL 93 M 11, 4 May 1917; M 1066, 3 June 1917.

3. AN F7 12994, 23–29 June and 2 Sept. 1918; similar vote at Bourse, Saint-Etienne, 12 Sept. 1918.

4. AN F7 12994, 5 July 1918; ADL 93 M 13, 14 Aug. 1918; 14 M 15, 14 Aug. and 6–9 Sept. 1918; 93 M 11, 1–4 Sept. 1918; 93 M 46, 30 Sept. and 1 Oct. 1918. The metalworkers' congress is described in AN F7 13771, 13 July 1918; and in *Union des Métaux,* Sept. 1918.

5. On Frécon: ADL 93 M 70, 6 Jan., 24 Feb., and 28 Apr. 1919; AN F7 12994, 10 Jan., 11 Feb., and 5 Mar. 1919; F7 12995, 21 Mar. and 1 Apr. 1920. On Torcieux: Bourse, Saint-Etienne, 17 Jan. 1919; ADL 93 M 58, 21 Jan. and 19 Apr. 1919; AN F7 12994, 23 Feb. 1920. On Torcieux in 1916–17, see ch. 3.

6. ADL 10 M 180, 10–11 Dec. 1918; 10 M 182, 13 Apr. 1919.

7. *Flamme,* 21 Dec. 1918 ("Communiqué de l'Union des Ouvriers sur Métaux de Saint-Etienne").

8. AN F7 12994, text of CI resolution for meeting of 25 Aug., with report of 22 Aug. 1918. See also ADL 93 M 69, 23 Oct. and 18 Dec. 1918.

9. On the issue of amnesty: ADL 93 M 69, 27 Aug. 1918; AN F7 12994, 22 Aug. and 18 Nov. 1918, and 5 Mar. and 15 Apr. 1919; ADL 92 M 252, 11 Mar. 1919; 92 M 251, 17 July and 25 Nov. 1919. On Merrheim and Blanchard: AN F7 13771, 11 July 1918; ADL 93 M 46, 30 Sept. 1918.

10. ADL 10 M 180, 14 Dec. 1918.

11. AN F7 12994, 14 Aug. 1918 and 27 Mar. 1919.

12. *O. Céram.,* May 1919; ADHV 10 M 135, 20 Nov. 1919; annual reports on industry and commerce, 1919–20, in *Bull. CCL,* no. 70 (1919), p. 1760, and no. 73 (1920), pp. 331–32; also session of 2 Mar. 1920, in no. 72 (1920), p. 70. For general trends see also Larivière, *Industrie à Limoges,* pp. 76–79.

13. *R. Tiss.,* Feb. to Nov. 1920; annual report on industry and commerce, 1920, in *Bull. CCSE,* 1e année, no. 7 (1921), pp. 419–24; also Guitton, *Rubans,* pp. 150, 175–77, 198–200, 256–58.

14. Synd. Chaussures, Limoges, 30 Dec. 1920 and 29 Jan. 1921; reports for 1919–20 in *Bull. CCL,* no. 70 (1919), p. 1761, and no. 73 (1920), p. 333; also general trends in Larivière, *Industrie à Limoges,* pp. 70–73, 88–89.

15. ADL 93 M 19, 20 Dec. 1918, and 28 Jan. and 19 May 1919; report for 1920, in *Bull. CCSE,* 1e année (1921), pp. 426–30; Beaud, "Etablissements Holtzer," pp. 17–23; Devun, "Cycle," pp. 39–48, 61; Arbogast, *Armes,* pp. 169–71, 193–95; Perrin, *Saint-Etienne,* pp. 229–62. Wartime developments, documented in AN F7 13356 and ADL M 1066, are discussed here in ch. 3.

16. Compare Bertrand Abherve, "Les origines de la grève des métallurgistes parisiens, juin 1919," *M. Social,* no. 93 (1975), p. 76; and Kemp, *French Economy,* pp. 54, 85–91.

17. ADL Houillères, carton 2480, dossier 1919, text of letter from the Comité des Houillères de la Loire to the Minister of Industrial Reconstruction, 18 Apr. 1919; carton 822, *Rapports de l'Ingénieur Divisionnaire,* Houillères de Montrambert et de la Béraudière (Division de Montrambert), 1919, pp. 1–4, and

1920, pp. 1–4. On conditions in the mines, see also Guillaume, "Mines de la Loire," pp. 21–39; Gras, *Mines,* 2:884–910; and Perrin, *Saint-Etienne,* pp. 93–107.

18. Employers' views in reports for 1919–20, *Bull. CCL,* no. 70 (1919), pp. 1760, 1772–76, and no. 73 (1920), pp. 331–32, 347–50; *Saint-Etienne et sa Région. Industrie — Commerce* (industrial journal), Feb. 1920, p. 51 ("Nos industries"), and June 1920, p. 150 ("Le mois industriel"); M. R. Touchard, *La journée de huit heures dans l'industrie de la métallurgie et du travail des métaux* (Saint-Etienne, 1925); and documents from ADL Houillères, cited in n. 17. Labor views in *Pop. C.,* 16 Apr. 1919 ("Le chômage"), and 26 Feb. 1920 ("La crise des transports et les cheminots"); *Flamme,* 6–13 Sept. 1919 ("Chez les cheminots"), 24 Jan. 1920 ("Pour avoir du charbon: 8 heures et production"), and 4 Sept. 1920 ("A propos du charbon"); and *Peuple L.,* 22 Sept. 1919 ("Chez les mineurs"), 24 Sept. 1919 ("La crise des transports"), and 8 Oct. 1919 ("Crise du charbon").

19. *Pop. C.,* 3 June 1918 ("Vie chère — Cercle vicieux"); for other examples of labor views in Limoges, see *Pop. C.,* 17 Feb. 1919 (L. Betoulle's speech to the Chamber), and 11 Jan. 1921 ("Crise de chômage"); *O. Céram.,* Sept. 1918, Jan. 1919, and May 1919; AN F7 13622, 20 Oct. 1919; ADHV 10 M 146, 31 Mar. 1920; Synd. Chaussures, Limoges, 28 Jan. and 30 Dec. 1920, and 29 Jan. 1921.

20. *Peuple L.,* 28 Aug. 1921 ("Guerre des salaires"); for other examples of labor views in the Loire, see *Peuple L.,* 10 Apr. 1920 ("Ce qu'il faut pour vivre à un ménage ouvrier"); *Flamme,* 14 June 1919 ("Chronique régionale"), 24 July 1920 ("Vie chère"), 14 Aug. 1920 ("Variations sur le même air: La vie restera chère"), and 19 Mar. 1921 ("Les salaires et les prix"); *R. Tiss.,* Aug. 1919 ("Augmentation du tarif"), Dec. 1919 ("1920"), Feb. 1920 and Jan. 1921 ("Congrès régional du tissage"), Feb. 1921 ("Le chantage patronal"), Apr. 1921 ("La crise du tissage"), and Jan. 1922 ("Diminution des salaires"); ADL 92 M 252, 11 Mar. 1919; 93 M 55, 18 Mar. 1919; AN F7 12995, 1 Apr. 1920.

21. AN F7 12994, chart of food prices tabulated by CI Loire, 7 Sept. 1918.

22. *Bulletin du Ministère du Travail,* nos. 11–12 (1919), p. 548; summary here in Figure 17, p. 304. These figures represented an increase over two quarters of 12.8 percent, compared to 15.4 percent for the same time period in 1918 and 16.1 percent in 1917. Figures for the Loire in 1920 are in *Bull. CCSE,* 1ᵉ année, no. 7 (1921), pp. 448–51. These and later figures are summarized here in Figure 18, p. 305.

23. *Bulletin du Ministère du Travail,* nos. 11–12 (1919), p. 548; also figures for Limoges cited in Sabourdy, "Conditions de la scission," pp. 131–32. Sabourdy calculates that the index for food prices in 1919 stood at 332, with the wage index at only 228, compared to constants of 100 in 1914. On wages and prices, see also Sauvy, *Histoire économique,* 1:349, 357–59.

24. This argument is drawn from the English example but appears to be valid also for France. See Waites, "Effects of First World War," pp. 6–8; Knowles and Robertson, "Wages of Skilled and Unskilled Workers," pp. 110–14; and Sauvy, *Histoire économique,* 1:508.

25. Cronin, "Labor Insurgency," pp. 134–35. Cronin also cites figures (p.

134) to show that inflation was worse in postwar France than in Britain or Italy, after being relatively less severe there during the war.

26. Cited in Abherve, "Grève des métallurgistes," p. 78.

27. On the Loire: weekly statistics for Saint-Etienne, May to Nov. 1919 and Dec. 1920 to Dec. 1921, in ADL 91 M 24; also general observations in M 1066, dossier on "Chômage," reports of 28 Jan. and 19 Apr. 1919; 92 M 252, 5–7 Mar. 1919; and *Flamme,* 10 May 1919. On the Limoges group of *"démobilisés chômeurs"*: ADHV 1 M 167, 7 Feb. 1919; AN F7 13369, 14–28 Feb. 1919. On veterans' organizations, see also Antoine Prost, *Les anciens combattants et la société française, 1914–1939,* 3 vols. (Paris, 1977), vol. 1, ch. 2, and vol. 3, chs. 3–4; and Robert Soucy, "France: Veterans' Politics between the Wars," in *The War Generation,* ed. Stephen R. Ward (Port Washington, N.Y., 1975), esp. pp. 60–68. On unemployment in Limoges: no official statistics are available, but see observations in *Pop. C.,* 16 Apr. 1919; Synd. Imprimeurs-Lithographes, Limoges, 5 Apr. 1919; Synd. Chaussures, Limoges, 20 June 1919; ADHV 10 M 49, 5 Aug. and 1 Nov. 1919; 10 M 135, 20–22 Nov. 1919.

28. Compare Waites, "Effects of First World War," p. 19. On the regulations governing unemployment compensation in France, see AN F22 681, reports on the Fonds National de Chômage, 1919 and 1921.

29. On the effect of unemployment on organized labor, see John A. Garraty, *Unemployment in History: Economic Thought and Public Policy* (New York, 1978), pp. 182–87, 189–91; Dufraisse, "Mouvement ouvrier 'rouge,' " in *Mouvements ouvriers,* ed. Fauvel-Rouif, pp. 180–84; and, on the late nineteenth century, Perrot, *Ouvriers en grève,* 1:158–64. This question is further discussed here in ch. 8, concerning the economic crisis of 1921.

30. For example, ADL 93 M 9, 28 Aug. 1918; *O. Céram.,* Sept. 1918.

31. Synd. Chaussures, Limoges, 11 July 1918 and 6 June 1919; *O. Céram.,* May 1919 ("Révision de tarifs à Limoges"); ADHV 10 M 135, 22 Feb. 1919; 10 M 63, 16 Dec. 1920; ADL 93 M 9, 28 Aug. 1918; AN F7 12994, 15 May 1919. The contrary view was expressed by Lyon's "yellow" unionists in *L'Indépendance Ouvrière,* July 1920 ("Chômage et vie chère"), and by Loire glassworkers in AN F7 12995, 2 June 1919.

32. Examples of labor sentiment for the Haute-Vienne: *O. Céram.,* May 1919 ("Journée de huit heures") and Apr. 1922 ("Défendez les 8 heures"); Synd. Chaussures, Limoges, 6–20 June 1919; ADHV 10 M 194, 7 June 1919; AN F7 13622, 12 June 1919; ADHV 10 M 63, 16 Dec. 1920. For the Loire: AN F7 12994, 16 Mar. 1919; *Union des Métaux,* Apr.–May 1919 ("La Fédération et la journée de huit heures"); *R. Tiss.,* July 1919 ("Journée de 8 heures" and "Assemblée générale des tisseurs"), and Aug. 1920 ("Nouvel horaire"). For similar reasons, some groups later demanded a six-hour day: ADL M 540, dossier on "CGT/CGTU," report of 7 Sept. 1922, and Circulaire from the Fédération des Syndicats Interindustriels (Paris); also *Combat Syndicaliste* (CGTSR), Feb. 1927.

33. P. Monatte in *VO,* 30 Apr. 1919; ADL 93 M 14, 1 May 1919; 93 M 11, 15 May 1919; also Monatte at CGT Lyon congress, speech reprinted in Monatte, *Lutte syndical,* pp. 169–70. On the eight-hour day and surrounding issues, see also *L'Hum.* and *Pop.* (Paris), 30 Mar. to 9 Apr., and 2–4 May 1919; *Voix du*

Peuple (CGT), Mar.–May 1919; and *Union des Métaux,* Apr.–May 1919. On the acquittal of Jaurès's assassin, see also ADHV 1 M 167, 6 Apr. 1919.

34. On the strikes generally, see *Union des Métaux,* June–July 1919; Papayanis, "Masses révolutionnaires," pp. 51–73; Abherve, "Grève des métallurgistes," pp. 75–85; and Brunet, *Saint-Denis,* pp. 210–32. The strikes and the political issues involved are further discussed later in this chapter.

35. AN F7 13576, 26 Aug. 1919; report for 1920 in *Bull. CCL,* no. 73 (1920), pp. 331–32; Touchard, *Journée de huit heures,* passim; *Indép. O.,* Feb. to June 1919, July 1920, Apr. 1922, and Nov.–Dec. 1923.

36. *Indép. O.,* Apr. 1919 and Apr. 1922; *R. Tiss.,* Sept. 1919 and Feb. to June 1920. The special provisions for taxation of weavers as workers were not included in the tax laws of 1917 or 1920 but were added in the revisions of 1923. See Zdatny, "Artisanal Movement," p. 286.

37. *Flamme,* 31 Jan. 1920; *Peuple L.,* 17 Apr. and 8 May 1920; ADL M 540, dossier on "L'impôt sur les salaires," reports of 12 Mar. and 19 Dec. 1919, 25 Jan. 1920, and 12 Dec. 1921; 93 M 26, 10 Mar. 1919; AN F7 12994, 28 Feb. to 15 Mar. 1919; F7 12995, 27 Jan. and 23 Feb. 1920.

38. "Programme Minimum de Revendications," issued on 24 Nov. and approved by the CGT on 16 Dec. 1918, reprinted in Léon Jouhaux, *Le syndicalisme et la CGT* (Paris, 1920), pp. 205–13. For commentary, see also Picard, *Mouvement syndical,* pp. 173–81.

39. ADL 93 M 70, minutes of UD meeting, 8 Dec. 1918, with report of 6 Jan. 1919.

40. ADL 93 M 68, 23 Feb. 1919; 93 M 66, 1 Mar. 1919; AN F7 12994, 1 Mar., 15 Apr., and 14 May 1919.

41. Jouhaux, *Syndicalisme et la CGT,* pp. 205–13; Jouhaux, *Les travailleurs devant la paix* (Paris, Dec. 1918); *Voix du Peuple,* Mar.–Apr. 1919. Jouhaux did get a seat at the Peace Conference, but he resigned it after the violent events of May Day 1919. *L'Hum.,* 4 May 1919; *Voix du Peuple,* May 1919.

42. *Indép. O.,* Feb. 1919 and Nov.–Dec. 1923.

43. Jouhaux in *La Bataille,* 5 Apr. 1919, cited in Abherve, "Grèves des métallurgistes," p. 80; see also Fine, "Toward Corporatism," pp. 70–73.

44. Albert Thomas, preface to Marcel Bidegaray's *L'exploitation d'aujourd'hui par les compagnies, l'exploitation de demain par la nationalisation des chemins de fer* (Paris, n.d.), cited in Fine, "Toward Corporatism," p. 68; also Bidegaray in *Pop. C.,* 29 Feb. 1920. For similar views, see M. Cachin in *Flamme,* 8 May 1920; C. Bartuel (miners' general secretary) in *Flamme,* 4 Sept. 1920; and *Peuple L.,* 3–10 July 1920. On the question of nationalization, see also Picard, *Mouvement syndical,* pp. 186–91, and Georges Lefranc, "Les origines de l'idée de nationalisation industrielle en France (1919–1920)," *Information Historique,* 21e année (1959), pp. 139–45.

45. On the criticisms by some leftists: *VO,* 16 Apr. and 14 May 1920; ADL 92 M 259, 6 May 1920; and Léon Blum, text of speech at SFIO National Congress, 21 Apr. 1919, in *L'Hum.,* 22 Apr. 1919; also published separately as *Commentaires sur le Programme d'Action du Parti Socialiste* (Paris, 1925), pp. 6–8. For the views of moderates and Radical Socialists: ADL 92 M 262, 14 May 1920;

Peuple L., 30 Sept. and 30 Oct. 1919; 6 Mar., 22 May, 19 June, and 3–10 July 1920; *Flamme,* 6 Mar., 8–15 May, and 4 Sept. 1920; *Pop. C.,* 26 Jan. and 22 Apr. 1920.

46. On Keufer, see Lefranc, *Mouvement syndical,* pp. 64–84; and Maitron, *Dictionnaire biographique,* 13:143–45.

47. Report by A. Keufer, "L'organisation des relations entre patrons et ouvriers," June 1919, in Ministère du Travail, Comité Permanent d'Etudes Relatives à la Prévision des Chômages Industriels, *Compte-rendu des travaux, années 1917–1920* (Paris, 1920), pp. 173–80.

48. AN F7 12994, 12 Mar. 1920; see also the later debate on "compulsory conciliation" (an alternative to arbitration) in *Le Travail* (CGT, Haute-Vienne), Nov. 1928; *O. Céram.* (CGT), Oct.–Dec. 1928; and *Céramiste Limousin* (CGTU, then autonomous), Dec. 1928.

49. Text of speech in CGT, XXᵉ Congrès National Corporatif, tenu à Lyon, du 15 au 21 septembre 1919, *Compte-rendu des travaux* (Villeneuve-Saint-Georges, n.d.), pp. 97–103; quoted passage, p. 103. Rougerie's speech is also summarized in *Pop. C.,* 19 Sept. 1919.

50. A. Reynard in *Flamme,* 24 Aug. 1918 ("Questions économiques et sociales"), 19 Oct. 1918 ("Lutte de classes"), and 10 May 1919 ("Ce que les électeurs pensent").

51. Rougerie at SFIO National Congress, in *Pop. C.,* 14 Apr. 1919.

52. Rougerie at CGT Confederal Congress, in *Pop. C.,* 19 Sept. 1919.

53. Cited in Christian Gras, "Merrheim et le capitalisme," *M. Social,* no. 63 (1968), p. 163.

54. Reynard in *Flamme,* 24 Aug. 1918 ("Questions économiques et sociales").

55. Text of Jouhaux's speech at CGT National Council, in *Voix du Peuple,* July 1919.

56. Blum, *Programme d'Action,* pp. 6–8, and text of majority motion at SFIO National Congress, in *L'Hum.,* 23 Apr. 1919. See also Merrheim's speech at the CGT National Council, in *Voix du Peuple,* July 1919; and Merrheim's pamphlet, *La révolution économique,* cited in Edouard Dolléans, *Alphonse Merrheim* (Paris, 1939), pp. 44–45.

57. Blum, *Programme d'Action,* pp. 6–8. Later on, party leftists similarly criticized the CGT program, which was then so reformist that even the Radical Party had adopted it. AN F7 13580, 22 Dec. 1927 and 19 Jan. 1928; *Réveil* (SFIO, Loire), 8 Apr. 1928; *Petit Limousin* (SFIO, Haute-Vienne), 16–30 May 1928. This question is further discussed here in ch. 10.

58. Parvy in *Pop. C.,* 1 Dec. 1918.

59. Wohl, *French Communism,* pp. 139–40.

60. Dumoulin, "Syndicalistes français." On Dumoulin's earlier evolution, see ch. 4 of this study. On Dumoulin's idea of a labor party (discussed in ch. 10), see also AN F7 13578, 8 Nov. 1922 and 19 Mar. 1923; F7 13579, 26 Nov. 1925.

61. Kriegel, *Aux origines,* 1:529–30, 538.

62. P. Monatte in *VO,* 30 Apr., 11 June, and 23 July 1919; also *Flamme,* 21 Dec. 1918 ("Communiqué de l'Union des Ouvriers sur Métaux de Saint-Etienne").

63. On the postwar radicalization, see Wohl, *French Communism,* pp. 117–22; Kriegel, *Aux origines,* 1:238–47, 297–307; Kriegel, *Croissance de la C.G.T.;* and Cronin, "Labor Insurgency," pp. 125–45.

64. Kriegel persuasively debunks the "age" hypothesis in *Aux origines,* 1:244–46, and *Croissance de la C.G.T.,* pp. 165–77.

65. See Kriegel, *French Communists,* pp. 47–59, 98–135; Wohl, *Generation of 1914,* esp. ch. 6; Wohl, *French Communism,* pp. 428–32, 442, 453; Prost, *La C.G.T.,* pp. 156–61; Wheeler, "German Labor," pp. 304–21; and Dan S. White, "Reconsidering European Socialism in the 1920s," *JCH* 16 (1981): 251–72. The question of age in the labor movement is further discussed here in ch. 11.

66. The social composition of the labor force is discussed here in ch. 1; on the age factor among anarchists, especially in the Loire, see ch. 2.

67. Robert and Chavance, "Syndicalisation en France," pp. 1103–5; and Robert, *Scission syndicale,* pp. 166–68.

68. See Prost, *La C.G.T.,* chs. 3–4.

69. Data in Labi, *Grande division des travailleurs,* pp. 248–49; similar figures in Robert, *Scission syndicale,* pp. 159–62. Annie Kriegel cites higher prewar and lower postwar membership figures, but these may be based on erroneous sources or methods of calculation. See Kriegel, *Croissance de la C.G.T.,* pp. 65–67; Robert, *Scission syndicale,* pp. 53–55; and Prost, *La C.G.T.,* chs. 2–3.

70. Labi, *Grande division des travailleurs,* pp. 248–49; also AN F7 13576, 10 Apr. 1919, on the metalworkers' federation; and Guy Chaumel, *Histoire des cheminots et de leurs syndicats* (Paris, 1948), chs. 7–8.

71. ADHV 10 M 77, report on trade unions in the Haute-Vienne, 1 Jan. 1920; ADL 93 M 58, 26 Aug. 1919. These figures do not agree with those of Labi (*Grande division des travailleurs,* pp. 250–53), but those are based on the UDs' periodic purchases of CGT membership stamps, which may not reflect actual memberships at any point in time.

72. AN F7 12994, 2 Sept. 1918; ADL 93 M 9, 22 Dec. 1918; 93 M 82, 8 Sept. 1919.

73. ADHV 1 M 167, 6 Apr. 1919; 10 M 177, report on trade unions, 1 Jan. 1920; 10 M 135, 11 Sept. and 20 Nov. 1919, and 7 Apr. 1920. (The issues of *O. Céram.* for the period of the strikes are missing from the ADHV's collection.)

74. ADHV 10 M 177, reports on trade unions, 1 Jan. 1914 and 1 Jan. 1920. A report for 1911 in AN F7 13622 similarly estimated the union's membership at 240 at that time.

75. ADHV 10 M 194, 4 Mar. 1919; 10 M 177, report on trade unions, 1 Jan. 1920.

76. ADHV 10 M 177–79, reports on trade unions, 1921, 1924–26, and 1936. (Reports for 1922–23 give no membership figures.) By adding together the figures for the CGT, CGTU, and independent or autonomous unions in each of the three industries, one may obtain the following totals:

	1 Jan. 1920	1 Jan. 1921	1 Jan. 1924	1 Jan. 1925	1 Jan. 1926	1936
Porcelain	3200	2550	2000	2000	2050	2150
Shoes	3446	1000	560	560	755	2200
Railroads	1675	1300	600	600	820	?

Problems of unionization and factional strengths in the 1920s are discussed here in ch. 11.

77. ADHV 10 M 177, reports on trade unions, 1914 and 1920; 10 M 165, list of unions created in 1919; 10 M 194, report of 1 Sept. 1919, on the creation of the Union Locale at Saint-Junien; also Bourse, Limoges, 22 May 1919, on the reorganization of the Bourse.

78. AN F7 12994, 31 Mar. 1919; F7 12995, 18 Jan. and 23 Feb. 1920; F22 73–74, lists of unions dissolved from 1914 to 1935 (including date of formation), Saint-Etienne and other Loire cities; ADL 93 M 72, reports of 18 June 1919 and of 1920–25 on the Catholic and other independent unions; M 540, reports of 1921–25 on the CFTC; also *R. Tiss.*, July 1919, on the creation of "Un nouveau syndicat ouvrier du textile." In 1913–14 the Bourse at Saint-Etienne had fifty-nine member unions and the UD had seventy-seven. ADL 93 M 52, report on "L'organisation ouvrière," 1913–14; AN F7 13570, Feb. 1914.

79. ADHV 10 M 178, report on trade unions, 1 Jan. 1925; AN F22 73–74, lists of Loire unions dissolved from 1914 to 1935. On the problem of "ephemeral" unions, see also Kriegel, *Croissance de la C.G.T.*, pp. 71, 112–25.

80. ADL 93 M 58, 17 Mar. 1919; AN F7 12994, 31 Mar. 1919. This deliberate creation of unions, even if only on paper, throws into question the method used by Kriegel in *Croissance de la C.G.T.* The author defends (pp. 11–12) her use of the *"syndicat"* as the basic unit for measuring the growth of the labor movement, by arguing that while unions or federations might wish to exaggerate their memberships, they would not seek to exaggerate the number of unions as such.

81. ADL 93 M 97, 28 Mar. 1919. The strategy depended, of course, on the fact that most UDs and federations voted by union, not by membership size. The issues of proportional representation and the problems of measuring factional strengths are further discussed here in ch. 9, on the consummation of the CGT split.

82. AN F7 12994, 1 Mar. 1919.

83. AN F7 12994, 1–5 Mar. 1919.

84. AN F7 12994, 27 Mar. 1919; also compare P. Monatte in *VO*, 11 June 1919.

85. ADL 10 M 184, 22 Dec. 1919; 93 M 59, 18 Jan. 1920; 92 M 262, 5 Feb. 1920; 93 M 26, 19 Oct. 1920.

86. ADL 93 M 70, 6 Feb. 1919; AN F7 12994, 5 Mar. 1919.

87. ADL 92 M 251, 19 May 1919; 92 M 252, 11 Mar. and 5 June 1919; 19 M 39, 12 Aug. 1919; 93 M 13, 21 Aug. and 23 Oct. 1919; 93 M 70, 26 July 1920; M 539, 17 Apr. 1921. Andrieu's departure and later activities are further discussed here in ch. 7.

88. ADL 93 M 9, 21 Mar. 1919. There is no record of the proportion of wartime union members who were mobilized soldiers.

89. AN F7 13576, 2 June 1919; *VO*, 4 June and 23 July 1919; see also Kriegel, *Aux origines*, 1:297–303; Wohl, *French Communism*, pp. 120–22, 136–38; Cronin, "Labor Insurgency," pp. 129, 132–33; Papayanis, "Masses révolutionnaires," pp. 51–52, 71–73; Abherve, "Grève des métallurgistes," pp.

83–85; Shorter and Tilly, *Strikes in France,* pp. 122–26. More nuanced views of these strikes are offered by Brunet in *Saint-Denis,* pp. 218–22, and by Robert in "Origines du P.C.F.," pp. 27–28.

90. The "strike-proneness" of miners and metalworkers is defined here in terms of both strike frequency and number of participants. Strike frequency rose by a factor of 6.2 for miners and by 5.1 for metalworkers, from 1918 to 1919, while the number of strikers rose by factors of 44.1 for miners and 6.6 for metalworkers in the same period. See graphs in Figure 11, p. 286, or data in the *Statistique des grèves,* 1915–19. On the goals of the miners: ADL 93 M 26, 10 Mar. 1919; 93 M 50, 26 June 1920; *Flamme,* 28 June 1919; *Peuple L.,* 3–6 Oct. and 17 Nov. 1919, and 19 June and 10 July 1920; and Bartuel and Rullière, *Mine et mineurs,* pp. 453–60.

91. *Statistique des grèves,* 1919. A total of 63 percent of the Loire's strikes, 58 percent of the Haute-Vienne's strikes, and 56 percent of the nation's strikes in 1919 began in this three-month period. The issues of wages and/or the application of the eight-hour day were the stated causes in 86 percent of the Loire's strikes and 92 percent of those in the Haute-Vienne in 1919.

92. AN F7 12994, 26–28 Feb. and 25–27 Mar. 1919; ADL 92 M 252, 11 Mar. 1919; 93 M 55, 18 Mar. 1919.

93. Cited in Abherve, "Grève des métallurgistes," p. 78; see also *L'Hum.,* 2–3 May 1919, and *Voix du Peuple,* May 1919. No such disturbances were reported in the Haute-Vienne or the Loire: see AN F7 13622, 5 May 1919; *Flamme,* 10 May 1919.

94. Cited in Arno J. Mayer, *Politics and Diplomacy of Peacemaking: Containment and Counterrevolution at Versailles, 1918–1919* (New York, 1967), p. 670. A similar observation, not concerning May Day specifically, can be found in Wohl, *French Communism,* p. 121.

95. On the strikes: ADHV 10 M 135, 27 May and 16 June 1919; AN F7 13622, 12 June 1919; F7 12994, 14 May 1919; ADL 92 M 251, 12 May 1919; 93 M 11, 8 June 1919; *Pop. C.,* 1–23 June 1919; *Flamme,* 7–21 June 1919; *L'Hum.,* 1–25 June 1919. On the attitudes of the CGT and the metalworkers' federation: *Voix du Peuple,* June–July 1919; *Union des Métaux,* June–July 1919; AN F7 13576, 5 June 1919; and Papayanis, "Masses révolutionnaires," pp. 62–64. On the reorganization and role of the Comité Intercorporatif in the Loire: ADL 93 M 70, 24 Feb. 1919; 92 M 252, 1 Mar. and 1 May 1919; 93 M 55, 18 Mar. 1919; AN F7 12994, 5 Mar. and 3 May 1919. The Comité Intercorporatif was finally dissolved in Dec. 1919 by order of the UD. ADL 93 M 59, 6 Dec. 1919.

96. Monatte in *VO,* 11 June 1919; also cited (in translation) in Cronin, "Labor Insurgency," p. 129. The political issues raised by the strikes are discussed later in this chapter.

97. On the planned demonstration of 21 July, see Kriegel, *Aux origines,* 1:301–3, and Mayer, *Peacemaking,* ch. 25. The repercussions of its cancellation are further discussed later in this chapter.

98. Merrheim at CGT Lyon congress (Sept. 1919), cited in Picard, *Mouvement syndical,* p. 212.

99. Cited in Papayanis, "Masses révolutionnaires," pp. 63–64.

100. Cassin (of Nantes) and Labbe (assistant federal secretary) at the metal-workers' congress: Féd. Métaux, *Congrès Extraordinaire, 1919,* pp. 50–51, 104. On the problem of weak unionization, see also Brunet, *Saint-Denis,* pp. 227–30.

101. Andrieu in *Peuple L.,* 10 Oct. 1919 ("Impressions du congrès"); in response to J. Bonnefonds, "Après le congrès confédéral," in *Peuple L.,* 28 Sept. 1919. See also Monatte's critique of the CGT's role in the earlier strikes, in *VO,* 23 July 1919.

102. ADL 92 M 251, 12 May 1919; AN F7 12995, 14 May 1919.

103. AN F7 12995, 2–19 June 1919.

104. AN F7 12995, 1 Apr. 1920.

105. *Statistique des grèves,* 1919–20. The percentages in Figure 12 refer to those strikes that failed to reach a successful or compromise settlement. The Loire's failures in 1919 included five of eleven (45 percent) of its strikes of metal-workers, as compared to 27 percent of the metalworkers' strikes in France as a whole. For the period of January to April 1920 (until the eve of the May general strike), 22 percent of the Loire's strikes were recorded as failures, as compared to 8 percent for the Haute-Vienne and 25 percent for the country. Although this rate was slightly lower than the national average, it included five of seven (71 percent) of the metalworkers' strikes in the Loire, as compared to 30 percent of those in France as a whole.

106. On Rougerie's and Bonnet's conciliatory policies: Synd. Chaussures, Limoges, 6 June 1919; ADHV 10 M 135, 27 May and 11 Sept. 1919; 10 M 194, 7 June 1919; AN F7 13622, 26 June 1919. The two men were finally replaced as Bourse secretaries after the general strike of May 1920. Bourse, Limoges, 24 May 1920; ADHV 10 M 99, 25 May 1920. Rougerie had already stepped down as secretary of the shoe workers' union, but Bonnet remained head of the porcelain workers' union until the eve of the CGT schism in 1921. Synd. Chaussures, Limoges, 28 Jan. 1920; *O. Céram.,* June–July 1921.

107. ADL 93 M 70, 24 Feb. and 28 Apr. 1919; 93 M 82, 4 Apr. 1919; 93 M 9, 3 May 1919; 93 M 58, 1–26 Aug. 1919; AN F7 12995, 25 Jan., 23 Feb., and 1 Apr. 1920. Frécon resigned as UD secretary in June 1920, and Torcieux stepped down as Bourse secretary (apparently because of illness) the following December. ADL 19 M 39, 21 June 1920; AN F7 12995, 7 Dec. 1920; Bourse, Saint-Etienne, 3 Dec. 1920.

108. Compare Kriegel, *Croissance de la C.G.T.,* pp. 24, 56–60. According to her figures, the national average was one Socialist to every five trade unionists.

109. This question is discussed earlier in this chapter, as well as briefly in ch. 4.

110. R. Lefebvre in *Vérité,* 29 Jan. 1918, cited in Shaul Ginsburg, "Du Wilsonisme au communisme: L'itinéraire du pacifiste Raymond Lefebvre en 1919," *RHMC* 23 (1976): 585. According to Ginsburg (p. 587), Lefebvre still held the same views through early 1919.

111. In response to Albert Thomas's famed question ("Wilson or Lenin?"), Blum answered, "I choose Jaurès." Thomas in *L'Hum.,* 9 Nov. 1918 ("Démocratie ou Bolchevisme"); Blum in *L'Hum.,* 15 Nov. 1918 ("Il faut s'entendre").

Also on these issues: Arno J. Mayer, *Wilson vs. Lenin: The Political Origins of the New Diplomacy, 1917–1918* (New Haven, Conn., 1959); Mayer, *Peacemaking;* and Kathryn E. Amdur, "The French Left and the 'American Peace,' " unpublished paper.

112. Bourse, Limoges, 11 Dec. 1918; *Pop. C.,* 5–17 Dec. 1918.

113. *Flamme,* 21 Dec. 1918 ("Les cheminots et les problèmes de la paix"); ADL 93 M 40, 24 Dec. 1918; 10 M 180, 14 Dec. 1918.

114. *Flamme,* 14 Dec. 1918 ("Pour le Président Wilson" and "Chronique régionale: Firminy"); ADL 10 M 180, 10–16 Dec. 1918; 93 M 70, 6 Jan. 1919.

115. Compare D. Renoult in *Pop.* (Paris), 11 May 1919; and F. Loriot in *VO,* 2 July 1919. On the varied responses to the treaty, see also Pierre Miquel, *La paix de Versailles et l'opinion publique française* (Paris, 1972), esp. pp. 133–46; and E. Beau de Loménie, *Le débat de ratification du Traité de Versailles: A la Chambre des Députés et dans la presse en 1919* (Paris, 1945).

116. A. Pressemane in *Pop. C.,* 14 Apr. 1919 (report on Haute-Vienne SFIO federal congress); *Flamme,* 24 May 1919 ("Leur paix et la nôtre"), and 12 July 1919 (resolution at Loire SFIO federal congress); ADL 10 M 183, 5 July 1919.

117. ADL 10 M 182, 27 Jan. 1919; *Pop. C.,* 23 June 1919 (resolution at porcelain workers' congress); AN F7 13622, 4 Dec. 1919. On Allied intervention in Russia, see also *L'Hum.,* 17 May to 29 June 1919; *Pop.* (Paris), 30 June and 1 July 1919; *VO,* 4–18 June 1919; Kriegel, *Aux origines,* 1:276–79; Mayer, *Peacemaking,* chs. 10, 13–14; and John M. Thompson, *Russia, Bolshevism, and the Versailles Peace* (Princeton, 1967).

118. AN F7 13576, 26 June and 5 July 1919; *Voix du Peuple,* July 1919 (report on CGT National Council); see also P. Monatte in *VO,* 23 July 1919.

119. Bourse, Limoges, 9 July and 8 Aug. 1919.

120. *Pop. C.,* 20 July 1919 ("Tous au travail le 21").

121. *L'Hum.,* 19 July 1919; and commentary in Ginsburg, "Lefebvre," p. 600.

122. Rougerie at CGT Confederal Congress, in *Pop. C.,* 19 Sept. 1919.

123. ADHV 10 M 100, 26 Apr. 1920.

124. ADHV 10 M 135, 11 Sept. 1919; 10 M 194, 5–9 Sept. 1919.

125. ADHV 10 M 194, 18 July 1919.

126. ADHV 1 M 168, report on Louis Bert, 8 Apr. 1919; Bourse, Limoges, 24 May 1920; AN F7 13023, 23 June and 20 Oct. 1920. There is also a biographical sketch of Bert in Maitron, *Dictionnaire biographique,* 19:51–52. Bert's role in the labor movement and in the nascent CP is further discussed here in chs. 6–7.

127. ADL 92 M 251, 17 July and 21 Aug. 1919; *Flamme,* 19 July 1919.

128. ADL 93 M 58, 16 July 1919; 93 M 70, 11 July 1919. The moderate unions of miners and railroad workers had voted in advance to support the strike: 93 M 58, 16 July 1919; 92 M 251, 17–19 July 1919; 92 M 257, 18 July 1919. According to Papayanis, left-wingers in Paris refused to support the strike so as to retaliate against moderates for their failure to support the strikes in June. "Masses révolutionnaires," p. 64.

129. *Peuple L.,* 6 Oct. 1919 ("Réunion corporative des mineurs"); ADL 93 M

70, report of 23 Sept. 1920 (list of votes at Lyon CGT congress, as background information for the forthcoming congress at Orléans). According to this list, 4 of the 7 miners' unions in the Loire voted with the left, excluding the union at Firminy but including those at La Ricamarie and Saint-Etienne. In all, only 43 Loire unions were cited as present at the Lyon congress, out of a supposed total of 118 member unions in the UD. These totals are consistent with but not identical to those reported by Labi, who credits the left with 32 of 53 votes by the Loire at the Lyon congress. Labi also reports that the Haute-Vienne voted with the majority, by a margin of 16 to 3 (2 abstentions); the national total was 1,393 to 588 (42 abstentions) in favor of the existing leadership and policies of the CGT. *Grande division des travailleurs,* pp. 273–75.

130. Andrieu in *Peuple L.,* 10 Oct. 1919 ("Impressions du congrès"), quoted earlier in this chapter. The question of schism was raised by Gaston Monmousseau, railroad workers' delegate, at a meeting in Limoges: ADHV 10 M 194, 9 Sept. 1919. The idea of schism is further discussed here in ch. 7.

131. The results of the legislative elections are tabulated in ADHV 3 M 164, and *Pop. C.,* 17–18 Nov. 1919, for the Haute-Vienne; and in ADL 3 M 63, and *Peuple L.,* 18 Nov. 1919, for the Loire. See also Lenoble et al., *La Gauche au pouvoir,* pp. 81–84, 90–91; and Pierre Jamet, "Les élections de 1919 dans la Loire," *Bulletin du Centre d'Histoire Régionale* (Université de Saint-Etienne), no. 2 (1977), pp. 27–53.

132. F. Faure in *Peuple L.,* 18 Nov. 1919. The old electoral system, by individual districts *("scrutin d'arrondissement"),* had enabled Socialists to benefit from electoral pacts with Radical candidates on the second round. The change helps to explain how the SFIO lost so many seats while increasing its total vote to 1.8 million from 1.4 million in 1914.

133. Membership reported in *Peuple L.,* 25 Sept. 1919. In this same period, the Haute-Vienne SFIO Federation reported an increase from 1,100 members in Aug. 1919 to 2,700 members in Jan. 1920. Lenoble et al., *La Gauche au pouvoir,* pp. 81, 84.

134. On the Radicals and Radical-Socialists in the Haute-Vienne: ADHV 3 M 164, "Appel de la Fédération Républicaine d'Union Nationale aux Electeurs de la Haute-Vienne" (Sept. 1919); also *Pop. C.* and *Courrier du Centre,* 4 Sept. 1919. On electoral alliances in the Loire: ADL 10 M 183, 26 Aug., 4 Oct., and 20 Nov. 1919; *Peuple L.,* 30 Sept. 1919 (letter from the Loire's Radical and Radical-Socialist Federation to SFIO Federation, 23 Sept. 1919); 1 Oct. 1919 (response by SFIO Federation, 29 Sept. 1919); and 19–21 Nov. 1919.

135. ADHV 3 M 164, results of legislative elections (1919), by city and by arrondissment; 3 M 531, results of municipal elections (1919), departmental totals; 3 M 526, results of municipal elections (1919), Limoges. In the legislative elections, the Haute-Vienne Socialists would have won only the two seats for the Limoges district if the old electoral system had still been in force. Lenoble et al., *La Gauche au pouvoir,* p. 82.

136. Results of legislative elections in *Peuple L.,* 18 Nov. 1919, and in ADL 3 M 63.

137. Jamet, "Elections de 1919," p. 49. The gap for the SFIO (between

20,403 and 21,866 votes) was indeed proportionally wider than for the Loire's conservative candidates (who ranged from 52,319 to 53,185 votes) but narrower than for the Haute-Vienne's Socialist candidates (who ranged between 39,687 and 43,043 votes). ADL 3 M 63; ADHV 3 M 164. There is no evidence as to which groups of voters most often split their tickets.

138. ADL 10 M 183, 22–30 Nov. 1919; *Flamme,* 29 Nov. 1919; *Peuple L.,* 25 Nov. to 8 Dec. 1919. (The dossiers in ADL 5 M 169 and 6 M 53, on the municipal elections and municipal councils in this period, are missing the files for Saint-Etienne.) The Radical candidates also outdrew, on the average, their Socialist allies in all four cantons of the Saint-Etienne arrondissement, but by a rather small margin (from 0.2 to 0.5 percent, according to canton, of the total votes cast). Tabulated results per candidate in ADL 10 M 183.

139. ADHV 3 M 164, 7 Aug. to 3 Nov. 1919; 10 M 127, 26 Sept. 1919; 10 M 135, 11 Sept. 1919.

140. ADHV 3 M 164, 13–17 Nov. 1919; ADL 10 M 182, 9 Feb. 1919; *Flamme,* 8 Nov. 1919 ("[Chez les cheminots] Le remède: Le bulletin rouge"). On the party's reliance on the *"bulletin de vote,"* see also *Peuple L.,* 3 July 1920.

141. AN F7 13576, 21 Nov. 1919; also P. Monatte in *VO,* 19 Dec. 1919.

142. On the anarchists: ADL 19 M 39, 8 Aug. and 21 Nov. 1919, and 28 May 1920; AN F7 12995, 27 Aug. 1920. For a contrary view by "yellow" unionists, see *Indép. O.,* Nov. 1919, which reported "with joy" the defeat of "the partisans of Bolshevism" in the Loire and around the nation.

143. Lists of legislative and municipal candidates of the SFIO and the Bloc des Gauches in ADL 10 M 183, 6 Sept. 1919; 6 M 53 (for the Loire basin but excluding Saint-Etienne); and *Flamme,* 29 Nov. 1919. On the UD and political candidatures: ADL 93 M 70, 18–20 June 1920; 19 M 39, 19–21 June 1920. This problem is further discussed here in ch. 7.

144. ADL 92 M 252, 11 Mar. 1919.

145. ADHV 3 M 164, 2 Sept. 1919; 3 M 526, results of municipal elections (1919), Limoges. There is no evidence as to which groups of voters failed to vote for Rougerie and Bonnet.

146. ADL 93 M 58, 7 Sept., 19 Oct., and 13 Dec. 1919; 93 M 82, 25 Dec. 1919; 93 M 59, 18 Jan. 1920; 92 M 259, 27 Feb. and 9 Aug. 1920.

147. F. Faure in *Peuple L.,* 20 Nov. 1919.

Chapter 6. May 1920: Mass Unionism on Trial

1. Archives of the PLM railway line, cited by Kriegel, in *Aux origines,* 1:434. Kriegel devotes Part Two of her work (1:355–547) to a discussion of the strike and its repercussions. For a brief summary, see also Wohl, *French Communism,* pp. 161–68.

2. On the postwar stabilization and its impact on French labor, see especially Maier, *Recasting Bourgeois Europe,* pp. 135–58. On the political context of the strike, in addition to Kriegel and Wohl, see Labi, *Grande division des travailleurs,* pp. 141–58; Charles, "Scission syndicale," pp. 59–74; and Charles, "Temps des scissions," pp. 1–45.

3. This argument most explicitly counters that of Adrian Jones in "The French Railway Strikes of January–May 1920: New Syndicalist Ideas and Emergent Communism," *FHS* 12 (1982): 517–19.

4. This is Kriegel's thesis in *Aux origines,* 1:522–47. It is upheld in Wohl, *French Communism,* pp. 166–67; and also in Moissonnier, "Octobre," pp. 46–47; Pinol, "Communisme à Lyon," pp. 184–85, 210–16; and M[aurice] Demouveau, "La scission de la C.G.T. à Lille-Roubaix-Tourcoing (1920–1922)," *Revue du Nord* 54 (1971): 460. Others have questioned the importance of May 1920 as the turning point, which they prefer to place earlier (1914–18) or later (1922), but they still accept Kriegel's view of the strike as a failure of revolutionary syndicalist strategy and a contributing factor in the labor movement's ultimate Bolshevization. See Charles, "Temps des scissions," pp. 8–14, 27–28; Robert, *Scission syndicale,* pp. 177–79; Moissonnier et al., "Débat," pp. 152–82; and M. Neely Young, "*La Vie Ouvrière* and International Communism, 1919–1924: Analysis of a Revolutionary Trade Union Newspaper" (Ph.D. diss., Emory Univ., 1975), esp. pp. 119–28, 359–65.

5. Note that, like the railway lines, the unions were organized by sector or *"réseau."* The Limoges workers were in the Union PO, and the Saint-Etienne workers in the Union PLM. On the background and organization of the railroad unions, see Kriegel, *Aux origines,* vol. 1, pt. 2; and Chaumel, *Cheminots,* esp. ch. 8.

6. Gaston Monmousseau [Jean Brécot], *La grande grève de mai 1920* (Paris, n.d.), esp. pp. 13–14, 49, 64–69; compare Monmousseau, *Syndicalisme devant la révolution,* pp. 7–32.

7. Compare Kriegel, *Aux origines,* 1:359–76; and Jones, "French Railway Strikes," pp. 511–15. On the demographic changes in the railroad industry, see the discussion here in ch. 1 and the statistics in Figure 8, p. 294. On the wartime role of military workers in the defense industries, see ch. 3.

8. Figures from Labi, *Grande division des travailleurs,* p. 248; a similar magnitude is cited in Robert, *Scission syndicale,* p. 208.

9. On the question of nationalization, see ch. 5 of this study, with reference to the variety of viewpoints expressed in *VO,* 16 Apr. and 14 May 1920; *Peuple L.,* 30 Sept. and 30 Oct. 1919; 6 Mar., 19 June, and 3–10 July 1920; *Flamme,* 6 Mar., 8–15 May, and 14 Sept. 1920; and *Pop. C.,* 26 Jan. and 22 Apr. 1920. The "independent" or "yellow" unionists opposed nationalization, however, as harmful to the general interest. *Indép. O.,* Apr. 1920.

10. See discussion here of the 1919 elections in ch. 5, with reference to ADHV 3 M 164, 13–17 Nov. 1919; ADL 10 M 182, 9 Feb. 1919; and *Flamme,* 8 Nov. 1919. The railroad workers' role in the later PCF is discussed here in chs. 9–10.

11. ADL 93 M 40, 4 Nov. 1916; 30 Jan., 15 Sept., and 31 Dec. 1917; and 4 Mar. and 24 Dec. 1918; 10 M 178, 25 Apr. 1918; and *Flamme,* 30 Mar. 1918 ("La guerre et la paix," by M. Guillot), 6 Apr. 1918 ("Chez les cheminots"), and 21 Dec. 1918 ("Les cheminots et les problèmes de la paix," by P. Chovet).

12. *Flamme,* 25 Jan. and 1 Feb. 1919 ("Chez les cheminots"); ADL 93 M 41, 25 Jan. and 3–19 Mar. 1919; 92 M 257, 18 July and 10 Sept. 1919.

13. ADHV R 258–59, 2–4 Nov. 1917; 10 M 194, 4–30 Mar. 1919.

14. ADHV 10 M 194, 30 Mar. 1919; *Pop. C.,* 5 Mar. 1919.

15. On Périgueux and its strike, see Kriegel, *Aux origines,* 1:379–84; and Jones, "French Railway Strikes," pp. 515–18.

16. ADHV 10 M 146, 15–26 Jan. and 31 Mar. 1920; *Pop. C.,* 26–27 Jan. 1920.

17. ADHV 10 M 146, 15 Mar. to 29 Apr. 1920; *Pop. C.,* 10–14 Apr. 1920.

18. On the origins of the PLM strike, see Kriegel, *Aux origines,* 1:389–94. On the participation of Limoges strikers: *Pop. C.,* 27 Feb. to 4 Mar. 1920; ADHV 10 M 146, 4–6 Mar. 1920. On the response at Saint-Etienne: ADL 92 M 257, 24 Feb. to 26 Mar. 1920; 93 M 41, 22 Mar. 1920.

19. Kriegel, *Aux origines,* 1:417–23. Contrast the views of Jones in "French Railway Strikes," pp. 533–37.

20. Kriegel, *Aux origines,* 1:421–22.

21. AN F7 12995, 29 Mar. 1920.

22. Monmousseau [Brécot] in *VO,* 30 July 1920; see also his *Grande grève,* pp. 13–14, 49, 64–69. Wohl does, however, cite the more intemperate hopes, at least before the fact, of some other militants; see his *French Communism,* p. 163n.

23. AN F7 13023, 31 Mar. 1920; F7 12995, 29 Mar. 1920.

24. AN F7 12995, 23 Feb. 1920; ADHV 10 M 186, 29 Aug. 1920. The issue of local organization in the CGT and CGTU is further discussed here in chs. 9–10.

25. AN F7 12995, 11 Apr. 1920.

26. ADHV 10 M 146, telegrams, 1–15 May 1920.

27. *Pop. C.,* 17 May 1920; ADHV 10 M 99, 18 May 1920; 10 M 146, 3 June 1920.

28. ADHV 10 M 99, 8 May 1920.

29. Kriegel, *Aux origines,* 1:483–85. Even the miners' national secretary, Casimir Bartuel, hesitated to launch his federation into the strike. AN F7 13577, 2–3 May 1920.

30. Frachon, *Pour la CGT,* p. 89. Frachon cites Monatte's article in *VO,* 23 July 1919, as an example of his condemnation of the strategy. The passage, however, refers to the strikes of May–June 1919 and concerns strategic problems apart from the *vagues d'assaut.* In the 14 May 1920 issue of *VO,* Monatte said that the tactic was all right in itself but badly applied, in that it was not sufficiently explained to "the troops" who hesitated to comply.

31. The number of workers in each industry who participated in the strike may be charted in ADHV 10 M 99, daily reports and telegrams, 8–27 May 1920.

32. ADHV 10 M 135, reports of May to Nov. 1919 and 7–14 Apr. 1920; 10 M 146, 23 May 1920; *C. Rouge,* 4 Dec. 1920. The union's contribution to the strike fund was more than half of the total (60,730 francs) collected.

33. ADHV 10 M 99, 21–25 May 1920; Bourse, Limoges, 24 May 1920. On Bonnet's vote at the CGT National Committee (in violation of his mandate from Limoges): AN F7 13577, 20 May 1920.

34. ADHV 1 M 168, report on Louis Bert, 8 Apr. 1919. Bert's activities are also reported in Bourse, Limoges, 22 Apr. and 8 Aug. 1919; ADHV 10 M 194,

18 July, 5–9 Sept., 3 Oct., and 15 Dec. 1919; and the biographical sketch in Maitron, *Dictionnaire biographique,* 19:51–52. There is also personal data on Rivet in ADHV 1 M 168, individual report, 24 June 1920. Rivet had been active in the strikes of 1919 but was less visible in those of 1920. He was nominated for the Bourse position by construction workers' secretary Pierre Rossignol, who had first been selected, and who was expected to act as Rivet's mentor in the new post.

35. AN F7 12995, 1 Apr. and 10 May 1920; ADL 92 M 257, 16–26 Mar. and 23–25 May 1920; 92 M 258, 7–23 May 1920; 92 M 259, 24 May and 4 June 1920. The succession to Frécon is further discussed below. Chovet—and Bert—also quit the CP, along with renegade secretary L.-O. Frossard, in early 1923; see ch. 10.

36. *Peuple L.,* 6 Mar. 1920 (minutes of railroad workers' meeting, with speeches by Chovet and by miners' secretary Pascal Duranton); AN F7 12995, 1 Apr. and 10 May 1920; ADL 92 M 258–59, 6–9 May 1920; 92 M 262, 14 May 1920.

37. ADL Houillères, carton 2480, notes, 3 June 1920. The report noted 19,351 striking miners, of the basin's total of 25,150 miners cited in similar notes for 24 Sept. 1921. On the railroad workers: ADL 92 M 257, 27–28 May and 15 June 1920.

38. ADL 92 M 257, 23–24 May 1920; 92 M 262, 20–24 May and 26 July 1920. The question of sanctions and arrests is further discussed below.

39. ADL 93 M 3, 16 Jan. to 17 Feb. 1920; 92 M 260, 6–28 Feb. 1920; *R. Tiss.,* Jan. to June 1920.

40. AN F7 12995, 23 Feb. and 22 Mar. 1920; *Peuple L.,* 27 Mar. 1920 (resolution by UD Loire, 21 Mar.). Frécon's vote at the CGT National Committee meeting of Dec. 1918 was approved by the UD Loire by a margin of forty-two to ten, with twenty-five abstentions.

41. AN F7 12995, 1–2 Apr. 1920; ADL 92 M 257–59, 4–11 May 1920; 19 M 39, 19–21 May 1920.

42. AN F7 12995, 2 Apr. and 10 May 1920; ADL 92 M 259, 5–10 May 1920.

43. ADL 92 M 259, 9–11 May 1920.

44. AN F7 13791, 28 June 1920 (quoted passage); ADL 92 M 262, 24 May to 26 July 1920; 92 M 257, 27 May to 15 June 1920. Frécon's reports were apparently not false: the railroad workers on the Nord and Est lines indeed resisted the strike. Kriegel, *Aux origines,* 1:481–83, 499.

45. ADL 92 M 257, 26–31 July, 27 Aug., and 4 Sept. 1920.

46. ADL 93 M 70, 18–20 June and 9 July 1920. The succession to Frécon is further discussed below.

47. AN F7 14608, reports of 16 Mar. (Loire) and 30 Mar. (Haute-Vienne) 1920, and ministerial circulars of 14 Apr. and 2 May 1920; extracts from *La Liberté,* 10 Feb. and 11 May 1920, and from *L'Intransigeant,* 10 Apr. 1920; text of the resolution of the Union Civique at Lyon, sent with report (Rhône) of 17 Jan. 1920. On the Loire, see also AN F7 12995, 9 Apr. 1920; and *Extraits des délibérations de la Chambre de Commerce de Saint-Etienne pendant l'année 1920* (Saint-Etienne, 1920), sessions of 31 Mar. and 14 May 1920, pp. 47, 89. A fuller

account of the Union Civique at Lyon is in Millevoye, "Grèves révolutionnaires," pp. 103–30. On the left's response to these organizations (questioning their legality or legitimacy), see *VO*, 27 Feb. 1920; *Peuple L.*, 1 May 1920; *Pop C.*, 19 July 1920; *Pop.* (Paris), 8 Oct. 1920; and *L'Hum.*, 22 Oct. 1920.

48. AN F7 14608, 16 Mar. (Loire) and 30 Mar. (Haute-Vienne) 1920. The Limoges Chamber of Commerce did, however, issue an antirevolutionary resolution: text in AN F7 13023, 4 May 1920.

49. Bourse, Saint-Etienne, 4 June 1920; ADL 92 M 258, 12 July 1920. The Parisian militants Monmousseau, Monatte, Loriot, and others were also arrested, and the government initiated, though never carried out, plans to dissolve the CGT as a whole. On these measures, see Kriegel, *Aux origines*, 1:461–75.

50. AN F7 12995, extract from *Action Française*, 25 May 1920 ("Le Bolchévisme dans l'administration").

51. ADHV 10 M 146, copy of resolution by PO railway company, 22 May 1920; report of 18 June 1920; list of *"cheminots révoqués"* in the Haute-Vienne; also ADL 92 M 258, 12 July 1920. On later demands for the "reintegration" of these dismissed workers: ADHV 10 M 147, 12 Feb. 1924; ADL 93 M 42, 23–24 May 1924.

52. AN F7 14608, 16 Mar. 1920; F7 12995, 1 Apr. 1920.

53. ADHV 10 M 195, 25 June 1920; 10 M 186, 13 July 1920; 10 M 146, 22–27 July 1920; 142 M, 18 Aug., 20 Sept., 16 Oct., and 27 Nov. 1920.

54. Synd. Chaussures, Limoges, 30 May 1920; Bourse, Limoges, 13 Aug. 1920; AN F7 13023, 13 Sept. 1920; *O. Céram,* Nov.–Dec. 1920. The reference to the "bastion of reformism"—and to its final collapse—is from *L'Hum.*, 6 July 1921.

55. ADHV 10 M 177, reports on trade unions in the Haute-Vienne, 1 Jan. 1920 and 1 Jan. 1921; also *O. Céram.*, June–July 1921; and Synd. Chaussures, Limoges, 28 Oct. 1921.

56. Figures from Labi, *Grande division des travailleurs,* pp. 248–49; a similar magnitude is cited in Robert, *Scission syndicale,* pp. 159–62. It is difficult to distinguish the effects of the 1920 strike failure from those of the 1921 recession, except for individual unions for which statistics were issued more than once a year. See discussion here in ch. 8 for the impact of the recession of 1921 on unionization and labor politics.

57. ADHV 10 M 186, 13 July 1920; 10 M 194, 5 June 1920; 10 M 135, 21 Sept. and 3–6 Oct. 1920. Bonnet remained union secretary until May 1921. *O. Céram.,* June–July 1921.

58. *Pop. C.,* 14 June 1920 ("Contre les calomniateurs"); ADHV 142 M, 19 June and 12 Sept. 1920. Note that Chauly was no left-winger within the party.

59. *Pop. C.,* 13 May 1920 ("L'ordre impossible"); 2 July 1920 ("Syndicalisme et socialisme"); and 8 Sept. 1920 (excerpt from *Pop.* [Paris], 29 Aug., by Paul Faure). The question of adhesion to the Third International is discussed here in ch. 7.

60. AN F7 13023, 1 June 1920.

61. Bourse, Limoges, 10 July 1920; ADHV 10 M 186, 20 June to 26 Nov. 1920; 142 M, 12 Sept. 1920; and *VO,* 17 Sept. 1920. A similar idea of schism

was raised by the construction workers' union at Marseille, as reported (and condemned) by P. Monatte [Lémont] in *VO,* 3 Sept. 1920.

62. L. Bert in *C. Rouge,* 18 Oct. and 13 Nov. 1920. The relations between communism and revolutionary syndicalism are discussed here in ch. 7, for 1919–21, and in chs. 9–10 for the period after 1921.

63. ADL 93 M 50, 26–29 June 1920; 93 M 26 and 93 M 30, 11–13 Dec. 1920; *Peuple L.,* 18 Sept. 1920.

64. ADL 19 M 39, 28 May, 4 June, 14 Sept., 22 Oct., and 24 Dec. 1920. The issues of anarchism and trade unionism are further discussed here in ch. 7.

65. ADL 92 M 257, 8 June and 26 July 1920.

66. ADL 92 M 257, 9 Nov. 1920. The vote was forty-five to five in favor of "class collaboration" and Chovet.

67. AN F7 12995, 20 Oct. and 16 Nov. 1920; ADL 93 M 10, 5 Nov. 1920.

68. On Lorduron's election to the UD: ADL 93 M 70, 9–26 July 1920. On his earlier activities: 93 M 82, Apr. 1917, Jan.–Mar. 1918, Apr. 1919, and May–June 1920. His relations with the SFIO and the CP are further discussed here in chs. 7 and 9–10.

69. ADL 93 M 70, 10 June 1920; 19 M 39, 18 June and 6 Aug. 1920; 93 M 82, 17 July 1920. A native of Terrenoire, Arnaud headed the metalworkers' union at Mâcon (Saône-et-Loire) during World War I and was active in the antiwar movement. 93 M 59, 27 Apr. 1921.

70. ADL 93 M 70, 26 July 1920; 92 M 259, 9 Aug. 1920; 93 M 10, 5 Nov. 1920; AN F7 12995, 16 Nov. 1920.

71. ADHV 142 M, 12–15 Sept. 1920; *VO,* 17 Sept. 1920; and AN F7 13577, 9 Oct. 1920.

72. AN F7 12995, 6–23 Aug. 1920; ADL 93 M 10, 4 Sept. 1920; also *VO,* 10–17 Sept. 1920. Lorduron himself favored participation in the conference, but his union voted it down. 93 M 82, 11 Sept. 1920.

73. ADL 93 M 70, 23 Sept. 1920; M 540, 13 Jan. 1921. These reports list the votes of each union at the two congresses.

74. CGT, XXIe Congrès National Corporatif, tenu à Orléans, du 27 septembre au 2 octobre 1920, *Compte-rendu des travaux* (Villeneuve-Saint-Georges, n.d.), pp. 428–86, results of votes on the Rapport Moral. Votes also tabulated in Labi, *Grande division des travailleurs,* pp. 274–77.

75. Monatte [Lémont] in *VO,* 21 May 1920. Monatte's "Communist-syndicalist" faction is further discussed here in chs. 7 and 9–10.

Chapter 7. Misalliance: Syndicalists and Communists in 1920–21

1. Kriegel, *Aux origines;* Wohl, *French Communism;* Labi, *Grande division des travailleurs;* Charles, "Scission syndicale," pp. 59–74; Charles, "Temps des scissions," pp. 1–45; and Robert, *Scission syndicale,* esp. pp. 182–87.

2. See Sinanoglou, "Frenchmen and the Russian Revolution," pp. 566–84; Mayer, *Wilson vs. Lenin;* and Amdur, " 'American Peace.' "

3. ADL 10 M 180, 10 Dec. 1918. See also the discussion of "defeatism" in ch. 4 of this study.

4. AN F7 12994, 1–24 Mar. 1919.

5. L. Bert [Trebs] in *Pop. C.,* 18 Feb. 1919 ("Encore le Bolchévisme"). Compare the interchange between A. Thomas and L. Blum in *L'Hum.,* 9–15 Nov. 1918, cited here in ch. 5, n. 111.

6. On Bert: ADHV 1 M 167, 22 Feb. 1919; 10 M 187, 11 Apr. 1922; *Prol. C.,* 4 Nov. 1923. On Andrieu: ADL 93 M 13, 30 Jan. and 2 Feb. 1917, and 4 Mar. 1923; 93 M 70, 26 July 1920; AN F7 12996, 14 Sept. 1923 and 24 Aug. 1925. On Andrieu's role in the CGTSR, see Samuel Jospin, "La C.G.T.S.R.: A travers son journal 'Le Combat Syndicaliste' (1926–1937)" (Mémoire de maîtrise, Paris I, 1974), p. 8; or the biographical sketch in Maitron, *Dictionnaire biographique,* 17:157–58. The politics of Bert (who left Limoges for Paris in 1922) are further discussed here in ch. 10, as is the early history of the CGTSR. Andrieu left the Loire for Lyon in late 1920 but still maintained occasional contacts with former associates in Firminy and Saint-Etienne.

7. André Roulot [Lorulot], *Le Soviet* (1919), in AN F7 12994, with the report of 6 Mar. 1919.

8. Lorulot in *L'Idée Libre* (Nov. 1918), quoted in Maitron, *Mouvement anarchiste,* 2:42; see generally pp. 41–55 on the anarchists and the Russian Revolution. Lorulot left Saint-Etienne to live in Paris as of Sept. 1919. ADL 19 M 39, 4 Sept. 1919.

9. See ch. 4 of this study.

10. On the question of schism, see Péricat's articles in *L'Internationale,* Feb. to Sept. 1919, and *VO,* 1 Oct. 1920; see also the assessment by Pierre Monatte in *Trois scissions syndicales* (Paris, 1958), pp. 151–52. Monatte's section on "La scission syndicale de 1921" is also reprinted in his *Lutte syndicale,* pp. 175–205. On the Marseille group (which grew to some 500 members but then folded in Apr. 1922), see also Kriegel, *Aux origines,* 2:747–48; and Maitron, *Mouvement anarchiste,* 2:59n. Benoît Frachon, the later CGTU leader from the Loire, was also briefly involved in this group. Frachon, *Pour la CGT,* p. 87.

11. Wohl, *French Communism,* p. 142.

12. On the "ultra-left," compare Kriegel, *Aux origines,* 1:282–307. Kriegel explains the multiplicity of postwar leftist currents as a succession from the "ultra-left" (anarcho-communism) to the "extreme left" (revolutionary syndicalism), and finally, after the failure of each, to Bolshevism (1:275–353). This image, however, understates the durable support, especially in certain localities, for any "earlier" form. It may be true that a succession of alternatives dominated the left on a national level, but local movements showed far greater continuity, even if they failed to win lasting national support.

13. ADHV 1 M 167, 22 Feb., 8 Mar., and 3–12 May 1919; 1 M 168, 28 May 1919, and 3 Jan. and 11 Feb. 1921.

14. ADL 19 M 39, 28 Apr. 1919. On Moulin's later role in the CP: M 541, 15 Feb. and 21 Oct. 1924; see also chs. 10–11 of this study.

15. ADL 19 M 39, 26 May and 7–19 July 1919; 10 M 183, 19 July, 1 Aug.,

and 27 Oct. 1919; 10 M 184, 22 Dec. 1919. On the Committee for the Third International, see also Wohl, *French Communism*, pp. 134, 158–61. The composition of the committee was at first heavily anarchist but soon became "overwhelmingly Socialist," according to a government estimate; by late 1920, 80 percent of the group were SFIO members and 20 percent were revolutionary syndicalists. AN F7 13090, 24 Aug. 1920.

16. On the Haute-Vienne: ADHV 1 M 167, 2 Aug. 1919; 10 M 146, 31 Mar. 1920; 1 M 168, 30 June 1920. On the Loire: ADL 3 M 66, 27 Dec. 1919 and 3 Jan. 1920; 10 M 184, 19–26 Jan., 4–30 June, and 19 Oct. 1920.

17. ADL 19 M 39, 8–12 Aug. and 21 Nov. 1919; and 31 Mar., 28 May and 4 June 1920.

18. ADHV 1 M 167, 12 May 1919; 142 M, 19 June 1920. The question of generational conflict is further discussed here in ch. 11.

19. ADL 92 M 251, 11 Mar. 1919.

20. ADL 10 M 184, 7 Mar. 1920; *Peuple L.,* 13 Mar. 1920 ("Congrès de Strasbourg," by Ferdinand Faure, and "Au travail maintenant," by Paul Faure). On the origins of the CP in the Haute-Vienne, see also Sabourdy, "Conditions de la scission," pp. 188–208; and Lenoble et al., *La Gauche au pouvoir*, pp. 85–86, 92–93. On the Congress of Strasbourg, see Kriegel, *Aux origines,* 1:335, 340–47; and Wohl, *French Communism,* pp. 152–57.

21. *Pop. C.,* 29 Oct. 1920 ("Tous ensemble et sans conditions!" by S. Valière); also Editorials, 27–31 Dec. 1920. For a survey of views on the merits of party schism, see Charles, "Temps des scissions," pp. 2–4. On the Twenty-One Conditions (issued by the Comintern in July–Aug. 1920 and published in *L'Hum.* on 8 Oct. 1920), see Kriegel, *Aux origines,* 2:649–51, and Wohl, *French Communism,* pp. 182–95 passim.

22. ADHV 1 M 168, 23 Dec. 1920; *Pop. C.,* 19 Oct. 1920 ("Conditions de l'adhésion," by R. Barret).

23. *Pop. C.,* 21 Oct. 1920 (text of Pressemane's speech at Limoges, 14 Oct.); ADHV 142 M, 15 Oct. 1920, with account of discussion after Pressemane's speech.

24. See ch. 10 of this study.

25. Compare Cousteix, "Doctrines anarchistes," pp. 26–34.

26. ADL 10 M 184, 8–11 Feb. and 7 Mar. 1920; *Peuple L.,* 13 Mar. 1920 ("Congrès de Strasbourg," by F. Faure); also 13 Feb. and 24 Apr. 1920 (reports on local congresses at Roanne and Saint-Etienne).

27. *Peuple L.,* 14 Aug. 1920 ("Conséquences de l'adhésion," by D. Renoult). On the views of Cachin, Frossard, and Renoult, see also Wohl, *French Communism,* pp. 153, 174–90. Renoult's arguments weaken the force of his claim (dated a few weeks later) that "[the Russian] cause is *ours.*" Renoult in *L'Hum.,* 30 Sept. 1920, quoted in Wohl, p. 190.

28. On Lafont, who was traveling in Russia on his own (not as part of Cachin's and Frossard's delegation): *Peuple L.,* 7 Aug. 1920; ADL M 556, 11 Jan. 1921. The Comintern later recommended that Lafont's expulsion be canceled, in acknowledgment of his "disciplined" behavior as a Communist since Tours. *Peuple L.,* 7 Aug. 1921.

29. ADL 10 M 184, 19 Nov. and 3 Dec. 1920; M 556, 11 Jan. 1921; *Peuple L.,* 6 Nov. 1920 to 9 Jan. 1921 (reports on preliminary votes of SFIO sections). Pétrus Faure, who quit the party in 1929, expressed a similar motive for having joined it, in *Un témoin raconte,* p. 43.

30. See ch. 10 of this study.

31. ADHV 1 M 167, 22 Jan. 1921; Decouty, "Opinion politique," pp. 370–72. Leading Communist politicians in the department included Joseph Lasvergnas, mayor of Saint-Junien, and Jules Fraisseix, *conseiller général* (and later deputy) for the canton of Eymoutiers.

32. Lenoble et al., *La Gauche au pouvoir,* pp. 93, 109; Cousteix, "Mouvement ouvrier limousin," pp. 84–87; Perrier, "Esquisse," p. 387.

33. L. Bert in *VO,* 24 Sept. 1920; *C. Rouge,* 8 Jan. 1921; ADHV 1 M 168, 10 Apr. 1921.

34. *Pop. C.,* 15 Jan. 1921 ("Nos deux actions," by A. Chauly).

35. The social composition of the two parties is further discussed here in ch. 11; see also Robert, "Origines du P.C.F.," pp. 32–34; Robert, ed., "Le Parti Communiste en 1923: Rapport du Secrétariat du Parti Français au Comité Exécutif Elargi de l'I.C. (Mai–Juin 1923)," *Cahiers IMT,* n.s., no. 6 (1974), p. 222; and Wohl, *French Communism,* pp. 216–18, 428–32.

36. ADHV 1 M 168, 30 Nov. 1921.

37. See ch. 10 of this study.

38. *Peuple L.,* 16 Jan. and 6 Mar. 1921; ADL M 541, dossier on "SFIO," reports of 6 Oct. and 11 Dec. 1922. The Briandist group (Independent Socialists) also debated rejoining the SFIO but chose instead to join the PSF. M 541, dossier on "Bloc Républicain et Socialiste," reports of 18 Sept. to 6 Nov. 1922.

39. AN F7 13090, 25 Apr. 1921; *Peuple L.,* 15 May 1921.

40. ADL M 556, dossier on "PCF," reports of 7–16 Jan. 1922. The social composition of the new party, in the Loire as in the Haute-Vienne, is further discussed here in ch. 11.

41. The Saint-Etienne section had an estimated 469 members in Sept. 1921 and 480 in Jan. 1922; the Limoges section had some 600 members in Dec. 1921 but lost more than half by the end of 1922, reportedly as part of a nationwide party crisis that probably also touched Saint-Etienne. ADL M 556, dossier on "PCF," reports of 2 Sept. 1921 and 7 Jan. 1922; ADHV 1 M 168, 21 Dec. 1921 and 9 Oct. 1922. On teachers and other public employees in the Saint-Etienne party: ADL M 556, dossier on "PCF," report of 11 Jan. 1923; AN F7 13110, 4 Mar. 1927.

42. See chs. 10–11.

43. Trotsky in *VO,* 26 Nov. 1920; P. Monatte in *VO,* 28 Jan. and 19 Aug. 1921; R. Louzon in *VO,* 8 July 1921; declaration by CSR Central Committee in *L'Hum.,* 21 May 1921.

44. *VO,* 10 Sept. 1919 (A. Rosmer), 1 Oct. 1920 (A. Dunois), 10 Dec. 1920 and 19 Aug. 1921 (Monatte), 2 Dec. 1921 (Monatte and G. Monmousseau), and 17–24 Mar. 1922 (Monmousseau and M. Chambelland). Compare Trotsky's view, in a letter to Monatte (13 July 1921), reprinted in *Archives de Monatte,* ed. Chambelland and Maitron, pp. 296–97: "Is it possible that in 1921 we are to re-

turn to the positions of 1906 and to 'reconstruct' the syndicalism of prewar days? (. . .) That position is amorphous; it is conservative; it risks becoming reactionary. (. . .) Prewar revolutionary syndicalism was the embryo of the Communist Party. To return to the embryo would be a giant step backward. In contrast, the active participation in a Communist Party would mean the continuation and development of the best traditions of French syndicalism."

45. "Circulaire de lancement de 'La Vie Ouvrière,' " reprinted in Monatte, *Lutte syndicale,* pp. 151–60; *VO,* 30 Apr. 1919 (Monatte), 10 Sept. 1919 (Rosmer), 15 Oct. 1919 (Louzon), 5 Mar. 1920 (M. Leblanc), and 30 Apr. 1920 (G. Verdier). Tom Mann was an English syndicalist who sympathized with Bolshevism and served as delegate to the first Profintern congress. His slogan appeared in the first postwar issue of *VO,* 30 Apr. 1919.

46. Compare the interpretations of Wohl, in *French Communism,* pp. 134–36, and Young, *"Vie Ouvrière,"* pp. 92–99.

47. "Circulaire de lancement," in Monatte, *Lutte syndicale,* p. 159. Note that Wohl seems to base his interpretation on a mistranslation of this passage, which reverses its meaning. See his *French Communism,* p. 135.

48. *VO,* 30 Apr. 1919 (Monatte), 10 Sept. 1919 (Rosmer), 20 Aug. 1920 (Monatte), and 1 Oct. 1920 (Dunois); *L'Hum.,* 3 Apr. 1921 (Montmayeur, of UD Isère); also Monmousseau, *Syndicalisme devant la révolution.*

49. *VO,* 1 Oct. 1920 (A. Dunois citing V. Griffuelhes); similar statement by Monatte in *VO,* 21 Dec. 1921. Compare the argument by Charles in "Temps des scissions," p. 8. The issues of adhesion to Moscow are further discussed here in chs. 9–10.

50. On the Orléans congress, see Wohl, *French Communism,* pp. 238–39, and Labi, *Grande division des travailleurs,* pp. 162, 170–76 passim. The issue of adhesion to the Profintern was not put to a vote until the CGT congress at Lille in July 1921.

51. Quoted passage in *Pop. C.,* 2 July 1920 ("Syndicalisme et socialisme," by Dr. L. Martin-Bihourd); similar statements by Paul Faure in *Pop. C.,* 13 May 1920 ("L'ordre impossible"), and in *Peuple L.,* 8 May 1920 ("Aux côtés de la classe ouvrière"). On the 1919 elections, see ch. 5 of this study.

52. AN F7 13023, 20 Oct. 1920. The UD later voted adhesion to the International, on the eve of the Lille congress, by a margin of forty-eight to five. F7 13023, 7–10 July 1921.

53. ADHV 142 M, tract by the Committee for the Third International, with report of 11 Sept. 1920; also AN F7 13023, 3–18 Jan. 1921.

54. *C. Rouge,* 30 Oct. 1920.

55. *C. Rouge,* 18 Oct. 1920 (Editorial; and "La IIIᵉ Internationale Syndicale," by L. Bert).

56. *C. Rouge,* 13 Nov. 1920.

57. *C. Rouge,* 29 Jan. 1921 (final issue). The new Communist newspaper for the region was *Le Prolétaire du Centre* (published at Périgueux); it was succeeded in turn by *Le Travailleur du Centre-Ouest* (published at Limoges) in Mar. 1924.

58. *C. Rouge,* 11 Dec. 1920 ("Le syndicalisme révolutionnaire et l'Internationale Syndicale de Moscou," by J. Accary, of CSR Rhône). The article's use of

the phrase *"il faut choisir"* echoed that of L. Bert in Feb. 1919 and of Thomas and Blum in Nov. 1918; see n. 5 above.

59. *C. Rouge,* 20 Nov. 1920 (Editorial).

60. ADL 93 M 70, 6–23 Aug. and 20 Sept. 1920; 92 M 258, 6 Sept. 1920; AN F7 12995, 1 Feb. and 6 June 1921.

61. ADL 93 M 97, 7 Oct. 1920. On the teachers' unionists, compare the interchange between Péricat and Mayoux at the minoritarian congress at Saint-Etienne in May 1918, cited here in ch. 4. The sometimes controversial role of teachers in the later CP is discussed in ch. 11.

62. ADL M 540, 23 May and 4 July 1921.

63. *Peuple L.,* 3 July 1920 (Communication from SFIO Firminy); ADL 10 M 184, 14 May, 21–22 June, and 13 Sept. 1920; 92 M 258, 18 Nov. 1920. On the 1919 elections, see ch. 5.

64. ADL 19 M 39, 1 Oct. 1920; AN F7 12995, 30 Oct. 1920. On Cachin, whom Wohl describes as a party centrist "out of political agility," not principle, see Wohl, *French Communism,* pp. 174–75.

65. Bourse, Saint-Etienne, 16 Apr. 1920; ADL 10 M 184, 1 May and 21–22 June 1920; 92 M 258, 19 Aug. 1920; AN F7 12995, 16–27 Aug. 1920. For attempts at collaboration on the national level, see F7 13577, 8 Oct. to 9 Nov. 1920.

66. ADL 93 M 70, 20 June 1920; 19 M 39, 21 June 1920; 10 M 184, 7 Aug. and 13 Sept. 1920. On the UD elections, see also ch. 6.

67. Bourse, Saint-Etienne, 3 Dec. 1920 and 15 Apr. 1921; AN F7 12995, 7 Dec. 1920 and 28–30 Apr. 1921. Torcieux resigned apparently for health reasons and may have supported Arnaud's candidacy. Arnaud later joined the CP, but he seems not to have been in the SFIO before the schism. His later political evolution is discussed in ch. 9.

68. ADL 19 M 39, 28 June 1919 and 14 Sept. 1920.

69. ADL 19 M 39, 28 May, 4 June, 14 Sept., 22–29 Oct., and 13 Nov. 1920. On the tactic of factory seizures, see ch. 8; this idea was especially current during the recession of 1921.

70. AN F7 12994, 5 Mar. 1919; ADL 19 M 39, 12 Aug. 1919. Flageollet died, after an illness, in late 1921: ADL M 539, dossier on "Anarchistes et Libertaires," report of 23 Oct. 1921.

71. ADL 19 M 39, 11 June and 6–27 Aug. 1920.

72. ADL 93 M 59, 18 Jan. and 14–22 Feb. 1920; 19 M 39, 19–23 Feb. 1920; 92 M 259, 27 Feb. and 25 July 1920; 93 M 70, 10–21 June 1920.

73. ADL 93 M 70, 26 July 1920; 92 M 259, 25 July and 9 Aug. 1920; 93 M 10, 28 Aug. and 5 Nov. 1920; AN F7 12995, 20 Oct., 16 Nov., and 20 Dec. 1920. See also ch. 6 on Lorduron's early leadership of the UD.

74. On the CSRs generally, see Kriegel, *Aux origines,* 1:322–23, 2:750–53; and Wohl, *French Communism,* pp. 140, 238–42. The CSRs were descended from an earlier Comité des Syndicats Minoritaires formed after the Lyon congress in 1919.

75. ADL 10 M 184, 7–19 Oct. and 8–28 Nov. 1920; see also *L'Hum.,* 8 June 1921 (Monatte's speech to CSR Centre-Est).

76. ADHV 1 M 168, 3–19 Jan. 1921.

77. ADL 10 M 184, 19 Oct. and 19–22 Nov. 1920; AN F7 12995, 30 Oct. 1920. Lorduron and Torcieux soon did join the CSR: F7 12995, 16 Jan. and 2 Feb. 1921.

78. ADL 19 M 39, 31 Dec. 1920; M 539, dossier on "CSR," report of 16 Jan. 1921; AN F7 12995, 16 June 1921.

79. AN F7 12995, 10–22 Nov. 1920; ADL M 539, dossier on "CSR," report of 6 June 1921.

80. ADL M 539, dossier on "CSR," report of 23 Mar. 1921; 93 M 97, 2 Mar. 1921; 93 M 10, 5 Mar., 1 July, and 21 Oct. 1921.

81. Besnard succeeded Monatte as CSR secretary in May 1921; his role is further discussed below.

82. *Peuple L.,* 14 Aug. 1921 ("Démocratie et dictature," by C.-E. Labrousse).

83. ADL M 539, dossier on "Anarchistes et Libertaires," report of 28 Oct. 1921; see also Maitron, *Mouvement anarchiste,* 2:49–54.

84. *Peuple L.,* 30 Jan. 1921 (declaration by CSR Saint-Etienne).

85. *Prol. C.,* 13 Nov. 1921; ADL M 556, dossier on "PCF," reports of 20 Jan. and 3 Feb. 1922; see also Jean Charles, ed., "L'intervention du P.C.F. dans les luttes ouvrières (1921)," *Cahiers IMT,* n.s., nos. 8–9 (1974), pp. 280–308. The PCF's union strategy, elaborated at the party congress at Marseille in Dec. 1921, is further discussed here in ch. 10.

86. ADL M 539, dossier on "Anarchistes et Libertaires," report of 2 Dec. 1921. On their subsequent debates: M 539, 13 Jan. and 7 Feb. 1922.

87. As argued by Lorduron and local Communist-syndicalists: AN F7 12995, 18 Jan. 1921; ADL 93 M 59, 23 Feb., 12 Mar., and 28 May 1921; M 540, dossier on "CGT/CGTU," report of 15 June 1922. On the prewar anarchists, see ch. 2.

88. Monatte, *Trois scissions,* p. 159, or his *Lutte syndicale,* p. 192.

89. AN F7 12995, 12–17 Oct. and 8 Nov. 1920, and 18 Jan. 1921; ADL 10 M 184, 8 Nov. 1920; 19 M 39, 13–19 Nov. and 24 Dec. 1920; M 539, dossier on "CSR," reports of 16 Jan. and 23 Mar. 1921; also VO, 17 June 1921.

90. ADL 19 M 39, 19 Nov. and 24–31 Dec. 1920; M 539, dossier on "Anarchistes et Libertaires," reports of 21 June and 13 Aug. 1921, and 19 Oct. and 1 Dec. 1922.

91. ADL 93 M 70, 20 Dec. 1920. An approximate translation: "One must appear revolutionary without being so, while being so nonetheless."

92. See ch. 4 of this study concerning May 1918; the parallel is also implied in H. Lorduron's recollections of the May 1918 congress, in VO, 24 Sept. 1920 and 23 Dec. 1921.

93. Monatte's reasons for not joining the party are in VO, 28 Jan. 1921; similar arguments by Aigueperse of Saint-Etienne are in VO, 11 Jan. 1921. Monatte's subsequent exclusion from the party (late 1924) is sketched here in ch. 10.

94. ADL 93 M 59, 12 Mar. and 28 May 1921. A similar conflict occurred the next year over the anarchists' group of Jeunesses Syndicalistes, which Arnaud expelled from the Bourse: Bourse, Saint-Etienne, 14 Apr. 1922; ADL M 539, dossier on "Anarchistes et Libertaires," reports of 8 Mar., 13–27 Apr., 19 Aug., 20

Sept., and 12–19 Oct. 1922; M 540, dossier on "CGT/CGTU," report of 15 June 1922.

95. ADL M 539, dossier on "CSR," report of 9 Oct. 1921; compare Lorduron's earlier views in AN F7 12995, 23 Mar. 1921; and Lorduron at CSR congress, in *VO*, 21 Oct. 1921. The circumstances of the schism and the events following the Lille congress are discussed here in ch. 9.

96. AN F7 13023, 21 Oct. 1920.

97. *C. Rouge*, 20 Nov. 1920 ("Leur audace et leur impuissance," by L. Bert).

98. *Prol. C.*, 9 Oct. 1921 ("La fin du neutralisme syndical," by A. Dunois).

99. Ibid. On Dunois (a leftist who quit the party leadership in 1924 when fellow leftist Boris Souvarine was expelled), see also *Prol. C.*, 15 Jan. 1922, and Wohl, *French Communism*, pp. 257, 261, 393–94, 427. The "united front" strategy is further discussed here in ch. 10.

100. *VO*, 10 Sept. 1920 ("Dehors ou dedans? Moscou et la scission dans les syndicats," by V. I. Lenin); reprinted from *L'Internationale Communiste* (May 1920) as a response to Paul Faure's articles in *Pop.* (Paris), 29 Aug. and 2 Sept. 1920. Faure's arguments were also reprinted in *Pop. C.*, 8 Sept. 1920. Despite Lenin's supposed opposition to a trade-union schism, he still condemned the reformist Amsterdam International and set up the rival Profintern, whose existence triggered if it did not actually cause the union split. See Gras, *Rosmer*, p. 221; and Wayne Westergard-Thorpe, "Syndicalist Internationalism and Moscow, 1919–1922: The Breach," *Canadian Journal of History* 14 (1979): 222, 227.

101. V. I. Lenin, *"Left-Wing" Communism: An Infantile Disorder* (New York, 1940); also B. Souvarine [Varine] and V. Méric in *L'Hum.*, 18–20 Jan. 1921. Lenin's work, first published in Apr. 1920, was issued in France that same year; see Danielle Tartakowsky, "Les conditions de la pénétration du Marxisme en France," *Cahiers IMT*, o.s., no. 28 (1972), p. 35.

102. Rosmer, cited in Charles, "Scission syndicale," p. 66; similar citations in Charles, "Temps des scissions," p. 4; and Gras, *Rosmer*, pp. 217–18. Rosmer was a left-wing Communist with views of syndicalism similar to Monatte's, but he was not a union member. He served as French delegate to the Comintern in 1921, but he quit the party, with Monatte, in 1924.

103. Rosmer in 1915, cited in Gras, *Rosmer*, p. 145.

104. Monatte in *L'Hum.*, 17 Apr. 1922; cited in Charles, "Temps des scissions," p. 4.

105. Monatte in *VO*, 3 Sept. and 29 Oct. 1920, and 17 June and 5–16 Sept. 1921; compare opposing views in *VO*, 1 Oct. 1920, and 18 Nov. to 16 Dec. 1921. See also Monatte, *Trois scissions*, pp. 138, 152–54, 165–68, or his *Lutte syndicale*, pp. 175, 186–87, 197–99. The Congress of Paris (which consummated the schism) is discussed here in ch. 9.

106. *VO*, 17 Sept. 1920, 4 Mar. and 16 Sept. 1921; *L'Hum.*, 8 July 1921; AN F7 13023, 8 July 1921; *Prol. C.*, 18 Sept. 1921. On Bert and Saint-Junien, see ch. 6.

107. AN F7 12995, 23 Mar. 1921; *VO*, 16 Sept. 1921; see also ch. 4 on the events of May 1918 and ch. 6 on the opposition to schism in late 1920.

108. See ch. 4 on the events of May 1918.

109. AN F7 12995, 12 Oct. 1920; ADL 93 M 10, 12–18 Oct. 1920.

110. AN F7 12995, 18 Jan., 23 Mar., 6 June, and 13 Oct. 1921; F7 13577, 19 Mar. 1921; ADL M 539, dossier on "CSR," reports of 1–9 May 1921; M 539, dossier on "Anarchistes et Libertaires," report of 28 Oct. 1921; *Peuple L.,* 6 June 1921 (congress of CSR Centre-Est) and 23 Oct. 1921 (declaration by CSR Saint-Etienne).

111. Monatte, *Trois scissions,* pp. 152–53, or his *Lutte syndicale,* p. 187. Similar views of Besnard are expressed by "P.L." [Lémont/Monatte?] in *VO,* 2 Mar. 1923, and by Théo Argence (syndicalist from the Isère) as cited in Maitron, *Mouvement anarchiste,* 2:60.

112. The CGTSR is discussed here in chs. 10–11. There is also a biographical sketch of Besnard in Maitron, *Dictionnaire biographique,* 19:110–11.

113. Text of "Pacte" (first published in *Bataille Syndicaliste,* 15 June 1922), reprinted in *Archives de Monatte,* ed. Chambelland and Maitron, pp. 277–78; see also Maitron, *Mouvement anarchiste,* 2:59, 62–65, and Charles, "Scission syndicale," pp. 68–69.

114. ADL 10 M 184, 7 Oct. 1920; AN F7 12995, 22 Nov. 1920.

115. Monatte [Lémont] at Orléans congress, in *VO,* 1 Oct. 1920; Monatte at Lille congress in *L'Hum.,* 31 July 1921; also Monatte, Foreword (June 1921) to his "Reflections on the Future of French Trade-Unionism" (1917), reprinted in his *Left-Wing Trade-Unionism in France* (London, 1922). The 1917 document (without the Foreword) is also in Monatte, *Lutte syndicale,* pp. 133–50.

116. Monatte, Foreword, in *Left-Wing Trade-Unionism;* compare Théo Argence and Auguste Herclet, "Workers' Control and Workshop Committees," in the same volume, pp. 75–127; Herclet in *VO,* 10 Sept. 1920, and 14 Jan. and 11 Mar. 1921; Monmousseau in *VO,* 31 Dec. 1920; Herclet in *L'Hum.,* 11–17 Feb. 1921; and Besnard in *L'Hum.,* 8–17 July 1921. The issues of "workers' control" and "workshop committees" are further discussed here in chs. 8 and 10.

117. Monatte, "Reflections," in *Left-Wing Trade-Unionism,* pp. 25–28, or in his *Lutte syndicale,* pp. 133–35.

Chapter 8: Unionism in Crisis

1. A characteristic view is that of Yves Trotignon in *La France au XXe siècle* (Paris, 1968), p. 107: he describes the event as "a small worldwide crisis of over-production" that had "little impact in France." For other brief summaries see Jacques Néré, *La crise de 1929* (Paris, 1973), pp. 15–23; Sauvy, *Histoire économique,* 1:218, 261, 334–35, 360–61; and (more from the British and American perspectives) Derek H. Aldcroft, *From Versailles to Wall Street, 1919–1929* (Berkeley, 1977), pp. 67–77. Fuller descriptions are in works from the period: Roger Picard, *La crise économique et la baisse des salaires* (Paris, 1921); and S. Arwas, *La crise économique de 1920 en France* (Paris, 1923).

On labor politics, there is little discussion of the impact of the crisis in the previously cited works by Wohl, Kriegel, Labi, Charles, Robert, Collinet, or Fine. Charles S. Maier does link the economic crisis to the postwar decline in proletarian militancy, but with little reference to the details of French labor politics, in *Re-*

casting Bourgeois Europe, pp. 148–50, 158. The impact of the Great Depression has been further studied, but with little reference to the earlier crisis; see Fauvel-Rouif, ed., *Mouvements ouvriers.*

2. Compare Kriegel, *Croissance de la C.G.T.,* pp. 165–77; the postwar recruitment is discussed here in ch. 5.

3. AN F7 13973, monthly reports, Apr.–May 1921; Picard, *Crise économique,* pp. 1–22; Sauvy, *Histoire économique,* 1:334–35.

4. Compare Trotignon, *La France,* p. 107; Sauvy, *Histoire économique,* 1:261–62; Néré, *Crise de 1929,* pp. 63–68, 74; also Paul Louis in *L'Hum.,* 15 Jan. 1921, and in *Pop. C.,* 26 Jan. 1921; and R. Picard in *R. Tiss.,* May 1921.

5. AN F7 12967, monthly report, Aug. 1920; F7 13973, monthly reports, Dec. 1920 and Apr. 1921; ADHV 9 M 2, "La crise économique à Limoges," 1921; *L'Hum.,* 8 Mar. 1921 ("Chômage dans la chaussure"); annual reports for 1921, in *Bull. CCL,* no. 75 (1921), pp. 863–68, and in *Bull. CCSE,* 2ᵉ année (1922), pp. 339–45; *R. Tiss.,* Mar.–May 1921 and Dec. 1922. See also the discussion of postwar industry in chs. 1 and 5.

6. Report for 1921 in *Bull. CCSE,* 2ᵉ année (1922), pp. 339–45; ADL Houillères, carton 823, *Rapports de l'Ingénieur en Chef,* Houillères de Montrambert et de la Béraudière, 1921, pp. 1–2, 82; and *Trav. S-S* (CGT), July 1922.

7. Report for 1921 in *Bull. CCL,* no. 75 (1921), pp. 861–63; *O. Céram.,* Apr.–May 1921.

8. ADL Houillères, carton 823, *Rapports de l'Ingénieur en Chef,* 1921, pp. 69, 81; *R. Tiss.,* Dec. 1920, Feb. 1921, and May–June 1921; ADL 93 M 26, 19 July 1921; 93 M 3, 20–21 May 1921; Synd. Chaussures, Limoges, 29 Jan. and 9 Mar. 1921; ADHV 10 M 195, 28 May and 27 Aug. 1921. According to Sauvy, wage cuts averaged 10 percent for France overall. *Histoire économique,* 1:360.

9. For general patterns, see Jean Lhomme, "Le pouvoir d'achat de l'ouvrier français au cours d'un siècle: 1840–1940," *M. Social,* no. 63 (1968), pp. 55–58; and Sauvy, *Histoire économique,* 1:357–61. Sauvy also sees (pp. 361–62) a correlation between high real wages and unemployment: as prices fall, wages must also fall to avoid throwing workers out of work. Living costs in the Loire are reported in *Bull. CCSE,* 1ᵉ année (1921), pp. 448–52, 551, 655; 2ᵉ année (1922), pp. 166–67. These figures indicate that regional living costs declined by only 16 percent from Oct. 1920 to Oct. 1921, or by 19 percent to their low point in Apr. 1922. There are no overall figures on wages in the region to compare to the prices for this period.

10. As Sauvy points out, wages are typically less volatile than prices; thus, they rise (and decline) less quickly in times of economic change. *Histoire économique,* 1:334, 359. Labor's response to the wage cuts is further discussed below.

11. Waites, "Effects of First World War," pp. 6–8; Knowles and Robertson, "Wages of Skilled and Unskilled Workers," pp. 110–14; Sauvy, *Histoire économique,* 1:508.

12. Sauvy, *Histoire économique,* 1:226–27, 236–37; 3:32–33 ("La population," by André Armengaud); also Garraty, *Unemployment,* p. 149.

13. ADHV 10 M 60, 24 July and 26 Aug. 1920; AN F7 12967, monthly

report, Aug. 1920; F7 13973, monthly reports, Dec. 1920 to May 1921; F7 13520, weekly reports, Mar. to Nov. 1921.

14. Sauvy, *Histoire économique,* 1:218–19, 229; 3:43 ("La population," by Armengaud); *Recensement,* 1921. According to these sources, unemployment nationwide hit 2.1 percent of the total active population in 1931 and 4.7 percent in 1936; departmental figures for 1921 were 1.8 percent in the Haute-Vienne and 3.6 percent in the Loire. These figures are based on those who identified themselves as unemployed at the time of the census (Mar. 1921); although such reports are in part a matter of self-perception, they are more accurate than reports that count only those who apply to public authorities for jobs or financial assistance. The impact of later economic crises is discussed here in chs. 10–11.

15. ADHV 10 M 64, weekly reports on unemployment in the Limoges shoe, clothing, and textile industries, 1921; these reports also estimate that unemployment peaked at one-half of the clothing workers and two-thirds of the textile workers in Limoges. Figures published in the census are much lower (they range from 5 to 10 percent for these industries throughout the department), but are still higher than the departmental average. In the porcelain industry, where unemployment was reportedly low but not measured in the weekly tables, the census reported a figure of 3.3 percent. ADHV 10 M 195, 27 Aug. 1921; *Recensement,* 1921.

16. *R. Tiss.,* Dec. 1920 to June 1921 ("Le travail"); ADL 93 M 3 and 93 M 45, 30 May 1921; 93 M 112, 14 May and 26 Dec. 1921; 93 M 10, 11 June 1921 and 10 June 1922; AN F7 13520, 22–27 Apr. and 11–18 July 1921, and 3 July 1922; *Trav. S-S* (CGT), Mar. and July 1922. Note that the number of inactive looms is not an exact measure of unemployment in the textile industry, since many weavers, especially those who owned their own shops, normally operated more than one loom. Except for these reports, there are no general figures on unemployment in Saint-Etienne; the reports in ADL 19 M 24 tabulate only those few who received aid from the city's *fonds de chômage.* Nor does the published census reveal the full extent of unemployment, except in relative terms: these figures ranged from 9.0 percent in textiles (for the department) down to 2.1 percent in the mines. *Recensement,* 1921.

17. Sauvy, *Histoire économique,* 3:43–44 ("La population," by Armengaud); Garraty, *Unemployment,* p. 211. The published census for 1921 does not distinguish unemployment rates for French and foreign workers, but it does do so by sex: the average rates for women were approximately half again those for men in both the Haute-Vienne and the Loire. *Recensement,* 1921.

18. ADHV 10 M 64, weekly reports on unemployment in the Limoges shoe industry, 1921; ADL 91 M 24, weekly reports on unemployed workers receiving compensation in Saint-Etienne, 1921; *Recensement,* 1921. The Limoges figures show only the number of women employed (not those unemployed) in the shoe industry in 1921; this varied from 50 to 55 percent of the total work force (full- or part-time) during the crisis. "Normal" female employment in the shoe industry at Limoges is not indicated here, but for the department it totaled some 48 percent of the work force; thus, the women appear to have weathered the crisis more easily than the men. According to the published census figures, however, unemployed

women outnumbered the men by nearly two to one in the Haute-Vienne shoe industry, and represented 14 percent of the industry's total female labor force, as against 7 percent for the men.

The Saint-Etienne reports do give figures for each sex, if one can assume that the sex ratio of those who received compensation is comparable to that of all unemployed workers in the city. In May 1921, at the peak of the crisis, unemployed women (on these lists) outnumbered the men by nearly five to one in textiles; this ratio was far higher than that for "normal" female employment in the industry (approximately two to one). The published census showed similar results: unemployment affected 11 percent of the women normally employed in textiles, as against 4 percent of the men.

19. Even in 1919, unemployed women (at least those on public assistance) had far outnumbered the men, according to reports in ADL 91 M 24, May 1919, and ADHV 10 M 49, Nov. 1919. The problem of unemployment immediately after the war is discussed here in ch. 5.

20. AN F7 13520, 11 Oct. and 8 Nov. 1921.

21. ADHV 10 M 64, weekly reports on unemployment (by company) in the Limoges shoe industry, 1921. A similar pattern in the coal mines was observed by the Loire's deputy Antoine Durafour, as reported in *L'Hum.*, 12 Feb. 1921.

22. Compare the tables on company size (and unemployment levels) in the Limoges shoe industry during a subsequent economic crisis: ADHV 10 M 63, 18 Dec. 1926. Also see the discussion of the shoe industry here in chs. 1 and 5.

23. For the Loire, the only figures available are from the published census (*Recensement, 1921*). These do show that the unemployment rate in "metallurgy" exceeded that in "metal work" by more than three to one. Still, this difference, however significant, is not directly related to company size. Many of the Loire's larger manufacturers of heavy steel machinery are classed in the latter category. For further discussion, see ch. 1.

24. *R. Tiss.*, Apr., June, Oct., and Nov. 1921 ("Le travail"). The published census also reports about a one-third higher unemployment rate for artisanal *"passementiers"* than for the rest of the textile industry. *Recensement*, 1921.

25. *R. Tiss.*, Aug. 1923, Feb. and Dec. 1924, and Feb.–Mar. 1925; see also Guitton, *Rubans*, pp. 198–255; and Zdatny, "Artisanal Movement," pp. 284–92.

26. The "red" textile union, founded in 1919, soon dissolved in mid-1922. A new one appeared briefly in 1928–30, and a third one emerged in 1934. Bourse, Saint-Etienne, 7 June 1922; AN F22 73, list of Saint-Etienne unions dissolved from 1914 to 1935; ADL 93 M 13, 30 Aug. 1922; M 592, reports on trade unions in the Loire, 1 Jan. 1926, 1 Jan. 1930, and 1 Jan. 1936.

27. *L'Hum.*, 30–31 Jan. 1921 (opinion poll); *R. Tiss.*, Feb. 1921 ("Chantage patronal"); *Peuple L.*, 28 Aug. 1921 ("La guerre des salaires"); *Flamme*, 19 Mar. and 3 Sept. 1921; *Prol. C.*, 6 Feb. 1921 ("Chômage criminel"); *Pop. C.*, 18–19 Aug. 1921 and 12 Feb. 1922; *O. Céram.*, Apr. 1922; *Trav. S-S* (CGT), July 1922 ("La baisse des salaires et les arguments patronaux").

28. In addition to the above references, see the articles on the patronal "Unions Civiques" by A. Herclet, in *VO*, 26 May and 2–16 June 1922; and the

report of 14 Feb. 1921 in AN F7 14608. These organizations, first active during the May 1920 general strike, are discussed here in ch. 6.

29. *Indép. O.,* Feb. to Apr. 1919, July 1920, and Jan. to Apr. 1922. On the eight-hour-day law, see also ch. 5.

30. *R. Tiss.,* Apr.–May 1921 and Dec. 1922; ADL 92 M 45, 30 May 1921; ADHV 10 M 195, 14 Feb. 1921; *Pop. C.,* 11 Jan. and 22 July 1921; *L'Hum.,* 8 Mar. 1921 ("Chômage dans la chaussure"); *O. Céram.,* Apr.–May 1921; *Céram. Lim.,* Apr. 1922; and *Trav. S-S,* July 1922; see also Picard, *Crise économique,* pp. 28–30. The question of industrial modernization is further discussed here in chs. 5 and 11.

31. *R. Tiss.,* Feb. 1921.

32. See discussion in ch. 5.

33. *Peuple L.,* 26 June 1920 ("La blague de baisse," by V. Méric), and 28 Aug. and 18 Sept. 1921; *Flamme,* 19 Mar. 1921 ("Les salaires et les prix"), and 3 Sept. 1921 ("La vague de baisse jusqu'à présent ne s'est attaqué qu'aux salaires," by H. Prete); *R. Tiss.,* Mar. and May 1921, and Jan. 1922; *Pop. C.,* 26 Jan. 1921; *L'Hum.,* 28 Mar. 1921 ("La crise des salaires et la cherté de la vie," by Paul Louis). According to *La Flamme,* 10 Sept. 1921, food prices in Saint-Etienne actually rose (not fell) from June to Sept. 1921. See earlier in this chapter on price variations during the recession.

34. Paul Louis in *L'Hum.,* 15 Jan. 1921; *Pop. C.,* 30 Jan. 1921.

35. Synd. Chaussures, Limoges, 29 Jan. and 9 Mar. 1921; ADHV 10 M 63, 29 Jan. 1921. The shoe factory in question, Monteux, faced wage cuts of up to 45 percent.

36. ADL 93 M 26, 19 July 1921; *Peuple L.,* 24 July and 18 Sept. 1921. Later on, a one-day strike—called by the national federation—did protest the pay cuts: AN F22 181, 12 Dec. 1921.

37. ADL 93 M 3, 20–30 May 1921; *R. Tiss.,* Mar. to June 1921. The weavers' *tarif* or pay scale, first instituted in 1912, was in fact nullified by the courts in 1922, as a violation of unionists' "right to work." 93 M 3, 21–22 Feb. 1922; *R. Tiss.,* Feb.–Mar. 1922.

38. *L'Hum.,* 28 Mar. 1921; *Pop. C.,* 11–30 Jan. 1921 and 12 Feb. 1922; *Prol. C.,* 6 Feb. 1921; AN F7 13973, monthly report, Mar. 1921; F7 13520, 7 July 1921; ADHV 10 M 63, 29 Jan. 1921; 10 M 195, 28 May 1921; ADL 93 M 82, 18 Apr. 1921; 93 M 59, 15 Oct. 1921.

39. A. Herclet in *VO,* 11 Mar. 1921 ("Contre le chômage"); see also Garraty, *Unemployment,* pp. 182–87; Dufraisse, "Mouvement ouvrier 'rouge,' " in *Mouvements ouvriers,* ed. Fauvel-Rouif, pp. 180–84; and Perrot, *Ouvriers en grève,* 1:158–64.

40. On foreign workers: *L'Hum.,* 31 Jan. 1921 (opinion poll); *Trav. du Papier* (Limoges), July–Aug. 1922; *Pop. C.,* 30 Dec. 1922. On the limitation of apprentices: ADHV 10 M 137, 31 Jan. to 26 Aug. 1922; *Céram. Lim.,* May–July 1922; *O. Céram,* July–Aug. 1922. Although foreign workers were numerous in the Loire, there were no reports of complaints against them at this time, perhaps because they were mostly employed in mining and metallurgy, where unemployment was still rare. On foreign labor during later economic crises, see ch. 11 of

this study, and Gary S. Cross, *Immigrant Workers in Industrial France: The Making of a New Laboring Class* (Philadelphia, 1983), ch. 9.

41. *L'Hum.*, 2 Feb. 1921; *Peuple L.*, 4 Sept. 1921; *Pop. C.*, 12–21 Feb. 1922; ADHV 10 M 63, 16 Dec. 1920; 1 M 167, 19 Mar. 1921; ADL 93 M 10, 21 Jan. 1921; AN F7 13520, 28 June 1921.

42. Figures in Labi, *Grande division des travailleurs*, pp. 248–53, or comparable figures in Robert, *Scission syndicale*, pp. 159–62, 206–7. The two authors use different means of calculation but similarly estimate UD membership in late 1921 at 14,000 to 16,000 in the Loire and 5,000 to 5,200 in the Haute-Vienne (down from some 26,000 and 14,000, respectively, in 1919–20).

43. AN F7 12995, 16 Nov. 1920 and 3 Apr. 1921; ADL 93 M 50, 26 Sept. 1921; 93 M 9, 22 Dec. 1918; 93 M 10, 1 July 1921.

44. ADHV 10 M 177, report on trade unions in the Haute-Vienne, 1 Jan. 1921 (there is no similar report for early 1922); Synd. Chaussures, Limoges, 28 Oct. 1921.

45. AN F7 12994, 31 Mar. 1919; F7 12995, 18 Jan. and 23 Feb. 1920, and 10 Jan. 1922. The problem of the Loire's "ephemeral" unions, created in 1919–20, is discussed here in ch. 5.

46. AN F22 73, list of Saint-Etienne unions dissolved from 1914 to 1935; ADL M 540, dossier on "CGT/CGTU," report of 2 Sept. 1921; 93 M 13, 30 Aug. 1922.

47. ADHV 10 M 177, reports on trade unions in the Haute-Vienne, 1 Jan. 1920 and 1 Jan. 1924; 10 M 187, 7 Jan. 1922; 10 M 195, 27 Aug. and 27 Sept. 1921; 10 M 107, 27 Sept. 1921.

48. *Statistique des grèves*, 1921. Participation in the Loire miners' strike is not cited separately in the published report but is estimated at some 15,000 in AN F22 181, 13 Dec. 1921.

49. *Statistique des grèves*, 1921. Nor were any shoe workers' strikes reported in ADHV 10 M 113, although the shoe workers' own archives mentioned an attempted conflict. Synd. Chaussures, Limoges, 29 Jan. and 9 Mar. 1921.

50. *Statistique des grèves*, 1920–21; ADHV 10 M 136, 9 Sept. to 28 Nov. 1920.

51. *Statistique des grèves*, 1921.

52. Although strikes normally occur (and succeed) more frequently in prosperous times, more strikes arose in hard times after than before the war in France; this may show an increased tendency to protest hardships, as labor organization developed and politicized after the war. See Shorter and Tilly, *Strikes in France*, pp. 81–92. Similar patterns are observed for the post-1945 period by Richard F. Hamilton, in *Affluence and the French Worker in the Fourth Republic* (Princeton, 1967), ch. 9.

53. On the Italian case: *VO*, 13 Feb. 1920 ("Contrôle ouvrier?"); and Paolo Spriano, *The Occupation of the Factories: Italy 1920* (London, 1975).

54. Herclet in *VO*, 14 Jan. 1921 ("Occupons les usines"); *L'Hum.*, 11 Feb. 1921; ADL M 540, dossier on "CGT/CGTU," reports of 18 Jan. and 28 Mar. 1921; 93 M 10, 11 June 1921. On Flageollet: ADL 19 M 39, 29 Oct. 1920.

55. ADL 93 M 10, 10 June 1922; M 540, dossier on "CGT/CGTU," report

of 24 Aug. 1922; AN F7 12995, 23–28 Oct. 1922. Arnaud's defection from the party is discussed here in ch. 9.

56. *VO*, 14 Jan. 1921 ("Bulletin des CSR"); AN F7 13023, 22 Jan. 1922. Haute-Vienne CSR leaders Bert and Beaubelicout did, however, later quit the CP; see ch. 10.

57. Herclet in *VO*, 13 Dec. 1920, and 14 Jan. and 11 Mar. 1921; Herclet in *L'Hum.*, 25 Sept. 1921.

58. ADL M 540, dossier on "CGT/CGTU," reports of 18 Jan. and 28 Mar. 1921.

59. *L'Hum.*, 13–27 Apr. 1921; *VO*, 15 Apr. and 13 May 1921; also Herclet in *VO*, 31 Dec. 1920 and 14 Jan. 1921.

60. Herclet in *VO*, 31 Dec. 1920.

61. Théo Argence and Auguste Herclet, "Le contrôle ouvrier et les comités d'ateliers," *Cahiers du Travail* [1921], pp. 5–7, 40–44, or the English version in Monatte, *Left-Wing Trade-Unionism,* pp. 75–127. For similar views see also *L'Hum.*, 17 Feb. 1921 (Herclet), 26 Apr. 1921 (P. Dumas), and 8 July 1921 (P. Besnard); ADL M 540, dossier on "CSR," report of 6 Feb. 1921; 93 M 10, 11 June 1921; Synd. Chaussures, Limoges, 9 Mar. 1921 and 6 Nov. 1923; *Céram. Lim.,* June 1922; and *Trav. S-S* (CGT), July 1922.

62. G. Monmousseau in *VO*, 31 Dec. 1920; Monmousseau, "Le contrôle syndical et les comités d'usine," *Cahiers du Travail* [1921]; Monatte, Foreword, in *Left-Wing Trade-Unionism.* On Herclet, see Wohl, *French Communism,* pp. 347n, 423. On the perceived similarities between *"soviets"* and *"syndicats,"* see also ch. 7 of this study.

63. Compare Kriegel, *Aux origines,* especially 1:522–47; and Young, *"Vie Ouvrière,"* especially pp. 163–69, 359–65. The problems of May 1920 and the subsequent conversion to communism are discussed in chs. 6–7 of this study.

64. *L'Hum.*, 17 Feb. 1921 (Herclet), 5–8 July 1921 (Besnard), and 10 July 1921 (resolution of UD Haute-Vienne); AN F7 13023, 10 July 1921; Synd. Chaussures, Limoges, 9 Mar. 1921 and 6 Nov. 1923; *Céram. Lim.,* Apr.–June 1922. Similar constructive reforms were accepted by the later CGTSR; see ch. 10.

65. Compare Monatte, "Reflections" (1917), in his *Left-Wing Trade-Unionism,* pp. 25–28; and Monatte in *VO*, 1 Oct. 1920, and 19 Aug. and 2 Dec. 1921.

66. *C. Rouge,* 20 Nov. 1920 ("Les réalisations immédiates et l'esprit révolutionnaire").

67. *L'Hum.*, 15 Mar. 1921 ("Les réformes et l'action révolutionnaire"), and, on the eight-hour day, 2 Feb. 1921, and 6 Feb. to 8 Mar. 1922.

68. ADL 93 M 10, 13 Mar. and 10 June 1922.

69. ADL M 540, dossier on "CGT/CGTU," reports of 13 May and 7 Sept. 1922, and Circulaire from the Fédération des Syndicats Interindustriels (Paris), "La journée de six heures." This demand was also later adopted by the CGTSR. *Combat Synd.,* Feb. 1927.

70. *L'Hum.*, 13 Sept. 1921 and 14 Jan. 1922; also Chambelland in *VO*, 13–20 Jan. and 10 Feb. 1922. This plan seems to have been actually carried out in the Paris region.

71. AN F7 12995, 5 Dec. 1921; ADL M 540, dossier on "L'impôt sur les salaires," report of 12 Dec. 1921.

72. For example, *L'Hum.*, 2 Feb. and 7–13 Mar. 1922; *Peuple L.*, 4 Dec. 1921 and 2 Apr. 1922; and *Prol. C.*, 7 May 1922. On the party's attitude toward strikes in this period (though with no reference to the recession), see also Badie, *Stratégie de la grève*, pp. 30–36.

73. ADL M 540, dossier on "L'impôt sur les salaires," reports of 10–12 Dec. 1921 and 19 Feb. 1922; dossier on "CGT/CGTU," report of 28 Mar. 1922; *VO*, 18 Nov. 1921; *Peuple L.*, 4 Dec. 1921 and 2 Apr. 1922; *Trav. S-S*, June 1922; *Pop. C.*, 16 July 1922. The CGT demanded especially that the tax exemption be raised from its wartime level to compensate for inflation; so did the "yellow" union of Loire weavers, who also objected to being taxed as employers rather than as workers. *R. Tiss.*, Sept. 1919, Feb. to June 1920, July 1923, and Jan. 1924.

74. *Peuple L.*, 24 July 1921.

75. *L'Hum.*, 19 July 1921 ("Pour le contrôle ouvrier," by A. Ker).

76. On Vardelle (secretary of paper workers' federation, and later UD secretary and SFIO deputy): ADHV 10 M 195, 24 Sept. 1921. On Dubreuil (secretary of UD Seine in 1919 and later author of works praising German and English trade unionism and American industrial methods): articles reprinted in *R. Tiss.*, Jan. 1922 ("Méditations ouvrières") and Jan. 1924 ("Contrôle ouvrier"); see also Fine, "Toward Corporatism," pp. 281–95. On the CFTC: ADL M 540, dossier on "CFTC," reports of 9 Apr. and 14 Nov. 1921 (speeches by national president Jules Zirnheld).

77. Dufraisse, "Mouvement ouvrier 'rouge,' " in *Mouvements ouvriers*, ed. Fauvel-Rouif, pp. 166–73; Fine, "Toward Corporatism," pp. 174–80; Jean Charles, "S.F.I.O. et C.G.T. dans la période de 'prospérité' — 1921–1931," in *Histoire du réformisme*, by Blum et al., 1:62–71; and Collinet, *Esprit du syndicalisme*, pp. 53–61. The issue of "rationalization" is further discussed here in ch. 10.

78. Summary report of Marseille congress in *L'Hum.*, 26–28 Dec. 1921; commentaries on trade-union policy in *L'Hum.*, 13 Oct. 1921 (F. Loriot) and 5 Nov. 1921 (A. Dunois), and in *VO*, 6 Jan. 1922 (M. Chambelland); text of Dunois's report to the congress on trade-union policy in Charles, ed., "Intervention du P.C.F.," pp. 280–308. On the Marseille congress, see also Wohl, *French Communism*, pp. 244–51. The issues of trade-union policy are further discussed here in chs. 9–10.

79. ADL M 539, dossier on "Anarchistes et Libertaires," report of 13 Jan. 1922.

80. ADL M 540, dossier on "CGT/CGTU," report of 13 Sept. 1921; *L'Hum.*, 17 Sept. 1921. The switch to proportional representation had been proposed in the Loire by the large textile workers' union at Roanne. Proportional representation was finally adopted by the CGT in 1925 and by the CGTU in 1927, with effects that are discussed in ch. 11. See also Prost, *La C.G.T.*, p. 19.

81. Voting results for the two congresses are summarized in *VO*, 5 Aug. 1921;

in Labi, *Grande division des travailleurs,* pp. 267–68; and detailed in the congress reports: CGT, *XXIᵉ Congrès, 1920,* pp. 429–86; XXIIᵉ Congrès National Corporatif, tenu à Lille, du 25 au 30 juillet 1921, *Compte-rendu des travaux* (Paris, n.d.), pp. 339–406. The results for the Loire are also detailed in ADL M 540, 2 Sept. 1921. According to these reports, the minority's biggest gains since the Orléans congress—both in numbers and in percentage of total votes—were in the federations of small unions, such as in metals, construction, leathers, and furniture making; the only exception was the railroad workers' federation, where large unions were the rule. By contrast, the large unions of miners, transport workers, textile workers, printers, and commercial and public employees remained centers of majoritarian strength. Similar results are observed by Robert in *Scission syndicale,* pp. 169, 174.

Chapter 9. A Schism of Desperation

1. ADHV 1 M 167, 18 Mar. 1921; *O. Céram.,* Apr.–May 1921 ("Re-mise au point," by L. Bonnet); *Pop. C.,* 3–13 Dec. 1921; ADL M 540, dossier on "CGT/CGTU," reports of 1–10 Oct. 1921; 93 M 59, 15 Oct. 1921; AN F7 12995, 23 Oct. and 19 Dec. 1921.

2. Cited in Labi, *Grande division des travailleurs,* pp. 177–78.

3. *Pop. C.,* 20 July 1920 and 20–25 Jan. 1921.

4. *Peuple L.,* 11 Sept. 1920; *C. Rouge,* 18 Oct., 20 Nov., and 11 Dec. 1920; *Prol. C.,* 30 Oct. 1921; *L'Hum.,* 30 July 1921.

5. *L'Hum.,* 18–31 July 1921; an example of the use of the term "anarcho-reformism" is in *Le Cri du Peuple* (PC, Loire), 12 Oct. 1929. This idea is further discussed here in ch. 10.

6. As charged in *L'Hum.,* 14 Mar. 1921. The court order to dissolve the CGT was never enforced, but there is no evidence that this was because of the expulsions.

7. CGT resolutions reprinted in *Voix du Peuple,* Nov. 1920 and Mar. 1921; left-wingers' reponses reported in *VO,* 12 Nov. 1920 and 11 Feb. 1921, and in *L'Hum.,* 11 Feb. 1921.

8. *VO,* 20 May 1921.

9. ADL 93 M 70, 20 Dec. 1920; M 539, dossier on "CSR," report (citing Legrain of Le Havre) of 16 Jan. 1921.

10. UD resolution, 16 Dec. 1920, in *L'Hum.,* 6 Jan. 1921.

11. ADL 93 M 82, 18 Feb. 1921; 93 M 26, 18 Apr., 27 June, and 7 Nov. 1921; M 540, dossier on "CGT/CGTU," reports of 2 Feb. and 1–10 Oct. 1921; 93 M 59, 15 Oct. 1921; AN F7 12995, 23 Oct. and 19 Dec. 1921. These issues were also discussed in the Bourse, Saint-Etienne, 9 Sept. to 14 Oct. 1921. (The protest resolution was presented to the UD by the Bourse at Saint-Etienne.) The teachers' union did later join the CGTU, but the delegate who had approved the exclusions quickly formed a rival CGT union. 93 M 97, 27 Apr. 1922.

12. ADL M 540, dossier on "CGT/CGTU," report of 24 Oct. 1921.

13. *VO,* 12 Nov. 1920; *L'Hum.,* 30 Mar. and 26 May 1921. On Dumoulin in 1918, see ch. 4 of this study.

14. *L'Hum.*, 3–10 June 1921; *VO*, 10–17 June 1921; see also Labi, *Grande division des travailleurs*, p. 205.

15. *VO*, 21–28 Sept. 1921; ADL 93 M 82, 7–23 Mar., 28 Apr., 6 June, 3 Sept., and 19 Nov. 1921, and 2 Feb. 1922.

16. *L'Hum.*, 24 Dec. 1921.

17. *VO*, 5 Sept. 1921 (Monatte), 18 Nov. 1921 (Herclet), 25 Nov. 1921 (Bouët), and 2 Dec. 1921 (Aigueperse); *L'Hum.*, 1 Jan. 1922; and Monatte, *Trois scissions*, pp. 159–61. Monatte's views on labor schism are discussed here in ch. 7.

18. Monmousseau in *VO*, 23 Dec. 1921; also *L'Hum.*, 23 Dec. 1921.

19. *L'Hum.*, 23 Dec. 1921 and 1 Jan. 1922; *VO*, 30 Dec. 1921 and 6 Jan. 1922. The latter claimed 1,564 unions were represented at the congress, but the congress's own report gave the figure of 1,528; 1,348 had voted with the minority at Lille. Figures tallied by individual union also show that the new total included 356 unions simply not represented at the Lille congress; 200 were previously majoritarian or undecided, and 972 had previously voted with the left. Robert, *Scission syndicale*, pp. 197–202.

20. Voting statistics (parallel though not identical) in Robert, *Scission syndicale*, pp. 197–202; and in Labi, *Grande division des travailleurs*, pp. 269–70, 280–81.

21. *L'Hum.*, 6 July 1921; *O. Céram.*, June–July 1921 and Jan.–Mar. 1922. The statistics in Robert and Labi also point to fifteen UDs and six federations in which fewer unions (even if still a majority) attended the Paris congress than had voted with the left at Lille; the differences, however, were rarely of more than one or two unions.

22. Voting results in Robert, *Scission syndicale*, pp. 151, 197–202; and in Labi, *Grande division des travailleurs*, pp. 269–70, 280–81; record of adhesions to the new confederation in CGTU, *Premier congrès tenu à Saint-Etienne du 25 juin au 1er juillet 1922: Rapports moral et financier* (n.p., n.d.), p. 7. The left's "losses" after the Paris congress numbered six of the nine UDs that had shifted leftward only after the Lille congress, plus three federations, one of which (glass) had also voted with the majority at Lille, and two (porcelain and metals) that had remained aligned with the majority until right before Lille. *L'Hum.*, 23–25 July 1921.

23. *Peuple L.*, 25 Dec. 1921 (H. Lorduron) and 1 Jan. 1922 (response by J. Bonnefonds); ADL M 540, dossier on "CGT/CGTU," reports of 19 Dec. 1921 and 10 Jan. 1922. The UD vote was forty-six to three, with one abstention; forty-two of these unions actually sent representatives to the congress.

24. *O. Céram.*, Jan. 1922 (quoted comment). On those unions that stayed in the CGT: Synd. Imprimeurs-Lithographes, Limoges, 22 Dec. 1921 and 17 Jan. 1922; ADHV 10 M 187, 7 Jan. and 1 Feb. 1922; ADL 93 M 26, 19 Dec. 1921 and 16 Jan. 1922; M 540, dossier on "CGT/CGTU," report of 4 Mar. 1922; M 540, dossier on "UD Confédérale," report of 31 Oct. 1922.

25. *L'Hum.*, 8–26 May and 1–7 June 1921; and Labi, *Grande division des travailleurs*, p. 205. Note that the majoritarian leaders had been restored to office after the failure of the May 1920 general strike; see ch. 6 of this study.

26. *L'Hum.*, 23–29 July 1921. The metalworkers' federation did *not* originally join the CGTU, although its "reconstituted" CGTU faction did soon outnum-
ber those who had stayed in the CGT. Statistics for the 1920s and 1930s are in
Prost, *La C.G.T.*, pp. 201–2. The relative sizes of the CGT and CGTU factions
are further discussed below.

27. *L'Hum.*, 25 July 1921. The porcelain workers' federation did vote with
the minority at Lille but then did not join the CGTU; its "reconstituted" CGTU
faction outnumbered the CGT's for a short time but then fell behind after the Limoges union quit the CGTU for autonomy. See figures in Prost, *La C.G.T.*, pp.
201–2. The autonomous unions are discussed here in chs. 10–11.

28. Monatte in *VO*, 29 July 1921. The moderates also held a small lead in the
textile and leather workers' federations, and a larger lead among printers and
various groups of civil and commercial employees, all of which continued to side
primarily with the CGT. Statistics in Labi, *Grande division des travailleurs*, pp.
268–69; and Prost, *La C.G.T.*, pp. 201–2.

29. Demouveau, "Scission de la C.G.T.," p. 477.

30. Calculations in Robert, *Scission syndicale*, p. 110; on the postwar creation
of "ephemeral" unions, see ch. 5 of this study.

31. Sémard in *VO*, 2 Sept. 1921; Monatte in *L'Hum.*, 21 Sept. 1921; also
ADL M 540, dossier on "CGT/CGTU," circular from UD Loire, 1 Oct., with
report of 10 Oct. 1921. Note that, although each UD and federation had one
vote, the UDs far outnumbered the federations, by ninety-two to forty-three. The
issue of representation in the new CGTU is discussed later in this chapter.

32. Compare the argument of Jean-Louis Robert, who discounts the influence
of anarcho-syndicalism but attributes the left's strength in the UDs to the big role
of the railroad workers (pro-Communist and pro-CGTU) in UDs all over the
country. Moissonnier et al., "Débat," p. 180. On the contrasts between UDs and
industrial federations, see also Robert, *Scission syndicale*, esp. pp. 174–75.

33. *L'Hum.*, 19 Jan. 1922; *Prol. C.*, 29 Jan. 1922.

34. *Voix du Peuple*, Jan. 1922; *Peuple L.*, 5–22 Jan. 1922; *VO*, 3 Feb. 1922.
The debate on the new statutes, which began in March, is discussed later in this
chapter.

35. Figures for 1922 cited in Wohl, *French Communism*, p. 280; compare to
estimates of 1.6 million in 1920 and 800,000 in 1921, cited in Labi, *Grande division des travailleurs*, pp. 248–49, or in Robert, *Scission syndicale*, pp. 159–62.
Figures for 1924–34, based on mandates at congresses, are in Prost, *La C.G.T.*,
pp. 35, 201–2; similar figures for 1923–26, based on the sale of cards and
stamps, are in AN F7 13580 (for the CGT), 12 Apr. 1926 and 30 Sept. 1927; and
F7 13584 (for the CGTU), 29 Apr. 1927. The relative strength of the CGT and
the CGTU later in the 1920s is further discussed here in ch. 11.

36. Demouveau, "Scission de la C.G.T.," pp. 487–88.

37. Synd. Imprimeurs-Lithographes, Limoges, 25 Feb. 1921 and 19 May
1922. The union's membership—fifty-two in Jan. 1921 and fifty in 1922—is cited
in ADHV 10 M 177, report on trade unions in the Haute-Vienne, 1 Jan. 1921;
and 10 M 151, report on UD Confédérale, "exercice 1922" (1923).

38. *Bulletin du Syndicat des Typos* (Limoges), Mar. and June 1922.

39. ADL M 540, dossier on "CGT/CGTU," reports of 4–13 Mar. 1922; 93 M 10, 23 Jan. and 8 Feb. 1922.

40. ADL M 540, dossier on "CGT/CGTU," reports of 10–16 Jan. and 28 Mar. 1922; Bourse, Saint-Etienne, 23 Jan., 10 Feb., and 21 Mar. 1922; *Peuple L.*, 22 Jan. 1922.

41. Tinel of railroad workers (CGTU) at Bourse, Saint-Etienne, 3 Mar. 1922; also *Peuple L.*, 5 Feb. 1922 ("Aux syndicats neutres," by H. Lorduron); *Pop. C.*, 17 Jan. 1922 ("Quelques solutions de moindre effort"), and 19 Jan. 1922 ("Les neutres").

42. *O. Céram.*, Mar. 1922 ("Ma faute," by F. Déry). Similar arguments are presented in the CGT circular printed in *Trib. R.* (Saint-Etienne), 21 Mar. 1922.

43. Lorduron at CSR, in *VO*, 21 Oct. 1921; Lorduron in *Peuple L.*, 22 Jan. 1922; ADL M 540, dossier on "CGT/CGTU," reports of 16 Jan. and 11 Feb. 1922; 93 M 27, 29 July 1922; and *R. Peuple* (successor to *Peuple L.*), 16–30 July 1922.

44. ADL 93 M 26, 10–26 July 1922.

45. *Pop. C.*, 13 Dec. 1921 ("Rupture syndicale," by P. Renaudel); *Union des Métaux*, Feb.–Apr. 1922.

46. *Prol. C.*, 22 Jan. 1922 (UD resolution); *Bull. Synd. Typos*, Sept. 1922.

47. *Le Travail* (PC, Sud-Est), 15 Apr. 1922.

48. ADL M 556, 20 Jan. 1922; *Peuple L.*, 22 Jan. 1922. The controversies over the united-front tactic are discussed later in this chapter.

49. Cited in Gras, *Rosmer*, p. 313.

50. Monatte in *Prol. C.*, 21 May 1922; Monatte in *L'Hum.*, 22 June 1922; Monatte, *Trois scissions*, pp. 138, 152–53.

51. *O. Céram.*, Aug. 1922 ("Leur congrès").

52. ADL 92 M 261, 18 Mar. 1920; 93 M 82, 26 May and 17 June 1920, and 2 Feb. and 27 July 1922; 93 M 84, 22 July 1922.

53. ADHV 1 M 167, 3 Feb. 1922.

54. *O. Céram.*, Jan. 1922 ("Action confédérale," by J. Tillet).

55. *L'Hum.*, 5 Mar. 1922 (declaration by CGTU National Committee); see also the statistics in Prost, *La C.G.T.*, pp. 201–2.

56. AN F7 12995, 24 Apr. 1922; F7 12997, 8–22 Feb. 1927; ADL M 540, dossier on "UD Confédérale," reports of 31 Oct. and 10 Nov. 1922. The new UD's original member unions (those whose majorities stayed in the CGT) included the postal employees, the miners at Firminy, and the typographers at Saint-Etienne. The UD's later growth is discussed here in ch. 11.

57. Commune de Limoges, *Procès-verbaux des séances du Conseil Municipal*, année 1922, session of 30 Jan. 1922, pp. 62–65; ADHV 10 M 187, 7 Jan. and 1 Feb. 1922; 1 M 167, 3 Feb. 1922; 10 M 151, report on UD Confédérale, "exercice 1922" (1923); *Prol. C.*, 12–19 Feb. 1922; *Bull. Synd. Typos*, Mar. 1922.

58. List of member unions, which also included the lithographers and the postal and municipal employees, in ADHV 10 M 187, 1 Feb. 1922. Membership figures are given as of 1 Jan. 1921 (and thus may not be accurate for 1922), from data in 10 M 177, report on trade unions in the Haute-Vienne.

59. *L'Hum.*, 12 Feb. 1922; *Prol. C.*, 19 Feb. 1922.

60. *Prol. C.,* 19 Feb. 1922. These alleged union leaders, and those longest in-active in the industry, included (in the leftists' estimation) Socialist deputies Pressemane and Parvy.

61. On unionization in the different labor groups, see Prost, *La C.G.T.,* pp. 52–55, 201–2. According to Prost's figures, unionization in the "tertiary" sector represented the following proportions of total CGT and CGTU memberships:

1921*		1926		1930		1934	
CGT	CGTU	CGT	CGTU	CGT	CGTU	CGT	CGTU
39%	42%	58%	57%	70%	66%	72%	64%

*factions prior to schism

Prost includes certain industrial workers in this "tertiary" sector, but the percentages are comparable even if these groups are excluded. On unionization of the *"fonctionnaires,"* see also Judith Wishnia, "The French *Fonctionnaires:* The Development of Class Consciousness and Unionization, 1884–1926" (Ph.D. diss., SUNY at Stony Brook, 1978), as well as the literature on teachers, railroad workers, and other individual groups.

62. General data on unionization in the two departments are in ADHV 10 M 177–79, reports on trade unions in the Haute-Vienne, 1 Jan. 1921, 1 Jan. 1924, and 1 Jan. 1927; ADL M 592, reports on trade unions in the Loire, 1 Jan. 1926 and 1 Jan. 1930. In addition, scattered figures for Limoges are in *Céram. Lim.,* July 1922; ADHV 10 M 137 and 10 M 187 for Feb.–June 1922; and 1 M 171, 10 M 115, and 10 M 191 for 1929–36. For the Loire: ADL 93 M 10, 93 M 13, 93 M 26, and 93 M 50 for 1921–23; AN F7 13782 and F7 13125 for 1928–31; and articles by U. Thévenon in *RP,* Apr. 1927 and July 1931.

63. ADL 93 M 59, 30 Nov. 1922; 93 M 26, 19 Sept. 1922; ADHV 10 M 187, 15 Feb. 1922. According to the latter two reports, the Catholic unions of railroad workers at Limoges and of miners at Saint-Etienne had 450 and 200 members, respectively. Total UD membership in 1922–23 was some 8,000 in the CGTU and 1,500 in the CGT in the Loire, and some 2,000 in the CGTU (no figure available for the CGT) in the Haute-Vienne. ADL M 540, dossier on "CGT/CGTU," report of 29 Aug. 1922; AN F7 12996, 14 Sept. 1923; ADHV 1 M 168, 29 June 1922. For UD memberships in 1921, see ch. 8, n. 42.

64. Prost, *La C.G.T.,* p. 64.

65. *Pop. C.,* 9 Feb. 1922; ADHV 10 M 177, report on trade unions in the Haute-Vienne, 1 Jan. 1924. The new CGT union of shoe workers was established in June 1923. The CGTU's later rupture is discussed here in ch. 10.

66. Interview with Jean Seigne, Saint-Etienne, 8 Feb. 1975. According to figures for 1920, the mining company of Roche-la-Molière and Firminy had 4,460 employees, second only to the Loire mining company at Saint-Etienne (4,700 employees). ADL Houillères, carton 2480, notes, 3 June 1920.

67. ADL M 556, 22 Sept. 1925; AN F7 13110, 4 Mar. 1927. For further discussion of unionization in the post-1922 period, see ch. 11.

68. ADHV 10 M 136, 9 Sept. to 28 Nov. 1920; *O. Céram.,* June–July 1921.

69. ADL 93 M 26, 16 Jan. and 6 Feb. 1922; *R. Peuple,* 16 July 1922. On the

earlier wage cuts (discussed in ch. 8): ADL 93 M 26, 19 July 1921; *Peuple L.,* 24 July and 18 Sept. 1921.

70. ADL M 540, dossier on "CGT/CGTU," reports of 28 Mar. and 24 Apr. 1922, and copy of poster by CGTU Saint-Etienne.

71. *L'Hum.,* 18 July 1921 (Frossard), and 21 July 1921 (Launat); similar phraseology by Monmousseau in *L'Hum.,* 30 July 1921.

72. Dunois in *L'Hum.,* 5 Nov. 1921; text of report to congress in Charles, ed., "Intervention du P.C.F.," pp. 280–308. For related viewpoints, see *Bull. C.,* 1 Sept. 1921 (F. Loriot); and *L'Hum.,* 13 Oct. 1921 (Loriot), 6 Nov. 1921 (A. Ker), and 27 Dec. 1921 (Comintern message to Marseille congress).

73. P. Besnard and A. Ker in *L'Hum.,* 13 Nov. 1921. Besnard's activities are further discussed below.

74. *Bull. C.,* 1 Dec. 1921; cited in Wohl, *French Communism,* pp. 243–44.

75. *Prol. C.,* 25 Dec. 1921.

76. ADL M 556, 9 Dec. 1921; Lafont at Marseille congress, in *L'Hum.,* 27 Dec. 1921.

77. See especially Victor Joannès, "La tactique du front unique et le Parti Communiste Français (1922–1924)," *Cahiers IMT,* o.s., no. 22 (1971), pp. 43–52; Jean-Louis Robert and Danielle Tartakowsky, "1921–1924: Internationale, Parti et Front Unique," *Cahiers IMT,* n.s., no. 1 (1972), pp. 32–44; and Jane Degras, "United Front Tactics in the Comintern, 1921–1928," in *International Communism,* ed. David Footman (London, 1960), pp. 9–22.

78. *L'Hum.,* 21 Jan. 1922 (Frossard and V. Méric), 23 Jan. 1922 (Lafont), 18 Apr. 1922 (Renoult), and 23–24 Apr. 1922 (Frossard and Lafont); *Peuple L.,* 22–29 Jan. and 26 Mar. 1922; *R. Peuple,* 1–22 Oct., and 5 Nov. 1922; ADL M 556, 20 Jan., 7 Apr., 7 Oct., and 17 Dec. 1922.

79. Degras cites results of a Comintern questionnaire in 1922 that showed 69 percent of the French party opposed to the new tactic, compared to 40 percent in Germany, 26 percent in Italy, and 24 percent in Britain. "United Front Tactics," p. 12.

80. Bouthonnier in *L'Hum.,* 23 Jan. and 23 Apr. 1922, and in *Prol. C.,* 16 Apr. 1922; similar views by Loriot in *L'Hum.,* 7 Feb. 1922, and by Treint in *Travail* (PC, Sud-Est), 29 July 1922. Bouthonnier was the Communist mayor of Périgueux in nearby Dordogne; his role in the Haute-Vienne is further discussed below.

81. *Prol. C.,* 16 June 1922 (Souvarine) and 30 July 1922 (Bouthonnier); also *Travail* (PC), 19 Aug. and 23 Sept. 1922.

82. Treint in *Bull. C.,* 13 Apr. 1922, quoted in part in *L'Hum.,* 5 May 1922, and in full in *Petit Lim.* (SFIO, Haute-Vienne), 23 Dec. 1922; Loriot in *Correspondance Internationale,* no. 9 (1922), quoted in Joannès, "Front unique," p. 50. Joannès claims that Loriot and Treint exaggerated the tactic's aggressive intentions; similar terms, however, were employed by Russia's Karl Radek at the Comintern Congress (". . . we shall stifle them [the Social Democrats] in our embrace") and by Lenin himself (the Communists should "support" the Social Democrats "as the rope supports a hanged man"). Radek quoted in Degras, "United Front Tactics," p. 11; Lenin in *"Left-Wing" Communism,* p. 70.

83. Monatte in *Prol. C.*, 21 May 1922; Monmousseau in *VO*, 3–10 Feb. and 28 Apr. 1922, and 2 Feb. 1923; see also P. Sémard in *VO*, 3 Nov. 1922, and CGTU resolutions in *VO*, 24 Nov. 1922. On "unity of action," see ch. 11.

84. ADL M 556, 7 Oct. 1922; *Prol. C.*, 1–15 Oct. 1922; Synd. Chaussures, Limoges, 29 Dec. 1922 and 24 Apr. 1923.

85. F. Faure in *Peuple L.*, 8 Jan. 1922; Dunois in *Prol. C.*, 15 Jan. 1922; Fernand Loriot, *Un an après Tours* (Paris, n.d.), esp. pp. 4, 12.

86. M. Chambelland in *VO*, 6 Jan. 1922.

87. Monmousseau in *VO*, 29 Sept. and 27 Oct. 1922.

88. Merrheim at Lille congress, in *L'Hum.*, 30 July 1921.

89. CSR resolution and Monatte's comments in *VO*, 7 July 1921; see also Labi, *Grande division des travailleurs*, pp. 202–3, on the Lille congress.

90. See Kriegel, *Aux origines*, 2:732n, 736; Wohl, *French Communism*, pp. 237–38; and Jean Charles, "Les débuts de l'Internationale Syndicale Rouge et le mouvement ouvrier français (1920–1923)," *Cahiers IMT*, n.s., nos. 25–26 (1978), pp. 162, 167.

91. *L'Hum.*, 22–27 June and 20–28 July 1921; *VO*, 3 June 1921 (resolution by CSR Loire) and 22 July 1921 (resolution by CSR Seine). The text of the ISR resolution (voted by 282 to 25) is reprinted in *Archives de Monatte*, ed. Chambelland and Maitron, pp. 298–99. On the international response, see also Westergard-Thorpe, "Syndicalist Internationalism," pp. 220–26.

92. Frossard in *L'Hum.*, 18 July 1921; Monatte in *VO*, 22 July 1921; Frossard at Saint-Etienne CGTU congress, in *L'Hum.*, 29 June 1922. Frossard's remarks are also printed in CGTU, *Premier congrès, 1922*, p. 218 (full text of speech, pp. 208–21).

93. A. Ker in *L'Hum.*, 22–23 June 1921; F. Faure in *Peuple L.*, 24 July 1921; Monmousseau in *VO*, 10 Mar. 1922.

94. Besnard in *L'Hum.*, 27 June to 30 July 1921; Besnard and Ker in *L'Hum.*, 13 Nov. 1921.

95. Besnard resolutions for CGTU in *VO*, 17 Feb. 1922, and in *L'Hum.*, 27 June 1922; text of CGTSR's "Lyon Charter" (Nov. 1926), reprinted in Pierre Besnard, *L'éthique du syndicalisme* (Paris, 1938), pp. 129–39; *Voix du Travail* (CGTSR), Jan. 1927. For the views of Monmousseau, Monatte, and other Communist-syndicalists (discussed in ch. 7), see *VO*, 5–12 Dec. 1919, 31 Dec. 1920, 19 Aug. and 2 Dec. 1921, and 17–24 Mar. 1922.

96. On the Berlin International (founded in Dec. 1922), see Lefranc, *Mouvement syndical*, p. 261; and Westergard-Thorpe, "Syndicalist Internationalism," pp. 229–34. On Besnard's role, see AN F7 12996, 24 July 1923. Note also that *La Voix du Travail*, founded in 1926 as AIT organ, became the CGTSR's monthly bulletin in 1927. On Besnard and the "Pacte," see ch. 7; the CGTSR is further discussed in chs. 10–11.

97. Communist views of Besnard and the Berlin International in *Bull. C.*, 25 Aug. 1921 ("Amsterdam ou Moscou," by A. Dunois); *VO*, 22 July 1921, and 21 Apr., 14 July, and 15 Sept. 1922; *L'Hum.*, 13 Mar., 6 Apr., and 10–19 June 1922; ADL M 540, dossier on "Congrès CGTU," report of 27 June 1922; and M 540, dossier on "CGT/CGTU," report of 25 Nov. 1922.

98. ADL M 540, dossier on "Congrès CGTU," reports of 26–30 June 1922; *L'Hum.*, 28–29 June 1922 (speeches by Frossard, Lozovsky, and Monmousseau). Lozovsky's views are also detailed in letters to Monatte, Jan. and May 1922, reprinted in *Archives de Monatte,* ed. Chambelland and Maitron, pp. 336–47.

99. *C. Rouge,* 18 Oct., 13 Nov., and 11 Dec. 1920, and 29 Jan. 1921; AN F7 13023, 7–10 July 1921; ADHV 1 M 168, 29 June 1922; Synd. Chaussures, Limoges, 18 June 1922; *Prol. C.,* 25 June 1922.

100. CGTU, *Premier congrès, 1922,* voting results, pp. 487–513; ADHV 1 M 168, 18–25 July 1922. The votes at Saint-Etienne are also tabulated by UD and federation, but not by union, in Robert, *Scission syndicale,* pp. 200–202.

101. Bert at congresses of PO rail line and national federation, in *L'Hum.*, 5 May and 18 June 1922.

102. *L'Hum.*, 27 June 1922 (congress of ceramics federation); *Céram. Lim.,* July 1922. The federation approved adhesion by a vote of nine to six.

103. CGTU, *Premier congrès, 1922,* voting results, pp. 487–513.

104. ADL 93 M 10, 1 July 1921.

105. Report on CGTU meeting in *L'Hum.*, 6 Mar. 1922. For earlier debates on this issue (discussed in ch. 7), see *C. Rouge,* 20 Nov. 1920, and *Peuple L.,* 30 Jan. and 14 Aug. 1921.

106. Monatte in *L'Hum.*, 17 Apr. 1922.

107. Monmousseau in VO, 14 Apr. 1922, and in *L'Hum.*, 16 Apr. 1922.

108. Monmousseau tract and statutes in VO, 12 May 1922, and in *L'Hum.*, 25 May 1922.

109. Frossard at Saint-Etienne congress, in *L'Hum.*, 28 June 1922.

110. Besnard in *L'Hum.*, 13 Nov. 1921.

111. Discussion of statutes in *L'Hum.*, 16 Apr. 1922, and in VO, 21 Apr. and 12 May 1922. Besnard's statutes are also reprinted in *Archives de Monatte,* ed. Chambelland and Maitron, pp. 328–34. The debate on the role of UDs and federations before the schism is discussed earlier in this chapter.

112. Metalworkers' congress, in ADL M 540, dossier on "Congrès CGTU," report of 23 June 1922, and in *L'Hum.*, 24 June 1922.

113. A. Ker in *L'Hum.*, 13 Nov. 1921; similar views are expressed by Monmousseau in VO, 31 Mar. 1922, and in *L'Hum.*, 16 Apr. 1922.

114. Sémard in VO, 2–16 Sept. 1921. Sémard later headed the PCF, from 1924 to 1929.

115. *L'Hum.*, 23 Apr., 25 May, and 4 June 1922 ("Fédéralisme centralisateur," by Monatte); VO, 12 May 1922.

116. Monmousseau in VO, 21 Apr. 1922; Monmousseau at Saint-Etienne congress, in *L'Hum.*, 29 June 1922.

117. CGTU resolution in VO, 27 July 1923; further changes in AN F7 13584, 1 Feb. 1926. Compare Merrheim's critique of regional autonomy, and Dumoulin's proposal to abolish the UDs, reported in AN F7 12995, 23 Feb. 1920, and ADHV 10 M 186, 29 Aug. 1920 (and discussed in ch. 6).

118. VO, 12–26 May 1922; *L'Hum.*, 25 May 1922. The miners' and glassworkers' federations did adopt proportional representation in 1922, and the

CGTU as a whole instituted it in 1927 (the CGT in 1925). ADL M 540, dossier on "Congrès CGTU," reports of 22–25 June 1922; Prost, *La C.G.T.,* p. 19. On the question of reeligibility, see also Collinet, *Esprit du syndicalisme,* p. 173: the author claims that the change, instituted by the CGTU in 1925, reflected the Communists' aim "to consolidate at the head of the unions a caste of professional revolutionaries."

119. ADL M 540, dossier on "Congrès CGTU," reports of 30 June and 1 July 1922.

120. *L'Hum.,* 28 June 1922; text of letter from M. Chambelland to Monatte, 27 June 1922, reprinted in *Archives de Monatte,* ed. Chambelland and Maitron, pp. 348–49.

121. CGTU, *Premier congrès, 1922,* voting results, pp. 487–513. The tables in Robert, *Scission syndicale,* pp. 200–202, do not list separately the results of the two votes.

122. Synd. Chaussures, Limoges, 18 June 1922.

123. ADHV 3 M 232, 9–10 June 1923; *Prol. C.,* 22 July 1923; *Trav. C-O,* 12 Dec. 1924 and 4 Apr. 1925; Synd. Chaussures, Limoges, 13 July 1923 to 7 Jan. 1925. The future evolution of the shoe workers' union (and other Limoges unions) is discussed here in ch. 10.

124. See Besnard, "Le syndicalisme est en danger," in *Libertaire,* 14 July 1922; cited in Maitron, *Mouvement anarchiste,* 2:65. Note that Besnard's CDS had no direct link to Péricat's wartime organization of the same name, discussed here in chs. 3–4. Péricat's group had aimed to "save" syndicalism not from a Bolshevik danger but from the threat of repression on the right. Still, the names do suggest a parallel fear of collaboration with governments or leftist parties, which the CGT majority pursued during the war.

125. *VO,* 7–14 July 1922 (Chambelland) and 15 Sept. 1922 (Monmousseau); *Prol. C.,* 23 July 1922 (Delagrange). Monatte's article, first published in *Clarté,* is reprinted in *R. Peuple,* 10 Sept. 1922. The question posed by the title was in reference to Besnard's cry, at the Saint-Etienne congress, "Il [le syndicalisme] est mort!" CGTU, *Premier congrès, 1922,* p. 425.

126. Synd. Chaussures, Limoges, 18 June 1922 (on the small "anti-statist" faction in the union); and on Saint-Junien: AN F7 13023, 13 Nov. and 27 Dec. 1922; ADHV 1 M 168, 19 Oct. 1923; 4 M 316, 12 June 1924. The anarchist and anarcho-syndicalist factions in Limoges are further discussed in chs. 10–11.

127. *Bull. C.,* 1 Dec. 1921; Bert at railroad congresses, in *L'Hum.,* 5 May and 18 June 1922; and further activities in the railroad federation, in *L'Hum.* and *Prol. C.,* Sept. 1923 to Feb. 1924. Bert's later activities in the CGT, in favor of syndicalist reunification, are discussed in ch. 10. Bert also eventually rejoined the Socialist Party; see his biographical sketch in Maitron, *Dictionnaire biographique,* 19:51–52.

128. ADHV 10 M 147, 24 Jan. 1922; 1 M 167, 10 Jan. 1922; 1 M 168, 29 June and 12–21 Nov. 1922.

129. *Prol. C.,* 18 Dec. 1921, 15 Oct. 1922, and 7–21 Jan. 1923; *L'Hum.,* 18 Jan. 1923; ADHV 1 M 168, 15 Jan. 1923; 3 M 232, 8 June 1923. Beaubelicout

was expelled for having signed (with other syndicalists) a party motion opposing the united front.

130. ADHV 1 M 168, 6 July 1923; 10 M 187, 16–18 July 1923; *Prol. C.,* 22 July 1923.

131. ADHV 1 M 168, 12–21 Nov. 1922, and 29 Mar. and 6 July 1923; Bouthonnier in *L'Hum.,* 23 Apr. 1922, and in *Prol. C.,* 10–24 Oct. and 24–31 Dec. 1922, and 8 Apr., 5 Aug., and 11 Nov. 1923; also compare Bouthonnier's response to the united-front tactic, discussed above.

132. ADHV 1 M 168, 17 Sept., 1 Oct., and 5 Nov. 1923; 1 M 169, 26 May, 25 Aug., and 18 Sept. 1924, and 31 Jan. 1925; 1 M 170, 3 Feb. 1926; 1 M 171, 25 Aug. 1929.

133. ADL M 539, dossier on "Anarchistes et Libertaires," reports of 2 Dec. 1921, and 13 Jan. and 7–10 Feb. 1922.

134. ADL M 539, dossier on "Anarchistes et Libertaires," reports of 13 Sept. 1921, and 7 Feb., 4 Mar., 20 July, and 7 Oct. 1922; and M 540, dossier on "CGT/CGTU," report of 13 May 1922.

135. ADL M 539, dossier "CDS," report of 6 Oct. 1922.

136. ADL M 539, dossier on "Anarchistes et Libertaires," reports of 13 Aug. 1921, 19 Oct. and 1 Dec. 1922, and 25 Jan. 1923; 93 M 10, 7 Aug. 1922 and 13 July 1923. Seigne had in fact quit the anarchist group in 1921; see ch. 7.

137. Bourse, Saint-Etienne, 14 Apr. 1922; AN F7 12995, 24 Apr. 1922; ADL M 539, dossier on "Anarchistes et Libertaires," reports of 8–23 Mar., 13–27 Apr., 19 Aug., 20 Sept., and 12–19 Oct. 1922; M 540, dossier on "CGT/CGTU," report of 15 June 1922. A group of "Jeunesses Syndicalistes" was reconstituted in 1924: M 556, 20 June 1924; M 540, 17 July 1925. See also the group's journal *Le Cri des Jeunes* (Oullins [Rhône], then Saint-Etienne), which included articles by Pierre Besnard and Jean Seigne on federalist labor organization and the Amiens Charter.

138. ADL M 556, 4 July 1922 and 9 Jan. 1923; M 540, dossier on "CGT/CGTU," report of 24 Aug. 1922; 93 M 10, 7 Aug. and 14–17 Sept. 1922. Arnaud also soon quit as Bourse secretary, but he was replaced by another leader of the same syndicalist tendency. Bourse, Saint-Etienne, 7 Aug. 1922; 93 M 59, 17 Aug. and 23–28 Oct. 1922, and 23 Jan. 1923.

139. ADL M 540, dossier on "CGT/CGTU," report of 28 Aug. 1922; M 556, dossier on "USC," report of 5 Feb. 1923.

140. *Peuple L.,* 22–29 July, 2–30 Sept., and 30 Dec. 1923; 10–17 Aug., 21 Sept., and 30 Nov. 1924; AN F7 12996, 24 July, 18 Aug., and 1–25 Sept. 1923; ADL M 539, dossier on "CDS," report of 7 Nov. 1923; M 540, dossier on "CGTU," reports of 4 Sept., 17–27 Nov., and 9 Dec. 1924. Lorduron's defeat and Frachon's politics are further discussed in ch. 10.

141. CGTU, *Premier congrès, 1922,* p. 457. It was Lorduron who was at first alleged to have protested the "death" of syndicalism at the Saint-Etienne congress; commentary in *Travail* (PC), 22 July 1922. In fact, it was Besnard who launched the protest, while Lorduron stressed the need for continued unity in the CGTU, even though his own faction had lost.

142. ADL M 556, dossier on "USC," reports of Jan. to Mar. 1921; AN F7 12996, 23 Aug. 1923; *Peuple L.* (now USC), Feb. 1923 to July 1927. The role of the USC in the Loire and the party's few signs of life in the Haute-Vienne are further discussed in chs. 10–11.

143. *R. Peuple,* 24 Sept. to 5 Nov. 1922; *Travail* (PC), 7–28 Oct. and 25 Nov. 1922; ADL M 556, 7 Oct. and 17 Dec. 1922, and 2 Jan. 1923.

144. Lafont and Faure in *L'Hum.,* 27 Dec. 1921; Vardelle in *Trav. du Papier* (CGT, Limoges), Nov.–Dec. 1922. On Lafont, Frossard, and Jaurès, see also Wohl, *French Communism,* pp. 31, 216–17, 236, 282. There are also two volumes of Frossard's memoirs, but neither stresses the syndicalist issue: *De Jaurès à Lénine: Notes et souvenirs d'un militant* (Paris, 1930), and *De Jaurès à Léon Blum: Souvenirs d'un militant* (Paris, 1943).

145. AN F7 12996, 23 Aug. 1923; ADL M 539, dossier on "Anarchistes et Libertaires," reports of 26 Jan. 1924 and 28 Feb. 1925; *Travail* (PC), 17 Mar. and 23 Apr. 1923; *Prol. C.,* 8 Apr. and 11 Nov. 1923; *L'Hum.,* 20 June 1924; *Cri du Peuple* (PC, Loire), 23 July to 12 Aug. 1927.

146. A. Rosmer in *Lutte de Classes,* 5 July 1922, quoted in Charles, "Débuts de l'I.S.R.," p. 162.

Chapter 10. After 1922: Syndicalists vs. Communists

1. The phrase was Limoges Bourse and shoe worker secretary Jean Rougerie's, in 1918: Synd. Chaussures, Limoges, 11 July 1918.

2. Racamond in *VO,* 12 May 1922; AN F7 13023, 5 Dec. 1929 (Congress of UR Unitaire of the Haute-Vienne).

3. On the party's evolution, see Wohl, *French Communism,* chs. 10–12; Ronald Tiersky, *French Communism, 1920–1972* (New York, 1974), ch. 2; A. Ferrat, *Histoire du P.C.F.* (Paris, 1931), chs. 4–6; and Jedermann [pseud.], *La 'bolchévisation' du P.C.F. (1923–1928)* (Paris, 1971).

4. On Monatte, see the documents in his *Lutte syndicale,* pp. 206–19; on other dissidents from the Communist-syndicalist faction, see Gras, *Rosmer,* pp. 276–307.

5. *VO,* 9 Mar. 1923; on the CDS and the AIT, see ch. 9.

6. *VO,* 13 July 1923 (GSR declaration); AN F7 13584, Aug. 1923.

7. Wohl, *French Communism,* p. 346; see also Monmousseau in *VO,* 20 July 1923.

8. The votes at Bourges are detailed in CGTU, *Congrès national extraordinaire, 2ᵉ congrès de la CGTU, tenu à Bourges du 12 au 17 novembre 1923* (Paris, n.d.), pp. 552–86, and are summarized, by UD and industrial federation, in Robert, *Scission syndicale,* pp. 200–2. According to these figures, the Loire's vote at Bourges was nineteen for the CGTU majority, twenty-six for the CDS, and seventeen for the GSR; the Haute-Vienne's vote was fourteen for the majority, six for the CDS, and one for the GSR. The social and geographic composition of the various factions is discussed later in this chapter.

9. ADHV 10 M 187, 16–18 July 1923 and 24 Sept. 1925; *Prol. C.,* 2 Sept. 1923 to 17 Feb. 1924; *Trav. C-O,* 21 June 1924, and 12 Dec. 1924 to 3 Jan.

1925; *O. Céram.*, Aug. 1923 and Feb. 1925; *Céram. Lim.*, Jan.–Feb. 1925; Synd. Chaussures, Limoges, 13 July to 6 Nov. 1923, 6 June to 12 Nov. 1924, and 7 Jan. 1925; *O. Chaussures*, Jan.–Feb. 1925. On the future importance of autonomous unionism, see *Bataille Synd. Lim.*, Jan. 1933 to Oct. 1935.

10. ADL 93 M 10, 13 July to 18 Aug. 1923; AN F7 12996, 18 Aug. 1923.

11. *Peuple L.*, 30 Nov. 1924 to 10 May 1925; ADL M 540, dossier on "CGTU," reports of 4 Sept. 1924 to 30 Mar. 1925; AN F7 12996, 2 Jan. to 16 Feb. 1925; F7 12741, 3 Dec. 1924 and 31 July 1927. On the CGTSR, see also AN F7 13060, 26 Feb. to 25 Apr. 1927; *Combat Synd.*, Jan. 1927 and Apr. 1928; *Silence du Peuple*, 15 Mar. and 1 June 1929; and Thévenon in *RP*, July 1931.

12. ADL M 539, dossier on "CDS," reports of 23–31 Oct. 1924; AN F7 12996, 9 Jan. and 30 Mar. 1925, and 29 Nov. 1926; F7 12997, 6 Feb. and 29 Nov. 1928, and 5 Nov. 1929; *RP*, Oct. 1925, Mar. to July 1926, and July 1927. On the "Ligue Syndicaliste," see also Gras, *Rosmer*, pp. 318–19, 350–51. The Ligue later merged with a group of minority syndicalists from within the CGTU, the "Comité pour l'Indépendance du Syndicalisme" (CIS). That group published its own weekly, *Le Cri du Peuple*, in Paris beginning 4 Dec. 1929. This publication should not be confused with the Loire Communists' newspaper of the same name.

13. AN F7 13784, 3–11 Dec. 1929; F7 13125, 16 Dec. 1931; *Cri* (Loire), 21–28 Dec. 1929 and 19 Dec. 1931.

14. AN F7 12997, 9 Nov. and 7–9 Dec. 1929; F7 13116, 6 Oct. 1929; *Cri* (Loire), 12 Oct. 1929, and 28 Jan. and 4 Feb. 1933; ADL M 517, 31 Dec. 1932; M 516, 19 Jan. 1933; *Trav. S-S* (CGT), Jan.–Feb. 1933. Note that miner Pierre Arnaud was apparently not related to metalworker Emile Arnaud, Bourse secretary at Saint-Etienne in 1921–22.

15. For example, *Trav. C-O*, 12 Dec. 1924, and 10 Jan. and 19 Sept. 1925; *Cri* (Loire), 12 Oct. 1929; *Réveil* (SFIO, Loire), 10 Mar. 1929; *Travail* (CGT, Haute-Vienne), Feb. 1929, and Apr. and July 1930; and *O. Céram.*, May 1930.

16. The CGTSR explicitly called itself "anarcho-syndicalist" in *Combat Synd.*, 11 Sept. 1936. The anarchists' role in the CGTSR is discussed in *Voix Libertaire* (Paris, then Limoges), especially Dec. 1928 and 4 Jan. to 8 Feb. 1930 (the latter a series of articles on the question, "A quelle CGT doit adhérer un anarchiste syndicable?"); see also Maitron, *Mouvement anarchiste*, 2:65–72. The CGTSR's activities can also be traced in *Voix du Travail* (Paris), Aug. 1926 to Dec. 1927, and *Combat Synd.* (Lyon, then Saint-Etienne, then Limoges), Dec. 1926 through the 1930s; see also Besnard, *Ethique du syndicalisme*. Besnard, who founded the CGTSR in 1926, had been secretary of the anarchistic AIT since mid-1923.

17. On the Ligue Syndicaliste: *RP*, 15 Dec. 1929; *Trib. R.* (Saint-Etienne), 6 Oct. and 1 Dec. 1929; AN F7 13116, 6 June and 9 Nov. 1929; and Gras, *Rosmer*, pp. 315–16. On the autonomists: *Céram. Lim.*, Mar.–Apr. 1926 and Aug. 1930; *O. Chaussures*, May 1926 and Sept. 1930; and *Bataille Synd. Lim.*, Mar. and May 1933, and Jan. 1934.

18. AN F7 13579, 7 Nov. 1924; *Voix du Travail*, Aug. 1926. In 1924–25 the autonomist federation had its own newspaper, *La Bataille Syndicaliste*, formerly

an organ of the anarcho-syndicalist wing of the CGTU. Note the similarity in title to that of the Limoges autonomists' newspaper.

19. Text of CGTSR's "Lyon Charter," reprinted in Besnard, *Ethique du syndicalisme,* pp. 129–39; *Voix du Travail,* Jan. 1927; *O. Chaussures,* May 1926; *Bataille Synd. Lim.,* May 1933; *RP,* Oct. 1925 and 15 Dec. 1929; and *Trib. SMUL,* Mar. 1930. For the views of the Communist-syndicalists, see also Monatte, *Lutte syndicale,* pp. 151–74, 206–19; and *VO,* 1919–24 passim. This question is also discussed here in chs. 7 and 9.

20. The text of the Amiens Charter is reprinted in Lefranc, *Mouvement syndical,* p. 406. For commentaries, see Julliard, "Théorie syndicaliste révolutionnaire," p. 56, on prewar syndicalism (which he prefers to call not "revolutionary" but "direct action" syndicalism); and Jean Rabaut, *Tout est possible! Les "gauchistes" français, 1929–1944* (Paris, 1974), pp. 32–33, on the postwar Ligue Syndicaliste (which mentioned only "resistance," not "revolution," among its four stated aims as published in *RP,* July 1927). That newspaper's title, and the CGTSR's name, of course included the word "revolution," as did the CGTSR's "Lyon Charter," reprinted in Besnard, *Ethique du syndicalisme,* pp. 129–39. The claim that rejecting party leadership meant abandoning the revolution was part of the Communists' own propaganda, as further discussed below.

21. *Cri* (Loire), 12 Oct. 1929; *Trav. C-O,* 25 May 1929. Similar views of Monatte and his friends as "counterrevolutionaries" or "right-oppositionists" are in *Bull. C.,* 8 Apr. 1924 (cited in *Peuple L.,* 11 May 1924); and *Trav. C-O,* 19 Sept. 1925 and 28 Sept. 1929. Monatte and Rosmer affirmed their claim to be, if classification were needed, on not the right but the left of the party, in an open letter to party members, published in the *Cahiers du Bolchévisme,* 12 Dec. 1924, and reprinted in *Le Parti communiste français pendant l'entre-deux-guerres,* ed. Nicole Racine and Louis Bodin (Paris, 1972), p. 135. Rosmer's biographer concedes, however, some truth to the orthodox Communists' allegations, in that if the party abandoned its union operations it would remain primarily an electoral institution. Gras, *Rosmer,* p. 296. Note also that Socialists liked to cite in turn the cases of dissident Communists who rallied to fascism. As one Limoges Socialist warned, many an apparent "communiste libertaire exasperé" was really an "autoritaire violent qui n'a pas encore trouvé sa voie." *Petit Lim.,* 6 Mar. 1926.

22. ADHV 1 M 168, 15 Jan. 1923; 3 M 232, 8 June 1923; ADL M 556, dossier on "USC," reports of 2 Jan. to 5 Feb. 1923; *Prol. C.,* 7–21 Jan. and 22 July 1923; *Trav. C-O,* 4 Apr. 1925; *Peuple L.,* 2 Sept. 1923, 26 Oct. 1924, and 22 Feb. to 19 Apr. 1925. On the later history of the USC in the Loire, see also ADL M 556, dossier on "USC," scattered documents from Mar. 1923 to Oct. 1925; and *Peuple L.,* May 1925 to July 1927. No membership figures are available for the USC, but PCF membership reportedly dropped by 140 at Saint-Etienne and by 335 throughout the Loire from late 1922 to 1924; many of these may have joined the USC. ADL M 556, dossier on "PCF," report of 9 Jan. 1923; M 541, 11 Jan. and 30 Aug. 1924.

23. *Peuple L.,* 22 July 1923. Not all observers were convinced of the sincerity of the group's syndicalist convictions; see Rosmer's critique of Ernest Lafont in

Lutte de Classes, 5 July 1922, quoted in Charles, "Débuts de l'I.S.R.," pt. 2, p. 162.

24. Trotsky in *Lutte de Classes,* Jan. 1930, cited in Rabaut, *Tout est possible!* pp. 56–57. Rosmer was much closer to Trotsky than was Pierre Monatte, who called himself "a friend and admirer" of Trotsky "but not a disciple." *RP,* 1 Jan. 1930, cited in Rabaut, pp. 28–29. On Rosmer's Trotskyism, and his break with the movement in 1931, see also Gras, *Rosmer,* pp. 350–73.

25. Gras, *Rosmer,* pp. 358–59; see also Jean-François Kesler, "Le communisme de gauche en France (1927–1947)," *RFSP* 28 (1978): 740–57; Michel Dreyfus, "Sur l'histoire du mouvement trotskyste en Europe de 1930 à 1952," *M. Social,* no. 96 (1976), pp. 111–24; and Rabaut, *Tout est possible!* pp. 23–26. Rabaut's bibliography also cites a Limoges Trotskyist newspaper, *La Vérité,* published in 1930–32 and available only in private collections. Beyond this, there are few local references to a Trotskyist movement, other than reports on the expulsion of an alleged Trotsky supporter from the Limoges Communist Party; see ADHV 1 M 170, 9 May 1928, and *Trav. C-O,* 23 Feb. 1929. The individual in question was expelled primarily for his violation of party tactics during the recent legislative elections; he had no evident syndicalist ties.

26. *Peuple L.,* 12 Sept. 1926 and 24 July 1927; *Cri* (Loire), 23 July to 13 Aug. 1927; AN F7 13110, 27 July and 25 Aug. 1927.

27. AN F7 13113, 9–25 May 1928; F7 13116, 9 Oct. to 19 Dec. 1929; *Cri* (Loire), 19 Oct. to 14 Dec. 1929, and 1 Mar. 1930; and *Trib. R.,* 16–25 Oct. and 28 Dec. 1929, and 31 Dec. 1930. The party had its own newspaper, *Ça Ira* (Paris), as of Jan. 1930, plus a local mimeographed newsletter, *Le Chambon Rouge,* published by Pétrus Faure at Le Chambon-Feugerolles in 1929–30. Faure later published a larger-scale political weekly, *Le Courrier de l'Ondaine,* beginning in Sept. 1932. There is also a collection of Paul Louis's personal papers and other PUP documents in the Bibliothèque Municipale of Roanne (Loire): carton 7 M⁴ 18. Paul Louis's own *Histoire du socialisme en France* (Paris, 1950) refers only briefly (pp. 397–98) to the USC and the PUP. There is no direct evidence of a PUP in the Haute-Vienne, although there were several expulsions from the party after the 1928 legislative elections and some signs of an unnamed new grouping of local Communist dissidents; see *Trav. C-O,* 2–16 June 1928 and 4 Jan. 1930; ADHV 1 M 170, 9 May and 15 June 1928; 1 M 185, 6 Aug. 1928. The group disappeared quickly, according to AN F7 13130, 5 Aug. 1932.

28. AN F7 12759, 6 Dec. 1929; F7 12997, 9 Dec. 1929; *Cri* (Loire), 1 Mar. 1930 and 21 Oct. 1933.

29. ADHV 1 M 170, 15 June 1928; AN F7 13123, 18 Jan. 1930; ADHV 10 M 186, report on CGT Haute-Vienne, 1934.

30. On Comintern policy, see Kermit E. McKenzie, *Comintern and World Revolution, 1928–1943: The Shaping of Doctrine* (New York, 1964), esp. ch. 5; and Degras, "United Front Tactics," pp. 9–22.

31. On the French context, see especially Danielle Tartakowsky, "Autour de la 'bolchévisation' du P.C.F.," and Serge Wolikow, "Analyse des classes et stratégie du P.C.F.: Période 'classe contre classe' au Front Populaire," in *La classe*

ouvrière française et la politique: Essais d'analyse historique et sociale, by Michel Dion et al. (Paris, 1980), pp. 87–108 and 109–36; and Wolikow, "L'orientation 'classe contre classe,' 1927–1928: Le processus complexe de son élaboration et de sa mise en oeuvre," *Cahiers IMT,* n.s., nos. 25–26 (1978), pp. 14–65.

32. AN F7 13100, 16 Feb. 1929, report on Comintern tactics after the Sixth World Congress in 1928.

33. On Comintern tactics, see Degras, "United Front Tactics," pp. 9–22; and McKenzie, *Comintern and Revolution,* pp. 132–33. On the application of these tactics to France, see Tiersky, *French Communism,* pp. 35–49; and Robert and Tartakowsky, "Front Unique," pp. 32–44.

34. ADHV 1 M 170, 22 July 1927; 10 M 138, 22 Sept. 1928; see also Ferrat, *Histoire du P.C.F.,* pp. 200–201.

35. A. Treint in *Bull. C.,* 13 Apr. 1922, cited in *L'Hum.,* 5 May 1922, and by Paul Faure in *Petit Lim.,* 23 Dec. 1922; see also ADHV 10 M 147, 9 June 1925; ADL M 556, 9 Feb. 1925; AN F7 13584, 1 Feb. 1926; and discussion here in ch. 9.

36. *Pop. C.,* 3 Mar. 1924; *Petit Lim.,* 23 June 1926.

37. On the new election tactics, see William A. Hoisington, Jr., "Class against Class: The French Communist Party and the Comintern. A Study of Election Tactics in 1928," *IRSH* 15 (1970): 19–42; on the elections of 1924, see Wohl, *French Communism,* pp. 383–86. The application of these tactics in the Haute-Vienne and the Loire is detailed in ADHV 1 M 169 and 3 M 166 (for 1924), and 1 M 170–71 and 3 M 167 (for 1928); ADL M 541 and 3 M 67 (for 1924), and 3 M 70 (for 1928); and AN F7 13110 and F7 13113 (for 1927–28). The various party strategies may also be traced in the press, especially *Pop. C.* (SFIO), *Petit Lim.* (SFIO), and *Trav. C-O* (PCF) for the Haute-Vienne; and *Peuple L.* (USC, 1924), *Bloc Ouvrier et Paysan* (PCF, 1924), *Réveil* (SFIO, 1928), and *Cri* (PCF, Loire, 1928), for the Loire.

38. F. Faure in *Réveil,* 25 Mar. 1928.

39. Gérard Walter, *Histoire du Parti communiste français* (Paris, 1948), pp. 191–92. Such calculations do not take into account the votes gained for the party by the withdrawal of Socialist candidates, as in the Haute-Vienne and the Loire, which raised the party's totals on the second round.

40. Local election results are tabulated in ADHV 3 M 167 and ADL 3 M 70, as well as in the local press. Note also that the Communists lost eleven seats nationwide in the 1928 elections, although they won 180,000 more votes and nearly two more percentage points of the total than in 1924. One factor that affected both parties was the switch back to single-member voting districts, a system that strengthens the center against the left and the right.

41. ADHV 3 M 167, 10 Mar. 1928; see also Lenoble et al., *La Gauche au pouvoir,* pp. 107, 113.

42. ADL 3 M 70, 30 Jan. and 7 Apr. 1928; see also the account in Jacques Surgey, "Saint-Etienne et son arrondissement face à la crise des années 30 (1930–1936)" (Thèse de 3e cycle, Saint-Etienne, 1980), pp. 70, 74.

43. ADL 3 M 70, 17 Mar. and 24 Apr. 1928; AN F7 13113, 9–25 May 1928.

Note that there had in fact been no second round in the Loire in 1924, because the Cartel candidates had won all seats outright in the first round.

44. On the Comintern's union strategy, see McKenzie, *Comintern and Revolution,* pp. 133–34; on its application in Britain, see James Hinton and Richard Hyman, *Trade Unions and Revolution: The Industrial Politics of the Early British Communist Party* (London, 1975), pp. 48–49.

45. *Trav. C-O,* 17 Dec. 1927; ADHV 10 M 167, report on the creation of new unions, 1928; 10 M 196, 18 Feb. 1928; 1 M 171, 13 Mar. and 5 Dec. 1929.

46. *Trav. C-O,* 24 Jan. 1925.

47. *Céram. Lim.,* Oct. 1926; *Trav. C-O,* 20 Nov. 1926. The course of collaboration between the CGT and the autonomists is discussed here in ch. 11.

48. *Trav. C-O,* 21 June and 24 July 1924. Similar controversies surrounded the autonomous unions in the Loire; see *Peuple L.,* 24 May 1925 (protest by Coster of the furniture makers' union).

49. See H. Borel, "La stratégie des grèves," in *Bull. C.,* 28 Mar. and 4 Apr. 1924; B. Vassart, *La stratégie des grèves* (Paris, 1926); also Badie, *Stratégie de la grève,* pp. 30–54.

50. See especially AN F7 13100, 16 Feb. 1929, report on Comintern tactics after the Sixth World Congress in 1928.

51. Monmousseau in *Mineur U.* (CGTU), 20 Oct. 1924; Monmousseau and Cellier in *Cri* (Loire), 23 June 1928 and 31 Aug. 1929.

52. Cited in Badie, *Stratégie de la grève,* p. 46.

53. *Cahiers du Bolchévisme,* 1 May 1925; AN F7 13100, 16 Feb. 1929.

54. Wolikow, "Analyse des classes," pp. 114–16; also Danielle Tartakowsky, "Le 'tournant' des années trente," in *Le P.C.F.,* by Bourderon et al., pp. 56–59.

55. *Cri* (Loire), 20 Oct. to 15 Dec. 1928; *Mineur U.,* Nov.–Dec. 1928.

56. AN F7 13797, 31 July and 22 Dec. 1928; F7 13798, 23 Mar. and 17 Oct. 1929; *Cri* (Loire), 5 Oct. 1929 and 21 Feb. 1931; *Mineur U.* (Loire ed.), Feb. 1931.

57. ADL M 1128, 26 Apr. 1929; Frachon in *L'Hum.,* 10 Feb. 1929. The point is also observed, and criticized, by dissident unionists in *Réveil,* 17 Feb. 1929; *Trav. S-S* (Loire ed.), May 1929; and *Trib. SMUL,* July 1930.

58. AN F7 13783, 19 Jan. 1929; F7 13100, 16 Feb. 1929; *Cri* (Loire), 23 Feb. 1929.

59. Criticisms by P. Arnaud in AN F7 13116, 5 Feb. and 20 Mar. 1929; see also *Réveil,* 17 Feb. 1929.

60. U. Thévenon and M. Chambelland in *RP,* 15 Feb. and 15 May 1929; R. Darcis in *Ça Ira* (PUP), 28 June 1930; P. Arnaud in *Trib. SMUL,* June and July 1930; also ADL M 517, 26 Jan. 1930; M 516, 31 Oct. 1931.

61. AN F7 13584, 19 Sept. 1928; F7 13904, text of CGT poster, Dec. 1928; *Réveil,* 17 Feb. and 24 Mar. 1929; *Trav. S-S* (Loire ed.), May 1929.

62. AN F7 13904, 26 Dec. 1928; *Réveil,* 24 Mar. 1929; *Trav. S-S* (Loire ed.), May 1929; *Cri* (Loire), 8 June 1929. The authorities had similarly claimed that agitation for a general strike in metallurgy (which did not reach fruition) in May 1928 was mostly for electoral purposes. AN F7 13782, 31 May 1928.

63. AN F7 13895, 30 Mar. to 8 Apr. 1924; ADL M 541, 11 Apr. 1924; 93 M 10, 7 July 1924; *Peuple L.,* 23 Mar. to 13 Apr. 1924; *Bloc Ouvrier et Paysan,* 12–19 Apr. 1924. The party's apparent electoral preoccupations also contributed to Monatte's and Rosmer's opposition, as they explained in *Bull. C.,* 23 May 1924; cited in Gras, *Rosmer,* p. 299.

64. ADL M 539, dossier on "Anarchistes et Libertaires," reports of 9 Feb. and 29 Mar. 1924.

65. AN F7 13895, 30 Mar. to 8 Apr. 1924.

66. AN F7 13579, 16 Feb. 1924; F7 12996, 23 Feb. 1924; F7 13023, 22 Mar. 1924.

67. AN F7 13895, 17 Mar. to 18 Apr. 1924.

68. As claimed by Frachon in *Pour la CGT,* pp. 107–9; and by Georges Séguy (CGT general secretary) in his preface to Frachon's book, p. x.

69. AN F7 13895, 4 Apr. 1924.

70. AN F7 12967, monthly report, Mar. 1924.

71. *Combat Synd.* (CGTSR), Mar. and Dec. 1928.

72. *Mineur U.,* Nov.–Dec. 1928.

73. ADHV 4 M 174, 25 Feb. 1924; *Trav. S-S* (Loire ed.), May 1929.

74. *VO,* 8 Feb. 1924 ("Plus de grève partielle!"); *Mineur U.,* 20 Oct. 1924; AN F7 13579, 16 Feb. 1924; F7 13584, 13 Feb. 1928; F7 13792, 31 Mar. 1924; F7 13795, 23 Jan. 1926; F7 13797, 31 July 1928.

75. *L'Hum.,* 29 Feb. 1928; AN F7 13584, 2 Mar. 1928.

76. AN F7 13797, 31 July 1928; F7 13798, 23 Mar. and 17 Oct. 1929; F7 13905, 25 Feb. 1931; *Trib. SMUL,* Feb. 1930 and Mar.–Apr. 1931; see also the similar argument by CGT miners in *Trav. S-S* (Loire ed.), May 1929. For the local Communists' position, see *Cri* (Loire), 21 Feb. 1931.

77. On CP membership, see Annie Kriegel, "Le Parti communiste français sous la IIIᵉ République (1920–1939): Mouvement des effectifs et structures d'organisation," in her *Le pain et les roses: Jalons pour une histoire des socialismes* (Paris, 1968), pp. 187–92 (article reprinted from *RFSP* 16 [1966]: 5–35). On CGTU membership, see Prost, *La C.G.T.,* pp. 34–36. Strike activity in the late 1920s is discussed here in ch. 11.

78. B. Souvarine in *Bull. C.,* Jan.–Mar. 1928 (reprinted in *Réveil,* 6 May 1928); *Trav. C-O,* 16 June 1928, 7 Dec. 1929, and 1 Mar. 1930; P. Arnaud and Pétrus Faure in *Trib. R.,* 17–19 Oct. 1929; M. Chambelland in *RP,* 15 May 1929; L. Sellier in *Ça Ira* (PUP), 21 Jan. 1930; Chambelland in *Cri* (Paris), 11–18 Feb. 1931.

79. *Trav. C-O,* 28 Sept. 1929; *Réveil,* 27 Jan. 1929; *Cri* (Loire), 19 Jan. 1929 and 21 Feb. 1931; *Mineur U.* (Loire ed.), Mar. and May 1930.

80. See the discussion of Merrheim's politics in ch. 4 of this study and in Papayanis, "Masses révolutionnaires," pp. 71–72.

81. AN F7 13121, 9 Sept. and 6 Oct. 1930; F7 13125, 20 May and 18 Sept. 1931; see also Danielle Tartakowsky, "1927–1931: Pour la conquête des masses," *Cahiers IMT,* n.s., no. 5 (1973), pp. 14–33; Tartakowsky, " 'Tournant,' " pp. 41–74; and Badie, *Stratégie de la grève,* pp. 55–60.

82. The circumstances of the party's strategic shift after 1930 are further discussed here in ch. 11; see also Serge Wolikow, "Le P.C.F. devant la crise (1929–1931): Les positions sur l'économie, leur place dans la politique du P.C.F.," *Cahiers IMT*, n.s., no. 11 (1975), pp. 32–94.

83. AN F7 13113, 17 Mar. 1928; F7 13116, 21 Jan. to 6 Oct. 1929; *Cri* (Loire), 12 Oct. and 23 Nov. 1929.

84. AN F7 13113, 9–25 May 1928; F7 13116, 25 Sept. and 14 Oct. 1929; F7 12997, 9 Nov. 1929; *Cri* (Loire), 9 Nov. and 14 Dec. 1929. The election controversy also led to CP exclusions in the Haute-Vienne: ADHV 1 M 170, 9 May and 15 June 1928. Unlike Pétrus Faure, however, mayor Léon Texier of Ambazac went ahead with plans for the illegal 1 Aug. 1929 demonstration and was therefore discharged from his mayoral functions. 1 M 173, 29 July to 2 Aug. 1929, and 23 June to 29 Oct. 1930.

85. AN F7 13116, 19 Dec. 1929; *Cri* (Loire), 4 Jan. and 1 Mar. 1930; *Trib. R.*, 31 Dec. 1930; *Ça Ira*, 21 Jan. and 13–27 Dec. 1930.

86. Faure, *Un témoin raconte*, p. 43.

87. AN F7 12996, 14 Apr. 1924.

88. AN F7 13792, 26 Aug. 1924.

89. On these action committees, see Wohl, *French Communism*, pp. 318, 328–30, 343–45; and Ferrat, *Histoire du P.C.F.*, pp. 128, 146–48.

90. ADL M 539, dossier on "Comité d'Action," reports of 14 Jan. and 2 Feb. 1923, and 17 Nov. 1924; M 539, dossier on "Anarchistes et Libertaires," reports of 28 July and 25 Aug. 1923; 26 July, 10 Oct., and 22 Nov. 1924; and 7 Aug. and 5–11 Dec. 1925; M 540, dossier on "Antimilitarisme," reports of 10–14 May, 17 July, and 7–24 Aug. 1925.

91. AN F7 13116, 14 Sept. 1929; *Cri* (Loire), 12 Oct. 1929.

92. Danielle Tartakowsky, *Les premiers communistes français: Formation des cadres et bolchévisation* (Paris, 1980), pp. 125–26. Tartakowsky's assessment is based on statistics for students enrolled in the CP's *"écoles des cadres."* The questions of membership and recruitment in the party and the CGTU are further discussed here in ch. 11.

93. Pierre Monatte, "Les commissions syndicales" (25 Nov. 1923), in his *Lutte syndicale*, p. 211; see also Monmousseau, "Contrôle syndical"; AN F7 13578, 14 Mar. 1923; F7 13579, 8 Sept. 1925; F7 12967, Apr. 1924.

94. AN F7 13102, 27 July 1923; F7 13584, Aug. 1923; F7 12996, 14 Sept. 1923; *VO*, 3 Aug. 1923; *Prol. C.*, 5 Aug. 1923; *Peuple L.*, 30 Sept. 1923.

95. Bouthonnier in *Prol. C.*, 5 Aug. 1923; compare Monmousseau in *VO*, 29 Sept. 1922; and Monatte in *Lutte syndicale*, p. 208.

96. AN F7 13578, text of CGTU's "Rapport sur les Comités d'Usine," 15 Oct. 1922; Monmousseau, "Contrôle syndical"; Synd. Chaussures, Limoges, 4 July and 6 Nov. 1923.

97. ADHV 1 M 168, 17 Mar. and 22 June 1923. A local Communist similarly proposed that the party's later "factory cells" be organized by workers outside the industry in question; that would have made them simple party agencies with no union ties. 1 M 169, 18 Sept. 1924.

98. *VO,* 28 Mar. 1924; compare AN F7 13100, report of 16 Feb. 1929.

99. *Prol. C.,* 6 May and 8 July 1923; *Synd.* Chaussures, Limoges, 19 Sept. 1924; ADL 93 M 10, 21 Sept. 1923; AN F7 13895, 30 Mar. and 1 Apr. 1924; F7 13116, 5 Feb. and 20 Mar. 1929.

100. Kriegel, "Le P.C.F.," in her *Le pain et les roses,* pp. 216–18; Tartakowsky, " 'Bolchévisation,' " pp. 97–101. Kriegel also discusses the party's structural reorganization (pp. 204–15); see also Wohl, *French Communism,* pp. 400–403. The weaknesses of cell organizaton and party implantation in the Loire and the Haute-Vienne are discussed here in ch. 11.

101. Union secretary Matline, of the Parisian hat-makers, interviewed in 1973 and quoted in Tartakowsky, *Premiers communistes,* p. 98.

102. Open letters to party members by P. Monatte with A. Rosmer and V. Delagarde, published in the *Cahiers du Bolchévisme,* 5–12 Dec. 1924, and reprinted in *Le P.C.F.,* ed. Racine and Bodin, pp. 133, 137.

103. ADHV 1 M 169, 9 Aug. and 22 Oct. 1924, and 16–31 Jan. 1925; 1 M 171, 25 Aug. 1929. Compare earlier protests discussed here in ch. 9.

104. *Peuple L.,* 21–28 Sept. 1924; Pétrus Faure in *Trib. R.,* 20 Oct. 1929.

105. As argued by Michel Collinet in "Masses et militants: La bureaucratie et la crise actuelle du syndicalisme ouvrier français," *RHES* 29 (1951): 69; see also his *Esprit du syndicalisme,* pp. 92–98. The earlier debates on the proposed switch from UDs to URs are discussed here in ch. 9.

106. AN F7 12997, 20 Aug. 1928; *Cri* (Loire), 12 Oct. and 21 Dec. 1929.

107. For example, *O. Céram.,* Aug. 1922, Aug. 1923, and Jan.–Feb. 1925; *Pop. C.,* 29 June 1922, and 14 Aug., 22 Nov., and 11 Dec. 1923; *Réveil,* 19 Feb. 1928; AN F7 13580, 3 Sept. 1925.

108. P. Sémard in *L'Hum.,* 7 Apr. 1924; similar views in *VO,* 14 July 1922, and 6 Apr. and 20 July 1923; *L'Hum.,* 20 June 1924; *Prol. C.,* 19–26 Aug. and 23–30 Sept. 1923; *Cri* (Loire), 14 Dec. 1929 and 1 Mar. 1930; AN F7 12996, 23 Aug. 1923.

109. Dumoulin in *Pop. C.,* 12 July 1922; AN F7 13578, 8 Nov. 1922 and 19 Mar. 1923; F7 13579, 26 Nov. 1925. For Dumoulin's later views, which came to question some of these earlier ideas, see *Cri* (Paris), esp. 17 Dec. 1930, 17 June 1931, and 6 Feb. 1932; and Marie-France Rogliano, "L'anticommunisme dans la C.G.T.: 'Syndicats,' " *M. Social,* no. 87 (1974), esp. pp. 77–78.

110. AN F7 13578, 19 Mar. 1923; Vardelle in *Trav. du Papier,* Nov.–Dec. 1922; Vardelle at CGT Congress of 1927, in CGT, Congrès Confédéral de Paris, 1927, *Compte-rendu des débats* (Paris, n.d.), pp. 100–101; *Petit Lim.,* 6 Jan. 1926 and 16 May 1928; *Travail* (CGT, Haute-Vienne), July 1932.

111. Dumoulin in *Pop. C.,* 7 Nov. 1924; AN F7 13580, 21 Feb. 1927. The evolution of closer CGT-SFIO relations is also traced by Charles, in "S.F.I.O. et C.G.T.," pp. 47–84. The author points out that the SFIO was far less centralized than the PCF and thus seemed closer to the federalist traditions of the CGT (pp. 49–50).

112. Jouhaux at CGT congresses of 1925 and 1927, quoted in Bernard Georges et al., *Léon Jouhaux dans le mouvement syndical français* (Paris, 1979),

pp. 29, 34. The issue of the *"politique de présence"* was one of the grounds for Dumoulin's ambivalence toward CGT strategy; see *Cri* (Paris), 17 Dec. 1930 and 28 Jan. 1931.

113. AN F7 13579, 3 Sept. and 26 Nov. 1925; F7 13580, 22 Dec. 1927 and 19 Jan. 1928; *Réveil,* 8 Apr. 1928; *Petit Lim.,* 16–30 May 1928. On the SFIO's left-wing faction, led nationally by Jean Zyromski, see also Baker, "Left Wing of Socialist Party," pp. 12–15.

114. L. Dumond, of CGT miners, in *Réveil,* 1 Apr. 1928.

115. CGT viewpoints in AN F7 13580, 20 Nov. 1926 and 22 Dec. 1927; *Trav. S-S,* May–Aug. 1927 and May–June 1929; and *Travail* (Haute-Vienne), Aug. 1928; opposing viewpoints in AN F7 13584, 3 May 1927; F7 13110, 31 Aug. 1927; F7 13082, 22 May 1928; *Trav. C-O,* 18 Dec. 1926; *Métallurgiste* (CGTU), June 1927, Jan. 1928, Sept.–Dec. 1929, and June 1930; and *Mineur U.,* Oct. 1927. On the issue of "rationalization" see also Charles, "S.F.I.O. et C.G.T.," pp. 62–71; Michel Margairaz, "La S.F.I.O. face au capitalisme (1920–1940): Eléments pour un dossier," *Cahiers IMT,* n.s., no. 14 (1975), pp. 87–116; Fine, "Toward Corporatism," pp. 174–80; and Dufraisse, "Mouvement ouvrier 'rouge,' " in *Mouvements ouvriers,* ed. Fauvel-Rouif, pp. 166–73. The economic impact of rationalization is further discussed here in ch. 11.

116. CGT viewpoints in *Travail* (Haute-Vienne), Nov. 1928, and *O. Céram.,* Oct.–Dec. 1928; opposing viewpoints in *Céram. Lim.,* Dec. 1928; *Trav. C-O,* 24 Oct. 1928; *RP,* 15 May 1929; and AN F7 12997, 6 Feb. 1929.

117. Evaluation in Georges et al., *Jouhaux,* pp. 34, 85.

118. Dumoulin, "Syndicalistes français"; AN F7 13584, 19 Sept. 1928. The CGT's (and its rivals') actual strike strategy is further discussed here in ch. 11.

119. AN F7 13579, 8 Jan. 1923 and 27 Aug. 1925; F7 13580, 21 Feb., 5–6 Apr., and 28 July 1927; F7 13584, 1 Feb. 1926 and 23 Apr. 1927; *Voix du Peuple,* July–Aug. 1925, July–Aug. 1927, and Sept. 1931; compare the views of the Haute-Vienne's CGT leaders in *Travail,* Feb. 1932, and *O. Céram.,* Mar. and May 1930, Dec. 1932, and Aug. 1934. In addition to the above reports, the CGTU's position was expressed in its pamphlet *Pour une C.G.T. et une Internationale uniques: Vers l'unité syndicale* (Paris, [1925]). The attempts at "unity of action" are discussed here in ch. 11.

120. See *Cri* (Paris), esp. 31 Dec. 1931 and 6 Feb. 1932; and Daniel Guérin, "Une tentative de réunification syndicale, 1930–31," *RHES* 44 (1966): 107–21.

121. *Cri* (Paris), 10 Dec. 1930, 22 July 1931, and (for Monatte's view), 31 Dec. 1931; *Trib. R.,* 11 Dec. 1930 and 29 May 1931; *Trib. SMUL,* Feb. 1931; ADL M 516, 17–25 Mar. 1931. For the local CGT's views—mostly negative— see *Echo Syndical* (published at Lyon), Aug. 1931.

122. See lists of supporters published in *Cri* (Paris), esp. 21–28 Jan., 4 Feb., and 29 July 1931. On the teachers, see also the debates in their journal *L'Effort* (CGTU, Haute-Vienne), esp. Dec. 1929, July 1930, and Jan. 1931.

123. *Cri* (Paris), 22 Apr. 1931; *Travail* (Haute-Vienne), Aug. 1931.

124. For example, *O. Céram.,* Mar. and July 1930, Dec. 1932, and Aug. 1934.

125. *Petit Lim.,* 6 Mar. 1926; *Travail* (Haute-Vienne), Feb. 1929, and Apr. and July 1930; *O. Céram.,* May 1930; compare the Communists' views in *Trav. C-O,* 27 Dec. 1924 to 10 Jan. 1925, and 19 Sept. 1925; and *Cri* (Loire), 12 Oct. 1929.

126. It should be remembered that most unions that quit the CGTU remained in autonomy in the Haute-Vienne (until 1936) but quickly returned to the CGT in the Loire.

127. *Réveil,* 10–31 Mar. 1929; compare *Trav. C-O,* 5 Oct. 1935.

128. ADHV 3 M 166, 29–30 Apr. 1924; *Petit Lim.,* 7 May 1924. The autonomous porcelain workers urged simple abstention in the 1928 legislative elections; see *Céram. Lim.,* Mar. 1928. The anarchists in Saint-Etienne also debated the issue, and many opposed abstentionism in favor of positive action to defeat right-wing candidates, who were more of a danger there than in Limoges. ADL M 539, dossier on "Anarchistes et Libertaires," report of 27 Nov. 1925.

129. Arnaud in *Trib. R.,* 6 Oct. 1929; similar viewpoint in *Trib. SMUL,* Mar. 1930.

130. For example, *O. Chaussures,* Jan. 1925.

131. *Céram. Lim.,* Dec. 1928; *O. Chaussures,* Oct.–Nov. 1929 and Apr.–June 1930; *Bataille Synd. Lim.,* Jan. 1935; Arnaud in *Cri* (Loire), 22 Dec. 1928; Chambelland in *RP,* 15 May 1929; and *Trib. SMUL,* Sept. 1930.

132. *O. Chaussures,* Feb. 1928; *Céram. Lim.,* June–Aug. 1928; *Trib. SMUL,* Mar. 1930; *Combat Synd.,* Jan.–Feb. 1927, 1 Mar. 1928, and 23 June 1933. The CGTU refused to endorse the six-hour day and, at its congress in 1929, specifically rejected the hope that technological progress might permit a shorter work day. Lefranc, *Mouvement syndical,* p. 276. This may have been because the Soviet Union did not have a shortened work day. *Combat Synd.,* 1 June 1927.

133. *RP,* 15 Feb. and 15 May 1929; *Cri* (Loire), 12 Oct. and 23 Nov. 1929; *O. Chaussures,* Aug. 1931.

134. ADHV 10 M 187, 29 Mar. 1927; *Céram. Lim.,* Mar.–July 1922, Oct.–Dec. 1924, and Mar.–Apr. 1926; *Bataille Synd. Lim.,* Mar. 1933 and Feb. 1934; ADL M 539, dossier on "CDS," report of 8 Oct. 1923; 93 M 26, 26 Apr. 1924; AN F7 13798, 31 May 1929; *Cri* (Loire), 22 Dec. 1928 and 12 Oct. 1929.

135. *O. Chaussures,* June 1930.

136. M. Lepoil in *Libertaire,* 17 Aug. 1924 (extract in AN F7 13579); see chs. 7 and 9 on the anarchists' views of the schism. Lepoil's views were countered by the anarchist Le Pen in *Libertaire,* 28 Aug. 1924, and in *Voix Libertaire,* 1 Feb. 1930.

137. AN F7 12996, 28 Jan. 1924; ADL M 539, dossier on "CDS," reports of 23–31 Oct. 1924; *RP,* Oct. 1925 and 15 May 1929. There is no evidence that Lorduron actually rejoined the CGT before reunification, although he did rejoin the SFIO along with most of the Loire's USC. AN F7 13082, 17 Jan. 1929.

138. AN F7 13799, 17 Nov. 1930; *Cri* (Loire), 5 July and 22 Nov. 1930; *Trib. SMUL,* Sept.–Dec. 1930, Feb. 1931, and July and Oct. 1932.

139. Compare the "Opposition Unitaire" in the CGTU teachers' federation, as described in Bernard et al., *Syndicalisme dans l'enseignement,* 3:107–10, 170–83.

140. *Peuple L.,* 22 Feb. and 16 May 1925; *O. Chaussures,* Jan.–Feb. 1925 and Jan.–Mar. 1931; *Bataille Synd. Lim.,* Mar. 1933.

141. *Trav. C-O,* 14 Feb. 1925.

142. *Combat Synd.,* 8 Sept. 1933 and 13 Mar. 1936; also CGTSR poster, 1936, in ADHV 10 M 189.

143. *Combat Synd.,* 25 Aug. 1933 and 20 Dec. 1935.

144. Besnard's views in ADHV 10 M 147, 17 Oct. 1933; text of CGTSR's "Lyon Charter," in Besnard, *Ethique du syndicalisme,* pp. 129–39; *Voix du Travail,* Aug. 1926; *Voix Libertaire,* 4 Jan. and 8 Feb. 1930, 28 Aug. and 8 Oct. 1932; and *Combat Synd.,* 16 Mar., 22 June, 17 Aug., and 9 Nov. 1934.

145. *Céram. Lim.,* Aug. 1925; *O. Chaussures,* May 1926, Nov. 1929, and Dec. 1932; *Bataille Synd. Lim.,* Feb. 1934 and Oct. 1935.

146. *Cri des Jeunes* (Saint-Etienne), Feb. 1924; *Voix Libertaire* (Limoges), July and Dec. 1928; *O. Chaussures,* Jan. to Aug. 1929.

147. Synd. Chaussures, Limoges, 29 Apr. 1924.

148. Ibid., 28 Jan. and 13 Aug. 1926.

149. *Peuple L.,* 19 Dec. 1926; AN F7 13584, 19 Sept. 1928; see also Frachon, *Pour la CGT,* pp. 10, 40–41.

150. Monmousseau, *Syndicalisme devant la révolution,* p. 6.

151. On prewar syndicalism, see Julliard, "Théorie syndicaliste révolutionnaire," p. 56; the quotation here is a summary by Jean Charles of postwar Communist theory, in "La C.G.T.U. et la greffe du communisme sur le mouvement syndical français: Fragments de thèse" (Paris I, 1969), p. 157.

152. For example, *Cri des Jeunes,* Feb. to July 1924; Monatte in *RP,* 15 Dec. 1929. Compare the Communists' views, in *VO,* 19 Aug. 1921 (Sémard), and 20 Apr. 1923 (Trotsky); and Lenin, *"Left-Wing" Communism.*

153. *Voix du Travail,* Jan. 1927; *O. Chaussures,* May 1926; *Bataille Synd. Lim.,* May 1933; *Combat Synd.,* esp. Mar. 1927 and 8 Sept. 1933; also CGTSR's "Lyon Charter," in Besnard, *Ethique du syndicalisme,* pp. 129–33.

154. Monmousseau in *VO,* 17 Mar. 1922; Sémard in *VO,* 24 Aug. 1923; Willard, ed., "Souvenirs de Frachon," pp. 63–72; and Frachon, *Pour la CGT,* pp. 25, 40–41, 57–58, 69.

155. *VO,* 2 Dec. 1921 (Monatte), 24 Mar. 1922 (Chambelland), and 13 July 1923 (GSR declaration); *RP,* Oct. 1925 (Chambelland) and 15 Dec. 1929 (Monatte); also CGTSR's "Lyon Charter," in Besnard, *Ethique du syndicalisme,* p. 129.

Chapter 11. Syndicalism in Action

1. Compare Stearns, *Revolutionary Syndicalism* ("A Cause without Rebels").

2. Figures in Prost, *La C.G.T.,* pp. 200–202; see also discussion here in ch. 9, and table in ch. 9, n. 61.

3. Prost, *La C.G.T.,* pp. 34–35. On Communist Party membership, which declined steadily from 1921 to 1933 except for a brief rebound in 1924, see Kriegel, "Le P.C.F.," in her *Le pain et les roses,* pp. 187–204. Scattered local figures show similar declines in the Haute-Vienne from 1921 to 1928, with a partial rebound

in 1930 and another decline by 1932; there was a more constant decline from 1921 to 1932 in the Loire. ADHV 1 M 168–71, reports for 1921–30; ADL M 556 (dossier on "PCF") and M 541, reports for 1922–24; AN F7 13106, F7 13129, and F7 13130, reports for 1926 and 1932.

4. See the reports on union elections in the Loire coal mines, in AN F7 13795, 12 Feb. 1926, and F7 13798, 30 May 1929. The record of strike activity is detailed in a later section of this chapter.

5. As argued by Prost, *La C.G.T.,* pp. 34–35; and by Charles, "S.F.I.O. et C.G.T.," p. 52. A similar argument was made by J. Racamond of the CGTU in *Trav. C-O,* 7 Sept. 1929.

6. A. Porte (of autonomists) in *Peuple L.,* 22 Feb. 1925; and P. Sémard in *VO,* 16 Jan. 1925. See also J. Racamond in AN F7 13113, report of 11 Sept. 1928; and Racamond in *Trav. C-O,* 7 Sept. 1929.

7. On this shift, see especially Tartakowsky, " 'Tournant,' " p. 59; and Tartakowsky, "Conquête des masses," pp. 23–25.

8. Figures for 1922–25 from Robert, *Scission syndicale,* pp. 117–19 (the number of abstentions has been added to the total vote for 1922); figures for 1927 from Lefranc, *Mouvement syndical,* p. 271.

9. Jospin cites (without references) various estimates of CGTSR membership that range from 1,000 to 6,000, in his "La C.G.T.S.R.," p. 116.

10. A. Herclet in *Trav. C-O,* 19 Sept. 1925.

11. There were approximately 1,000 subscribers to *RP* in 1927, according to Rabaut, *Tout est possible!* p. 31. On the size and composition of the *VO* group, see Young, *"Vie Ouvrière,"* pp. 38–48, 172–81, 300–308.

12. See lists of signers published in *Cri* (Paris), 7 Jan. to 15 July 1931; of these, a total of twenty-four signers were from the Haute-Vienne and ninety-two were from the Loire. On the "Comité des 22," see also Guérin, "Tentative de réunification," and discussion here in ch. 10.

13. See Guérin, "Tentative de réunification"; and Monatte in *Cri* (Paris), 31 Dec. 1931 and 6 Feb. 1932. Note that the journal, which had had a peak of some 5,000 subscribers (according to its 4 Nov. 1931 issue), ceased publication soon after the failure of the attempted reunification; the last issue was that of 6 Feb. 1932.

14. UD votes tabulated in Robert, *Scission syndicale,* pp. 200–201. At the CGTU congress of 1925 there were only two dissenting votes from the Loire and none from the Haute-Vienne.

15. AN F7 12996, 7 Nov. 1925. The victorious UD secretary, Frachon, also made this argument in his *Pour la CGT,* p. 115.

16. AN F7 12996, 16 Feb. and 7 Nov. 1925; F7 13023, 18 Sept. 1925.

17. Tabulated UD votes in Robert, *Scission syndicale,* pp. 200–201; votes by each union in CGTU, *Premier congrès, 1922,* pp. 487–513; and CGTU, *2e congrès, 1923,* pp. 552–86.

18. *Prol. C.,* 2 Sept. 1923 to 17 Feb. 1924; ADHV 1 M 171, 23 Oct. 1929. Other syndicalist currents also existed among railroad workers, including an autonomous federation led by Pierre Besnard (with some 50 members) and the mi-

nority wing of the CGTU federation; the latter rejoined the CGT in 1932. There are no signs, however, of support for either current at Limoges. See AN F7 13669, 21 Oct. 1926; F7 13671, 13 June 1929, 25 Nov. 1930, 15 Dec. 1931, and 29 Mar. 1932.

19. On Gaillard: *Prol. C.,* 22 July 1923; ADHV 1 M 168, 19 Oct. 1923; 4 M 174, 25 Feb. 1924; and 10 M 187, 18 Oct. 1926. On the elections of 1928, see tabulated results in 3 M 167. The Communist candidate, Joseph Lasvergnas, took the lead in the city of Saint-Junien, but he trailed narrowly in the canton and lost by a wide margin in the district as a whole.

20. Lists of votes in CGTU, *Premier congrès, 1922,* pp. 487–513; and CGTU, *2ᵉ congrès, 1923,* pp. 552–86.

21. Compare Robert, *Scission syndicale,* pp. 180–81; Wohl, *French Communism,* p. 346; and Maitron, *Mouvement anarchiste,* 2:65–72.

22. Union membership figures in ADHV 10 M 178–79, reports on trade unions in the Haute-Vienne, 1 Jan. 1924 and 1 Jan. 1927; and scattered figures in 10 M 115, 21 Oct. 1930; 10 M 191, 1 Jan. 1936; and AN F7 13023, 1 Mar. 1929. The CGT finally surpassed the autonomous unions in both industries on the eve of unity in 1936.

23. On the CGTSR: ADHV 10 M 189, 30 Nov. 1929 and 22 Mar. 1934; 4 M 316, 17 Sept. and 30 Nov. 1936; and *Combat Synd.,* Feb.–Mar. 1933. On the autonomists: *O. Chaussures,* July–Sept. 1930 and Dec. 1932; and *Bataille Synd. Lim.,* May 1933 and Jan. 1934. On the shoe union's expectations concerning membership after autonomy: Synd. Chaussures, Limoges, 29 Apr. 1924, and 28 Jan. and 13 Aug. 1926.

24. Tabulated UD votes in Robert, *Scission syndicale,* pp. 200–201.

25. Lists of votes in CGTU, *Premier congrès, 1922,* pp. 487–513; and CGTU, *2ᵉ congrès, 1923,* pp. 552–86. For the votes by industrial federation, see the tabulated results in Robert, *Scission syndicale,* p. 202.

26. AN F7 12996, 16 Feb. and 7 Nov. 1925, and 8 Feb. 1926; F7 12741, 31 July 1927.

27. AN F7 13060, 26 Feb. to 25 Apr. 1927; *Combat Synd.,* Jan. 1927 and Apr. 1928; *Silence du Peuple,* 15 Mar. and 1 Apr. 1929; ADL M 592, trade-union statistics, 1 Jan. 1930; M 516, 20 Mar. 1937 and 11 Feb. 1938.

28. AN F7 12997, 28 Feb. and 19 July 1927, and 29 Nov. 1928. Further information on the UD-CGT is in *Echo Syndical* (published at Lyon) for Apr. 1929 through Dec. 1936. The UD claimed 69 member unions and a total membership of 7,000 unionists in the Loire in Nov. 1935.

29. AN F7 12996, 14 Sept. 1923, 4 Sept. and 9 Dec. 1924, and 7 Nov. 1925; F7 12741, 4 Oct. 1924; and Frachon, *Pour la CGT,* p. 115.

30. AN F7 12996, 14 Sept. 1923 and 14 Apr. 1924; ADL 93 M 26, 26 Aug. 1924; CGTU, *2ᵉ congrès, 1923,* p. 579. Unlike the Saint-Etienne miners' union, those at Firminy, La Ricamarie, and Le Chambon did support the CGTU majority at Bourges.

31. AN F7 12996, 1 Mar. 1923, 28 Jan. 1924, and 26 June 1926; F7 12997, 20 Feb. 1927. The "unity" of confederal and autonomous unions in the Saint-

Etienne Bourse is discussed in the final section of this chapter.

32. AN F7 13116, 6 Oct. 1929; *Trib. R.,* 6 Oct. 1929; *Cri* (Loire), 23 Nov. 1929.

33. ADL M 517, 10 June and 31 Dec. 1932. Earlier signs of dissension among miners outside Saint-Etienne are reported in AN F7 12997, 20 July 1927; F7 13904, 26 Dec. 1928; F7 13799, 4 Feb. 1930; F7 13801, 2 Dec. 1931; by U. Thévenon in *RP,* 15 Feb. 1929 and July 1931; and in *Trib. SMUL,* Mar. 1930 and June 1932.

34. *Cri* (Loire), 25 July 1932; *Mineur U.* (Loire ed.), Apr. 1933; ADL M 513, 3 Jan. 1935.

35. Prost, *La C.G.T.,* pp. 52–54, 201–2; according to his figures, the ratio of CGT to CGTU miners stood at more than three to one in 1924, further widened by 1932, and only then began to narrow as Communist membership slowly rebounded while CGT membership continued to decline (until 1936).

36. *Trib. R.,* 11 Dec. 1930 and 29 May 1931; *Trib. SMUL,* Feb. 1931 and Oct. 1932; *Cri* (Paris), 22 July 1931; ADL M 516, 25 Mar. 1931; M 517, 3 Apr. and 17 Nov. 1930, 28 Jan. 1931, and 14 Nov. 1935.

37. ADL M 517, 5 Mar. 1937; M 516, 23 Jan. 1939; and Bourse, Saint-Etienne, 14 May 1936 and 3 Feb. 1939. Bourse reports for 1 Aug. 1941 and 30 May 1947 cite Arnaud as assistant secretary and then general secretary of the organization during and after World War II.

38. ADL 93 M 97, 5 Feb. 1925; the circumstances surrounding the reorganization of separate Communist unions in Limoges are discussed earlier in this chapter.

39. AN F7 12996, 29 Nov. 1926; F7 12997, 29 Nov. 1927; ADL M 516, 17 Mar. 1931 and 23 Jan. 1939; M 515, 5 June 1939. On the politics of the teachers' unions, see also *Bulletin de l'Union Fraternelle* (CGT, Loire), for 1929–30; *Le Travailleur de l'Enseignement* (CGTU, Loire), for 1931–35; *L'Effort* (CGTU, Haute-Vienne), for 1928–33; and AN F7 13747–49 for 1925–29 and 1935–36. The role of the "Opposition Unitaire" in the teachers' federation before reunification is further discussed in Bernard et al., *Syndicalisme dans l'enseignement,* 3:170–72. After reunification, the teachers' federation was a main supporter of the anti-Bolshevik and pro-autonomy "Syndicats" faction; see Prost, *La C.G.T.,* pp. 147–48; and Rogliano, " 'Syndicats,' " pp. 64, 75.

40. See Jospin, "La C.G.T.S.R.," pp. 117–19, on the organization's appeal to workers in *"la petite industrie,"* including leather, clothing, hairdressing, building, and some metalworking trades.

41. A useful index of the proportion of skilled labor in the principal French industrial sectors (for 1948) is in Collinet, *Condition ouvrière,* pp. 88–89. Other highly skilled or technologically traditional industries were printing, clothing, and construction, which were also bastions of revolutionary syndicalism. Collinet's figures further distinguish between "metallurgy" and "metalworking" or "mechanical" trades; the latter were, of course, the more highly skilled and also the most characteristic of Saint-Etienne. On the nature of the Loire's metals industries, see discussion here in ch. 1.

42. See *R. Tiss.*, Jan. 1926 to Dec. 1932; Arbogast, *Armes*, pp. 177–79; and discussion of prewar weavers and gunsmiths in ch. 2 of this study.

43. *Peuple L.*, 9 Mar. 1924; compare the Communists' own views in ADL 3 M 67, 11 May 1924.

44. Arnaud in *Trib. R.*, 6–17 Oct. 1929, and in *Trib. SMUL*, Apr. 1930. The role of teachers in the Saint-Etienne party leadership is documented in ADL M 556, 11 Jan. 1923; M 541, 15 Feb. and 22 Dec. 1924; AN F7 13110, 4 Mar. 1927; F7 13113, 27 Sept. 1928; and F7 13125, 15 June 1931. Their role in the Limoges party leadership is reported in ADHV 1 M 172, 6 Dec. 1930, and 23 Feb. and 13 Mar. 1931.

45. *Cri* (Loire), 26 Oct. 1929; AN F7 13121, 14 Feb. and 17 Dec. 1930; F7 13125, 15 June 1931.

46. See discussion in ch. 4 of this study.

47. On the Communist Party, see Robert, ed., "P.C. en 1923," p. 222 (figures based on a survey by the party's Seine Federation); Tartakowsky, *Premiers communistes*, p. 112, n. 30 (figures based on a survey by *L'Hum.*, 17 Feb. 1929); and Prost, *La C.G.T.*, p. 131 (figures based on a survey by the *Cahiers du Bolchévisme*, 1 Feb. 1934). On the CGTU, see also Prost, pp. 52–55, 201–2, and discussion here in ch. 9.

48. Kriegel, "Le P.C.F.," in her *Le pain et les roses*, pp. 214–18; and Tartakowsky, " 'Bolchévisation,' " p. 101.

49. On the Haute-Vienne: ADHV 1 M 170, 29 Apr. to 18 Aug. 1926, and 14 Feb. and 12 May 1927; 1 M 171, 13 Mar. 1929; and AN F7 13130, 5 Aug. 1932. On the Loire: ADL M 556, 22 Sept. 1925; AN F7 13105, 7 Jan. and 27 Feb. 1926; F7 13106, 26 July 1926; F7 13110, 4 Mar. and 27 July 1927; F7 13125, 2 Feb. 1931; F7 13129, summary report, 1932.

50. ADL M 556, 22 Sept. 1925; AN F7 13110, 4 Mar. 1927; F7 13121, 13 Mar. and 9 Sept. 1930; *Cri* (Loire), 11 Jan. 1930.

51. Cited in Gras, *Rosmer*, pp. 251–52. (The context concerned the issue of proportional representation.) On the CP's growth, see the regional case studies in *Sur l'implantation du Parti communiste français dans l'entre-deux-guerres*, ed. Jacques Girault (Paris, 1977). In his introduction, Girault acknowledges (p. 37) that Communist implantation would still be difficult in the Loire in the 1930s because of high unemployment and the shrinking labor force in the mines.

52. ADHV 1 M 169, 2 Oct. 1924; 10 M 147, 3 June 1925, and 25 Mar. and 13 Sept. 1927; 1 M 170, 14 Feb. and 13 Mar. 1927; 1 M 171, 18 Jan. and 23 Oct. 1929; AN F7 13130, 5 Aug. 1932.

53. ADHV 1 M 171, 16–23 Oct. 1929; 10 M 147, 25 Nov. 1934 and 9 Apr. 1938.

54. AN F7 13670, 22 Jan. to 2 Mar. 1928; ADHV 10 M 147, 5 July 1928; 3 M 167, tabulated results of the legislative elections of 1928. There are no reports on the proportion of industrial workers generally who voted for the CP in the department or at Limoges.

55. See Figure 20, p. 307, for CGTU and CGT membership figures. On the vote in 1929 (50 "yes" to 40 "no," of the 90 present—out of some 900 members):

AN F7 13687, 13 Sept. 1929. The union also voted against the federation's attempt to call a brief work stoppage in 1930; see F7 13688, 15 Mar. 1930; F7 13671, 26 Apr. 1930. Nonetheless, the union's public position was one of apparently unambiguous support for the CGTU line; see *L'Emancipation du Rail* (CGTU, Loire), Jan. 1931 to Oct. 1934.

56. ADL 93 M 10, 13 July to 5 Nov. 1923, and 28 Jan. to 21 July 1924; M 541, 23 July 1923; AN F7 12996, 1 Sept. 1923; ADL M 556, 6 Nov. 1925; and interview with Jean Seigne, Saint-Etienne, 8 Feb. 1975.

57. ADHV 10 M 138, 3 May 1929; 1 M 171, 5 Dec. 1929.

58. AN F7 13518, 6 Mar. 1925; F7 13106, 12 Aug. 1926; F7 13525, 20 Dec. 1926.

59. ADL 93 M 29, 3 Nov. 1922; AN F7 13903, 14–20 Nov. 1923; ADL M 541, 6 Dec. 1924; F7 13904, 12 Jan. 1929.

60. See, for example, Gratton, "Communisme rural en Corrèze," pp. 123–45; Anne-Marie Pennetier and Claude Pennetier, "Les militants communistes du Cher," in *Implantation du P.C.F.,* ed. Girault, pp. 244–46; and Stephen Vincent Gallup, "Communists and Socialists in the Vaucluse, 1920–1939" (Ph.D. diss., UCLA, 1971), chs. 3–5.

61. Tabulated election results for 1924 and 1928 in ADHV 3 M 166–67; see also the electoral maps for the Haute-Vienne for 1924–73 in Lenoble et al., *La Gauche au pouvoir,* pp. 99, 111, 121, 139, 151–68.

62. ADHV 1 M 170, 18 Jan. 1926; 1 M 171, 13 Mar. 1929. The activity of rural cells in 1932 is also reported in AN F7 13130, 5 Aug. 1932. The proportion of members from Limoges was higher (but still half or less of the total) in 1922–24, before the local unions quit the CGTU. ADHV 1 M 168, 8 Oct. 1922; 1 M 169, 30 June and 18 Sept. 1924.

63. Fraisseix himself recognized the role of personality in his election, since his Socialist rival had also run as a "labor" candidate; see Fraisseix, *Au long de ma route,* p. 88.

64. ADHV 1 M 170, 15 June 1928; 1 M 171, 12 Sept. 1929.

65. AN F7 13130, 5 Aug. 1932.

66. *Peuple L.,* 22 July 1923; AN F7 13110, 19 Dec. 1927. Even at Le Chambon, where the Communists nearly won a parliamentary seat in 1928, they had won only a maximum of 7.2 percent of the vote in the 1924 elections. (This was higher than the peak of 3.8 percent at Saint-Etienne, or 3.0 percent for the department.) Tabulated results in ADL 3 M 67 and 3 M 70. On labor politics at Le Chambon, see also Hanagan, *Logic of Solidarity,* ch. 6; Faure, *Chambon Rouge;* and Frachon, *Pour la CGT,* chs. 3–4.

67. AN F7 12997, 9 Nov. and 7 Dec. 1929. On Faure's election as mayor, see also ADL 10 M 187, 3 May and 21 July 1925. It was Faure who had nearly won the party a parliamentary seat in 1928; those votes remained with him, not with the party, in 1932 and 1936. Tabulated results in 3 M 70–71 and 3 M 75.

68. Annual reports for 1923–29, in *Bull. CCL,* nos. 81–93 (1924–30); ADHV 10 M 98, 25 Jan. and 22 Mar. 1924; 10 M 61, 12 Dec. 1926 to 13 Sept. 1927; AN F7 13527, 18 Jan. 1927; F7 12750, monthly reports, Apr. 1926 to Mar. 1928. The evolution of Limoges industries is also discussed here in chs. 1

and 5. The record of labor activism and strikes in the two industries is discussed in the last section of this chapter.

69. Annual reports for 1923–29, in *Bull. CCSE,* 4e to 10e années (1924–30); Comité des Forges de la Loire et al., *La situation de l'industrie lourde dans la Loire (Métallurgie, Mines, Verrerie), 1927–1928* (Saint-Etienne, 1928), pp. 3–10; AN F7 12741, monthly reports, Jan. 1926 to Apr. 1928; F7 13525, weekly reports, Dec. 1926 to Dec. 1927. The evolution of Loire industries is also discussed here in chs. 1 and 5.

70. Robert, *Scission syndicale,* esp. pp. 151–53, 174–82. This study correlates voting patterns of UDs and federations at CGT and CGTU congresses from 1918 to 1925.

71. Ibid., pp. 33–38, 162–65; also Robert and Chavance, "Syndicalisation en France," pp. 1099, 1104–7.

72. Compare Prost, *La C.G.T.,* ch. 4.

73. Robert, *Scission syndicale,* pp. 180–81.

74. Ibid., pp. 124–25, 176–82.

75. AN F7 13121, 3 Jan. 1930; *Cri* (Loire), 11 Jan. 1930.

76. *Trav. S-S* (CGT), Sept.–Dec. 1928; Odette Hardy-Hemery, "Rationalisation technique et rationalisation du travail à la Compagnie des Mines d'Anzin (1927–1938)," *M. Social,* no. 72 (1970), pp. 6–11, 16; Lequin, "Rationalisation," pp. 115, 121–24.

77. Some employers acknowledged their own inaction: reports for 1925–28, *Bull. CCSE,* 6e année (1926), p. 357 (on the ribbon industry); and 8e année (1928), pp. 339–40, and 9e année (1929), pp. 303–4 (on small machine construction). Workers also sometimes criticized their employers for their failure to adopt new technology: *Trav. S-S* (CGT), May–June 1927; *Mineur U.* (CGTU), Oct. 1927 and Aug.–Sept. 1928; *Le Métallurgiste* (CGTU), Jan. 1928; *Cri* (PC, Loire), 19 June and 8–15 Oct. 1927, 20 July and 21 Sept. 1929, 8 Mar. and 5 Apr. 1930; *Le Travailleur du Cuir et de la Peau* (CGTU), Jan. and Mar. 1928; *Trav. C-O* (PC, Haute-Vienne), 29 Mar. and 19 Apr. 1930. This did not necessarily mean an acceptance of "rationalization," but it showed a preference at least for those measures that would lessen the workers' burdens. On attitudes toward rationalization by the various labor factions, see ch. 10.

78. AN F7 13035, 4 July and 4 Aug. 1933; ADL M 1063, 29 Sept., 29 Oct., and 29 Nov. 1935; M 1070, 28 Aug. 1935; *Cri* (Loire), 29 June, 27 July, 24 Aug., and 21 Sept. 1935; *Trib. SMUL,* 10 Jan. 1936. There is also a series of articles on the Bedaux system in the *Revue de l'Industrie Minérale* (Saint-Etienne), no. 304 (Aug. 1933), pp. 355–85; no. 358 (Nov. 1935), pp. 553–62; and no. 408 (Jan. 1938), pp. 26–31.

79. On employers' campaigns for tax and tariff concessions, see the reports for 1926 and 1929, *Bull. CCL,* no. 85 (1926), p. 1182, and no. 91 (1929), p. 2351 (on the porcelain industry); and Comité des Forges de la Loire et al., *Industrie lourde,* pp. 10–11. On the general goals of patronal associations in the 1920s, see Caron and Bouvier, "Structure des firmes," in *Histoire économique et sociale,* ed. Braudel and Labrousse, vol. 4, pt. 2, pp. 789–91.

80. *Bull. CCL,* no. 85 (1926), pp. 1182–84; no. 91 (1929), pp. 2351–53; no.

93 (1930), pp. 2743–45; and no. *95* (1931), pp. 3131–33 (on the porcelain and shoe industries); *Bull. CCSE,* 6ᵉ année (1926), pp. 364, 373; 8ᵉ année (1928), pp. 282–86, 350–51; and 13ᵉ année (1933), pp. 427–29 (on heavy metallurgy, mining, and small machine construction); *Saint-Etienne et sa Région,* Jan.–Feb. 1928; also general observations by François Caron, "Dynamiques et freinages de la croissance industrielle," in *Histoire économique et sociale,* ed. Braudel and Labrousse, vol. 4, pt. 1, pp. 242–44, 263–64.

81. The economic difficulties of weavers and gunsmiths are discussed in the annual reports for 1926–30 in the *Bull. CCSE,* 7ᵉ to 11ᵉ années (1927–31); in *R. Tiss.,* 1926–30; in *Cri* (Loire), 17 Dec. 1927, 3–31 Mar. 1928, and 14 Dec. 1929; and in AN F7 13526, 25 Nov. 1930. On the artisanal attitudes of weavers and gunsmiths, see Guitton, *Rubans,* pp. 256–60; Arbogast, *Armes,* pp. 161–68, 193–98; and discussion here in chs. 1–2.

82. AN F7 13121, 3 Jan. 1930. The published census measures industrial concentration by reporting the distribution of companies by size but not, at the departmental level, the proportion of workers in each size range. It shows, nonetheless, that as late as 1931, only 6 of the Loire's 2,210 metalworking companies (7 of 14 companies in heavy metallurgy) employed more than 500 workers. *Recensement,* 1931, 2:123. See also the discussion of industrial concentration in ch. 1 of this study.

83. AN F7 13525, 21 Dec. 1926, 11 Jan. and 11 Apr. 1927; F7 13527, 18 Jan. 1927; see also the reports in the *Bull. CCL* and *Bull. CCSE; Saint-Etienne et sa Région,* Jan.–Feb. 1928; and the account in François Caron and Jean Bouvier, "Guerre, crise, guerre, 1914–1939," in *Histoire économique et sociale,* ed. Braudel and Labrousse, vol. 4, pt. 2, pp. 639–46.

84. AN F7 13799, 29 Apr. 1930; ADL M 1065, Rapport de l'Ingénieur en Chef des Mines de la Loire, 3 Jan. 1931; Comité des Forges de la Loire et al., *Industrie lourde,* pp. 10–11; *Bull. CCSE,* 8ᵉ année (1928), pp. 282–86, 350–51. The tariff issue was also addressed in *Mineur U.* (CGTU), Sept. 1927; in *Trav. S-S* (CGT), Mar.–Apr. 1928; and by all factions, including *Trib. SMUL,* in 1931–33.

85. AN F7 13525, 11 Jan. 1927; F7 13536, 30 Dec. 1930 and 15 Jan. 1931.

86. AN F7 13525, 20 Dec. 1926; 5–13 Jan., 22 Feb., and 11 Oct. 1927.

87. *Bull. CCL,* no. 87 (1927), pp. 1524–25; AN F7 13528, 16 Jan. 1928; F7 13536, 30 Dec. 1930.

88. ADHV 10 M 63, unemployment figures by company (porcelain and shoe industries), Dec. 1926; also reports on individual companies in difficulty in AN F7 13543, 26–27 Nov. 1931 (Monteux shoe company); F7 13525, 17 Sept. and 11 Oct. 1927 (Villeboeuf mines); F7 13547, 13 Feb. 1932 (various cycle companies); and ADL M 1067 bis, 4 Nov. 1931 (Verdié steelworks). See ch. 8 on the recession of 1921.

89. AN F7 13796, 27 Apr. 1927 (on a strike movement that never materialized); F7 13782, 27 Feb. and 17 Mar. 1928; *Trav. S-S* (CGT), Mar.–Apr. 1927; *Mineur U.,* Sept. 1927; *Métallurgiste* (CGTU), Aug.–Sept. 1928; *Cri* (Loire), 21 May 1927, and 23 June and 11 Aug. 1928. The question of strike activity is further discussed below.

90. *Trav. C-O,* 18 Aug. 1928; *Cri* (Loire), 11 Aug. 1928 and 19 Apr. 1930; AN F7 13100, 16 Feb. 1929.

91. On the CGT: *Trav. S-S,* Aug.–Sept. 1931 and June 1932; *Travail* (Haute-Vienne), 1 Oct. 1931. On the syndicalists and other dissidents: *Cri* (Paris), 11–18 Feb. 1931; *Trib. SMUL,* May and Dec. 1930, and Mar.–Apr. 1931; *Céram. Lim.,* Feb. 1931; *Ça Ira* (PUP), 21 Jan. and 15 Nov. 1930, and 28 Feb. 1931. On the CGTU and the Communists: *Mineur U.* (Loire ed.), Dec. 1930; *Cri* (Loire), 8–15 Nov. 1930; *Trav. C-O,* 1 Mar. and 23 Aug. 1930, and 3 Jan. 1931. On the Communists' views, and on debates within the party and the Comintern, see also Wolikow, "P.C.F. devant la crise," pp. 46–57, 67–75.

92. *Ça Ira* (PUP), 21 Jan. 1930; compare Wolikow, "Analyse des classes," pp. 109–36.

93. AN F7 13528, 16 Jan. 1928; F7 12757–59, 5 July, 6 Aug., and 4 Nov. 1929; annual reports in *Bull. CCSE,* 9e to 11e années (1929–31). The biggest change, as industrial concentration progressed in this period, was the drop in the number of companies with fewer than ten employees. See Caron and Bouvier, "Structure des firmes," in *Histoire économique et sociale,* ed. Braudel and Labrousse, vol. 4, pt. 2, pp. 770–73; and discussion here in ch. 1.

94. This is the reverse of the process usually said to have occurred during World War I, when all labor was scarce enough to have bargaining power, and when employers granted cost-of-living increases either at uniform rates for all workers or at regressive rates, with the largest sums going to those at the low end of the scale. See Robert, "Luttes ouvrières," pp. 42–43; Cronin, "Labor Insurgency," pp. 140–41; and Knowles and Robertson, "Wages of Skilled and Unskilled Workers," pp. 110–14.

95. ADHV 4 M 174, 25 Feb. 1924; *Trav. S-S* (CGT, Loire ed.), May 1929; see also discussion here in ch. 10.

96. Compare Wohl, *Generation of 1914,* ch. 6.

97. Compare Lenin, *"Left-Wing" Communism;* and Lenin, *What Is To Be Done?* (New York, 1929). The latter work, written in 1902, was not issued in France until 1925, when the Comintern sought to reemphasize its argument; see Tartakowsky, *Premiers communistes,* pp. 63–64.

98. Faure, *Un témoin raconte,* p. 42; also Frachon, *Pour la CGT,* pp. 10, 25, 40–41, 58.

99. Wohl, *French Communism,* pp. 216, 442.

100. White, "European Socialism," pp. 253–54; Robert, "Origines du P.C.F.," pp. 32–33 (age data on Socialist Party members in the Cher, 1921); Tartakowsky, *Premiers communistes,* pp. 125–26 (data on students at the Communist Party's *"écoles des cadres,"* 1924–30).

101. ADHV 1 M 171, 13 Mar. 1929; also individual information in report of 28 Aug. 1929, and in AN F7 13023, 12 Feb. 1929; ADL M 556, 13 Apr. and 19 Oct. 1923; F7 12997, 14 Mar. 1927; F7 13110, 16 June 1927; F7 13129, annual report, 1932.

102. AN F7 12996, 1 Mar. 1923; ADHV 4 M 316, 17 May 1923 and 1 June 1935. Compare the age patterns of prewar anarchists, recorded in 4 M 316, 13 Sept. 1910, and in ADL 19 M 37, Etat nominatif, 1914, as discussed in ch. 2.

103. *Cri* (Loire), 12 Sept. 1926.

104. *Trav. C-O*, 13 June 1931.

105. As shown by Kriegel, *Aux origines*, 1:244–46; and Kriegel, *Croissance de la C.G.T.*, pp. 165–77. Wheeler did see more correlation of political orientation to age; see his "German Labor," pp. 304–21.

106. See the discussion of age structure in ch. 1, and figures 3, 6, and 8, pp. 286, 290, and 294.

107. See Daniel Cohn-Bendit, *Le Gauchisme, remède à la maladie sénile du communisme* (Paris, 1968). The title is, of course, a parody of the title of Lenin's earlier work.

108. Prost, *La C.G.T.*, pp. 156–61; also Collinet, *Esprit du syndicalisme*, p. 99.

109. See especially Tiersky, *French Communism*, pp. 30–32; and Jean-Paul Brunet, "Une crise du Parti communiste français: L'affaire Barbé-Célor," *RHMC* 16 (1969): 439–61.

110. Pétrus Faure in *Le Chambon Rouge*, Dec. 1929 (in AN F7 13116); Dmitri Manuilsky (Manouilski) of the Comintern, cited in Brunet, "Barbé-Célor," p. 450.

111. Kriegel, *French Communists*, pp. 55–59; Gilbert Allardyce, "French Communism Comes of Age: Jacques Doriot, Henri Barbé, and the Disinheritance of the *Jeunesses Communistes*, 1923–1931," *Durham Univ. Journal* 66 (1974): 129–45. On the *"tournant"* (Thorez's word) in party strategy, see also Tartakowsky, " 'Tournant,' " pp. 41–74.

112. On Frachon, see AN F7 13125, 24 Nov. 1931; and Frachon, *Pour la CGT*, pp. 150–51, 159–60. On Thorez, see Wohl, *French Communism*, pp. 430, 442–43; Brunet, "Barbé-Célor," pp. 452–54, 457–60; and Allardyce, "French Communism," pp. 134, 139, 144–45. As Brunet and Allardyce note, Thorez had initially approved Barbé's actions and accepted the "class against class" line; see also Wolikow, " 'Classe contre classe,' " pp. 229–30.

113. Tartakowsky, *Premiers communistes*, pp. 125–26. See also the discussion here in ch. 10.

114. Pierre Monatte, "La scission syndicale de 1921," in his *Lutte syndicale*, pp. 187–88; a similar idea was expressed by Monatte [Lémont] in his "Avant-propos" to Monmousseau [Brécot], *Grande grève*, p. 5.

115. Monatte in *RP*, Aug. 1925 and 15 Dec. 1929; a similar idea was expressed by Besnard in his "Introduction" to *Ethique du syndicalisme*.

116. An exception was the year 1930, when strike size and intensity were unusually high. Strike statistics from *Statistique des grèves*, 1922–30.

117. Compare the general patterns of strikes in this period as described in Shorter and Tilly, *Strikes in France*, ch. 3. The authors detect a trend toward increased frequency and participation but decreased length since the late nineteenth century. Still, the phenomenon of brief (and highly politicized) conflicts did not emerge fully until after the onset of the Popular Front.

118. The correlation of strike duration with militancy is subject to some dispute. Shorter and Tilly link strike brevity with politicization because party-led conflicts often aimed at a show of strength rather than at a negotiated settlement.

Many of these strikes rallied a large number of participants but lasted for a period of twenty-four hours or less. See *Strikes in France,* ch. 3. Unlike these strikes, however, those in the Loire tended to be both short (two or three days) and small in size, so there is no reason to assume a high degree of militancy. In addition, a study of contemporary trends has found a statistical relationship between ideological orientation (according to declared aims) and strike length, which presumably applies except in cases of one-day strikes. See Durand and Dubois, *La grève,* p. 357.

119. *Statistique des grèves,* 1922–30. The eleven strikes at Le Chambon in this period (3.9 percent of the department's total) comprised 1.3 percent of the total strikers and 5.2 percent of the total working-days lost. These strikes averaged forty-eight days lost per striker, as against thirty for the Loire's metalworkers generally and twelve for the department as a whole.

120. *Statistique des grèves,* 1922–30. The fifteen strikes at Saint-Junien in this period (10.1 percent of the department's total) comprised 14.6 percent of the total strikers and 41.8 percent of the total working-days lost. These strikes averaged sixty-nine days lost per striker, as against twenty-four for the department as a whole.

121. See especially Shorter and Tilly, *Strikes in France,* pp. 227–35. Similar patterns are noted for the late nineteenth century in Perrot, *Ouvriers en grève,* 1:55.

122. See especially Lagrange, "Dynamique des grèves," pp. 690–91.

123. As argued by Shorter and Tilly, *Strikes in France,* pp. 228–31. Strike results from the Loire and the Haute-Vienne confirm this pattern: of the four major industries, only metalworking (Loire) had a failure rate that was lower in the largest companies than in those with 500 or fewer workers. This exception may have resulted in part from the fact that many metalworkers' strikes were of small professional groups within larger establishments, so that relative participation rates (and capacity for effective organization) were rather high. The failure rates in local strikes by company size (for the years 1912–30) are as follows:

	1–20 Workers	21–100 Workers	101–500 Workers	1–500 Workers (total %)	Over 500 Workers (no. and %)
Mines:	—	4 of 4	7 of 20	(46%)	9 of 18 (50%)
Metals:	5 of 14	25 of 51	19 of 42	(46%)	16 of 39 (41%)
Porcelain:	0 of 1	4 of 10	5 of 21	(28%)	2 of 6 (33%)
Shoes:	2 of 2	10 of 16	6 of 20	(47%)	1 of 2 (50%)

Note that, as in the discussion of strike success rates below, "failures" are those strikes that did not reach even a compromise settlement.

124. *Statistique des grèves,* 1922–30. Shorter and Tilly explain the relatively high failure rate in this period as a consequence not only of unfavorable economic conditions but of the greater tendency to launch strikes in such conditions (a result in turn of the strikes' heightened political leadership), rather than to limit strike activity mostly to favorable periods as in the past. *Strikes in France,* pp. 86–93.

125. See especially *Mineur U.* (CGTU), 15 Dec. 1923. For the strike record,

see the *Statistique des grèves,* 1923; and reports in AN F7 13791 and F7 13903.

126. ADHV 10 M 107, 4 June to 23 July 1925; 10 M 178, report on trade unions in the Haute-Vienne, 1 Jan. 1926.

127. ADHV 1 M 169, 8 Aug. 1925; 10 M 98, 3 Nov. 1925 to 15 Jan. 1926.

128. Synd. Chaussures, Limoges, 28 Jan. and 13 Aug. 1926.

129. ADHV 10 M 178–79, reports on trade unions in the Haute-Vienne, 1 Jan. 1926 and 1 Jan. 1927; 10 M 115, 21 Oct. 1930; 10 M 191, 1 Jan. 1936.

130. Reports in *Trib. SMUL,* Jan. 1931; *RP,* July 1931; also AN F7 13800, 7 Mar. 1931; F7 13801, 11 Feb. 1931; and ADL M 513, 3 Jan. 1935.

131. On the autonomists and minority syndicalists: ADHV 10 M 114, 12–24 July 1926; 10 M 138, 3 May 1929; Synd. Chaussures, Limoges, 13 Aug. 1926; *O. Chaussures,* Mar. 1929 and Aug. 1931; *Trib. SMUL,* Feb. and July 1930; ADL M 517, 26 Dec. 1930; and AN F7 13801, 9 Feb. 1931. On the CGT: *O. Céram.,* Mar. to Dec. 1928; *Trav. S-S,* Jan.–Feb. 1929; and AN F7 12997, 6 Feb. 1929.

132. See ch. 10 of this study for a discussion of "unity of action" from a theoretical perspective.

133. AN F22 183, 3 Feb. and 27 Nov. 1923; F7 13791, 8 Nov. 1923; F7 13903, 13–20 Nov. 1923; 93 M 26, 26 Nov. 1923; also *Trav. S-S,* Oct.–Dec. 1923; and *Mineur U.,* 15 Dec. 1923 ("Leçons de la grève du 15 novembre"). The employers' view of the strike is recorded in Comité des Houillères de la Loire, *Note sur l'agitation ouvrière et les grèves dans la Loire au cours de l'année 1923* (Saint-Etienne, 1924).

134. AN F7 13904, 21 Dec. 1928 to 18 Jan. 1929; F7 13797–98, 22 Dec. 1928 to 23 Jan. 1929.

135. *Mineur U.,* 15 Dec. 1923, and Nov.–Dec. 1928 to Apr.–May 1929; *Trav. S-S,* Jan.–Feb. 1929.

136. ADHV 10 M 137, 7 Apr. to 11 Aug. 1922; F. Masbatin (CGTU union secretary) in *L'Hum.,* 4 July 1922; *Céram. Lim.,* July 1922; *O. Céram.,* July to Oct. 1922; *Pop. C.,* 22 July, 20–26 Nov., and 9 Dec. 1922.

137. AN F7 12996, 30 Mar., 14 May, and 26 June 1926; F7 12997, 28 Feb. 1927, 29 Nov. 1928, and 29 May and 8 June 1929.

138. Bourse, Saint-Etienne, 9 Apr. to 25 June 1937, and 4 Feb. 1938.

139. *Trib. SMUL,* Sept. 1930 and Apr. 1931; *Trav. S-S,* Nov. 1930 and Jan. 1931; *Mineur U.* (Loire ed.), July–Aug. 1930 and Apr. 1931; also reports for 1930–31 in AN F7 13799–801, F7 13905–6, and ADL M 517.

140. For example, *Pop. C.,* July to Sept. 1934; and ADHV 10 M 139, 5 July to 7 Sept. 1934.

141. *Trav. C-O,* 28 Sept. 1929 and 1 Oct. 1932; ADHV 1 M 171, text of annual report of UR Unitaire (CGTU), Dec. 1929.

142. *O. Chaussures,* Oct. 1928, Mar. and Nov. 1929, and Aug. 1931; *Céram. Lim.,* Sept. to Nov. 1932.

143. ADHV 10 M 115, 11 Aug. 1931.

144. Synd. Chaussures, Limoges, 28 Sept. 1928; ADHV 10 M 114, 29 Dec. 1928; 10 M 115, 11 Aug. 1931; *O. Chaussures,* Sept. 1930; *Combat Synd.,* Mar. and May 1933.

145. ADHV 10 M 115, 5–20 Oct. 1930; *O. Chaussures*, June 1930. The CP's attitude is expressed in *Trav. C-O*, 13 Sept. and 4 Oct. 1930; the CGT's in *Travail*, June 1931.

146. *Céram. Lim.*, Feb. 1933; *Bataille Synd. Lim.*, Jan., Mar., and Oct. 1932, and Mar.–Apr. 1935; *O. Céram.*, Dec. 1932, June 1933, and Aug. 1934; and *Travail*, Jan. and Apr. 1935.

147. See discussion in the first part of this chapter.

Conclusion

1. Shorter and Tilly, *Strikes in France*, pp. 252–55; also Prost, *La C.G.T.*, pp. 118–25.

2. On the repercussions of "the revolution that failed," see Wohl, *French Communism*, Conclusion (pp. 433–54).

3. Compare Lagrange, "Dynamique des grèves," pp. 690–91; and Collinet, *Esprit du syndicalisme*, pt. 1.

4. See especially Jean Bouvier, "Le mouvement ouvrier et la conjoncture économique," *M. Social*, no. 48 (1964), pp. 3–30; and Cronin, *Industrial Conflict*, pp. 64–66. Cronin cites V. L. Allen in *The Sociology of Industrial Relations* (London, 1971, p. 47), as arguing that " 'trade unions are patently not initiators'. They 'have always been sluggish in their assessment of circumstances', and leaders usually cling to worn-out slogans and antiquated policies."

5. See James E. Cronin, "Strikes, 1870–1914," in *A History of British Industrial Relations, 1875–1914*, ed. Chris J. Wrigley (Amherst, Mass., 1982), p. 81. According to him, British labor historians tend "to overemphasize elements of continuity over those of change, to denigrate and minimize the genuine achievements of labour, and to stress the strength of tradition, sectionalism and conservatism among workers rather than the secular increase in class awareness and organization." Cronin would no doubt perceive the same tendency among historians of other national labor movements, particularly among those with moderate or conservative outlooks of their own.

6. Compare Tartakowsky, " 'Bolchévisation,' " pp. 106–7; Tartakowsky, "Conquête des masses," pp. 14–16; Wolikow, "Analyse des classes," pp. 118–26; and Hinton and Hyman, *Trade Unions and Revolution*, pp. 9, 41, 72–74.

7. Compare Kriegel in *Aux origines;* and the discussion by Kriegel's critics in Moissonnier et al., "Débat," pp. 160–69.

8. Compare Wolikow, "P.C.F. devant la crise," pp. 32–94; Wolikow, "Le P.C.F. et le Front Populaire," plus essays on the later period, in *Le P.C.F.*, by Bourderon et al., pp. 99–197, 199–552.

9. Compare Tartakowsky, " 'Bolchévisation,' " pp. 106–7; and Tartakowsky, *Premiers communistes.*

10. For general views of this problem, see Sabel, *Work and Politics;* Stearns, "Unskilled and Industrialization," pp. 249–82; and Rancière, "Myth of the Artisan," pp. 1–16, plus commentaries, pp. 17–25.

11. See Sabel, *Work and Politics*, pp. 176–78; Hinton, *First Shop Stewards' Movement;* Cronin, "Labor Insurgency," pp. 125–52; and (on the "labor aristoc-

racy"), E. J. Hobsbawm, "The Labour Aristocracy in Nineteenth-Century Britain," in his *Labouring Men: Studies in the History of Labour* (London, 1964), pp. 272–315.

12. As acknowledged by Hinton, *First Shop Stewards' Movement,* p. 337; also noted by Christopher H. Johnson, response to Rancière's "Myth of the Artisan," p. 24.

13. Compare Hinton and Hyman, *Trade Unions and Revolution;* Girault, ed., *Implantation du P.C.F.;* and Yves Lequin, "Social Structures and Shared Beliefs: Four Worker Communities in the 'Second Industrialization,' " *ILWCH,* no. 22 (1982), esp. pp. 8–12.

14. See Mayer, *Persistence of the Old Regime,* especially Preface and Introduction; and Maier, "Two Postwar Eras," pp. 327–67.

15. On the timing of the "turning point," compare Wohl, *French Communism,* pp. 42–43, 433–54; Kriegel, *Aux origines,* 2:757–58; Charles, "Temps des scissions," pp. 8–14, 27–28; Robert, "Origines du P.C.F.," pp. 28, 34–39; and Robert, *Scission syndicale,* pp. 177–79. On later Communist implantation, see the case studies in *Implantation du P.C.F.,* ed. Girault; Brunet, *Saint-Denis,* chs. 12–15; and Prost, *La C.G.T.,* chs. 4–6.

16. See Shorter and Tilly, *Strikes in France,* pp. 55, 75, 127–37.

17. See Prost, *La C.G.T.,* pp. 127–52; and Daniel R. Brower, *The New Jacobins: The French Communist Party and the Popular Front* (Ithaca, N.Y., 1968), chs. 1–4.

18. According to figures in Prost, *La C.G.T.,* p. 196, total membership dropped from some 4.3 million in 1938 to 2.9 million in 1939. Other reports indicate that Loire membership also dropped by about one-third between Jan. 1938 and June 1939. ADL M 515, 5 June 1939.

Sources

1. Documents available at the National Archives in Paris now include all items catalogued in the Ministry of Interior's F7 series. Gaps are frequent for the 1930s but are said to have resulted from the hazards of time and warfare, not from a policy of keeping these materials from public view. The archives of the Prefecture of Police in Paris have also been used in other studies of French labor history, but for the twentieth century these materials are mostly national rather than local in scope.

2. On the police use of paid informants, see Calhoun, "Politics of Internal Order," p. 126. The author reports that the quality of the information provided by informants was in general "surprisingly high."

3. The Ministry of Interior criticized the reporting techniques of the Limoges police in AN F7 13023, report of 17 Jan. 1923. The ample funding for surveillance at Saint-Etienne is reported in F7 12994, 19 Mar. 1919. The Saint-Etienne police reports, which cite all informants by number, indicate their presence at private meetings of all major party and union groups.

4. Private union and party documents available at Limoges and Saint-Etienne are listed in the bibliography. In general the groups contacted seemed willing to

share any documents available, but these documents rarely covered more than a few years of the period under study. The national headquarters of the CGT and the Force Ouvrière in Paris had little of use on local activities for the period prior to 1936.

5. Interviews and private collections of letters or other personal papers are listed in the bibliography.

6. Newspapers used in this study can be found in the departmental archives or municipal libraries at Limoges and Saint-Etienne or in the Bibliothèque Nationale (Versailles annex).

7. The police reports on trade unions and politics and the Labor Ministry's reports on strike activity are included in the M series of the departmental archives. Specific code numbers are identified in the bibliography. Summary graphs of strike data, prepared from the Ministry of Labor's annual *Statistique des grèves,* are provided in the appendix. The published statistics are also analyzed in Shorter and Tilly, *Strikes in France.*

8. These documents are cited in the notes as ADL Houillères; detailed indications of their contents are given in the bibliography. The S series ("Public Works") in the departmental archives also includes scattered documents on the mining industry in the Loire.

9. The economic historian Bertrand Gille discusses the use of business archives for the study of the labor force, in "Les archives de l'industrie houillère," *Histoire des Entreprises,* no. 2 (1958), pp. 78–103. Except for the mining records in the Loire departmental archives, the business archives consulted in Limoges and Saint-Etienne were of no direct use in this study and are not listed in the bibliography. Special thanks are due nonetheless to the managements of the Haviland porcelain company and the Heyraud and Vincent shoe companies at Limoges, who made their pay lists and other documents from the period available for whatever use to which they might be put.

10. The method of analysis of the census data is described in a separate "Note on Methodology."

Methodology

1. The manuscript censuses used in this study are available in the municipal archives at Limoges and in the departmental archives at Saint-Etienne; full citations are given in the bibliography. The analysis of these data is presented in ch. 1 of this study. For a discussion of the choice of census dates, see ch. 1, n. 16.

2. The industries studied are the Limoges porcelain, shoe, and railroad industries and the Saint-Etienne textile, metals, mining, and railroad industries.

3. A useful discussion of sampling techniques and problems is in Charles M. Dollar and Richard J. Jensen, *Historian's Guide to Statistics: Quantitative Analysis and Historical Research* (Huntington, N.Y., 1971), pp. 11–15.

4. Note that the extrapolated sample figures are of no intrinsic value except as a guide to the samples' comparability to other labor force estimates. Among the limitations on sampling techniques is the fact that observations apply statistically only to the sample, not to the entire city population. But the better the sample,

the closer the sample values will be to the real values, and the more accurately one can generalize from the sample to the entire population. See Dollar and Jensen, *Statistics,* p. 8.

5. The cantonal population in 1911, according to the manuscript census, was 39,305, or 42.6 percent of the total city population of 92,181. The cantonal population in 1921 was 39,363, or 43.6 percent of the total city population of 90,187. For the purpose of these extrapolations, it is assumed that the portion of the population engaged in industry was the same in the canton as in the entire city.

6. Figures for 1891 are from ADL 54 M 8, Classement de la population par profession, Saint-Etienne, 1891; estimates for the early 1920s are from M 1066, 25 Oct. 1920 (for textiles), and M 1068, 12 Oct. and 10 Nov. 1925 (for metals and mines); estimates for the later 1920s are from AN F7 13525, 11 Jan. 1927 (for textiles and metals), and F7 13904, 27–28 Dec. 1928 (for mines). The estimates for railroad workers are not drawn from any archival reports but are based both on the peak unionization (2,500) at Saint-Etienne in early 1920 and on the departmental totals of some 6,800 railroad workers in 1921 and some 8,000 in 1931. ADL 92 M 257, 26 July 1920; *Recensement,* 1921 and 1931. On the ribbon industry and its prewar crisis, see Clerc, *Crise du ruban,* ch. 3; and Guitton, *Rubans,* pp. 50–80, 164–97. General trends in the ribbon and other industries are described here in ch. 1.

7. Estimated employment figures in the prewar and early postwar shoe and porcelain industries are from "Les villes françaises: Limoges," p. 12; later estimates for these industries are from ADHV 10 M 138, 10 Jan. 1926 (for porcelain), and 10 M 63, 15 Jan. 1927 (for shoes). The estimates for the railroads in the 1920s are from 10 M 146, dossier on "Agents révoqués, 1920," and from 10 M 147, 13 Nov. 1927. Although supposedly for the city alone, the figures for shoes and porcelain may well be for the entire department because they are very close to those in the published census: 6,568 in porcelain and 7,354 in the shoe industry in 1921; slightly more in 1931. *Recensement,* 1921 and 1931.

8. The city census recorded 220 glassworkers in Saint-Etienne in 1891, according to figures in ADL 54 M 8. The estimate for the mid-1920s is from Gras, *Verrerie,* pp. 227–30. Postwar economic problems in the industry are documented in ADL M 1066, dossier on "Chômage dans les verreries"; and in *Bull. CCSE,* annual reports, 1928–32.

9. For the Haute-Vienne, "neighbor departments" include Corrèze, Creuse, Indre, Vienne, Charente, and Dordogne; for the Loire, the group includes (other than the Haute-Loire) the Rhône, Saône-et-Loire, Allier, Puy-de-Dôme, Ardèche, and Isère.

10. See, for example, Schnetzler, "Evolution démographique (1820–1876)," p. 157. Perrin's definition of the Saint-Etienne region also includes an unspecified part of the Haute-Loire department, as well as part of the Rhône. *Saint-Etienne,* p. 59.

Bibliography

1. Manuscript Sources

PUBLIC ARCHIVES

ARCHIVES MUNICIPALES DE LIMOGES (AM LIMOGES)
Département de la Haute-Vienne, Arrondissement de Limoges. Liste nominative des habitants de la commune de Limoges, canton du Nord. Dénombrement(s) de 1911, 1921, 1931.

ARCHIVES DEPARTEMENTALES DE LA HAUTE-VIENNE (ADHV), LIMOGES

M Series (Police)

142 M	(old series) Origins of the Third International, 1920–21
1 M 167	Socialist Party, 1916–38
1 M 168–71	Communist Party, 1921–29
1 M 172	Communist Party, 1930–39
1 M 173	Communist Party, miscellaneous affairs, 1925–30
1 M 174	Communist Party, annual demonstrations, 1929–33
1 M 180–81	Demonstrations on 1 May, 1900–1930
1 M 183–85	Antimilitarism, 1891–1939
1 M 186	Pacifism, 1900–1939
1 M 187	Antifascism, 1900–1939
1 M 188	Anticlericalism, 1900–1939
1 M 189	Comité de Défense Sociale, 1909–27
3 M 164	Results of legislative elections, 1919
3 M 166	Results of legislative elections, 1924
3 M 167	Results of legislative elections, 1928
3 M 169	Results of legislative elections, 1932
3 M 170	Results of legislative elections, 1936
3 M 230–34	Results of cantonal elections, 1920–28
3 M 526	Results of municipal elections, 1919

3 M 531	Lists of municipal councillors, 1919–25
3 M 538	Results of municipal elections, 1925
4 M 174	Public opinion, monthly reports, 1924–29
4 M 201	Foreign labor, 1924–26
4 M 211	Foreign labor, 1914–16
4 M 316	Anarchism, 1910–38
6 M 393	Meat prices, 1911–40
6 M 398	Bread prices, 1914–38
9 M 2	Industries, diverse reports, 1800–1924
10 M 22	Labor demands concerning inflation, 1917–28
10 M 49	Unemployment, 1919–22
10 M 60–66	Unemployment, reports and statistics, 1920–39
10 M 72–73	Wages, diverse statistics, 1908–36
10 M 98	Miscellaneous strikes, 1901–38
10 M 99	General strikes, Limoges, 1895 and 1920
10 M 100	General strikes, Saint-Junien, 1919–23
10 M 106–7	Strikes and meetings, construction industry, 1908–38
10 M 113–17	Strikes and meetings, shoe industry, 1917–38
10 M 119	Strikes and meetings, glove industry, 1908–35
10 M 122	Strikes and meetings, leather industries, 1880–1935
10 M 124	Strikes and meetings, metallurgy, 1895–1938
10 M 127–29	Strikes and meetings, printing and paper industries, 1901–38
10 M 135–39	Strikes and meetings, porcelain industry, 1908–37
10 M 140	Strikes and meetings, textile industry, 1907–33
10 M 146–47	Strikes and meetings, railroad industry, 1920–40
10 M 148	Strikes and meetings, transport industry, 1920–35
10 M 151–52	Bourses du Travail, 1896–1936
10 M 165–69	Reports on the creation of unions, 1919–39
10 M 170	"Mixed" unions, 1889–1936
10 M 177–80	Annual reports on trade-union organizations, 1900–1936
10 M 186	CGT, 1895–1939
10 M 187	CGTU, 1921–38
10 M 188	CFTC, 1929–35
10 M 189	CGTSR, 1929–38
10 M 190	Autonomous unions, 1934
10 M 191	Reunification of CGT, 1934–38
10 M 192–96	Labor movement, meetings and demonstrations, 1879–1940

R Series (Military Affairs)

R 258	Labor movement, 1916–18
R 259	Pacifism and anarchism, 1914–18
R 261	Suspects, 1914–18

ARCHIVES DEPARTEMENTALES DE LA LOIRE (ADL), SAINT-ETIENNE

Département de la Loire, Arrondissement de Saint-Etienne. Liste nominative des habitants de la commune de Saint-Etienne. Dénombrement(s) de 1911, 1921, 1931.

M Series (Police)

M 432	(old series) Anarchists and antimilitarists deleted from the departmental surveillance list, 1911–20
M 446	(old series) Strikes, diverse industries, 1923
M 452–54	(old series) Living costs, diverse statistics, 1926–39
M 513–17	(old series) CGT and CGTU, miscellaneous reports, 1926–39
M 539	(old series) Political affairs, diverse anarchist and syndicalist groups, 1921–25
M 540	(old series) Political affairs, diverse trade-union groups, 1921–25
M 541	(old series) Political affairs, diverse Socialist groups, 1921–25
M 548	(old series) Foreign population, statistics, 1927–28
M 556	(old series) Political affairs, diverse Communist groups, 1921–25
M 592	(old series) Trade-union statistics, 1926–36
M 640	(old series) Living costs, diverse statistics, 1920–29
M 1063–65	(old series) Unemployment, diverse statistics, 1927–36
M 1066	(old series) War industries, 1917
M 1067	(old series) Unemployment, diverse statistics, 1930–31
M 1067 bis	(old series) Unemployment, diverse statistics, 1930–31
M 1068–70	(old series) Strikes, diverse industries, 1923–35
M 1128	(old series) Strikes, diverse industries, 1927–28
M 2023	(old series) Wartime political affairs, 1914–18
M 2033	(old series) Feminist agitation, 1913–18
M 2059	(old series) Strikes, diverse industries, 1907–31
3 M 63	Results of legislative elections, 1919
3 M 67	Results of legislative elections, 1924
3 M 70	Results of legislative elections, 1928
3 M 71	Results of legislative elections, 1932
3 M 75	Results of legislative elections, 1936
4 M 119–20	Results of cantonal elections, 1922–25
6 M 53	Results of municipal elections, 1919–25
10 M 154–55	Political affairs, 1913
10 M 161	Political affairs, Jan.–July 1914
10 M 166–84	Political affairs, Aug. 1914 to Dec. 1920
10 M 187	Municipal elections, 1925
14 M 15	Personal archives, Police Commissioner of Saint-Chamond, 1916–18
15 M 22	Foreign population, diverse statistics, 1914–20
19 M 33–37	Anarchism and antimilitarism, 1913–14
19 M 38	Anarchists during the war, 1914–18
19 M 39	Anarchist movement, 1919–20

54 M 8	Saint-Etienne population, statistics, 1891
56 M 10	Saint-Etienne industries, statistics, 1889
85 M 3	Wages and prices, diverse statistics, 1879–1920
91 M 5	Unemployment, diverse statistics, 1915
91 M 24	Unemployment, reports and statistics, 1914–26
92 M 240–41	Strikes, metallurgy and diverse industries, 1917
92 M 247–49	Strikes, metallurgy and diverse industries, 1918
92 M 250	Movements for a general strike, 1918
92 M 251	Strikes, metallurgy, 1919
92 M 252	Movements for a general strike, 1919
92 M 257	Strikes, railroad industry, 1920
92 M 258	Movements for a general strike, 1920
92 M 259–62	Strikes, metallurgy and diverse industries, 1920
93 M 3	Textile unions, Saint-Etienne and the Loire, 1874–1924
93 M 8–10	Metalworkers' unions, Saint-Etienne, 1911–26
93 M 11–14	Metalworkers' unions, Loire basin (by locality), 1880–1924
93 M 18	Gunsmiths' unions, Saint-Etienne, 1872–1920
93 M 19	Unions at the Manufacture Nationale d'Armes, 1892–1925
93 M 25–26	Miners' unions, Saint-Etienne, 1909–25
93 M 27–31	Miners' unions, Loire basin (by locality), 1869–1925
93 M 38–42	Railroad workers' unions, 1891–1925
93 M 44	Interdepartmental congresses, 1917–18
93 M 45	Congresses, textile unions, 1893–1923
93 M 46	Congresses, metalworkers' federation, 1894–1924
93 M 50	Congresses, miners' federation, 1912–24
93 M 52	Unions and the Bourse du Travail, Saint-Etienne, 1876–1914
93 M 53–55	Labor movement, 1880–1926
93 M 56–59	Bourse du Travail, Saint-Etienne, 1887–1925
93 M 65–68	Bourses du Travail, Loire department (by locality), 1892–1925
93 M 69–70	Departmental federations and Unions Départementales, 1880–1926
93 M 71	Independent unions, 1903–13
93 M 72	Catholic unions and the CFTC, 1887–1926
93 M 81–82	Construction workers' unions, 1880–1926
93 M 84	Masons' unions, 1873–1924
93 M 86	Cement workers' unions, 1888–1923
93 M 93	Leather workers' unions, 1883–1921
93 M 94	Commercial employees' unions, 1891–1925
93 M 96	Public employees' unions, 1913–25
93 M 97	Teachers' unions, 1907–25
93 M 98	Postal workers' unions, 1911–25
93 M 99	Municipal employees' unions, 1912–25

93 M 100	Gas workers' unions, 1912–25
93 M 101	Electrical workers' unions, 1912–25
93 M 103	Printers' unions, 1885–1924
93 M 111	Transport workers' unions, 1913–25
93 M 112	Glassworkers' unions, 1878–1925

S Series (Public Works)

| S 2154 | Miners, lists of employees, 1920 |
| S 2206 | Miners, lists of employees, 1921 |

Series Houillères (Archives of the nationalized mining industry in the Loire)

Carton 822	*Rapports de l'Ingénieur Divisionnaire,* S. A. des Houillères de Montrambert et de la Béraudière (Division de Montrambert), 1917–20
Carton 823	*Rapports de l'Ingénieur en Chef,* S. A. des Houillères de Montrambert et de la Béraudière, 1921–25
Carton 2480	Comité des Houillères de la Loire, diverse correspondence, 1917–30

BIBLIOTHÈQUE MUNICIPALE DE ROANNE (BM ROANNE)

| 7 M⁴ 18 | Personal papers of Paul Louis: Archives of the Parti d'Unité Prolétarienne (PUP) in the Loire |

ARCHIVES NATIONALES (AN), PARIS

F7 Series (Police and Ministry of Interior)

F7 12741	Public opinion (Loire), monthly reports, 1924–28
F7 12750	Public opinion (Haute-Vienne), monthly reports, 1924–28
F7 12756–63	Public opinion (all depts.), monthly reports, 1929–30
F7 12892	Socialist Party, diverse reports, 1920
F7 12893	Socialist and Communist parties, diverse reports, 1921
F7 12897	Communist Party, diverse reports, 1924–25
F7 12936	Response to the mobilization for war, 1914
F7 12939	Response to the mobilization (Haute-Vienne), 1914 (Dossier for the Loire is missing from the appropriate file.)
F7 12951	Public opinion, diverse reports, 1918–22
F7 12967–69	Public opinion, monthly reports, 1920–27
F7 12994–97	Labor movement and politics (Loire), 1917–29
F7 13023	Labor movement and politics (Haute-Vienne), 1915–29
F7 13030	Diverse political affairs (Haute-Vienne), 1919–24
F7 13035	Public opinion (Loire), monthly reports, 1931–34
F7 13042	Public opinion (Haute-Vienne), monthly reports, 1931–34
F7 13053	Anarchist movement, 1897–1914
F7 13060	Anarchist movement (Loire and Haute-Vienne), 1912–32
F7 13082	Socialist Party, diverse reports, 1926–32
F7 13085	Socialist Party (Haute-Vienne), 1924–32
F7 13086	Pacifist propaganda, diverse reports, 1916–19
F7 13091	Communist Party, diverse reports, 1918–24

F7 13096	Reorganization of the Communist Party (Loire), 1924–26
F7 13097	Reorganization of the Communist Party (Haute-Vienne), 1924–26
F7 13100	Communist Party, diverse reports, 1925–29
F7 13102	Communist Party, diverse reports, 1923–24
F7 13105–6	Communist Party (Loire), 1926
F7 13110	Communist Party (Loire), 1927
F7 13113	Communist Party (Loire), 1928
F7 13116	Communist Party (Loire), 1929
F7 13118	Communist Party (Haute-Vienne), 1929
	(Earlier dossiers for the Haute-Vienne are missing from the appropriate files.)
F7 13121	Communist Party (Loire), 1930
F7 13123	Communist Party (Haute-Vienne), 1930
F7 13125	Communist Party (Loire), 1931
F7 13127	Communist Party (Haute-Vienne), 1931
F7 13129	Communist Party (Loire), 1932
F7 13130	Communist Party (Haute-Vienne), 1932
F7 13136	Communist Party, recruitment campaign, June 1928
F7 13193	Radical Socialist Party, diverse reports, 1922–30
F7 13348–49	Antimilitarism, diverse reports, 1914–16
F7 13356	War industries, diverse reports, 1917
F7 13369	War industries (Haute-Vienne), 1915–19
	(Dossier for the Loire is missing from the appropriate file.)
F7 13372	Pacifist propaganda, summary report, 1914–18
F7 13518	Foreign population, diverse reports, 1925–29
F7 13520	Unemployment (Haute-Vienne and Loire), statistics, 1921–22
F7 13525	Unemployment (Loire), diverse reports, 1926–27
F7 13527	Unemployment (Haute-Vienne), 1926–27
F7 13528	Unemployment (Loire), 1928–30
F7 13536	Unemployment (Loire), 1931
F7 13543	Unemployment (Haute-Vienne), 1931
F7 13547	Unemployment (Loire), 1932
F7 13551	Unemployment (Haute-Vienne), 1932
F7 13571	CGT and politics, diverse reports, 1906–16
F7 13574–80	CGT, 1914–28; 1935
F7 13584	CGTU, 1922–28
F7 13585	CGTU, 1933–35
F7 13586	CGTU congresses, 1921–23
F7 13605	Bourses du Travail (Loire), 1890–1918
F7 13622	Bourses du Travail (Haute-Vienne), 1895–1919
F7 13659	Porcelain workers' unions, 1920–28
F7 13668–71	Railroad workers' unions, 1923–32
F7 13685–88	Railroad workers' unions, PLM line, 1921–32
F7 13690–92	Railroad workers' unions, PO line, 1921–29

F7 13697–98	Leather workers' unions, 1907–31
F7 13745–49	Teachers' unions, 1922–29; 1935–36 (intervening years are missing from these files)
F7 13771	Metalworkers' federation, congresses, 1918–19
F7 13775–86	Metalworkers' unions, 1918–36
F7 13791–801	Miners' unions, 1920–31
F7 13823–24	Textile workers' unions, 1922–29
F7 13891–902	Metalworkers' strikes, 1910–35
F7 13903–6	Miners' strikes, 1923–34
F7 13973	Public opinion, monthly reports, Dec. 1920 to May 1921
F7 13975	Communism and foreign labor, diverse reports, 1925–26
F7 14607	Strikes (Loire), 1917
F7 14608	General strike, 1920

F22 Series (Ministry of Labor)

F22 73–74	Unions dissolved from 1914 to 1935 (Loire)
F22 155	Unions dissolved from 1914 to 1935 (Haute-Vienne)
F22 177–96	Strikes, diverse industries, 1920–28
F22 288	Conflicts, mining industry, 1918–19
F22 292–93	Wages and working conditions, mining industry, 1917–23
F22 542	Unemployment, 1914
F22 593	Wages, diverse industries, 1918–21
F22 681	Unemployment, 1918–21

PRIVATE COLLECTIONS

ARCHIVES OF THE SYNDICAT CGT DE LA CHAUSSURE, LIMOGES

Bourse du Travail, Limoges. Procès-verbaux des délibérations de la Commission Administrative et du Comité Général, 11 Oct. 1905 to 13 Aug. 1920.

Syndicat des ouvriers et ouvrières en Chaussures de Limoges. Procès-verbaux de l'Assemblée Générale et du Conseil Syndical, 17 Aug. 1905 to 16 Apr. 1931.

ARCHIVES OF THE SYNDICAT CGT DU LIVRE, LIMOGES

Chambre Syndicale des ouvriers Imprimeurs-Lithographes, Limoges. Procès-verbaux des séances du Comité Syndical et des Assemblées Générales. 2 vols. 4 Nov. 1910 to 17 Jan. 1922; 11 Mar. 1922 to 2 Sept. 1932.

ARCHIVES OF THE UNION LOCALE CGT, SAINT-ETIENNE

Bourse du Travail, Saint-Etienne. Procès-verbaux des délibérations du Conseil d'Administration, 16 Jan. 1914 to 7 Aug. 1922.

——. Procès-verbaux des délibérations du Conseil d'Administration et de la Commission Exécutive, 5 July 1935 to 6 Oct. 1947.

BIBLIOTHÈQUE DE LA CHAMBRE DE COMMERCE DE SAINT-ETIENNE

Comité des Forges de la Loire, Comité des Houillères de la Loire, et Syndicat de la Verrerie. *La situation de l'industrie lourde dans la Loire (Métallurgie, Mines, Verrerie), 1927–1928.* Saint-Etienne: Théolier, 1928.

Comité des Houillères de la Loire. *Note sur l'agitation ouvrière et les grèves dans la Loire au cours de l'année 1923.* Saint-Etienne: Théolier, 1924.

Touchard, M. R. *La journée de huit heures dans l'industrie de la métallurgie et du travail des métaux.* Rapport de l'Association des Syndicats Métallurgistes Patronaux de la Loire. Saint-Etienne, 1925.

PERSONAL COLLECTIONS

Comité d'Action du Prolétariat Organisé de Saint-Etienne. *Rapport Général du Comité d'Action présenté à l'Assemblée Générale du 24 janvier 1917.* Papers of the late Urbain Thévenon. Personal files of Michelle Zancarini, Saint-Etienne.

Desmoulins, Martial. (Anarchist shoe worker, Limoges, 1905–14.) Set of letters to Michel Laguionie, Limoges, 20 Mar. 1972 to 3 May 1974. Personal files of Michel Laguionie, Limoges.

Laguionie, Michel. "Le groupe Sébastien Faure, Limoges." Draft article. Personal files of Michel Laguionie, Limoges.

Thévenon, Urbain. (Teachers' unionist, Saint-Etienne, 1920s–30s.) Biographical sketches of Loire militants. Personal files of Michelle Zancarini, Saint-Etienne.

INTERVIEWS

Laguionie, Michel. (Assistant secretary [as of 1974] of the UD Haute-Vienne of the Force Ouvrière, and member of the anarchistic Libre Pensée, Limoges.) Interview at Limoges, 10 July 1974.

Penot, Roger. (Former secretary of the UD Haute-Vienne of the Force Ouvrière.) Interview at Limoges, 22 Feb. 1974.

Perrier, Antoine. (Former unionist and author of works on Limoges labor history.) Interview at Limoges, 11 Sept. 1974.

Pralong, Jean. (Former secretary of the UD Loire of the CFTC.) Interview at Saint-Etienne, 5 Feb. 1975.

Seigne, Jean. (Former secretary of the metalworkers' union, the CSR, and the anarchist group, Saint-Etienne.) Interviews at Saint-Etienne, 8–12 Feb. 1975.

2. Printed Sources

GOVERNMENT DOCUMENTS

Commune de Limoges. *Procès-verbaux des séances du Conseil Municipal.* Année 1922. Meeting of 30 Jan. 1922.

Ministère du Travail et de la Prévoyance Sociale. *Bulletin du Ministère du Travail et de la Prevoyance Sociale.* 1919.

_____. Direction du Travail. *Annuaire des syndicats professionnels industriels, commerciaux et agricoles déclarés conformément à la loi du 21 mars 1884 en France et aux colonies.* 18ᵉ année (1912). Paris: Imprimerie Nationale, 1912.

————. Direction du Travail. *Statistique des grèves et des recours à la conciliation et à l'arbitrage.* 1912 to 1930. Paris: Imprimerie Nationale, 1913–34.

————. Statistique Générale de la France. *Annuaire Statistique.* T. 34 (1914–15).

————. Statistique Générale de la France. *Résultats statistiques du recensement général de la population.* 1906, 1921, and 1931. Paris: Imprimerie Nationale, 1908–35.

————. Statistique Générale de la France et Service d'Observation des Prix. Comité Permanent d'Etudes Relatives à la Prévision des Chômages Industriels. *Compte-rendu des travaux, années 1917–1920.* Paris: Imprimerie Nationale, 1920. Report by A. Keufer, "L'organisation des relations entre patrons et ouvriers," June 1919.

Ministère du Travail, de l'Hygiène, de l'Assistance et de la Prévoyance Sociales. Direction du Travail. *Règlement amiable des conflits collectifs du travail. Enquête et documents.* Paris: Imprimerie Nationale, 1924.

PARTY AND TRADE-UNION DOCUMENTS

Confédération Générale du Travail. *Compte-rendu de la Conférence Extraordinaire des Fédérations Nationales, Bourses du Travail, et Unions de Syndicats, tenue à Clermont-Ferrand les 23, 24, 25 décembre 1917.* Paris: Maison des Syndicats, n.d.

————. Congrès Confédéral 1925. *Compte-rendu des débats du XXIVᵉ Congrès National Corporatif (XVIIIᵉ de la C.G.T.) tenu à Paris, Salle Japy, du 26 au 29 août 1925.* Paris: Edition de la C.G.T., n.d.

————. Congrès Confédéral de Paris, 1927. *Compte-rendu des débats du XXVᵉ Congrès National Corporatif (XIXᵉ de la C.G.T.) tenu à la Salle Bullier les 26, 27, 28, et 29 juillet 1927.* Paris: Edition de la C.G.T., n.d.

————. XIXᵉ Congrès National Corporatif (XIIIᵉ de la C.G.T.), tenu à Paris, du 15 au 18 juillet 1918. *Compte-rendu des travaux.* Paris: Imprimerie Nouvelle, 1919.

————. XXᵉ Congrès National Corporatif (XIVᵉ de la C.G.T.), tenu à Lyon, du 15 au 21 septembre 1919. *Compte-rendu des travaux.* Villeneuve-Saint-Georges: Imprimerie "L'Union Typographique," n.d.

————. XXIᵉ Congrès National Corporatif (XVᵉ de la C.G.T.), tenu à Orléans, du 27 septembre au 2 octobre 1920. *Compte-rendu des travaux.* Villeneuve-Saint-Georges: Imprimerie "L'Union Typographique," n.d.

————. XXIIᵉ Congrès National Corporatif (XVIᵉ de la C.G.T.), tenu à Lille, du 25 au 30 juillet 1921. *Compte-rendu des travaux.* Paris: Edition de la C.G.T., n.d.

[C.G.T.]. Fédération des ouvriers sur Métaux. 4ᵉ Congrès National. *Rapport moral et compte-rendu du Congrès Extraordinaire, tenu à Lyon les 10, 11, 12, et 13 septembre 1919.* Paris, 1919.

[C.G.T.]. Fédération des ouvriers des Métaux et similaires de France. Ve Congrès National, tenu à Lille les 20, 21, 22, et 23 juillet 1921. *Rapport moral et compte-rendu des débats.* N.p., n.d.

Confédération Générale du Travail Unitaire. *Congrès National Extraordinaire, 2e Congrès de la C.G.T.U., tenu à Bourges du 12 au 17 novembre 1923.* Paris: Maison des Syndicats, n.d.

————. *Premier congrès tenu à Saint-Etienne du 25 juin au 1er juillet 1922. Rapports moral et financier.* N.p., n.d.

[C.G.T.U.]. *Pour une C.G.T. et une Internationale uniques. Vers l'unité syndicale.* Paris: Editions de la C.G.T.U., [1925].

Parti Communiste Français. *Les Communistes et les syndicats.* Paris: Bureau d'Editions, 1932.

NEWSPAPERS AND PERIODICALS

Limoges and its Region (published at Limoges unless otherwise noted)

La Bataille Syndicaliste Limousine. "Organe mensuel de l'Union Régionale des Syndicats Autonomes." Jan. 1933 (first issue) to Oct. 1935 (last available).

Bulletin de la Chambre de Commerce de Limoges. Bi-monthly, then semi-annually. Jan. 1918 to July–Dec. 1936.

Bulletin du Syndicat des Typos, Imprimeurs et partis similaires de Limoges [CGT, then CGTU]. Monthly. July 1921 (first issue) to Jan. 1924 (last issue).

Le Centre Rouge. "Organe hebdomadaire de Défense Syndicaliste Révolutionnaire, sous le contrôle des C.S.R. du Centre-Ouest." 30 Oct. 1920 (first issue) to 29 Jan. 1921 (last issue). Succeeded by *Le Prolétaire du Centre.*

Le Céramiste Limousin. "Organe mensuel du Syndicat Général de la Céramique" [CGTU, then autonomous]. March 1922 (first issue) to July 1922; Oct. 1924 (publication resumed) to Feb. 1933 (last issue).

L'Effort. "Bulletin mensuel des Syndicats de l'Enseignement Laïque de la Haute-Vienne et la Creuse" [CGTU]. Oct. 1928 (first issue) to Mar. 1933 (last available).

L'Ouvrier Céramiste. "Organe officiel de la Fédération Nationale de la Céramique" [CGT]. Monthly. Jan. to May 1914; Sept. 1918 (publication resumed) to Dec. 1936.

L'Ouvrier en Chaussures Limousin. "Organe mensuel du Syndicat des ouvriers et ouvrières en Chaussures de Limoges" [autonomous]. Jan. 1925 (first issue) to Dec. 1932 (last issue).

Le Petit Limousin. "Journal bi-hebdomadaire régional du Parti Socialiste." Dec. 1920 to Dec. 1936.

Le Populaire du Centre. "Journal quotidien régional sous le contrôle des Fédérations Socialistes du Centre (SFIO)." 1914 to 1936 (selected dates).

Le Prolétaire du Centre (Périgueux, then Nîmes). "Journal hebdomadaire, communiste et syndicaliste, sous le contrôle des organisations ouvrières, urbaines et rurales." 18 Sept. 1921 (first issue) to 15 Mar. 1924 (last issue). Succeeded by *Le Travailleur du Centre-Ouest.*

Le Travail. "Organe de l'Union Départementale des Syndicats Confédérés de la

Haute-Vienne" [CGT]. Monthly. Aug. 1928 (first issue) to June 1935 (last available).

Le Travailleur du Centre-Ouest. "Hebdomadaire régional du Parti Communiste." 22 Mar. 1924 (first issue) to 26 Dec. 1936.

Le Travailleur du Papier. "Organe de la Fédération Nationale des Ouvriers fabriquant le Papier et le Carton" [CGT]. Bi-monthly. May–June 1922 (first issue) to Nov.–Dec. 1928.

SAINT-ETIENNE AND ITS REGION (published at Saint-Etienne unless otherwise noted)

Annuaire Administratif, Commercial, Industriel, et Statistique du Département de la Loire. 1913, 1920, and 1925.

Le Bloc Ouvrier et Paysan. "Organe hebdomadaire de la Fédération Communiste de la Loire." 29 Mar. 1924 (first issue) to 10 May 1924 (last issue).

Bulletin de la Chambre de Commerce de Saint-Etienne. Semi-annually. 1921 (first year) to 1936.

Bulletin de l'Union Fraternelle. "Bulletin des Membres de l'Enseignement Primaire de la Loire" [CGT]. Oct. 1929 (first available) to Dec. 1930 (last available).

Le Courrier de l'Ondaine. "Journal politique hebdomadaire et d'informations locales." (Political director: Pétrus Faure.) 3 Sept. 1932 (first issue) to 26 Dec. 1936.

Le Cri des Jeunes (Oullins [Rhône], then Saint-Etienne). "Organe mensuel des Jeunesses Syndicalistes de France." Dec. 1922 (first available) to Aug. 1925 (last available).

Le Cri du Peuple (Lyon, then Saint-Etienne). "Organe hebdomadaire des Ouvriers et Paysans de la Région de la Loire, publié par le Parti Communiste." 13 Dec. 1925 (first issue) to 25 Dec. 1936.

L'Echo Syndical (Lyon). "Journal officiel des Unions Départementales Confédérées du Sud-Est (Rhône, Loire, Isère, Drôme, Ardèche)" [CGT]. Monthly. Apr. 1929 (first issue) to Dec. 1936 (last issue to include the Loire).

L'Emancipateur du Rail. "Organe des Cheminots Unitaires du 3ème Secteur P.L.M." [CGTU]. Monthly. Jan. 1931 (first issue) to Oct. 1934 (last available).

La Flamme. "Hebdomadaire régional, social, artistique." 22 Sept. 1917 (first issue) to 6 Jan. 1923 (last issue). Succeeded by *La Flamme Républicaine et Socialiste* ("Grand journal politique et littéraire").

L'Indépendance Ouvrière (Lyon). "Journal Professionel du Monde du Travail. Organe mensuel des syndicats indépendants de Lyon et du Sud-Est." Jan. 1918 (first issue after wartime suspension) to Dec. 1928.

Le Métallo. "Organe mensuel du Syndicat Régional des Métaux de la Région Forézienne" [CGTU]. May 1927 (first issue) to Oct.–Nov. 1927 (last issue).

Le Mineur Unitaire. "Journal de la majorité de la Fédération Unitaire du Sous-Sol et de la C.G.T.U."; then, after 1933, organ of the Syndicat Unitaire des Mineurs de la Loire. Loire edition of national mineworkers' publication. Monthly. Mar. 1930 (first issue) to Nov. 1935 (last issue).

Le Peuple de la Loire. Socialist then Communist weekly. Succeeded in 1922 by *Le*

Réveil du Peuple, then resumed in 1923 under its old title as "Organe officiel de la Fédération Communiste Unitaire de la Loire." 16 Sept. 1919 (first issue) to 2 July 1922; 11 Feb. 1923 (publication resumed) to 31 July 1927 (last issue).

Le Réveil. "Organe hebdomadaire de la Fédération Socialiste (SFIO) de la Loire." 19 Feb. 1928 (first issue) to 19 May 1929 (last issue before publication suspended); May to Dec. 1930 (monthly) and 12 Mar. to 21 May 1932 (weekly, during electoral campaigns).

Le Réveil des Tisseurs. "Organe mensuel du Comité Général pour le Relèvement des Salaires du Tissage"; then, as of Aug. 1902, "Organe des travailleurs de l'industrie textile de Saint-Etienne et de la région." Sept. 1898 (first issue) to Dec. 1914; July 1919 (publication resumed) to Dec. 1936.

Le Réveil du Peuple. "Organe hebdomadaire de la Fédération de la Loire du Parti Communiste (SFIC)." 9 July 1922 (first issue) to 28 Jan. 1923 (last issue). Succeeded by *Le Peuple de la Loire.*

Le Réveil Libertaire (Lyon). "Organe de la Fédération Anarchiste du Sud-Est." Monthly. June 1923 (first issue) to Apr. 1924 (last issue).

Revue de l'Industrie Minérale. Bi-weekly. 1930–38 (selected issues).

Saint-Etienne et sa Région. "Industrie—Commerce." Monthly. Jan. 1920 (first issue) to Dec. 1936.

Le Silence du Peuple. "Organe bi-mensuel des travailleurs libertaires." 13 Jan. 1929 (first issue) to 1 Aug. 1929 (last issue).

Le Syndicaliste. "Bulletin bi-mensuel de l'Union Départementale des Syndicats ouvriers de la Loire." Issues for Jan. to May 1918 available in AN F7 12994.

Le Travail (Lyon). "Organe de l'Interfédération Communiste du Sud-Est." Weekly. 8 Apr. 1922 (first issue) to 26 May 1923 (last issue).

Le Travailleur de l'Enseignement. "Organe du Syndicat de l'Enseignement de la Loire" [CGTU]. Monthly, then quarterly. Nov. 1931 (first available) to Apr. 1935 (last available).

Le Travailleur du Sous-Sol. "Organe de la Fédération Confédérée des Mineurs du Bassin de la Loire." Loire edition of national mineworkers' publication (CGT). May 1929 (first issue) to June 1932 (last issue).

La Tribune Républicaine. "Journal républicain quotidien." 1914 to 1930 (selected dates).

La Tribune Syndicaliste des Mineurs Unitaires de la Loire. Organ of local union in the minority wing of the national miners' federation (CGTU); then, with *"Unitaires"* deleted from the title, organ of the reunified miners' union of the Loire. Monthly. Feb. 1930 (first issue) to Dec. 1936.

NATIONAL PUBLICATIONS (published at Paris unless otherwise noted)

La Bataille Syndicaliste. "Hebdomadaire prolétarien" (unofficially of CGTU); then, as of 20 Nov. 1924, "Organe de l'Union fédérale des syndicats autonomes de France et des minorités syndicalistes adhérentes aux deux C.G.T." 1 May 1922 (first issue) to 25 Oct. 1925 (last issue).

Le Bulletin Communiste. "Organe du Comité de la IIIᵉ Internationale," then of the Communist Party. Weekly. 1920 to 1924 (selected dates). Succeeded after 1924 by the *Cahiers du Bolchévisme.*

Ça Ira. "Organe Central du Parti Ouvrier-Paysan," then of the "Bloc Ouvrier-Paysan" [PUP]. Weekly. 21 Jan. 1930 (first issue) to 11 Apr. 1931 (last issue).

Cahiers du Bolchévisme. "Organe du Parti communiste français." Weekly. 1925 to 1930 (selected dates).

Le Combat Syndicaliste (Lyon, then Saint-Etienne, then Limoges). "Organe officiel de la Confédération Générale du Travail Syndicaliste Révolutionnaire." Monthly. Dec. 1926 (first issue) to Dec. 1928; Oct. 1932 to Dec. 1936. (Intervening issues unavailable.)

Le Cri du Peuple. "Hebdomadaire Syndicaliste Révolutionnaire publié sous le contrôle du Comité pour l'Indépendance du Syndicalisme." 23 July 1930 (first available) to 6 Feb. 1932 (last issue).

L'Humanité. "Organe central du Parti Socialiste (SFIO)"; then, as of 1921, "Organe central du Parti Communiste Français." Daily. 1914 to 1930 (selected dates).

Le Métallurgiste. "Organe mensuel de la Fédération Unitaire des Métaux et de la Voiture-Aviation" [CGTU]. June 1927 (first available) to Feb. 1936 (last issue).

Le Mineur Unitaire. "Organe mensuel de la Fédération Unitaire des Travailleurs du Sous-Sol" [CGTU]. Dec. 1923 (first available) to Mar.–Apr. 1931 (last available).

Le Populaire de Paris. Left-wing Socialist daily. 1918 to 1920 (selected dates).

La Révolution Prolétarienne. "Revue mensuelle syndicaliste communiste." Jan. 1925 (first issue) to Dec. 1936.

Le Travailleur de la Céramique et des Industries Chimiques. "Organe de la Fédération Nationale" [CGTU]. Approximately monthly. June–July 1927 (first available) to May 1929 (last available).

Le Travailleur du Cuir et de la Peau. "Organe mensuel de la Fédération Unitaire des Cuirs et Peaux" [CGTU]. June 1927 (first available) to Dec. 1928; Mar. 1934 to Aug. 1935 (last available; intervening issues unavailable).

Le Travailleur du Sous-Sol. "Organe de la Fédération Nationale des Travailleurs du Sous-Sol" [CGT]. Monthly. Sept. 1919 (first issue after wartime suspension) to Dec. 1924; Mar.–Apr. 1927 to Nov.–Dec. 1936. (Intervening issues unavailable.)

L'Union des Métaux. "Organe de la Fédération des ouvriers sur Métaux et similaires de France" [CGT]. Monthly (sporadic). May–Dec. 1915 (first issue after wartime suspension) to Nov.–Dec. 1925.

La Vie Ouvrière. "Hebdomadaire syndicaliste révolutionnaire." 2e série. Apr. 1919 (first issue after wartime suspension) to Dec. 1924.

La Voix du Peuple. "Bulletin officiel de la C.G.T." Monthly. 2e série. Jan. 1919 (first issue after wartime suspension) to Dec. 1930 (selected dates).

La Voix du Travail. "Bulletin mensuel de l'A.I.T."; then, as of Apr. 1927, "Bulletin mensuel de la C.G.T.S.R." Aug. 1926 (first issue) to Oct. 1927 (last issue).

La Voix Libertaire (Paris, then Limoges). "Organe des Fédéralistes Anarchistes." Monthly, then weekly. May 1928 (first issue) to Dec. 1936.

MEMOIRS AND CONTEMPORARY EXPRESSIONS OF OPINION

Argence, Théo, and Auguste Herclet. "Le contrôle ouvrier et les comités d'ateliers." *Cahiers du Travail* [1921].

Besnard, Pierre. *L'éthique du syndicalisme.* Paris: Librairie CGTSR, 1938.

Blum, Léon. *Commentaires sur le Programme d'Action du Parti Socialiste.* Discours prononcé le 21 avril 1919 au Congrès National Extraordinaire. Paris: Librairie Populaire, 1925.

Chambelland, Colette, and Jean Maitron, eds. *Syndicalisme révolutionnaire et communisme: Les archives de Pierre Monatte, 1914–1924.* Paris: Maspero, 1968.

Cohn-Bendit, Daniel. *Le Gauchisme, remède à la maladie sénile du communisme.* Paris: Editions du Seuil, 1968.

Dumoulin, Georges. *Carnets de route: Quarante années de vie militante.* Lille: Editions de "L'Avenir," [1938].

———. "Les syndicalistes français et la guerre," June 1918. *Cahiers du Travail* [1921].

Faure, Pétrus. *Un témoin raconte . . .* Saint-Etienne: Imprimerie Dumas, 1962.

Frachon, Benoît. *Pour la CGT: Mémoires de lutte, 1902–1939.* Preface by Georges Séguy. Paris: Editions Sociales, 1981.

Fraisseix, Docteur [Jules]. *Au long de ma route: Propos anecdotiques d'un militant limousin.* Limoges: Rivet, 1946.

Frossard, L.-O. *De Jaurès à Lénine: Notes et souvenirs d'un militant.* Paris: Bibliothèque de Documentation Sociale, 1930.

———. *De Jaurès à Léon Blum. Souvenirs d'un militant.* Paris: Flammarion, 1943.

Georges, Bernard, and Denise Tintant, eds. *Léon Jouhaux: Cinquante ans de syndicalisme.* Vol. 1: "Des origines à 1921." Paris: Presses Universitaires de France, 1962.

Jouhaux, Léon. *Le syndicalisme et la CGT.* Paris: Editions de la Sirène, 1920.

———. *Les travailleurs devant la paix.* Paris: Editions de "La Bataille," Dec. 1918.

Lenin, V. I. *"Left-Wing" Communism: An Infantile Disorder.* New York: International Publishers, 1940.

———. *What Is To Be Done?* New York: International Publishers, 1929.

Loriot, Fernand. *Un an après Tours.* Discours prononcé le 5 février 1922 au Compte-rendu du Congrès de Marseille à la Fédération de la Seine. Paris: Cahiers Communistes, n.d.

Monatte, Pierre. *Left-Wing Trade-Unionism in France.* London: Labour Publishing Co., 1922.

———. *La lutte syndicale.* Edited by Colette Chambelland. Paris: Maspero, 1976.

———. *Trois scissions syndicales.* Paris: Editions Ouvrières, 1959.

Monmousseau, Gaston. "Le contrôle syndical et les comités d'usine." *Cahiers du Travail* [1921].

——— [Jean Brécot]. *La grande grève de mai 1920.* Paris: Librairie du Travail, n.d.

———. *Le syndicalisme devant la révolution.* Discours prononcé à la 2ᵉ session du Congrès de l'Union des Syndicats de la Seine, le 27 novembre 1921. Paris: Editions de "La Vie Ouvrière," 1922.

Roulot, André [Lorulot]. *Le Soviet.* 1919. Pamphlet in AN F7 12994.

Soulié, Louis. *Pro Domo: Quarante-cinq ans de vie publique.* Saint-Etienne: Imprimerie de la "Tribune Républicaine," 1934.

Vassart, B. *La stratégie des grèves.* Paris: Editions de la CGTU, 1926.

Willard, Claude, ed. "Souvenirs de Benoît Frachon. A l'appel d'Octobre: Premiers pas d'un militant ouvrier de l'anarcho-syndicalisme au communisme." *Cahiers d'Histoire de l'Institut Maurice Thorez,* o.s., no. 5 (1967), pp. 63–72.

3. Secondary Works

Abherve, Bertrand. "Les origines de la grève des métallurgistes parisiens, juin 1919." *Le Mouvement Social,* no. 93 (Oct.–Dec. 1975), pp. 75–85.

Accampo, Elinor. "Entre la classe sociale et la cité: Identité et intégration chez les ouvriers de Saint-Chamond, 1815–1880." Translated by Claire Auzias. *Le Mouvement Social,* no. 118 (Jan.–Mar. 1982), pp. 39–59.

Aldcroft, Derek H. *The European Economy, 1914–1970.* New York: St. Martin's Press, 1978.

———. *From Versailles to Wall Street, 1919–1929.* History of the World Economy in the Twentieth Century. Berkeley: University of California Press, 1977.

Allardyce, Gilbert. "French Communism Comes of Age: Jacques Doriot, Henri Barbé, and the Disinheritance of the *Jeunesses Communistes,* 1923–1931." *Durham University Journal* 66 (1974): 129–45.

Amdur, Kathryn E. "The French Left and the 'American Peace.' " Unpublished paper.

———. "From Schism to Reunification: Conflict and Compromise in Provincial French Labor Politics, 1922–1936." *Proceedings of the Western Society for French History* 8 (Oct. 1980): 464–80.

———. "La politique de désunion syndicale: Les origines du schisme de la CGT à Saint-Etienne, 1914–1922." *Cahiers d'Histoire* 27 (1982): 329–44.

Arbogast, Marcel. *L'industrie des armes à Saint-Etienne.* Saint-Etienne: Théolier, 1937.

Archer, Julian. "The Crowd in the Lyon Commune." *International Review of Social History* 17 (1972): 183–88.

Arum, Peter M. "Du syndicalisme révolutionnaire au réformisme: Georges Dumoulin (1903–1923)." *Le Mouvement Social,* no. 87 (Apr.–June 1974), pp. 35–62.

Arwas, S. *La crise économique de 1920 en France.* Paris: Presses Universitaires de France, 1923.

Badie, Bertrand. *Stratégie de la grève: Pour une approche fonctionnaliste du Parti communiste français.* Paris: Presses de la Fondation Nationale des Sciences Politiques, 1976.

Baker, Donald Noel. "The Politics of Socialist Protest in France: The Left Wing of the Socialist Party, 1921–39." *Journal of Modern History* 43 (Mar. 1971): 2–41.

_____. "The Surveillance of Subversion in Interwar France: The Carnet B in the Seine, 1922–1940." *French Historical Studies* 10 (Fall 1978): 486–516.

Baker, Robert Parsons. "A Regional Study of Working-Class Organization in France: Socialism in the Nord, 1870–1924." Ph.D. diss., Stanford University, 1966.

Barjonet, André. *La C.G.T.: Histoire, Structure, Doctrine.* Paris: Editions du Seuil, 1968.

Bartuel, C., and H. Rullière. *La mine et les mineurs.* Paris: Librairie Octave Doin, 1923.

Beau de Loménie, E. *Le débat de ratification du Traité de Versailles: A la Chambre des Députés et dans la presse en 1919.* Paris: Société des Editions Denoël, 1945.

Beaud, Claude. "La première guerre mondiale et les mutations d'une entreprise métallurgique de la Loire: Les établissements Jacob Holtzer." *Bulletin du Centre d'Histoire Economique et Sociale de la Région Lyonnaise,* no. 2 (1975), pp. 1–29.

Beaugitte, André. *Le Chemin de Cocherel.* Paris: Alphonse Lemerre, 1960.

Becker, Jean-Jacques. *Le Carnet B: Les pouvoirs publics et l'antimilitarisme avant la guerre de 1914.* Paris: Editions Klincksieck, 1973.

_____. *1914: Comment les Français sont entrés dans la guerre.* Paris: Presses de la Fondation Nationale des Sciences Politiques, 1977.

Bernard, Charles L., ed. *Revolutionary Situations in Europe, 1917–1922: Germany, Italy, Austria-Hungary.* Proceedings of the Second International Conference, Mar. 25–27, 1976. Montreal: Interuniversity Center for European Studies, 1977.

Bernard, François, Louis Bouët, Maurice Dommanget, and Gilbert Serret. *Le syndicalisme dans l'enseignement: Histoire de la Fédération de l'Enseignement des origines à l'unification de 1935.* 3 vols. Grenoble: Institut d'Etudes Politiques, 1966 (orig. ed. 1938).

Bernard, Philippe. *La fin d'un monde, 1914–1929.* Nouvelle Histoire de la France Contemporaine. Paris: Editions du Seuil, 1975.

Bezucha, Robert J. *The Lyon Uprising of 1834: Social and Political Conflict in the Early July Monarchy.* Cambridge, Mass.: Harvard University Press, 1974.

Biétry, Pierre. *Les Jaunes de France et la question ouvrière.* Paris: Paclot, 1907.
———. *Le socialisme et les Jaunes.* Paris: Plon, 1906.
Bobe, Bernard. "Contribution à l'histoire de l'idée socialiste durant la Seconde Internationale: Essai sur le département de la Haute-Vienne." D.E.S., Paris, 1969.
Boissieu, Henri de. "La rubanerie stéphanoise." In *Le mouvement économique et social dans la région lyonnaise,* 2 vols., edited by Paul Pic and Justin Godart, 1:69–126. Lyon: Storck, 1902.
Bonnet, Jean-Charles. "Histoire de la main-d'oeuvre étrangère dans l'agglomération économique stéphanoise." D.E.S., Lyon, 1960.
———. "Les travailleurs étrangers dans la Loire sous la IIIe République." *Cahiers d'Histoire* 16 (1971): 67–80.
Bourdelle, Francine. "Evolution du syndicalisme ouvrier à Limoges, 1870–1905." Mémoire de maîtrise, Limoges, 1973.
Bourderon, Roger, et al. *Le P.C.F., étapes et problèmes, 1920–1972.* Paris: Editions Sociales, 1981.
Bourgoin, J. *Les antitout: De l'éveil de l'industrie à la naissance douloureuse du syndicalisme.* Paris: Nouvelles Editions Debesse, 1964.
Boutaud, Roger. "Les ouvriers porcelainiers de Limoges de 1884 à 1905." Mémoire de maîtrise, Poitiers, 1970.
Bouvier, J. "Le mouvement ouvrier et la conjoncture économique." *Le Mouvement Social,* no. 48 (July–Sept. 1964), pp. 3–30.
Bouvier-Ajam, Maurice. *Histoire du travail en France depuis la Révolution.* Paris: Librairie Générale de Droit et de Jurisprudence, 1969.
Boxer, Marilyn J. "Foyer or Factory? Working Class Women in Nineteenth Century France." *Proceedings of the Western Society for French History* 2 (Nov. 1974): 192–203.
Braudel, Fernand, and Ernest Labrousse, eds. *Histoire économique et sociale de la France.* 4 vols. Vol. 4: "L'ère industrielle et la société d'aujourd'hui (siècle 1880–1980)." 2 parts. Paris: Presses Universitaires de France, 1979–80.
Braybon, Gail. *Women Workers in the First World War: The British Experience.* Totowa, N.J.: Barnes and Noble Books, 1981.
Brécy, Robert. *Le mouvement syndical en France (1871–1921). Essai bibliographique.* Paris: Mouton, 1963.
Bron, Jean. *Histoire du mouvement ouvrier français.* 2 vols. Paris: Editions Ouvrières, 1968–70.
Broué, Pierre, and Jean Machu. "Le mouvement ouvrier dans l'Isère de 1919 à 1939." *Cahiers d'Histoire* 16 (1971): 175–80.
Brower, Daniel R. *The New Jacobins: The French Communist Party and the Popular Front.* Ithaca, N.Y.: Cornell University Press, 1968.
Brunet, Jean-Paul. "Une crise du Parti communiste français: L'affaire Barbé-Célor." *Revue d'Histoire Moderne et Contemporaine* 16 (July–Sept. 1969): 539–61.
———. *Saint-Denis, la ville rouge: Socialisme et communisme en banlieue ouvrière, 1890–1939.* Paris: Hachette, 1980.

Burk, Kathleen, ed. *War and the State: The Transformation of British Government, 1914–1919.* Boston: Allen and Unwin, 1982.

Cahen, M. "La concentration des établissements en France de 1896 à 1936." *Etudes et Conjonctures* 9 (1954): 840–81.

Calhoun, A. Fryar. "The Politics of Internal Order: French Government and Revolutionary Labor, 1898–1914." Ph.D. diss., Princeton University, 1973.

Callon, G. "Le mouvement de la population dans le département de la Haute-Vienne au cours de la période 1821–1920 et depuis la fin de cette période." 2 parts. *Revue Scientifique du Limousin,* no. 356 (1929), pp. 330–48; no. 357 (1930), pp. 13–26.

Caron, François. *An Economic History of Modern France.* Translated by Barbara Bray. The Columbia Economic History of the Modern World. New York: Columbia University Press, 1979.

Carsten, F. L. *War against War: British and German Radical Movements in the First World War.* Berkeley: University of California Press, 1982.

Cass, Millard. "The Relationship of Size of Firm and Strike Activity." *Monthly Labor Review* 80 (Nov. 1957): 1330–34.

Cavignac, J., ed. *La classe ouvrière bordelaise face à la guerre (1914–1918): Receuil de textes.* Bordeaux: Institut Aquitain d'Etudes Sociales, 1976.

Charles, Jean. "La C.G.T.U. et la greffe du communisme sur le mouvement syndical français: Fragments de thèse." Typescript, Paris I, 1969.

———. "Les débuts de l'Internationale Syndicale Rouge et le mouvement ouvrier français (1920–1923)." *Cahiers d'Histoire de l'Institut Maurice Thorez,* n.s., nos. 25–26 (1978), pp. 161–99; no. 28 (1978), pp. 125–64.

———. *Les débuts du mouvement syndical à Besançon: La fédération ouvrière, 1891–1914.* Paris: Editions Sociales, 1962.

———. "A propos de la scission syndicale de 1921." In *Mélanges d'histoire sociale offerts à Jean Maitron,* pp. 59–74. Paris: Editions Ouvrières, 1976.

———. "S.F.I.O. et C.G.T. dans la période de 'prospérité'—1921–1931." In *Histoire du réformisme en France depuis 1920,* 2 vols., by Daniel Blum et al., 1:47–103. Paris: Editions Ouvrières, 1976.

———. "Le temps des scissions." In *Histoire du réformisme en France depuis 1920,* 2 vols., by Daniel Blum et al., 1:1–45. Paris: Editions Ouvrières, 1976.

———, ed. "L'intervention du P.C.F. dans les luttes ouvrières (1921)." *Cahiers d'Histoire de l'Institut Maurice Thorez,* n.s., nos. 8–9 (1974), pp. 280–308.

Chatelain, Abel. "La formation de la population lyonnaise: L'apport d'origine montagnarde (XVIIIe–XXe siècles)." *Revue de Géographie de Lyon* 29 (1954): 91–116.

———. "La main-d'oeuvre dans l'industrie française du bâtiment aux XIXe et XXe siècles." *Revue de l'Enseignement Technique,* no. 101 (Oct. 1956), pp. 35–42.

———. *Les migrants temporaires en France de 1800 à 1914.* 2 vols. Lille: Publications de l'Université de Lille III, 1977.

Chatelard, Claude. "La misère à Saint-Etienne entre 1870 et 1914." D.E.S., Lyon, 1966.

Chaumel, Guy. *Histoire des cheminots et de leurs syndicats*. Paris: Librairie Marcel Rivière, 1948.

Chouvel, Marie-Anne. "Les Croix de Feu et le P.S.F. en Haute-Vienne et sur la bordure occidentale du Massif Central." Mémoire de maîtrise, Paris, [1973].

Clancier, Georges-Emmanuel. *La vie quotidienne en Limousin au XIXe siècle*. Paris: Hachette, 1976.

Clerc, Gabriel. *Passementiers stéphanois en 1912: La crise du ruban*. Saint-Etienne: Théolier, 1912.

Collinet, Michel. *Essai sur la condition ouvrière (1900–1950)*. Paris: Editions Ouvrières, 1951.

———. "Masses et militants: La bureaucratie et la crise actuelle du syndicalisme ouvrier français." *Revue d'Histoire Economique et Sociale* 29 (1951): 65–73.

———. "Masses et militants: Quelques aspects de l'évolution des minorités agissantes au syndicalisme de masse." *Revue d'Histoire Economique et Sociale* 28 (1950): 200–211.

———. *L'ouvrier français: L'esprit du syndicalisme*. Paris: Editions Ouvrières, 1951.

Corbin, Alain. *Archaïsme et modernité en Limousin au XIXe siècle, 1845–1880*. 2 vols. Paris: Marcel Rivière, 1975.

———. "Prélude au Front Populaire. Etude de l'opinion publique dans le département de la Haute-Vienne (Février 1934–Mai 1936)." Thèse de 3e cycle, Poitiers, 1968.

Cousteix, Pierre. "Le catholicisme social en Haute-Vienne sous la IIIe République." *Information Historique,* 16e année (May–June 1954), pp. 100–107.

———. "Influence des doctrines anarchistes en Haute-Vienne sous la IIIe République." *L'Actualité de l'Histoire,* no. 13 (Nov. 1955), pp. 26–34.

———. "Le mouvement ouvrier limousin de 1870 à 1939." *L'Actualité de l'Histoire,* nos. 20–21 (Dec. 1957), pp. 27–96.

Cronin, James E. *Industrial Conflict in Modern Britain*. Totowa, N.J.: Rowman and Littlefield, 1979.

———. "Labor Insurgency and Class Formation: Comparative Perspectives on the Crisis of 1917–1920 in Europe." *Social Science History* 4 (Feb. 1980): 125–52.

———. "Strikes, 1870–1914." In *A History of British Industrial Relations, 1875–1914,* edited by C. J. Wrigley, pp. 74–98. Amherst: University of Massachusetts Press, 1982.

Cronin, James E., and Jonathan Schneer, eds. *Social Conflict and the Political Order in Modern Britain*. New Brunswick, N.J.: Rutgers University Press, 1982.

Cross, Gary S. *Immigrant Workers in Industrial France: The Making of a New Laboring Class*. Philadelphia: Temple University Press, 1983.

Dabouis, Frédéric. "Le Parti Ouvrier-Paysan: Une scission de droite du PCF pendant la Troisième Période." Mémoire de maîtrise, Paris VIII, 1971.

Davis, Joseph S. *The World between the Wars, 1919–39: An Economist's View*. Baltimore: Johns Hopkins University Press, 1975.

Decouty, Guy. "Introduction à l'étude de l'évolution de l'opinion politique dans le département de la Haute-Vienne." Thèse, Institut d'Etudes Politiques, Paris, 1950.

Degras, Jane. "United Front Tactics in the Comintern, 1921–1928." In *International Communism,* edited by David Footman, pp. 9–22. St. Antony's Papers, no. 9. London: Chatto and Windus, 1960.

Delatour, Yvonne. "Le travail des femmes pendant la première guerre mondiale et ses conséquences sur l'évolution de leur rôle dans la société." *Francia,* Band 2 (1974), pp. 482–501.

Delaveau, Françoise, Eric Till, and Marcel Lecourt. "La C.G.T.U. à travers les grèves (1930–1933): Le problème du syndicalisme rouge." Mémoire de maîtrise, Paris I, 1970.

Delon, Pierre. *Le syndicalisme chrétien en France.* Paris: Editions Sociales, 1961.

Demouveau, M[aurice]. "La scission de la C.G.T. à Lille-Roubaix-Tourcoing (1920–1922)." *Revue du Nord* 54 (July–Sept. 1971): 459–93.

_____. "La scission du parti socialiste à Lille-Roubaix-Tourcoing (1918–1921)." *Revue du Nord* 56 (Apr.–June 1974): 215–19.

Dereymez, Jean-William. "Les usines de guerre (1914–1918) et le cas de la Saône-et-Loire." *Cahiers d'Histoire* 26 (1981): 150–81.

Desforges, R. "Limoges. Essai d'analyse démographique, économique et sociale. Etude sommaire." Typescript. INSEE, Apr. 1958.

Désiré-Vuillemin, Geneviève. "Une grève révolutionnaire: Les porcelainiers de Limoges en avril 1905." *Annales du Midi* 83 (Jan.–Mar. 1971): 25–86.

_____. "Les grèves dans la région de Limoges de 1905 à 1914." *Annales du Midi* 85 (Jan.–Mar. 1973): 51–84.

Destours, Henri. "Les syndicalistes révolutionnaires et le mouvement syndical dans le département de la Loire entre les deux guerres mondiales. Aperçu des luttes de tendances dans les syndicats ouvriers de la Loire entre les deux guerres mondiales." Mémoire de maîtrise, Saint-Etienne, 1971.

Devun, M. "L'industrie du cycle à Saint-Etienne." *Revue de Géographie Alpine* 35 (1947): 5–61.

Dion, Michel, et al. *La classe ouvrière française et la politique: Essais d'analyse historique et sociale.* Paris: Editions Sociales, 1980.

Dollar, Charles M., and Richard R. Jensen. *Historian's Guide to Statistics: Quantitative Analysis and Historical Research.* Huntington, N.Y.: Robert E. Krieger Publishing Co., 1971.

Dolléans, Edouard. *Alphonse Merrheim.* Conférences de l'Institut Supérieur Ouvrier, Série Histoire Syndicale, no. 11. Paris, 1939.

_____. *Histoire du mouvement ouvrier.* 3 vols. Paris: Colin, 1939–53.

Dollinger, Philippe, ed. *Bibliographie d'histoire des villes de France.* Paris: Klincksieck, 1967.

Dorna, Louis [Abbé]. *Histoire de Saint-Etienne.* Saint-Etienne: Editions Dumas, 1970.

Dreyfus, Michel. "Sur l'histoire du mouvement trotskyste en Europe de 1930 à 1952." *Le Mouvement Social,* no. 96 (July–Sept. 1976), pp. 11–24.

Dubief, Henri. *Le syndicalisme révolutionnaire.* Collection U, Series "Idées Politiques." Paris: Colin, 1969.

Dubofsky, Melvin. *We Shall Be All: A History of the Industrial Workers of the World.* Chicago: Quadrangle Books, 1969.

Ducray, Gaston. *Le travail porcelainier en Limousin: Etude économique et sociale.* Angers: Burdin, 1904.

Dujacques, Andrée. "Le mouvement anarchiste à Limoges, 1880–1920." Mémoire de maîtrise, Limoges, 1975.

Durand, Claude, and Pierre Dubois. *La grève: Enquête sociologique.* Paris: Colin, 1975.

Duroselle, Jean-Baptiste. *La France de la 'Belle Epoque': La France et les Français, 1900–1914.* Paris: Richelieu-Bordas, 1972.

_____. *La France et les Français, 1914–1920.* Publications de l'Université de Paris I. Paris: Editions Richelieu, 1972.

Durousset, Maurice. "La vie ouvrière dans la région stéphanoise sous la Monarchie de Juillet et la Seconde République." D.E.S., Lyon, n.d.

Dyer, Colin. *Population and Society in Twentieth-Century France.* New York: Holmes and Meier, 1978.

Estienne, Pierre. *Villes du Massif Central.* Publications de la Faculté de Clermont-Ferrand. Paris: Presses Universitaires de France, 1963.

Faure, Pétrus. *Le Chambon Rouge: Histoire des organisations ouvrières et des grèves au Chambon-Feugerolles.* Le Chambon-Feugerolles: Edition du Syndicat Unitaire des Métaux, 1929.

_____. *Histoire de la métallurgie au Chambon-Feugerolles.* Le Chambon-Feugerolles: Edition de la Chambre syndicale des ouvriers métallurgistes du Chambon-Feugerolles, 1931.

_____. *Histoire du mouvement ouvrier dans le département de la Loire.* Saint-Etienne: Imprimerie Dumas, 1956.

Fauvel-Rouif, Denise, ed. *Mouvements ouvriers et dépression économique, 1929–1939.* Assen: Van Gorcum, 1966.

Ferrat, A. *Histoire du P.C.F.* Paris: Editions Git-Le-Coeur, 1931.

Fine, Martin. "Albert Thomas: A Reformer's Vision of Modernization, 1914–1932." *Journal of Contemporary History* 12 (1977): 545–64.

_____. "Toward Corporatism: The Movement for Capital-Labor Collaboration in France, 1914–1936." Ph.D. diss., University of Wisconsin, 1971.

Flonneau, Jean-Marie. "Crise de vie chère et mouvement syndical, 1910–1914." *Le Mouvement Social,* no. 72 (July–Sept. 1970), pp. 49–81.

Fohlen, Claude. *La France de l'Entre-Deux-Guerres (1917–1939).* 2nd ed. Paris: Casterman, 1972.

Fontaine, Arthur. *French Industry during the War.* Publications of the Carnegie Endowment for International Peace. New Haven, Conn.: Yale University Press, 1926.

Fournial, Etienne, ed. *Saint-Etienne: Histoire de la ville et de ses habitants.* Saint-Etienne: Editions Horvath, 1976.

Fridenson, Patrick. "L'idéologie des grands constructeurs dans l'entre-deux-guerres." *Le Mouvement Social,* no. 81 (Oct.–Dec. 1972), pp. 51–68.

———, ed. *1914–1918: L'autre front.* Paris: Editions Ouvrières, 1977.

Gallo, Max. "Quelques aspects de la mentalité et du comportement ouvriers dans les usines de guerre, 1914–1918." *Le Mouvement Social,* no. 56 (July–Sept. 1966), pp. 3–33.

Gallup, Stephen Vincent. "Communists and Socialists in the Vaucluse, 1920–1939." Ph.D. diss., University of California at Los Angeles, 1971.

Garraty, John A. *Unemployment in History: Economic Thought and Public Policy.* New York: Harper and Row, 1978.

Garrier, Gilbert. *Paysans du Beaujolais et du Lyonnais, 1800–1970.* 2 vols. Grenoble: Presses Universitaires, 1973.

Gaudemar, Jean-Paul de. *La mobilisation générale.* Paris: Editions du Champ Urbain, 1979.

Gaudy, Georges. *La ville rouge.* Paris: Nouvelle Librairie Nationale, 1925.

Geary, Dick. "Radicalism and the Worker: Metalworkers and Revolution, 1914–1923." In *Society and Politics in Wilhelmine Germany,* edited by Richard J. Evans, pp. 267–86. London: Croom Helm, 1978.

Georges, Bernard, Denise Tintant, and Marie-Anne Renauld. *Léon Jouhaux dans le mouvement syndical français.* Paris: Presses Universitaires de France, 1979.

Gerest, Henri. "Problèmes posés par le ravitaillement d'une population ouvrière pendant la Grande Guerre: Le cas de l'agglomération stéphanoise en 1917–1918." *Actes du 98ᵉ Congrès National des Sociétés Savantes,* Saint-Etienne, 1973. Section histoire moderne, 2:253–70.

Gignoux, C.-J. *Bourges pendant la guerre.* Publications of the Carnegie Endowment for International Peace. Paris: Presses Universitaires de France, 1926.

Gille, Bertrand. "Les archives de l'industrie houillère." *Histoire des Entreprises,* no. 2 (1958), pp. 78–103.

———. *La sidérurgie française au XIXᵉ siècle.* Geneva: Librairie Droz, 1968.

Ginsburg, Shaul. "Du Wilsonisme au communisme: L'itinéraire du pacifiste Raymond Lefebvre en 1919." *Revue d'Histoire Moderne et Contemporaine* 23 (1976): 583–605.

Girault, Jacques, ed. *Sur l'implantation du Parti communiste français dans l'entre-deux-guerres.* Paris: Editions Sociales, 1977.

Goetz-Girey, Robert. *Le mouvement des grèves en France, 1919–1962.* Paris: Editions Sirey, 1965.

———. *La pensée syndicale française: Militants et théoriciens.* Paris: Colin, 1948.

Gordon, David M. *Merchants and Capitalists: Industrialization and Provincial Politics in Mid-Nineteenth-Century France.* University, Ala.: University of Alabama Press, 1985.

Goujon, Pierre. "Militants du mouvement ouvrier en Saône-et-Loire entre les deux guerres." *Le Mouvement Social,* no. 99 (Apr.–June 1977), pp. 63–76.

Gras, Christian. *Alfred Rosmer et le mouvement révolutionnaire international.* Paris: Maspero, 1971.

———. "La Fédération des Métaux en 1913–1914 et l'évolution du syndicalisme révolutionnaire français." *Le Mouvement Social,* no. 77 (Oct.–Dec. 1971), pp. 85–112.

———. "Merrheim et le capitalisme." *Le Mouvement Social,* no. 63 (Apr.–June 1968), pp. 143–63.

Gras, L.-J. *Essai sur l'histoire de la quincaillerie et la petite métallurgie à Saint-Etienne.* Saint-Etienne: Théolier, 1904.

———. *Histoire de l'armurerie stéphanoise.* Saint-Etienne: Théolier, 1905.

———. *Histoire des eaux minérales du Forez, suivie de notes historiques sur l'industrie de la verrerie en Forez et en Jarez.* Saint-Etienne: Théolier, 1923.

———. *Histoire économique de la métallurgie de la Loire, suivie d'une notice sur la construction mécanique et l'industrie des cycles et automobiles dans la région stéphanoise.* Saint-Etienne: Théolier, 1908.

———. *Histoire économique générale des mines de la Loire.* 2 vols. Saint-Etienne: Théolier, 1922.

Gratton, Philippe. "Le communisme rural en Corrèze." *Le Mouvement Social,* no. 67 (Apr.–June 1969), pp. 123–45.

———. *Les luttes de classes dans les campagnes.* Paris: Editions Anthropos, 1971.

Greenwald, Maurine Weiner. *Women, War and Work: The Impact of World War I on Women Workers in the United States.* Westport, Conn.: Greenwood Press, 1980.

Guérin, Daniel. "Une tentative de réunification syndicale, 1930–31." *Revue d'Histoire Economique et Sociale* 44 (1966): 107–21.

Guilbert, Madeleine. *Les femmes et l'organisation syndicale avant 1914.* Paris: Editions du C.N.R.S., 1967.

———. *Les fonctions des femmes dans l'industrie.* Paris: Mouton, 1966.

Guillaume, Pierre. *La Compagnie des Mines de la Loire, 1846–1854.* Paris: Presses Universitaires de France, 1966.

———. "Les mines de la Loire après la première guerre mondiale." *Histoire des Entreprises,* no. 5 (May 1960), pp. 21–39.

Guitton, Henri. *L'industrie des rubans de soie en France.* Paris: Librairie du Receuil Sirey, 1928.

Hamilton, Richard F. *Affluence and the French Worker in the Fourth Republic.* Princeton: Princeton University Press, 1967.

Hanagan, Michael P. *The Logic of Solidarity: Artisans and Industrial Workers in Three French Towns, 1871–1914.* Urbana: University of Illinois Press, 1980.

———. "Organisation du travail et action revendicative: Verriers et métallurgistes de Rive-de-Gier à la fin du XIXe siècle." Translated by Yves Lequin. *Cahiers d'Histoire* 26 (1981): 3–25.

Hardach, Gerd. *The First World War, 1914–1918.* History of the World Economy in the Twentieth Century. Berkeley: University of California Press, 1977.

Hardy-Hémery, Odette. "Rationalisation technique et rationalisation du travail à la Compagnie des Mines d'Anzin (1927–1938)." *Le Mouvement Social,* no. 72 (July–Sept. 1970), pp. 3–48.

Hatry, Gilbert. *Renault, Usine de Guerre, 1914–1918.* Paris: Lafourcade, 1978.

Héritier, P., R. Bonnevialle, J. Ion, and C. Saint-Sernin. *150 ans de luttes ouvrières dans le bassin stéphanois.* Saint-Etienne: Editions Le Champ du Possible, 1979.

Herriot, Edouard. *Lyon pendant la guerre.* Publications of the Carnegie Endowment for International Peace. Paris: Presses Universitaires de France, 1926.

Hinton, James. *The First Shop Stewards' Movement.* London: Georges Allen and Unwin, 1973.

Hinton, James, and Richard Hyman. *Trade Unions and Revolution: The Industrial Politics of the Early British Communist Party.* London: Pluto Press, 1975.

Hobsbawm, E. J. *Labouring Men: Studies in the History of Labour.* London: Weidenfeld and Nicolson, 1964.

_____. "Peasants and Rural Migrants in Politics." In *Politics of Conformity in Latin America,* edited by Claudio Veliz, pp. 43–65. New York: Oxford University Press, 1967.

Hobsbawm, E. J., and Joan Wallach Scott. "Political Shoemakers." *Past and Present,* no. 89 (Nov. 1980), pp. 86–114.

Hoisington, William A., Jr. "Class against Class: The French Communist Party and the Comintern. A Study of Election Tactics in 1928." *International Review of Social History* 15 (1970): 19–42.

Holter, Darryl. "Mineworkers and Nationalization in France: Insights into Concepts of State Theory." *Politics and Society* 11 (1982): 29–49.

Holton, Bob. *British Syndicalism 1900–1914: Myths and Realities.* London: Pluto Press, 1976.

Horne, John. "Le Comité d'Action (CGT-PS) et l'origine du réformisme syndical du temps de guerre." Translated by Michel Garel. *Le Mouvement Social,* no. 122 (Jan.–Mar. 1983), pp. 33–60.

Huard, R. "Aspects du mouvement ouvrier gardois pendant la guerre de 1914–18: Les grèves de 1917." *Annales du Midi* 80 (1968): 305–18.

Huber, Michel. *La population de la France pendant la guerre.* Publications of the Carnegie Endowment for International Peace. Paris: Presses Universitaires de France, 1931.

Ion, Jacques. "Les perspectives d'évolution socio-économique du bassin stéphanois et leurs relations avec les besoins de formation professionnelle et culturelle." Typescript. Saint-Etienne, Sept. 1969.

Jacobs, Janet. "A Community of French Workers: Social Life and Labour Conflicts in the Stéphanois Region, 1890–1914." Ph.D. diss., Oxford University, 1973.

Jamet, Pierre. "Les élections de 1919 dans la Loire." *Bulletin du Centre d'Histoire Régionale* (Université de Saint-Etienne), no. 2 (1977), pp. 27–53.

Jedermann [pseud.]. *La 'bolchévisation' du P.C.F. (1923–1928).* Paris: Maspero, 1971.

Joannès, Victor. "La tactique du front unique et le Parti Communiste Français (1922–1924)." *Cahiers de l'Institut Maurice Thorez,* o.s., no. 22 (1971), pp. 43–52.

Jones, Adrian. "The French Railway Strikes of January–May 1920: New Syndicalist Ideas and Emergent Communism." *French Historical Studies* 12 (Fall 1982): 508–40.

Jospin, Samuel. "La Confédération Générale du Travail Syndicaliste Révolutionnaire: A travers son journal 'Le Combat Syndicaliste' (1926–1937)." Mémoire de maîtrise, Paris I, 1974.

Jozefowicz, Rosa. "Le travail des femmes et des enfants dans la région stéphanoise de 1850 à 1914." Mémoire de maîtrise, Lyon II, 1961.

Judt, Tony. "The French Socialists and the Cartel des Gauches of 1924." *Journal of Contemporary History* 11 (July 1976): 199–215.

_____. *Socialism in Provence, 1871–1914: A Study in the Origins of the Modern French Left.* London: Cambridge University Press, 1979.

Julliard, Jacques. "Théorie syndicaliste révolutionnaire et pratique gréviste." *Le Mouvement Social,* no. 65 (Oct.–Dec. 1968), pp. 55–69.

Kemp, Tom. *The French Economy 1913–1939: The History of a Decline.* London: Longman Group, 1972.

Kesler, Jean-François. "Le communisme de gauche en France (1927–1947)." *Revue Française des Sciences Politiques* 28 (Aug. 1978): 740–57.

Klaerr, Michèle. "La scission syndicale et la formation de la C.G.T.U., dans le bassin de Saint-Etienne, de 1921 à 1925." Mémoire de maîtrise, Paris-Nanterre, 1969.

Kletch, Georges. "L'organisation syndicale des travailleurs étrangers en France." Mimeographed. Paris: Société d'Etudes et d'Informations Economiques, Jan. 1937.

Knowles, K. G. J. C. *Strikes: A Study in Industrial Conflict.* New York: Philosophical Society, 1952.

Knowles, K. G. J. C., and D. J. Robertson. "Differences between the Wages of Skilled and Unskilled Workers, 1880–1950." *Bulletin of the Oxford University Institute of Statistics* 13 (1951): 109–27.

Koenker, Diane. *Moscow Workers and the 1917 Revolution.* Princeton: Princeton University Press, 1981.

_____. "Urban Families, Working-Class Youth Groups, and the 1917 Revolution in Moscow." In *The Family in Imperial Russia: New Lines of Historical Research,* edited by David L. Ransel, pp. 280–304. Urbana: University of Illinois Press, 1978.

Kriegel, Annie. *Aux origines du communisme français, 1914–1920: Contribution à l'histoire du mouvement ouvrier français.* 2 vols. Paris: Mouton, 1964.

_____. *La croissance de la C.G.T., 1918–1921: Essai statistique.* Paris: Mouton, 1966.

_____. *The French Communists: Profile of a People.* Translated by Elaine P. Halperin. Chicago: University of Chicago Press, 1972.

_____. "L'opinion publique française et la Révolution russe." In *La Révolution d'Octobre et le mouvement ouvrier européen,* by Victor Fay et al., pp. 75–104. Paris: Etudes et Documentation Internationales, 1967.

_____. *Le pain et les roses: Jalons pour une histoire des socialismes.* Paris: Presses Universitaires de France, 1968.

Kriegel, Annie, and Jean-Jacques Becker. *1914: La guerre et le mouvement ouvrier français*. Paris: Colin, 1964.

Kuisel, Richard F. *Capitalism and the State in Modern France: Renovation and Economic Management in the Twentieth Century*. New York: Cambridge University Press, 1981.

Kupferman, Fred. "L'opinion française et le défaitisme pendant la Grande Guerre." *Relations Internationales*, no. 2 (1974), pp. 91–100.

Labi, Maurice. *La grande division des travailleurs: Première scission de la C.G.T. (1914–1921)*. Paris: Editions Ouvrières, 1964.

Lagrange, Hugues. "La dynamique des grèves." *Revue Française des Sciences Politiques* 29 (Aug.–Oct. 1979): 665–92.

Larivière, Jean-Pierre. *L'industrie à Limoges et dans la vallée limousine de la Vienne*. Publications de la Faculté de Clermont-Ferrand. Paris: Presses Universitaires de France, 1968.

————. *La population du Limousin*. 2 vols. Lille: Atelier de Reproduction des Thèses, 1975.

Laux, J.-M. "Travail et travailleurs dans l'industrie automobile jusqu'en 1914." *Le Mouvement Social*, no. 81 (Oct.–Dec. 1972), pp. 9–26.

Le Balle, Yves. *L'ouvrier paysan en Lorraine mosellane*. Paris: Montchrestien, 1958.

Le Bras, Gabriel. *Etudes de sociologie réligieuse: Sociologie de la pratique réligieuse dans les campagnes françaises*. Paris: Presses Universitaires de France, 1955.

Lefranc, Georges. *Le mouvement socialiste sous la Troisième République (1875–1940)*. Paris: Payot, 1963.

————. *Le mouvement syndical sous la Troisième République*. Paris: Payot, 1967.

————. *Les organisations patronales en France, du passé au présent*. Paris: Payot, 1976.

————. "Les origines de l'idée de nationalisation industrielle en France (1919–1920)." *Information Historique*, 21e année (Sept.–Oct. 1959), pp. 139–45.

Le Marec, Gérard. "La C.G.T.U.: Expérience du syndicalisme bolchévique en France des origines à 1929." Thèse, Institut d'Etudes Politiques, Paris, 1953.

Lenoble, Jean. "L'évolution politique du socialisme en Haute-Vienne sous la IIIe République." Thèse, Institut d'Etudes Politiques, Paris, 1950.

Lenoble, Jean, Maurice Robert, Serge Dunis, and Jean-Paul Gendillou. *Etudes sur la vie politique et les forces électorales en Limousin (1871–1973): La Gauche au pouvoir depuis un siècle*. Limoges: Editions de la S.E.L.M., 1978.

Lequin, Yves. "Classe ouvrière et idéologie dans la région lyonnaise à la fin du XIXe siècle." *Le Mouvement Social*, no. 69 (Oct.–Dec. 1969), pp. 3–20.

————. "1914–1916: L'opinion publique en Haute-Savoie devant la guerre." *Revue Savoisienne* 107 (1967): 125–41.

————. *Les ouvriers de la région lyonnaise (1848–1914)*. 2 vols. Lyon: Presses Universitaires de Lyon, 1977.

_____. "Social Structures and Shared Beliefs: Four Worker Communities in the 'Second Industrialization.' " *International Labor and Working Class History,* no. 22 (Fall 1982), pp. 1–17.

Lequin, Yves-Claude. "La rationalisation du capitalisme français: A-t-elle eu lieu dans les années vingt?" *Cahiers d'Histoire de l'Institut Maurice Thorez,* n.s., no. 31 (1979), pp. 115–43.

_____. "Le Taylorisme avant 1914: Réponse technique et idéologique aux exigences du monopolisme." *Cahiers d'Histoire de l'Institut Maurice Thorez,* n.s., no. 16 (1976), pp. 14–37.

Lhomme, Jean. "Le pouvoir d'achat de l'ouvrier français au cours d'un siècle: 1840–1940." *Le Mouvement Social,* no. 63 (Apr.–June 1968), pp. 41–69.

Lichtheim, Georges. *Marxism in Modern France.* New York: Columbia University Press, 1966.

Ligou, Daniel. *Histoire du socialisme en France, 1871–1961.* Paris: Presses Universitaires de France, 1962.

Lorcin, J. "Un essai de stratigraphie sociale: Chefs d'atelier et compagnons dans la grève des passementiers de Saint-Etienne en 1900." *Cahiers d'Histoire* 13 (1968): 179–92.

Lorwin, Val R. *The French Labor Movement.* Cambridge, Mass.: Harvard University Press, 1954.

_____. "The Red and the Black: Socialist and Christian Labor Organization in Western Europe." Paper delivered at the Fourteenth International Congress of Historical Sciences, San Francisco, Aug. 22–29, 1975. Offprint.

_____. "Syndicalism." *International Encyclopedia of the Social Sciences,* 1968 ed., 15:447–52.

Loubère, Leo. "Coal Miners, Strikes, and Politics in the Lower Languedoc, 1880–1914." *Journal of Social History* 2 (Fall 1968): 25–50.

Louis, Paul. *Histoire du mouvement syndical en France.* Vol. 2: "De 1910 à 1958." Paris: Librairie Valois, 1948.

_____. *Histoire du socialisme en France.* Paris: Marcel Rivière, 1950.

Luirard, Monique. *La région stéphanoise dans la guerre et dans la paix (1936–1951).* Saint-Etienne: Centre d'Etudes Foréziennes, 1980.

Maier, Charles S. "Between Taylorism and Technocracy: European Ideologies and the Vision of Industrial Productivity in the 1920s." *Journal of Contemporary History* 5 (1970): 27–61.

_____. *Recasting Bourgeois Europe: Stabilization in France, Germany, and Italy in the Decade after World War I.* Princeton: Princeton University Press, 1975.

_____. "The Two Postwar Eras and the Conditions for Stability." *American Historical Review* 86 (Mar. 1981): 327–67.

Maitron, Jean. *Le mouvement anarchiste en France.* 2 vols. Paris: Maspero, 1975.

Maitron, Jean, and Claude Pennetier, eds. *Dictionnaire biographique du mouvement ouvrier français.* Part 3, vols. 10–15: "De la Commune à la Grande Guerre (1871–1914)." Part 4, vols. 16–: "De la Première à la Seconde

Guerre Mondiale." Paris: Editions Ouvrières, 1972–.

Marcieu, Gaston de. *Les syndicats catholiques du commerce et de l'industrie.* Paris: Editions de la Vie Universitaire, [1921].

Margairaz, Michel. "La S.F.I.O. face au capitalisme (1920–1940): Eléments pour un dossier." *Cahiers d'Histoire de l'Institut Maurice Thorez,* n.s., no. 14 (1975), pp. 87–116.

Martin, Jean-Paul. "Une culture militante à l'époque du syndicalisme révolutionnaire: Les métallurgistes de l'Ondaine." *Cahiers d'Histoire* 27 (1982): 313–27.

Massard, Marcel. "Syndicalisme et milieu social (1900–1940)." *Le Mouvement Social,* no. 99 (Apr.–June 1977), pp. 23–38.

Mauco, Georges. *Les étrangers en France: Leur rôle dans l'activité économique.* Paris: Colin, 1932.

Mayer, Arno J. *The Persistence of the Old Regime: Europe to the Great War.* New York: Pantheon Books, 1981.

———. *Politics and Diplomacy of Peacemaking: Containment and Counterrevolution at Versailles, 1918–1919.* New York: Knopf, 1967.

———. *Wilson vs. Lenin: The Political Origins of the New Diplomacy, 1917–1918.* New Haven, Conn.: Yale University Press, 1959.

McCord, Norman. *Strikes.* New York: St. Martin's Press, 1980.

McDougall, Mary Lynn. "Consciousness and Community: The Workers of Lyon, 1830–1850." *Journal of Social History* 12 (Fall 1978): 129–45.

McKenzie, Kermit E. *Comintern and World Revolution, 1928–1943: The Shaping of Doctrine.* New York: Columbia University Press, 1964.

Meaker, Gerald H. *The Revolutionary Left in Spain, 1914–1923.* Stanford: Stanford University Press, 1974.

Ménard, François. *Antoine Durafour, 1876–1932.* Saint-Etienne: Comité pour la Commémoration du Centenaire de la Naissance d'Antoine Durafour, 1976.

Merkle, Judith A. *Management and Ideology: The Legacy of the International Scientific Management Movement.* Berkeley: University of California Press, 1980.

Merley, Jean. "La contribution de la Haute-Loire à la formation de la population stéphanoise au milieu du XIXe siècle." *Cahiers de la Haute-Loire* 2 (1966): 165–80.

Merlin, Pierre. *L'exode rural.* Cahiers de l'Institut National d'Etudes Démographiques, no. 59. Paris: Presses Universitaires de France, 1971.

Merriman, John M. "Incident at the Statue of the Virgin Mary: The Conflict of Old and New in Nineteenth-Century Limoges." In *Consciousness and Class Experience in Nineteenth-Century Europe,* edited by John M. Merriman, pp. 129–48. New York: Holmes and Meier, 1979.

———. "Social Conflict in France and the Limoges Revolution of April 27, 1848." *Societas* 4 (Winter 1974): 21–38.

Millevoye, M.-J. "Une page d'histoire contemporaine lyonnaise: Les grèves révolutionnaires de 1920." *Mémoires de l'Académie des Sciences, Belles-Lettres et Arts de Lyon. Sciences et Lettres,* 3e Série, 18 (1924): 103–30.

Miquel, Pierre. *La paix de Versailles et l'opinion publique française.* Paris: Flammarion, 1972.

Mitchell, Harvey, and Peter N. Stearns. *Workers and Protest: The European Labor Movement, the Working Classes and the Origins of Social Democracy, 1890–1914.* Itasca, Ill.: F. E. Peacock, 1971.

Moissonnier, Maurice. "Octobre et le mouvement ouvrier de la région lyonnaise." *Cahiers d'Histoire de l'Institut Maurice Thorez,* o.s., nos. 7–8 (1967), pp. 37–47.

———. "La province et la Commune." *International Review of Social History* 17 (1972): 152–82.

Moissonnier, Maurice, et al. "Naissance du P.C.F. et traditions ouvrières (Débat)." *Cahiers d'Histoire de l'Institut Maurice Thorez,* n.s., no. 3 (1973), pp. 152–82.

Monds, Jean. "Workers' Control and the Historians: A New Economism." *New Left Review,* no. 97 (May 1976), pp. 81–104.

Montgomery, David. "The 'New Unionism' and the Transformation of Workers' Consciousness in America, 1909–22." *Journal of Social History* 7 (Summer 1974): 509–29.

———. "Quels Standards? Les ouvriers et la réorganisation de la production aux Etats-Unis (1900–1920)." *Le Mouvement Social,* no. 102 (Jan.–Mar. 1978), pp. 101–27.

———. "Workers' Control of Machine Production in the Nineteenth Century." *Labor History* 17 (Fall 1976): 485–509.

Montoux, Emile. *La vie économique dans la région de la Loire de 1916 à 1919.* Paris: Edition de l'Union Technique et Commerciale, n.d.

Morichon, René, ed. *Histoire du Limousin et de la Marche.* 3 vols. Limoges: Editions René Dessagne, 1976.

Moss, Bernard H. *The Origins of the French Labor Movement: The Socialism of Skilled Workers, 1830–1914.* Berkeley: University of California Press, 1976.

Mosse, George L. "The French Right and the Working Classes: 'Les Jaunes.' " *Journal of Contemporary History* 7 (1972): 185–208.

Moutet, Aimée. "Les origines du système de Taylor en France: Le point de vue patronal (1907–1914)." *Le Mouvement Social,* no. 93 (Oct.–Dec. 1975), pp. 3–49.

Naville, Pierre. *L'entre-deux-guerres. La lutte des classes en France, 1926–1939. Matériaux pour l'histoire du mouvement communiste en France.* Paris: Etudes et Documentation Internationales, 1975.

Néré, Jacques. *La crise de 1929.* Paris: Colin, 1973.

Nicot, Jean, and Philippe Schillinger. "L'opinion face à la guerre: L'influence de la Révolution Russe d'après les archives du contrôle postal." *Actes du 97ᵉ Congrès National des Sociétés Savantes,* Nantes, 1972. Section histoire moderne, 2:451–71.

———. "L'opinion publique et les grèves de la Loire, Mai 1918." *Actes du 98ᵉ Congrès National des Sociétés Savantes,* Saint-Etienne, 1973. Section histoire moderne, 2:239–52.

Nogaro, B., and Lucien Weil. *La main-d'oeuvre étrangère et coloniale pendant la guerre.* Publications of the Carnegie Endowment for International Peace. Paris: Presses Universitaires de France, n.d.

Nouailhat, Yves-Henri. "L'opinion à l'égard des Américains à Saint-Nazaire en 1917." *Revue d'Histoire Moderne et Contemporaine* (special issue, "Colloque sur l'année 1917"), 15 (Jan.–Mar. 1968): 97–102.

Oualid, William. "The Effect of the War upon Labour in France." In *Effects of the War upon French Economic Life,* edited by Charles Gide, pp. 139–91. Publications of the Carnegie Endowment for International Peace. Oxford: Clarendon Press, 1923.

Oualid, William, and Charles Picquenard. *Salaires et tarifs. Conventions collectives et grèves. La politique du Ministère de l'Armement et du Ministère du Travail.* Publications of the Carnegie Endowment for International Peace. Paris: Presses Universitaires de France, 1928.

Papayanis, Nicholas. "Collaboration and Pacifism in France during World War I." *Francia,* Band 5 (1977), pp. 425–51.

———. "Masses révolutionnaires et directions réformistes: Les tensions au cours des grèves des métallurgistes français en 1919." *Le Mouvement Social,* no. 93 (Oct.–Dec. 1975), pp. 51–73.

Paraf, Pierre. *Le syndicalisme pendant et après la guerre.* Paris: Editions de la Vie Universitaire, 1923.

Pedroncini, Guy. *Les mutineries de 1917.* Paris: Presses Universitaires de France, 1967.

Pelé, Edmond. "Le mouvement ouvrier lyonnais pendant la première guerre mondiale, 1914–1918." Mémoire de maîtrise, Lyon, 1970.

Penot, Roger. "Comment Limoges vota socialiste en 1912, 'Betoullistes' contre 'Goujadistes.' " *Limousin Magazine,* Dec. 1974, pp. 10–13.

Perrier, Antoine. "Esquisse d'une sociologie du mouvement socialiste dans la Haute-Vienne et en Limousin." *Actes du 87ᵉ Congrès National des Sociétés Savantes,* Poitiers, 1962. Section histoire moderne et contemporaine, pp. 377–98.

——— [A. Pittle]. *Une esquisse du mouvement ouvrier à Limoges depuis le XIXᵉ siècle.* Angoulême: Imprimerie Populaire, 1929.

———. "Une industrie limousine: la porcelaine. La crise économique vue d'un centre porcelainier." *Revue du Centre-Ouest de la France,* Mar. 1937, pp. 1–30.

———. *Limoges: Etude de géographie urbaine.* Toulouse: Ateliers Apta-France, 1939.

Perrin, Maxime. *Saint-Etienne et sa région économique: Un type de la vie industrielle en France.* Tours: Arrault, 1937.

Perrot, Michelle. "Archives policières et militants ouvriers sous la Troisième République. Un exemple: le Gard." *Revue d'Histoire Economique et Sociale* 37 (1959): 219–39.

———. "Grèves, grévistes, et conjoncture: Vieux problème, travaux neufs." *Le Mouvement Social,* no. 63 (Apr.–June 1968), pp. 109–24.

———. *Les ouvriers en grève: France, 1871–1890.* 2 vols. Paris: Mouton, 1974.

Peterson, Larry. "The One Big Union in International Perspective: Revolutionary

Industrial Unionism, 1900–1925." *Labour/Le Travail* 7 (Spring 1981): 41–66.

Picard, Roger. *Le contrôle ouvrier sur la gestion des entreprises.* Paris: Marcel Rivière, 1922.

———. *La crise économique et la baisse des salaires.* Paris: Marcel Rivière, 1921.

———. *Le mouvement syndical durant la guerre.* Publications of the Carnegie Endowment for International Peace. Paris: Presses Universitaires de France, 1926.

Pierre, Roger. *Les origines du syndicalisme et du socialisme dans la Drôme (1850–1920).* Paris: Editions Sociales, 1973.

Pigenet, M., P. Pigenet, R. Rygiel, and M. Picard. *Histoire du mouvement ouvrier dans le Cher.* 2 vols. Paris: Editions Sociales, 1977.

Pinol, Jean-Luc. "Origines et débuts du communisme à Lyon, 1918–1923." Mémoire de maîtrise, Lyon, 1972.

Pompon, André. *Les ouvriers porcelainiers de Limoges: Etude d'économie sociale.* Paris: Librairie de Receuil Sirey, 1910.

Posselle, Michel. "Face à l'économie moderne, une industrie traditionnelle: La porcelaine de Limoges." Mimeographed. Mémoire de stage, Ecole Nationale d'Administration, Dec. 1961.

Pressac, Pierre de. *Les forces historiques de la France: La tradition dans l'orientation politique des provinces.* Paris: Hachette, 1928.

Prost, Antoine. *Les anciens combattants et la société française, 1914–1939.* 3 vols. Paris: Presses de la Fondation Nationale des Sciences Politiques, 1977.

———. *La C.G.T. à l'époque du Front Populaire: Essai de description numérique.* Paris: Colin, 1964.

Rabaut, Jean. *Tout est possible! Les "gauchistes" français, 1929–1944.* Paris: Editions Denoël, 1974.

Rachidi, Malika. "La population minière immigrée à Saint-Etienne de 1920 à 1940." Mémoire de maîtrise, Saint-Etienne, 1973.

Racine, Nicole, and Louis Bodin, eds. *Le Parti communiste français pendant l'entre-deux-guerres.* Fondation Nationale des Sciences Politiques, collection "Archives de Notre Temps." Paris: Colin, 1972.

Raffaelli, Gérard. "Les mouvements pacifistes dans les usines d'armement de la région de Saint-Etienne (1914–1918)." *Actes du 98ᵉ Congrès National des Sociétés Savantes,* Saint-Etienne, 1973. Section histoire moderne, 2:221–37.

Raffaelli, Michelle [Zancarini], and Gérard Raffaelli. "Introduction bibliographique, méthodologique et biographique à l'étude de l'évolution économique et sociale du département de la Loire, 1914–1920. Le mouvement ouvrier contre la guerre." Mémoire de maîtrise, Paris-Nanterre, 1969.

Rancière, Jacques. "The Myth of the Artisan: Critical Reflections on a Category of Social History." *International Labor and Working Class History,* no. 24 (Fall 1983), pp. 1–16. With comments by William H. Sewell, Jr., and by Christopher H. Johnson, pp. 17–25.

Rebérioux, Madeleine, and Patrick Fridenson. "Albert Thomas, pivot du réformisme français." *Le Mouvement Social,* no. 87 (Apr.–June 1974), pp. 85–97.

Reid, Donald. "Guillaume Verdier et le syndicalisme révolutionnaire aux usines de Decazeville (1917–1920)." *Annales du Midi* 96 (Apr.–June 1984): 171–98.

Renouvin, Pierre. "L'opinion publique en France pendant la guerre, 1914–1918." *Revue d'Histoire Diplomatique* 84 (Oct.–Dec. 1970): 289–336.

———, ed. "Colloque sur l'année 1917" (special issue). *Revue d'Histoire Moderne et Contemporaine* 15 (Jan.–Mar. 1968).

Renshaw, Patrick. *The Wobblies: The Story of Syndicalism in the United States.* Garden City, N.Y.: Doubleday, 1967.

Reynaud, J.-D. *Les syndicats en France.* Paris: Colin, 1966.

Reynaud, Serge. "L'industrie de la chaussure en Haute-Vienne." Mimeographed. Limoges, Ministère du Travail, 1970.

———. "L'industrie de la porcelaine en Haute-Vienne." Mimeographed. Limoges, Ministère du Travail, 1971.

Ridley, F. F. *Revolutionary Syndicalism in France: The Direct Action of Its Time.* Cambridge: Cambridge University Press, 1970.

Robert, Jean-Louis. "Une analyse d'implication: L'évolution du groupe des Temps Nouveaux en 1915." *Le Mouvement Social,* no. 122 (Jan.–Mar. 1983), pp. 61–74.

———. "La CGT et la famille ouvrière, 1914–1918: Première approche." *Le Mouvement Social,* no. 116 (July–Sept. 1981), pp. 47–66.

———. "Les luttes ouvrières en France pendant la première guerre mondiale." *Cahiers d'Histoire de l'Institut Maurice Thorez,* n.s., no. 23 (1977), pp. 28–65.

———. "Les origines du P.C.F." In *Le P.C.F., étapes et problèmes, 1920–1972,* by Roger Bourderon et al., pp. 13–39. Paris: Editions Sociales, 1981.

———. *La scission syndicale de 1921: Essai de reconnaissance des formes.* Paris: Publications de la Sorbonne, 1980.

———. "Le syndicalisme en mouvement: Essai d'information historique, 1918–1925." Mémoire de maîtrise, Paris, 1970.

———, ed. "Le Parti Communiste en 1923: Rapport du Secrétariat du Parti Français au Comité Exécutif Elargi de l'I.C. (Mai-Juin 1923)." *Cahiers d'Histoire de l'Institut Maurice Thorez,* n.s., no. 6 (1974), pp. 213–38.

Robert, Jean-Louis, and Michel Chavance. "L'évolution de la syndicalisation en France de 1914 à 1921: L'emploi de l'analyse factorielle des correspondances." *Annales: Economies, Sociétés, Civilisations* 29 (1974): 1092–1107.

Robert, Jean-Louis, and Danielle Tartakowsky. "1921–1924: Internationale, Parti et Front Unique." *Cahiers d'Histoire de l'Institut Maurice Thorez,* n.s., no. 1 (1972): 32–44.

Robert, Maurice, "La société limousine, 1870–1914." Mimeographed. Limoges, 1971.

Rogliano, Marie-France. "L'anticommunisme dans la C.G.T.: 'Syndicats.' " *Le Mouvement Social,* no. 87 (Apr.–June 1974), pp. 63–84.

Rosmer, Alfred. *Le mouvement ouvrier pendant la guerre.* 2 vols. Paris: Librairie du Travail, 1936–56.

Sabel, Charles F. *Work and Politics: The Division of Labor in Industry.* Cambridge: Cambridge University Press, 1982.

Sabourdy, Yves. "Approche des conditions de la scission de 1920 dans le mouvement socialiste de la Haute-Vienne." Mémoire de maîtrise, Paris I, 1971.

Sagnes, Jean. *Le mouvement ouvrier en Languedoc: Syndicalistes et Socialistes de l'Hérault de la fondation des Bourses du Travail à la naissance du Parti Communiste.* Toulouse: Privat, 1980.

Sauvy, Alfred. *Histoire économique de la France entre les deux guerres.* 4 vols. Paris: Fayard, 1965–75.

Schaper, B. W. *Albert Thomas: Trente ans de réformisme social.* Translated by Louis Dupont. Assen: Van Gorcum, 1959.

Schnetzler, J. "Un demi-siècle d'évolution démographique (1820–1876)." *Etudes Foréziennes* 1 (1968): 157–89.

———. "L'évolution démographique de la région de Saint-Etienne de 1876 à 1946." *Etudes Foréziennes* 4 (1971): 157–95.

———. *Les industries et les hommes dans la région stéphanoise: Etude de géographie humaine.* Saint-Etienne: Imprimerie "Le Feuillet Blanc," 1975.

Scott, Joan Wallach. *The Glassworkers of Carmaux: French Craftsmen and Political Action in a Nineteenth-Century City.* Cambridge, Mass.: Harvard University Press, 1974.

Shorter, Edward, and Charles Tilly. *Strikes in France, 1830–1968.* London: Cambridge University Press, 1974.

Siegfried, André. *Tableau politique de la France de l'Ouest sous la Troisième République.* Paris: Colin, 1964.

Sinanoglou, Ioannis. "Frenchmen, Their Revolutionary Heritage, and the Russian Revolution." *International History Review* 2 (Oct. 1980): 566–84.

Sirianni, Carmen J. "Workers' Control in the Era of World War I: A Comparative Analysis of the European Experience." *Theory and Society* 9 (Jan. 1980): 29–88.

Slater, Catherine. *Defeatists and Their Enemies: Political Invective in France, 1914–1918.* London: Oxford University Press, 1981.

Smith, Harold. "The Issue of 'Equal Pay for Equal Work' in Great Britain, 1914–19." *Societas* 3 (Winter 1978): 39–51.

Sohn, Anne-Marie. "Exemplarité et limites de la participation féminine à la vie syndicale: Les institutrices de la C.G.T.U." *Revue d'Histoire Moderne et Contemporaine* 23 (July–Sept. 1977): 391–414.

Sokoloff, Sally. "Peasant Leadership and the French Communist Party, 1921–1940." *Historical Reflections/Réflexions Historiques* 4 (Winter 1977): 153–70.

Sorlin, Pierre. *La société française, 1840–1968.* 2 vols. Paris: Arthaud, 1969.

Soucy, Robert. "France: Veterans' Politics between the Wars." In *The War Generation,* edited by Stephen R. Ward, pp. 59–103. Port Washington, N.Y.: Kennikat Press, 1975.

Spriano, Paolo. *The Occupation of the Factories: Italy 1920.* Translated by Gwyn A. Williams. London: Pluto Press, 1975.

Stearns, Peter N. "Against the Strike Threat: Employer Policy toward Labor Agitation in France, 1900–1914." *Journal of Modern History* 40 (1968): 474–500.

———. *Lives of Labor: Work in a Maturing Industrial Society.* New York: Holmes and Meier, 1975.

———. "Measuring the Evolution of Strike Movements." *International Review of Social History* 19 (1974): 1–27.

———. *Revolutionary Syndicalism and French Labor: A Cause without Rebels.* New Brunswick, N.J.: Rutgers University Press, 1971.

———. "The Unskilled and Industrialization: A Transformation of Consciousness." *Archiv für Sozialgeschichte* 16 (1976): 249–82.

Stearns, Peter N., and Daniel Walkowitz, eds. *Workers in the Industrial Revolution.* New Brunswick, N.J.: Transaction Books, 1974.

Stein, Margot. "The Meaning of Skill: The Case of the French Engine-Drivers, 1837–1917." *Politics and Society* 8 (1979): 399–427.

Suarez, Georges. *Briand. Sa vie — son oeuvre.* 6 vols. Vol. 1: "Le révolté circonspect, 1862–1904." Paris: Plon, 1938–52.

Surgey, Jacques. "Saint-Etienne et son arrondissement face à la crise des années 30 (1930–1936)." Thèse de 3ᵉ cycle, Saint-Etienne, 1980.

Tartakowsky, Danielle. "Autour de la 'bolchévisation' du P. C. F." In *La classe ouvrière française et la politique: Essais d'analyse historique et sociale,* by Michel Dion et al., pp. 87–108. Paris: Editions Sociales, 1980.

———. "Les conditions de la pénétration du Marxisme en France." *Cahiers d'Histoire de l'Institut Maurice Thorez,* o.s., no. 28 (Sept.–Oct. 1972), pp. 32–43.

———. "1927–1931: Pour la conquête des masses." *Cahiers d'Histoire de l'Institut Maurice Thorez,* n.s., no. 5 (1973), pp. 14–33.

———. *Les premiers communistes français: Formation des cadres et bolchévisation.* Paris: Presses de la Fondation Nationale des Sciences Politiques, 1980.

———. "Le 'tournant' des années trente." In *Le P.C.F., étapes et problèmes, 1920–1972,* by Roger Bourderon et al., pp. 41–74. Paris: Editions Sociales, 1981.

Tenand, D. "Les origines de la classe ouvrière stéphanoise." Mémoire de maîtrise, Lyon II, 1972.

Thomas, Jean-Paul. "La C.G.T.U. et la stratégie des grèves (1922–1926)." Mémoire de maîtrise, Paris I, 1972.

Thompson, John M. *Russia, Bolshevism, and the Versailles Peace.* Princeton: Princeton University Press, 1967.

Tiersky, Ronald. *French Communism, 1920–1972.* New York: Columbia University Press, 1974.

Touraine, Alain, and Orietta Ragazzi. *Ouvriers d'origine agricole.* Paris: Travaux du Laboratoire de Sociologie Industrielle de l'Ecole Pratique des Hautes Etudes, VIᵉ Section, 1961.

Trempé, Rolande. *Les mineurs de Carmaux, 1848–1914.* 2 vols. Paris: Editions Ouvrières, 1971.

_____. "Le réformisme des mineurs français à la fin du XIXe siècle." *Le Mouve-ment Social,* no. 65 (Oct.–Dec. 1968), pp. 93–107.

Trotignon, Yves. *La France au XXe siècle.* Paris: Bordas-Mouton, 1968.

Université de Saint-Etienne, ed. *Les villes du Massif Central.* Actes du Colloque de Saint-Etienne. Saint-Etienne: Publications du Centre d'Etudes Forézien-nes, 1971.

Vant, André. "L'industrie du cycle dans la région stéphanoise." *Revue de Géo-graphie de Lyon* 49 (1974): 155–84.

Vaudant, Albert. "La main-d'oeuvre dans le bassin industriel stéphanois." D.E.S., Lyon, 1955.

Verynaud, Georges. *Histoire de Limoges.* Limoges: Centre Régional de Recher-che et de Documentation Pédagogiques, 1973.

Vidalenc, Jean. "La main-d'oeuvre étrangère en France et la première guerre mondiale." *Francia,* Band 2 (1974), pp. 524–50.

"Les villes françaises: Limoges." *Notes et Etudes Documentaires,* 10 Apr. 1970.

"Les villes françaises: Saint-Etienne et son agglomération." *Notes et Etudes Do-cumentaires,* 12 Oct. 1973.

Waites, Bernard. "The Effects of the First World War on the Economic and So-cial Structure of the English Working Class." *Journal of the Scottish Labour History Society* 10 (1978): 3–33.

Walter, Gérard. *Histoire du Parti communiste français.* Paris: A. Somogy, 1948.

Weber, Eugen. *Action Française: Royalism and Reaction in Twentieth-Century France.* Stanford: Stanford University Press, 1962.

_____. *Peasants into Frenchmen: The Modernization of Rural France, 1870–1914.* Stanford: Stanford University Press, 1976.

Westergard-Thorpe, Wayne. "Syndicalist Internationalism and Moscow, 1919–1922: The Breach." *Canadian Journal of History* 14 (Aug. 1979): 199–234.

Wheeler, R[obert] F. "German Labor and the Comintern: A Problem of Genera-tions?" *Journal of Social History* 7 (1974): 304–21.

White, Dan S. "Reconsidering European Socialism in the 1920s." *Journal of Con-temporary History* 16 (Apr. 1981): 251–72.

Willard, Claude. "La connaissance de la Révolution Russe et de l'expérience sovi-étique par le mouvement ouvrier français en 1918–1919." *Cahiers d'Histoire de l'Institut Maurice Thorez,* n.s., nos. 12–13 (1975), pp. 318–30.

_____. *Le mouvement socialiste en France (1893–1905): Les Guesdistes.* Paris: Editions Sociales, 1965.

Wishnia, Judith. "The French *Fonctionnaires:* The Development of Class Con-sciousness and Unionization, 1884–1926." Ph.D. diss., SUNY at Stony Brook, 1978.

Wohl, Robert. *French Communism in the Making, 1914–1924.* Stanford: Stan-ford University Press, 1966.

_____. *The Generation of 1914.* Cambridge, Mass.: Harvard University Press, 1979.

Wolfe, Martin. "French Interwar Stagnation Revisited." In *From the Ancien Régime to the Popular Front: Essays in the History of Modern France in*

Honor of Shepard B. Clough, edited by Charles K. Warner, pp. 159–80. New York: Columbia University Press, 1969.

Wolikow, Serge. "Analyse des classes et stratégie du P.C.F.: Période 'classe contre classe' au Front Populaire." In *La classe ouvrière française et la politique: Essais d'analyse historique et sociale,* by Michel Dion et al., pp. 109–36. Paris: Editions Sociales, 1980.

──────. "Conjoncture économique et intervention de l'état (1926–1932)." *Cahiers d'Histoire de l'Institut Maurice Thorez,* n.s., no. 6 (1974): 17–46.

──────. "Economie et société: L'analyse et la pratique du P.C.F. (1926–1939). Première partie." *Cahiers d'Histoire de l'Institut Maurice Thorez,* n.s., no. 10 (1974), pp. 22–54.

──────. "Le P.C.F. devant la crise (1929–1931): Les positions sur l'économie, leur place dans la politique du P.C.F." *Cahiers d'Histoire de l'Institut Maurice Thorez,* n.s., no. 11 (1975), pp. 32–94.

──────. "Le P.C.F. et le Front Populaire." In *Le P.C.F., étapes et problèmes, 1920–1972,* by Roger Bourderon et al., pp. 99–197. Paris: Editions Sociales, 1981.

──────. "Les rapports du P.C.F. et de l'Internationale Communiste (1925–1935)." Part 1: "Remarques méthodologiques et théoriques." Part 2: "L'orientation 'classe contre classe,' 1927–1928: Le processus complexe de son élaboration et de sa mise en oeuvre." *Cahiers d'Histoire de l'Institut Maurice Thorez,* n.s., nos. 25–26 (1978), pp. 14–65; no. 27 (1978), pp. 224–71.

Wright, Gordon. *Rural Revolution in France.* Stanford: Stanford University Press, 1964.

Young, M. Neely. "*La Vie Ouvrière* and International Communism, 1919–1924: Analysis of a Revolutionary Trade Union Newspaper." Ph.D. diss., Emory University, 1975.

Zdatny, Steven M. "The Origins of the Artisanal Movement in France, 1919–1925." *Proceedings of the Western Society for French History* 9 (Oct. 1981): 284–92.

Zeldin, Theodore. *France 1848–1945.* 2 vols. London: Oxford University Press, 1973–77.

Index

Note on the Author

KATHRYN E. AMDUR is a member of the History Department faculty at Emory University. She received her B.A. degree from Cornell University and her M.A. and Ph.D. degrees from Stanford University. She is a contributor to the *Historical Dictionary of the French Third Republic,* edited by Patrick Hutton (Greenwood Press, 1986), and the author of articles and reviews in the *Cahiers d'Histoire, Le Mouvement Social,* the *Journal of Economic History, International Labor and Working Class History,* and the *American Historical Review.*